# Prose and Poetry of America

## St. Thomas More Series

# PROSE AND POETRY
# OF AMERICA

SECOND EDITION

## Julian L. Maline, Ph.D.

PROFESSOR OF EDUCATION, WEST BADEN COLLEGE OF LOYOLA UNIVERSITY

## Frederick P. Manion, A.M.

FORMERLY INSTRUCTOR IN ENGLISH AT LOYOLA ACADEMY, CHICAGO, ILLINOIS

CHARLES J. CAGNEY, A.M.

ROBERT J. KEARNS, A.M.

JOSEPH G. MILUNAS, PH.D.

ALBERT J. WILZBACHER, A.B.

JOSEPH R. ZUBRICKY, A.M.

SYRACUSE, NEW YORK

## The L. W. Singer Company, Inc.

THE COVER DESIGN:

"Enthroned Madonna and Child" was painted around 1200 in Constantinople, then called Byzantium. The artist is unknown, but the painting is a colorful example of early religious art. This picture is more formal than later art, and is reminiscent of the classical sculptures of Greece. It is reprinted by permission of the National Gallery of Art, Washington, D. C. (Mellon Collection). The Kodachrome is by Francis G. Mayer Art Color Slides, Inc., New York City.

IMPRIMATUR:

✠ Paul C. Schulte, Archbishop of Indianapolis

THE DESIGN:

Stefan Salter

*5 2799*

# PREFACE

## THE PLAN OF THIS BOOK

The purposes of the first two books in this PROSE AND POETRY Series, St. Thomas More Edition, are to enable the student to *enjoy and to evaluate* what he reads. The purpose of this third book is to have students enjoy and evaluate the literature of America taken in its *historical significance.* "History tells us what men did and were. Literature tells us what their aspirations, hopes, and ideals were." Just as a modern mother and father by using a movie camera can make a pictorial record of their child's first toddling steps, his bright-eyed interest and innocence, his gradual maturing process, so the printed page of American history gives us a picture of our nation's first steps, its growing pains of war, its early enthusiasms and keen disappointments. But no matter how many feet of film a father may shoot of his son or daughter, all he can put on celluloid are the external physical actions of his child. The thoughts, fears, and secret ambitions and joys can never be recorded on a mere strip of film. These are the things of the soul. But they can be caught and imbedded on the pages of literature. For literature is the communication of man's most secret, profound, and universal thoughts through the medium of language.

This anthology presents selections which are representative pieces of each period in American history. As our ancestors fought their wars to give us the freedom we enjoy today, what did they think about? What were they fighting for? A composite picture of our nation's literature is the answer. A distillation of their many and varied thoughts will give us a clear picture of the soul of America.

Why, then, begin our study with the period of the twentieth century if this book is to examine American literature in its historical setting? The reasons are two. First, by placing the products of the modern era at the beginning of the book the editors feel that a student will see the more interesting works of American prose and poetry at the beginning of the year when his appetite is sharp and his scholastic zeal more easily fed. Difficult essays, famous historical documents though they be, have often ruined a student's taste for literature before the school year was a month old. Second, it is good for the pupil to see American literature as it *now* is, to study its trends and attitudes, and then go back to examine how the whole development took place. To recall our movie-metaphor, would not a visitor who is to be entertained by a showing of the film presenting the baby-and-boyhood antics of some favorite son, first see and converse with the young fellow, now grown to manhood? It seems only natural that an outsider would first meet and appraise the young man as he now is, then sit back and enjoy watching this man's development from a four-months-old baby to a twenty-one-year-old man at graduation from college. So, too, in this book of literature. First we meet a composite young man of the twentieth century whose main characteristics are thorough-going realism tinged with romanticism, materialism mixed with religion, wisdom diluted with cynicism, optimism coupled with pessimism. Our composite man depicting the modern era of literature is a strange Hamlet containing many contradictions. How did he develop these characteristics? Snap on the movie machine of American literature and see his toddling steps during the period of Revolution. Behold his open boyishness, his love of action, his love of mysterious things as he grows in wisdom during the Romantic or National era. Follow him in the Transition period where his experiences involving a Civil War and "wild-west days" have given him a hard-bitten wisdom. As the literary-film nears its end we see that he is beginning to "wise-up" to the world. He is adopting a more realistic attitude towards life; he is facing bitter facts, and soon he will become bitter himself, but not wholly so. Then the student turns again to our young twentieth-century man—a man with an intense joy of life, a lover of democracy and freedom, a generous optimist, yet secretly a partially embittered and unhappy man, searching always higher, but content too often with false values and standards. This young nation's composite literary works tell us these things about him. But contradictions are difficult to reconcile. How then shall we interpret him?

## A CATHOLIC INTERPRETATION OF AMERICAN LITERATURE

It may seem strange that St. Thomas More, a model of the Catholic cultured gentleman, should be the patron of a book which presents the essence of American culture—a culture which on many points is directly opposed to Catholic culture. One wonders what St. Thomas More would think of our modern America were he suddenly to be reincarnated here in the United States today, complete with his medieval attitudes and characteristics. Of course, he would be amazed at our scientific progress, our ability to build higher, move faster, destroy more completely than man has ever done before. But we think he would be more astonished at the complete reversal of man's attitude toward God. The spirit of St. Thomas' age, especially the few centuries preceding it, was centered in God. It was an era of Catholic culture in which the seven sacraments and the sacramentals permeated the lives of all people. The people may have disobeyed God, but they knew there was a God. Every king and peasant welcomed the grace of the sacraments at each turning point of his life. Today St. Thomas would be hard put to find the direct influence of God-centered lives (though there are many) in the affairs of the world. He would see that by and large the creed of modern men is no longer that of Christ's Apostles, but that of the secularists who teach that man can get along perfectly well without God or religion.

Yes, St. Thomas More would shed bitter tears over our civilization and culture, but, balanced intellect that he was, he would not find it wholly bad. He would recognize the generosity, the honesty, the optimism, the spirit of democracy, the whole-hearted desire of most Americans to build a better world. And he would rejoice. But he would also breathe a prayer that our justice and charity might become more supernatural in their motivation.

If St. Thomas More had been given the task of editing this anthology, he would not have demanded that only those works be represented which were written by Catholic authors, or works which are of a specifically religious nature. True literature is always in accord with the heart of man—and the heart of a completely rounded man, socially, intellectually, and religiously, is always

looking towards God. As in the other books of this series, Catholic and non-Catholic authors will be found following one another in perfect step, the works of all subject to the searching standards of Catholic Faith and Catholic ideals.

## TYPE DIVISION

A glance at the table of contents shows that this book has a twofold division: it is divided both according to time and to type-study. These divisions are especially true of the twentieth century. Stress has been given to two main types which are typically American: the short story and journalistic writing. In each period the various types are kept more or less separate (orations are sometimes interspersed between essays), a division which should help the teacher in drawing up a study schedule.

All teachers are urged to link constantly the literature with the history of America. There is no better way in which to give a just appraisal of our literary culture.

JULIAN L. MALINE, S.J.
FREDERICK P. MANION, S.J.
AND THE EDITORS

# CONTENTS

# CONTENTS

# CONTENTS

# CONTENTS

# CONTENTS

# CONTENTS BY TYPES

# CONTENTS BY TYPES

# CONTENTS BY TYPES

# CONTENTS BY TYPES

# CONTENTS BY TYPES

## NARRATIVE POETRY

# THE TWENTIETH CENTURY

## *1 9 0 0 –*

We live in swiftly changing times. How many of the "necessities" of today would have seemed sheer impossibilities only fifty years ago! All of us know people who can remember when the automobile was a novelty and the airplane a dream; when there were no motion pictures and no hint of radio or television with their endless stream of entertainment.

Yet all these changes have not altered the basic nature of mankind. We still are curious about ourselves and each other. We still enjoy a good story. We may not spend much time sitting by the fire telling tales; but we pick up the paper or turn on the radio to see "what's doing," or we go off to a movie or settle down with a magazine for an evening's entertainment.

It is typical of the present-day American that his first interest in literature is with the writings of today. From periodicals and from books fresh from the press he learns the names of living writers—journalists, statesmen, popular story-writers. Radio and television bring him addresses direct from the lips of men and women who are molding world events. The dramas of the airways are built out of yesterday's headlines; and much modern fiction is as up-to-the-minute as the March of Time.

In range, current writing is country-wide. It deals with Americans everywhere, and it is being produced in every section of the United States. In form it is equally diverse. An author chooses any style that suits his fancy or his subject; he writes in slang or in dialect; in poetic prose or in unrhymed verse, or in sonnets; in old forms revived or in new ones invented. Radio and television drama are new forms, and these media have renewed the importance of an early American favorite—the public address.

In its wealth and complexity, modern American literature is almost overwhelming. Like the country that produces it, it is vigorous and diversified.

There is much of it, however, that is not touched with the Catholic spirit. Much of it is either openly or secretly against it. This is not surprising, for once men cut themselves off from the teachings of Him Who pointed to Himself as the Way, the Truth, and the Life, they wander into the myriad paths of error. Hence, it is imperative that we train ourselves to think, to read critically, for many an author with a persuasive style has only a husk of truth to offer the reader, or he may even be spreading the deadly virus of positive error.

# TWENTIETH-CENTURY FICTION

By the time the student has reached the senior high school level, his experience in reading will have shown him that all literature is divided into groups or *types* depending upon differences in form and in purpose. The two major classifications as to form are *prose* and *poetry*; the two general classifications as to purpose or content are *fiction* and *nonfiction*. There is some overlapping in these main divisions. Libraries use an arbitrary system: under the heading "Fiction" they classify all prose stories and novels; under the heading "Nonfiction" they catalogue everything else, including poetry and drama. Studies in literature actually follow the library precedent; and for practical purposes the term "fiction" is understood to include all prose stories written, not to give information, but to entertain.

Strictly speaking, *fiction* is that sort of literary prose which, through the imagination of the author, presents lifelike situations in the form of stories. The usual classifications within the field are made on the basis of length. Thus book-length fiction is called a *novel*; a story which can be read at a single sitting is called a *short story*; a narrative considerably longer, yet not book length, is called a *novelette*; and a short story compressed to about a thousand words is called a *short short story*. There are, however, certain other qualifications which distinguish each type. These we shall consider briefly.

## THE NOVEL

We have said that a piece of book-length fiction is commonly called a novel, yet there are, of course, several types of novels. In general, we should be familiar with two distinct classifications of novels—the romantic novel and the realistic novel. Originally, prose fiction was little more than a series of highly imaginative adventures often quite unrelated to each other. However, when writers discovered the possibilities of the long tale in which events and characters were bound together by a framework or plot, the growth of the novel was assured.

Reflecting a growing spirit of the age in which they developed, the early novels were romantic in tone. Their authors looked at life through rose-colored spectacles, seeing it as they wished it to be rather than as it actually was.

It should be explained that the term *romantic* when applied to fiction does not designate, as boys and girls often think it does, a story with a strong love interest; it applies rather to any story highly colored by the imagination. For *romanticism* in literature denotes a tendency on the part of the author to get away from harsh or sober realities of life. It reflects love of nature, desire for freedom and individualism, escape from unpleasant facts, idealism in religion and politics, interest in distant times and places, patriotism, sentimentalism, and emotion rather than reason. The modern romantic novel may be a fantasy like Morley's *Where the Blue Begins*; it may be a wild-west adventure tale; or it may be a complicated murder mystery in which nice people are dropped off like flies. Such fiction may be entertaining reading. It may be delightfully written. But it is not to be confused with the more realistic story which characterizes the true novel.

*Realism*, like romanticism, has its distinguishing characteristics. It, too, is a viewpoint or a way of looking at life. It deals with commonplace, everyday happenings; it shuns the weird and strange; it stresses actuality and infinite detail. It is a direct look at life as it is, uncolored by a bizarre imagination. Such novels as *Silas Marner*, *The Rise of Silas Lapham*, and *Main Street* are typical realistic novels. *Giants in the Earth* is also a good example of the realistic novel because, although the characters and events are imaginary, they are so lifelike as to seem real. Men like Per Hansa did settle in North Dakota. Their wives did suffer from lonesomeness and privation. Blizzards still sweep across the prairies; and men have died in them. One can almost believe he is reading a biography in Rolvaag's masterpiece.

Early American literature, as we shall see in later chapters of this book, was almost entirely romantic in tone. Early twentieth-century fiction, on the other hand, was dominantly realistic. Today the excesses of each are being tempered by the inclusion of the other. The novel, because it is an extended work of fiction, is well suited to presenting life as it is or may be. A book like *Ethan Frome* or *The Yearling* makes us think deeply about the problems of human relations, with the result that each reader then sees himself and his own problems more clearly. Historical novels like those of Walter D. Edmonds and Kenneth Roberts not only make the past live for us but also show the people of long ago to have been men and women like ourselves. Books of our own day have the opportunity of presenting critical issues fairly and of helping the reader to reach right judgments. The true novel— of all literary forms—gives the most compelling representations of life.

## THE NOVELETTE

A genuine novelette partakes of all the characteristics of the novel, but in abbreviated form. It is not only longer than a short story; it takes a fuller view. Our interest is not confined to a single character. We are concerned with the community which forms its setting and with the interplay of characters. It is a novel in miniature, rather than a short story.

## THE SHORT SHORT STORY

The very newest child in the fiction family is the short short story. It owes its popularity to the magazine. It is designed to tell its tale on one page or less. The first short shorts followed one pretty definite pattern, a pattern not unlike that devised by O. Henry in which the incidents lead up to a surprise ending with an ironic twist. The chief character was often a criminal, and the surprise usually made him the victim of a trap of his own setting. Recently patterns have been changing; and some magazines are featuring short shorts that meet, in limited fashion, the requirements of a good short story. They are like miniature etchings from life.

## THE SHORT STORY

One way to clarify the special qualities of the short story is to contrast it with the novel. Both forms tell a story through the use of characters, dialogue, and action. But whereas the novel may take as many as a thousand pages to develop its theme, the short story must unfold within the limits of a dozen pages or less.

Brander Matthews in 1885 said this about the short story: "A true short story differs from a novel chiefly in its essential unity of impression. . . . It deals with a single character interest, a single event, a single emotion, or the series of emotions called forth by a single situation. . . . Thus the short story has what the novel cannot have, the effect of 'totality,' as Poe called it, the unity of impression." Characters and scene should be introduced briefly, vividly. Every element should work toward one predetermined effect.

Until recently, there was almost a formula for building a short story, beginning with the setting, or background, and working carefully through the action to climax and *denouement,* or solution. Today the requirements for short-story construction have been much relaxed. Perhaps the only restriction left is that there must be some opposition or struggle involved and that in the presentation of this struggle some single emphasis be made. Some modern stories have little action. Stories like "The Sculptor's Funeral" by Willa Cather and "The Trouble" by J. F. Powers are concerned not so much with incidents as with interplay of character.

Each story must be appraised for what it has to offer. Stories that focus on character may be as thrilling as tales of action, for they raise a quiet excitement that comes with seeing deeply into human nature. Like the novel, the good story presents a picture from life. And like all true literature, it must carry the reader outside and beyond himself.

Much popular fiction lacks this artistic touch, following rather some pattern that the public likes. The average reader wants to be pleasantly amused, frightened, or saddened for a while, with everything coming out right in the end. And hundreds of writers cater to these tastes. But when any story leaves upon the reader the unforgettable impression that he has touched life itself—then that story qualifies as real literature.

A final consideration enters into one's appreciation of a good story. It is this: What is the viewpoint of the author? Stories are the work of people like ourselves. Authors differ in manner or purpose. When we read one man's story, we see life —for a space—through his eyes. Our sense of appreciation deepens in proportion to our feeling that an author's view is right and valid. If a writer's mind is clouded with hate, despair, unbelief, he cannot completely prevent his feelings from coloring the story he tells. If a writer tries to see the world through the eyes of Christ, he will see things truly, and his stories will reveal the real values of life.

The whirl of circumstance that eddies about us does not alter eternal truths. The man of every age who would be in touch with reality says with the poet Hopkins, "Thee, God, I come from; to Thee I go." Even the dizzy merry-go-round of the twentieth century has not changed the fact that man comes from God and is made for God. One should judge the modern author's picture of man in terms of this relationship between man and God. Does the writer have his values right? Brilliant technique, mastery of expression—these are not enough to make a writer great. There must be essential truth besides. An author does not always treat such matters explicitly, but his awareness of truth should light up all his work.

The stories offered in this section have been chosen for their skillful interweaving of plot and character and for the light they shed on the marvelous handiwork of God—man. Some names well known in modern fiction are not included. The omission is not a denial of talent. If the genius of a writer has not been matched with grandeur of vision, we have passed him by, believing that it is best to read the works of those who can deal with truth and at the same time be artists with words.

Recent trends among writers both Catholic and non-Catholic give promise of great fiction to come. Authors are rediscovering heroic qualities in men and women. The vogue for the sordid is passing. It is encouraging to note the emergence of such promising Catholic writers as J. F. Powers, Brendan Gill, Harry Sylvester, Albert Eisele, and Maureen Daly. And a dip into two fine volumes of short stories, *They Are People* and *Our Father's House*, selected by Sister Mariella Gable, O.S.B., reveals the possibilities for story material on Catholic themes.

---

7

# FIFTY MISSIONS

*JOSEPH DEVER*

*This is a story about a nun and a soldier who loved her. Its unusual ending is probably the main reason why it won the short story contest sponsored by* YANK, THE ARMY WEEKLY.

I am on my way to see my girl in Boston, and it has been a long time. It has been twenty-six months since I said good-bye to her in Boston.

Fifty missions always seemed incredible to me. How could anyone ever come back to the States after fifty missions? How could anyone step off a DC-4 in East Boston and quietly take a taxicab to the Hotel Statler after having been over Europe fifty times?

I'm doing it, though; I'm home in Boston. And I'm not being sentimental when I say that it's damned good to be here.

I'm just like them now; I mean the gunners I knew at armament school— the exotic GIs with fifty missions, with their wings, their rainbow service ribbons, their medals, and the quiet, easy way they had about them. They'd say: "You'll get your chance, kid." "Yeah, it's kinda rough up there." I wanted some day to be wordless, humble and friendly with other eager kids the way the gunners were with me. How far away it all seemed then: fifty missions, the ribbons and the quiet, easy manner.

And now I'm riding through East Boston; I'm just like they were. I know a hell of a lot of things, but I would

rather turn my face away and ask about your brother John who is in the ASTP. I know what flak is now. I know how a gunner can make a chapel out of the Sperry lower ball; I know that he can pray with rich eloquence. I know what the enemy looks like. There is also, of course, the blood fleck, the mother-mercy-calling and the blubbering, steel-given death of the nice guys who were hilariously drunk with you just a few nights before.

And now I'm looking at Boston. My taxi-driver is a maniac at the wheel, as all taxi-drivers are. He is doing forty-seven miles an hour through this big-city street. On a street in Berlin he would listen for the menacing wail of the air-raid sirens.

"This is it," the Boston taxi-driver says.

I get out, I pay him, I walk into a beautiful thick-rugged Boston hotel, and I get a room.

It is a room on the seventh floor. My stuff is all unpacked, and I stand by a window looking out. I stand looking out at downtown Boston, and I see only the white face of a nun.

My girl Jane is a nun now. We were going to be married, but something struck her, some kind of spiritual ack-ack, I guess. And now she's gone off and become a nun.

She's here in Boston now, in some kind of a cloister, and I'm on my way to see her. I figured the fifty missions wouldn't let me see her again, I was almost sure of it, but here I am in Boston looking out a window.

The Copley Plaza is over that way. And on the other side of it, about four stories high and facing Copley Square and the Boston Public Library, there is a little marble balcony. The night of my college senior prom I threw highball glasses into the square. I liked to hear the tinkling clatter of the glass against the cobbles, and I wanted to do it again and again.

"Jay, come inside," was all Jane had said.

I went inside; I loved her greatly, more than even the sound of breaking glass, and I always did what she said.

And over there to the right is Beacon Hill. We liked that place very much. When I was a feather merchant, Jane and I used to walk all over it in the blackout. We knew all the places—the quaint, cobbled, snaky alleys, the huddled coffee nooks, the little barny theaters where you could see Philip Barry's plays for twenty cents, the H. M. Pulham doorways with the white marble steps and the shiny brass door plates. We used to sit in those doorways at midnight, on our way home; I used to kiss her there a lot. We'd pretend we were locked out, and sometimes we'd yell loudly for Nana or Jeeves. If anybody came to the door we'd jump to our feet and run like scared rabbits all the way down the hill to the Charles Street elevated station.

And there, across the Charles River, is Cambridge. That's where I used to live; that's where Jane lived. Our playground's there, too.

In the summertime Jane and I worked on the playground. She was my boss—and did we have a time! There was a big brick schoolhouse called the Peary. There was a playground in back of it, a sun-baked macadam rectangle, and there were kids, hundreds of kids, from the stinking Cambridge tenements.

She wouldn't say a thing when I'd come in, maybe an hour and a half late. Sometimes she'd pretend she was peeved and go on with her jigsaw project. She'd sit there in the sun wearing a colossal straw bonnet, and she'd prattle merrily but exclusively to the little girls who were gathered busily about her feet.

I'd keep teasing her. I'd hit a softball out to my outfielders from a place right near her; I'd make the ball roll right over to her sometimes and in retrieving it I'd get myself all tangled up in her and the jigsaw plywood animals she and the girls were making. After a while she would burst out laughing and come after me with a bat, a shrill chorus of girl voices urging her on.

It was on the playground that I really became infected with the planes. The P-38s would go over at about 8,000, and I'd stand down there by shortstop and crane my neck until the planes were little silver winks way out to the west.

I never knew about Jane leaving me then, but I did know that someday I was going to be up there in a plane.

About four-thirty in the afternoon we'd quit for the day and lock up. That was when Jane and I played our own little game. I'd go in the front door of the school and she'd go in the back. We'd both slam the doors and run quickly towards each other.

I'd take her in my arms, then I'd kiss her hair, her eyes, her lips and the very tip of her nose. I'd hold her close in my arms and we'd talk about being married and having a place of our own; we'd wonder what our children would look like and if they'd be scampering off to a playground like the Peary every day.

Then the kids would start banging on the door and hollering for us to come out. We'd kiss a few times more and walk innocently out to them. They used to escort us part of the way home, and they never said a thing about the kissing, even though they knew, as all kids know, even when you think they do not.

That was the way it was. It was a good way to be living and loving. Now it is all changed.

Well, anyway, I am going out to the convent to see her. It is a place called Mission Hill, which is in Roxbury. Roxbury's a part of Boston and only a short ride from the hotel.

A girl who used to double-date with Jane and me wrote to me when I was in England. She said she'd seen Jane and that Jane told her to tell me that if I ever got back to the States I was to be sure and make a visit to the convent. I wrote to the girl and said I would.

I am in a taxi again, riding very fast along Huntington Avenue.

The taxi climbs up Mission Hill, and the convent is at the top. It is red brick with a red brick wall around it. It is low and quadrangular, and there are those cylindrical clay shingles all over its roof and on the top of the brick wall.

I ring the front-door bell. You only ring once in a convent because that ring, however slight, is amplified by the silence and the distance that fills the inside of a cloister until the ring becomes something like an echoing clap of thunder.

A little nun lets me in. I ask for Jane. Jane's nun name is Sister Felicitas. I pretend I don't notice, but I see the little nun who let me in eat up the gunner's wings and the service ribbons. I go into the parlor and wait. There is always a large wall clock in this kind of parlor, and it always says: "Wait, wait, wait." It says this over and over again. You hear a door softly open and softly close way off in a cool interminable distance. You know then someone is coming.

Jane comes into the parlor.

She is just as I pictured she'd be. Her face is white, her eyes are sparkling blue pools of goodness and mischief, the backs of her hands have little red and creamy blotches as though she does a lot of dishes and scrubs a lot of floors.

She is all swaddled up as I was afraid she'd be, wound in endless and oppressive reams of black cloth; she wears a tremendous white starched collar and a black veil over her head. But she is my Jane all right, she is my Jane.

She stands in the middle of the room and looks right at me for about a minute.

"Hello, Jane," I say.

She doesn't say a thing. She walks over to me and takes hold of both my hands; she comes up as close to me as a nun ever can and squeezes both my hands until they sting.

She stays close to me that way for what seems a long time; she eases the pressure on my hands and looks strongly at me so I can see that everything is there just as it had always been: all the love and the light and the music are there for me in just the way they used to be, and even though these things are God's now, I can somehow see and know they are still mine, too.

"Oh, Jay," she says, and her eyes are a little wet, "I'm so very, very glad to see you. Let me look at you."

She steps away from me, and I notice that her step, although as light and graceful as ever, is now a swish instead of the swirl that it had once been. A girl has become a nun; an elfin skirt has become a ponderous petticoat.

"My, what a handsome soldier you are! You know, I've never seen you in your uniform before. And the wings, and the ribbons. Jay, you're really a man now, aren't you!"

"Am I, Jane?" I gulp, fumbling desperately for words. "Wasn't I one before?" I finally ask.

"Of course you were," she says, "but you were a boy's man then, Jay. You're a man's man now. The kind I always knew you'd be. But come, let's sit down."

We sit down in separate, straight-backed wooden chairs. The chairs are cold, unyielding symbols of poverty, chastity and obedience. We sit in them a while and, although she does not come right out and say it, I think she wants me to talk.

But I don't want to talk. I want to be with her, to be near her, to hear her voice and watch her eyes. I want to sit with Sister Felicitas and think about my Jane.

She kind of guesses that I don't want to talk.

She says she likes it here; she has prayed for me night and day; she is happy teaching fourth grade to the little Roxbury urchins; she is proud of me and tells the little kids in her class stories about me all the time; she had read everything in the Cambridge *Clarion* which someone sent her, and she doesn't care if I never utter so much as a syllable about airplanes.

I have not changed greatly, she says;

the wonder and the impudence are still in my face; my eyes have a distance in them that wasn't there before; I'm not as loquacious— "Glory," she says, "things have happened!"

I have had enough of looking at her. I begin to ache for her like when I was across. I begin to want her in my arms, and I know that it is time for me to go.

I say I have to be going. We stand up. She looks at me a while and takes both my hands; she makes them sting again.

"What happens now, Jay?" she asks.

"They're sending me out to Denver as an armament instructor. I don't want to go, but you just go, that's all."

"Well, I guess this is good-bye, Jane," I stammer. "I hope you'll be very happy, kid." She hasn't heard me call her "kid" for a long time.

I turn to go.

"Wait," she says quickly. "Come in the chapel with me, Jay, and we'll say a prayer together. It's down here."

We walk down the hall toward the chapel.

"You can leave me inside," she whispers when we are about to enter the chapel. "You can go out the front door of the chapel and into the street."

She hesitates a little, then she says quietly: "I love you, Jay; I'll always love you and I'll pray for you constantly, all the days of my life."

She turns away swiftly and moves into a pew about three yards from me. She begins to pray.

I kneel down and I pray, too. I tell God I am sorry for not wanting to come back from fifty missions; I thank Him for bringing me back even though I had not wanted to come. I say three Hail Marys. I take a long look at Jane. I genuflect and walk out of the chapel and into the street.

———

## FOR DISCUSSION

1. What is the quiet, easy way that the flyers with fifty missions have, and what causes such an attitude?

2. Why doesn't a soldier usually want to talk about his experiences? Why would he rather turn his face away and ask about your brother John?

3. Why are past events like the prom and the playground incidents put into this story?

4. What kind of girl do you think Jane was before she entered the convent? If Jane still loves Jay and always will, why did she enter the convent? Explain whether or not it was the right thing to do. Was it fair to Jay?

5. Many popular authors today sacrifice artistic principles for popular appeal. If the author had had Jane leave the convent and marry Jay, would he have been guilty of this fault? Why? How would such an ending have cheapened Jane's character? With such an ending, do you think this story would still have been able to win the short story contest? Explain.

## STUDYING THE SHORT STORY

1. The story is told in the first person. What effect does this have?

2. The present tense is constantly used throughout the story. What effect does this achieve?

# APPOINTMENT WITH LOVE

## S. I. KISHOR

*Both character and plot have been developed in this short short story even though the story required less than half a page in* COLLIER'S.

Six minutes to six, said the great round clock over the information booth in Grand Central Station. The tall young Army lieutenant who had just come from the direction of the tracks lifted his sunburned face, and his eyes narrowed to note the exact time. His heart was pounding with a beat that shocked him because he could not control it. In six minutes, he would see the woman who had filled such a special place in his life for the past thirteen months, the woman he had never seen, yet whose written words had been with him and sustained him unfailingly.

He placed himself as close as he could to the information booth, just beyond the ring of people besieging the clerks. . . .

Lieutenant Blandford remembered one night in particular, the worst of the fighting, when his plane had been caught in the midst of a pack of enemy fighters. He had seen the grinning face of one of the enemy pilots.

In one of his letters, he had confessed to her that he often felt fear, and only a few days before this battle, he had received her answer: "Of course you fear . . . all brave men do. Didn't King David know fear? That's why he wrote the Twenty-third Psalm. Next

time you doubt yourself, I want you to hear my voice reciting to you: 'Yea, though I walk in the valley of the shadow of death, I shall fear no evil, for Thou art with me.' . . ." And he had remembered; he had heard her imagined voice, and it had renewed his strength and skill.

Now he was going to hear her real voice. Four minutes to six. His face grew sharp.

Under the immense, starred roof, people were walking fast, like threads of color being woven into a gray web. A girl passed close to him, and Lieutenant Blandford started. She was wearing a red flower in her suit lapel, but it was a crimson sweet pea, not the little red rose they had agreed upon. Besides, this girl was too young, about eighteen, whereas Hollis Meynell had frankly told him she was thirty. "Well, what of it?" he had answered. "I'm thirty-two." He was twenty-nine.

His mind went back to that book— the book the Lord Himself must have put into his hands out of the hundreds of Army library books sent to the Florida training camp. *Of Human Bondage*, it was; and throughout the book were notes in a woman's writing. He had always hated that writing-in habit, but these remarks were different. He had never believed that a woman could see into a man's heart so tenderly, so understandingly. Her name was on the bookplate: Hollis Meynell. He had got hold of a New York City tele-

shall see me and then you shall make your decision. Remember, both of us are free to stop or to go on after that— whichever we choose. . . ."

One minute to six . . . he pulled hard on a cigarette.

Then Lieutenant Blandford's heart leaped higher than his plane had ever done.

A young woman was coming toward him. Her figure was long and slim; her blond hair lay back in curls from her delicate ears. Her eyes were blue as flowers, her lips and chin had a gentle firmness. In her pale green suit, she was like springtime come alive.

He started toward her, entirely forgetting to notice that she was wearing no rose, and as he moved, a small, provocative smile curved her lips.

"Going my way, soldier?" she murmured.

Uncontrollably, he made one step closer to her. Then he saw Hollis Meynell.

She was standing almost directly behind the girl, a woman well past forty, her graying hair tucked under a worn hat. She was more than plump; her thick-ankled feet were thrust into low-heeled shoes. But she wore a red rose in the rumpled brown lapel of her coat.

The girl in the green suit was walking quickly away.

Blandford felt as though he were being split in two, so keen was his desire to follow the girl, yet so deep was his longing for the woman whose spirit had truly companioned and upheld his own; and there she stood. Her pale, plump face was gentle and sensible; he could see that now. Her gray eyes had a warm, kindly twinkle.

Lieutenant Blandford did not hesitate. His fingers gripped the small, worn, blue leather copy of *Of Human*

phone book and found her address. He had written, she had answered. Next day he had been shipped out, but they had gone on writing.

For thirteen months, she had faithfully replied, and more than replied. When his letters did not arrive, she wrote anyway, and now he believed he loved her, and she loved him.

But she had refused all his pleas to send him her photograph. That seemed rather bad, of course. But she had explained: "If your feeling for me has any reality, any honest basis, what I look like won't matter. Suppose I'm beautiful. I'd always be haunted by the feeling that you had been taking a chance on just that, and that kind of love would disgust me. Suppose I'm plain (and you must admit that this is more likely) then I'd always fear that you were only going on writing to me because you were lonely and had no one else. No, don't ask for my picture. When you come to New York, you

*Bondage* which was to identify him to her. This would not be love, but it would be something precious, something perhaps even rarer than love—a friendship for which he had been and must ever be grateful. . . .

He squared his broad shoulders, saluted and held the book out toward the woman, although even while he spoke he felt choked by the bitterness of his disappointment.

"I'm Lieutenant John Blandford, and you—you are Miss Meynell. I'm so glad you could meet me. May—may I take you to dinner?"

The woman's face broadened in a tolerant smile. "I don't know what this is all about, son," she answered. "That young lady in the green suit, who just went by, she begged me to wear this rose on my coat. And she said that if you asked me to go out with you, I should tell you that she's waiting for you in that big restaurant across the street. She said it was some kind of a test. I've got two boys with Uncle Sam myself, so I didn't mind to oblige you."

## FOR DISCUSSION

1. How was Hollis Meynell testing the lieutenant?

2. What kind of character do you think the lieutenant had? Explain. What kind of character did Hollis Meynell have?

## STUDYING THE SHORT STORY

Even though a short short story is limited, do you think this one meets all the requirements of a good short story? Explain.

## THE AUTHOR'S WORDS

Find in the text the following words and then write synonyms of your own in their place: *besieging, provocative, tolerant*. Whose words express the ideas better, the author's or yours?

## A PROJECT

Have the lieutenant follow the girl when she says, "Going my way, soldier?" Write your own conclusion after that.

# THE GIFT OF THE MAGI

## O. HENRY

*To the sophisticated of their day, the Magi must have appeared foolish and addle-pated old men. What man in his senses would have undertaken their long journey to find an infant in a poor cave in Bethlehem! But we know that the Magi truly deserve their title of wise men, for at the end of their hard road they were rewarded with the sight of the Infant Jesus, God become one of us. To some, Jim and Della in this story may appear foolish and absurdly wasteful of their treasures. O. Henry shows us that Jim and Della are truly the "Magi."*

One dollar and eighty-seven cents. That was all. And sixty cents of it was in pennies. Pennies saved one and two at a time by bulldozing the grocer and the vegetable man and the butcher until one's cheeks burned with silent imputation of parsimony [1] that such close dealing implied. Three times Della counted it. One dollar and eighty-seven cents. And the next day would be Christmas.

There was clearly nothing to do but flop down on the shabby little couch and howl. So Della did it. Which instigates the moral reflection that life is made up of sobs, sniffles, and smiles, with sniffles predominating.

While the mistress of the home is gradually subsiding from the first stage to the second, take a look at the home. A furnished flat at $8 per week. It did not exactly beggar description, but it certainly had that word on the lookout for the mendicancy [2] squad.

In the vestibule below was a letter box into which no letter would go, and an electric button from which no mortal finger could coax a ring. Also appertaining thereunto was a card bearing the name "Mr. James Dillingham Young."

The "Dillingham" had been flung to the breeze during a former period of prosperity when its possessor was being paid $30 a week. Now, when the income was shrunk to $20, the letters of "Dillingham" looked blurred, as though they were thinking seriously of contracting to a modest and unassuming D. But whenever Mr. James Dillingham Young came home and reached his flat above, he was called "Jim" and greatly hugged by Mrs. James Dillingham Young, already introduced to you as Della. Which is all very good.

Della finished her cry and attended to her cheeks with the powder rag. She stood by the window and looked out dully at a gray cat walking a gray fence in a gray back yard. Tomorrow would be Christmas Day, and she had only $1.87 with which to buy Jim a present. She had been saving every penny she could for months, with this result. Twenty dollars a week doesn't go far. Expenses had been greater than she had calculated. They always are. Only $1.87 to buy a present for Jim. Her Jim. Many a happy hour she had spent planning something nice for him. Something fine and rare and sterling—something just a little bit near to being worthy of the honor of being owned by Jim.

There was a pier-glass [3] between the windows of the room. Perhaps you have seen a pier-glass in an $8 flat. A very thin and very agile person may, by observing his reflection in a rapid sequence of longitudinal strips, obtain a fairly accurate conception of his looks. Della, being slender, had mastered the art.

Suddenly she whirled from the window and stood before the glass. Her eyes were shining brilliantly, but her face had lost its color within twenty seconds. Rapidly she pulled down her hair and let it fall to its full length.

Now, there were two possessions of the James Dillingham Youngs in which they both took a mighty pride. One was Jim's gold watch that had been his father's and his grandfather's. The other was Della's hair. Had the Queen of Sheba lived in the flat across the airshaft, Della would have let her hair hang out the window some day to dry just to

---

[1] PARSIMONY—Closeness, stinginess.

[2] MENDICANCY—(měn′dĭ·kăn·sĭ) The state of being a beggar.

"The Gift of the Magi" from *The Four Million* by O. Henry, copyright, 1906, by Doubleday & Company, Inc.

[3] PIER-GLASS—An ornamental mirror, usually narrow.

depreciate her majesty's jewels and gifts. Had King Solomon been the janitor, with all his treasures piled up in the basement, Jim would have pulled out his watch every time he passed, just to see him pluck at his beard from envy.

So now Della's beautiful hair fell about her, rippling and shining like a cascade of brown waters. It reached below her knee and made itself almost a garment for her. And then she did it up again nervously and quickly. Once she faltered for a minute and stood still while a tear or two splashed on the worn red carpet.

On went her old brown jacket; on went her old brown hat. With a whirl of skirts and with the brilliant sparkle still in her eyes she fluttered out the door and down the stairs to the street.

Where she stopped the sign read: "Mme. Sofronie. Hair Goods of All Kinds." One flight up Della ran, and collected herself, panting. Madame, large, too white, chilly, hardly looked the "Sofronie."

"Will you buy my hair?" asked Della.

"I buy hair," said Madame. "Take yer hat off and let's have a sight at the looks of it."

Down rippled the brown cascade.

"Twenty dollars," said madame, lifting the mass with a practiced hand.

"Give it to me quick," said Della.

Oh, and the next two hours tripped by on rosy wings. Forget the hashed metaphor.[4] She was ransacking the stores for Jim's present.

She found it at last. It surely had been made for Jim and no one else. There was no other like it in any of the stores, and she had turned all of them inside out. It was a platinum fob chain, simple and chaste in design, properly proclaiming its value by substance alone and not by meretricious [5] ornamentation —as all good things should do. It was even worthy of The Watch. As soon as she saw it she knew that it must be Jim's. It was like him. Quietness and value—the description applied to both. Twenty-one dollars they took from her for it, and she hurried home with the 87 cents. With that chain on his watch Jim might be properly anxious about the time in any company. Grand as the watch was, he sometimes looked at it on the sly on account of the old leather strap that he used in place of a chain.

When Della reached home her intoxication gave way a little to prudence and reason. She got out her curling irons and lighted the gas and went to work repairing the ravages made by generosity added to love. Which is always a tremendous task, dear friends—a mammoth task.

Within forty minutes her head was covered with tiny, close-lying curls that made her look wonderfully like a truant schoolboy. She looked at her reflection in the mirror long, carefully, and critically.

"If Jim doesn't kill me," she said to herself, "before he takes a second look at me, he'll say I look like a Coney Island chorus girl. But what could I do—oh! what could I do with a dollar and eighty-seven cents?"

At seven o'clock the coffee was made and the frying pan was on the back of the stove hot and ready to cook the chops.

Jim was never late. Della doubled the fob chain in her hand and sat on the corner of the table near the door that he always entered. Then she heard his step

---

[4] HASHED METAPHOR—The mixed figure of speech in the preceding sentence.

[5] MERETRICIOUS (měr′ê·trĭsh′ŭs)—Tawdry, showy; gaudily and deceitfully ornamental.

on the stair, way down on the first flight, and she turned white for just a moment. She had a habit of saying little silent prayers about the simplest everyday things, and now she whispered: "Please, God, make him think I am still pretty."

The door opened and Jim stepped in and closed it. He looked thin and very serious. Poor fellow, he was only twenty-two—and to be burdened with a family! He needed a new overcoat and he was without gloves.

Jim stopped inside the door, as immovable as a setter at the scent of quail. His eyes were fixed upon Della, and there was an expression in them that she could not read, and it terrified her. It was not anger, nor surprise, nor disapproval, nor horror, nor any of the sentiments that she had been prepared for. He simply stared at her fixedly with that peculiar expression on his face.

Della wriggled off the table and went for him.

"Jim, darling," she cried, "don't look at me that way. I had my hair cut off and sold it because I couldn't have lived through Christmas without giving you a present. It'll grow out again—you won't mind, will you? I just had to do it. My hair grows awfully fast. Say 'Merry Christmas!' Jim, and let's be happy. You don't know what a nice—what a beautiful, nice gift I've got for you."

"You've cut off your hair?" asked Jim, laboriously, as if he had not arrived at that patent fact yet even after the hardest mental labor.

"Cut it off and sold it," said Della. "Don't you like me just as well, anyhow? I'm me without my hair, ain't I?"

Jim looked about the room curiously.

"You say your hair is gone?" he said, with an air almost of idiocy.

"You needn't look for it," said Della. "It's sold, I tell you—sold and gone, too. It's Christmas Eve, boy. Be good to me, for it went for you. Maybe the

18

hairs of my head were numbered," she went on with a sudden seriousness, "but nobody could ever count my love for you. Shall I put the chops on, Jim?"

Out of his trance Jim seemed quickly to wake. He enfolded his Della. For ten seconds let us regard with discreet scrutiny some inconsequential object in the other direction. Eight dollars a week or a million a year—what is the difference? A mathematician or a wit would give you the wrong answer. The Magi brought valuable gifts, but that was not among them. This dark assertion will be illuminated later on.

Jim drew a package from his overcoat pocket and threw it upon the table.

"Don't make any mistake, Della," he said, "about me. I don't think there's anything in the way of a haircut or a shave or a shampoo that could make me like my girl any less. But if you'll unwrap that package you may see why you had me going a while at first."

White fingers and nimble tore at the string and paper. And then an ecstatic scream of joy; and then, alas! a quick feminine change to hysterical tears and wails, necessitating the immediate employment of all the comforting powers of the lord of the flat.

For there lay The Combs—the set of combs, side and back, that Della had worshiped for long in a Broadway window. Beautiful combs, pure tortoise shell, with jeweled rims—just the shade to wear in the beautiful vanished hair. They were expensive combs, she knew, and her heart had simply craved and yearned over them without the least hope of possession. And now they were hers, but the tresses that should have adorned the coveted adornments were gone.

But she hugged them to her bosom, and at length she was able to look up

with dim eyes and a smile and say: "My hair grows so fast, Jim!"

And then Della leaped up like a little singed cat and cried, "Oh, oh!"

Jim had not yet seen his beautiful present. She held it out to him eagerly upon her open palm. The dull precious metal seemed to flash with a reflection of her bright and ardent spirit.

"Isn't it a dandy, Jim? I hunted all over town to find it. You'll have to look at the time a hundred times a day now. Give me your watch. I want to see how it looks on it."

Instead of obeying, Jim tumbled down on the couch and put his hands under the back of his head and smiled.

"Della," said he, "let's put our Christmas presents away and keep 'em a while. They're too nice to use just at present. I sold the watch to get the money to buy your combs. And now suppose you put the chops on."

The Magi, as you know, were wise men—wonderfully wise men—who brought gifts to the Babe in the manger. They invented the art of giving Christmas presents. Being wise, their gifts were no doubt wise ones, possibly bearing the privilege of exchange in case of duplication. And here I have lamely related to you the uneventful chronicle of two foolish children in a flat who most unwisely sacrificed for each other the greatest treasures of their house. But in a last word to the wise of these days let it be said that of all who give gifts these two were the wisest. Of all who give and receive gifts, such as they are wisest. Everywhere they are wisest. They are the Magi.

FOR DISCUSSION

1. How did Della manage to scrape together one dollar and eighty-seven cents?

2. By what specific details does O. Henry bring out the hard conditions under which Jim and Della lived? Why does the author spend time describing Jim's name card?

3. Why was Della not satisfied with getting just any kind of present for Jim? What requirements did the present have to meet?

4. What does the author mean when he says that it is always a tremendous task to repair "the ravages made by generosity added to love"? Was Della's sacrifice of her hair an act of generosity added to love?

5. How did Della explain to Jim what she had done? Why did Jim act so strangely when he learned that Della's hair was gone? Do you think Jim appreciated the love behind Della's sacrifice?

6. In the closing paragraph O. Henry states that he has related "the uneventful chronicle of two foolish children in a flat who most unwisely sacrificed for each other the greatest treasures of their house. But in a last word to the wise of these days let it be said that of all who give gifts these two were the wisest. Of all who give and receive gifts, such as they are wisest. They are the Magi." Do you agree with the author in his estimate of Jim and Della? Explain.

7. Why are the virtues of generosity and self-sacrifice more important than money as a basis for a happy marriage?

## THE ART OF THE SHORT STORY

1. The first paragraph of the story emphasizes the meager amount of money in Della's possession. Why is this an effective opening for the story?

2. Who is telling the story? What details in a story give you the clue to the identity of the narrator?

3. O. Henry is noted for his surprise endings. Does he give you sufficient hints of the way in which the story is to turn out? Point out details which prepare you for the ending of the story.

## WORDS TO STUDY

Explain the meaning of the following words as they are used in the story: *instigates, depreciate, mammoth, discreet, inconsequential.*

## RELATED READING

One of O. Henry's best stories is "A Municipal Report" which he wrote to prove that material for a good short story can be found in any city. His collected works contain many stories that will hold your interest.

◇◇◇◇◇

# THE SCULPTOR'S FUNERAL

## WILLA CATHER

*Many people measure a man's success by the yardstick of money. This story will give you a clue to the qualities of a truly successful life.*

A group of the townspeople stood on the station siding of a little Kansas town, awaiting the coming of the night train,

"The Sculptor's Funeral" is reprinted from *Youth and the Bright Medusa* by Willa Cather, by permission of Alfred A. Knopf, Inc. Copyright 1904, 1932 by Willa Cather.

which was already twenty minutes overdue. The snow had fallen thick over everything; in the pale starlight the line of bluffs across the wide, white meadows south of the town made soft, smoke-colored curves against the clear sky.

The men on the siding stood first on one foot and then on the other, their hands thrust deep into their trousers pockets, their overcoats open, their shoulders screwed up with the cold; and they glanced from time to time toward the southeast, where the railroad track wound along the river shore. They conversed in low tones and moved about restlessly, seeming uncertain as to what was expected of them. There was but one of the company who looked as if he knew exactly why he was there, and he kept conspicuously apart; walking to the far end of the platform, returning to the station door, then pacing up the track again, his chin sunk in the high collar of his overcoat, his burly shoulders drooping forward, his gait heavy and dogged. Presently he was approached by a tall, spare, grizzled man clad in a faded Grand Army suit,[1] who shuffled out from the group and advanced with a certain deference, craning his neck forward until his back made the angle of a jack-knife three-quarters open.

"I reckon she's a-goin' to be pretty late again tonight, Jim," he remarked in a squeaky falsetto. "S'pose it's the snow?"

"I don't know," responded the other man with a shade of annoyance, speaking from out an astonishing cataract of red beard that grew fiercely and thickly in all directions.

The spare man shifted the quill toothpick he was chewing to the other side of his mouth. "It ain't likely that anybody from the East will come with the corpse, I s'pose," he went on reflectively.

"I don't know," responded the other, more curtly than before.

[1] GRAND ARMY SUIT—The uniform of the G.A.R. (Grand Army of the Republic), an organization of men who served in the Union army during the Civil War.

"It's too bad he didn't belong to some lodge or other. I like an order funeral myself. They seem more appropriate for people of some reputation," the spare man continued, with an ingratiating concession in his shrill voice, as he carefully placed his toothpick in his vest pocket. He always carried the flag at the G.A.R. funerals in the town.

The heavy man turned on his heel, without replying, and walked up the siding. The spare man rejoined the uneasy group.

"Jim's ez full ez a tick, ez ushel," he commented, commiseratingly.

Just then a distant whistle sounded, and there was a shuffling of feet on the platform. A number of lanky boys, of all ages, appeared as suddenly and slimily as eels wakened by the crack of thunder; some came from the waiting room, where they had been warming themselves by the red stove, or half asleep on the slat benches; others uncoiled themselves from baggage trucks or slid out of express wagons. Two clambered down from the driver's seat of a hearse that stood backed up against the siding. They straightened their stooping shoulders and lifted their heads, and a flash of momentary animation kindled their dull eyes at that cold, vibrant scream, the world-wide call for men. It stirred them like the note of a trumpet; just as it had often stirred the man who was coming home tonight, in his boyhood.

The night express shot, red as a rocket, from out the eastward marsh lands and wound along the river shore under the long lines of shivering poplars that sentineled the meadows, the escaping steam hanging in gray masses against the pale sky and blotting out the Milky Way. In a moment the red glare from the headlight streamed up the snow-covered track before the siding and glittered on the wet, black rails. The burly man with the dishevelled red beard walked swiftly up the platform toward the approaching train, uncovering his head as he went. The group of men behind hesitated, glanced questioningly at one another, and awkwardly followed his example. The train stopped, and the crowd shuffled up to the express car just as the door was thrown open, the man in the G.A.R. suit thrusting his head forward with curiosity. The express messenger appeared in the doorway, accompanied by a young man in a long ulster and traveling cap.

"Are Mr. Merrick's friends here?" inquired the young man.

The group on the platform swayed uneasily. Philip Phelps, the banker, responded with dignity: "We have come to take charge of the body. Mr. Merrick's father is very feeble and can't be about."

"Send the agent out here," growled the express messenger, "and tell the operator to lend a hand."

The coffin was got out of its rough-box and down on the snowy platform. The townspeople drew back enough to make room for it and then formed a close semicircle about it, looking curiously at the palm leaf which lay across the black cover. No one said anything. The baggage man stood by his truck, waiting to get at the trunks. The engine panted heavily, and the fireman dodged in and out among the wheels with his yellow torch and long oil can, snapping the spindle boxes. The young Bostonian, one of the dead sculptor's pupils who had come with the body, looked about him helplessly. He turned to the banker, the only one of that black, uneasy, stoop-shouldered group who seemed enough of an individual to be addressed.

"None of Mr. Merrick's brothers are here?" he asked, uncertainly.

The man with the red beard for the first time stepped up and joined the others. "No, they have not come yet; the family is scattered. The body will be taken directly to the house." He stooped and took hold of one of the handles of the coffin.

"Take the long hill road up, Thompson; it will be easier on the horses," called the liveryman as the undertaker snapped the door of the hearse and prepared to mount to the driver's seat.

Laird, the red-bearded lawyer, turned again to the stranger. "We didn't know whether there would be anyone with him or not," he explained. "It's a long walk, so you'd better go up in the hack." He pointed to a single battered conveyance, but the young man replied, stiffly: "Thank you, but I think I will go up with the hearse. If you don't object," turning to the undertaker, "I'll ride with you."

They clambered up over the wheels and drove off in the starlight up the long, white hill toward the town. The lamps in the still village were shining from under the low, snow-burdened roofs; and beyond on every side the plains reached out into emptiness, peaceful and wide as the soft sky itself, and wrapped in a tangible, white silence.

When the hearse backed up to a wooden sidewalk before a naked, weather-beaten frame house, the same composite, ill-defined group that had stood upon the station siding was huddled about the gate. The front yard was an icy swamp, and a couple of warped planks, extending from the sidewalk to the door, made a sort of rickety footbridge. The gate hung on one hinge, and was opened wide with difficulty. Steavens, the young stranger, noticed that something black was tied to the knob of the front door.

The grating sound made by the casket, as it was drawn from the hearse, was answered by a scream from the house; the front door was wrenched open, and a tall, corpulent woman rushed out bareheaded into the snow and flung herself upon the coffin, shrieking: "My boy, my boy! And this is how you've come home to me."

As Steavens turned away and closed his eyes with a shudder of unutterable repulsion, another woman, also tall, but flat and angular, dressed entirely in black, darted out of the house and caught Mrs. Merrick by the shoulders, crying, sharply: "Come, come, mother; you mustn't go on like this." Her tone changed to one of obsequious solemnity as she turned to the banker. "The parlor is ready, Mr. Phelps."

The bearers carried the coffin along the narrow boards, while the undertaker ran ahead with the coffin-rests. They bore it into a large, unheated room that smelled of dampness and disuse and furniture polish, and set it down under a hanging lamp ornamented with jingling glass prisms and before a "Rogers group"[2] of John Alden and Priscilla,[3] wreathed with smilax. Henry Steavens stared about him with the sickening conviction that there had been a mistake and that he had somehow arrived at the wrong destination. He looked at the clover-green Brussels, the fat plush upholstery, among the hand-painted china plaques and panels and vases, for some mark of identification—for something that might once conceivably have belonged to Harvey Merrick. It was not

[2] ROGERS GROUP—Small figures by the American sculptor, John Rogers.
[3] JOHN ALDEN AND PRISCILLA—Characters in Longfellow's poem, "The Courtship of Miles Standish."

until he recognized his friend in the crayon portrait of a little boy in kilts and curls, hanging above the piano, that he felt willing to let any of these people approach the coffin.

"Take the lid off, Mr. Thompson. Let me see my boy's face," wailed the elder woman between her sobs. This time Steavens looked fearfully, almost beseechingly into her face, red and swollen under its masses of strong, black, shiny hair. He flushed, dropping his eyes, and then, almost increduously, looked again. There was a kind of power about her face—a kind of brutal handsomeness, even; but it was scarred and furrowed by violence, and so colored and coarsened by fiercer passions that grief seemed never to have laid a gentle finger there. The long nose was distended and knobbed at the end, and there were deep lines on either side of it; her heavy, black brows almost met across her forehead, her teeth were large and square and set far apart—teeth that could tear. She filled the room; the men were obliterated, seemed tossed about like twigs in an angry water, and even Steavens felt himself being drawn into the whirlpool.

The daughter—the tall, rawboned woman in crepe, with a mourning comb in her hair which curiously lengthened her long face—sat stiffly upon the sofa, her hands, conspicuous for their large knuckles, folded in her lap, her mouth and eyes drawn down, solemnly awaiting the opening of the coffin. Near the door stood a mulatto woman, evidently a servant in the house, with a timid bearing and an emaciated face pitifully sad and gentle. She was weeping silently, the corner of her calico apron lifted to her eyes, occasionally suppressing a long, quivering sob. Steavens walked over and stood beside her.

Feeble steps were heard on the stairs, and an old man, tall and frail, odorous of pipe smoke, with shaggy, unkempt gray hair and a dingy beard, tobacco stained about the mouth, entered uncertainly. He went slowly up to the coffin and stood rolling a blue cotton handkerchief between his hands, seeming so pained and embarrassed by his wife's orgy of grief that he had no consciousness of anything else.

"There, there, Annie, dear, don't take on so," he quavered, timidly, putting out a shaking hand and awkwardly patting her elbow. She turned and sank upon his shoulder with such violence that he tottered a little. He did not even glance toward the coffin, but continued to look at her with a dull, frightened, appealing expression, as a spaniel looks at the whip. His sunken cheeks slowly reddened and burned with miserable shame.

When his wife rushed from the room, her daughter strode after her with set lips. The servant stole up to the coffin, bent over it for a moment, and then slipped away to the kitchen, leaving Steavens, the lawyer, and the father to themselves. The old man stood looking down at his dead son's face. The sculptor's splendid head seemed even more noble in its rigid stillness than in life. The dark hair had crept down upon the wide forehead; the face seemed strangely long, but in it there was not that repose we expect to find in the faces of the dead. The brows were so drawn that there were two deep lines above the beaked nose, and the chin was thrust forward defiantly. It was as though the strain of life had been so sharp and bitter that death could not at once relax the tension and smooth the countenance into perfect peace—as though he were still guarding something precious, which might even yet be wrested from him.

The old man's lips were working under his stained beard. He turned to the lawyer with timid deference: "Phelps and the rest are comin' back to set up with Harve, ain't they?" he asked. "Thank 'ee, Jim, thank 'ee." He brushed the hair back gently from his son's forehead. "He was a good boy, Jim; always a good boy. He was ez gentle ez a child and the kindest of 'em all—only we didn't none of us ever onderstand him." The tears trickled slowly down his beard and dropped upon the sculptor's coat.

"Martin! Martin! Oh, Martin! come here," his wife wailed from the top of the stairs. The old man started timorously: "Yes, Annie, I'm coming." He turned away, hesitated, stood for a moment in miserable indecision; then reached back and patted the dead man's hair softly, and stumbled from the room.

"Poor old man, I didn't think he had any tears left. Seems as if his eyes would have gone dry long ago. At his age nothing cuts very deep," remarked the lawyer.

Something in his tone made Steavens glance up. While the mother had been in the room, the young man had scarcely seen anyone else; but now, from the moment he first glanced into Jim Laird's florid face and bloodshot eyes, he knew that he had found what he had been heartsick at not finding before— the feeling, the understanding, that must exist in someone, even here.

The man was red as his beard, with features swollen and blurred by dissipation, and a hot, blazing blue eye. His face was strained—that of a man who is controlling himself with difficulty—and he kept plucking at his beard with a sort of fierce resentment. Steavens, sitting by the window, watched him turn down the glaring lamp, still its jangling pendants with an angry gesture, and then stand with his hands locked behind him, staring down into the master's face. He could not help wondering what link there had been between the porcelain vessel and so sooty a lump of potter's clay.

From the kitchen an uproar was sounding; when the dining room door opened, the import of it was clear. The mother was abusing the maid for having forgotten to make the dressing for the chicken salad which had been prepared for the watchers. Steavens had never heard anything in the least like it; it was injured, emotional, dramatic abuse, unique and masterly in its excruciating cruelty, as violent and unrestrained as had been her grief of twenty minutes before. With a shudder of disgust the lawyer went into the dining room and closed the door into the kitchen.

"Poor Roxy's getting it now," he remarked when he came back. "The Merricks took her out of the poorhouse years ago; and if her loyalty would let her, I guess the poor old thing could tell tales that would curdle your blood. She's the mulatto woman who was standing in here a while ago, with her apron to her eyes. The old woman is a fury; there never was anybody like her. She made Harvey's life a hell for him when he lived at home; he was so sick ashamed of it. I never could see how he kept himself sweet."

"He was wonderful," said Steavens, slowly, "wonderful; but until tonight I have never known how wonderful."

"That is the eternal wonder of it, anyway; that it can come even from such a dung heap as this," the lawyer cried, with a sweeping gesture which seemed to indicate much more than the four walls within which they stood.

"I think I'll see whether I can get a little air. The room is so close I am beginning to feel rather faint," murmured Steavens, struggling with one of the windows. The sash was stuck, however, and would not yield, so he sat down dejectedly and began pulling at his collar. The lawyer came over, loosened the sash with one blow of his red fist and sent the window up a few inches. Steavens thanked him, but the nausea which had been gradually climbing into his throat for the last half hour left him with but one desire—a desperate feeling that he must get away from this place with what was left of Harvey Merrick. Oh, he comprehended well enough now the quiet bitterness of the smile that he had seen so often on his master's lips!

Once when Merrick returned from a visit home, he brought with him a singularly feeling and suggestive bas-relief [4] of a thin, faded old woman, sitting and sewing something pinned to her knee; while a full-lipped, full-blooded little urchin, his trousers held up by a single gallows, [5] stood beside her, impatiently twitching her gown to call her attention to a butterfly he had caught. Steavens, impressed by the tender and delicate modeling of the thin, tired face, had asked him if it were his mother. He remembered the full flush that had burned up in the sculptor's face.

The lawyer was sitting in a rocking chair beside the coffin, his head thrown back and his eyes closed. Steavens looked at him earnestly, puzzled at the line of the chin, and wondering why a man should conceal a feature of such

[4] BAS-RELIEF—Sculpture in which the figure stands out very slightly from the background.
[5] GALLOWS—Suspenders for the trousers.

distinction under that disfiguring shock of beard. Suddenly, as though he felt the young sculptor's keen glance, Jim Laird opened his eyes.

"Was he always a good deal of an oyster?" he asked, abruptly. "He was terribly shy as a boy."

"Yes, he was an oyster, since you put it so," rejoined Steavens. "Although he could be very fond of people, he always gave one the impression of being detached. He disliked violent emotion; he was reflective, and rather distrustful of himself—except, of course, as regarded his work. He was sure enough there. He distrusted men pretty thoroughly, and women even more, yet somehow, without believing ill of them. He was determined, indeed, to believe the best; but he seemed afraid to investigate."

"A burnt dog dreads the fire," said the lawyer, grimly, and closed his eyes.

Steavens went on and on reconstructing that whole miserable boyhood. All this raw, biting ugliness had been the portion of the man whose mind was to become an exhaustless gallery of beautiful impressions—so sensitive that the mere shadow of a poplar leaf flickering against a sunny wall would be etched and held there for ever. Surely, if ever a man had the magic word in his finger tips, it was Merrick. Whatever he touched, he revealed its holiest secret; liberated it from enchantment and restored it to its pristine loveliness. Upon whatever he had come in contact with, he had left a beautiful record of the experience—a sort of ethereal signature; a scent, a sound, a color that was his own.

Steavens understood now the real tragedy of his master's life; neither love nor wine, as many had conjectured, but a blow which had fallen earlier and cut deeper than anything else could have done—a shame not his, and yet so un-escapably his, to hide in his heart from his very boyhood. And without—the frontier warfare; the yearning of a boy, cast ashore upon a desert of newness and ugliness and sordidness, for all that is chastened and old, and noble with tradi-tions.

At eleven o'clock the tall, flat woman in black announced that the watchers were arriving, and asked them to "step into the dining room." As Steavens rose, the lawyer said, dryly: "You go on —it'll be a good experience for you. I'm not equal to that crowd tonight; I've had twenty years of them."

As Steavens closed the door after him he glanced back at the lawyer, sitting by the coffin in the dim light, with his chin resting on his hand.

The same misty group that had stood before the door of the express car shuffled into the dining room. In the light of the kerosene lamp they sepa-rated and became individuals. The minister, a pale, feeble-looking man with white hair and blond chin whiskers, took his seat beside a small side table and placed his Bible upon it. The Grand Army man sat down behind the stove and tilted his chair back comfortably against the wall, fishing his quill tooth-pick from his waistcoat pocket. The two bankers, Phelps and Elder, sat off in a corner behind the dinner table, where they could finish their discussion of the new usury [6] law and its effect on chattel security loans.[7] The real-estate agent, an old man with a smiling, hypo-critical face, soon joined them. The coal-and-lumber dealer and the cattle-shipper sat on opposite sides of the hard-

[6] USURY (ū′zhŏō·rĭ)—Interest that exceeds the legal rate charged to a borrower for the use of money.

[7] CHATTEL SECURITY LOANS—Loans made on personal property as security.

coal burner, their feet on the nickel-work. Steavens took a book from his pocket and began to read. The talk around him ranged through various topics of local interest while the house was quieting down. When it was clear that the members of the family were in bed, the Grand Army man hitched his shoulders and, untangling his long legs, caught his heels on the rounds of his chair.

"S'pose there'll be a will, Phelps?" he queried in his weak falsetto.

The banker laughed disagreeably, and began trimming his nails with a pearl-handled pocket knife.

"There'll scarcely be any need for one, will there?" he queried in his turn.

The restless Grand Army man shifted his position again, getting his knees still nearer his chin. "Why, the ole man says Harve's done right well lately," he chirped.

The other banker spoke up. "I reckon he means by that Harve ain't asked him to mortgage any more farms lately, so as he could go on with his edu-cation."

"Seems like my mind don't reach back to a time when Harve wasn't bein' edy-cated," tittered the Grand Army man.

There was a general chuckle. The minister took out his handkerchief and blew his nose sonorously. Banker Phelps closed his knife with a snap. "It's too bad the old man's sons didn't turn out better," he remarked, with re-flective authority. "They never hung together. He spent money enough on Harve to stock a dozen cattle farms, and he might as well have poured it into Sand Creek. If Harve had stayed at home and helped nurse what little they had, and gone into stock on the old man's bottom farm, they might all have been well fixed. But the old man had to trust everything to tenants and was cheated right and left."

"Harve never could have handled stock none," interposed the cattleman. "He hadn't it in him to be sharp. Do you remember when he bought Sander's mules for eight-year-olds, when everybody in town knew that Sander's father-in-law give 'em to his wife for a wedding present eighteen years before, an' they was full-grown mules then?"

The company laughed discreetly, and the Grand Army man rubbed his knees with a spasm of childish delight.

"Harve never was much account for anything practical, and he shore was never fond of work," began the coal-and-lumber dealer. "I mind the last time he was home; the day he left, when the old man was out to the barn helpin' his hand hitch up to take Harve to the train, and Cal Moots was patchin' up the fence; Harve he come out on the step and sings out, in his lady-like voice; 'Cal Moots! Cal Moots! please come cord my trunk.'"

"That's Harve for you," approved the Grand Army man. "I kin hear him howlin' yet, when he was a big feller in long pants and his mother used to whale him with a rawhide in the barn for lettin' the cows get foundered in the cornfield when he was drivin' 'em home from pasture. He killed a cow of mine that-a-way onct—a pure Jersey and the best milker I had, an' the old man had to put up for her. Harve, he was watchin' the sun set acrost the marshes when the anamile got away."

"Where the old man made his mistake was in sending the boy East to school," said Phelps, stroking his goatee and speaking in a deliberate, judicial tone. "There was where he got his head full of nonsense. What Harve needed, of all people, was a course in some

first-class Kansas City business college."

The letters were swimming before Steaven's eyes. Was it possible that these men did not understand, that the palm on the coffin meant nothing to them? The very name of their town would have remained forever buried in the postal guide had it not been now and again mentioned in the world in connection with Harvey Merrick's. He remembered what his master had said to him on the day of his death, after the congestion of both lungs had shut off any probability of recovery, and the sculptor had asked his pupil to send his body home. "It's not a pleasant place to be lying while the world is moving and doing and bettering," he had said with a feeble smile, "but it rather seems as though we ought to go back to the place we came from, in the end. The townspeople will come in for a look at me; and after they have had their say, I shan't have much to fear from the judgment of God!"

The cattleman took up the comment. "Forty's young for a Merrick to cash in; they usually hang on pretty well. Probably he helped it along with whisky."

"His mother's people were not long lived, and Harvey never had a robust constitution," said the minister, mildly. He would have liked to say more. He had been the boy's Sunday-school teacher and had been fond of him; but he felt that he was not in a position to speak. His own sons had turned out badly, and it was not a year since one of them had made his last trip home in the express car, shot in a gambling-house in the Black Hills.

"Nevertheless, there is no disputin' that Harve frequently looked upon the wine when it was red, also variegated, and it shore made an oncommon fool of him," moralized the cattleman.

Just then the door leading into the parlor rattled loudly and everyone started involuntarily, looking relieved when only Jim Laird came out. The Grand Army man ducked his head when he saw the spark in his blue, bloodshot eye. They were all afraid of Jim; he was a drunkard, but he could twist the law to suit his client's needs as no other man in all western Kansas could do, and there were many who tried. The lawyer closed the door behind him, leaned back against it, and folded his arms, cocking his head a little to one side. When he assumed this attitude in the courtroom, ears were always pricked up, as it usually foretold a flood of withering sarcasm.

"I've been with you gentlemen before," he began in a dry, even tone, "when you've sat by the coffins of boys born and raised in this town; and, if I remember rightly, you were never any too well satisfied when you checked them up. What's the matter, anyhow? Why is it that reputable young men are as scarce as millionaires in Sand City? It might almost seem to a stranger that there was, some way, something the matter with your progressive town. Why did Ruben Sayer, the brightest young lawyer you ever turned out, after he had come home from the university as straight as a die, take to drinking and forge a check and shoot himself? Why did Bill Merrit's son die of the shakes in a saloon in Omaha? Why was Mr. Thomas' son, here, shot in a gambling-house? Why did young Adams burn his mill to beat the insurance companies and go to the pen?"

The lawyer paused and unfolded his arms, laying one clenched fist quietly on the table. "I'll tell you why. Because you drummed nothing but money and knavery into their ears from the time they wore knickerbockers; because you

carped away at them as you've been carping here tonight, holding our friends Phelps and Elder up to them for their models, as our grandfathers held up George Washington and John Adams. But the boys were young, and raw at the business you put them to, and how could they match coppers with such artists as Phelps and Elder? You wanted them to be successful rascals; they were only unsuccessful ones—that's all the difference. There was only one boy ever raised in this borderland between ruffianism and civilization who didn't come to grief, and you hated Harvey Merrick more for winning out than you hated all the other boys who got under the wheels. Lord! Lord, how you did hate him! Phelps, here, is fond of saying that he could buy and sell us all out any time he's a mind to; but he knew Harve wouldn't have given a hoot for his bank and all his cattle farms put together; and a lack of appreciation, that way, goes hard with Phelps.

"Old Nimrod thinks Harve drank too much; and this from such as Nimrod and me!

"Brother Elder says Harve was too free with the old man's money—fell short in filial consideration, maybe. Well, we can all remember the very tone in which brother Elder swore his own father was a liar, in the county court; and we all know that the old man came out of that partnership with his son as bare as a sheared lamb. But maybe I'm getting personal, and I'd better be driving ahead at what I want to say."

The lawyer paused a moment, squared his heavy shoulders, and went on: "Harvey Merrick and I went to school together, back East. We were dead in earnest, and we wanted you all to be proud of us some day. We meant to be

great men. Even I, and I haven't lost my sense of humor, gentlemen, I meant to be a great man. I came back here to practice, and I found you didn't in the least want me to be a great man. You wanted me to be a shrewd lawyer—oh yes! Our veteran here wanted me to get him an increase of pension, because he had dyspepsia; Phelps wanted a new county survey that would put the widow Wilson's little bottom farm inside his south line; Elder wanted to lend money at five per cent a month, and get it collected; and Stark here wanted to wheedle old women up in Vermont into investing their annuities in real-estate mortgages that are not worth the paper they are written on. Oh, you needed me hard enough, and you'll go on needing me!

"Well, I came back here and became the shyster [8] you wanted me to be. You pretend to have some sort of respect for me; and yet you'll stand up and throw mud at Harvey Merrick, whose soul you couldn't dirty and whose hands you couldn't tie. Oh, you're a discriminat-

[8] SHYSTER—A lawyer who uses underhand or tricky methods.

ing lot of Christians! There have been times when the sight of Harvey's name in some Eastern paper has made me hang my head like a whipped dog; and, again, times when I liked to think of him off there in the world, away from all this hog-wallow, climbing the big, clean up-grade he'd set for himself.

"And we? Now that we've fought and lied and sweated and stolen, and hated as only the disappointed strugglers in a bitter, dead little Western town know how to do, what have we got to show for it? Harvey Merrick wouldn't have given one sunset over your marshes for all you've got put together, and you know it. It's not for me to say why, in the inscrutable wisdom of God, a genius should ever have been called from this place of hatred and bitter waters; but I want this Boston man to know that the drivel he's been hearing here tonight is the only tribute any truly great man could have from such a lot of sick, side-tracked, burnt-dog, land-poor sharks as the here-present financiers of Sand City —upon which town may God have mercy!"

The lawyer thrust out his hand to Steavens as he passed him, caught up his overcoat in the hall, and had left the house before the Grand Army man had had time to lift his ducked head and crane his long neck about at his fellows.

Next day Jim Laird was drunk and unable to attend the funeral services. Steavens called twice at his office, but was compelled to start East without seeing him. He had a presentiment that he would hear from him again, and left his address on the lawyer's table; but if Laird found it, he never acknowledged it. The thing in him that Harvey Merrick had loved must have gone underground with Harvey Merrick's coffin; for it never spoke again, and Jim got the oold he died of driving across the Colorado mountains to defend one of Phelps's sons who had got into trouble out there by cutting government timber.

◇◇◇◇◇◇◇◇◇◇◇◇◇◇◇◇◇◇◇◇◇◇◇◇◇◇◇◇

## FOR DISCUSSION

1. What details in the opening paragraphs foreshadow the differences of opinion about the life and character of Harvey Merrick which are revealed more fully as the story develops? Contrast the behavior of Jim Laird and the Grand Army man as they wait for the approaching train.

2. What is the significance of the palm leaf?

3. Why did Steavens turn away and close his eyes "with a shudder of unutterable repulsion"?

4. Why did Steavens feel that there had been a mistake and that he had arrived at the wrong destination?

5. Point out the details by which the author brings out the differences in character between Mr. and Mrs. Merrick.

6. What makes Steavens say that "until tonight I have never known how wonderful"?

7. Explain the statement: "He could not help wondering what link there had been between the porcelain vessel and so sooty a lump of potter's clay."

8. Give reasons why Harvey Merrick was an "oyster." What does Jim Laird mean when he says that "a burnt dog dreads the fire"? How does this remark apply to Harvey Merrick?

9. What was the real tragedy of Harvey Merrick's life?

10. One way of knowing a person is to find out what others think of him. However, in discussing others, people often tell us more about themselves than about the person they are describing. Is this true of some of the characters in the story? Do the watchers at the funeral understand the true character of the sculptor and the significance of his life? Point out how their comments on Harvey betray their own meanness of spirit.

11. Why does Jim Laird denounce the ideals and practices of his fellow townsmen? Would his criticisms apply to your own community? What ideals are held up to American youth today?

12. How do you explain Jim's actions after Harvey's funeral? Point out the irony in the manner of his death. Do you think that the author in this story wished merely to entertain or did she wish to bring home an important truth? Give reasons for your answer.

## STUDYING THE SHORT STORY

1. How does the author manage to cover so long a period of time in the life of the sculptor within the limits of the short story?

2. Point out the details by which the author reveals the character of the people in the story.

3. Write a short summary of the plot of the story.

## WORDS TO KNOW

1. *Obsequious* is derived from the Latin word, *obsequor*, which means *to follow*. How would you describe an *obsequious* person?

2. *Unkempt* has for its basic meaning *not combed*. What other meanings does the word have?

3. *Florid* comes from a Latin word meaning *flower*. What color is a *florid* face? What is *florid* speech?

## RELATED READING

Willa Cather's two volumes of short stories, *Youth and the Bright Medusa* and *Obscure Destinies*, contain some of the best short stories written in our time. To deepen your appreciation of Miss Cather's art read "Paul's Case," "A Wagner Matinee," and "Neighbor Rosicky."

# THE BISHOP'S BEGGAR

### STEPHEN VINCENT BENÉT

*The Bishop disliked being the patron of a beggar. In face of the situation, however, he felt helpless. For many years he endured the sting to his pride. When the beggar lay dying, though, the bishop heard a marvelous thing! And wept.*

It seems that in the old days there was a bishop of Remo, and he was a heedless and proud young man, though of good intentions. Now that was possible in those days, when the fire and light of the new learning had spread through Italy and men drank, as if intoxicated, at a new spring. There were bishops who cared less for the Word of God than for their own splendor, and cardinals who were rather men of the world—and of no good world—than sons of the Church. I do not say that our bishop was as idle and self-seeking as some of these; I do say that he was a child of his time. He would have liked to be a lord, but his eldest brother was the lord; he would have liked to be a soldier, but his second brother was the soldier. So he went into the Church, for there, too, a man who bore a great name could rise. He was clever; he was ambitious; he had great connections. Now and then, to be sure, he asked a disquieting question; but the Baldis had always been original. The path that is rugged for many was made smooth for him from the first.

When he was made bishop of Remo at an early age, the fact did not surprise him. Since he was to be neither lord nor soldier, he found that pleasant enough.

All went well for him at first. They were glad to have a young and handsome bishop at Remo, for the bishop before him had been old and ill-favored. It was a pleasure to no one to kiss his ring, and he frightened the children with his peering eyes. With the coming of our bishop, all this was changed. There was a great to-do and refurbishing of the bishop's palace; the smells of good cooking drifted again from the bishop's kitchens; when the bishop drove through the city, men threw their caps in the air. There were fine new frescoes [1] in the cathedral, a new way of chanting in the choir. As for sin and suffering—well they are always with us. The people of Remo liked to sin pleasantly and be reminded of it as little as possible.

Nevertheless, at times a grayness would come over our bishop's spirit. He could not understand why it came. His life was both full and busy. He was a friend to art, a host to the gay and the

"The Bishop's Beggar" by Stephen Vincent Benét reprinted from *The Saturday Evening Post*, copyright, 1942, by Curtis Publishing Company. Reprinted by permission of Brandt & Brandt.

[1] FRESCOES—Paintings made on freshly spread plaster before it dries.

learned, a ruler of men. He did not meddle in things which did not concern him; he felt in his heart that there was no prize in the Church which might not be within his grasp. And yet at times there was a grayness within him. It was singular.

He could not show that grayness before the world; he could not show it to his secretary or the witty company that gathered at his table. He could wrestle with it in prayer; and so he did. But he found it no easy task. Had the Devil appeared before him with horns and a tail, he would have known what to do. But a grayness of spirit—a cool little voice in the mind which said to him now and then, "What do you in these robes at this place, Gianfrancesco Baldi?"—that was another matter.

He came to find by experience that motion in the open air helped him as much as anything. When the grayness oppressed him too severely, he would summon his coach and drive about the countryside. So one day as he drove through a small country village in the hills beyond Remo, it happened. It was nobody's fault, the bishop's least of all. He saw to it that he had a skillful coachman and good horses as he saw to all such matters. But when a tall, gangling boy darts across the street right under the nose of the horses, the most skillful coachman cannot always save him. There was a cry and a scream and a soft jar. Then where the coach had passed, the boy lay writhing in the street.

The bishop always showed at his best in emergency. When he got out of the coach, the angry shouts of the crowd died away to a respectful murmur. He lifted the boy into the coach with his strong arms and drove back with him to Remo. On the way he talked to him soothingly, though the boy was in too

much pain to pay much attention to this graciousness. When they got to Remo, he had the boy carried to a servant's room in the palace and doctors summoned for him. Later on he gave instructions about cleaning the coach.

At dinner his secretary recounted the little incident, and all men praised the kindliness of the bishop. The bishop passed it off pleasantly, but at heart he felt a trifle irritated. He had not felt particularly drawn toward the boy; on the other hand, he could not have left him lying in the road.

By the next day, as such things do, the story had gone all over Remo; and there were unusual demonstrations of good will as the bishop passed to the cathedral. The bishop received them with dignity, but his irritation remained. He disliked ostentatious shows of virtue and distrusted the fickleness of crowds. Nevertheless, it was his duty to see the boy, and he did so.

Washed, combed, and rid of his vermin, the boy looked ordinary enough, though somewhat older than the bishop had thought him. His body was slight and emaciated, but he had a well-shaped head and large liquid eyes. These stared at the bishop with some intensity; indeed with such intensity that the bishop wondered at first if the boy might not be an idiot. But a little conversation proved him sound of mind, though rustic in speech.

His name was Luigi, and he was an orphan living as best he could. In the summer he tended goats; in the winter he lived with his uncle and aunt, the tavern keepers, who fed him and beat him. His age was about nineteen. He had made his Easter duty as a Christian. He would never walk again.

Such were the facts of the case, and the bishop thought them over clearheadedly. He wondered what to do with the boy.

"Luigi," he said, "would you like to go back to your village?"

"Oh, no," said the boy. "It is a very good village; but now that I can no longer herd goats, there is no place in it for me. Besides, one eats better in Remo—I have had white cheese twice already." And he smacked his lips. His voice was remarkably strong and cheerful, the bishop noticed with surprise.

"Very well," said the bishop patiently. "You need not go back if you do not choose. You are now in some sense a ward of the Church, and the wings of the Church are sheltering." He looked at the boy's legs, lying limp and motionless under the covers, and felt, though against his will, the natural distaste of the hale man for the maimed. "You might learn some useful trade," he said thoughtfully. "There are many trades where the hands do all—a cobbler's, a tailor's, a basket weaver's."

The boy shook his head joyfully. "Oh, no, your lordship," he said. "Trades take so long to learn, and I am very stupid. It would not be worth the expense; your lordship would be embarrassed."

"My lordship perhaps is the best judge of that," said the bishop a trifle grimly. He kept thinking of the boy's remark about white cheese; it must be a spare life indeed where white cheese was such a treat. "But we are reasonable," he said. "Come, what would you be?"

"A beggar!" said the boy, and his dark eyes shone with delight.

"A beggar?" said the bishop, astonished and somewhat revolted.

"Why, yes," said the boy as if it were the most natural thing in the world. "For ten years my father begged on the cathedral steps. That was before your

lordship's time, but he was an excellent beggar and a master of his craft. True, he was subject to continual persecutions and jealousies from the honorable corporation of the beggars of Remo, coming as he did from outside the city. It was that which caused the ruin of our fortunes; for in the end when he had begun to fail, they threw him down a well, where he caught a bad cold and died of it. But in his good days he could outbeg any two of them. If your lordship would care to have me demonstrate his celebrated fainting fit, when his eyeballs rolled backward in his head—"

"I can think of nothing I should like less," said the bishop, shocked and disgusted, for it seemed to him an unworthy thing that a sturdy young man, though a cripple, should think of nothing better than beggary. "Besides," he said, "these other beggars you speak of— if they persecuted your father, no doubt they would persecute you."

"Me?" said the boy and laughed. "Oh, once they understood, they would not dare touch me—not even Giuseppe the Hook. I would be your lordship's beggar—the bishop's beggar!" And a light of great peace and contentment spread over his countenance.

The bishop stared at him for a long time in silence. "That is what you wish?" he said, and his voice was dry.

"That is what I wish, your lordship," said the boy, nodding his head.

"So be it," said the bishop with a sigh, and left him. But when his coachman came to him the next morning for orders, it was all he could do to keep from reviling the man.

The bishop was not the sort of man who liked beggars. Indeed, were it not for custom and Christian charity, he would long since have cleared them from the steps of his cathedral. He could not very well do that; he knew what an impression such a move would make. Nevertheless, when he passed among them, as he must at times, he saw to it that his almoner [2] made a suitable distribution of small coins, but he himself did his best to see and smell them as little as possible. Their whines and their supplications, their simulated sores and their noisome [3] rags—these were a fret and a burden to him.

Now, it seemed he was to have a beggar of his own. He would have taken it as a suitable humiliation for pride, but he did not feel himself to be a proud man. Nor could he think of the accident as anything but an accident. Had he deliberately trodden the lad beneath the hoofs of his horses—but he had not. He was well liked, able, decisive, a rising son of the Church. Nevertheless, he was to have a beggar—every day he must see his beggar on the steps of the cathedral, a living reproach, a living lesson in idleness and heedlessness. It was a small thing to be sure, but it darkened his dinner and made him sore at heart.

Therefore, being the man he was, he put a mask upon his face. He meant to speak of the thing, so it should be known—at least that might ward off ridicule. He spoke of it to his secretary; the secretary agreed that it was a very seemingly and Christian idea of his lordship's, while the bishop wondered if the man laughed at him in his sleeve. He spoke of it to others; there were compliments, of course. Each time he spoke of it, it turned a small knife in his breast. But that did not keep him from speaking of it nor from seeing that every care was given Luigi.

Nevertheless, he dreaded the day when Luigi would take up his post on the steps of the cathedral. He dreaded and yearned for it, both. For then at last the thing would be done. After that like many things it would become a custom, and in time Luigi himself would fade into the mass of whining beggary that haunted the steps of the cathedral. But things were not to be quite that way.

He admired, while he detested, the thoroughness with which Luigi prepared himself for his profession. He heard the whine ring out from the servants' quarters—"ten scudi [4] for Luigi!"—he saw the little cart and the crutches Luigi had made for himself. Now and then he heard his own servants laugh at the beggar's stories. This was hard enough to bear. But at last the day of parting came.

To his disgust the bishop found the boy neither clean nor well clad, as he had been since his accident, but dirty and dressed in tatters. He opened his mouth to reprove the boy; then he shut it again, for it seemed pitifully true that a beggar must dress his part. Nevertheless, the bishop did not like it. He asked Luigi cooly how he meant to live.

"Oh, your lordship's secretary has found me a very suitable chamber," said Luigi eagerly. "It is on the ground floor of a rookery [5] by the river, and it has room for my crutches, my gear, and my cart. He will move me there tonight. Tomorrow I will be at my post on the steps of the cathedral." And he smiled

---

[2] ALMONER—A servant whose duty it is to distribute alms.

[3] NOISOME (noi′sŭm)—Offensive to the smell or other senses.

[4] SCUDI—Italian coins, silver or gold, valued at about 97 cents each, used from the seventeenth to the ninteenth centuries.

[5] ROOKERY—A dilapidated building with many rooms and occupants.

gratefully at the bishop. "That will be a great day," he said.

"So," said the bishop, who could not trust himself to say anything further.

"Yet before I go," said Luigi, "I must thank your lordship for his kindness and ask your lordship's blessing on my work. That is only suitable."

The bishop stiffened. "I may bless you, Luigi," he said, "but your work I cannot bless. I cannot give the blessing of the church to the work of a man who lives by beggary when he might live otherwise."

"Well, then I must go unblessed," said Luigi cheerfully. "After all, your lordship has already done so much for me! The bishop's beggar! How my uncle and aunt will stare!"

*Now of all the vainglorious, self-seeking, worthless, rascally sons of iniquity —and to think that I stand your sponsor,* said the bishop; but fortunately he did not say it aloud. Silently he extended his ring, and Luigi kissed it with such innocent reverence that the bishop was sorely moved to give him his blessing after all. But he summoned up his principles and departed in silence.

The bishop slept ill that night, tormented by dreams of Luigi. He dreamed that for his sins he must carry Luigi on his back all the way up the steps of the cathedral. And as he mounted each step, the weight upon his back became more crushing till at last he awoke, unrefreshed.

The next day he went to the cathedral in great state, though it was an ordinary Sunday. Yet he felt the state to be in some measure a protection. When he passed by the steps of the cathedral, the beggars set up their usual supplications. He sent his almoner among them; it was over quicker than he thought. He did not look for Luigi, and yet he felt Luigi's

eyes upon him as he stood there for a moment, splendid in robe and miter. Then the thing was finished.

In the cathedral that same day, he preached passionately against the sins of idleness and heedlessness. Seldom had he been so moving—he could feel that from his congregation. When Mass was over, he retired to his palace, exhausted. Yet it was pleasant for him to walk about the palace and know that Luigi was not there.

It was just after vespers when his secretary came to him and told him that a man called Giuseppe, self-styled provost [6] of the company of the beggars of Remo, requested an audience. The bishop sighed wearily and ordered the man brought before him. He was a squat fellow of great strength and an evil cast of countenance, for one side of his face had been so burned in a fire that it was as if he had two faces, one of them inhuman. Also, his left arm terminated in an iron hook.

"This is Giuseppe, the beggar, your lordship," said the secretary with repugnance.

"Giuseppe, called Double-Face, also called the Hook, provost of the honorable company of the beggars of Remo," said Giuseppe in a rusty voice and plumped on his knees.

The bishop raised him and asked his business.

"Well, your lordship, it's this new fellow, Luigi Lamelegs," said Giuseppe. "I've got nothing against him personal— I wouldn't hurt a fly myself in a personal way," and he grinned horribly—"but there he is in a good place on the steps, and your lordship's servants put him there. Well, now if he's your lordship's beggar, that's one thing—though, even

---

[6] PROVOST (prŏv′ŭst)—Superintendent; official head.

so, there's fees and vails [7] to be paid, for that's the custom. But if he isn't your lordship's beggar—and your lordship paid him no attention this morning—"

"Stop!" said the bishop with anger. "Do you mean to tell me that the very steps of the cathedral are bartered and sold among you? Why, this is simony [8] —this is the sin of simony!"

"Your lordship can call it hard words," said Giuseppe stolidly, "but that's been the way it's been done ever since there were beggars in Remo. I paid twenty crowns for my own place and fought old Marco too. But that's beside the point. Your lordship has a right to a beggar if your lordship wants one—we're all agreed on that. But the question is: Is this man your lordship's beggar or isn't he?"

"And supposing I said he was not my beggar?" said the bishop, trembling.

"Well, that's all we'd want to know," said Giuseppe. "And thank your lordship kindly. I had my own suspicions of the man from the first. But we've got him down by the river now—Carlo and Benito and old blind Marta; she's a tough one, old blind Marta—and once we're through with him, he'll trouble your lordship no more." And sketching a clumsy salute, the man turned to go.

"Stop!" said the bishop again. "Would you have the guilt of murder upon your conscience?"

"Oh, your lordship takes it too hard," said Giuseppe, shuffling his feet. "What's one beggar more or less? We're not rich folk or learned folk to bother a mind like your lordship's. We breed and we die, and there's an end. And even at the best it's no bed of roses on the steps of the cathedral."

[7] VAILS—Tips.
[8] SIMONY—Buying and selling sacred things, especially ecclesiastical preferment.

The bishop wished to say many things, but he could think of only one.

"I declare to you that this man is my beggar," he said. "I stretch my hand over him."

"Well, that's very nicely spoken of your lordship," said Giuseppe in a grumbling voice, "and I dare say we can make room for him. But if the man's to keep a whole skin, your lordship had best come with me—old Marta was talking of ear slitting when I left her."

So they found Luigi, bound but cheerful, in his first-floor chamber by the river, guarded by the persons Giuseppe had described—a hunchback, a dwarf, and a blind woman. The window which gave upon the river was open, and a large sack weighted with stones lay in one corner of the room. The bishop's arrival produced a certain consternation on the part of all but Luigi, who seemed to take it as a matter of course. After the boy had been unbound, the bishop addressed the beggars with some vivacity, declared that Luigi was his beggar, and gave him a piece of silver before them all in token. This seemed to satisfy the company, who then crept away in silence.

"And yet have I done right? Have I done right?" said the bishop, striding up and down the chamber. "I greatly fear I have condoned the sin of simony! I have spent Mother Church's substance among the unworthy! And yet, even so, your blood may be upon my head!" and he looked at Luigi doubtfully.

"Oh, your lordship need not take it so hard," said Luigi, rubbing his arms. "All is safe enough now. I arranged about the dues and vails with Giuseppe while your lordship was discussing her state of grace with Marta. He's an honest fellow enough, and his point is reasonable. One should not take a good place with-

out money to keep it up. Had your lordship given me alms with your own hand this morning, our little difficulty would never have arisen. That was my fault—I assumed that your lordship knew."

"Knew?" said the bishop. "What should I know of such things? And yet, God forgive me, I am a priest and I should have knowledge of evil."

"It is merely a difference in knowledge," said Luigi gently. "Now, your lordship, doubtless, has never been in a room quite like this before."

The bishop stared at the damp walls and the mean chamber. He smelled the smell that cannot be aired from a room, the smell of poverty itself. He had never doubted his own experience before—when he had been first made a priest, he had gone on certain works of charity. Now it seemed to him that those works must have been rather carefully selected.

"No," he said, "I have never been in a room just like this one."

"And yet there are many of us who live in such rooms—and not all beggars," said Luigi. He changed his tone. "That was a fine rousing sermon your lordship gave us on idleness and heedlessness this morning," he said. "Hey, it brought the scudi forth from the good folks' pockets! An admirable sermon!"

"I am grateful for your encomiums,"[9] said the bishop bitterly. He glanced around the room again. "Is there nought else I can do?" he said unwillingly.

"No, thank your lordship," said Luigi, and his eyes were smiling. "I have a woman to cook my dinner—it is true she is a thief, but she will not steal from a cripple—and soon with your lordship's patronage I shall be able to afford a

9 ENCOMIUMS   (ĕn·kō′mĭ·ŭmz)—Words or speeches of high praise.

charcoal brazier.[10] Moreover, my friends seem to have left me a sack. So after dinner I shall say my prayers and go to bed to refresh myself for tomorrow's labor."

*I shall say mine too, for I need them,* said the bishop, though he did not say it to Luigi.

So that was how it began. Soon enough the bishop's beggar was a familiar figure on the steps of the cathedral—one of the admitted curiosities of the town. He was well liked in his trade, for he always had a merry word or a sharp one for his clients—and it passed around until "Luigi says" became a by-word. The bishop became used to him as one becomes used to a touch of rheumatism. Other men had their difficulties; he had his beggar. Now and then it seemed odd to the bishop that he had ever thought of the beggars on the steps as a vague and indistinguishable heap of misery and rags. He knew them all by now—blind Marta and Carlo, the dwarf, Giuseppe Double-Face and Benito, the hunchback. He knew their ways and their thoughts. He knew the hovels where they lived and the bread they ate. For every week or so he would slip from his palace to visit Luigi's chamber.

It was necessary for him to do so, for to him Luigi represented the gravest problem of the soul that he had yet encountered. Was the man even a Christian? The bishop was not sure. He professed religion; he followed the rites of the Church. Yet sometimes when he confessed him, the bishop was appalled. Every sin that could ravage the human heart was there—if not in act then in desire—and all told so gaily! Sometimes the bishop angrily would tax him with

willful exaggeration, and Luigi with a smile would admit the charge and ask for still another penance. This left the bishop confused.

Yet through the years there grew up between the two men a singular bond. The bishop may have been heedless; he was not stupid. Very soon he began to realize that there was another Remo than the city he had come to first—a city not of lords and scholars and tradesmen and pious ladies but a city of the poor and the ignorant, the maimed and the oppressed. For, as Luigi said, when one lay all day on the steps of the cathedral, one heard stories; and anyone will talk to a beggar. Some of the stories struck the bishop to the heart. He could hardly believe them at first; yet when he investigated them, they were true. When he was convinced they were true, he set himself stubbornly to remedy them. He was not always successful—pleasant sinners like the Church to keep its own place. Now and then he discussed his efforts with Luigi, who listened, it seemed to the bishop, with an air of perfect cynicism.[11] His attitude seemed to be that it was all very well for a man like the bishop to concern himself about these things, but he was the bishop's beggar; and if other folk starved and died, it was none of his concern. This irritated the bishop inordinately and made him more determined than ever.

Gradually he noticed the composition of his table changed. There were fewer courtiers and scholars; there were more priests from the country, smelling of poverty and chestnut bread. They came in their tattered cassocks with their big red wrists; at first they were strange and

[10] BRAZIER (brā′zhēr)—A pan for holding burning coals.

[11] CYNICISM—Disbelief. Cynics are persons who question the sincerity or unselfishness of the motives of others.

ill at ease at his table. But the bishop was able to talk to them. After all, were they not like the old parish priest that Luigi talked of so often? When the ceremony of his table disturbed them, he saw to it that there was less ceremony. Luigi mocked him for this and told him bluntly what his richer clients were saying. The bishop rebuked him for impertinence to his spiritual director and persisted.

It is strange how time flies when the heart is occupied. In no time at all it seemed to the bishop he was a middle-aged man with gray at his temples, and Luigi a man in his thirties. That seemed odd to the bishop; he did not know where the time had gone. He thought of it one morning with a sense of loss. He had meant to do many things—he was still ambitious. Now when night came, he was often too tired to think. The troubles of many people weighed upon his heart—the troubles of the peasants in the hills, who lived from hand to mouth; the troubles of Domenico, the shoemaker, who had too pretty a daughter; the troubles of Tessa, the flower seller, whose son was a thief. When he had first come to Remo, he had not had all these troubles. He picked up a letter on his desk—a letter that had lain there for days—and, having read it, sat staring.

The dreams of his youth came back to him, doubly hot, doubly dear. While he idled his life away in Remo, his brother and his friends had been busy. They had not forgotten him, after all. Cardinal Malaverni, the great sage statesman whose hand was ever upon the strings of policy, meant to pass by Remo on his way to Rome. The bishop knew the cardinal—once, long ago, he had been one of the cardinal's promising young men. There was a letter also

from the bishop's brother, the lord—a letter that hinted of grave and important matters. The bishop almost sobbed when he thought how long both letters had lain unanswered. He summoned his secretary and set himself about an unaccustomed bustle of preparation.

It often occurred to him sorrowfully within the next few days how foolish it was to leave one's letters unopened. The preparations went forward for the cardinal's visit; yet it seemed to him that they went forward ill, though he could not put his finger upon the cause. Somehow he had got out of the way of the world where such things go forward smoothly; he was more used to his country priests than to entertaining distinguished visitors. Nevertheless, he botched together a few Latin verses, saw to it that the hangings in the guest chambers were cleaned and mended, drove his choirmaster nearly frantic, and got in the way of his servants. He noticed that these were no longer afraid of him but treated him with tolerant patience, more like a friend than a master; and this irked him oddly. What irked him even more perhaps was Luigi's shameless undisguised self-interest in the whole affair.

"Ah, your lordship, we've waited a long time for this," he said, "but it's come at last. And everyone knows that a great man like Cardinal Malaverni doesn't come to a place like Remo for nothing. So all we have to do is to play our cards well; and then when we move on, as we doubtless shall—well, I for one, won't be sorry."

"Move on?" said the bishop, astonished.

The beggar yawned.

"But how else?" he said. "I have been the bishop's beggar. When your lordship is made a cardinal, I will be the cardinal's beggar. The post will entail new responsibilities, no doubt; but I have confidence in my abilities. Perhaps I shall even employ an assistant for my actual begging—after all, it is often drafty on the steps of the cathedral."

The bishop turned and left him without a word. Yet what Luigi had said caused trouble and disquiet in his heart, for he knew that Luigi often had news of things to come before even the count of Remo had an inkling of them.

At last the great day of the cardinal's visit came.

Like all such days, it passed as a dream passes, with heat and ceremony and worry about small things. The Latin verses of welcome were unexpectedly well read; on the other hand, the choristers were nervous and did not sing their best. Two gentlemen of the cardinal's suite had to be lodged over the stables, much to the bishop's distress, and the crayfish for dinner had been served without sauce.

The bishop hoped that all had gone well, but he did not know. As he sat at last alone with his old friend in his study that overlooked the garden, he felt at once wrought up and drowsy.

This should be the real pleasure of the day, to sit with his old friend in the cool of the evening and renew contact with the great world. But the bishop was used to country hours by now, and the feast had broken up late. He should be listening to the cardinal with the greatest attention, and yet those accursed crayfish kept coming into his mind.

"Well, Gianfrancesco," said the cardinal, sipping delicately at his wine, "you have given your old tutor a most charming welcome. Your wine, your people, your guests—it reminds me somehow of one of those fine Vergilian eclogues [12] we used to parse together. 'Tityre, tu patulae recubans—' " [13]

"The choir," said the bishop—"the choir usually is—"

"Why, they sang very well!" said the cardinal. "And what good, honest, plain-spoken priests you have in your charge!" He shook his head sadly. "I fear that we do not always get their like in Rome. And yet each man to his task."

"They have a hard charge in these hills," said the bishop wearily. "It was a great honor for them to see Your Eminence."

"Oh, honor!" said the cardinal. "To see an old man with the gout—yes, I have the gout these days, Gianfrancesco—I fear we both are not so young as we were." He leaned forward and regarded the bishop attentively. "You too have altered, my old friend," he said softly.

"Your Eminence means that I have rusticated," said the bishop a trifle bitterly. "Well, it is true."

"Oh, not rusticated," said the cardinal with a charming gesture. "Not at all. But there has been a change—a perceptible one—from the Gianfrancesco I knew." He took a walnut and began to crack it. "That Gianfrancesco was a charming and able young man," he said. "Yet I doubt if he would have made the count of his city do penance in his shirt for his sins before the doors of his cathedral."

"I can explain about that," said the bishop hurriedly. "The shirt was a silk one and the weather by no means inclement. Moreover, the count's new

[12] VERGILIAN ECLOGUES—Pastoral poems written by Vergil, a famous Roman poet in the time of Augustus.
[13] Tityre . . . recubans—The opening words of the first eclogue: "You, Tityre, lying 'neath the spreading beech's cover."

tax would have ruined my poor. It is true we have not always seen eye to eye since then; yet I think he respects me more than he did before."

"That is just what I said to your brother Piero," said the cardinal comfortably. "I said, 'you are wrong to be perturbed about this, Piero; it will have a good effect.' Yes, even as regards the beggar."

"My beggar?" said the bishop and sighed.

"Oh, you know how small things get about," said the cardinal. "Some small thing is seized upon; it even travels to Rome. The bishop's beggar—the beggars' bishop—the bishop who humbles his soul to protect the poor."

"But it was not like that at all," said the bishop. "I—"

The cardinal waved him aside. "Do not hide your good works beneath a bushel, Gianfrancesco," he said. "The Church herself has need of them. These are troubled times we live in. The French king may march any day. There is heresy and dissension abroad. You have no idea what difficult days may lie ahead." He watched the bishop intently. "Our Holy Father leans much upon my unworthy shoulder," he said, "and our Holy Father is beginning to age."

"That is sore news for us all," said the bishop.

"Sore indeed," said the cardinal. "And yet one must face realities. Should our Holy Father die, it will be necessary for those of us who truly love the Church to stand together—more especially in the college of cardinals." He paused and with a silver nutpick extracted the last meat from the walnut. "I believe that our Holy Father is disposed to reward your own labors with the see of Albano," he said.

"The see of Albano?" said the bishop as if in a dream; for, as all men knew, Albano was an old and famous diocese outside the walls of Rome, and he who was bishop of Albano wore a cardinal's hat.

"It might have a most excellent effect," said the cardinal. "I myself think it might. We have clever and able men who are sons of the Church. Indeed. And yet just at this moment with both the French and the German parties so active—well, there is perhaps need for another sort of man—at least as regards the people." He smiled delightfully. "You would be very close to me as cardinal-bishop of Albano—very close to us all," he said. "I should lean upon you, Gianfrancesco."

"There is nought that would please me more!" cried the bishop like a boy. He thought for a moment of the power and the glory of the great, crowded streets of Rome and the Church that humbles kings. "I would have to leave Remo?" he said.

"Well, yes, naturally it would mean your having to leave Remo," said the cardinal. "Your new duties would demand it."

"That would be hard," said the bishop. "I would have to leave Luigi and all my people." He thought of them suddenly—the lame, the halt, the oppressed.

"Your people perhaps," said the cardinal, "but certainly not Luigi. He should come with you by all means as a living example."

"Oh, no, no, that would never do," said the bishop. "Your Eminence does not understand. Luigi is difficult enough as a bishop's beggar. As a cardinal's beggar he would be overweening. You have no idea how overweening he would be."

The cardinal regarded him with a puzzled stare.

"Am I dreaming, Gianfrancesco?" he said. "Or are you declining the see of Albano and a cardinal's hat for no more reason than that you are attached to a beggar?"

"Oh, no, no, no!" cried the bishop in an agony. "I am not in the least attached to him—he is my cross and my thorn. But you see, it would be so bad for him if I were to be made a cardinal. I tremble to think what would happen to his soul. And then there are all his companions—Giuseppe the Hook is dead, but there is still blind Marta, and Benito, the hunchback, and the new ones. No, I must stay in Remo."

The cardinal smiled—a smile of exasperation. "I think you have forgotten something, Gianfrancesco," he said. "I think you have forgotten that obedience is the first law of the Church."

"I am five times obedient," said the bishop. "Let our Holy Father do with me as he wills. Let him send me as a missionary to savages; let him strip me of my bishopric and set me to work in the hills. I shall be content. But while I have been given Remo, I have work to do in Remo. I did not expect it to be so when I first came here," he said in a low voice, "and yet somehow I find that it is so."

The cardinal said nothing at all for a long time.

Then at last he rose, and, pressing the bishop's hand, he retired to his own quarters. The bishop hoped that he was comfortable in them, though it occurred to him in the uneasy sleep before dawn that the chimney smoked.

Next morning the cardinal departed on his journey toward Rome without speaking of these matters further. The bishop felt sorry to see him go and yet relieved. He had been very glad to see his old friend again—he told himself that. Yet from the moment of the cardinal's arrival there had been an unfamiliar grayness upon his spirit, and now that grayness had gone. Nevertheless, he knew that he must face Luigi—and that thought was hard for him.

Yet it went well enough, on the whole.

The bishop explained to him, as one explains to a child, that it did not seem as if God had intended him to be a cardinal, only bishop of Remo, and with that Luigi had to be content. He grumbled about it frequently and remarked that if he had known all this in the first place, he might never have accepted the position of bishop's beggar. But he was not any more overweening than before, and with that the bishop had to be satisfied.

Then came the war with the French, and that was hard upon the bishop. He did not like wars; he did not like the thought of his people being killed. Yet when the count of Remo fled with most of his soldiery and the mayor locked himself in his house and stayed there shaking, there was no one to take over the rule of the town but the bishop. The very beggars in the streets cried out for him; he could not escape the task.

He took it with a heavy heart under the mocking eyes of Luigi. With Luigi in his cart he inspected the walls and defenses.

"Well, your lordship has a very pretty problem," said Luigi. "Half a dozen good cannon shot and the city will be taken by storm."

"I thought so, I feared so," said the bishop, sighing. "And yet my people are my people."

"Your lordship might easily compromise with the enemy," said Luigi. "They are angry with the count, it is true—they thought they had him bought over. Yet it would mean but two score hangings or so and a tribute properly assessed."

"I cannot permit my flock to be harried and persecuted," said the bishop.

"Well, if your lordship must die, I will die with your lordship," said Luigi. "Meanwhile, we might set the townsfolk to work on the walls—at least it will give them something to do. And yet there may be another way."

So it was done, and the bishop worked day and night enheartening and encouraging his people. For once, all Remo was one, and the spirit and will that burned within it were the bishop's. Yet it seemed no time at all before the French sat down before Remo.

They sent a trumpet and a flag to de-mand the surrender of the city. The bishop received the young officer who came with the trumpet—a dark-faced man he was with a humorous twist to his mouth. The bishop even took him on a tour of the walls, which seemed to surprise him a little.

"You are well defended," said the Frenchman politely.

"Oh, no, we are very ill defended," said the bishop. "My good children have been trying to strengthen the wall with sandbags, but, as you perceive, it is rotten and needs rebuilding. Moreover, the count was badly cheated on his powder. I must speak to him of it sometime, for hardly a gun we have is fit to fire."

"I do not wish to doubt your lord-ship's word," he said, "but if those things are so, how does your lordship propose to defend Remo?"

"By the will of God," said the bishop very simply. "I do not wish my poor people killed; neither do I wish them oppressed. If needs must, I shall die in their stead, but they shall go scatheless. Ere you hang one man of Remo, I shall take the noose from around his neck and put it around my own."

"Your lordship makes things very difficult," said the Frenchman thoughtfully. "My king has no desire to attack the Church—and indeed the walls of Remo seem stronger than your lordship reckons."

Then he was conscious of a plucking at his sleeve. It was Luigi, the beggar, in his little cart, who by signs and grimaces seemed to wish the Frenchman to follow him.

"What is it, Luigi?" said the bishop wearily. "Ah, yes, you wish to show our friend the room where we store the powder. Very well. Then he may see how little we have."

When the Frenchman rejoined the bishop, he was wiping sweat from his forehead and his face was white. The bishop pressed him to stay for a glass of wine, but he said he must return to his camp and departed, muttering something incoherent about it being indeed the will of God that defended Remo.

When he had gone, the bishop looked severely upon Luigi. "Luigi," he said sternly, "I fear you have been up to some of your tricks."

"How your lordship mistakes me," said the beggar. "It is true I showed him three of my fellow beggars—and they did not seem to him in the best of health. But I did not say they had plague; I let him draw his own conclusions. It took me four days to school them in their parts, but that I did not tell him either."

"That was hardly honest, Luigi," said

the bishop. "We know there is no plague in the town."

"We know also that our walls are rotten," said Luigi, "but the French will not believe that either. Men of war are extremely suspicious—it is their weakness. We shall wait and see."

They waited and saw, for that night a council of war was held in the French camp and the officer who had come with the trumpet reported (a) that Remo was held in great force and strongly defended; (b) that its bishop was resolved to die in the breach; and (c) that there was a plague in the city. Taking all these factors into account, the French wisely decided after some forty-eight hours' delay to strike camp and fall back on their main army—which they did just in time to take part in the historic defeat of the whole French invasion a week later. This defeat sealed for all time the heroic defense of Remo; for had the part of the French army occupied before Remo rejoined their main body before, the historic defeat might have been as historic a victory for the French. As it was, all Italy rang with the name of the bishop of Remo.

But of all this the bishop knew nothing, for his beggar, Luigi, was dying.

As the French moved away, they had loosed off a few cannon shot, more in irritation than for any real military purpose. However, one of the cannon shot, heedlessly aimed, struck the steps of the cathedral; and you may still see the scars. It also struck the cart wherein Luigi lay directing his beggars at one task of defense or another. When the bishop first heard that his beggar was hurt, he went to him at once. But there was little that man could do but wait, and the waiting was long. It was not until seven weeks later that Luigi passed from this earth. He endured indeed till the messengers came from Rome.

After they had talked with the bishop, the bishop went alone to his cathedral and prayed. Then he went to see Luigi.

"Well?" said the dying man earnestly, staring at him eagerly with limpid eyes.

"His Holiness has been graciously pleased to make of me the first archbishop of Remo, placing under my staff, as well, the dioceses of Ugri and Soneto," said the bishop slowly. "But I have the news from Cardinal Malaverni, and I may remain here till I die." He stared at Luigi. "I do not understand," he said.

"It is well done. You have stood by the poor in their poverty and the wretched in their hour of trial," said Luigi, and for once there was no trace of mockery in his voice.

"I do not understand. I do not understand at all," said the bishop again. "And yet I think you deserve recompense rather than I, Luigi."

"No," said Luigi, "that I do not."

The bishop passed his hand across his brow. "I am not a fool," he said. "It was well done, to humble my spirit. And yet why did you do so, Luigi?"

"Why, that was my great sin," said Luigi. "I have confessed many vain and imaginary sins but never the real one till now." He paused as if the words hurt him. "When your lordship's coach rolled over my legs, I was very bitter," he said. "A poor man has little. To lose that little—to lose the air on the hills and the springing step, to lie like a log forever because a bishop's coachman was careless—that made me very bitter. I had rather your lordship had driven over me again than taken me back to your palace and treated me with kindness. I hated your lordship for your indifferent kindness—I hated you for everything."

"Did you so, Luigi?" said the bishop.

"Yes," said Luigi. "And I could see that your lordship hated me—or, if not hated, loathed, like a crippled dog that one must be kind to without liking. So I set myself out to tease and torment your lordship—at first by being your beggar, then in other ways. I could not believe in goodness; I could not believe there would not come a moment when your lordship would turn upon me and drive me forth."

He paused a moment and wiped his mouth with a cloth.

"Yes, I could not believe that at all," he said. "But you were not to be broken, Gianfrancesco, my brother. The evil I showed you daily was like a knife in your heart and a burden on your back, but you bore the knife and the burden. I took delight in showing you how ill things went in your city—how below the fair surface there was misery and pain. And had you once turned aside from that misery and pain, I would have been satisfied; for then, bishop or no bishop, you would have lost your soul. Was that evil of me, Gianfrancesco?"

"Very evil in intent," said the bishop steadily, "for while it is permitted to be tempted, it is evil to tempt. And yet proceed."

"Well," said Luigi, with a sudden and childlike stare, "it did not work. The more I tried to make you a bad man, the better man you became. You would not do what was ill; you would not depart from your poor, once you had known them—not even for a red hat or a count's favor. You would not do ill at all. So now we have defended Remo, the two of us, and I am dying." He stirred uneasily in his bed. "It is just as well," he said with a trace of his old mockery. "I told my uncle I would live to be a cardinal's beggar, but I am not

are a multitude of beggars, lame, halt, and misshapen, yet all praising God. And there are words in Latin which say, "It is not enough to have knowledge— these also are my sheep." Of the tomb of Luigi, the beggar—that no man knows. They say it was beside the bishop's, but in one war or another it was destroyed and there is no trace of it now. Yet Luigi was an arrogant spirit; perhaps he would have liked that best.

◇◇◇◇◇◇◇◇◇◇◇◇◇◇◇◇◇◇◇◇◇◇◇◇◇

## FOR DISCUSSION

1. What do you understand by the grayness which often came over the bishop's spirit? What was the cause of this grayness?

2. After the accident, what characteristics does the bishop show of an aristocrat who has been "inconvenienced" by the poor?

3. The bishop did not at first think himself a proud man. What signs of pride do you think he showed? Is it natural that we should be blind to our own faults? Why? Why is it hard to admit that we have the faults that our friends or enemies point out?

4. In view of Luigi's death-bed confession, do you think he would have died cheerfully when in the power of Giuseppe and the beggars? Why or why not?

5. Why did the grayness of spirit again come upon the bishop during the cardinal's visit?

6. What was unusual about the bishop's treatment of the French officer? What effect did the treatment have? Do you think that the bishop foresaw the effect? Was Luigi's trick of scaring the French an honest one? Why or why not?

7. What made Luigi's tempting of the bishop so horrible a sin?

8. If this story were told as a sermon, as it might well be, what conclusion or moral would you draw from it?

sure that I would have liked it. I have been the bishop's beggar so long. And yet from the first I have loved you also, Gianfrancesco. Will you give me your blessing now, on me and my work—the blessing you denied me once?"

The bishop's face was wrung. Yet he lifted his hand and absolved and blessed Luigi. He blessed Luigi and his work in the name of the Father and of the Son and of the Holy Ghost. When that had been done, a smile appeared on Luigi's face.

"A very fine blessing," he said. "I must tell that to the Hook when I see him; he will be envious. I wonder is it drafty on the steps of heaven? A very fine blessing, your lordship . . . ten . . . scudi . . . for . . . Luigi." And with that his jaw dropped and it was over. But the bishop knelt beside the bed with streaming eyes.

And all that, to be sure, was a long time ago. But they still tell the story in Remo when they show the bishop's tomb. He lies upon it fairly carven in marble. But carved all around the tomb

## THE CRAFT OF THE SHORT STORY

1. What is the most dramatic scene in the story? Why?

2. Where does the main interest of the story lie—in the plot, character development, or setting? Give reasons for your answer.

3. Point out how the author prepares you for the bishop's change of heart.

## WORDS TO STUDY

Before you answer the following questions, make sure that you know the meaning of the italicized words.

1. Why is a well-fed man more apt to be *vivacious* than an *emaciated* one?

2. If you lived in the country all your life, why would you not go to the city to become *rusticated*?

3. Was Giuseppe *stolid* because he was *squat*?

4. When the French officer departed muttering something *incoherent*, why would it have been impossible for the bishop to understand him?

5. Are *limpid* eyes a sign of life or of death?

6. The bishop's spirit was overcast by grayness. The mood was *singular*. Was it also *unique*?

## PROJECTS—THINGS TO WRITE ABOUT

1. Write a short story in which a disastrous accident turns out to be a blessing for one or more of the persons involved.

2. Write an imaginary account of the bishop's difficulty with the count of Remo.

3. Imagine that you are Cardinal Malaverni, and that you have very little sympathy with the changes you find in the bishop. Describe your thoughts, criticizing the bishop's reception, the lodgings, and the dinner.

## RELATED READING

Bishop Francis C. Kelley wrote a pleasant autobiography, *The Bishop Jots It Down*. You will find in it many amusing anecdotes and interesting pictures of modern ecclesiastical life. *Tales from the Rectory*, also by Bishop Kelley, tells fascinating stories of Catholic life.

# THE TROUBLE

### *J. F. POWERS*

*The author tells us that his story is "an attempt to focus hearts upon the devilish irony of race today; it is my belief that the Church alone, holding within herself divine direction and cure, can combat evil of a preternatural order in its most fierce and subtle forms." The story puts in a clear light the way in which a Catholic can help along the devil's work and get in the way of the work of Christ. It challenges you to face the problem of race in the light of the Church's teaching and to put to one side all the miserable, petty, hateful side issues that promote race hatred.*

*Neither the slavers' whip*
*nor the lynchers' rope*
*nor the bayonet*
*could kill our black belief.*
—Margaret Walker, *For My People.*

We watched at the window all that afternoon.

Old Gramma came out of her room and said, Now you kids get away from there this very minute, and we would until she went back to her room. We could hear her old rocking-chair creak when she got up or sat down and so we always ran away from the window before she came into the room to see if we were minding her good or looking out. Except once she went back to her room and didn't sit down, or maybe she did and got up easy so the chair didn't creak, or maybe we got our signals mixed, because she caught us all there and shooed us away and pulled down the green shade. The next time we were very sure she wasn't foxing us before we went to the window and lifted the shade just enough to peek out.

It was like waiting for rats as big as cats to run out from under a tenement so you could pick them off with a .22. Rats are about the biggest live game you can find in ordinary times and you see more of them than white folks in our neighborhood—in ordinary times. But the rats we waited for today were white ones and they were doing most of the shooting themselves. Sometimes some coloreds would come by the guns, but not often; they mostly had clubs. This morning we'd seen the whites catch up with a shot-in-the-leg colored and throw bricks and stones at his black head till

it got all red and he was dead. I could still see the wet places in the alley. That's why we kept looking out the window. We wanted to see some whites get killed for a change, but we didn't much think we would, and I guess what we really expected to see was nothing, or maybe them killing another colored.

There was a rumpus downstairs in front and I could hear a mess of people tramping up the stairs. They kept on coming after the second floor and my sister Carrie, my twin, said maybe they were whites come to get *us* because we saw what they did to the shot-in-the-leg colored in the alley. I was scared for a minute, I admit, but when I heard their voices plainer I knew they were coloreds and it was all right, only I didn't see why there were so many of them.

Then I got scared again, only different now, empty scared all over, when they came down the hall on our floor, not stopping at anybody else's door. And then there they were, banging on our door, of all the doors in the building. They tried to come right on in, but the door was locked.

Old Gramma was the one locked it and she said she'd clean house if one of us kids so much as looked at the knob even. She threw the key down her neck somewhere and I went and told her that was our door the people were pounding on and where was the key. She reached down her neck and there was the key all right. But she didn't act much like she intended to open the door. She just stood there staring at it like it was somebody alive, saying the litany to the Blessed Virgin: *Mère du Christ, priez pour nous, Secours des chrétiens, priez.*[1] Then all the

---

"The Trouble" from *Prince of Darkness and Other Stories* by J. F. Powers, reprinted by permission of Doubleday and Company, Inc.

[1] *Mère du . . . priez*—Mother of Christ, pray for us. Help of Christians, pray.

sudden she was crying, tears were blurry in her old yellow eyes, and she put the key in the lock, her veiny hands shaking, and unlocked the door.

They had Mama in their arms. I forgot all about Old Gramma, but I guess she passed out. Anyway, she was on the floor and a couple of men were picking her up and a couple of women were saying, Put her here, put her there. I wasn't worried as much about Old Gramma as I was about Mama.

A bone, God it made me sick, had poked through the flesh of Mama's arm, all bloody like a sharp stick, and something terrible was wrong with her chest. I couldn't look any more and Carrie was screaming. That started me crying. Tears got in the way, but still I could see the baby, one-and-a-half, and brother George, four-and-a-half, and they had their eyes wide open at what they saw and weren't crying a bit, too young to know what the hell.

They put Old Gramma in her room on the cot and closed the door on her and some old woman friend of hers that kept dipping a handkerchief in cold water and laying it on Old Gramma's head. They put Mama on the bed in the room where everybody was standing around and talking lower and lower until pretty soon they were just whispering.

Somebody came in with a doctor, a colored one, and he had a little black bag like they have in the movies. I don't think our family ever had a doctor come to see us before. Maybe before I was born Mama and Daddy did. I heard the doctor tell Mr. Purvine, that works in the same mill Daddy does, only the night shift, that he ought to set the bone, but honest to God he thought he might as well wait as he didn't want to hurt Mama if it wasn't going to make any difference.

He wasn't nearly as brisk now with his little black bag as he had been when he came in. He touched Mama's forehead a couple of times and it didn't feel good to him, I guess, because he looked tired after he did it. He held his hand on her wrist of the good arm, but I couldn't tell what this meant from his face. It mustn't have been any worse than the forehead, or maybe his face had nothing to do with what he thought and I was imagining all this from seeing the shape Mama was in. Finally he said, I'll try, and he began calling for hot water and other things and pretty soon Mama was all bandaged up white.

The doctor stepped away from Mama and over to some men and women, six or seven of them now—a lot more had gone—and asked them what had happened. He didn't ask all the questions I wanted to ask—I guess he already knew some of the answers—but I did find out Mama was on a streetcar coming home from the plant—Mama works now and we're saving for a cranberry farm—when the riot broke out in that section. Mr. Purvine said he called the mill and told Daddy to come home. But Mr. Purvine said he wasn't going to work tonight himself, the way the riot was spreading and the way the coloreds were getting the worst of it.

As usual, said a man with glasses on, the Negroes ought to organize and fight the thing to a finish. The doctor frowned at that. Mr. Purvine said he didn't know. But one woman and another man said that was the right idea.

If we must die, said the man with glasses on, let it not be like hogs hunted and penned in an inglorious spot! The doctor said, Yes, we all know that, but the man with glasses on went on, because the others were listening to him, and I was glad he did, because I was listening to him too: We must meet the common foe; though far outnumbered, let us still be brave, and for their thousand blows deal one death-blow! What though before us lies the open grave? Like men we'll face the murderous, cowardly pack, pressed to the wall, dying, but—fighting back!

They all thought it was fine and a woman said that was poetry and I thought if that is what it is I know what I want to be now, a poetryman. I asked the man with glasses on if that was his poetry, though I did not think it was for some reason, and the men and women all looked at me like they were surprised to see me there and like I ought not hear such things, except the man with glasses on, and he said, No, son, it was not his poetry, he wished it was, but it was Claude McKay's, a Negro, and I could find it in the public library. I decided I would go to the public library when the riot was over and it was the first time in my life I ever thought of the public library the way I did then.

They all left about this time, except the doctor and the old woman friend of Old Gramma's. She came out of Old Gramma's room, and when the door opened I saw Old Gramma lying on the cot with her eyes closed. The old woman asked me if I could work a can opener and I said, Yes, I can, and she handed me a can of vegetable soup from the shelf. She got a meal together and us kids sat down to eat. Not Carrie, though. She sat in our good chair with her legs under her and her eyes closed. Mama was sleeping and the doctor rolled up the shade at the window and looked out while we ate. I mean brother George and the baby. I couldn't eat. I just drank my glass of water. The old woman said, Here, here, I hadn't ought to let good food go to

waste and was that any way to act at the table and I wasn't the first boy in the world to lose his mother.

I wondered was she crazy and I yelled I wasn't going to lose my mother and I looked to see and I was right. Mama was just sleeping and the doctor was there in case she needed him and everything was taken care of and—everything. The doctor didn't even turn away from the window when I yelled at the old woman and I thought at least he'd say I'd wake my mother up shouting that way, or maybe that I was right and the old woman was wrong. I got up from the table and stood by the doctor at the window. He only stayed there a minute more then and went over to feel Mama's wrist again. He did not touch her forehead this time.

Old Gramma came out of her room and said to me, Was that you raising so much cain in here, boy? I said, Yes, it was, and just when I was going to tell her what the old woman said about losing Mama I couldn't. I didn't want to hear it out loud again. I didn't even want to think it in my mind. Old Gramma went over and gazed down at Mama. She turned away quickly and told the old woman, Please, I'll just have a cup of hot water, that's all, I'm so upset. Then she went over to the doctor by the window and whispered something to him and he whispered something back and it must've been only one or two words, because he was looking out the window the next moment.

Old Gramma said she'd be back in a minute and went out the door and slip-slapping down the hall. I went to the window; the evening sun was going down, and I saw Old Gramma come out the back entrance of our building. She crossed the alley and went in the back door of the grocerystore.

A lot of racket cut loose about a block up the alley. It was still empty, though. Old Gramma came out of the grocery-store with something in a brown bag. She stopped in the middle of the alley and seemed to be watching the orange evening sun going down behind the buildings. The sun got in her hair and somehow under her skin kind of and it did a wonderful thing to her. She looked so young for a moment that I saw Mama in her, both of them beautiful New Orleans ladies.

The racket cut loose again, nearer now, and a pack of men came running down the alley, about three dozen whites chasing two coloreds. One of the whites was blowing a bugle—*tan tivvy tan tivvy tan tivvy*—like the white folks do when they go fox-hunting in the movies or Virginia. I looked down, quick, to see if Old Gramma had enough sense to come inside and I guess she did because she wasn't there. The

two coloreds ran between two buildings, the whites ran after them and then the alley was quiet again. Old Gramma stepped out and I watched her stoop and pick up the brown bag that she had dropped before.

Another big noise made her drop it again. A whole smear of men swarmed out of the used-car lot and came galloping down the alley like wild buffaloes. Old Gramma scooted inside our building and the brown bag stayed in the alley. This time I couldn't believe my eyes, I saw what I thought I'd never see, I saw what us kids had been waiting to see ever since the riot broke out—a white man that was fixing to get himself nice and killed. A white man running —running, God Almighty, from about a million coloreds. And he was the one with the tan-tivvy bugle too. I hoped the coloreds would do the job up right.

The closer the white man came the worse it got for him, because the alley

comes to a dead end when it hits our building. All at once, I don't know why, I was praying for that fool white man with the bugle to get away. But I didn't think he had a Chinaman's chance, the way he was going now, and maybe that's what made me pray for him.

Then he did a smart thing. He whipped the bugle over his shoulder like you do with a horseshoe for good luck and it hit the first colored behind him smack in the head, knocking him out, and that slowed up the others. The white man turned into the junkyard behind the furniture warehouse and the Victory Ballroom. Another smart thing, if he used his head. The space between the warehouse and the Victory is just wide enough for a man to run through. It's a long piece to the street, but if he made it there he'd be safe probably.

The long passageway must've looked too narrow to him, though, because the fool came rushing around the garage next to our building. For a moment he was the only one in the alley. The coloreds had followed him through the junkyard and probably got themselves all tangled up in garbage cans and rusty bed springs and ashpiles. But the white man was a goner just the same. In a minute they'd be coming for him for real. He'd have to run the length of the alley again to get away and the coloreds have got the best legs.

Then Old Gramma opened our back door and saved him.

I was very glad for the white man until suddenly I remembered poor Mama all broken to pieces on the bed and then I was sorry Old Gramma did it. The next moment I was glad again that she did. I understood now I did not care one way or the other about the white man. Now I was thinking of Mama—not of myself. I did not see what difference it could make to Mama if the white man lived or died. It only had something to do with us and him.

Then I got hold of a very strange idea. I told myself the trouble is somebody gets cheated or insulted or killed and everybody else tries to make it come out even by cheating and insulting or killing the cheaters and insulters and killers. Only they never do. I did not think they ever would. I told myself that I had a very big idea there and when the riot was over I would go to the public library and sit in the reading room and think about it. Or I would speak to Old Gramma about it, because it seemed like she had the same big idea and like she had had it a long time too.

The doctor was standing by me at the window all the time. He said nothing about what Old Gramma did, and now he stepped away from the window and so did I. I guess he felt the same way I did about the white man and that's why he stepped away from the window. The big idea again. He was afraid the coloreds down below would yell up at us, did we see the white man pass by. The coloreds were crazy mad all right. One of them had the white man's bugle and he banged on our door with it. I was worried Old Gramma had forgot to lock it and they might walk right in and that would be the end of the white man and the big idea.

But Old Gramma pulled another fast one. She ran out into the alley and pointed her yellow finger in about three wrong directions. In a second the alley was quiet and empty, except for Old Gramma. She walked slowly over against our building, where somebody had kicked the brown bag, and picked it up.

Old Gramma brought the white man right into our room, told him to sit down and poured herself a cup of hot water. She sipped it and said the white man could leave whenever he wanted to, but it might be better to wait a bit. The white man said he was much obliged, he hated to give us any trouble, and Oh, oh, is somebody sick over there, when he saw Mama, and that he'd just been passing by when a hundred nig—when he was attacked.

Old Gramma sipped her hot water. The doctor turned away from the window and said, Here they come again, took another look, and said, No, they're going back. He went over to Mama and held her wrist. I couldn't tell anything about her from his face. She was sleeping just the same. The doctor asked the white man, still standing, to sit down. Carrie only opened her eyes once and closed them. She hadn't changed her position in the good chair. Brother George and the baby stood in a corner with their eyes on the white man. The baby's legs buckled then—she'd only been walking about a week—and she collapsed softly to the floor. She worked her way up again without taking her eyes off the white man. He even looked funny and out of place to me in our room. I guess the man for the rent and Father Egan were the only white people come to see us since I could remember and now it was only the man for the rent since Father Egan died.

The doctor asked the white man did he work or own a business in this neighborhood. The white man said, No, glancing down at his feet, no, he just happened to be passing by when he was suddenly attacked like he said before. The doctor told Old Gramma she might wash Mama's face and neck again with warm water.

There was noise again in the alley, windows breaking and fences being pushed over. The doctor said, You could leave now, to the white man, it's a white mob this time, you'd be safe.

No, the white man said, I should say not, I wouldn't be seen with them, they're as bad as the others almost.

It is quite possible, the doctor said.

Old Gramma asked the white man if he would like a cup of tea.

Tea? No, he said, I don't drink tea, I didn't know you drank it.

I didn't know you knew her, the doctor said, looking at Old Gramma and the white man.

You colored folks, I mean, the white man said, Americans, I mean. Me, I don't drink tea, always considered it an English drink and bad for the kidneys.

The doctor did not answer. Old Gramma brought him a cup of tea.

And then Daddy came in. He ran over to Mama and fell down on his knees like he was dead, like seeing Mama with her arm broke and her chest so pushed in killed him on the spot. He lifted his face from the bed and kissed Mama on the lips; and then, Daddy, I could see, was crying, the strongest man in the world was crying with tears in his dark eyes and coming down the side of his big hard face. Mama called him her John Henry sometimes and there he was, her John Henry, the strongest man, black or white, in the whole damn world, crying.

He put his head down on the bed again. Nobody in the room moved until the baby toddled over to Daddy and patted him on the ear like she wanted to play the games those two make up with her little hands and his big ears and eyes and nose. But Daddy didn't move or say anything, if he even knew she was there, and the baby got a blank look in her eyes and walked away from Daddy and sat down, *plump*, on the floor across the room, staring at Daddy and the white man, back and forth, Daddy and the white man.

Daddy got up after a while and walked very slowly across the room and got himself a drink of water at the sink. For the first time he noticed the white man in the room. Who's he, he said, who's he? None of us said anything. Who the hell's he? Daddy wanted to know, thunder in his throat like there always is when he's extra mad or happy.

The doctor said the white man was Mr. Gorman and went over to Daddy and told him something in a low voice.

Innocent! What's he doing in this neighborhood then? Daddy said, loud as before. What's an *innocent* white man doing in this neighborhood now, answer me that! He looked at all of us in the room and none of us that knew what the white man was doing in this neighborhood wanted to explain to Daddy. Old Gramma and the doctor and me, none of us that knew, would tell.

I was just passing by, the white man said, as they can tell you.

The scared way he said it almost made me laugh. Was this a white *man*, I asked myself. Alongside Daddy's voice the white man's sounded plain foolish and weak, a little old pink tug squeaking at a big brown ocean liner about the right of way. Daddy seemed to forget all about him and began asking the doctor a lot of questions about Mama in a hoarse whisper I couldn't hear very well. Daddy's face got harder and harder and it didn't look like he'd ever crack a smile or shed a tear or anything soft again. Just hard, it got, hard as four spikes.

Old Gramma came and stood by Daddy's side and said she had called the priest when she was downstairs a while ago getting some candles. She was worried that the candles weren't blessed ones. She opened the brown bag then and that's what was inside, two white candles. I didn't know grocerystores carried them.

Old Gramma went to her room and took down the picture of the Sacred Heart all bleeding and put it on the little table by Mama's bed and set the candles in sticks on each side of it. She lit the candles and it made the Sacred Heart, punctured by the wreath of thorns, look bloodier than ever and made me think of that song, To Jesus' Heart All Burning, the kids sing at Our Saviour's on Sundays.

The white man went up to the doctor and said, I'm a Catholic too. But the doctor didn't say anything back, only nodded. He probably wasn't one himself, I thought, not many of the race are. Our family wouldn't be if Old Gramma and Mama didn't come from New Orleans, where Catholics are thicker than flies or Baptists.

Daddy got up from the table and said to the white man, So help me God, mister, I'll kill you in this room if my wife dies! The baby started crying and the doctor went to Daddy's side and turned him away from the white man and it wasn't hard to do because now Daddy was kind of limp and didn't look like he remembered anything about the white man or what he said he'd do to him if Mama . . . or anything.

I'll bet the priest won't show up, Daddy said.

The priest will come, Old Gramma said, the priest will always come when you need him, just wait. Her old lips were praying in French.

I hoped he would come like Old Gramma said, but I wasn't so sure.

Some of the priests weren't much different from anybody else. They knew how to keep their necks in. Daddy said to Mama once if you only wanted to hear about social justice you could turn on the radio or go to the nearest stadium on the Fourth of July and there'd be an old white man in a new black suit saying it was a good thing and everybody ought to get some and if they'd just kick in more they might and anyway they'd be saved. One came to Our Saviour's last year and Father Egan said this is our new assistant and the next Sunday our new assistant was gone—poor health. But Daddy said he was transferred to a church in a white neighborhood because he couldn't stand to save black souls. Father Egan would've come a-flying, riot or no riot, but he was dead now and we didn't know much about the one that took his place.

Then he came, by God, the priest from Our Saviour's came to our room while the riot was going on. Old Gramma got all excited and said over and over she knew the priest would come. He was kind of young and skinny and pale, even for a white man, and he said, I'm Father Crowe, to everybody in the room and looked around to see who was who.

The doctor introduced himself and said Old Gramma was Old Gramma, Daddy was Daddy, we were the children, that was Mr. Gorman, who was just passing by, and over there was poor Mama. He missed Old Gramma's old woman friend; I guess he didn't know what to call her. The priest went over and took a look at Mama and nodded to the doctor and they went into Old Gramma's room together. The priest had a little black bag too and he took it with him. I suppose he was getting ready to give Mama Extreme Unction. I didn't think they would wake her up for Confession

or Holy Communion, she was so weak and needed the rest.

Daddy got up mad as a bull from the table and said, Remember what I said, mister, to the white man.

But why me, the white man asked, just because I'm white?

Daddy looked over at Mama on the bed and said, Yeah, just because you're white, yeah, that's why . . . Old Gramma took Daddy by the arm and steered him over to the table again and he sat down.

The priest and the doctor came out of Old Gramma's room and right away the priest faced the white man, like they'd been talking about him in Old Gramma's room, and asked him why he didn't go home. The white man said he'd heard some shouting in the alley a while ago that didn't sound so good to him and he didn't think it was safe yet and that was why.

I see, the priest said.

I'm a Catholic too, Father, the white man said.

That's the trouble, the priest said.

The priest took some cotton from his little black bag, dipped his fingers in holy oil and made the sign of the cross on Mama's eyes, nose, ears, mouth, and hands, rubbing the oil off with the cotton, and said prayers in Latin all the time he was doing it.

I want you all to kneel down now, the priest said, and we'll say the rosary. But we mustn't say it too loud because she is sleeping.

We all knelt down except the baby and Carrie. Carrie said she'd never kneel down to God again. Now Carrie, Old Gramma said, almost crying. She told Carrie it was for poor Mama and wouldn't Carrie kneel down if it was for poor Mama?

No! Carrie said, it must be a white

THE TROUBLE

God too! Then she began crying and she did kneel down after all.

Even the white man knelt down and the doctor and the old woman friend of Old Gramma's, a solid Baptist if I ever saw one, and we all said the rosary of the five sorrowful mysteries.

Afterwards the white man said to the priest, Do you mind if I leave when you do, Father? The priest didn't answer and the white man said, I think I'll be leaving now, Father. I wonder if you'd be going my way?

The priest finally said, All right, all right, come along, you won't be the first one to hide behind a Roman collar.

The white man said, I'm sure I don't know what you mean by that, Father. The priest didn't hear him, I guess, or want to explain, because he went over to Mama's bed.

The priest knelt once more by Mama and said a prayer in Latin out loud and made the sign of the cross over Mama! *In nomine Patris et Filii et Spiritus Sancti.* He looked closer at Mama and motioned to the doctor. The doctor stepped over to the bed, felt Mama's wrist, put his head to her chest, where it wasn't pushed in, and stood up slowly.

Daddy and all of us had been watching the doctor when the priest motioned him over and now Daddy got up from the table, kicking the chair over he got up so fast, and ran to the bed. He sank, shaking all over, to his knees, and I believe he must've been crying again, although I thought he never would again and his head was down and I couldn't see for sure.

I began to get an awful bulging pain in my stomach. The doctor left the bed and grabbed the white man by the arm and was taking him to the door when Daddy jumped up, like he knew where they were going, and said, Wait a minute, mister!

The doctor and the white man stopped at the door. Daddy walked draggily over to them and stood in front of the white man, took a deep breath, and said in the stillest kind of whisper, I wouldn't touch you. That was all. He moved slowly back to Mama's bed and his big shoulders were sagged down like I never saw them before.

Old Gramma said *Jésus!* and stumbled down on her knees by Mama. Then the awful bulging pain in my stomach exploded and I knew that Mama wasn't just sleeping now and I couldn't breathe for a long while and then when I finally could I was crying like the baby and brother George and so was Carrie.

◇◇◇◇◇◇◇◇◇◇◇◇◇◇◇◇◇◇◇◇◇◇◇◇◇◇

FOR DISCUSSION

1. Sister Mariella Gable, O.S.B., included this story in *Our Father's House,* an excellent anthology of short stories on Catholic themes. In her introduction to "The Trouble" she urges the reader not "to pass over in haste the quietly ironic moment when the white man, who has been taking violent part in a race riot, announces to the priest, 'I am a Catholic, too.' 'That is the trouble,' answers the priest; and according to Mr. Powers, that indeed is the key to all our grief—the Catholic who does not live according to the sublime doctrine of the Church." What is the doctrine of the Church on race? Why is the failure of Catholics to live up to the teaching of the Church the key to all our grief?

2. Point out details which show that the person who is telling the story is young.

3. "I told myself the trouble is somebody gets cheated or insulted or killed and everybody else tries to make it come out even by cheating or insulting or killing the cheaters and insulters and killers. Only they never do. I did not think they

ever would." Do you consider this a "big" idea? The boy in the story did. Why?

4. What does the priest mean when he says that ". . . you won't be the first one to hide behind a Roman collar"?

5. You have noticed the lack of quotation marks in the story. Explain why you like or dislike this style which is used by a few modern writers.

## STUDYING THE SHORT STORY

1. Why does the author present the incidents in the story from the point of view of the young boy?

2. Is there any struggle or conflict in the story? If so, point it out.

3. What is the main interest of the story—plot, character, or setting?

4. What was the author's purpose in writing the story?

## PROJECTS ON RACE PROBLEMS

1. Where would you go to find the Church's teaching on race? Prepare a list of writings which contain these teachings.

2. Write an account of your own opinions regarding other races. Where do your opinions come from? Are they the result of personal observation and experience? Are your opinions formed by what the Church has to say or are they snap judgments and the repetition of the prejudices of others?

3. What is your city or town doing to help the relations between the races? Make a report to the class on what is being done.

## RELATED READING

The race question is one of our major social problems. We should appreciate its importance and accent the responsibility of working toward a solution of it. Elizabeth Laura Adams, a talented and sensitive Negro girl, gives an inside view of how it feels to face a world of prejudice in her *Dark Symphony*. Art Kuhl's *Royal Road* and James Hyland's *The Dove Flies South* are fine novels on race problems.

❖❖❖❖❖

# SIXTEEN

*MAUREEN DALY*

*Sixteen is an age with a magic and a sorrow all its own. Maureen Daly in this story has captured both the laughter and the tears of a girl of sixteen.*

Now don't get me wrong. I mean, I want you to understand from the beginning that I'm not really so dumb. I know what a girl should do and what she

"Sixteen" by Maureen Daly, reprinted by permission of the author and *Scholastic Magazines*.

shouldn't. I get around. I read. I listen to the radio. And I have two older sisters. So you see, I know what the score is. I know it's smart to wear tweedish skirts and shaggy sweaters with the sleeves pushed up and pearls and ankle socks and saddle shoes that look as if they've seen the world. And I know that your hair should be long, almost to your shoulders, and sleek as a wet seal, just a little fluffed on the ends, and you should wear a campus hat or a dink or else a peasant hankie if you've that sort of face. Properly, a peasant hankie should make you think of edelweiss, mist and sunny mountains, yodeling and Swiss cheese. You know, that kind of peasant. Now, me, I never wear a hankie. It makes my face seem wide and Slavic and I look like a picture always in one of those magazine articles that run—"And Stalin says the future of Russia lies in its women. In its women who have tilled its soil, raised its children—" Well, anyway. I'm not exactly too small-town either. I read Winchell's column. You get to know what New York boy is that way about some pineapple princess on the West Coast and what Paradise pretty is currently the prettiest, and why someone, eventually, will play Scarlett O'Hara. It gives you that cosmopolitan feeling. And I know that anyone who orders a strawberry sundae in a drugstore instead of a lemon coke would probably be dumb enough to wear colored ankle socks with high-heeled pumps or use Evening in Paris with a tweed suit. But I'm sort of drifting. This isn't what I wanted to tell you. I just wanted to give you the general idea of how I'm not so dumb. It's important that you understand that.

You see, it was funny how I met him. It was a winter night like any other winter night. And I didn't have my Latin done, either. But the way the moon tinseled the twigs and silver-plated the snowdrifts, I just couldn't stay inside. The skating rink isn't far from our house—you can make it in five minutes if the sidewalks aren't slippery—so I went skating. I remember it took me a long time to get ready that night because I had to darn my skating socks first. I don't know why they always wear out so fast—just in the toes, too. Maybe it's because I have metal protectors on the toes of my skates. That probably *is* why. And then I brushed my hair—hard, so hard it clung to my hand and stood up around my head in a hazy halo.

My skates were hanging by the back door all nice and shiny, for I'd just gotten them for Christmas and they smelled so queer—just like fresh smoked ham. My dog walked with me as far as the corner. She's a red chow, very polite and well mannered, and she kept pretending it was me she liked when all the time I knew it was the ham smell. She panted along beside me and her hot breath made a frosty little balloon balancing on the end of her nose. My skates thumped me good-naturedly on my back as I walked and the night was breathlessly quiet and the stars winked down like a million flirting eyes. It was all so lovely.

It was all so lovely I ran most of the way and it was lucky the sidewalks had ashes on them or I'd have slipped surely. The ashes crunched like crackerjack and I could feel their cindery shape through the thinness of my shoes. I always wear old shoes when I go skating.

I had to cut across someone's back garden to get to the rink and last summer's grass stuck through the thin ice, brown and discouraged. Not many people came through this way and the crusted snow broke through the little hollows between corn stubbles frozen hard in the ground. I was out of breath when I got to the shanty—out of breath with running and with the loveliness of the night. Shanties are always such friendly places. The floor all hacked to wet splinters from skate runners and the wooden wall frescoed with symbols of dead romance. There was a smell of singed wool as someone got too near the glowing isinglass grin of the iron stove. Girls burst through the door laughing, with snow on their hair, and tripped over shoes scattered on the floor. A pimply-faced boy grabbed the hat from the frizzled head of an eighth-grade blonde and stuffed it into an empty galosh to prove his love and then hastily bent to examine his skate strap with innocent unconcern.

It didn't take me long to get my own skates on and I stuck my shoes under the bench—far back where they wouldn't get knocked around and would be easy to find when I wanted to go home. I walked out on my toes and the shiny runners of my new skates dug deep into the sodden floor.

It was snowing a little outside—quick, eager little Luxlike flakes that melted as soon as they touched your hand. I don't know where the snow came from, for there were stars out. Or maybe the stars were in my eyes and I just kept seeing them every time I looked up into the darkness. I waited a moment. You know, to start to skate at a crowded rink is like jumping on a moving merry-go-round. The skaters go skimming round in a colored blur like gaudy painted horses and the shrill musical jabber re-echoes in the night from a hundred human calliopes. Once in, I went all right. At least after I found out exactly where that rough ice was. It was "round, round, jump the rut, round, round, round, jump the rut, round, round—"

And then he came. All of a sudden his arm was around my waist so warm and tight and he said very casually, "Mind if I skate with you?" and then he took my other hand. That's all there was to it. Just that and then we were skating. It wasn't that I'd never skated with a boy before. Don't be silly. I told you before I get around. But this was different. He was a smoothie! He was a big shot up at school and he went to all the big dances and he was the best dancer in town except Harold Wright, who didn't count because he'd been to college in New York for two years! Don't you see? This was different.

I can't remember what we talked about at first; I can't even remember if we talked at all. We just skated and skated and laughed every time we came to that rough spot and pretty soon we were laughing all the time at nothing at all. It was all so lovely.

Then we sat on the big snowbank at the edge of the rink and just watched. It was cold at first even with my skating pants on, sitting on that hard heap of snow, but pretty soon I got warm all over. He threw a handful of snow at me and it fell in a little white shower on my hair and he leaned over to brush it off. I held my breath. The night stood still.

The moon hung just over the warming shanty like a big quarter slice of muskmelon and the smoke from the pipe chimney floated up in a sooty fog. One by one the houses around the rink twinked out their lights and somebody's hound wailed a mournful apology to a star as he curled up for the night. It was all so lovely.

Then he sat up straight and said, "We'd better start home." Not "Shall I take you home?" or "Do you live far?" but "We'd better start home." See, that's how I know he wanted to take me home. Not because he *had* to but be-

cause he *wanted* to. He went to the shanty to get my shoes. "Black ones," I told him. "Same size as Garbo's." And he laughed again. He was still smiling when he came back and took off my skates and tied the wet skate strings in a soggy knot and put them over his shoulder. Then he held out his hand and I slid off the snowbank and brushed off the seat of my pants and we were ready.

It was snowing harder now. Big, quiet flakes that clung to twiggy bushes and snuggled in little drifts against the tree trunks. The night was an etching in black and white. It was all so lovely I was sorry I lived only a few blocks away. He talked softly as we walked, as if every little word were a secret. "Did I like Wayne King, and did I plan to go to college next year, and had I a cousin who lived in Appleton and knew his brother?" A very respectable Emily Post sort of conversation, and then finally "how nice I looked with snow in my hair and had I ever seen the moon so—close?" For the moon was following us as we walked and ducking playfully behind a chimney every time I

turned to look at it. And then we were home.

The porch light was on. My mother always puts the porch light on when I go away at night. And we stood there a moment by the front steps and the snow turned pinkish in the glow of the colored light and a few feathery flakes settled on his hair. Then he took my skates and put them over my shoulder and said, "Good night now. I'll call you." "I'll call you," he said.

I went inside then and in a moment he was gone. I watched him from my window as he went down the street. He was whistling softly and I waited until the sound faded away so I couldn't tell if it was he or my heart whistling out there in the night. And then he was gone, completely gone.

I shivered. Somehow the darkness seemed changed. The stars were little hard chips of light far up in the sky and the moon stared down with a sullen yellow glare. The air was tense with sudden cold and a gust of wind swirled his footprints into white oblivion. Everything was quiet.

But he'd said, "I'll call you." That's

what he said—"I'll call you." I couldn't sleep all night.

And that was last Thursday. Tonight is Tuesday. Tonight is Tuesday and my homework's done, and I darned some stockings that didn't really need it, and I worked a crossword puzzle, and I listened to the radio, and now I'm just sitting. I'm just sitting because I can't think of anything else to do. I can't think of anything, anything but snowflakes and ice skates and yellow moons and Thursday night. The telephone is sitting on the corner table with its old black face turned to the wall so I can't see its leer. I don't even jump when it rings any more. My heart still prays, but my mind just laughs. Outside the night is still, so still I think I'll go crazy, and the white snow's all dirtied and smoked into grayness and the wind is blowing the arc light so it throws weird, waving shadows from the trees onto the lawn—like thin, starved arms begging for I don't know what. And so I'm just sitting here and I'm not feeling anything; I'm not even sad, because all of a sudden I know. All of a sudden I know. I can sit here now forever and laugh and laugh and laugh while the tears run salty in the corners of my mouth. For all of a sudden I know, I know what the stars knew all the time —he'll never, never call—never.

◇◇◇◇◇◇◇◇◇◇◇◇◇◇◇◇◇◇◇◇◇◇◇◇◇◇◇◇◇

## FOR DISCUSSION

1. In the first paragraph the girl who is telling the story tells you that she is "not really so dumb." Why is it important that you understand that fact about her? By what details does she try to prove that she knows the right things to do?

2. Why does the girl remember clearly and in great detail everything about that particular night?

3. Read through the story to note the different changes in mood. In what way do her different moods change her surroundings? Pick out four examples of the way in which she reads her moods into the things about her, similar to her description of the telephone "with its old black face turned to the wall so I can't see its leer."

4. Do you think that the story gives a true picture of the way in which a girl of sixteen would react to a disappointment over a broken "date"?

## THE WRITER'S CRAFT

1. What changes in the emotional tone, incidents, and climax would take place in the story if it were told from the point of view of the girl's mother or a younger sister?

2. Is there any plot to the story? In what does it consist?

3. Did the story hold your attention? Why or why not?

## USING EFFECTIVE WORDS

The story is packed with crisp, accurate observations. Study the following phrases and point out the words which help to make this story not just an ordinary bit of writing but a kind of prose poem.

1. ". . . the way the moon tinseled the twigs and silver-plated the snowdrifts."

2. The dog's hot breath "made a frosty little balloon balancing on the end of her nose."

3. "The ashes crunched like crackerjack."

4. "Luxlike flakes."

5. ". . . to start to skate at a crowded rink is like jumping on a moving merry-go-round."

## A PROJECT—FINISH THE STORY

The telephone *does* ring! It is the boy who is calling. He had been called out of town and has just returned. The very first thing he did was to call the girl. Continue Maureen Daly's story from there.

# MODERN JOURNALISM

We have spoken briefly of various kinds of fiction. Much of our literature, however is *nonfiction prose*. Such writing deals chiefly with facts and opinions. The material is usually informational, though it may also be entertaining. But it concerns actual rather than imagined experiences. Nonfiction prose comprises such different types of writing as *history, biography, travel accounts, journals, public addresses, news stories*, and *editorial writing*. Almost all journalistic writing is nonfiction.

The current literature most widely read throughout the world is American. The credit for the fact goes chiefly to first-class American papers and magazines. Our periodicals have introduced many great writers to the world. They make liberal payments to writers who have "arrived," and reach an encouraging hand to unknown writers of promise. In fact, most present-day writers in America are either active journalists or men and women who got their start in journalism.

The press of a nation may be likened to its rivers that laugh in the sunlight, twirl turbines, or gather filth and slime. It can be pure and strong, or ugly and polluted. It can be useful or terrible in its power. Consider the speed with which news is gathered and interpreted; and consider the volume of daily print. Nikolai Bulganin clasps the hand of a visitor in Moscow. The interview is scarcely over before the headlines are being read on every Main Street from San Diego, California, to Aroostook County, Maine. The incident is analyzed, interpreted, and made the basis of prediction by journalists large and small.

The volume of newsprint is amazing. Daily the *New York Times* comes out in twenty-four pages, a hundred thousand words; Sundays it appears in nine sections with a total of half a million words. The *Saturday Evening Post, Colliers,* and the *Ladies' Home Journal* call at millions of homes; and magazines like *Harper's, Fortune,* and the *Atlantic Monthly* have tens of thousands of subscribers. But—sadly —at the same time ten million Americans a month draw entertainment from subliterary pulps and near-pulps. The flood of sensational journalism and cheap fiction today is appalling.

Newsprint is a powerful influence. It can inform the public mind, elevate taste, safeguard ideals, arouse worthy action. Or it can misrepresent the facts, persuading men to believe what is false, do what is wrong, hope for what is unattainable, and fear what is nonexistent. We cannot live in a mental monastery today. Whatever we read—like this page—has been designed to impress our minds or sway our feelings. No wonder it has been said, "If St. Paul were alive today, he would be a journalist!"

Our Holy Father Pope Pius XII emphasized the need for professional integrity in an address to a group of American newspaper correspondents: "An editor, writer, or speaker conscious of his vocation and its responsibilities is always alive to the obligations he has to the millions of people who may be strongly affected by his words, to give them nothing but the truth so far as he has been able to ascertain it."

What is the assignment of the journalist? As Pope Pius has said, he is not free "to print what is wrong, what is known to be false, or calculated to undermine the moral and religious fiber in individuals and the peace and harmony of nations." His assignment is to build up a nation united under God in the brotherhood of man; to deepen the channels of sympathy, respect, love of harmony and fair-dealing which flow from a consideration of the grandeur of each human soul; to direct us to and provide that richer life for which millions came to our shores. Confidence that we can become such a nation is not a new or passing thought. It is rooted in our deepest and oldest traditions.

Nearly one hundred and forty Catholic newspapers and two hundred Catholic magazines have determined to work for the realization of these ideals. Two weeklies interpreting current events are *America* and *Commonweal,* the latter edited by laymen. Other leading periodicals are the *Catholic World,* the *Sign,* the *Messenger of the Sacred Heart,* the *Catholic Mind*—oldest of the reprint magazines—and the

*Catholic Digest.* *Today* and *Integrity* are two forthright publications of promise. For these and other publications, Catholic writers are needed—and Catholic readers. Should not 25,000,000 Catholics be able to support a daily paper that would put religion where it belongs—in first place?

## LITERARY JOURNALISM

Journalism concerns itself with the publication of news and views. It is not always "literature." The news story, the editorial typed to fit the latest problem in transportation or taxes, the dramatic criticism dashed off while the copy boy races it a paragraph at a time to the pressroom—this writing is mostly for the moment rather than for all time.

Who, then, is the *literary journalist?* He is the newspaper or magazine writer who, through gifts of imagination and insight, makes the reader feel the significance of truth in the world of men and events. He deals not with bare bones of fact and principle; rather, he reveals "the substantial flesh that grieves upon the bones"— the heart that beats beneath the judge's gown, the face of the man beneath the make-up of a clown. He does not just report statistics; he interprets statistics in human terms—the tragic and the farcical, the beautiful and the sublime.

In what form does he write? The answer is hard to give. Journalism is a miscellany. It takes many forms. The enduring essay, "Mary White," was written as an editorial by her father; sixty of O. Henry's stories appeared first as features in a New York newspaper. The columns of Ernie Pyle will rank with the great literature of the Second World War. The literary journalist may be a reporter, a critic, an editor, a columnist.

The various journalistic forms are pretty well set. The editorial is impersonal, usually unsigned, and is evaluated principally for its thought. The best editorial writing uses simple diction, orderly discussion, vigorous and clear expression. Occasionally it becomes great writing. The editor, ideally, passes honest judgment on men and events. But there are considerations which often tempt him to temper his views—the pressure of advertisers, of political powers, of business enterprises. Indeed, such influences may touch in one way or another the work of any journalist. The writer of integrity must be a person of courage.

The columnist is usually an outspoken man. Sometimes his stint for the day has a footnote from the editor: "The views in this column do not necessarily represent those of the editor." The columnist is a combination reporter, critic, and essayist. He should be a person of broad learning and experience; he should be versatile, turning easily from humor to satire, from triviality to deep seriousness. And he must be original. "A vaudeville performer can go out with one act and get it booked for forty weeks solid. . . . A column hound must have a new act every day."

The feature article is a third type that gives real opportunity to the literary journalist. The feature may be a news story of special interest, a personality study, a sidelight on history or art or science—anything new or old dressed up to catch the present public fancy.

Like the feature writer is the "popularizer"—the writer who reduces the secrets of learning to simple terms, who talks in the language of the crowd. James Truslow Adams has done it in history and Paul de Kruif in medicine. Such writing often achieves wide and swift popularity. If it is to live as literature it must be done with fineness of touch.

In summary one may say that any journalist—reporter, reviewer, critic, editor—may write with such insight and such freshness and originality that his work becomes literature. Thus newspapers and magazines that make no claims to being "literary" often find themselves playing host to truly literary men. Then journalism becomes an art; and the story, comment, or verse struck off for the hour becomes a piece of reading for all time.

The writers whose work appears in this section of American journalism are all columnists. The columnist has unusual opportunity to instruct and to point up our ideals. When the "little man" seemed in danger of being counted a nobody in the late war, the beloved Ernie Pyle reminded us of an American and Christian principle—a belief in the dignity and worth of every man. Dorothy Thompson in "The Lesson of Dachau" points out where that worth lies. Walter Lippman, one of the greatest of the columnists, states the truth this way: "It is just here that the issue is joined. For in the recognition that there is in each man a final essence—that is to say, an immortal soul—which only God can judge, a limit was set upon the dominion of men over men."

Other columnists like John B. Kennedy and Marquis Childs probe the meaning of the news as it breaks about the world. Paul Mallon interprets it for the milkman and the butcher. Westbrook Pegler, strident and acid in his wrath, has a large following. Diplomatic Sumner Welles in his syndicated articles adheres unrelentingly to his clear-cut principles regarding international affairs; and George Sokolsky has joined in holy ire in the struggle between paganism and the "essential need for man to walk again in the image of God, unafraid and without shame."

# CHAPLAIN COURAGEOUS

*QUENTIN REYNOLDS*

*Perhaps the most recent type of journalistic writing to become popular is the digest article. Since a digest magazine condenses into an abbreviated form the best articles appearing in various periodicals and newspapers, the American people look upon it as a valuable timesaver.*

*In the article printed below, the left-hand column represents the original article as it appeared in COLLIER'S. In the right-hand column is the same article as it appeared in the READER'S DIGEST.*

*Here is the great war story telling how Father Joseph O'Callahan, S.J. helped to save the flaming carrier "Franklin" from one of the worst tragedies of our navy. For his bravery he received the Congressional Medal of Honor, the first one ever to be given to a chaplain of the U. S. armed forces.*

There had been twelve "General Quarters" during the night but no enemy planes had got through, and now the dawn had sent the Japs scurrying back to their bases on Okinawa and Kyushu. It looked like just another routine day for the big Essex-class carrier U.S.S. Franklin, rolling along 53 miles east of Shikoku, on Japan's doorstep.

The Franklin was named after a famous but indecisive battle of our Civil War, the Battle of Franklin, Tennessee, in which casualties were 10,000. But most of the crew of the big carrier didn't know that; they thought she was named after Benjamin Franklin and they called her the Big Ben. She had

There had been 12 "General Quarters" during the night but no enemy planes had got through, and now the dawn had sent the Japs scurrying back to their bases on Okinawa and Kyushu. March 19 looked like just another routine day for the big Essex-class carrier U.S.S. Franklin, rolling along 53 miles east of Shikoku, on Japan's doorstep. At 7 A.M., fighters zoomed off her deck for a strike at Kobe, and then the whole ship was quiet.

"Chaplain Courageous" by Quentin Reynolds, reprinted from the June 23–30, 1945 issues of *Collier's* and the September 1945 issue of *Reader's Digest,* reprinted by permission of the author and *Reader's Digest.*

been out in the Pacific almost a year and was in the Marianas and Philippines campaigns, and she knew her way around. Now, at 7 A.M., fighters zoomed off her deck for a strike at Kobe, and then the whole ship was quiet.

Down in the ready room, pilots lounged about drinking coffee. Everyone felt pretty secure. They were in the midst of a huge task force commanded by Vice-Admiral Marc Mitscher. American air-combat patrol circled above. Thirty Helldivers warmed up on the big flight deck and twenty-eight more planes were down below in the hangar deck, all bombed and gassed.

Aft on the fantail, Methodist Chaplain Grimes W. Gatlin of Grandview, Texas, murmured the soft words of the funeral service for a crewman who had died during the night.

Captain Leslie E. Gehres, of La Mesa, California, stood on the bridge with his air officer, Commander Henry Henderson Hale, and his navigator, Commander Stephen Jurika. Gehres is not an Annapolis man. He is a veteran fighter pilot, a large man with a strong face, and the big hands and cold eyes of a pilot. He's hard on himself and hard on his men, but he is cautious, too; and now he peered ahead at a low-hanging bank of clouds about 2,000 feet above the sea. He picked up a phone.

"What does the plot show?" he asked the Combat Information Center (CIC).

"No bogies, sir," the answer came from below. In the dark clouds ahead, they watched our own planes forming up for the strike.

Down in the wardroom, Lieutenant Commander Joseph Timothy O'Callahan was having breakfast with a few of-

Everyone felt pretty secure. The ship was in the midst of a huge task force. American air-combat patrol circled above. Thirty Helldivers warmed up on the big flight deck.

Captain Leslie E. Gehres stood on the bridge with his air officer and his navigator, peering at a low-hanging cloud bank. Down in the wardroom Lieut. Commander Joseph Timothy O'Callahan, the Catholic chaplain, was having breakfast with a few officers. The padre was a dark, slight-built man with the face of a perennial altar boy.

ficers. The padre is a dark, slight-built man with wavy black hair and the face of a perennial altar boy. He felt pretty good because he had collected four dollars during the night. Father O'Callahan had made it a ship's rule that he would impose a fine of fifty cents on anyone who swore. Twelve times during the night the crew had been routed out by air alarms, and the padre's sharp ear had caught seven officers swearing at the interruption of their sleep. And he had caught the captain himself. He always felt good when he caught the skipper. But now he was giving his fellow officers a little lecture on logic.

Father O'Callahan knew his logic the way he knew his mathematics and his philosophy. He had taught these subjects at Georgetown and at Holy Cross, and often, just for the sheer pleasure of hearing the brilliant Jesuit, his fellow officers would draw him into discussions.

"Look, Padre," one of them said, "theology and logic are full of contradictions. It is hard to reconcile some of these contradictions."

"Not at all." The eyes of the chaplain twinkled behind his glasses. "Sometimes life is filled with contradictions but logic never is. Now what are we having for breakfast?" The padre picked up his fork and tasted his hot cakes. "They're cold," he said triumphantly. "Now how can hot cakes be cold? If they are cold they are obviously not hot cakes. These miserable cold hot cakes are a contradiction. Life is filled with such contradictions. Hear those planes leaving the flight deck? They are nothing but heavy masses of steel and fabric. They have no right to rise above the deck and float in the air as they do. But they do just the same. Every time they take off, it is an apparent contradiction of the law of gravity."

"A fine way to start the day, arguing about logic," an officer laughed. "We're fifty miles off the coast of Japan and we sit here and talk about hot cakes."

"This is a day that long ago was dedicated to peace," the padre said, serious now. "It is March 19th. Do you know what feast we celebrate today? I see you don't. It is the feast of Saint Joseph. He is the patron saint of a happy death. We pray to him that we will die peacefully and without sin. . . ."

That's when it happened. It was 7:07 A.M. There was no warning—just an explosion that shook the ship and bounced the plates off the table, and then before the sound of it had died away, there was another, so quickly that it might have been an echo. Father O'Callahan and the other officers leaped to their feet. The wardroom is just aft of the forward hangar deck and above it. Smoke began to stream in through the port ventilator. The men choked and groped toward the doors.

It was quiet now, ominously quiet. It was quiet for thirty seconds, and no one knew the quiet was merely the prelude to the most horrifying hours any ship ever had to face; no one knew that this interlude was to usher in the most violent tragedy in the history of the United States Navy. What had happened? No one in the wardroom knew.

Captain Gehres, up on the bridge, knew. He saw—dead ahead—a single-engined Judy flash out of that cloud bank, diving at 360 miles an hour. Our own planes had been so close to it that the lookouts didn't spot it. It came over the bows of the Franklin at 75-foot height, dropped one 500-pounder near the deck edge, swung around the island,

Then it happened. It was 7:07 A.M. There was no warning—just an explosion that shook the ship and, before the sound had died away, there came another, so quickly that it might have been an echo.

What had happened? No one in the wardroom knew. But Captain Gehres, up on the bridge, knew. He saw a single-engined Judy flash out of the cloud bank, diving at 360 miles an hour. It came over the bows of the *Franklin* at 75-foot height, dropped one 500-pounder near the deck edge, swung around the island, and dropped another aft. As the skipper said later, "It was a Jap pilot's dream."

and dropped another aft of the island. The first sliced through the steel plate of the deck and hit the hangar deck. It exploded and threw metal all over the deck, went through the gas tanks, and a lick of flame crept over the planes.

The second bomb landed among the planes that were warming up on deck aft of the island. Their propellers were whirring, and their pilots were in their cockpits. The concussion blew planes against one another, threw turning steel-bladed propellers against fuselages and gas tanks, and a heavy billow of smoke covered the planes and the men and the deck. The Franklin, still under control, steamed ahead. The smoke was bad up on the bridge. You could chew it and spit it out.

Ordinarily, a big carrier can sustain several hits of the 500-pound kind, and perhaps take a torpedo hit or two without being in grave danger. But, as the skipper said later: "This was a Jap pilot's dream."

Commander Edwin Parker of San Francisco had just taken off in his Corsair. Parker is cool in combat and coldly efficient. He banked sharply, got on the tail of the Judy, let go a burst, and the Judy (to use carrier language) splashed. It splashed but it had done its work well—very well indeed.

And then the merciful interlude of thirty seconds was gone. Under the flight deck, the flames in the forward hangar deck had reached the bombs and the rockets, and then it was as though the world had come to an end. The explosion lifted the huge Franklin and spun it sharply to starboard. A burst of flame 400 feet high leaped out of the deck edge. One explosion followed another. The flight deck burst upward in a dozen places. The planes

It was ominously quiet now—for 30 seconds. No one knew that the quiet was merely the prelude to the most violent tragedy in the history of the U. S. Navy.

The first bomb, slicing through steel plate to the hangar deck, exploded among gas tanks and planes. The second, landing in the midst of planes warming up on deck, blew them against one another, threw turning steel-bladed propellers against fuselages. Flame and a heavy billow of smoke covered the planes and the men and the deck.

Commander Edwin Parker, who had just taken off in his Corsair, banked sharply, got on the tail of the Judy, let go a burst, and the Jap splashed. But he had done his work very well indeed.

For now the merciful interlude of 30 seconds was gone. Under the flight deck, the flames reached the bombs and rockets, and it was as though the world had come to an end. The explosion lifted the huge *Franklin* and spun it sharply to starboard. A burst of flame 400 feet high leaped out of the deck edge. The exploding flight deck burst upward in a dozen places. Huge rockets went off with weird swooshes, zooming through the holes in the deck high into the sky like giant Roman candles.

that were aft now began to burn fiercely. Every man of the more than 3,000 on board was knocked down. Before the day was done, 832 of them were dead, and 270 were wounded—the most tragic casualty list ever sustained by a U. S. Navy ship. The second terrific blast crippled the ship; it destroyed fifty-eight planes, and severed practically all communications—except by word of mouth.

Gehres could talk to the aft steering room and the engine room only. In the aft steering room, 20 by 25 feet and jammed with machinery, five men were trapped. There were four decks below topside. The explosions had warped their bulkhead exit. It wouldn't open. One of the trapped sailors—Holbrook R. Davis, 24, of Marstons Mills, Mass., thought that five trapped men among more than 3,000 stood very little chance of getting out alive. Steering aft is at

the water line. The compartment is airtight and watertight. When the lights failed, they were in darkness.

Hot bombs tore loose from the burning planes and rolled about the flight deck. Then the flames reached the plane ammunition, and .50-caliber belts went off like firecrackers, their staccato barking cutting through the explosion of the big bombs. Every few seconds the leaping flames would find another bomb or rocket. Men lay stunned all over the flight deck. Men lay dead on the hangar deck.

The CIC is the heart of the ship. On the Franklin, it lies between the flight deck and the hangar deck, in the "gallery" deck. This tremendous explosion burst right under it. The deck burst upward, hurling the men against the steel overhead. Every man there died instantly, except one. Lieutenant W. A. Simon was the only man in either compartment who was wearing a helmet. It saved his life. Close by, in the ready room, a dozen pilots who had been talking of the strike the day before died instantly. The skippers of the cruisers and destroyers for miles around the Franklin watched and winced as they saw the orange flames leap high into the blue. They saw her racked by thirty-one major explosions. Fifty tons of bombs and rockets tore her guts apart and fifty tons of ready ammunition drilled through her decks and zoomed into the sky. Twelve thousand gallons of gasoline burned fiercely inside.

Father O'Callahan tried to get aft from the wardroom. He was met by barriers of flame and twisted metal. Being cursed with a mathematical mind, he knew the Franklin the way he knew his way around the Gospels. He knew what the chances of survival were.

The planes that were aft now began to burn fiercely. Hot bombs tore loose from them and rolled about. Fifty-caliber belts went off like firecrackers. Men lay stunned all over the flight deck. Men lay dead on the hangar deck.

The CIC (Combat Information Center) on the gallery deck burst upward in a tremendous explosion, hurling the men in it against the steel overhead. Every man there died instantly, except Lieut. W. A. Simon, the only one wearing a helmet. Close by, in the ready room, a dozen pilots died instantly. Fifty tons of stored bombs and rockets tore the Franklin's guts apart, 50 tons of ready ammunition drilled through her decks. Twelve thousand gallons of gasoline burned fiercely inside her. The skippers of the cruisers and destroyers for miles around watched and winced as they saw the Franklin racked by 31 major explosions.

Father O'Callahan tried to make his way aft, to get to the flight deck where the wounded were. He was met by barriers of flame and twisted metal. He knew how much dynamite and gasoline the ship carried, and that it was probably only a few minutes before the

He knew them as a mathematician knows them. "About one in two hundred," he calculated instinctively. He knew how much dynamite and gasoline the ship carried. It was only a question of a few minutes before the flames would reach a magazine that would blow the ship sky high. He knew and he accepted the prospect of death calmly.

He accepted it almost joyously because he had just seen a miracle. Every man on that ship had been granted thirty seconds of life; those precious thirty seconds between the explosion of the two Jap bombs and the complete explosions of the bombs, rockets and aircraft on the hangar deck. Those were, he felt, thirty seconds in which to repent and prepare for death.

"The feast day of St. Joseph, patron saint of a happy death," he murmured, as he groped his way forward through corridors heavy with smoke. He reached a group of frantic men trying to climb through a hatchway that led up to the deck. They were jammed in the hatchway, shocked numb.

"One at a time, boys!" Father O'Callahan said crisply, and, recognizing the authority in his voice, some of the tenseness left them, and reason returned.

"We'll all get out. Take it easy, take it easy. One at a time," he repeated, and one by one they hoisted themselves through the hatchway. Father O'Callahan was trying to get to the flight deck. That's where the wounded were. He went farther aft and there he stumbled over a dozen wounded. One by one he bent over them. Catholic? Jew? Protestant? He didn't know. He didn't care. These were his men and this was the moment for which he had trained all his life. Two pharma-

flames would reach a magazine that would blow the ship sky high. He knew and he accepted the prospect of death calmly.

Groping his way through corridors heavy with smoke, he reached a group of frantic men trying to climb through a hatchway to the deck. They were jammed in the hatchway, shocked numb.

"One at a time, boys!" Father O'Callahan called crisply, and when they recognized the authority in his voice some of the tenseness left them and reason returned. "Take it easy. One at a time," he repeated, and one by one they hoisted themselves through the hatchway.

cist's mates were puncturing the arms of the men with morphine needles and hauling the worst injured into quarters now converted into an emergency hospital.

"Say the Our Father with me," Father O'Callahan would say, and the men would repeat it after him.

"Say an Act of Contrition, boy," he'd murmur. Sometimes the men would look blank. "Repeat this after me, son: 'O my God, I am heartily sorry for having offended Thee. . . .'"

He went from one to another, and to those who were obviously dying he gave the last rites of the Church, absolution. If he gave them to some who were not of his faith, it did not matter. He went into the emergency hospital. There was a doctor there now, Lieutenant Commander "Sam" Sherman. He was working. In addition to Sherman, there were three other medicos on board, James Fuelling, F. K. Smith and J. W. Fox. Fox died in the first explosion. The padre went from bunk to bunk. . . .

One boy in great pain burst out, "Jesus Christ!" and then through the mist of agony that clouded his eyes he saw Father O'Callahan. "I owe you half a dollar, Padre," he said.

"No. That's a free word today, son," the padre said gently, and the boy smiled as though at a secret joke he and the padre shared.

Every man on the ship shared something with Joseph Timothy O'Callahan. He talked their language, and they admired him and they knew he was their friend and it didn't matter to what church they belonged. When you got into trouble he was always there with a word in your defense. Besides, he was more than a cleric somehow. Why, he played poker with you

Every man on the ship shared something with Joseph Timothy O'Callahan. He talked their language, and they knew he was their friend. When you got into trouble he was always there with a word in your defense. Besides, he was somehow more than a cleric. He played poker with you and he wrote and he wrote songs for the band and in port he'd have a glass of beer with you. "He only believes in two things," they'd chuckle. "He believes in God and the enlisted man."

On the bridge, Captain Gehres watched airplane engines and big chunks of deck sing through the air. He picked up the phone to the aft steering room where the five men were trapped. "Listen," he said. "Take it easy. We'll get you out of there. It may take a little time, but it's a promise."

Meanwhile, Commander Joe Taylor, executive officer and second in command of the ship, was trying to find his way to the bridge. The flight deck aft, covered with heavy smoke, was a wilderness, a jungle of debris and bodies, and the smoke so thick you couldn't keep your bearings. Taylor dropped to the deck and crawled, using the deck seams as guides. Finally he found the island. The bottom part of it was enveloped in smoke and flame and he couldn't get to the doors. But he found a chain ladder hanging down, and he scrambled up and tumbled over the side of the bridge. Gehres was there. "Your face is dirty as hell, Joe," he said. "That's what the admiral said last time you were bombed. Remember?"

"I remember," Taylor said grimly. "This is a bit worse though, Captain."

"It is indeed," Gehres said thoughtfully.

Gehres was thinking of that day in October off the Philippines when the Big Ben sustained a hit on her deck that killed twenty-five men. That was the Big Ben's baptism of fire, and it was nothing compared to this.

But when trouble comes to you in the Navy, you're never alone. Every ship in the task force was figuring out

songs for the band and in port he'd have a glass of beer with you. "He only believes in two things," they'd say, "—God and the enlisted man."

Meanwhile, Commander Joe Taylor, second in command of the ship, was trying to find his way to the bridge. The flight deck aft was a jungle of debris and bodies; the smoke was so thick "you could eat it and spit it." Taylor dropped to the deck and crawled, using the deck seams as guides. Finally he found the island. The bottom part of it was enveloped in smoke and flame and he couldn't get to the doors. But he found a chain ladder hanging down, and he scrambled up and tumbled over the side of the bridge. Gehres greeted him. "Your face is dirty as hell, Joe," he said.

By now every ship in the task force was figuring out some way to help the some way to help the Franklin. Carriers had sent their fighters up to protect the stricken ship from air attack. The billowing smoke from the ship could be seen forty miles away—almost to the Japanese mainland. The cruiser Santa Fe, Captain H. C. Fitz, U.S.N., commanding, came up on the starboard side.

"Are your magazines flooded?" he yelled through his megaphone to Gehres. He was thinking of the disaster that overtook the Birmingham last fall when she was taking survivors off the stricken Princeton. The Princeton exploded and inflicted horrible casualties on the Birmingham personnel.

"I think so," Gehres called back. He'd given orders to flood them. But were the valves which controlled that operation in working order? Gehres couldn't tell from the bridge and he had practically no communication with the men below except through the trapped men in steering aft.

There, Seaman Davis and his trapped companions watched drops of water hang for a moment to the hatchway above their heads, then drop to their feet. They watched it with their flashlights and they wondered if the skipper remembered his promise.

When a carrier is on fire and there seems little hope of saving her, there are a great many things that are done automatically. This is Navy routine, and the officers and men on board had been trained for such emergencies and they knew what to do. There is one order that must be obeyed as quickly as possible: "Get all unnecessary personnel off the ship."

There were two air admirals on board, Ralph Davison and Jerry Bogan. They and their staffs had to leave; they had no discretion in the matter. The

Franklin. Carriers had sent their fighters up to protect the stricken ship: the billowing smoke could be seen 40 miles away—almost to the Japanese mainland. The cruiser Santa Fe and the destroyer Miller had come up and begun to play hoses on the flames.

Gehres asked the Miller and Santa Fe to take off the seriously wounded and the whole air group aboard. There was no discretion in this matter. These pilots, the whole air group and radar experts had to leave. They must live to fight from another ship. The wounded, too, must be taken off.

The explosions kept coming. The huge rockets went off with weird swooshes, and then if their heads hit anything, the explosion would shake the big ship. Some rockets exploded and flew through holes in the flight deck and zoomed high in the sky like giant Roman candles and then fell back to explode in the water, sending huge geysers skyward.

The destroyer U.S.S. Miller came aft and began to play four streams of hose on the flames. Gehres asked her to come up on the port side so the two admirals and their staffs could leave. As Admiral Davison left the bridge he said to Gehres, "You'd better prepare to abandon ship."

"If you'll give me an air patrol and surface support, I think I can save her, sir," Gehres said. Admiral Davison shook hands and nodded. In the Navy, the captain of the ship is its boss. The admirals left. They had to.

Up on the bridge soft-spoken Commander Stephen Jurika, survivor of the carrier Hornet, was methodically keeping the log. As navigator, that was part of his job. Steve is a quiet man who hates the Japanese very much. He had lived among them as naval attaché in Tokyo. He speaks their language. A very quiet and a very dangerous man. He hates Japs more than any man on the ship—more than any man in the whole Pacific fleet. The Japs killed his mother in Manila.

"At 0952 (he wrote) the most terrific blast of the morning occurred resulting from a five-inch ready service magazine being set afire. The ship felt as though it were a rat being shaken by an angry

men must live to fight from another ship.

As Air Admiral Davison left he said to Gehres, "You'd better prepare to abandon ship."

"If you'll give me an air patrol and surface support, I think I can save her, sir," Gehres said. Admiral Davison shook hands and nodded. In the Navy, the captain of the ship is its boss.

cat. Whole aircraft engines with propellers attached, debris of all description, including pieces of human bodies were flung high into the air and descended in the general area like hail upon a roof. . . ."

Now the Franklin was dead in the water and drifting—toward Japan. She had a 14-degree list to starboard. She had drifted away from the Santa Fe, but the cruiser turned about and roared up at 22 knots to crunch hard and fast against the sagging side of the Franklin. "Greatest bit of seamanship I ever saw," Gehres said.

Jurika wrote: "She came alongside as though she were a well-handled gig making a liberty float at Long Beach."

The explosions continued, but Fitz, on the bridge of the Santa Fe, ignored them and ignored the debris that sprinkled his ship. Men from the Franklin jumped down to her decks. The pilots and technical personnel were sent aboard her. The wounded were transferred. There were fires all over the Big Ben now. Only one Diesel was working and that gave just enough power to send water through the hoses.

Father O'Callahan had given the last rites to dozens of men; he'd prayed with the wounded and now, for the moment, he was finished. A strong breeze came from starboard to pierce the heavy smoke, and from the bridge Gehres saw the padre manning a hose. Exhausted men numb from shock lay on the deck but when they saw the padre, with the white cross painted on his helmet, they climbed to their feet and followed him.

Hot bombs still rolled about the deck. They were all "armed;" that is, sharp contact would explode them. O'Callahan pointed his hose and led the men to them. He knew that if the heavy stream of the hose ever hit the

Now the *Franklin* was dead in the water and had a 14-degree list to starboard. She drifted away from the *Santa Fe*, but the cruiser, commanded by Captain H. C. Fitz, turned about and crunched hard and fast against the sagging side of the *Franklin*. "Greatest bit of seamanship I ever saw," Gehres said.

The explosions kept coming. A magazine containing five-inch shells blew up. But Fitz, on the bridge of the *Santa Fe*, ignored them and ignored the debris, including whole aircraft engines, that sprinkled his ship.

From the bridge, Gehres saw Father O'Callahan manning a hose. Exhausted men numb from shock lay on the deck but when they saw the padre with the white cross painted on his helmet they climbed to their feet and followed him.

Hot bombs still rolled about the deck. If the heavy stream of the hose hit the sensitive noses of the bombs

sensitive noses of the bombs they would explode. Cleverly he directed the stream to the deck a foot from the bombs and literally sprinkled and sprayed them, keeping them cool even though fires raged within feet of them and smoke occasionally hid them from view. A man could stand only a few minutes of that choking smoke. They would fall back gasping, and O'Callahan would cry for more men. He seemed made of iron.

Jurika wrote: "Fires on the flight deck were being fought with great courage and determination. O'Callahan was everywhere, leading men, officiating at last rites, manning hoses and doing the work of ten men."

Gehres asked the priest to phone the men in steering aft. He did. "Play cards and pray," he yelled. "The captain promised to get you out and he will!"

they would explode. So O'Callahan directed his hose at the deck a foot from the bombs and sprinkled and sprayed them, keeping them cool even though fires raged near them. The smoke was bad. Men could stand only a few minutes of it. They would fall back gasping, and O'Callahan would cry for more men. He seemed made of iron. Gehres said afterward that "O'Callahan is the bravest man I've ever seen in my life."

Gehres said afterward that "O'Callahan is the bravest man I've ever seen in my life."

Fire threatened a five-inch magazine below, loaded with shells. O'Callahan saw the danger and rushed into the magazine, calling for men to follow. Heat had blistered the paint off ammo lockers, and heavy greenish smoke poured out. The padre wet down the lockers and the shells, and then helped carry the stuff out and dump it overboard.

"The padre's praising the Lord and he's passing the ammunition," somebody yelled.

One man repeated it to another. It traveled all over the ship. The men grinned. The padre was all right. He didn't know it, but up on the bridge Gehres was saying to himself, "If we ever get out of this, I'll recommend that Irishman for the Congressional Medal."

The padre went from one part of the ship to another. He was always where things were hottest and he was smiling, and his good humor and his courage acted as a tonic to men who had almost reached the breaking point. Now flaming gasoline had broken out all over. It sluiced down the sloping deck, floating flames that licked everywhere. O'Callahan turned his hose on it and swept it overboard. The fight to survive went on.

One of many who waged the battle was Don Gary. Remember the name—Lieutenant (jg) Donald Gary of Oakland, California. A thin-faced man with a voice that could be soft on occasions but that could crack like a whip on others. Gary, an assistant engineering officer who had served thirty years at sea, somehow found his way down to the third deck aft. He knew that 300 men were trapped there in the mess-

Fire threatened a five-inch magazine below, loaded with shells. O'Callahan saw the danger and rushed into the magazine, calling for men to follow. Heat had blistered the paint off ammo lockers, and heavy greenish smoke poured out. The padre wet down the lockers and shells, and then helped carry the stuff out and dump it overboard.

Flaming gasoline sluiced down the sloping deck, floating flames that licked everywhere. O'Callahan turned his hose on it and swept it overboard. The fight to survive went on.

One of many who waged the battle was Lieut. (j.g.) Donald Gary, a former petty officer who had served 30 years at sea. Gary knew that many men were trapped in the messroom on the third deck aft. He walked through fire and water and blast to reach it—how, no one knows. In the messroom were 300 men. There were four entrances to the room. Three of the steel doors had been sprung by the heat and

room below on the third deck. He walked through fire and water and blast to reach it. How Gary got from the flight deck to the hangar deck and below that to the third deck, no one knows.

In the messroom were Lieutenant Commander James Fuelling of Woodburn, Indiana, and 300 men. There were four entrances to the room. Three of the steel doors had been sprung by the heat and blast. The other exit was blocked by fire.

"We'll get you out of here," Gary shouted, and the men recognized the whip in his voice. This was their kind of man, an old petty officer who knew the ropes. They quieted down and Gary said, "I'll be back in a few minutes." He went back through the smoke and flames to see if there was a safe way of getting topside.

Doctor Fuelling called through the smoke, "Oxygen's giving out, men. Lie on the floor. Don't talk. Say a prayer to yourselves and don't worry. Mr. Gary will get us out."

Gary came back. The smoke he'd swallowed didn't soften the whip in his voice. "Form a chain," he said crisply. "Each man grab another man and follow me. Come in groups of twenty."

Lieutenant Gary ordered the first group of twenty men to follow him. All lights had long since gone. Gary's small flashlight made no impression in the thick yellow smoke that filled the passageways. But he found a ventilator trunk. He led the men to it. He had removed the grate and now he shoved his body inside and began to climb. The men followed him and within a few minutes lay gasping on the flight deck. Gary went back many times. He brought every one of the three hundred men out to safety. The last to

blast. The other exit was seemingly blocked by fire, but Gary got through.

"Form a chain!" he shouted. "Each man grab another man and follow me. Come in groups of 20."

Gary's small flashlight made no impression in the thick yellow smoke that filled the passageways. But he found a ventilator trunk. He led the men to it, removed the grate, got inside and began to climb. The men followed him and within a few minutes lay gasping on the flight deck. Gary went back many times. He brought every one of the 300 men out to safety. Captain Gehres later recommended him for the Congressional Medal of Honor.

leave with him was Jim Fuelling, the medico.

"We'd have all been dead if it hadn't been for Gary," Fuelling said.

Gary blushed that off and joined the fire fighters. Oh, yes, Captain Gehres later recommended him for the Congressional Medal. But right then Gary was in a hurry to get back to the flight deck and the fire fighting and the Irishman, Father O'Callahan, who was writing history up there.

Young Lieutenant Stanley S. Graham was the fire marshal. Father O'Callahan was always at his elbow. They call the blond, good-looking fire marshal "Steamship" Graham. They say that's what the S in his name stands for.

"We all belonged to the padre's church that day," Graham said later. "And I'm a Baptist. The padre just doesn't know what fear is."

Father O'Callahan wasn't afraid. In fact, he is puzzled at anyone who is afraid of death. "It's stupid to fear death," he told me. "Yes, I thought we were all going that morning but I can't say I bothered to think much of it. To begin with, I was prepared. I was as ready as I'll ever be. If a man can be given the chance of picking a way to die —well, what better way than to die in the uniform of the United States Navy, fighting for your country? I don't remember being afraid. I've led an academic life for the most part. I often wondered if some of the things I've learned and some of the things I've taught were really of practical value. Well, that morning I found that everything I'd been taught was now helping me in one way or another. Yes, even logic and philosophy and mathematics and, of course, physics. They give you added strength when you're in the kind of situation we found ourselves in."

That's O'Callahan—fighting Navy priest—and that's the way he felt on that morning of March 19th when, at 11:15, Captain Gehres told Joe Taylor he had decided to accept a tow from the cruiser Pittsburgh.

Quite a man, Joe Taylor. He'd been christened prophetically enough Joseph Franklin Taylor in Danville, Illinois. But when they first asked his name when he entered the Naval Academy he blurted out "Joe Taylor," and he's been Joe Taylor on the rolls ever since. Every naval man in the Pacific knows about Taylor's two Navy Crosses, his Bronze Star, his Purple Heart and the green ribbon he wears, sign of a commendation from Admiral Nimitz.

"He's part Indian," the pilots will tell you, chuckling. "That's what makes him so tough. Used to be a test pilot. Hell, he can fly anything with wings! As a torpedo pilot he sank a carrier in the Coral Sea battle. Yeah, Joe was on the Yorktown when she got it, but nothing much happened to him. The guy is indestructible."

So it was Taylor who went forward and found thirty men and gave them the captain's orders. First they'd have to get rid of a starboard anchor so they could use the heavy anchor chain for the tow. You need a strong chain to tow 27,000 tons of dead weight. They found an emergency cutting outfit and soon the big anchor splashed into the sea. The Pittsburgh had come around to the Franklin's bow. She tossed a rope over and to it was attached what Navy men call an eight-inch messenger. That's a rope eight inches thick. They began to haul in the water-soaked rope. Ordinarily this would be done by winches, but there was no power.

"The men were Negro cooks and steward's mates but they worked like

Now, by transferring water and oil from starboard tanks to port, the ship was brought almost on an even keel. Captain Gehres decided to accept a tow from the cruiser *Pittsburgh*, and 30 men on the *Franklin* began to haul in the eight-inch rope. Ordinarily this would be done by winches, but there was no power.

real deck seamen," Taylor says. "It was an inspiring sight to watch the men and officers all pulling together, all chanting."

Tommy Frasure and Willie Cogman had a bright idea. They remembered an old Negro spiritual and they began to chant the chorus of it. "Yeave . . . Ho . . . Yeave . . . Ho," they chanted slowly, and the others took it up.

Joe Taylor grinned. How could you go wrong when even the messboys were turning into heroes? The huge rope slackened and then tightened and slackened and tightened, and, every time it tightened, a few extra precious feet came aboard. "Yeave . . . Ho . . . Yeave . . . Ho."

On the bridge, the captain watched the scene. He phoned the five men trapped in steering aft and told them that he hadn't forgotten them. Young Holbrook Davis said thanks and told the skipper that someone—he didn't know who—had phoned from an engine room and asked permission to correct the 14-degree list to starboard by transferring water and oil from starboard tanks to port. The skipper said, "Tell him to proceed."

A little more than an hour later, the ship was on an almost even keel, listing slightly to port. No one has been able to find out the identity of the hero who eliminated the danger of capsizing.

Finally, everything was secured and the Pittsburgh, Captain John E. Gingrich in command, began to move ahead slowly. At least the Franklin wouldn't be a sitting duck in the water when Jap planes came over. And it was Jap planes that worried Gehres up there on the bridge. Most of his guns were out of commission or in parts of the ship where fires were blazing. Besides, the men were too busy with the fires to

"Yeave . . . Ho . . . Yeave . . . Ho," the men chanted as they hauled. The huge rope slackened and tightened and slackened and tightened, and every time it tightened a few extra precious feet came aboard.

When everything was secured, the *Pittsburgh* began to tow slowly. At least the *Franklin* wouldn't be a sitting duck when Jap planes came over. Most of her guns were out of commission, even if the men weren't too busy with the fires to man them.

man guns, and he knew that the Japs like nothing better than a shot at a blazing cripple. Gehres noticed that aft of the bridge there was a 40-millimeter battery that hadn't been touched. But could he spare the men to man it? Gehres sometimes thinks aloud. He was thinking of that battery, and his Marine orderly, Wally Klimciewicz, heard him thinking out loud.

"Begging the captain's pardon, but may I have permission to man the battery?" chunky Klimciewicz said.

"What do you know about forty-millimeters?" Gehres asked impatiently.

"I'm a Marine, sir," Klimciewicz said.

"All right, Marine. Go ahead."

The orderly scrambled down and half an hour later Gehres saw him with seven other men around the guns. Klimciewicz had gathered two cooks, one gunner's mate, a yeoman, two buglers from the band and another Marine orderly—and none too soon. Far above the horizon, black puffs dotted the sky. Enemy planes were coming in. The puffs blossomed closer as near-by ships began to fire. Klimciewicz hunched over the sights of his battery.

Then a Judy, squirming and escaping the ack-ack fire of the whole fleet, dived at the Franklin. She started to make her run from aft. Klimciewicz's forties popped at her. It was an unequal duel, because the makeshift crew had to shift the gun by hand; the electrical controls were out.

The Judy, coming at 300 miles an hour, was a hundred yards from the ship when she swerved sharply. The forties had hit her; hit her just enough to make her lose control. She dropped a bomb and missed the Franklin by twenty feet. The explosion raised the ship and shook her—but no real damage had been done. Klimciewicz and his makeshift

Gehres noticed one 40-mm. battery that hadn't been touched. But could he spare the men to man it? Gehres sometimes thinks aloud. His 19-year-old Marine orderly, Wally Klimciewicz, heard him thinking out loud now.

"Begging the Captain's pardon, but may I have permission to man the battery?" Klimciewicz said.

"What do you know about 40-millimeters?" Gehres asked impatiently.

"I'm a Marine, sir," Klimciewicz said.

"All right, Marine. Go ahead."

The orderly scrambled down and half an hour later Gehres saw him with seven other men at the battery. Klimciewicz had gathered two cooks, one gunner's mate, a yeoman, two buglers from the band and another Marine orderly—and none too soon. Far above the horizon, black puffs dotted the sky. Enemy planes were coming in. The puffs blossomed closer as nearby ships began to fire. Klimciewicz hunched over the sights of his battery.

Then a Judy dived at the Franklin. Klimciewicz's 40's popped at her. The makeshift crew had to shift the gun by hand; the electrical controls were out. The Judy, coming at 300 miles an hour, was a hundred yards from the ship when she swerved sharply. The 40's had hit her, just enough to make her lose control. She dropped a bomb and missed the Franklin by 20 feet. The explosion shook the ship—but no further damage was done. Klimciewicz and his makeshift crew had saved the Franklin from a hit that undoubtedly would have been fatal.

crew had saved the Franklin from a direct hit, a hit that undoubtedly would have been fatal.

"I'm a Marine, sir," Klimciewicz had said. That's enough—a 19-year-old Marine out of Jersey City.

The Pittsburgh kept a steady six knots, pulling the stricken carrier slowly away from Japan. Twice during the afternoon Jap planes made desperate efforts to get at her. But now the whole fleet was fighting to save this amazing ship that had lived through an experience that no ship in the history of naval warfare had ever been asked to live through. In truth, a large part of the fleet interposed itself between the Franklin and the coast of Japan, so that Nip bombers would be forced to run the gantlet of heavy AA fire before reaching the cripple.

Gehres received a report that a hundred Jap planes were approaching. He set his teeth a bit harder. He had confidence in this Navy. The planes were intercepted by our fighters far out beyond the horizon. A few got through but more than forty were "splashed." Now and then an odd one got through, and twice the Big Ben rattled and shook as bombs screamed down at her to explode in the sea.

In steering aft, Holbrook Davis and his four trapped companions sat in darkness and listened to the explosions. Someone said, "I don't think we ran into a mine field. We got bombed." The water dripped down from the hatchway above. That was their only means of escape but they did not yet know that the hatchway was flooded with ten feet of water. All they knew was that up above, the fight went on to save the Franklin.

"Every time a Judy dived at us," Lieutenant Commander Dave Berger of

Twice during the afternoon Jap planes made desperate efforts to get at her. But now the whole fleet was fighting to save this amazing ship that refused to die, and more than 40 Jap planes were "splashed."

Philadelphia, says, "we looked for fox-holes. We dug our noses in the deck all right. Once when one came close, I ducked behind a five-inch magazine. The Jap had opened his wing guns and was chewing up the deck. At that moment I looked up, and there was Father O'Callahan calmly walking along the flight deck carrying a hose. He was so busy he never noticed the Jap planes."

But everyone noticed the padre. By now everyone on board was talking about him. He walked through smoke and fire, and emerged unscathed. He tried to get a Filipino boy to help him dump a bomb overboard. The youngster took one look at the bomb and understandably shrank from it.

"Are you a Catholic, son?" Father O'Callahan asked.

The boy nodded.

"Then I'll give you the last rites of the church and, no matter what happens, if you truly repent your sins, you'll have a chance for heaven." Solemnly he repeated the ritual, and the fear left the face of the boy.

"And now, son, let's get to work," Father O'Callahan said crisply.

The boy was a good worker from then on. Good? Gehres recommended him for a Bronze Star.

That story ran around the ship. Men began to believe that if you were with Father O'Callahan you were safe. They crowded around him saying, "What next, Padre?" And he'd tell them.

Now and then Father O'Callahan would point to the bridge. The bulky figure of Gehres, megaphone in hand, leaned over the rail. When the wind cleared the smoke away, you could see him. Father O'Callahan would point up to Gehres and he'd cry out to the men, "You can't let the Old Man down. Look at him up there. He

Father O'Callahan still fought the fires, indefatigable after ten hours of it. The heat was so intense that, in spots, the steel itself seemed to be blazing. But the padre walked through smoke and fire with his hose, emerging unscathed. Men began to believe that if you were with him you were safe. They crowded around him saying, "What next, Padre?"

Now and then he would point to the bridge. The bulky figure of Gehres leaned over the rail. When the wind blew the smoke away you could see him, and Father O'Callahan would cry out, "Look at the Old Man up there!

doesn't look worried, does he? Have faith in the Old Man!"

In the long run, it was faith that saved that ship, the faith of the padre; the faith of the men in him and the faith of the men in Captain Gehres and Joe Taylor. Call it by some other name if you want but the men of the Franklin believe it was faith. Dusk began to fall, and no one was very happy about that. From now on, the fleet would have to depend almost entirely upon radar to defend the Franklin. The Santa Fe and two destroyers came in close, again directing their hoses on the flaming parts of the ship. The heat was so intense that, in some spots, the steel itself was blazing. The fires must be out by nightfall or the Franklin would be a flaming beacon visible fifty miles away. Father O'Callahan was still at it, indefatigable, and now, by virtue of ten hours of work, a veteran fire fighter.

The soft darkness had fallen to end a horrible day. The sick bay was crowded with wounded but the hands of Doctors Fuelling and Smith and Sherman weren't tired, or if they were, you'd never notice it. They had a great assistant with them, Chaplain Grimes W. Gatlin. He'd been with them since the first bomb struck early that morning. He'd been comforting the wounded and binding jagged cuts and using the morphine needles the way a doctor uses them. He had never left the wounded. He had some knowledge of medicine and considerable knowledge of men, and his knowledge and deft hands and sympathy were of great help that fearful day. Father O'Callahan is the first to say, "You can't write a story of the Franklin without telling of the great work Chaplain Gatlin did." He got the Silver Star.

He doesn't look worried, does he? Don't let him down!"

Holbrook Davis phoned to say that the engine-room crews were dropping from smoke and that the below-deck ventilators were out. They wanted permission to "secure station" and leave. Gehres told Davis to relay an order to each engine room to stand to station as long as possible, and then to leave without "securing station"—in sum, without dousing the boiler fires. Davis said "Aye, aye, sir." He didn't say a word about himself and his companions or how it felt to be imprisoned at the water line in an airtight compartment.

The Franklin was still moving ahead at six knots. She was listing slightly to port now. Her rudder control was gone, and nothing much on board was working, but her hull was sound and her heart was sound. Men brought food to the bridge—canned pork sausage and orange juice.

"Best damn' meal I ever tasted," Commander Taylor grinned.

The Hunt and the Marshall hovered close, their hoses ready to dim any fires that might break out. Twice they reported blazes that the men aboard couldn't get at. Twice they threw tons of water at the flames. Gehres received a report that Japs were approaching in large numbers. This time he could grin at Taylor. He felt by now that his ship was indestructible. And he was right.

"The Jap planes had been given the position we'd been at six hours before," Gehres explains. "But we had been towed forty miles since then. They went to that position, dropped flares, didn't see us—and returned home. We were sitting there with plenty of flames to guide them but they never went looking for us. Apparently the Jap just obeys orders. He doesn't take the initiative."

After dark Gehres received a report that Japs were approaching in large numbers. He grinned. He felt by now that his ship was indestructible. As Commander Taylor put it, "a ship that won't be sunk, can't be sunk." He was right. "Jap planes had been given the position we'd been at six hours before," Gehres explains. "But we had been towed 40 miles since then. They went to that position, dropped flares, didn't see us—and returned home."

The night wore on, and Gehres breathed easier. He lighted a cigarette and inhaled deeply. It was the first time since that morning he'd had a chance to smoke.

"Watch that butt, Captain. It's a 'darkened ship,'" a respectful voice said.

Gehres tossed the cigarette overboard automatically and then looked to see who on this ship had the temerity to reprimand the skipper. It was Wally "I'm-a-Marine" Klimciewicz. Gehres smiled. This is a good crew, he thought, standing there on the bridge. He thought with satisfaction of Lieutenant Melvin Tappen, officer of the deck and of Jurika and Taylor, and of Jortberg, the helmsman, of Ryan and Tarr and Bernard and O'Donovan. A great gang to have along when you're in trouble, Gehres said to himself. Gehres tried not to think of the dead.

As the fires grew less in number and size, the men fell to the deck and let the night breeze revive them. The skipper came down from the bridge and asked some of them if they would try to rescue the five men in steering aft. They got up wearily and some of them worked their way below decks into the blackness. They used their flashlights and came to the compartment above the five men.

They saw the ten feet of water. Heavy debris sloshed about as the carrier tossed. Power pumps would be useless. The rescuers knew that there was no power. So they went topside again and came back down with hand pumps and worked. One man managed to open a bulkhead door, and the pent-up water crashed out into the darkness.

When the compartment had less than a foot of water, the rescuers

The night wore on, and Gehres breathed easier. He lighted a cigarette and inhaled deeply. "Watch that butt, Captain. It's 'darkened ship,'" a respectful voice said.

Gehres tossed the cigarette overboard automatically and then looked to see who had the temerity to reprimand the skipper. It was Wally "I'm-a-Marine" Klimciewicz. Gehres smiled. This is a good crew, he thought, a great gang to have along when you're in trouble. He tried not to think of the dead.

tapped a message to Davis below. Then they swung the hatch open, and the water swirled down. It wasn't quite midnight when Holbrook Davis and his four friends, dripping, came topside, looking bewildered and asking, "What the hell happened?"

They had been trapped below for sixteen hours, but the skipper had kept his word.

The engineers reported that they might be able to get the engines running soon. They had stuck by their stations, although many had dropped unconscious in the 130-degree heat, and they had managed to turn over the engines. Now, through Holbrook Davis' telephone they said they were ready to proceed. This would give the bridge steering power. It would mean that Gehres could throw off the tow. He'd have a ship again, not just a huge battered hulk.

The dawn came finally, and Gehres looked down on what was left of his ship. The flight deck had jagged holes torn all over it—more than twenty gaping holes—and was littered with debris; broken aircraft, smashed guns, melted steel—and bodies. He looked around. It was comforting to see the Santa Fe, the Pittsburgh and four destroyers standing by.

At ten o'clock that morning Gehres sent this message to the Pittsburgh: "Ready to make fifteen knots on two engines. If okay desire to cast off tow lines. Request permission to go ahead."

An hour later the Franklin was moving along under her own power. Men on ships all around her yelled when they saw the battered giant, her flag snapping from her mast, move away alive. They'd seen this ship blazing from dozens of fires. They'd expected her to take the final plunge any minute,

The engineers below decks had stuck by their stations, although many had dropped unconscious in the 130-degree heat. By midmorning they managed to turn over the engines, and Gehres could throw off the tow.

Men on ships all around the *Big Ben* —as her crew affectionately call her— yelled when they saw the battered giant moving along under her own power, her flag snapping from her mast. They'd seen this ship blazing from dozens of fires. They'd expected her to take the final plunge any minute, yet here she yet here she was, a bit lopsided, with her island mast leaning forward like the feather in a hat, the smoke still coming from her hangar deck and through the holes in her flight deck—but she was moving. She was alive.

Down below, there was one persistent fire that wouldn't die. The thick smoke kept pouring from a room that held stores. Men with oxygen masks and asbestos suits finally got into the room to remove the smoldering stuff. They found that what had laughed at tons of water was the ship's supply of black shoe polish. The remains were hurriedly dumped overboard.

The ship was still listing to port. The only thing to do was to jettison everything possible from the port side. Five-inch guns were ripped up and rolled over the side. Down on the hangar deck, thousands of tons of still hot metal had shifted with the list. This had to be jettisoned. But there was no power to work hoists and cranes. Lieutenant (jg) Lindsay (Red) Morgan had the idea of using jeeps. There were four of them on board and, by some miracle, they were still intact. Red Morgan connected them by chains, and the masses of steel were pulled to the side. It was easy then for fifty men to shove the stuff overboard. They jettisoned the "Beast" (the huge hangar deck crane used to pick up wrecked planes).

Chaplains O'Callahan and Gatlin held burial services for hundreds of men. There were still many bodies under the smoldering tons of steel and on the hangar deck. Others had been blown overboard. It was impossible to know as yet what the casualities were.

Late that afternoon the men found a precious bit of cargo intact: several hundred cases of beer. There was no

was, a bit lopsided, smoke still coming from her hangar deck and through 20 jagged holes in her flight deck—but moving. She was alive.

fresh water left, so Gehres ordered one can of beer to be given to each man. It was a morale builder.

Father O'Callahan bumped into Saxy Dowell, the band leader, who began life in Raleigh, North Carolina. Saxy used to play with Hal Kemp's band and it was he who wrote the popular song, Three Little Fishes. Most of his instruments had been destroyed, Saxy told the padre sadly. He still had his saxophone and a couple of trumpets.

"We can use pots and pans, Saxy, instead of drums," Father O'Callahan said. "We've got to give the men something to laugh at. Get some whistles. We'll give them a concert, Saxy. I'll write some parodies for them to sing."

Just before nightfall, a dozen men, most of whom carried makeshift instruments, began to parade the flight deck. They played loudly if not beautifully, and their song was an old familiar American folk song, The Old Gray Mare, but the words were:

Oh, the Old Big Ben, she ain't what
　she used to be,
Ain't what she used to be, just a few
　hours ago. . . .

The men took up the song. Father O'Callahan was singing louder than any of them. Well, it was his song. The voices rang across the water to the men aboard the Santa Fe and the Pittsburgh.

"Those guys must be punch drunk," the cruiser crews said. The sound grew louder and louder until every man on the Franklin was singing. The voices were cracked from swallowing smoke.

"Give 'em this one, Saxy," the padre whispered in Dowell's ear, and then his band struck up probably the most appropriate song that any one could have imagined.

The men listened and then roared with laughter and they took up the words. It's the song that begins:

*Oh, give me land . . . lots of land . . .*
*and a starry sky above. . . .*
*Don't fence me in.*

In the morning Joe Taylor found a mimeograph that still worked. Gehres told him to get out a mimeographed plan of the day, and distribute copies to the crew. The mimeographed sheet was headed: "Big Ben bombed, battered, bruised and bent but not broken."

The plan for the day read: "(1) All hands wear clean dungarees, blue-dyed hats, black shoes to quarters. Chins up, chests out, tails over the dashboard. (2) Gun crews will wear helmets. All usable gun batteries will be manned. . . . Joe Taylor, Executive Officer."

Another night and another day, and now Gehres put the crew to clearing the hangar deck. It could never be entirely cleared but some of the debris could be shoved overboard. He worked them hard to keep their minds off the job they were doing, uncovering bodies of shipmates. He worked them hard to keep them sane, and then when they were ready to drop, Father O'Callahan took over. He made them play volley ball; he wrote more parodies, and he and Saxy Dowell and the band sang lustily, and then when darkness fell, men dropped where they were and slept; too tired for nightmares.

The next day Joe Taylor got out another mimeographed order of the day. It was headed: "A ship that won't be sunk, can't be sunk." It contained a message to Captain Gehres from Captain Fitz of the Santa Fe: "Congratulations on heroic work and outstanding efficiency of yourself and men in getting ship under way and saving her. It is an example we will never forget."

The orders for the day read: "(1) Due to our after gasoline system being damaged, smoking regulation must be strictly enforced. You may smoke on the forecastle during the daylight hours. You may smoke in the forward messing compartment between reveille and taps. Officers may smoke in the wardroom. *Never throw a lighted butt over the side.*

"(2) Keep busy doing something all the time. If you aren't on a scheduled working party, work anyway. We've got the world by the tail, hang on.

"(3) Do not throw *any usable article* over the side. If you think it can be salvaged, stack it neatly on the hangar deck just forward of No. 3 elevator on the starboard side.

"(4) Anyone knowing the whereabouts of any musical instrument, report to the chaplain.

"(5) Any personal effects such as wallets, watches, etc., shall be turned into the Executive Officer's cabin. . . . Joe Taylor, Commander, U. S. Navy, Executive Officer."

The men chuckled over Order No. 2. They chuckled over the message Admiral Davison had sent. It read: "Congratulations. I may be on a stranger's doorstep now but I claim you again with pride. Battered though you may be, you're still my child. Great work. Davison."

There were 704 men aboard the Big Ben as she slid through the waters toward Pearl Harbor. There had been more than 3,000 aboard the morning of March 19th. The cruisers had taken off hundreds of unnecessary personnel but 1,496 were dead or wounded or missing. The seriously wounded had been taken to shore hospitals by the Santa Fe and other ships. Seven hun-

There had been more than 3000 men aboard the *Franklin* the morning of March 19. Now 1496 were dead or wounded or missing—the most tragic casualty list ever sustained by a U. S. Navy ship. Since the "unnecessary personnel" had also been removed, just 704 officers and men brought the *Big*

dred and four officers and men brought her to port. Father O'Callahan organized the "704 Club." Today each man has a card of membership to this, the most exclusive club in the world whose members brushed elbows with death and shoved death aside.

Finally the Franklin steamed into Pearl Harbor. News of the disaster had reached the big naval base. Every admiral in Hawaii was there to pay his respects to this ship that had come back from the dead. As she approached her dock, every ship in the harbor saluted her. Men looked unbelieving at the huge holes in her. Thirty Waves had volunteered to sing the traditional song of the islands to welcome the Franklin —Aloha.

The crew of the Big Ben was drawn up smartly on deck. Yes—even the 270 slightly wounded. The clear voices of the girls rang out in the plaintive strains of the ancient Hawaiian song of welcome.

The Franklin slid to the dock. The girls looked . . . they faltered . . . they hesitated . . . they broke down,

Ben to Pearl Harbor. Today each man has a card of membership in the "704 Club," organized by Father O'Callahan —the most exclusive club in the world, whose members brushed elbows with death and shoved death aside.

At Pearl Harbor every admiral in Hawaii waited at the dock to pay his respects to the Franklin, every ship in the harbor saluted her. Men looked unbelievingly at the huge holes in her. Thirty Waves had volunteered to sing the welcome song of the islands— "Aloha"—and their clear voices rang out in the plaintive strains of the traditional Hawaiian song.

The Franklin slid to the dock. The crew was drawn up smartly on deck. Yes—even the 270 slightly wounded. The girls looked . . . they faltered . . . they broke down, and their song

and their song died. No one could look at this stricken ship without breaking down. No one but the crew—her own crew.

It was Father O'Callahan who started it, of course. And the whole crew took it up. The admirals waiting on the pier strained their ears.

Up on the bridge Gehres nudged Joe Taylor and grinned as these men who had returned from death sang lustily:

*The Old Big Ben, she ain't what she used to be,*
*Ain't what she used to be. . . ."*

died. No one could look at this stricken ship without breaking down. No one but her own crew.

It was Father O'Callahan who started it, and the whole crew took it up. Up on the bridge Gehres nudged Joe Taylor and grinned as these men who had returned from death sang lustily:

*"The Old Big Ben, she ain't what she used to be,*
*Ain't what she used to be . . ."*

---

## FOR DISCUSSION

1. What caused the thirty-second interlude between the explosions? Why was Father O'Callahan thankful for the interlude?

2. What did the padre mean when he said that to use the name of God was "a free word today?"

3. Why did Father O'Callahan tell the men in the steering aft to "play cards and pray?"

4. What does the author mean when he says that Father O'Callahan was writing history?

5. Why does the padre think "It's stupid to fear death?"

6. Why was it "faith" that saved the ship?

7. The author's choice of words and figures of speech add much life and interest to the article. Point out several examples of this and explain how they improve the story.

8. Under what type of journalistic writing would you classify this article?

## WORDS TO EXPLAIN

Explain the meaning of the following words. Their Latin source words should aid you in understanding their meanings.

1. *Prelude* comes from: *prae*, before; and *ludo*, to play.

2. *Indefatigable* is composed from: *in*, not; and *defatigo*, to tire out.

3. *Initiative* comes from: *initiatus*, the past participle of *initio*, to begin.

4. *Temerity* is from: *temeritas*, rashness.

## TYPE STUDY

1. Does the digest article leave out any important matter from the original? If it does, explain why you think the ideas left out should or should not be included in the digest.

2. Does the digest add anything new that was not in the original article?

3. The digest changes the paragraph and sentence structure and even the phrasing at times. Do you think this changes the author's style? Explain.

4. Point out several examples of sentences in which structure was changed.

## A PROJECT

Try to write a digest of a magazine article without changing the author's style or adding anything new.

# PASSION IN THE ANDES

*HEYWOOD BROUN*

*Heywood Broun spent the greater part of his life searching for the truth. A short while before his death he found what he was looking for. He became a Catholic. This essay shows how fresh and deep was his appreciation of our faith. He helps us to see its truths as if for the first time.*

Some few years ago I went on a spring cruise. The steamer touched the northern tip of South America and paused for a day at the port so that passengers might travel up the mountain to Caracas.[1] When we reached Venezuela word came that Gomez, the old dictator, lay dying in the capital. And as we went up the winding road, which drops a sheer two or three thousand feet at convenient corners, I noticed that all those who walked along the highway were clad in black or purple. Young and old all seemed to be hurrying to some central point. And, naturally, it was my notion that they were hurrying to the palace to learn the fate of Gomez.

Of course, we went faster than the pedestrians, much faster than was my will and pleasure. I remember mountains above me and hills leaping like waterfalls to meet the sea. Sky and sea and chasm pinwheeled across my vision. And all because an old dictator drew close to his appointed hour.

In the great square of the city these signs of mourning and of tribulation became banked into moving masses of peo-

ple, and I thought to myself, "Perhaps the potentate is already dead, and it is for that reason that the garb of grief is everywhere."

But at the door of the cathedral the driver stopped and said something to my companion. My friend translated and explained, "The driver says this is the service to mark the three hours of agony on the cross."

And it came to me that they mourned not for Gomez but for the Son of God. Out of bright sunlight I came into cool darkness flecked, but not wholly broken, by the light of many hundred candles. And all about the walls and statues and across the shoulders of the worshipers I saw the badge of purple. Holy Week had come to the foothills of the Andes.

I have seen church services in far and near places, and many were impressive, but here for the first time I saw a people who seemed to feel that the Passion of the Lord was actually occurring once again.

Pilate was not a famous dead procurator[2] of Judea who washed his hands in an ancient city long ago. It was but yesterday that Jesus stood before the Romans on trial for His life and was

[1] CARACAS—A city in Venezuela.

[2] PROCURATOR—An imperial administrator.

condemned. And at the very moment the living Christ hung on the cross.

An Indian woman, older than any being I have ever seen before, lifted her head from the floor as she prayed that death should not achieve its victory. Children in their purple smocks looked at the dancing lights and wondered. But they were silent.

It was as if someone of their own lay dying in a room at home. And all of them lived in a world in which each year Jesus again walked the earth and Judas brought betrayal in a pleasant garden. Many stood outside upon the steps under the hot sun and peered through the doors and down the dark aisles. They waited for some word from the mourners. Almost they seemed to say, "What is the news? How fares our Lord on Calvary!"

The faith of the faithful burns high along that mountain shelf. Some part of the agony is theirs, but the joy of resurrection bursts in their hearts like an apple tree suddenly come to bloom. To them the miracle is without question. They have lived through it, and rebirth becomes a part of their own experience.

Only one sleepy sentry stood outside the palace of Gomez. My friend spoke to him. "Gomez is very old," said the soldier, "and, like you and me and the beggar in the street, he must die some day. But he is of strong will. He will breathe until he has seen another Easter morning." I suppose that before death the old man wanted once again to dip his hands in life.

◇◇◇◇◇◇◇◇◇◇◇◇◇◇◇◇◇◇◇◇◇◇◇◇◇◇

## FOR DISCUSSION

1. Heywood Broun noted the mourning crowds of people and assumed that they were sorrowing for their dying leader, Gomez. What is the main impression made on the author when he learned that the people were commemorating the death of Christ?

2. By what means does the Church help us to re-live the life, sufferings, death, and resurrection of Christ? When does the Church year begin? When does it end?

3. The people acted "as if someone of their own lay dying in a room at home. And all of them lived in a world in which each year Jesus again walked the earth and Judas brought betrayal in a pleasant garden." Discuss this statement. Point out the ways in which Christ is truly a contemporary of every one of us. In what ways does Christ enter into our everyday life?

4. What is the force of the contrast between the crowd at the cathedral and the "one sleepy sentry outside the palace of Gomez"?

5. What is the meaning of the closing sentence: "I suppose that before death the old man wanted once again to dip his hands in life"?

## TYPE STUDY

1. Frequently a casual and entertaining article is better propaganda than direct editorials. Do you think Heywood Broun is propagandizing? If so, what idea? How do you think Father Gillis would have written these observations?

2. There are several striking metaphors and similes in this piece. Can you find two of them?

## WHERE WORDS COME FROM

Explain the meaning of the following words: *pedestrian, potentate, flecked.* Write a short account of their derivations.

## RELATED READING

*The Collected Works of Heywood Broun* contains many short essays on a variety of subjects.

# ON THE ROAD TO BERLIN

*ERNIE PYLE*

*The secret of Ernie Pyle's power as a war correspondent lay in his intense interest in the enlisted men. On principle he avoided mentioning generals and other high officers. His reporting is filled with details of what the men in battle saw and suffered. The battle scene as he saw it is devoid of the glamour sometimes associated with war. The curtain is lifted on waste, destruction, death, and the other horrors of modern warfare.*

I took a walk along the historic coast of Normandy in the country of France. It was a lovely day for strolling along the seashore. Men were sleeping on the sand, some of them sleeping forever. Men were floating in the water, but they didn't know they were in the water, for they were dead.

The water was full of squishy little jellyfish about the size of a man's hand. Millions of them. In the center of each of them was a green design exactly like a four-leafed clover. The good-luck emblem. Sure.

I walked for a mile and a half along the water's edge of our many-miled invasion beach. I walked slowly, for the detail on that beach was infinite.

The wreckage was vast and startling. The awful waste and destruction of war, even aside from the loss of human life, has always been one of its outstanding features to those who are in it. Anything and everything is expendable.[1] And we did expend on our beachhead in Normandy during those first few hours.

For a mile out from the beach there were scores of tanks and trucks and boats that were not visible, for they were at the bottom of the water—swamped by overloading, or hit by shells, or sunk by mines. Most of their crews were lost.

There were trucks tipped half over and swamped, partly sunken barges, and the angled-up corners of jeeps, and small landing craft half submerged. And at low tide you could still see those vicious six-pronged iron snares that helped snag and wreck them.

On the beach itself, high and dry, were all kinds of wrecked vehicles. There were tanks that had only just made the beach before being knocked out. There were jeeps that had burned to a dull gray. There were big derricks on caterpillar treads that didn't quite make it. There were half-tracks carrying office equipment that had been made into a shambles by a single shell hit, their interiors still holding the useless equipage of smashed typewriters, telephones, office files.

There were LCTs [2] turned completely

---

[1] EXPENDABLE—Pertaining to military equipment which can be sacrificed in order to attain an objective.

[2] LCT—Landing craft tank.

upside down, and lying on their backs, and how they got that way I don't know. There were boats stacked on top of each other, their sides caved in, their suspension doors knocked off.

In this shore-line museum of carnage there were abandoned rolls of barbed wire and smashed bulldozers and big stacks of thrown-away life belts and piles of shells still waiting to be moved. In the water floated empty life rafts and soldiers' packs and ration boxes, and mysterious oranges. On the beach lay snarled rolls of telephone wire and big rolls of steel matting and stacks of broken, rusting rifles.

On the beach lay, expended, sufficient men and mechanism for a small war. They were gone forever now. And yet we could afford it.

We could afford it because we were on, we had our toe hold, and behind us there were such enormous replacements for this wreckage on the beach that you could hardly conceive of the sum total. Men and equipment were flowing from England in such a gigantic stream that it made the waste on the beachhead seem like nothing at all, really nothing at all.

But there was another and more human litter. It extended in a thin little line, just like a high-water mark, for miles along the beach. This was the strewn personal gear, gear that would never be needed again by those who fought and died to give us our entrance into Europe.

There in a jumbled row for mile on mile were soldiers' packs. There were socks and shoe polish, sewing kits, diaries, Bibles, hand grenades. There were the latest letters from home, with the address on each one neatly razored out—one of the security precautions enforced before the boys embarked.

There were toothbrushes and razors, and snapshots of families back home staring up at you from the sand. There were pocketbooks, metal mirrors, extra trousers, and bloody, abandoned shoes. There were broken-handled shovels, and portable radios smashed almost beyond recognition, and mine detectors twisted and ruined.

There were torn pistol belts and can-

vas water buckets, first-aid kits, and jumbled heaps of life belts. I picked up a pocket Bible with a soldier's name in it, and put it in my jacket. I carried it half a mile or so and then put it back down on the beach. I don't know why I picked it up, or why I put it down again.

Soldiers carry strange things ashore with them. In every invasion there is at least one soldier hitting the beach at H-hour with a banjo slung over his shoulder. The most ironic piece of equipment marking our beach—this beach first of despair, then of victory—was a tennis racket that some soldier had brought along. It lay lonesomely on the sand, clamped in its press, not a string broken.

Two of the most dominant items in the beach refuse were cigarettes and writing paper. Each soldier was issued a carton of cigarettes just before he started. That day those cartons by the thousand, water-soaked and spilled out, marked the line of our first savage blow.

Writing paper and air-mail envelopes came second. The boys had intended to do a lot of writing in France. The letters—now forever incapable of being written—that might have filled those blank abandoned pages!

Always there are dogs in every invasion. There was a dog still on the beach, still pitifully looking for his masters.

He stayed at the water's edge, near a boat that lay twisted and half sunk at the waterline. He barked appealingly to every soldier who approached, trotted eagerly along with him for a few feet, and then, sensing himself unwanted in all the haste, he would run back to wait in vain for his own people at his own empty boat.

Over and around this long thin line

of personal anguish, fresh men were rushing vast supplies to keep our armies pushing on into France. Other squads of men picked amidst the wreckage to salvage ammunition and equipment that was still usable.

Men worked and slept on the beach for days before the last D-day victim was taken away for burial.

I stepped over the form of one youngster whom I thought dead. But when I looked down I saw he was only sleeping. He was very young, and very tired. He lay on one elbow, his hand suspended in the air about six inches from the ground. And in the palm of his hand he held a large, smooth rock.

I stood and looked at him a long time. He seemed in his sleep to hold that rock lovingly, as though it were his last link with a vanishing world. I have no idea at all why he went to sleep with the rock in his hand, or what kept him from dropping it once he was asleep. It was just one of those little things without explanation that a person remembers for a long time.

The strong, swirling tides of the Normandy coast line shifted the contours of the sandy beach as they moved in and out. They carried soldiers' bodies out to sea, and later they returned them. They covered the corpses of heroes with sand, and then in their whims they uncovered them.

As I plowed out over the wet sand, I walked around what seemed to be a couple of pieces of driftwood sticking out of the sand. But they weren't driftwood. They were a soldier's two feet. He was completely covered except for his feet; the toes of his GI shoes pointed toward the land he had come so far to see, and which he saw so briefly.

A few hundred yards back on the

beach was a high bluff. Up there we had a tent hospital, and a barbed-wire enclosure for prisoners of war. From up there you could see far up and down the beach, in a spectacular crow's-nest view, and far out to sea.

And standing out there on the water beyond all this wreckage was the greatest armada man has ever seen. You simply could not believe the gigantic collection of ships that lay out there waiting to unload. Looking from the bluff, it lay thick and clear to the far horizon of the sea and on beyond, and it spread out to the sides and was miles wide.

As I stood up there I noticed a group of freshly taken German prisoners standing near by. They had not yet been put in the prison cage. They were just standing there, a couple of doughboys leisurely guarding them with tommy guns.

The prisoners too were looking out to sea—the same bit of sea that for months and years had been so safely empty before their gaze. Now they stood staring almost as if in a trance. They didn't say a word to each other. They didn't need to. The expression on their faces was something forever unforgettable. In it was the final, horrified acceptance of their doom.

◇◇◇◇◇◇◇◇◇◇◇◇◇◇◇◇◇◇◇◇◇◇◇◇◇◇◇◇◇◇

## FOR DISCUSSION

1. Make a list of the various items of beach wreckage catalogued by Ernie Pyle.

2. What effect does the author gain by keeping back mention of the "human litter" until after he has described the wreckage of heavy equipment?

3. What is the significance of the incident in which the author picked up a soldier's Bible, carried it half a mile, and then put it down?

4. What were the two most prominent items of human litter? Why was the tennis racket the "most ironic" piece of equipment?

5. Why do you think the author ends this description with a view of the vast armada waiting off shore?

6. What is the outstanding feature of war as described by Ernie Pyle?

## TYPE STUDY

1. Column writing is the best example of personal journalism today. What devices can you find which "personalize" this description of the Normandy beachhead?

2. An *antithesis* is the expression of opposing or contrasting ideas. Find an instance or two of antithesis in the thoughts expressed by Ernie Pyle at the beginning of this article.

3. What is the principal method used to develop the idea: "The wreckage was vast and startling"?

## A PROJECT

Make a list of as many items as you can think of which would be necessary equipment for an army invading a hostile shore.

## RELATED READING

The following books are outstanding examples of reporting in World War II: *Here Is Your War, Brave Men,* and *The Last Chapter* by Ernie Pyle; *Dress Rehearsal* and *The Curtain Rises* by Quentin Reynolds; *Men of Bataan* by John Hersey; and *Many a Watchful Night* by John Mason Brown.

# THE LESSON OF DACHAU

## DOROTHY THOMPSON

*One of the greatest horrors of World War II was the phenomenon of concentration camps. They were a frightening revelation of the cruelties that man could inflict on man. Here, Dorothy Thompson writes an indictment of them and points the warning and lesson of their cruelties.*

Since the revelation from the German concentration camps burst upon the world, I have been wondering whether civilized nations have drawn the right conclusions from their horrors. I have heard over and over again the words, "Such things never happened before anywhere else in the world." But do people say, "Such things never happened before in *Germany?*" For that is also true. These monstrous crimes happened in our own civilization; in a white, European civilization, Christian for centuries, among a people in no way inferior to other western peoples in the things of which our civilization is especially proud: science, technology, organization, production, and a high standard of living. Indeed, in a bomb-wrecked Germany, whose entire urban life has been largely demolished, our Army and civilian authorities have been amazed at the material standards that Germany was able to maintain through six years of shattering war, and at the scientific and even cultural discoveries made there.

If only one could say, and dismiss it with that, "These people are savages." They are—but they are a new and terrifying kind of savage. The twentieth century and the white civilized world produced this savage. He can read and write—Germany is a totally literate nation. His brains can bring down fire from heaven and unchain the forces of the universe—German science is second to none in the world. He understands medicine and hygiene. He lives in beautiful and comfortable houses, equipped with labor-saving devices of every sort, set in beautiful parks and gardens, along magnificent highways.

The Germans are in many ways *like us*. That is what is terrifying about the concentration camps, with their millions of victims murdered en masse by the most modern and hygienic methods—gassed to death in ingeniously constructed chambers, disposed of in mass-produced crematories.

They are in many ways *like us*—these people, in whose country victims descended to cannibalism, cutting chunks out of the corpses of fellow victims to appease for a moment the wild hunger ravings of their dying bodies and fevered minds. While they did so, the administrators of the camps lived in pleasant and civilized villas; their tables were set with damask and crystal; they ate food carefully calculated as to vitamins, prepared in modern electric kitchens, served in courses by neat maids; and in the evenings they entertained themselves with sentimental songs played by skilled hands upon properly tuned pianos, or listened to the news of the world on radios, or read books, very often the same books familiar to you and to me—translations, for instance, of Jack London.

Nothing, to me, in visiting these camps, was so shattering as the sight of the homes of the SS administrators [2]—of the men who, in a modern bureaucratic manner, according to card catalogues, dossiers,[3] and files, gave the orders which resulted in tortures, carefully calculated famine, and corpses piled like cordwood, when the crematories were too full. Their homes were *civilized.* You or I would have enjoyed living in them. I pulled out of the library of one of them the lyric poems of Goethe,[4] which in my early encounters with the German language, as its beauties dawned upon me, filled me with a sense of magical beauty and spiritual grandeur. On the piano of one of them I found the lovely *Lieder* [5] of Schubert and the songs of Hugo Wolf.[6]

"When the soul goes, man goes." When civilized man, with his science, his technique, his organization, his power, loses his soul, he becomes the most terrible monster the world has ever seen. He is not the savage of the jungle; the wildest cannibals of the South Seas kill only to assuage a hunger they cannot otherwise still. But the modern savage—the twentieth-century savage—understands the most intimate secrets of nature.

In Germany I found a scientist who has developed a high-protein-content food out of wood. It has the consistency of corn flakes; it has the delicious taste of a delicate cheese. So the modern savage knows how to feed himself under the most adverse circumstances. He is about to discover, also, a new source of energy which will be universally available and can turn every wheel in the world. Indeed, he is so ingenious that *he thinks he is God.* His own fantastic achievements—or the achievements of his men of genius—free him, he thinks, from the ethical inhibitions imposed on all previous generations of men. He is the Ultimate Judgment; he is the Creator and Destroyer; he is the Thunder and the Hurricane. There *is* no "still, small voice."

When I surveyed Dachau, my soul trembled within me. "But for the grace of God," I thought, "there we could go."

For modern man has set himself up in his own image; or rather, he has set up his own creations as the image of God. He is "functional." The SS administrators were but bureaucratic cogs in a smoothly oiled and functioning machine.

Our political life—all twentieth-century political life—approaches the same "functional" concept. We are advised, even in our own country, to vote as "workers," or as "employers," to arrange ourselves in a "system," to fit ourselves into a "plan"—as though man is a steam riveter, or a manufacturer, or bureaucrat, or a salesman, and nothing else whatsoever. Is he a *conscience?* Can anyone *prove* conscience? Has anyone ever seen the soul? Can you

---

[2] SS ADMINISTRATORS—The chiefs of the Nazi storm troopers.

[3] DOSSIERS (dŏs′ĭ·ā)—Bundles of papers containing detailed information.

[4] GOETHE (1749–1832)—German poet and novelist, author of the drama, *Faust.*

[5] *Lieder* (lē′dēr)—German songs; these by the Austrian composer, Schubert, (1797–1828).

[6] HUGO WOLF—Austrian composer.

measure it? Put it under a microscope? Cure its illnesses with sulpha or penicillin? Do you know that it exists? So argues the modern savage.

The soul, says the modern savage, can be manipulated. We have "scientific psychology," which measures the exact reactions of man to suggestions of fear, sex, patriotism, ego, hunger. And the structure of societies is more and more created by careful and scientific manipulations of "mass psychology." The soul is not the subject, but the object; government is a "technique." Religion is an "opiate"—to be administered or withdrawn as any anodyne, according to the purpose to be served.

Even the Nazi concentration camps themselves were testing places of mass reactions. Does the world realize that some of the worst crimes in these camps were committed by the inmates? Reduce a man to the lowest level consistent with the maintenance of the spark of life; put him under carefully calculated pressures of hunger, fear, and sex, and play upon his ego, and you can make him, they argued—and successfully argued—what you will. You can make him the executioner of his fellow victims, the organizer of killing work brigades, the scientific experimenter on human bodies, turning them into guinea pigs, by elevating him an inch or two above them, in terms of relative comfort and relative freedom.

The physicians who inoculated concentration-camp victims with malaria and boil serum to test scientific formulas were prisoners of the Nazis themselves; the organizers of work-and-famine, whose object was to get the largest amount of "manpower" out of the smallest amount of nourishment, were prisoners themselves; the operators of gas chambers and crematories were pris-oners themselves. By assisting in the extermination of their fellow victims, they prolonged the lease on their own lives.

Some of them were hardened criminals, put among the political and racial prisoners for this purpose. But not all. Alas, not all. Many of them were "politicals." They came into the camps because they believed, or were suspected of believing, in democracy, or communism, or socialism, or because they were patriots, loving Poland, or France, or Belgium, or Holland.

Various agencies of the United States Government and armed forces have made a study of the behavior of the prisoners of Dachau. Under the terrible pressures under which they were put, did these beliefs determine their conduct? Did democrats or socialists or communists hold together to protect one another? Did Poles stick to Poles or Frenchmen to Frenchmen? Was political belief or patriotism a basis for morale or morality of behavior?

No. That is the most tremendous lesson of Dachau. No. There were communists who were saints—and communists who were stooges of the SS. There were Poles, Frenchmen, and Germans who, for the sake of an extra ration of meat, turned loose the cyanide gas on other Poles, Frenchmen, and Germans. There were socialists pledged to a philosophy of workers' solidarity, who organized the work brigades that sent tottering, half-dead men into the grueling sun where they dropped dead.

Under the pressure of life or death— life for an extra week, or an extra day —no political beliefs or economic theories, or physicians' Hippocratic oaths,[7]

---

[7] HIPPOCRATIC OATHS—An oath given to those entering the practice of medicine in early days. The oath is said to have originated with Hippocrates, a Greek physician (460–357 B.C.).

or national affiliations were decisive. What was decisive for behavior was the individual human soul. What separated the saint from the sinner-under-pressure was a spark in the breast, an admonition in the heart—was *conscience*. The old words of Charles Kingsley,[8] "He who will be pure, pure he will be," held good. And nothing else held good.

The concentration-camp victims gradually came to know who, among their own number, was a man, and who was a function. The OSS[9] report points out that they did not hate "all Germans." For among themselves were Germans who protected them—and Germans who exploited them. There were saints and heroes among the mass of helpless victims, as there were opportunists and savages. But the test was always individual. The words of Whitman were demonstrated daily. "Nothing survives, except personal character." Nothing is decisive when a man stands before torture and death, except his soul.

The lesson of Dachau is that no science, no technology, no political, social, or economic systems, neither patriotism nor race, nor material standards of liv-

[8] CHARLES KINGSLEY (1819–1875)—English novelist and evangelical minister.
[9] OSS—The Office of Strategic Services.

ing, nor learning, nor civilization will save mankind from relapse into the most monstrous savagery, but only the most careful nurture of his noblest instincts.

I asked an old friend who served twenty months in the dreadful death house of Mauthausen, issuing from it half mummy and half man, "Who behaved best among the inmates? Businessmen? Intellectuals? What race? What political parties?"

He answered, after thinking a long time, "Priests."

I shall remember that answer forever, and translate it into a larger generalization: They remained men, in conditions of lowest bestiality, who served an Image and an Ideal higher than the highest achievements of man; an Ideal in whom alone man attains significance and worth. They were those who knew that man, as man, is a soul.

FOR DISCUSSION

1. Why does the author emphasize the fact that the horrible crimes of Dachau happened in our own civilization? Why does she stress the high material standards, the scientific and cultural discoveries of Germany throughout the war?

2. Why is the new savage who is responsible for the crimes at Dachau much

worse than the old savage who was un-civilized?

3. What effect does the contrast between the horrible crimes these men committed and the cultured surroundings in which they lived have upon you? Why was the sight of the homes of the SS administrators so shattering to the author?

4. What does the author mean by her statement that "when the soul goes, man goes"?

5. Do you agree with the author when she says after her survey of Dachau that "but for the grace of God there we could go"? Why? Why not?

6. How does the author explain her statement that modern man is "functional"? What is wrong with the arguments of the modern savage against conscience? What misunderstanding of religion is betrayed by saying that religion is an "opiate"?

7. Who were responsible for some of the worst crimes committed in the concentration camps? For what beliefs and convictions were many of the prisoners confined to these camps? How did their beliefs influence their conduct?

8. What does the author say was decisive for human behavior? How would you complete her statement from your knowledge and practice of your Catholic faith?

9. What is the lesson of Dachau for America? for education? for the United Nations organization? Do you think the modern world is profiting from this lesson or is it going on just as if Dachau and the other horrors of World War II had never happened?

10. How does the author account for the fact that priests behaved best?

## TYPE STUDY: THE EDITORIAL

1. Prove that this article fits the requirements for an editorial: an interesting and timely comment on the significance of an event or idea.

2. Publishers sometimes print important words in red. What similar method of emphasis has Dorothy Thompson used?

3. Note the occasional use of interrogative sentences. Does their rising inflection heighten your attention? Are they well-spaced? Discuss.

## WORDS TO LEARN

1. What is meant by: "to *assuage* a hunger"?

2. Expain the difference between an *opiate* and an *anodyne*.

## RELATED READING

The columnists in our newspapers exert a tremendous influence on public opinion. You will find balanced studies of our chief columnists in *Molders of Opinion* by David Bulman.

# AND THE WORLD WAS PURIFIED

WESTBROOK PEGLER

*"And the World Was Purified" is a stinging, indignant, prophetic bit of writing. Pegler wrote it in 1938. Many of the events he predicted happened in World War II. Perhaps some of the others will be fulfilled in due time, if men continue following their own private schemes for bettering the world and turning a deaf ear to the Christian solution.*

So, at last, they totally obliterated the Jews from the face of the earth. The last few hundred thousand were taken to sea in old merchant boats, packed in cages and locked up tight, and when the rusty flotilla had reached the appointed spot, far down in the South Atlantic, the crews and jailers opened the cocks, abandoned ship, and made for the vessels of the International Navy, which took them aboard and then opened fire with their guns.

It was like shooting barnyard ducks. In less than an hour it was done. The mopping up was simple, but thorough. Picket boats went among the wreckage with sharpshooters in their bows to pick off the few half-conscious floaters who had been blown free by the explosions and had grasped fragments of furniture, doors, and booms. There was not one Jew left on earth, not one, and the remaining peoples of the world sighed with relief and said, "Now we shall have peace and progress and no more greed, lying, cheating, conspiracy, or theft."

The property of the Jews was distributed according to promise, and there was now no reason why the people should fail to prosper and get along as friends.

Yet there were alarms, and complete trust and co-operation were lacking. The Japanese had united all the Asiatics and were moving against the Russians. The Germans attacked the Poles to rescue an oppressed minority on the Sudeten precedent [1] and Mussolini pounced on Great Britain's lifeline because, even though they were indubitably Aryan, the British were arrogant, cunning, and acquisitive, and honor was not in them. "The Englishman," little Italian soldiers wrote on the blackboards in their schools, "is the scourge of the earth and must be destroyed."

These moves pitched the world into a general war in which it was difficult to distinguish friend from foe. The French fought the Germans with the slogan that there could never be permanent peace as long as any German

[1] SUDETEN PRECEDENT—The Sudeten region, a mountain range in northwestern Bohemia, was ceded to Germany in 1938.

lived, and verified the slogan to themselves by quotations from Herr Hitler's book to the effect that France must be destroyed.

The Americans held off a while, but finally pitched in against the Japanese, and the jumble became so confused that a bomber could unload his bombs almost anywhere outside his own country and find justification in some evil and menacing trait of the people living there.

Not only that, but within the warring countries individual and group hatred grew. There were still greed and lying, cheating, treachery, and theft. Men swindled one another, failed to pay their bills, seduced maidens, robbed, and stole. God had seemed to have the measure of their moral frailty, but they had always told themselves that it was the Jews alone to whom the Ten Commandments were addressed. With the Jews gone they thought the Ten Commandments would become superfluous if not even a little insulting, a sort of insinuation that even they were not above the sort of conduct for which the Jews, of course, were peculiar and notorious.

The Africans were wiped out early. In Asia starvation and disease destroyed millions, but the Western nations were no better off. They could feed themselves better and knew more of sanitation, but their weapons were much more deadly.

Still the world fought on long after the last Jew had gurgled beneath the waves until just two small bands were left, the freckle-faced people and the non-freckled, each claiming to be pure and to possess exclusively the virtues of honesty, honor, and clean blood, and each of them sworn to exterminate the other as the only guarantee of peace, progress, and decency on earth.

It ended with just two survivors, an old man and an old woman, together in a hut. He was one-eighth freckled, that is to say he had a few small freckles. She was of the pure, non-freckled strain.

So one night she slugged him with an axe as he slept and fell dead of the poison he had put in her soup that evening.

And the horses and asses romped in the fields, never again to be beaten or overburdened; deer walked in the open, unafraid of being shot by men; rabbits and birds took courage, cities moldered, and the world was purified of cruelty, dishonesty, treachery and greed.

❖❖❖❖❖❖❖❖❖❖❖❖❖❖❖❖❖❖❖❖❖❖❖❖❖❖❖

## FOR DISCUSSION

1. Give instances in yourself or others of a tendency to put the blame for everything that goes wrong on one class of people.

2. What was your reaction to this statement: "Now we shall have peace and progress and no more greed, lying, cheating, conspiracy, or theft"?

3. From your knowledge of history, show how much of the author's forecast of conflict of nations has been verified in the recent past.

4. Discuss the following statement: "God had seemed to have the measure of their moral frailty, but they had always told themselves that it was the Jews alone to whom the Ten Commandments were addressed."

5. What is the effect of the last paragraph?

## TYPE STUDY

1. A title may be good for a number of reasons: it may have a vivid verb; it may have the eye-value of color; it may be an allusion; or it may sound provocative. Jot down several titles for Pegler's article. In

what way are they better or worse than his title?

2. What examples of forceful repetition can you find in the selection?

3. Why are the first two paragraphs and the last especially effective descriptions? How has Pegler secured the effect of climax?

## WORDS FOR YOUR USE

1. *Obliterate* and *exterminate* are companion words. *Obliterate* means to wipe out so as to leave no trace, as when you thoroughly erase a word which you have misspelled; *exterminate* means to destroy entirely, to put an end to. Look up the words in the dictionary and show how the Latin words from which they are derived help you to distinguish the different shades of meaning contained in each.

2. *Notorious* once meant simply that a person was well known. As used today it means a person or fact that is publicly known in an unfavorable sense. Use the word *notorious* in an original sentence.

## PROJECTS

1. Write a short essay showing how much of Pegler's imaginative forecast of events has taken place. How were the big nations getting along in 1938? What great conflicts have arisen between them since that time? Do the nations seem to be getting along any better *now*?

2. Our Holy Father, the Head of the Universal Church, has made many important statements on peace and how it is to be achieved. Read at least one of his pronouncements and write a brief summary of it.

❖❖❖❖❖

# CHRISTMAS, A CATHOLIC CONQUEST

## JAMES M. GILLIS

*Christmas, the commemoration of the birthday of Our Lord, was not always celebrated as widely as it is today in the United States. Father Gillis describes how this most joyous day won the affections of more and more Americans, and he suggests a way of making Christmas a deeper Catholic conquest than it is at present.*

Those who know the history of Puritanism [1] in the United States, must marvel to see how completely the festival of Christmas has captured—and

[1] PURITANISM—The teachings characteristic of the Puritans.

"Christmas, a Catholic Conquest" from *This Our Day*, Vol. I, by James M. Gillis C.S.P., reprinted by permission of *The Catholic World*.

captivated—this country. Christmas is, beyond question, the favorite holiday of all the American people. It is more than a day, it is a season; and more than a celebration, a pervading spirit. It was not ever thus. In early days in New England, and indeed in almost all the colonies except Virginia, Christmas was considered a "papist" [2] festival; and to celebrate the day was an act of faith in Catholicism. Indeed, within the memory of living men, to ask for a holiday on Christmas was sufficient to warrant discharge from one's position, as well as to incur opprobrium as a "Romanist." [3]

The Puritans celebrated Thanksgiving Day. The Dutch celebrated New Year's. The Quakers in Pennsylvania and Delaware rather discouraged all such festivals. Besides the handful of Catholics scattered over the thirteen colonies, only the Anglicans [4] in Virginia made much of Christmas. Among the minor conquests of the Church in this country, therefore, is the universal enthusiastic celebration of the birthday of Our Lord.

There is always a danger when the multitude seizes upon a great idea— the danger of misapprehension and distortion. At this moment, there is a possibility that Christmas shall be secularized,[5] just as Thanksgiving Day has been robbed of almost all its religious meaning. The merchants will run away with our Christmas, if we are not careful. The impenetrable crowds in the streets and at the shops outnumber the crowds at the Crib of Jesus. There are already too many who give and receive Christmas presents, with perhaps no thought of Christ. As a matter of fact, the bestowing of gifts was originally associated with St. Nicholas' Day, or with Epiphany, rather than with Christmas. But Christmas has absorbed all the festivals in its vicinity, as a big city swallows up outlying villages and surrounds them. Of course, there is no harm in the custom of giving presents; it has become inseparably associated with the day. But the custom threatens to develop abnormally and unhealthily. Merchants too eagerly welcome the Christmas holidays as a mere stimulus to trade. Everything is bought and sold, given and received, at Christmas time; from a penny post-card to a Rolls-Royce; from a bag of cheap colored candy to a $300,000 pearl necklace; from knickknacks and gewgaws [6] that hang on Christmas trees to gilt-edged stocks and bonds; from a cotton handkerchief to a baby-lamb coat. Thousands of millions of dollars' worth of merchandise is marketed at Christmas time, and because of Christmas. To the merchants Christmas means simply Big Business.

If the birthday of Moses brought as much trade and as great profit, they would welcome the celebration of the birthday of Moses with equal, or perhaps even greater, enthusiasm. If it happened to be the American custom to exchange gifts on Washington's Birthday, or Lincoln's, the merchants would rejoice equally.

Then there are those (and unfortunately some of our own) who consider Christmas as an occasion not so much of religion as revelry. They are tenacious of traditions—and especially of traditions that favor the appetites. They have read that in "the good old days," it was the custom to go a-wassailing on Christmas Day, and they are determined that the hoary old habit of wassail [7] shall not die out in this drab

---

[2] "PAPIST"—A term used by non-Catholics in a non-complimentary sense to point out Catholic loyalty to the Pope.

[3] "ROMANIST"—A term used in a non-complimentary way to indicate members of the Roman Catholic Church.

[4] ANGLICANS—Members of the Church of England, numerous in colonial Virginia.

[5] SECULARIZED—Deprived of its religious character; made secular.

[6] GEWGAWS—Showy trifles.

[7] WASSAIL—An ancient expression of good wishes on a feast day. A drinking bout.

world. They make of it a day of dining and wining—with the accent chiefly on the wining. I have heard men boast that they have treasured for many years a goodly supply of an ancient vintage,[8] and that they have carefully selected a few dear old friends, to help them consume it on Christmas Day.

To such as these, Christmas means no more than any other occasion of jollification and carousal.[9] There are scholars (archaeologists and the like) who try to persuade us that all Christian customs and ceremonies are survivals of paganism. They tell us that there is no evidence that Christ was born in the winter season, and that Christmas is really the continuation of the Lupercalia,[10] which, like the Bacchanalia,[11] was a time of abandon and orgy. Perhaps the archaeologists got their theory not from scrutinizing ancient documents, but from observing the manners of some of our Catholic roisterers,[12] who are determined to prove to the world that religion and intoxicating drink are inseparably united, and that the abolition of the one would mean the ruin of the other. If Christmas means principally wassail, it is a pity that Christmas has conquered.

But, after all, there remains the unobtrusive, non-clamorous multitude of Catholics who rightly appreciate the meaning of Christmas. They, too, have memories of old traditions, not, however, of the bringing in of the boar's head, of lusty songs that make the smoky rafters ring, of the thumping of oaken tables with beer mugs, and all that sort of barbaric revelry, but of little processions of devout Catholics over the snow-covered hills, lighting their way with torches, to the midnight Christmas Mass. They love the "Adeste Fideles" and "Holy Night," hymns that stir old memories, bring a thrill to the heart and tears of joy to the eyes. They rejoice innocently about the Christmas tree, remembering that the day is consecrated to children. They practice the good old custom of family reunion, and all their Christmas pleasures are compatible with a childlike piety that is most appropriate on the day when Christ the Babe was born.

Further, there are Catholics—and doubtless other Christians—to whom Christmas has a mystical, as well as an historical meaning. Just as certain people listen to music, and hear only the succession of notes and the tunes, while others experience a sense of rapture; and as there are some who read poetry and catch only the prettiness of the verses, while others enjoy sheer ecstasy; so, while most of us are content to know that Christ was born of the Blessed Virgin in a stable at Bethlehem, the more sensitive spirits, upon contemplating that sacred event, are stricken with a feeling of awe and of rapture that cannot be expressed, unless by the song of angels. The historical fact that Christ was born in a stable long ago, is the outward symbol of the inner mystery that Christ is born in the heart today. For those to whom this mystery is revealed, heaven is come to earth. This, indeed, is Christmas.

◇◇◇◇◇◇◇◇◇◇◇◇◇◇◇◇◇◇◇◇◇◇◇◇◇◇◇◇◇

FOR DISCUSSION

1. What was the attitude of many non-Catholics to Christmas in the early days

---

[8] VINTAGE—A wine or other alcoholic drink which is of a particular type and is prized for its special qualities.

[9] CAROUSAL—A drunken revel.

[10] LUPERCALIA—An ancient religious ceremony of pagan Romans.

[11] BACCHANALIA—An ancient Roman festival of the god Bacchus, celebrated with frenzied dancing, singing, and revelry.

[12] ROISTERERS—Noisy and riotous revelers.

of our country? How do you account for their attitude?

2. What can happen when a great number of people seize upon a great idea? What signs are there in American life that Christmas may be stripped of its religious meaning?

3. Father Gillis is severe on the way businessmen use Christmas as an occasion for unloading their wares. Do you agree with him that they are a threat to the real meaning of Christmas? Point out some of the ways in which business has commercialized Christmas.

4. How do some Catholics misinterpret the meaning of Christmas? Why is their behavior worthy of blame?

5. In what way should Christmas be celebrated? What is the real meaning of Christmas?

6. In what way has Christmas changed every moment of our lives? Why is the birth of Christ the most important event that ever happened?

## TYPE STUDY

1. Richness of background and experience, an aggressive view of life, and a style forceful and flexible are some of the qualities demanded of the successful columnist. Can you find evidences of these qualities in the author of this selection?

2. Point out the transitional words in the last four paragraphs. Can you justify the inclusion of paragraphs five and six?

## WORDS TO STUDY

1. What difference in connotation is there between a *festival* and a *holiday?* Explain.

2. Define the following words: *distortion, abnormally, tenacious, drab, unobtrusive.*

## PROJECTS—WHAT DOES CHRISTMAS MEAN?

1. Look up the prayers for the Masses on Christmas Day in your Missal. What clues do they give you as to the proper way in which to celebrate Christmas?

2. Make a survey of the Christmas cards that are sold in the stores in your neighborhood. How many of them catch the true spirit of Christmas? Sketch or describe a Christmas card which you think best expresses the meaning of Christmas.

3. Write a report on the history of the feast of Christmas.

4. Bring a poem or short story to class that you think catches the meaning of Christmas.

## RELATED READING

Father Gillis is the former editor of the *Catholic World.* His editorials make interesting reading. Some of his best editorials have been collected in the volume entitled *This Our Day.* An excellent book of Christmas poems is *Twelfth Night and Other Poems* by Sister Mary Madeleva.

# CONTEMPORARY POETRY

Before trying to define poetry, let us think first about the question, "Why is there such a thing as poetry?" Or, as more than one boy or girl has put it, "Why does a person ever write poetry?" The question is fair enough. People do not *talk* poetry. They talk in prose. And all ordinary writing is done in prose. Then when anyone writes poetry, he must have a special reason for doing so. What is the reason? Why did not John Magee say in prose what he thought about flying? It would have been easier. But if he had, how many thousands of people would have missed the thrilling sense of *high flight* that sings in the words,

> "Oh, I have slipped the surly bonds of earth
> And danced the skies on laughter-silvered wings."

For poetry is like music and painting; it adds to our enjoyment of the things of life. When an artist sees a spread of summer landscape or a wind-torn tree against a mountain sky, he wants to transfer it to canvas, to hold it for future pleasure and to show it to others. When an idea for a design comes to him, he wants to work it out in color or clay and thus give it a permanence which he may share with someone else.

There are people who cannot reproduce beauty with brush or crayon, yet who have the skill to work with words. These are the poets. They too have a means of preserving loneliness or worth. The purpose of the poet is like the purpose of the painter—to preserve in artistic form a thought or experience or impression either so significant or so beautiful that it is worth being saved. Three months after John Magee wrote his sonnet, his life was gone. But as long as men can read they can share the ecstasy of that September flight when he had this moment—

> "Up, up the long, delirious, burning blue
> I've topped the wind-swept heights with easy grace,
> Where never lark, or even eagle flew;
> And while with silent, lifting mind I've trod
> The high, untrespassed sanctity of space,
> Put out my hand, and touched the face of God."

Since the content of a poem is of value, its form should be carefully wrought. And so the poet takes the materials of prose—words and sentences—and fashions them into a special form designed to fit his thought.

Another likeness may be drawn between poetry and the other arts. The true measure of greatness of any artistic creation lies not so much in the quality of the product itself as in the effect it produces. A symphony must do more than meet the requirements of musical composition; it must stir the feelings and set imaginations playing. The greatest pictures are those that suggest meanings beyond what actually appears on the canvas. The true poem reveals to its readers a new vision and some deeper appreciation of truth.

In summary, then, we may define poetry thus:

*Poetry is an artistic expression of a significant idea or experience, in words designed to delight the ear and appeal to the reader's imagination and feelings.*

Not all so-called "poems" measure up to every element of this definition. Some emphasize feeling rather than melody; others emphasize melody and imagination to the exclusion of meaning. Our definition describes the ideal which only the highest type of poetry attains.

## POETRY OF TODAY

Poetry in the first years of the present century gave little promise of new or startling developments. Most writers seemed content to mold their work into the patterns set by the earlier English poets. But within a dozen years some striking changes began to appear. Techniques and themes that we now take for granted exploded like literary bombs.

Even so there had been earlier influences at work to produce such changes. Walt Whitman had, in the later nineteenth century, broken new poetic ground. He had cut himself loose from conventional styles. He had boldly tried out as themes for his poems many aspects of American life which other poets had shied away from as "unpoetic." He had experimented with new verse forms and new rhythms. His revolutionary tactics encouraged later poets to blaze fresh trails.

A convenient date line for the rise of new qualities in twentieth-century American poetry is the year 1912. In that year Harriet Monroe founded in Chicago *Poetry,* a magazine devoted to the publication of verse. Many outstanding modern poets appeared in the pages of *Poetry*. Harriet Monroe's intelligent and nonpartisan editorial policies did much to promote the cause of the new poetry. The success of *Poetry* encouraged the appearance of other little magazines for the publication of verse and the discussion of problems connected with its writing. Poetry became a live issue, and an amazing amount of it was written.

Ezra Pound and Amy Lowell did much to stir up fresh interest in poetry. They headed the Imagist Movement. The imagists favored the use of language that had the flavor of common speech, unrestricted freedom in the choice of subject matter, the creation of new rhythms, concentration of effect, and the evocation of images in hard, clear poetry. A vigorous discussion of the subject matter and the forms appropriate to poetry followed the appearance of the imagist group. The merits of *free verse* were strenuously defended by one school of poets and vigorously denounced by the opposition.

The great flood of poetry that followed was not of equal value. Some of the attempts to write a "new" poetry were bizarre and freakish. However, when the controversy calmed, it was clear that some genuine and lasting poetry had resulted from the latest overhauling of poetic principles. Edwin Arlington Robinson's poems found an appreciative audience—especially his delicate and searching portraits of enigmatic figures and his reworking of the Arthurian romances. Robert Frost introduced a freshly colloquial note into American poetry with his poems on the New England scene and people. The subtle poetry of T. S. Eliot won recognition. Eliot, who was born an American and later became a British citizen, has influenced the course of modern poetry more than any other poet of our time.

## CONTEMPORARY CATHOLIC POETRY

The poetry written by Catholics in the past thirty years is impressive. A roll call of twentieth-century Catholic poets would reveal an array of richly varied talent. To verify this statement, one has only to sample the work of such poets as Joyce Kilmer, Aline Kilmer, Father Charles O'Donnell, Sister Madeleva, Sister Maris Stella, and Jessica Powers. Much excellent poetry has come from the pens of nuns. A good sampling of their poetry may be found in *Our Lady's Choir*, an anthology edited by William Stanley Braithwaite.

In 1931 the Catholic Poetry Society was established, and in 1934 the Society founded *Spirit*, a magazine devoted to the publication of Catholic poetry. The cause of Catholic poetry was greatly advanced by these two events. How fruitful has been their stimulus on the writing of Catholic verse may be judged from the two anthologies of poetry culled from the pages of *Spirit*—*From the Four Winds* and *Drink from This Rock*.

Catholic poetry is bright not only with achievement but also with promise of good things to come. Two young Catholic poets, Thomas Merton and Robert Lowell, have won much critical acclaim from all quarters. Thomas Merton, a Trappist monk, has to date published several volumes, including *Thirty Poems* and *Man in the Divided Sea*. Robert Lowell won the Pulitzer Prize in 1947 for his volume of poems, *Lord Weary's Castle*.

# Prayer to the Virgin of Chartres

### HENRY ADAMS

Alfred Noyes in his preface to THE GOLDEN BOOK OF CATHOLIC POETRY says of this poem: "I believe it to be among the greatest, perhaps itself the greatest, in American literature. It is one of the most remarkable pieces of self-revelation in modern times: the work of an outwardly skeptical and sophisticated man, disillusioned by a long 'education' in the realm of high politics and international affairs, acquainted with all the tendencies of modern materialistic thought; and it suddenly lays bare the profound hunger of a mind robbed of its spiritual heritage. . . . Written a good many years ago, it actually anticipates the fearful hour when man would tear out the secret springs of the atom."

Gracious Lady:—
Simple as when I asked your aid before;
Humble as when I prayed for grace in vain
Seven hundred years ago; weak, weary, sore
In heart and hope, I ask your help again.

You, who remember all, remember me;                    5
An English scholar of a Norman name,
I was a thousand who then crossed the sea
To wrangle in the Paris schools for fame.

When your Byzantine portal was still young,
I prayed there with my master Abélard,               10
When Ave Maris Stella was first sung,
I helped to sing it here with Saint Bernard.

Title—CHARTRES (shär'tr')—The magnificent Gothic cathedral at Chartres, France. The stained glass windows of the cathedral celebrate the glorification of the Virgin Mary.
   8. PARIS SCHOOLS—The University of Paris was in the twelfth century a center of learning to which students from all parts of the world came to take part in the philosophical disputations.
   10. ABÉLARD (1079–1142) was a famous and popular teacher of philosophy.
   11. AVE MARIS STELLA—The hymn "Ave Maris Stella" (Hail, Star of the Ocean) is attributed by the poet to Saint Bernard. It dates back, however, as far as the ninth century.

"Prayer to the Virgin of Chartres" from Letters to a Niece by Henry Adams, reprinted by permission of Houghton Mifflin Company.

When Blanche set up your gorgeous Rose of France,
I stood among the servants of the Queen;
And when Saint Louis made his penitence,                    15
I followed barefoot where the King had been.

For centuries I brought you all my cares
And vexed you with the murmurs of a child;
You heard the tedious burden of my prayers;
You could not grant them, but at least you smiled.          20

If then I left you, it was not my crime,
Or if a crime, it was not mine alone,
All children wander with the truant Time.
Pardon me too!   You pardoned once your Son!

For He said to you: "Wist ye not that I                     25
Must be about my Father's business?"   So,
Seeking His Father, He pursued His way
Straight to the Cross towards which we all must go.

So I too wandered off among the host
That racked the earth to find the Father's clue,            30
I did not find the Father, but I lost
What now I value more, the mother—you!

I thought the fault was yours that foiled my search;
I turned and broke your image on its throne,
Cast down my idol and resumed my march                      35
To claim the Father's empire for my own.

Crossing the hostile sea, our greedy band
Saw rising hills and forests in the blue;
Our Father's kingdom in the promised land!
We seized it and dethroned the Father too.                  40

And now we are the Father, with our brood,
Ruling the Infinite, not Three but One;
We made our world and saw that it was good;
Ourselves we worship, and we have no Son.

Yet we have gods, for even our strong nerve                 45
Falters before the Energy we own.

13. BLANCHE—Blanche of Castile, the mother of Saint Louis.  She was the donor of the famous rose window of the cathedral.
15. SAINT LOUIS—Saint Louis made a pilgrimage to Chartres.
32. Henry Adams laments the loss of devotion to the Blessed Virgin which the Protestant Revolt entailed.

Which shall be master?   Which of us shall serve?
Which wears the fetters?   Which shall bear the crown?

Brave though we be, we dread to face the Sphinx
Or answer the old riddle she still asks.                    50
Strong as we are, our reckless courage shrinks
To look beyond the piecework of our tasks.

But when we must, we pray as in the past
Before the Cross on which your Son was nailed.
Listen, dear lady!   You shall hear the last            55
Of the strange prayers Humanity has wailed.

49. SPHINX—The Sphinx of Thebes, who proposed a riddle to all passersby and destroyed them if they failed to answer it.  The riddle: "What walks in the morning on four feet, at noon upon two, at evening upon three?"  The answer is man, as a baby on his hands and feet, later on his feet, and as an old man with a staff.

---

## FOR DISCUSSION

1. In what attitude does the poet present himself to Our Lady?

2. The poet identifies himself with the men who lived in various ages.  Point out the lines which refer to the times when faith was strong.  Point out the lines which refer to the Protestant Revolt. What reason does the poet give for the rejection of Mary?

3. Contrast the attitudes of men during the ages of faith with those after the Protestant Revolt.  What does the man who has rejected Mary finally come to worship?

4. Point out how lines 45–48 truly describe the reaction of men today to the discoveries of atomic power.  Why should modern man "falter" before this energy?

5. Lines 53–56 give the solution to the problems of modern man, to the problems of men of all times.  Henry Adams himself never became a Catholic, but many men and women since his time have followed the path he indicates in the last line of his poem.  Can you name a number of famous recent converts to the faith in America and England?

6. Explain your interpretation of the following lines:

Line 20—You could not grant them, but at least you smiled.

Line 28—Straight to the Cross towards which we all must go.

Line 30—That racked the earth to find the Father's clue.

Line 36—To claim the Father's empire for my own.

7. To what historical event or series of events do lines 37–39 refer?

# The Man with the Hoe

## EDWIN MARKHAM

*"The Man with the Hoe" was inspired by the famous painting of Jean François Millet. Edwin Markham tells us that in that portrait of the stooped French peasant he saw "the landless, the soul-blighted workman of the world, the dumb creature that has no time to rest, no time to think, no time for the hopes that make us men." As you read the poem keep in mind that "the man with the hoe" stands for all men who have been ground down by the greed and cruelty of men grasping for power and wealth.*

> *God made man in his own image*
> *In the image of God he made him.*
> *—Genesis*

Bowed by the weight of centuries he leans
Upon his hoe and gazes on the ground,
The emptiness of ages in his face,
And on his back the burden of the world.

Who made him dead to rapture and despair,     5
A thing that grieves not and that never hopes,
Stolid and stunned, a brother to the ox?
Who loosened and let down this brutal jaw?
Whose was the hand that slanted back this brow?
Whose breath blew out the light within this brain?     10

Is this the Thing the Lord God made and gave
To have dominion over sea and land;
To trace the stars and search the heavens for power;
To feel the passion of Eternity?
Is this the dream He dreamed who shaped the suns     15
And marked their ways upon the ancient deep?
Down all the caverns of Hell to their last gulf
There is no shape more terrible than this—
More tongued with cries against the world's blind greed—
More filled with signs and portents for the soul—     20
More packed with danger to the universe.

"The Man with the Hoe" by Edwin Markham, reprinted by permission of Virgil Markham.

What gulfs between him and the seraphim!
Slave of the wheel of labor, what to him
Are Plato and the swing of Pleiades?
What the long reaches of the peaks of song,                  25
The rift of dawn, the reddening of the rose?
Through this dread shape the suffering ages look;
Time's tragedy is in that aching stoop;
Through this dread shape humanity betrayed,
Plundered, profaned and disinherited,                        30
Cries protest to the Powers that made the world,
A protest that is also prophecy.

O masters, lords and rulers in all lands,
Is this the handiwork you give to God,
This monstrous thing distorted and soul-quenched?           35
How will you ever straighten up this shape;
Touch it again with immortality;
Give back the upward looking and the light;
Rebuild in it the music and the dream;
Make right the immemorial infamies,                          40
Perfidious wrongs, immedicable woes?

O masters, lords and rulers in all lands,
How will the future reckon with this Man?
How answer his brute question in that hour
When whirlwinds of rebellion shake all shores?               45
How will it be with kingdoms and with kings—
With those who shaped him to the thing he is—
When this dumb Terror shall rise to judge the world,
After the silence of the centuries?

22. SERAPHIM—Angels; one of the choirs of angels.
24. PLATO—An outstanding Greek philosopher who lived about 428–348 B.C. He is the author of some of the world's greatest philosophical literature.
24. PLEIADES—A conspicuous loose cluster of stars in the constellation Taurus. Six stars are visible to the average eye, but the telescope reveals many hundreds more.

## FOR DISCUSSION

1. Lines 1–4 describe the sad state of the man with the hoe. The poet then asks who brought the man to this plight. Do the questions in lines 5–10 imply that other men are responsible? Who is responsible for the oppression of the people of whom the man with the hoe is a symbol? What lines give you the answer?

2. Lines 11–16 suggest what man is meant to be. Contrast these lines with the first ten lines of the poem. What details does the poet use to show what God intended man to be?

3. In what sense is the man's protest also a prophecy?

4. Mention one incident from history which supports the truth of line 45.

5. To what event do the last two lines

of the poem refer? Do you think it refers to the Last Judgment? Why or why not? *fidious wrongs, immedicable woes, brute question.*

## WORDS TO KNOW

To appreciate poetry you must get the full force and flavor of each word. What is the exact meaning of the following words and phrases: *stolid, signs and portents, profaned, immemorial infamies, per-*

## A PROJECT—THE CHURCH'S ATTITUDE

Look up the teachings of Popes Leo XIII and Pius XI on social justice. Do you see any similarities between what they say and what Edwin Markham presents in this poem?

⬥⬥⬥⬥

# Lincoln, the Man of the People

## EDWIN MARKHAM

*It is said that for every crisis in the history of America, a man has come forth to carry the country through the strenuous period. Washington and Lincoln are examples. With the thought of the great need for such a man as Lincoln during the Civil War period, read the following poem.*

When the Norn Mother saw the Whirlwind Hour
Greatening and darkening as it hurried on,
She left the Heaven of Heroes and came down
To make a man to meet the mortal need.
She took the tried clay of the common road—  5
Clay warm yet with the genial heat of Earth,
Dasht through it all a strain of prophecy,
Tempered the heap with thrill of human tears,
Then mixt a laughter with the serious stuff.
Into the shape she breathed a flame to light  10
That tender, tragic, ever-changing face;
And laid on him a sense of the Mystic Powers,
Moving—all husht—behind the mortal veil.
Here was a man to hold against the world,
A man to match the mountains and the sea.  15

1. NORN MOTHER—In Scandinavian mythology, a divine goddess who presides over the destinies of men.
1. WHIRLWIND HOUR—The approaching Civil War between the States.

"Lincoln, the Man of the People" by Edwin Markham, reprinted by permission of Virgil Markham.

The color of the ground was in him, the red earth,
The smack and tang of elemental things:
The rectitude and patience of the cliff,
The good-will of the rain that loves all leaves,
The friendly welcome of the wayside well,                    20
The courage of the bird that dares the sea,
The gladness of the wind that shakes the corn,
The pity of the snow that hides all scars,
The secrecy of streams that make their way
Under the mountain to the rifted rock,                       25
The tolerance and equity of light
That gives as freely to the shrinking flower
As to the great oak flaring to the wind—
To the grave's low hill as to the Matterhorn
That shoulders out the sky.  Sprung from the West,           30
He drank the valorous youth of the new world.
The strength of virgin forests braced his mind,
The hush of spacious prairies stilled his soul.


Up from log cabin to the Capitol,
One fire was on his spirit, one resolve—                     35
To send the keen ax to the root of wrong,
Clearing a free way for the feet of God,
The eyes of conscience testing every stroke,
To make his deed the measure of a man.
He built the rail-pile as he built the State,               40
Pouring his splendid strength through every blow:
The grip that swung the ax in Illinois
Was on the pen that set a people free.


So came the Captain with the mighty heart;
And when the judgment thunders split the house,             45
Wrenching the rafters from their ancient rest,
He held the ridgepole up, and spikt again
The rafters of the Home.  He held his place—
Held the long purpose like a growing tree—
Held on through blame and faltered not at praise—           50
Towering in calm rough-hewn sublimity.
And when he fell in whirlwind, he went down
As when a lordly cedar, green with boughs,
Goes down with a great shout upon the hills,
And leaves a lonesome place against the sky.                 55

29. MATTERHORN—A famous peak in the Alps between Switzerland and Italy.

## FOR DISCUSSION

Mr. Markham's poem, which celebrates Lincoln's passion for social justice, was chosen out of more than two hundred poems on Lincoln to be read aloud at the dedication of the Lincoln Memorial in Washington, D. C.

1. In lines 1–4 the poet uses a mythological figure to bring out the providential aspect of Lincoln's appearance in a time of crisis. What is the *mortal need* which Lincoln met?

2. What elements is the Norn Mother pictured as using to fashion Lincoln? Point out the lines in the first stanza which describe Lincoln's physical characteristics. What lines in the same stanza describe his spiritual qualities?

3. Describe the qualities of Lincoln as they are expressed in the second stanza.

4. What was the dominant ideal of Lincoln's life?

5. What is the meaning of line 45: "And when the judgment thunders split the house"?

## PROJECTS

1. Compare Markham's poem with Whitman's "O Captain, My Captain" and Vachel Lindsay's "Abraham Lincoln Walks at Midnight."

2. Look up the early life of Lincoln in Carl Sandburg's biography of Lincoln.

3. Make an anthology of poems on Lincoln.

◇◇◇◇◇

# The Kings

### LOUISE IMOGEN GUINEY

*Here is a dialogue between a man and his angel. The man is every man, and the angel's reply holds good for all men of all times.*

A man said unto his Angel:
"My spirits are fallen low,
And I cannot carry this battle:
O brother! Where might I go?

"The terrible Kings are on me     5
With spears that are deadly bright;
Against me so from the cradle
Do fate and my fathers fight."

Then said to the man his Angel:
"Thou wavering witless soul,     10
Back to the ranks! What matter
To win or to lose the whole,

"As judged by the little judges
Who hearken not well, nor see?
Not thus, by the outer issue,     15
The Wise shall interpret thee.

"Thy will is the sovereign measure
And only event of things:
The puniest heart defying,
Were stronger than all these Kings.     20

"Though out of the past they gather,
Mind's Doubt, and Bodily Pain,
And pallid Thirst of the Spirit
That is kin to the other twain,

"The Kings" by Louise Imogen Guiney, reprinted by permission of Houghton Mifflin Company.

"And Grief, in a cloud of banners,  25
And ringletted Vain Desires,
And Vice, with spoils upon him
Of thee and thy beaten sires,—

"While Kings of Eternal evil
Yet darken the hills about,  30
Thy part is with broken saber
To rise on the last redoubt;

"To fear not sensible failure,
Nor covet the game at all,
But fighting, fighting, fighting,  35
Die, driven against the wall."

◇◇◇◇◇◇◇◇◇◇◇◇◇◇◇◇◇◇◇◇◇◇◇◇◇◇◇◇◇◇◇◇◇◇◇◇◇◇◇◇◇◇◇◇◇◇◇◇◇◇

## FOR DISCUSSION

1. Of what does the man complain to his Angel? What is the man prepared to do? What does he mean by *fate and my fathers?*

2. Who are the *little judges* whom the Angel scorns? What is the *outer issue?*

3. Why is the will the *sovereign measure* of things? Why is it true that the *puniest heart,* if it stands fast in battle, is stronger than all the Kings? Who are the Kings?

4. What are the forces and weapons which the Kings gather for their attack?

5. In what way should the man oppose the snares and devices of the Kings? What is the significance of the *broken saber?* Why is a man truly successful if he dies fighting against the wall?

6. Do you agree with the Angel's view of success? How would someone who judged success by the *outer issue* reply to the Angel? Do you judge the success of your own actions according to the teaching of the Angel?

## WORDS

1. How would you describe a *witless* soul?

2. Why is *ringletted* a fitting word to use in connection with *Vain Desires?*

3. What is a *redoubt?*

4. What kind of failure is *sensible* failure? Why should it not be feared?

# An Old Story

## EDWIN ARLINGTON ROBINSON

*It is "an old story" with most of us that we fail to appreciate "that friend of mine" until it is too late for us to show him our appreciation.*

Strange that I did not know him then,
  That friend of mine!
I did not even show him then
  One friendly sign;

But cursed him for the ways he had   5
  To make me see
My envy of the praise he had
  For praising me.

    I would have rid the earth of him
      Once, in my pride!     10
    I never knew the worth of him
      Until he died.

"An Old Story" by Edwin Arlington Robinson, reprinted by permission of Charles Scribner's Sons.

---

## FOR DISCUSSION

1. What do lines 7–8 tell you of the character of "that friend of mine"? How would you explain the peculiar source of envy mentioned in the second stanza?

2. Why does the poet mention pride as the root of his blindness to the excellent qualities of his friend?

## WORDS TO LOOK UP

Look up the exact meaning of the following words: *cursed, envy, pride.*

# Richard Cory

## EDWIN ARLINGTON ROBINSON

*Even the people we know best surprise us at times by what they do. And time and time again the newspaper blazes in its headlines the unaccountable, desperate deeds of people who seem to have had everything. "Richard Cory" gives us a hint of the depths of human experience.*

"Richard Cory" by Edwin Arlington Robinson, reprinted by permission of Charles Scribner's Sons.

Whenever Richard Cory went down town,
    We people on the pavement looked at him:
He was a gentleman from sole to crown,
    Clean favored, and imperially slim.

And he was always quietly arrayed,                  5
    And he was always human when he talked;
But still he fluttered pulses when he said,
    "Good-morning," and he glittered when he walked.

And he was rich—yes, richer than a king—
    And admirably schooled in every grace:          10
In fine, we thought that he was everything
    To make us wish that we were in his place.

So on we worked, and waited for the light,
    And went without the meat, and cursed the bread;
And Richard Cory, one calm summer night,        15
    Went home and put a bullet through his head.

## FOR DISCUSSION

The contrast between the first three stanzas and the last stanza is violent and jolting. The poet does not fill in the gap between what Richard Cory seemed to be and the elements in his character which led to his final violent action. Complete the story of Richard Cory. What do you think was lacking in his life?

# Wind and Silver

AMY LOWELL

Greatly shining,
The Autumn moon floats in the thin sky;
And the fish-ponds shake their backs and flash their
      dragon scales
As she passes over them.

"Wind and Silver" by Amy Lowell, reprinted by permission of Houghton Mifflin Company.

◇◇◇◇◇◇◇◇◇◇◇◇◇◇◇◇◇◇◇◇◇◇◇◇◇◇◇◇◇◇◇◇◇◇◇◇◇◇◇◇◇◇◇◇◇◇◇◇◇◇◇◇◇◇◇◇◇◇◇

FOR DISCUSSION

1. The title of this poem is "Wind and Silver." What line suggests the *wind?* What line, or lines, *silver?*

2. What do you think Miss Lowell intended this poem to do—give a message, record an impression, or create a mood? Give reasons for your answer. Discuss this topic briefly in class.

◇◇◇◇◇

# Madonna of the Evening Flowers

AMY LOWELL

All day long I have been working,
Now I am tired.
I call: "Where are you?"
But there is only the oak-tree rustling in the wind.
The house is very quiet,                                          5
The sun shines in on your books,
On your scissors and thimble just put down,
But you are not there.
Suddenly I am lonely:
Where are you?                                                   10
I go about searching.

Then I see you,
Standing under a spire of pale blue larkspur,

"Madonna of the Evening Flowers" by Amy Lowell, reprinted by permission of Houghton Mifflin Company.

With a basket of roses on your arm.
You are cool, like silver,                                     15
And you smile.
I think the Canterbury bells are playing little tunes.

You tell me that the peonies need spraying,
That the columbines have overrun all bounds,
That the pyrus japonica should be cut back and rounded.     20
You tell me these things.
But I look at you, heart of silver,
White heart-flame of polished silver,
Burning beneath the blue steeples of the larkspur,
And I long to kneel instantly at your feet,                25
While all about us peal the loud, sweet *Te Deums* of the
    Canterbury bells.

## FOR DISCUSSION

1. What is the brief story of the poem? Who do you think is the "madonna of the evening flowers"? What do you learn about her appearance? About her habits? About her character and her personality?

2. How can the reader know from this single poem that Miss Lowell had the soul of a poet? Explain your answer.

3. Which lines show a practical knowledge of gardening? Which lines show especial appreciation of the loveliness of flowers?

4. What is a *Te Deum?* Explain the significance of the last two lines of the poem.

5. Show how the title of the poem gives added significance to these closing lines. What figures of speech in these and in earlier lines are especially appropriate to the theme of the poem?

6. How do Amy Lowell's outdoor subjects differ from Robert Frost's? Why do you think there is this difference?

## THE POET'S CRAFT

Since there is neither rhyme nor regular rhythm in "Wind and Silver" or in "Madonna of the Evening Flowers," how is the poetic effect secured? Make a list of the poetic devices Miss Lowell has used.

# Sea Lullaby

## ELINOR WYLIE

Many poets have written about the beauty and grandeur of the sea, or about its power and majesty. This poem considers the sea from an entirely different and unusual viewpoint.

The old moon is tarnished
With smoke of the flood,
The dead leaves are varnished
With color like blood,

A treacherous smiler                    5
With teeth white as milk,
A savage beguiler
In sheathings of silk,

The sea creeps to pillage,
She leaps on her prey;                   10
A child of the village
Was murdered today.

She came up to meet him
In a smooth golden cloak,
She choked him and beat him
To death, for a joke.                     16

Her bright locks were tangled,
She shouted for joy,
With one hand she strangled
A strong little boy.                      20

Now in silence she lingers
Beside him all night
To wash her long fingers
In silvery light.

## FOR DISCUSSION

1. When you read the title of the poem, what idea did you expect the poem to express? What idea does the poem actually express? Is "Sea Lullaby" a fitting title? Explain.

2. What is the mood of the first stanza? What words help set this mood? Is this the proper mood for the poem? Why?

3. What are the "teeth white as milk," the "smooth golden cloak," the tangled "bright locks"?

4. What idea is expressed in the last stanza? Is this compatible with the rest of the poem? Explain.

# Fire and Ice

## ROBERT FROST

*In a masterpiece of condensation Frost reflects on two natural elements and their part in the end of the world.*

> Some say the world will end in fire,
> Some say in ice.
> From what I've tasted of desire
> I hold with those who favor fire.
> But if it had to perish twice, 5
> I think I know enough of hate
> To say that for destruction ice
> Is also great
> And would suffice.

◇◇◇◇◇◇◇◇◇◇◇◇◇◇◇◇◇◇◇◇◇◇◇◇◇◇◇◇◇◇◇◇◇◇◇◇◇◇◇◇◇◇◇◇◇◇◇◇◇◇◇◇

FOR DISCUSSION

1. Is Frost talking about the end of the world described in the gospels by Christ? Is Frost talking about the world's end for the individual or for all men?

2. What are the qualities of desire which make Frost compare it to fire? Why does he feel fire is the most likely end?

3. How is ice related to destruction?

4. What is the rhyme scheme? Does the silent "e" add anything?

◇◇◇◇◇

# Mending Wall

## ROBERT FROST

*Two neighbors meet in the spring to repair a wall—one of those low walls made of loose stones which serve as fences in the New England states.*

> Something there is that doesn't love a wall,
> That sends the frozen-ground-swell under it,
> And spills the upper boulders in the sun;

And makes gaps even two can pass abreast.
The work of hunters is another thing: 5
I have come after them and made repair
Where they have left not one stone on a stone,
But they would have the rabbit out of hiding,
To please the yelping dogs.  The gaps I mean,
No one has seen them made or heard them made, 10
But at spring mending-time we find them there.
I let my neighbor know beyond the hill;
And on a day we meet to walk the line
And set the wall between us once again.
We keep the wall between us as we go. 15
To each the boulders that have fallen to each.
And some are loaves and some so nearly balls
We have to use a spell to make them balance:
"Stay where you are until our backs are turned!"
We wear our fingers rough with handling them, 20
Oh, just another kind of out-door game,
One on a side.  It comes to little more:
There where it is we do not need the wall:
He is all pine and I am apple orchard.
My apple trees will never get across 25
And eat the cones under his pines, I tell him.
He only says, "Good fences make good neighbors."
Spring is the mischief in me, and I wonder
If I could put a notion in his head:
"*Why* do they make good neighbors?  Isn't it 30
Where there are cows?  But here there are no cows.
Before I built a wall I'd ask to know
What I was walling in or walling out,
And to whom I was like to give offence.
Something there is that doesn't love a wall, 35
That wants it down."  I could say "Elves" to him,

134

But it's not elves exactly, and I'd rather
He said it for himself.  I see him there
Bringing a stone grasped firmly by the top
In each hand, like an old stone savage armed.               40
He moves in darkness as it seems to me,
Not of woods only and the shade of trees.
He will not go behind his father's saying,
And he likes having thought of it so well
He says again, "Good fences make good neighbors."           45

40. OLD STONE SAVAGE—A savage of the Stone Age, a stage in the development of human
culture in which stones were used as weapons and utensils.

## FOR DISCUSSION

1. What is the *something* that doesn't love a wall?

2. Why is the "work of hunters" mentioned in the poem?  Are the hunters regarded as praiseworthy in their work?  Give reasons for your answer.

3. Why is the man so impatient with the business of the wall?

4. Explain lines 18–19.

5. Do you agree with the sentiments expressed in lines 32–34?  Discuss.

6. Why doesn't the man suggest that it may be "elves" that do not love a wall?

7. Do you agree with the statement that "good fences make good neighbors"?  Why or why not?

8. Write a short character sketch of the two men.  Which of the two men would you prefer as a neighbor?  Why?  Explain your reasons fully.

# The Runaway

### ROBERT FROST

*The first touch of winter has sent a young colt into panic.  The poet, realizing the animal's genuine fright, is all sympathy.*

Once when the snow of the year was beginning to fall,
We stopped by a mountain pasture to say, "Whose colt?"
A little Morgan had one forefoot on the wall,
The other curled at his breast.  He dipped his head
And snorted at us.  And then he had to bolt.
We heard the miniature thunder where he fled,
And we saw him, or thought we saw him, dim and gray,
Like a shadow against the curtain of falling flakes.

"I think the little fellow's afraid of the snow.
He isn't winter broken.  It isn't play 10
With the little fellow at all.  He's running away.
I doubt if even his mother could tell him, 'Sakes,
It's only weather.'  He'd think she didn't know!
Where is his mother?  He can't be out alone."
And now he comes again with clatter of stone, 15
And mounts the wall again with whited eyes
And all his tail that isn't hair up straight.
He shudders his coat as if to throw off flies.
"Whoever it is that leaves him out so late,
When other creatures have gone to stall and bin, 20
Ought to be told to come and take him in."

---

FOR DISCUSSION

1. Lines 3–8 describe the little Morgan, one of the best breeds of horses.  Why did the colt have to bolt?

2. What explanation is given of the colt's behavior?  In what way do lines 12– 13 bring out the extreme fright of the colt?  Why?

3. Why do you think the colt came back?  Why did he "shudder his coat"?

4. Lines 19–21 contain a quiet but emphatic condemnation of the owner of the colt.  Do you agree with it?

# The Death of the Hired Man

## ROBERT FROST

*An old farm hand comes back to his "home" to die.  His return is the occasion of a quietly dramatic discussion between Warren and Mary.*

Mary sat musing on the lamp flame at the table
Waiting for Warren.  When she heard his step
She ran on tiptoe down the darkened passage
To meet him in the doorway with the news
And put him on his guard.  "Silas is back." 5
She pushed him outward with her through the door
And shut it after her.  "Be kind," she said.

She took the market things from Warren's arms
And set them on the porch, then drew him down
To sit beside her on the wooden steps.                    10

"When was I ever anything but kind to him?
But I'll not have the fellow back," he said.
"I told him so last haying, didn't I?
'If he left then,' I said, 'that ended it.'
What good is he?  Who else will harbor him                15
At his age for the little he can do?
What help he is there's no depending on.
Off he goes always when I need him most.
'He thinks he ought to earn a little pay,
Enough at least to buy tobacco with,                      20
So he won't have to beg and be beholden.'
'All right,' I say, 'I can't afford to pay
Any fixed wages, though I wish I could.'
'Someone else can.'  'Then someone else will have to.'
I shouldn't mind his bettering himself                    25
If that was what it was.  You can be certain,
When he begins like that, there's someone at him
Trying to coax him off with pocket money—
In haying time, when any help is scarce.
In winter he comes back to us.  I'm done."                30

"Sh! not so loud; he'll hear you," Mary said.

"I want him to; he'll have to soon or late."

"He's worn out.  He's asleep beside the stove.
When I came up from Rowe's I found him here,
Huddled against the barn door fast asleep,                35
A miserable sight, and frightening, too—
You needn't smile—I didn't recognize him—
I wasn't looking for him—and he's changed.
Wait till you see."

                    "Where did you say he'd been?"

"He didn't say.  I dragged him to the house,             40
And gave him tea and tried to make him smoke.
I tried to make him talk about his travels.
Nothing would do; he just kept nodding off."

"What did he say?  Did he say anything?"

"But little."                                             45

"Anything?  Mary, confess
He said he'd come to ditch the meadow for me."

"Warren!"

"But did he?  I just want to know."

"Of course he did.  What would you have him say?
Surely you wouldn't grudge the poor old man
Some humbled way to save his self-respect.                    50
He added, if you really care to know,
He meant to clear the upper pasture, too.
That sounds like something you have heard before?
Warren, I wish you could have heard the way
He jumbled everything.  I stopped to look              55
Two or three times—he made me feel so queer—
To see if he was talking in his sleep.
He ran on Harold Wilson—you remember—
The boy you had in haying four years since.
He's finished school, and teaching in his college.            60
Silas declares you'll have to get him back.
He says they two will make a team for work;
Between them they will lay this farm as smooth!
The way he mixed that in with other things.
He thinks young Wilson a likely lad, though daft        65
On education—you know how they fought
All through July under the blazing sun,
Silas up on the cart to build the load,
Harold along beside to pitch it on."

"Yes, I took care to keep well out of earshot."              70

"Well, those days trouble Silas like a dream.
You wouldn't think they would.  How some things linger!
Harold's young college boy's assurance piqued him.
After so many years he still keeps finding
Good arguments he sees he might have used.              75
I sympathize.  I know just how it feels
To think of the right thing to say too late.
Harold's associated in his mind with Latin.
He asked me what I thought of Harold's saying
He studied Latin like the violin                        80
Because he liked it—that an argument!
He said he couldn't make the boy believe
He could find water with a hazel prong—
Which showed how much good school had ever done him,

He wanted to go over that.  But most of all      85
He thinks if he could have another chance
To teach him how to build a load of hay—"

"I know, that's Silas' one accomplishment.
He bundles every forkful in its place,
And tags and numbers it for future reference,      90
So he can find and easily dislodge it
In the unloading.  Silas does that well.
He takes it out in bunches like big birds' nests.
You never see him standing on the hay
He's trying to lift, straining to lift himself."      95

"He thinks if he could teach him that, he'd be
Some good perhaps to someone in the world.
He hates to see a boy the fool of books.
Poor Silas, so concerned for other folk,
And nothing to look backward to with pride,      100
And nothing to look forward to with hope,
So now and never any different."

Part of a moon was falling down the west,
Dragging the whole sky with it to the hills,
Its light poured softly in her lap.  She saw      105
And spread her apron to it.  She put out her hand
Among the harplike morning-glory strings,
Taut with the dew from garden bed to eaves,
As if she played unheard the tenderness
That wrought on him beside her in the night.      110
"Warren," she said, "he has come home to die;
You needn't be afraid he'll leave you this time."

"Home," he mocked gently.

          "Yes, what else but home?
It all depends on what you mean by home.
Of course he's nothing to us, any more      115
Than was the hound that came a stranger to us
Out of the woods, worn out upon the trail."

"Home is the place where, when you have to go there,
They have to take you in."

          "I should have called it
Something you somehow haven't to deserve."      120

139

Warren leaned out and took a step or two,
Picked up a little stick, and brought it back
And broke it in his hand and tossed it by.
"Silas has better claim on us, you think,
Than on his brother?  Thirteen little miles          125
As the road winds would bring him to his door.
Silas has walked that far no doubt today.
Why didn't he go there?  His brother's rich,
A somebody—director in the bank."

"He never told us that."                               130

        "We know it though."

"I think his brother ought to help, of course.
I'll see to that if there is need.  He ought of right
To take him in, and might be willing to—
He may be better than appearances.
But have some pity on Silas.  Do you think          135
If he'd had any pride in claiming kin
Or anything he looked for from his brother,
He'd keep so still about him all this time?"

"I wonder what's between them."

                "I can tell you.
Silas is what he is—we wouldn't mind him—          140
But just the kind that kinsfolk can't abide.
He never did a thing so very bad.
He don't know why he isn't quite as good
As anyone.  He won't be made ashamed
To please his brother, worthless though he is."      145

"I can't think Si ever hurt anyone."

"No, but he hurt my heart the way he lay
And rolled his old head on that sharp-edged chair back.
He wouldn't let me put him on the lounge.
You must go in and see what you can do.              150
I made the bed up for him there tonight.
You'll be surprised at him—how much he's broken.
His working days are done; I'm sure of it."

"I'd not be in a hurry to say that."

"I haven't been.  Go, look, see for yourself.        155
But, Warren, please remember how it is:

He's come to help you ditch the meadow.
He has a plan.  You mustn't laugh at him.
He may not speak of it, and then he may.
I'll sit and see if that small sailing cloud          160
Will hit or miss the moon."

                 It hit the moon.
Then there were three there, making a dim row,
The moon, the little silver cloud, and she.
Warren returned—too soon, it seemed to her,
Slipped to her side, caught up her hand and waited.          165

"Warren?" she questioned.

              "Dead," was all he answered.

---

## FOR DISCUSSION

1. Why is Mary concerned to put Warren on his guard?

2. Note how much you find out about Silas from the conversation between Mary and Warren.  Why had Silas left?  Why did Silas offer to ditch the meadow? What was Silas' opinion of college education?  Why wouldn't Silas go to his brother's home to be taken in?

3. Is Warren really as gruff as he seems to be at first sight?

4. Warren and Mary both give their definitions of home.  What insight into their characters do these definitions give?

Which definition do you think is more nearly correct?  Express your own feeling about home.

5. Why does Mary ask Warren to "please remember how it is"?  What does Mary mean by this request?

6. Why does Warren catch up Mary's hand?  Do you think that Warren regretted his lack of sympathy for Silas when Mary first told him of his return?

7. How does the poet make the reader seem a part of the scene?

8. What great human values does the poem help one appreciate?  Name at least three and show how the poet brings them to our attention.

# The Latin Tongue

## JAMES J. DALY

*To give the rich and varied history of the Latin language in a poem of
fourteen lines seems an impossible achievement. Father Daly has done it
in the following sonnet, however, clearly and concisely.*

Like a loud-booming bell shaking its tower
  Of granite blocks, the antique Latin tongue
  Shook the whole earth: over all seas it flung
Triremes of war, and bade grim legions scour
The world's far verges. Its imperial dower      5
  Made Tullius a god: and Flaccus strung
  Its phrases into garlands, while among
The high enchanters it gave Maro power.

Then Latin lost its purple pomp of war,
  Its wine-veined laughter and patrician tears:     10
    It cast its fleshly grossness, won a soul,
And trafficked far beyond the farthest star
  With angel cohorts, echoing through the years
    In sacred Embassies from pole to pole.

4. TRIREMES—Galleys with three banks of oars.
5. VERGES—Margin, brink.
6. TULLIUS—Marcus Tullius Cicero (B.C. 106–43)—A famous Roman orator and writer.
6. FLACCUS—Quintus Horatius Flaccus (B.C. 65–8)—A Latin poet.
8. MARO—Publius Vergilius Maro (B.C. 70–19)—A Latin poet famed for his epic, *The
Aeneid*.

"The Latin Tongue" by James J. Daly from *Boscobel*, reprinted by permission of John F. Quinn, S.J.

---

## FOR DISCUSSION

1. By what details does the poet show
that the Latin tongue shook the whole
earth? In what sense did the *imperial
dower* of Latin make the orator, Cicero, a
god?

2. Point out the way in which lines 9–
10 refer to lines 5–8. A little research on
the works of Cicero, Horace, and Vergil

will help you to answer this question.

3. To what historical event do the last
four lines of the poem refer? When did
the Latin tongue win a soul? In what
sense is it true to say that it trafficked with
angel cohorts? What is meant by *sacred
Embassies*?

4. Write a brief prose account of the history of the Latin language. Use the poem
as an outline and give a more detailed ex-

planation of the main facts treated in the poem.  Use an encyclopedia.

## WORDS TO LEARN

Explain the following phrases: *imperial dower; wine-veined laughter; patrician tears; from pole to pole.*

## THE POET'S CRAFT

1. Is this an Elizabethan or an Italian sonnet?  How can you tell?
2. How do the last six lines differ in tone or spirit from the first eight?  How does this conform to the requirements for this type of sonnet?

# I Am the People, the Mob

### CARL SANDBURG

Carl Sandburg, a Midwestern American poet, brings to the minds of his readers the everyday happenings of the early Twentieth Century.  Using a free-verse, unrhymed style, he constantly attempts to highlight the new-found spirit and activity of Midwestern America and especially the growing city of Chicago.  Drawing on his own youthful experience, Sandburg emphasizes the role of the long-neglected part of society, the common man, the worker, the wage-earner.

I am the people—the mob—the crowd—the mass.
Do you know that all the great work of the world is done through me?
I am the workingman, the inventor, the maker of the world's food and clothes.

I am the audience that witnesses history.  The Napoleons come from me and the
    Lincolns.  They die.
And then I send forth more Napoleons and Lincolns.                    5
I am the seed ground.  I am the prairie that will stand for much plowing.
    Terrible storms pass over me.
I forget.  The best of me is sucked out and wasted.
I forget.  Everything but Death comes to me and makes me work and give up
    what I have.  And I forget.
Sometimes I growl, shake myself and spatter a few red drops for history to remem-
    ber.  Then—I forget.                    10

When I, the People, learn to remember, when I, the People, use the lessons of yesterday, and no longer forget who robbed me last year, who played me for a fool —then there will be no speaker in all the world say the name: "The People," with any fleck of a sneer in his voice or any far-off smile of derision.

The mob—the crowd—the mass—will arrive then.                15

---

FOR DISCUSSION

1. What do you think of Sandburg's use of the phrase, "the people"? Does he overlook the individual person in his usage of such a phrase?

2. Is the working man better off today than he was in Sandburg's time, the early 1900's? Contrast the conditions of these two periods.

3. What message or warning do you think Sandburg is trying to give here?

4. Does the common man, the workingman, exert any influence on American political, economic, and social life today? How?

5. Compare the thought in this poem with that in the poem, "The Man with the Hoe." Are they similar in any way? Explain.

A PROJECT

In a brief essay compare the achievements of Napoleon and Lincoln, their ambitions and aims.

# The Harbor

## CARL SANDBURG

Passing through huddled and ugly walls,
By doorways where women
Looked from their hunger-deep eyes,
Haunted by shadows of hunger-hands,
Out from the huddled and ugly walls,                5
I came sudden, at the city's edge,
On a blue burst of lake—
Long lake waves breaking under the sun
On a spray-flung curve of shore;
And a fluttering storm of gulls,                10
Masses of great gray wings
And flying white bellies
Veering and wheeling free in the open.

## FOR DISCUSSION

1. By focusing your attention on the ugliness and beauty that are found so intimately knit together in the harbor, does the poet wish to give merely a picture of striking contrasts? Or what more does he intend?

2. What details bring out the sordidness of the waterfront? What images suggest the cleanness and beauty of the lake? Are the opposing images effective?

◇◇◇◇◇

# Abraham Lincoln Walks at Midnight

## VACHEL LINDSAY

*Vachel Lindsay calls up the sorrowing figure of Abraham Lincoln to have him restlessly walk the streets of Springfield, his former home. The poem was written at the beginning of World War I and is Lindsay's way of expressing his horror at the insane folly of the war.*

It is portentous, and a thing of state
That here at midnight, in our little town,
A mourning figure walks, and will not rest,
Near the old court house pacing up and down.

Or by his homestead, or in shadowed yards          5
He lingers where his children used to play,
Or through the market, on the well-worn stones
He stalks until the dawn-stars burn away.

A bronzed, lank man! His suit of ancient black,
A famous high top-hat and plain worn shawl          10
Make him the quaint great figure that men love,
The prairie-lawyer, master of us all.

2. OUR LITTLE TOWN—Springfield, Illinois, Lindsay's home town; also Lincoln's home.

He cannot sleep upon his hillside now.
He is among us:—as in times before!
And we who toss and lie awake for long,          15
Breathe deep, and start, to see him pass the door.

His head is bowed.  He thinks of men and kings.
Yea, when the sick world cries, how can he sleep?
Too many peasants fight, they know not why;
Too many homesteads in black terror weep.          20

The sins of all the war-lords burn his heart.
He sees the dreadnaughts scouring every main.
He carries on his shawl-wrapped shoulders now
The bitterness, the folly and the pain.

He cannot rest until a spirit-dawn          25
Shall come;—the shining hope of Europe free:
The league of sober folk, the Workers' Earth,
Bringing long peace to Cornland, Alp, Sea.

It breaks his heart that kings must murder still,
That all his hours of travail here for men          30
Seem yet in vain.  And who will bring white peace
That he may sleep upon his hill again?

23. SHAWL-WRAPPED—Lincoln often wore a shawl or cape according to custom in dress then.

FOR DISCUSSION

1. Why is it a sign of evil to come and of great importance to the state that Lincoln walks the streets of the town?

2. What reasons does the poet give for the return of Lincoln?  What troubles Lincoln's great spirit?

3. When does the poet say Lincoln will be able to rest once more?  Do you think that time is near?  Do you believe the world will ever be completely at peace?

# The Leaden-Eyed

## VACHEL LINDSAY

*Like Edwin Markham's "The Man with the Hoe" this poem protests against the forces in society which quench and bruise the spirit of man.*

Let not young souls be smothered out before
They do quaint deeds and fully flaunt their pride.
It is the world's one crime its babes grow dull,
Its poor are ox-like, limp, and leaden-eyed.
Not that they starve, but starve so dreamlessly,          5
Not that they sow, but that they seldom reap,
Not that they serve, but have no gods to serve,
Not that they die, but that they die like sheep.

FOR DISCUSSION

1. Explain the exact meaning of "quaint" and "pride" in line 2. Are there two kinds of pride? Explain.

2. What does the poet intend to bring out by comparing the poor to animals?

3. Why is the poet more concerned over the way in which the people starve and die than over the fact that they do starve and die?

4. If you think the poet is describing a real state of affairs, what are the remedies for such a situation?

# Incident

## COUNTÉE CULLEN

*This short poem is more eloquent in its presentation of the cruel thoughtlessness behind name-calling and race prejudice than hundreds of pages of rational and eloquent logic could be.*

Once riding in Old Baltimore,
  Heart-filled, head-filled with glee,
I saw a Baltimorean
  Keep looking straight at me.

Now I was eight and very small,          5
   And he was no whit bigger,
And so I smiled, but he poked out
   His tongue and called me, "Nigger."

I saw the whole of Baltimore
   From May until December;          10
Of all the things that happened there
   That's all that I remember.

---

## FOR DISCUSSION

1. Which words in the first stanza give the mood of the little boy? How did he interpret the look of the Baltimorean? Why is this a natural interpretation?

2. What effect does the poet's mention of age and size have in the poem? What is the source of the Baltimorean's prejudice?

3. Why does the "incident" blot out everything else for the youngster?

# O Black and Unknown Bards

## JAMES WELDON JOHNSON

*A noted Negro poet pays his tribute to the unknown bards of his race.*

O black and unknown bards of long ago,
How came your lips to touch the sacred fire?
How, in your darkness, did you come to know
The power and beauty of the minstrel's lyre?
Who first from midst his bonds lifted his eyes?          5
Who first from out the still watch, lone and long,
Feeling the ancient faith of prophets rise
Within his dark-kept soul, burst into song?

Heart of what slave poured out such melody
As "Steal away to Jesus"? On its strains          10
His spirit must have nightly floated free,
Though still about his hands he felt his chains.
Who heard great "Jordan roll"? Whose starward eye
Saw chariot "swing low"? And who was he
That breathed that comforting, melodic sigh,          15
"Nobody knows de trouble I see"?

What merely living clod, what captive thing,
Could up toward God through all its darkness grope,
And find within its deadened heart to sing
These songs of sorrow, love, and faith, and hope?                    20
How did it catch that subtle undertone,
That note in music heard not with the ears?
How sound the elusive reed so seldom blown,
Which stirs the soul or melts the heart to tears?

Not that great German master in his dream                            25
Of harmonies that thundered amongst the stars
At the creation, ever heard a theme
Nobler than "Go down, Moses."  Mark its bars
How like a mighty trumpet-call they stir
The blood.  Such are the notes that men have sung                    30
Going to valorous deeds; such tones there were
That helped make history when Time was young.

There is a wide, wide wonder in it all,
That from degraded rest and servile toil
The fiery spirit of the seer should call                             35
These simple children of the sun and soil.
O black slave singers, gone, forgot, unfamed,
You—you alone, of all the long, long line
Of those who've sung untaught, unknown, unnamed,
Have stretched out upward, seeking the divine.                       40

You sang not deeds of heroes or of kings;
No chant of bloody war, no exulting pæan
Of arms-won triumphs; but your humble strings
You touched in chord with music empyrean.
You sang far better than you knew; the songs                         45
That for your listeners' hungry hearts sufficed
Still live,—but more than this to you belongs:
You sang a race from wood and stone to Christ.

FOR DISCUSSION

1. What is the meaning of "sacred fire"?  How do you interpret line 5?

2. In what way did the spirit of the slave find freedom?  What are the poems these unknown bards composed?  What lines give us the answer?

3. In the third stanza what line indicates the way in which the Negro was re-garded by those who had enslaved him?

4. Read "Go Down, Moses."  Do you agree with the author's estimate of it?

5. What is the "wide, wide wonder" mentioned in the fifth stanza?

6. What is the great achievement of the "black and unknown" poets?  How do their songs still live?  What is the meaning of: "You sang a race from wood and stone to Christ"?

# The Coin

## SARA TEASDALE

Into my heart's treasury
 I slipped a coin
That time cannot take
 Nor a thief purloin—

Oh, better than the minting     5
 Of a gold-crowned king
Is the safe kept memory
 Of a lovely thing.

---

FOR DISCUSSION

1. Explain how treasures of the memory are better than treasures of gold. Do you agree with the idea the poet states here?

2. Explain the following words and phrases: *heart's treasury, purloin, the minting of a gold-crowned king.*

# The Single-Track Mind

## ARTHUR GUITERMAN

*Arthur Guiterman is following a good tradition when he writes of the habits of a bird in order to illuminate the ways of men.*

Upon the reef that guards the palm-fringed sands
A heron stands.
Around him sweeps the azure Caribbean
Where cities Atlantean
Lie buried; through that strait to lasting fame     5
Columbus came,
And thousands on those shores where lizards glide
Have fought and died.
But little for such great and vast affairs
The heron cares.     10

Oblivious alike of Ocean's mystery
And Man's dark history,
He scans the foaming waves that seethe and—swish!
He gets his fish!

FOR DISCUSSION

1. What locality is described as the background for the heron?

2. What are the disadvantages of having a single-track mind? Are there any advantages? Explain fully the reasons for your answers.

# The Mountain Woman

## DUBOSE HEYWARD

*The lives of most of us are comfortably padded and gadget-ruled. We know very little about men and women whose lives are squeezed dry of beauty and filled with grinding toil. Here is a glimpse of such a life.*

> Among the sullen peaks she stood at bay
> And paid life's hard account from her small store.
> Knowing the code of mountain wives, she bore
> The burden of the days without a sigh;
> And, sharp against the somber winter sky,　　　　　5
> I saw her drive her steers afield that day.

Hers was the hand that sunk the furrows deep
Across the rocky, grudging southern slope.
At first youth left her face, and later hope;
Yet through each mocking spring and barren fall,     10
She reared her lusty brood, and gave them all
That gladder wives and mothers love to keep.

And when the sheriff shot her eldest son
Beside his still, so well she knew her part,
She gave no healing tears to ease her heart;     15
But took the blow upstanding, with her eyes
As drear and bitter as the winter skies.
Seeing her then, I thought that she had won.

But yesterday her man returned too soon
And found her tending, with reverent touch,     20
One scarlet bloom; and, having drunk too much,
He snatched its flame and quenched it in the dirt.
Then, like a creature with a mortal hurt,
She fell, and wept away the afternoon.

---

## FOR DISCUSSION

1. What words in lines 1–2 highlight the nature of the mountain woman's life?

2. What does the poem teach us about "the code of mountain wives"? Who makes the code?

3. What changes did the harshness of life work in the mountain woman? What was her reaction to the shooting of her son? What is the meaning of the line, "I thought that she had won"? Won what?

4. Does the last stanza surprise you? Why? Was it unreasonable to weep so long over "one scarlet bloom"?

5. Make a list of the adjectives used in the poem. Show how the author by the careful choice of words paints the whole background of mountain life.

# Rouge Bouquet

## JOYCE KILMER

*"Rouge Bouquet" is one of several war poems written by Joyce Kilmer before his own death in the First World War. Here the poet commemorates a company of men who died when their trench was buried with earth dislodged by exploding shells. Mass burial services were held over the spot and Kilmer's poem was written to be read at the ceremony.*

In a wood they call the Rouge Bouquet
There is a new-made grave today,
Built by never a spade nor pick
Yet covered with earth ten meters thick.
There lie many fighting men,    5
  Dead in their youthful prime,
Never to laugh nor love again
  Nor taste the Summertime.
For Death came flying through the air
And stopped his flight at the dugout
    stair,    10
Touched his prey and left them there,
  Clay to clay.
He hid their bodies stealthily
In the soil of the land they fought to
    free
  And fled away.    15
Now over the grave abrupt and clear
  Three volleys ring;
And perhaps their brave young spirits
    hear
  The bugle sing:
"Go to sleep!    20
Go to sleep!
Slumber well where the shell screamed
    and fell
Let your rifles rest on the muddy floor,
You will not need them any more.
Danger's past;    25
Now at last,
Go to sleep!"

There is on earth no worthier grave
To hold the bodies of the brave
Than this place of pain and pride    30
Where they nobly fought and nobly
    died.
Never fear but in the skies
  Saints and angels stand
Smiling with their holy eyes
  On this new-come band.    35
St. Michael's sword darts through the
    air
And touches the aureole on his hair
As he sees them stand saluting there,
  His stalwart sons:
And Patrick, Brigid, Columkill    40
Rejoice that in veins of warriors still
  The Gael's blood runs.
And up to Heaven's doorway floats,
  From the wood called Rouge Bou-
    quet,
A delicate cloud of bugle notes    45
  That softly say:
"Farewell! Farewell.

36. The Archangel Michael is represented as a military commander in the heavenly war against Satan.

40. PATRICK, BRIGID, COLUMKILL—Patron saints of Ireland.

42. GAEL'S BLOOD—Irish blood.

"Rouge Bouquet" from *Poems, Essays, and Letters*, Vol. 1, by Joyce Kilmer, reprinted by permission of Doubleday & Company, Inc.

Comrades true, born anew, peace to
  you!
Your souls shall be where the heroes are
And your memory shine like the morn-
  ing-star.                                    50

Brave and dear,
Shield us here.
Farewell!"

◇◇◇◇◇◇◇◇◇◇◇◇◇◇◇◇◇◇◇◇◇◇◇◇◇◇◇◇◇◇◇◇◇◇◇◇◇◇◇◇◇◇◇◇◇◇◇◇◇◇◇◇◇◇◇◇

FOR DISCUSSION

1. Explain the literal meaning of the first four lines of the poem.

2. Why is Death described as "flying through the air"? How do you interpret "clay to clay"?

3. Lines 20–27 fit words to a bugle song. What official bugle song do they suggest? What other group of lines suggests the same bugle song?

4. Why is there "no worthier grave" than the place where the soldiers fought and died? Why does St. Michael touch "the aureole on his hair"?

5. Lines 46–53 express the poet's praise of the dead soldiers. What line gives the strongest praise?

6. What comfort does the poem hold for the living kindred and friends of this company who have been buried here in the Rouge Bouquet?

◇◇◇◇◇

# Prayer of a Soldier in France

## JOYCE KILMER

*Every war brings great suffering in its train. World War I was no exception, and Joyce Kilmer, who gave his life in that struggle, had caught the meaning of the suffering of the soldier. Christ suffered and died for every man that comes into this world; and the sufferings of every man, if united to those of Christ, are an opportunity to "fill up those things that are wanting of the sufferings of Christ."*

My shoulders ache beneath my pack
(Lie easier, Cross, upon His back).

I march with feet that burn and smart
(Tread, Holy Feet, upon my heart).

Men shout at me who may not speak   5
(They scourged Thy back and smote
  Thy cheek).

I may not lift a hand to clear
My eyes of salty drops that sear.

"Prayer of a Soldier in France" from *Poems, Essays, and Letters*, Vol. 1, by Joyce Kilmer, reprinted by permission of Doubleday & Company, Inc.

(Then shall my fickle soul forget
Thy Agony of Bloody Sweat?)    10

My rifle hand is stiff and numb
(From Thy pierced palm red rivers
  come).

Lord, Thou didst suffer more for me
Than all the hosts of land and sea.

So let me render back again    15
This millionth of Thy gift.  Amen.

FOR DISCUSSION

1. Joyce Kilmer ended one of his last letters in this way: "Pray for me, dear Father, that I may love God more and that I may be unceasingly conscious of Him— that is the greatest desire I have."  After reading this poem would you say that he was attaining his "greatest desire"?

2. The poem lists some of the sufferings which a soldier endures.  How does the poet help himself to bear his sufferings?

# Christmas

## ALINE KILMER

*At Christmas-time we miss in a special way the presence of those who are dear to us.  Aline Kilmer wrote this poem when her husband, Joyce, was a soldier in France and her daughter, Rose, was dead.*

"And shall you have a tree," they say,
"Now one is dead and one away?"

Oh, I shall have a Christmas tree!
Brighter than ever it shall be;    4
Dressed out with colored lights to make
The room all glorious for your sake.

And under the Tree a Child shall sleep
Near shepherds watching their wooden
  sheep.
Threads of silver and nets of gold,
Scarlet bubbles the Tree shall hold,    10
And little glass bells that tinkle clear.
I shall trim it alone but feel you near.

And when Christmas Day is almost
  done,
When they all grow sleepy one by one,
When Kenton's books have all been
  read,    15
When Deborah's climbing the stairs to
  bed,

I shall sit alone by the fire and see
Ghosts of you both come close to me.
For the dead and the absent always stay
With the one they love on Christmas
  Day.    20

FOR DISCUSSION

1. Why will the tree be "brighter than ever" this year?

2. Who is the Child under the tree?

3. How do lines 19–20 link up with and explain lines 5–6?

4. To whom is the poet speaking when she says "for your sake"?

◇◇◇◇◇

# ℋare 𝒟rummer

### EDGAR LEE MASTERS

*The graveyard of Spoon River, a village in Illinois, is the scene of the poems in Edgar Lee Masters' SPOON RIVER ANTHOLOGY. The men and women buried there recount the stories of their lives. In this poem Hare Drummer calls up scenes from his boyhood.*

Do the boys and girls still go to Siever's
For cider, after school, in late September?
Or gather hazelnuts among the thickets
On Aaron Hatfield's farm when the frosts begin?
For many times with the laughing girls and boys      5
Played I along the road and over the hills
When the sun was low and the air was cool,
Stopping to club the walnut tree
Standing leafless against a flaming west.
Now, the smell of the autumn smoke,      10
And the dropping acorns,
And the echoes about the vales
Bring dreams of life. They hover over me.
They question me:
Where are those laughing comrades?      15
How many are with me, how many
In the old orchards along the way to Siever's,
And in the woods that overlook
The quiet water?

"Hare Drummer" by Edgar Lee Masters from *Spoon River Anthology*, reprinted by permission of Mrs. Ellen C. Masters.

◇◇◇◇◇◇◇◇◇◇◇◇◇◇◇◇◇◇◇◇◇◇◇◇◇◇◇◇◇◇◇◇◇◇◇◇◇◇◇◇◇◇◇◇◇◇◇◇◇◇◇◇◇◇◇◇◇◇◇◇

FOR DISCUSSION

1. Why does Hare Drummer wonder about the activities of the boys and girls he knew? List the details he remembers.

2. Do we tend to remember the happy or the sad things from the past? List the things you remember most about your early childhood.

# Meditation on Atlas

## SISTER MARY MADELEVA

According to Greek mythology Atlas was a god in charge of the pillars which held up the heavens. He supported the heavens on his head and his hands. This meditation on the giant who carried the burden of the world hints that it is possible to take oneself too seriously.

Atlas held the firmament
But could not see the sun;
He had the world between his hands
But did not have its fun.

He ate the bread of bitterness          5
Nor knew that bread is sweet;
Nor guessed the joy of outstretched
          arms,
The gayety of feet.

The earth was on his shoulders;
The sky was on the earth;          10
He did not know its wonder;
He did not know its mirth.

He knelt for aeons, burdened
With the whole unwieldy scheme
And he missed the point entirely          15
Of the grand, deific theme.

## FOR DISCUSSION

1. In what way did Atlas have so much and yet so little? Does his predicament remind you of yourself in certain moods?

2. What were the good things that Atlas missed? How can you apply his situation to yourself and others? What is the remedy for those states of mind when like Atlas we are completely wrapped up in our own importance? What virtue do we need most at such times?

3. What is the meaning of "deific theme"?

# The Ballad of William Sycamore

## STEPHEN VINCENT BENÉT

"So impatient, full of action, full of manly pride and friendship"—this
was the spirit of the pioneers according to Walt Whitman. Another great
poet-lover of America, Stephen Vincent Benét, expressed the same spirit
in the following stanzas. William Sycamore is typical of the restless, venturesome Western youths of the last century.

My father, he was a mountaineer,
  His fist was a knotty hammer;
He was quick on his feet as a running deer,
  And he spoke with a Yankee stammer.

My mother, she was merry and brave,     5
  And so she came to her labor,
With a tall green fir for her doctor grave
  And a stream for her comforting neighbor.

And some are wrapped in the linen fine,
  And some like a godling's scion;     10
But I was cradled on twigs of pine
  In the skin of a mountain lion.

And some remember a white, starched lap
  And a ewer with silver handles;
But I remember a coonskin cap     15
  And the smell of bayberry candles.

The cabin logs with the bark still rough,
  And my mother, who laughed at trifles,
And the tall, lank visitors, brown as snuff,
  With their long, straight squirrel-rifles.     20

I can hear them dance, like a foggy song,
  Through the deepest one of my slumbers,
The fiddle squeaking the boots along
  And my father calling the numbers.

10. SCION (sī'ŭn)—Son, heir.
14. EWER (ū'ēr)—A wide-mouthed jug.
24. NUMBERS—Dance steps.

"The Ballad of William Sycamore" from *Selected Works of Stephen Vincent Benét*, published by Rinehart &
Company, Inc., copyright, 1922, by Stephen Vincent Benét. Reprinted by permission of Brandt & Brandt.

The quick feet shaking the puncheon floor,     25
  And the fiddle squeaking and squealing,
Till the dried herbs rattled above the door
  And the dust went up to the ceiling.

There are children lucky from dawn till dusk,
  But never a child so lucky!     30
For I cut my teeth on "Money Musk"
  In the Bloody Ground of Kentucky!

When I grew tall as the Indian corn,
  My father had little to lend me,
But he gave me his great old powder horn     35
  And his woodsman's skill to befriend me.

With a leather shirt to cover my back,
  And a redskin nose to unravel
Each forest sign, I carried my pack
  As far as a scout could travel.     40

Till I lost my boyhood and found my wife,
  A girl like a Salem clipper!
A woman straight as a hunting knife
  With eyes as bright as the Dipper!

31. "MONEY MUSK"—An old popular song.
32. BLOODY GROUND—A name applied to Kentucky because of conflicts with the Indians which took place there.

We cleared our camp where the buffalo feed,          45
    Unheard-of streams for our flagons;
And I sowed my sons like the apple seed
    On the trail of the Western wagons.

They were right, tight boys, never sulky or slow,
    A fruitful, a goodly muster.          50
The eldest died at the Alamo.
    The youngest fell with Custer.

The letter that told it burned my hand.
    Yet we smiled and said, "So be it!"
But I could not live when they fenced the land,          55
    For it broke my heart to see it.

I saddled a red, unbroken colt
    And rode him into the day there;
And he threw me down like a thunderbolt
    And rolled on me as I lay there.          60

The hunter's whistle hummed in my ear
    As the city men tried to move me.
And I died in my boots like a pioneer
    With the whole wide sky above me.

Now I lie in the heart of the fat, black soil,          65
    Like the seed of a prairie thistle;
It has washed my bones with honey and oil
    And picked them clean as a whistle.

And my youth returns, like the rains of Spring,
    And my sons, like the wild geese flying:          70
And I lie and hear the meadow lark sing
    And have much content with my dying.

Go play with the towns you have built of blocks
    The towns where you would have bound me!
I sleep in my earth like a tired fox,          75
    And my buffalo have found me.

46. FLAGON—A pitcher with handle and spout; also, its contents.

FOR DISCUSSION

1. What kind of people were William Sycamore's mother and father?

2. Mention some of the earliest memories of William Sycamore. Do these memories indicate that his surroundings were happy despite the hardships?

3. Explain the ninth stanza.

4. Why did William Sycamore want to

push on farther west when he had lost his boyhood?

5. Was he proud of his wife and sons? Point out three stanzas which answer the question.

6. How did William Sycamore die? Why did he have "much content" with his way of dying?

7. How can a modern city-bred youth imitate the spirit of the pioneers?

## A PROJECT: WRITING A CHARACTER SKETCH

Write a character sketch of William Sycamore based on the ideas you caught from the poem.

## THE POET'S CRAFT

1. What figures of speech does the poet use in the first stanza to describe William Sycamore's father? Do you think these figures are expressive and effective? Why? Make a list of some other effective figures of speech in the poem.

2. Do you think that the rhythm Benét has written this poem in is fitting to the subject of the poem? Give reasons for your answer.

## WORDS TO KNOW

Interpret the following phrases as they are used in the poem: *knotty hammer; white, starched lap; bayberry candles; foggy song; puncheon floor; little to lend me; redskin nose; Salem clipper; right, tight boys; a good muster; into the day there.*

## RELATED READING

Locate and read "Pioneers! O Pioneers!" by Walt Whitman.

# Valentine

### THOMAS BUTLER

*The poem, "Valentine," brings a smile to our lips, but the lines have serious undercurrents. Pathos is here no less than humor. You will want to read the poem several times before discussing it.*

I'm Jerry the dope who never woiks,
The all-American flop . . .
Me best friend is a glass o' rye
Me woist one is a cop.

Not long ago I was good enough,    5
A very nifty lad . . .
I had a little sweetheart too . . .
At least I think I had.

She was the best kid in our block,
As pretty as anyone . . .    10
But she hoid a call, and went to be
A Missionary nun.

She was so young the day she sailed
So beautiful on a boat . . .
When I saw her eyes an elephant    15
Stood up inside me troat.

"Valentine" from *America* by Thomas Butler, reprinted by permission of The America Press.

| | |
|---|---|
| I makes a little rolling dice, | She thinks I'm quite a guy, I guess |
| And a little shooting pool, | She thinks I'm in the dough . . . |
| And I sends it all to Sister Jane | I asked a San Franciscan priest |
| To help her in her school.    20 | And he said she needn't know. |

Somehow she seems to be my gift    25
And it lifts me thoughts above!
"From Jerry the dope . . . a Valen-
    tine . . .
To Africa, wit love."

---

### FOR DISCUSSION

1. Is Jerry "the dope" altogether a good-for-nothing? You will have mixed feelings about Jerry. Explain them.

2. How do you account for the fact that the missionary nun influenced Jerry's life so much? How was she Jerry's gift? Was it because of her prayers, or because of Jerry's desire to do something worth while for her, or because of a combination of these things?

3. Do you think Jerry was the kind of fellow who could commit a really serious crime? Why or why not?

4. What was the question which Jerry asked the San Franciscan priest? Did that show that he was ashamed of the way he got the money?

5. How do you account for the fact that Jerry changed from a "nifty lad" to something of a bum? Was it because of hard luck, lack of education, lack of ability, weakness of will, or what?

### PROJECTS

1. Write a brief imaginative account of the downgrade history of some young fellow like Jerry. Show how one bad thing leads to another, all leading down hill.

2. Let some member of the class recite "Valentine" in character.

◇◇◇◇

# Loss of Faith

### ALFRED J. BARRETT

*The loss of faith here on earth is a tragedy and a casting away of one of our most prized possessions. However, the author is not speaking of this tragic waste but of the joyful possession of the soul in heaven which no longer needs to believe or hope because it now sees and possesses what on earth it knew only by the dim light of faith.*

"Loss of Faith" from *Mint by Night* by Alfred J. Barrett, reprinted by permission of The America Press.

The life of grace and glory is the same.
The life of grace is, by another name,
Heaven on earth, and death is but a change
In range—
And nothing strange!                                           5

There is between our dreaming and our seeing
One pulsing continuity of being.
Ah, when the life of glory we achieve
Why grieve?
We only lose our having to believe!                           10

FOR DISCUSSION

1. What is the meaning of *glory* in line
1? Make sure of the exact meaning of
the word as used in this poem.

2. In what way is the life of grace
"heaven on earth"?

3. What reason does the poet give for
saying that death is "nothing strange"?

4. How would you translate the words
"dreaming" and "seeing" into terms which
you use in your study of religion?

5. Why should we rejoice over the loss
of "our having to believe"?

6. What does the poet mean by line
seven, "One pulsing continuity of being"?
Can you explain his idea clearly in your
own words? What is the "continuity" of
which the poet speaks? Why does he describe it as "pulsing"?

# *High Flight*

## JOHN GILLESPIE MAGEE, JR.

*In September, 1941, while John Gillespie Magee, Jr., was in combat train-
ing, he wrote "High Flight" on the back of a letter to his mother. In
December he was killed while on active service in England. His sonnet
was made the official poem of the British flying forces.*

Oh, I have slipped the surly bonds of earth,
And danced the skies on laughter-silvered wings;
Sunward I've climbed and joined the tumbling mirth
Of sun-split clouds—and done a hundred things

You have not dreamed of—wheeled and soared and swung          5
High in the sunlit silence.  Hov'ring there,
I've chased the shouting wind along and flung
My eager craft through footless halls of air.
Up, up the long delirious, burning blue
I've topped the wind-swept heights with easy grace,          10
Where never lark, or even eagle, flew;
And, while with silent, lifting mind I've trod
The high untrespassed sanctity of space,
Put out my hand, and touched the face of God.

"High Flight" by John Gillespie Magee, Jr., reprinted by permission of Mrs. John G. Magee.

## FOR DISCUSSION

1. In the first five lines of the poem John Magee has used several different expressions to describe the experience of flight.  How many do you find?  Which seem to you to be especially appropriate?

2. What are some of the "hundred things you have not dreamed of" which the poet mentions?  What are the "footless halls of air"?

3. What lines show the boyish joy of the pilot?  What lines show his reverent spirit?

4. Why is this an appropriate poem for the flying forces?

## WORDS

1. Make a list of the adjectives which the author uses to describe his experiences in the air.  Do you think they are apt?

2. Explain the italicized words in the following quotation:

". . . while with silent, lifting mind I've trod
The high *untrespassed sanctity* of *space*."

# Ars Poetica

## ARCHIBALD MacLEISH

Many definitions of poetry have been proposed, but there is none upon which all are agreed.  Some of these proposed definitions would allow that much poetry has been written; others would narrow the field severely. The basic problem is to determine such a clear and concise definition that a line of division may be drawn between true poetry and that which approaches and resembles true poetry, but is not.

Among the modern poets, one of the first to take up this challenging question was Ezra Pound, who tried to elaborate a "mathematics of poetry," that is, to make poetry a science as rigid and exact as mathematics. Although unsuccessful in this, Pound has given direction to much of the modern thinking about what a true poem should be.

Two of the best contemporary spokesmen on this subject are Archibald MacLeish and T. S. Eliot. Although neither has fully developed and explained his theory, both would regard poetry as something objective, a crystallization of the experience and emotion of the poet. The poem itself, however, is neither the full concept of the author, because he is unable to express it fully, nor is it the full concept of the reader, since he brings his own personal experiences and associations to his reading of the poem. Consequently, the poem, that which is on paper, has its own proper identity which is separate from the minds of both author and reader. Rather than a communication of the author's concept to the reader, the poem is a being in itself, a thing, the objective expression of an emotional experience.

The objective of poetry, then, is simply to create with words this emotional experience. This can be achieved, according to Eliot, only by a series of images which crystallize and make objective such an experience; for example, rather than explaining what his grief is or even the fact that he is sad, the poet images his grief and sadness by:

"An empty doorway and a maple leaf."

In "Ars Poetica," Archibald MacLeish tells us what a poem should be.

A POEM should be palpable and mute
As a globed fruit

Dumb
As old medallions to the thumb

Silent as the sleeve-worn stone          5
Of casement ledges where the moss has
   grown—

A poem should be wordless
As the flight of birds

A poem should be motionless in time
As the moon climbs                               10

Leaving, as the moon releases
Twig by twig the night-entangled trees,

Leaving, as the moon behind the winter
   leaves,
Memory by memory the mind—

A poem should be motionless in time
As the moon climbs                               16

.   .   .   .

"Ars Poetica" from *Collected Poems 1917–1952* by Archibald MacLeish. Reprinted by permission of Houghton Mifflin Company, publishers.

A poem should be equal to:
Not true

For all the history of grief
An empty doorway and a maple leaf

For love                                                    21
The leaning grasses and two lights
  above the sea—

A poem should not mean
But be

◇◇◇◇◇◇◇◇◇◇◇◇◇◇◇◇◇◇◇◇◇◇◇◇◇◇◇◇◇◇◇◇◇◇◇◇◇◇◇◇◇◇◇◇◇◇◇◇◇◇◇◇

FOR DISCUSSION

1. What one thought is the author repeating when he says that a poem should be *mute, dumb, silent, wordless*?

2. If we interpret the words *leaving* and *releases*, in line 11 as *bringing out*, and *clarifying*, what do these lines mean?

3. In lines 17 and 18, the author suggests that the function of the poem is not to express a truth, but rather to be "equal to" what?

4. How do the last two lines summarize the author's thought and theory?

5. By the standards proposed in these lines, would *Ars Poetica* be a true poem?

◇◇◇◇◇

# The Young Cat and the Chrysanthemums

## WILLIAM CARLOS WILLIAMS

*William Carlos Williams writes his poetry about the plain, ordinary things of everyday life. This short poem merely gives us a description of a young cat in a plot of chrysanthemums and a very brief statement of the author's attitude toward the cat. Notice, however, how complete and accurate an idea of the picture he sees the author is able to give us in a very few words.*

You mince, you start
advancing indirectly—
your tail upright
knocking about among the
frail, heavily flowered                           5
sprays.

Yes, you are lovely
with your ingratiating
manners, sleek sides and
small white paws but                              10
I wish you had not come
here.

FOR DISCUSSION

1. William Carlos Williams was an imagist. That is, a poet who tries to give brief, impressionistic descriptions. What phrases in "The Young Cat and the Chrysanthemums" best show this tendency? Are his descriptions successful? Explain.

RELATED READING

Other excellent poems in this same style by Williams are "Metric Figure," "Dawn," "Daisy," "The Red Wheelbarrow," and "Flowers by the Sea." Other imagist poets you will enjoy are Amy Lowell and H. D.

◇◇◇◇◇

# For My Brother: Reported Missing in Action, 1943

## THOMAS MERTON

*A poet is a seer, that is, he looks into the very heart of things, and he shares his insights with others. In this poem Thomas Merton wakes us to a realization of how the Incarnation and the Redemption have entered into our lives.*

Sweet brother, if I do not sleep,
My eyes are flowers for your tomb;
And if I cannot eat my bread,
My fasts shall live like willows where
    you died.
If in the heat I find no water for my
    thirst,     5
My thirst shall turn to springs for you,
    poor traveler.

Where, in what desolate and smokey
    country,
Lies your poor body, lost and dead?

And in what landscape of disaster     9
Has your unhappy spirit lost its road?

Come, in my labor find a resting place
And in my sorrows lay your head,
Or rather take my life and blood
And buy yourself a better bed—     14
Or take my breath and take my death
And buy yourself a better rest.

When all the men of war are shot
And flags have fallen into dust,

Your cross and mine shall tell men still
Christ died on each, for both of us.   20

For in the wreckage of your April Christ
  lies slain;
And Christ weeps in the ruins of my
  spring:

The money of Whose tears shall fall
Into your weak and friendless hand   24
And buy you back to your own land:
The silence of Whose tears shall fall
Like bells upon your alien tomb.
Hear them and come: they call you
  home.

## FOR DISCUSSION

1. What is the meaning of lines 2, 4, and 6?  Show how the teaching of the Church on the relation between the living members of the Church and the souls in Purgatory explains the first stanza.

2. Point out how the title of the poem is linked with the second stanza.

3. Explain how the poet's brother can find a resting place in "my labor."  What is the "better bed" and "better rest" of which the poet makes mention in the third stanza?  Why is *buy* an appropriate word?

4. What is the meaning of lines 19–20?  Explain how Christ lies slain in "the wreckage of your April."

5. Explain how lines 23–25 refer to the Redemption.  Why must "home" in line 28 refer to heaven?

6. How does the teaching of the Church on the Mystical Body of Christ help towards an understanding of the last stanza of the poem?

# The Housewife's Prayer

## BLANCHE MARY KELLY

*Mary, the Mother of Our Lord, has been an inspiration to men and women of all ages.  Here is a simple, modern expression of devotion to Mary, a testimony to her power to mold thoughts and lives.*

Lady, who with tender word
Didst keep the house of Christ the Lord,
Who didst set forth the bread and wine
Before the Living Wheat and Vine,
Reverently didst make the bed        5
Whereon was laid the Holy Head
That such a cruel pillow prest
For our behoof, on Calvary's crest;
Be beside me while I go
About my labors to and fro.          10
Speed the wheel and speed the loom,
Guide the needle and the broom,
Make my bread rise sweet and light,
Make my cheese come foamy white,
Yellow may my butter be             15
As cowslips blowing on the lea.
Homely though my tasks and small,
Be beside me at them all.
Then when I shall stand to face
Jesu in the judgment place,          20
To me thy gracious help afford,
Who art the Handmaid of the Lord.

"The Housewife's Prayer" from *The Valley of Vision* by Blanche Mary Kelly, reprinted by permission of the author.

## FOR DISCUSSION

1. How are the first eight lines related to the rest of the poem?

2. To whom do the words "Living Wheat and Vine" refer?

3. Why does the housewife address her prayer to Mary? Was Mary's life in any way like that of the housewife?

4. In what way are the simple tasks which the housewife mentions an expression of love for Mary and her Son? Do you think that any kind of work can be made a prayer? How?

5. Compare this poem with Henry Adams' "Prayer to the Virgin of Chartres."

6. Bring to class five other poems written in praise of Mary.

◇◇◇◇◇

# The Ox Bone Madonna

## JAMES J. GALVIN

*A Polish soldier in a Russian concentration camp carved a statue of Mary from a bone plucked out of the soup.*

Once they minted Our Lady in multiple golden medallions
Commingling her glories in smouldering roses of glass;
From gale-bellied mainsails she nodded on numberless galleons
Accorded a salvo at sunset on cannon of brass.

Time was when her icon was blazoned on jewel-spun banners     5
When lancers went plunging to battle huzzahing her Name,
When guildsmen aspired to depict her ineffable manners
In spidery windows of moon-dappled amber and flame.

But now though the pitiless shock of artillery shake her
From lily-sprung pinnacles high on the spires of Cologne,     10
Though matchless madonnas be splinters of quincewood and nacre,
Her bell-plundered abbeys with clover and thorn overgrown,
Neither flogging nor hunger nor death can make captives forsake her:
From a castaway ox bone they carve her more splendid than stone.

1. MEDALLION—Something resembling a large medal, as a tablet bearing a figure in relief.
2. ROSES OF GLASS—A reference to the windows of cathedrals, for example, the famous Rose Window of Chartres.
4. SALVO—A salute given by firing all the guns.
5. ICON (ī′kŏn)—An image or representation.
7. GUILDSMEN—An association of men who have common interests or aims for mutual aid and protection. The reference here is to the guilds of medieval times.
10. COLOGNE—A reference to the famous cathedral of Cologne.
11. NACRE (nā′kẽr)—Mother-of-pearl.

"The Ox Bone Madonna" by James J. Galvin, C.SS.R., from *Spirit, A Magazine of Poetry*, copyrighted by The Catholic Poetry Society of America.

# The Ox Bone Madonna

## JOHN DUFFY

We have minted her beauty in multiple golden medallions,
Commingling her graces in smouldering roses of glass,
In banners have hued her that blazed over lancers and stallions,
And pared her in plumwood to smile on the perilous pass.

Her splendor has dimpled the darkness of rafter and moulding—     5
A luminous cheek in the cavernous dusk of Cologne!
From marvelous maple and marble her features unfolding,
Her face has anointed the timber and sweetened the stone.

But haloed and holy and folded in fretted apparel,
Incredibly crowned, with the Child in her snowy embrace—     10
Out of the silence of bone an ineffable carol,
Out of the thigh of an ox her unspeakable face!

Ah, none but Our Lady could blazon a bone into glowing,
Who stood without stain in the mire where the cattle had trod,
And kept in the stench and the dark and the din of the lowing,     15
In the squalor of oxen the mien of the Mother of God.

◇◇◇◇◇◇◇◇◇◇◇◇◇◇◇◇◇◇◇◇◇◇◇◇◇◇◇◇◇◇◇◇◇◇◇◇◇◇◇◇◇◇◇◇◇◇◇◇◇◇◇◇◇◇◇◇◇◇◇◇◇◇◇◇

## FOR DISCUSSION

1. Make a close study of these two poems on the "Ox Bone Madonna." In how many ways does the author of the first poem indicate the glories of Mary were celebrated?

2. Make a list of the ways in which Mary is pointed out as being honored in the second poem. Which of the two poems gives a more varied account of the honors shown to Our Lady?

## THE POET'S CRAFT

1. Which of these two poems is a sonnet? How can you tell? Do you think the sonnet form fits this theme better or worse than the form of the other poem? Explain.

2. What name is given to the poetic device used in the first line of each of these poems—the use of several words beginning with the same consonant? In the third line of the second poem the same vowel sound is repeated four times; what is this device called? What effect do you think these devices have? Read the poems aloud to see if these devices force you to accent certain words. Can you find other lines in these poems where these devices are employed? Which lines are they?

3. Using letters, as shown in the section "For Appreciation of Poetry," indicate the rhyme scheme of each poem.

# Now That Can Never Be Done

## SISTER MARIS STELLA

*Have you ever had the experience of wishing too late that you had done
something you had fully intended to do, but did not?*

I shall never forget my mother's voice singing.
It was a true voice that no one could forget
who had heard it once.  It came like water springing
from a deep spring that must be running yet
somewhere for someone else to sing from.   I                    5
could wish that spring were mine, for like no other
singing was my mother's singing.   Why
I never knew for sure.   Always my mother
had her songs by heart and sang them so—
old songs that everyone knew and dozens more—              10
but though I loved them it is only the tunes I know.
The words are half forgot.   I thought before,
while she still sang her songs, that one by one
I should write them down.   Now that can never be done.

◇◇◇◇◇◇◇◇◇◇◇◇◇◇◇◇◇◇◇◇◇◇◇◇◇◇◇◇◇◇◇◇◇◇◇◇◇◇◇◇◇◇◇◇◇◇◇◇◇◇◇◇◇◇◇◇◇◇◇

## FOR DISCUSSION

1. Is it stated anywhere in the poem that the mother's singing is missed?   Then how do you know that it is?

2. Was the poem written to express sorrow over the loss of the songs or the loss of the mother?   How does the title help to answer this question?   How are the two losses related?

3. Try to guess what some of the songs were; then discuss from what source, from what "deep spring" they flowed.

4. "My mother had her songs by heart and sang them so" could simply mean that the mother had a good memory.   What deeper meaning is there in the words?

5. How can you tell that this is a son-net?   What is the effect produced in lines 5 and 7 by starting a new sentence at the end of a line?   Does this device emphasize or deemphasize the rhyme scheme?   Do you or do you not like this effect?   Give reasons for your answer.

## A PROJECT

Express in a poem or essay or letter your feelings at the loss of a friend or a relative. Use the indirect way employed in the poem above: stress some quality or some repeated action that has endeared the person to you.   Let this quality or action be the symbol of your affection and your sense of loss.

# Laudate Pueri Dominum

## SISTER M. THÉRÈSE

*A seven-year-old climbs the organ loft and ripples out the tunes she knows best as praise to God.*

> Today God's organ shall have holiday
> From ritual mode and Palestrinian air
> Wedded to cloistered voices sweet in prayer—
> For Rita Alice climbs the loft to play . . .
> Strong in her blithe seven years, and seeming gay     5
> For such bold venture. Tunes from a gypsy-fair
> Ripple the reverent dusk, and debonair
> Snatches of childish dance and roundelay.
>
> Saints marble-gowned, and carven seraphim
> Start from their ancient niches, as such hymn     10
> Mellows the hush with magical lingerings—
> Where little cherubs smile behind their wings.
> One looks through tears—His parted lips abreath—
> Remembering songs and games at Nazareth.

Title: LAUDATE PUERI DOMINUM—Praise the Lord, ye children. Psalm 112.
8. ROUNDELAY—A song in which a simple strain is often repeated.

## FOR DISCUSSION

1. In what sense is the organ said to "have holiday"?

2. How would you contrast the music which is regularly played on the organ with the tunes that Rita Alice plays? By what words does the poet show the contrast?

3. The little cherubs are pictured as smiling. Line 13 pictures "one" as looking through tears. To whom do you think "one" refers? How do you account for the difference between the reaction of this one and the other cherubs?

## WORDS TO EXPLAIN

Explain the meaning of the following phrases: *ritual mode; cloistered voices; debonair snatches of childish dance.*

# You Are the Spikenard

## SISTER MARY ST. VIRGINIA

*Mutual understanding and deep love and friendship do not always need words and external actions to manifest themselves. A soul in close union with Jesus Christ, especially, shows a sympathy, a strength, and a sweetness that are voiceless, yet telling.*

You are the gaze He seeks for His delight
When enemies stare,
You are the secret hills wherein at night
He hides His prayer.

You are the stillness in a storm-strewn place     5
Where voices cry,
You are the anguish cloistered in a face
From the casual eye.

You are the word waiting upon His tongue
Yet never said,     10

You are the sharpened sabre never swung
Unscabbarded.

You are the harp confiscate and afar
No hand has swept,
You are the burning undiscovered star
The night has kept.     16

You are the spikenard redolent and rare
Disputed by men
That, unexplained, is spilled upon His hair
By Magdalen.

"You Are the Spikenard" by Sister Mary St. Virginia, originally published in *The Commonweal*, reprinted by permission of the author.

13. CONFISCATE—Seized, carried off as a forfeit.

---

FOR DISCUSSION

1. How many distinct metaphors are used to describe the character about whom this poem is written? What common element binds them together?

2. In what verses is the person described shown to be sympathetic? strong? ardent? overwhelmingly loving? What other qualities are suggested by the figures of speech used in the poem?

3. In what walk of life would you especially expect to find a person with the traits noted in the poem?

4. Give your reasons why the poet chose "You Are the Spikenard" for the title in preference to the other lines of the poem.

5. What impression does the poet hope to make on the reader by these images?
   a) "You are the secret hills . . ."
   b) "You are the sharpened sabre . . ."
   c) "You are the gaze He seeks . . ."

# Call to Stars

## SISTER MARY JEREMY

Stars! Stars for immortality. Stars to tell the weather. Stars to tell the future. Stars to tell of love. But above all, stars, God's good gentlemen-at-arms, stand steady in a changing sky, witnesses and pledges of our growing, glowing constancy.

O far and leagued with immortality,
Primer of distance to the prentice mind
That in neglect of learning counts you friend,
Affirms you kind,
Takes you for weather-sign and wishing spell,     5
Sets you above
The birth of kings, makes your integrity
An annotation for the night of love;

Or thorned and cold in the imperfect dawn,
Lost in the storm and found incredibly;     10
Unsure, ill-seen,
Yet mark of our extremest constancy:
"Bright star, would I were steadfast as thou art,"
Avers the young, undying voice again—
Thus we indenture you. Be witness still:     15
Our nights grow longer, God's good gentlemen.

3. NEGLECT—Absence, lack.
8. ANNOTATION—Note, comment.
13. "BRIGHT STAR . . . ART"—The title and opening line of a sonnet by the English poet, John Keats (1795–1821).

"Call to Stars" by Sister Mary Jeremy, reprinted by her permission and that of The America Press.

◇◇◇◇◇◇◇◇◇◇◇◇◇◇◇◇◇◇◇◇◇◇◇◇◇◇◇◇◇◇◇◇◇◇◇◇◇◇◇◇◇◇◇◇◇◇◇◇◇◇◇◇◇◇◇◇◇◇◇◇◇◇◇◇◇◇

## FOR DISCUSSION

1. Pagans believed that souls of illustrious people appear after death as new stars in the heavens. The Greek philosopher, Plato, said that each man has a star to which his soul returns after death. The Italian poet, Dante, peopled the planets with the souls of the just. Explain the phrase: "leagued with immortality."

2. What is a primer? Does "primer of distance" mean that men learn about distance from the stars, or that the stars are a primer in the distant sky from which men read? Explain your opinion.

3. Have you ever wished on a star? Explain. What songs or verses about stars do you know that contain wishing spells?

4. Recall from last year, two instances in which Shakespeare connects stars with man's destinies. One begins: "The fault, dear Brutus. . . ."; the other: "When beggars die. . . ." What is the most famous star announcing a royal birth?

5. How does the poet express the idea that lovers talk about the stars? What quality or qualities of love could the stars represent? Give reasons for your answer.

6. Why is the star called thorned? cold? What is an imperfect dawn? Why can the star always be found?

7. The stars are indentured, put to serve many purposes. What does the author of this poem make them do? How does the fact that our nights seem to grow longer show that we are more constant and loyal?

◇◇◇◇◇

# *Dea Roma*

## ROBERT LOWELL

*The poet, pained by the growing paganism of the modern world, looks at history to see what progress man has made in his efforts to find God. Using Rome as a symbol of the soul's struggle for peace, he shows us the part that the Rome of Augustus played in the struggle; then the part played by the Era of Persecutions; then what the Christian Era offers.*

Augustus mended you.  He hung the
  tongue
Of Tullius upon your rostrum, lashed
The money-lenders from your Senate-
  house;
And Brutus bled his forty-six per cent
For *Pax Romana*.  Quiet as a mouse  5

> 1-5. These are closely packed images drawn from Lowell's wide knowledge of Ancient Rome.  Augustus wished to revive the spirit of the Early Republic.  To do this, he restored the ancient shrines and allowed the cult of the goddess Roma to spread to Rome itself.  Religious revival alone would be insufficient and so political and financial reforms also were made—the first is represented by the reference to Cicero's execution and the subsequent nailing of his head to the rostrum. The gospel image of Christ and the Money-changers in the Temple add vigor to Augustus's efforts to relieve the burden of taxation resulting from Senatorial control of government officials.  Even so, Marcus Brutus could collect four times the legal interest on a loan.

Blood licks the king's cosmetics with its
  tongue.

Some years, your legions soldiered
  through this world
Under the eagles of Lord Lucifer;
But human torches lit the captains
  home
Where victims warped the royal cruci-
  fix:
How many roads and sewers led to
  Rome.  10
Satan is pacing up and down the world

> 8. EAGLES—The standards of the Roman Legions.
> 9. HUMAN TORCHES—Refers to the tarring and feathering of the Christians to make torches for the games at night.

These sixteen centuries, Eternal City,
That we have squandered since Maxen-
   tius fell
Under the Milvian Bridge; from the dry
   dome
Of Michelangelo, your fisherman      15

Walks on the waters of a draining Rome
To bank his catch in the Celestial City.

14. MAXENTIUS—had seized power in
Italy and was finally defeated by Constantine
the Great in 312 at the Milvian Bridge.
16. DRY DOME OF MICHELANGELO—
Michelangelo designed the Basilica of St.
Peter.

FOR DISCUSSION

1. The imagery of the poem is closely packed. What effect does this have on the emotion which the poet wishes to express? What kind of picture of the Roman Senate does line 3 create? What does this tell you of Augustus? How does this help us in our understanding of the soul's struggle for salvation?

2. Is the thought of line 11 "All roads lead to Rome"? What is the connection of this line with what has gone before? What is the poet trying to tell us of the vigor of the Christian spirit at that time?

3. What is the poet's estimate of Christianity since the time of Constantine? How do the images he uses help bring out this estimate? Do you think he is fair to Christians of the last 16 centuries?

4. What is the meaning contained in the following figures: "eagles of Lord Lucifer"; "dry dome of Michelangelo"; "draining Rome"; "To bank his catch"? What is the effect of contrasting "Eternal City" in line 13 with "Celestial City" in line 18?

# The Dead in Europe

## ROBERT LOWELL

*A prayer to Mary, our Mother, to aid those who died without an opportunity to receive the Last Sacraments. The last stanza is a personal plea for Mary's special help on Resurrection Day.*

> After the planes unloaded, we fell down
> Buried together, unmarried men and women;
> Not crown of thorns, not iron, not Lombard crown,
> Not grilled and spindle spires pointing to heaven
> Could save us. Raise us, Mother, we fell down      5
> Here hugger-mugger in the jellied fire:
> Our sacred earth in our day was our curse.

4. Monasteries and cathedrals are imaged here.
6. HUGGER-MUGGER—Slovenly; secret, sly.
6. JELLIED FIRE—Flame throwers; incendiary bombs.

Our Mother, shall we rise on Mary's day
In Maryland, wherever corpses married
Under the rubble, bundled together?  Pray          10
For us whom the blockbuster marred and buried;
When Satan scatters us on Rising-day,
O Mother, snatch our bodies from the fire:
Our sacred earth in our day was our curse.

Mother, my bones are trembling and I hear          15
The earth's reverberations and the trumpet
Bleating into my shambles.  Shall I bear,
(O Mary!) unmarried man and powder-puppet,
Witness to the Devil?  Mary, hear,
O Mary, marry earth, sea, air and fire;            20
Our sacred earth in our day is our curse.

## FOR DISCUSSION

1. This poem was written while Lowell was seriously asking himself whether he should take part in the war or not.  Does the poem reflect such thoughts?  If so, does it indicate what Lowell's answer was? Is the answer to be found in the words of the poem or rather in the poet's attitude toward the indiscriminate killing of civilians?  Is the poet more concerned with the death of the body or of the soul?

2. What is the meaning of the last line of the first stanza?  Why does the poet change the tense of the verb in the last line of the poem?  Why is the Resurrection pictured as Mary's day?  Why does the poet imagine that the Resurrection will be in Maryland?  Might not these refer to Mary's Queenship of the World?

# Said the Inn-Keeper

### MYLES CONNOLLY

I cannot take these poor;
They do not pay;
They brand the house, they bring dis-
    grace;
I had to send that pair away. . . .
And yet there was a strange look on her
    face,       5
This girl who kept her eyes upon the
    floor,
So strange I stopped a space
Before I sent them from the door.

What could I do?
A man must make a living while he
    may,       10
And sentiment is not, I say.

And yet this girl was strangely fair:
She shivered in the doorway there,
And once she raised her eyes to
    mine. . . .

I bowed; I would have knelt, I swear,
But at the table some poor lout    16
Made cry for wine
And broke the spell. . . .

I saw the poorness of the pair
And put them out.    20
And I did well.
Two merchants took the great room
    overhead.
It is my principle: I buy and sell
And give my pity to the dead.

And yet this girl, this girl. . . .    25
I turned her from my door,
But she looked back with kindly eyes
And fairer than before,
And went away
As if she walked with emperors    30
And was a queen, and all the world was
    hers!

"Said the Innkeeper" by Myles Connolly from *The Eternal Babe*, verses from *America*, copyright, 1927, by The America Press.

## FOR DISCUSSION

1. Explain what the "spell" was that was broken by the lout crying for wine.
2. What was it in this girl that made it seem as though she "walked with emperors"?
3. In what way is this inn-keeper similar to many business men today? If you were the inn-keeper, how would you have acted?

178

# The Mothers

## CHARLES L. O'DONNELL

*The sorrow a mother experiences when her son dies is always deep. However, it can make a world of difference whether her son dies a hero or a coward. Even though the three mothers in the following poem lose their sons on the same day and in the same town, their griefs differ.*

Three mothers met that woeful day;
One as her dead Son pale, one gray
With grieving, and one red with shame:
All called upon one blessed Name.

One from the sorrow of the Cross,       5
One by the woe of kindred loss,
And one cried out in agony
From shadow of a blacker tree.

One gave the Nazarean birth,
One brought the pardoned thief to
    earth,                                   10
While of that hopeless one begot
Was Judas the Iscariot.

"The Mothers" from *Collected Poems of Charles L. O'Donnell*, C.S.C. Published by the University Press, Notre Dame, Indiana, 1942. Reprinted with the permission of the University of Notre Dame.

◇◇◇◇◇◇◇◇◇◇◇◇◇◇◇◇◇◇◇◇◇◇◇◇◇◇◇◇◇◇◇◇◇◇◇◇◇◇◇◇◇◇◇◇◇◇◇◇◇◇◇

FOR DISCUSSION
   1. Who are the three mothers?
   2. Explain how the grief of the three mothers would differ.
   3. What is meant by the line, "All called upon one blessed Name."?

   4. Explain the words, "a blacker tree." Why is this tree "blacker," and to what other tree is it compared?
   5. Why is one mother "hopeless"?

◇◇◇◇◇

# The Temptations of St. Anthony

## PHYLLIS McGINLEY

*St. Anthony (c. 250–356) was the founder of Christian monasticism. While still a comparatively young man, he renounced his possessions and went into the Egyptian desert to live a life of solitude in prayer and self-denial. For fifteen years he waged incessant battles against the demons,* who appeared in the shapes of wild beasts to torment him. He made a few brief excursions back to the world, but after each trip returned to his cenobitic life with a great sigh of relief.

> Off in the wilderness bare and level,
> Anthony wrestled with the Devil.
> Once he'd beaten the Devil down,
> Anthony'd turn his eyes toward town
> And leave his hermitage now and then          5
> To come to grips with the souls of men.
>
> Afterward, all the tales agree,
> Wrestling the Devil seemed to be
> Quite a relief to Anthony.

FOR DISCUSSION

1. It is often suggested that the apostolate of the Contemplative life (e.g., Trappists, Discalced Carmelites, etc.) is the most difficult way of life that the Church offers. What does Phyllis McGinley say to this question? What do you think?

2. Compare this poem with the author's "Reflections Dental" in order to note how she varies her metrical scheme constantly for the sake of variety.

# $\mathcal{A}$ Gallery of Elders

## PHYLLIS McGINLEY

In "A Gallery of Elders," a section of THE LOVE LETTERS OF PHYLLIS McGINLEY, the reader sees limned in short verses older people whom he has really known—at least by hearsay. With a few deft strokes of her pen, the author lays bare the real heart behind an apparently benign façade.

### THE OLD REFORMER

Few friends he kept that pleased his
    mind.
  His marriage failed when it began,
Who worked unceasing for mankind
  But loathed his fellow man.

### THE OLD PHILANTHROPIST

His millions make museums bright;
  Harvard anticipates his will;
While his young typist weeps at night
  Over a druggist's bill.

# Reflections Dental

## PHYLLIS McGINLEY

*In this bit of humorous, satirical verse, Phyllis McGinley sums up the oft-unexpressed thought of the average television viewer, who is exposed day after day to thousands of sets of dentures leering at him from his television screen. This is Phyllis McGinley at her whimsical best.*

How pure, how beautiful, how fine
Do teeth on television shine!
No flutist flutes, no dancer twirls,
But comes equipped with matching
  pearls.
Gleeful announcers all are born    5
With sets like rows of hybrid corn.
Clowns, critics, clergy, commentators,
Ventriloquists and roller skaters,
M.C.'s who beat their palms together,
The girl who diagrams the weather,   10
The crooner crooning for his supper—
All flash white treasures, lower and up-
  per.
With miles of smiles the airwaves teem,
And each an orthodontist's dream.   15

'Twould please my eye as gold a mi-
  ser's—
One charmer with uncapped incisors.

## FOR DISCUSSION

1. Just for fun, how many television performers can you name who "never show their teeth"?

2. The author mentions the word *teeth* but once—in line 2. What different figures of speech does she use thereafter as substitutes for the word *teeth?*

3. This poem is in iambic tetrameter. But notice how the author skillfully substitutes different metrical feet to achieve variety. Point out examples, and explain why this variety is necessary.

# TWENTIETH-CENTURY DRAMA

A radio comedian once defined the United States as "a great open space between New York and Hollywood." That he was using the two cities as symbols of America's love of dramatic entertainment is obvious. And although we admit the exaggeration of the statement, it is true that since 1914 the stage and movie productions of Broadway and Hollywood have mirrored the people of this country and their doings. An occasional fling at historical drama has in no way deterred our dramatists from their main business of portraying present "life in these United States."

There have been presentations of the terrors and miseries of war. There have been plays spotlighting social evils of our times. There have been plays about the poor, about the rich; plays about farmers and ranchers and businessmen. There have been plays dealing with the powder-packed question of racial inequality. There have been plays of mystery and murder, of hope and happiness, of marriage and motherhood. And in recent years, because of the widespread interest in psychiatry, the stage has given us psychological dramas in which the audience watches normal, sub-normal, and abnormal workings of the human brain. Plays—weak and strong—have reflected, sometimes with confidence, sometimes in delusion, the spirit of our times.

The manner of presentation has been both realistic and romantic. Realistic plays have been at times shockingly brutal, even obscene. Romantic plays, on the other hand, have tended to escape even the mild realities and to live in a realm of frolic and fantasy. Both realistic and romantic plays have drawn their own particular audiences. Many dramatists seem to be writing with an eye on box-office appeal rather than from a burning desire to express their own convictions. Thus modern drama has become a field for wild experimentation. The experiments have produced sometimes mere sophomoric trash, occasionally a great and original play.

## DRAMATIC TERMS IN LITERATURE

The word *drama* names the literary classification which includes plays of all types. A drama is a piece of literature written to be acted, or—as the Greeks said—to be "done." The earliest plays were merely *done*, but the form eventually found its way into manuscript or printed record. Today successful dramas appear on the stage, in the movies, on television, over the radio, and in print almost simultaneously.

Literary drama aims to present a portion of life in rapid, vivid action. In production, it depends for expression on actors with their voices, movements, personalities. It is the assignment of each actor to interpret his role to the audience. The play itself must be planned so that characterization is developed swiftly and action moves rapidly to its conclusion.

Like fiction, drama is built around a plot or general scheme of events. The first chain of events, known as the *rising action,* leads to a dramatic moment known as the *climax* or turning point of the play. From the climax, a *falling action* brings the play to its *denouement,* or conclusion. Both characters and plot are developed in harmony with the *setting*—that is, with the place and time of the play.

In the written play, explicit directions are given for the setting and staging, sometimes also for acting and interpretation. Though the directions usually are printed in italic type, they are important; the reader must not skip them or he will lose much of the significance of the play.

## TYPES OF DRAMA

Dramatic productions fall into different classifications according to action and form.

If the plot of a play grows out of a conflict between two opposing forces, such as the conflict between a man and a personal weakness or between a woman and her environment, then the outcome of the conflict determines the classification. If the principal character wins out in the struggle, the play is a *comedy;* if he loses, it is a *tragedy.* A comedy, in the strictest sense, is not always funny; it does have a happy ending. Nor does a tragedy always end in violence and bloodshed; it does, however, leave one with a sense of defeat or loss.

Within these two main divisions there are other classifications. Comedies may be *romantic, melodramatic,* or *farcical.* A romantic comedy is a light play with a happy ending. A *fantasy* is a romantic comedy set in an imaginary scene and using whimsical or supernatural characters. A *melodrama* is a comedy characterized by rapid action, sentimental scenes, and thrilling situations. The solution of the difficulties is often unexpected or unexplained. Melodrama provides exciting but not profound entertainment. It is popular in motion pictures. A *farce* is a comedy which is out-and-out funny, with laughable characters getting involved in ridiculous situations.

Other kinds of drama are distinguished by their forms. A *pageant* is the presentation of a subject—usually historical—in a succession of short scenes touching relatively long periods of time. A pageant that portrays present-day scenes and that is characterized by music, dancing, and wit is called a *revue*.

A *one-act play* is a short play built around a single dramatic incident or situation. It has the same relation to the full-length play that a short story has to a novel. The *radio play* requires a special technique in writing and production. Its story is projected by unseen actors by means of dialogue and sound effects. Instead of stage directions, the radio play has an announcer to supplement the dialogue. Sometimes the announcer is woven into the plot and becomes an incidental character of the play. The *television play* also requires special techniques in writing and direction. Among other things, the variety of angles from which the action may be photographed and the ease with which close-ups may be interchanged with more distant views give the writer, directors, and actors new scope for their talents. Much excellent drama is being produced on television today, written by such men as Gore Vidal, Reginald Rose, and Paddy Chayefsky.

## A REVIEW OF AMERICAN DRAMA SINCE 1900

There was little original drama in America from 1900 to 1914. We were feeling the influence of the great European playwrights, Ibsen and Shaw; but it was not until 1915 that our own plays showed the effects. Then after the First World War came a flood of American satires—gloomy satires modeled after Ibsen's and impudent satires like Shaw's. Restlessness of spirit and an attempt to be different gave rise to such perversions as "Another Interior" by Edward Goodman. In this play, the setting is inside a man's stomach and the dashing hero is Gastric Juice. Not all productions were so weird; but playwrights were floundering, groping for ideas.

About this time the star of Eugene O'Neill began to rise. O'Neill's work is brutally frank and usually tragic. Yet situations which, handled by anyone else, might be revolting rise to literary excellence under his deft treatment. In many of his plays O'Neill is content to present a question but no answer and to leave his audience pondering. For a time in 1934, when O'Neill produced *Days Without End*, many believed that he was about to embrace the Catholic religion. In the play the hero, through the interposition of a priest, returns to God and in the end lies prostrate at the foot of the cross. Here is one apparent attempt by O'Neill to offer a solution to the human problem. But whether the solution has an autobiographical meaning lies in doubt since the appearance in 1946 of *The Iceman Cometh*. Once again O'Neill presents problems but no answers.

O'Neill died in 1953, but there are other contemporary dramatists who have been influenced by his work and who seem to be carrying on his tradition in American drama. Perhaps the most important of these are Arthur Miller and Tennessee Williams; several of their plays have received wide critical acclaim.

Most American dramatists, however, have been content to write comedies. George S. Kaufman, for example, writing in collaboration with other playwrights, has produced many mirth-provoking plays. With Marc Connelly he did *Merton of the Movies* and *Beggar on Horseback*; with Moss Hart, *You Can't Take It With You*; with Morrie Ryskind, *Of Thee I Sing*. He has worked also with Ring Lardner and Edna Ferber. He is mainly a "wisecracker," and one usually carries away from his plays only the piquant flavor of amusement. Philip Barry, too, has a reputation as a writer of clever dialogue. But his play *A Joyous Season* proves him also able to deal with philosophical and moral problems. Marc Connelly's Pulitzer prize winner, *The Green Pastures*, which appears in this book, proves that he, too, is successful in handling plays other than comedy. George Kelly is a promising writer, known chiefly for *The Torchbearers*, *The Showoff*, *Craig's Wife*, and *Philip Goes Forth*. George Abbott, S. N. Behrman, and Robert Sherwood are men of high dramatic ability; yet it is doubtful that any of their plays will live.

In the drama of social criticism the outstanding writers are Eugene O'Neill, Elmer Rice, John Lawson, and Clifford Odets. These men, all leftist in sympathies, have dramatized the many diverse problems of labor and capital, of the oppressed and the oppressor; but they do it in the blurry focus of men who feel strongly for the unfortunate but whose only solution, unhappily, is revolution. One pleasant but nonetheless penetrating picture of American social and family life is to be found in the play *Our Town* by Thornton Wilder.

T. S. Eliot and Archibald MacLeish have written plays in verse; but the dominant poetic dramatist of America is Maxwell Anderson. Be his vices what they may, his play *Joan of Lorraine* is evidence of his dramatic virtues.

The Little Theater Movement, which sprang up in America about 1900, has done much to develop and popularize the one-act play. It has become a favorite type with playwrights and with amateur producers.

## CONTEMPORARY CATHOLIC DRAMA

With the growth of the Little Theater Movement in the 1920's the Catholic Little Theater made its appearance. The purpose of the movement was to take the plays of the secular stage and to stamp them with a bold Catholic impression, to adapt the forms of plays as developed in the regular theater, and to write similar ones on Catholic themes. The art of this energetic group has been used mainly to further Catholic principles. There has been the added purpose of combating all dramatic entertainment that is indifferent, unsympathetic, or aggressively opposed to all that is good and wholesome. The members of the Catholic theater have made many noble gestures toward making Catholics and non-Catholics aware of Catholic historical background, Catholic doctrines and their application to life. This enterprising theatrical group deserves much praise for its spirit of independence which has brought fresh Catholic leaven to the American theater.

# MARTY

### PADDY CHAYEFSKY

Television drama is a comparatively new form of dramatic art. Although using devices from both the stage and the screen, T-V drama strives to appeal more to the man-in-the-street than do other forms of drama. Television, because of its vaster viewing audience, appeals to a larger class of American people today than either the stage or the movies.

MARTY is a story written precisely for television. It is an ordinary love story about ordinary persons, people you would expect to meet on any street-corner or in any drug store everyday. The hero is not handsome, nor is the heroine beautiful. To capture the full flavor of MARTY, the characters must be known as you would know your next-door neighbors; and the scenes must be imagined as vividly as you would your own home setting. This will not prove too difficult for either the reader or the T-V viewer, because Marty Piletti, together with the other natives of the Bronx who form the background for the story, is the type of person you see everyday in places that are most typical of our American way of life.

## ACT I

FADE IN: A butcher shop in the Italian district of New York City. Actually, we fade in on a close-up of a butcher's saw being carefully worked through a side of beef, and we dolly back to show the butcher at work, and then the whole shop. The butcher is a mild-mannered, stout, short, balding young man of thirty-six. His charm lies in an almost indestructible good-natured amiability.

The shop contains three women customers. One is a young mother with a baby carriage. She is chatting with a second woman of about forty at the door. The customer being waited on at the moment is a stout, elderly Italian woman who is standing on tiptoe, peering over the white display counter, checking the butcher as he saws away.

ITALIAN WOMAN. Your kid brother got married last Sunday, eh, Marty?

MARTY (absorbed in his work). That's right, Missus Fusari. It was a very nice affair.

ITALIAN WOMAN. That's the big tall one, the fellow with the mustache.

MARTY (sawing away). No, that's my other brother Freddie. My other brother Freddie, he's been married four years already. He lives down on Quincy Street. The one who got married Sunday, that was my little brother Nickie.

Reprinted from TELEVISION PLAYS, by Paddy Chayefsky, by permission of Simon and Schuster, Publishers. Copyright, ©, 1955 by Paddy Chayefsky. Copyright, ©, 1954 as an unpublished dramatic composition by Paddy Chayefsky.

ITALIAN WOMAN. I thought he was a big, tall, fat fellow. Didn't I meet him here one time? Big, tall, fat fellow, he tried to sell me life insurance?

MARTY (*sets the cut of meat on the scale, watches its weight register*). No, that's my sister Margaret's husband Frank. My sister Margaret, she's married to the insurance salesman. My sister Rose, she married a contractor. They moved to Detroit last year. And my other sister, Frances, she got married about two and a half years ago in Saint John's Church on Adams Boulevard. Oh, that was a big affair. Well, Missus Fusari, that'll be three dollars, ninety-four cents. How's that with you?

*The Italian woman produces an old leather change purse from her pocketbook and painfully extracts three single dollar bills and ninety-four cents to the penny and lays the money piece by piece on the counter.*

YOUNG MOTHER (*calling from the door*). Hey, Marty, I'm inna hurry.

MARTY (*wrapping the meat, calls amiably back*). You're next right now, Missus Canduso.

*The old Italian lady has been regarding Marty with a baleful scowl.*

ITALIAN WOMAN. Well, Marty, when you gonna get married? You should be ashamed. All your brothers and sisters, they all younger than you, and they married, and they got children. I just saw your mother inna fruit shop, and she says to me: "Hey, you know a nice girl for my boy Marty?" Watsa matter with you? That's no way. Watsa matter with you? Now, you get married, you hear me what I say?

MARTY (*amiably*). I hear you, Missus Fusari.

*The old lady takes her parcel of meat, but apparently feels she still hasn't quite made her point.*

ITALIAN WOMAN. My son Frank, he was married when he was nineteen years old. Watsa matter with you?

MARTY. Missus Fusari, Missus Canduso over there, she's inna big hurry, and . . .

ITALIAN WOMAN. You be ashamed of yourself.

*She takes her package of meat, turns, and shuffles to the door and exits. Marty gathers up the money on the counter, turns to the cash register behind him to ring up the sale.*

YOUNG MOTHER. Marty, I want a nice big fat pullet, about four pounds. I hear your kid brother got married last Sunday.

MARTY. Yeah, it was a very nice affair, Missus Canduso.

YOUNG MOTHER. Marty, you oughtta be ashamed. All your kid brothers and sisters, married and have children. When you gonna get married?

CLOSE-UP: *Marty. He sends a glance of weary exasperation up to the ceiling. With a gesture of mild irritation, he pushes the plunger of the cash register. It makes a sharp ping.*

DISSOLVE TO: *Close-up of television set. A baseball game is in progress. Camera pulls back to show we are in a typical neighborhood bar—red leatherette booths—a jukebox, some phone booths. About half the bar stools are occupied by neighborhood folk. Marty enters, pads amiably to one of the booths where a young man of about thirty-odd already sits. This is Angie. Marty slides into the booth across from Angie. Angie is a little wasp of a fellow. He has a news-paper spread out before him to the sports pages. Marty reaches over and pulls one of the pages over for himself to read. For a moment the two friends sit across from each other, reading the sports pages. Then Angie, without look-ing up, speaks.*

ANGIE.  Well, what do you feel like doing tonight?

MARTY.  I don't know, Angie. What do you feel like doing?

ANGIE.  Well, we oughtta do some-thing. It's Saturday night. I don't wanna go bowling like last Saturday. How about calling up that big girl we picked up inna movies about a month ago in the RKO Chester?

MARTY (*not very interested*).  Which one was that?

ANGIE.  That big girl that was sitting in front of us with the skinny friend.

MARTY.  Oh, yeah.

ANGIE.  We took them home alla way out in Brooklyn. Her name was Mary Feeney. What do you say? You think I oughtta give her a ring? I'll take the skinny one.

MARTY.  It's five o'clock already, Angie. She's probably got a date by now.

ANGIE.  Well, let's call her up. What can we lose?

MARTY.  I didn't like her, Angie. I don't feel like calling her up.

ANGIE.  Well, what do you feel like doing tonight?

MARTY.  I don't know. What do you feel like doing?

ANGIE.  Well, we're back to that, huh? I say to you: "What do you feel like doing tonight?" And you say to me: "I don't know, what do you feel like

doing?" And then we wind up sitting around your house with a couple of cans of beer, watching Sid Caesar on tele-vision. Well, I tell you what I feel like doing. I feel like calling up this Mary Feeney. She likes you.

*Marty looks up quickly at this.*

MARTY.  What makes you say that?

ANGIE.  I could see she likes you.

MARTY.  Yeah, sure.

ANGIE (*half rising in his seat*).  I'll call her up.

MARTY.  You call her up for yourself, Angie. I don't feel like calling her up.

*Angie sits down again. They both return to reading the paper for a moment. Then Angie looks up again.*

ANGIE.  Boy, you're getting to be a real drag, you know that?

MARTY.  Angie, I'm thirty-six years old. I been looking for a girl every Sat-urday night of my life. I'm a little, short, fat fellow, and girls don't go for me, that's all. I'm not like you. I mean, you joke around, and they laugh at you, and you get along fine. I just stand around like a bug. What's the sense of kidding myself. Everybody's al-ways telling me to get married. Get married. Get married. Don't you think I wanna get married? I wanna get married. They drive me crazy. Now, I don't wanna wreck your Saturday night for you, Angie. You wanna go some-where, you go ahead. I don't wanna go.

ANGIE.  Boy, they drive me crazy too. My old lady, every word outta her mouth, when you gonna get married?

MARTY.  My mother, boy, she drives me crazy.

*Angie leans back in his seat, scowls at the paper-napkin container. Marty returns to the sports page. For a moment a silence hangs between them.  Then . . .*

ANGIE.  So what do you feel like doing tonight?

MARTY (*without looking up*).  I don't know.  What do you feel like doing?

*They both just sit, Angie frowning at the napkin container, Marty at the sports page.*

*The camera slowly moves away from the booth, looks down the length of the bar, up the wall, past the clock—which reads ten to five—and over to the television screen, where the baseball game is still going on.*

DISSOLVE SLOWLY TO: *The television screen, now blank.  The clock now reads a quarter to six.*

*Back in the booth, Marty now sits alone.  In front of him are three empty beer bottles and a beer glass, half filled.  He is sitting there, his face expressionless, but his eyes troubled.  Then he pushes himself slowly out of the booth and shuffles to the phone booth; he goes inside, closing the booth door carefully after him.  For a moment Marty just sits squatly.  Then with some exertion—due to the cramped quarters—he contrives to get a small address book out of his rear pants pocket.  He slowly flips through it, finds the page he wants, and studies it, scowling; then he takes a dime from the change he has just received, plunks it into the proper slot, waits for a dial tone . . . then carefully dials a number. . . .  He waits.  He is beginning to sweat a bit in the hot little booth, and his chest begins to rise and fall deeply.*

MARTY (*with a vague pretense at good diction*).  Hello, is this Mary Feeney?  . . . Could I please speak to Miss Mary Feeney? . . . Just tell her an old friend . . .

*He waits again.  With his free hand he wipes the gathering sweat from his brow.*

. . . Oh, hello there, is this Mary Feeney?  Hello there, this is Marty Pilletti.  I wonder if you recall me . . . Well, I'm kind of a stocky guy.  The last time we met was inna movies, the RKO Chester.  You was with another girl, and I was with a friend of mine name Angie.  This was about a month ago . . .

*The girl apparently doesn't remember him.  A sort of panic begins to seize Marty.  His voice rises a little.*

The RKO Chester on Payne Boulevard.  You was sitting in front of us, and we was annoying you, and you got mad, and . . . I'm the fellow who works inna butcher shop . . . come on, you know who I am! . . . That's right, we went to Howard Johnson's and we had hamburgers.  You hadda milk shake . . . Yeah, that's right.  I'm the stocky one, the heavy-set fellow. . . .  Well, I'm glad you recall me, because I hadda swell time that night, and I was just wondering how everything was with you.  How's everything? . . . That's swell . . . Yeah, well, I'll tell you why I called . . . I was figuring on taking in a movie tonight, and I was wondering if you and your friend would care to see a movie tonight with me and my friend . . . (*his eyes are closed now*).  Yeah, tonight.  I know it's pretty late to call for a date, but I didn't know myself till . . . Yeah, I know, well how about . . . Yeah, I know, well maybe next Saturday night.  You free next Saturday night? . . . Well, how about the

Saturday after that? . . . Yeah, I know . . . Yeah . . . Yeah . . . Oh, I understand, I mean . . .

*He just sits now, his eyes closed, not really listening. After a moment he returns the receiver to its cradle and sits, his shoulders slack, his hands resting listlessly in the lap of his spotted white apron. . . . Then he opens his eyes, straightens himself, pushes the booth door open, and advances out into the bar. He perches on a stool across the bar from the bartender, who looks up from his magazine.*

BARTENDER. I hear your kid brother got married last week, Marty.

MARTY (*looking down at his hands on the bar*). Yeah, it was a very nice affair.

BARTENDER. Well, Marty, when you gonna get married?

*Marty tenders the bartender a quick scowl, gets off his perch, and starts for the door—untying his apron as he goes.*

MARTY. If my mother calls up, Lou, tell her I'm on my way home.

DISSOLVE TO: *Marty's mother and a young couple sitting around the table in the dining room of Marty's home. The young couple—we will soon find out—are Thomas, Marty's cousin, and his wife, Virginia. They have apparently just been telling the mother some sad news, and the three are sitting around frowning.*

*The dining room is a crowded room filled with chairs and lamps, pictures and little statues, perhaps even a small grotto of little vigil lamps. To the right of the dining room is the kitchen, old-fashioned, Italian, steaming, and over-crowded. To the left of the dining room is the living room, furnished in same fashion as the dining room. Just off the living room is a small bedroom, which is Marty's. This bedroom and the living room have windows looking out on front. The dining room has windows looking out to side alleyway. A stairway in the dining room leads to the second floor.*

*The mother is a round, dark, effusive little woman.*

MOTHER (*after a pause*). Well, Thomas, I knew sooner or later this was gonna happen. I told Marty, I said: "Marty, you watch. There's gonna be real trouble over there in your cousin Thomas' house." Because your mother was here, Thomas, you know?

THOMAS. When was this, Aunt Theresa?

MOTHER. This was one, two, three days ago. Wednesday. Because I went to the fruit shop on Wednesday, and I came home. And I come arounna back, and there's your mother sitting onna steps onna porch. And I said: "Catherine, my sister, wadda you doing here?" And she look uppa me, and she beganna cry.

THOMAS (*to his wife*). Wednesday. That was the day you threw the milk bottle.

MOTHER. That's right. Because I said to her: "Catherine, watsa matter?" And she said to me: "Theresa, my daughter-in-law, Virginia, she just threw the milk bottle at me."

VIRGINIA. Well, you see what happen, Aunt Theresa . . .

MOTHER. I know, I know . . .

VIRGINIA. She comes inna kitchen, and she begins poking her head over my

shoulder here and poking her head over my shoulder there . . .

MOTHER. I know, I know . . .

VIRGINIA. And she begins complaining about this, and she begins complaining about that. And she got me so nervous, I spilled some milk I was making for the baby. You see, I was making some food for the baby, and . . .

MOTHER. So I said to her, "Catherine . . ."

VIRGINIA. So, she got me so nervous I spilled some milk. So she said: "You're spilling the milk." She says: "Milk costs twenny-four cents a bottle. Wadda you, a banker?" So I said: "Mama, leave me alone, please. You're making me nervous. Go on in the other room and turn on the television set." So then she began telling me how I waste money, and how I can't cook, and how I'm raising my baby all wrong, and she kept talking about these couple of drops of milk I spilt, and I got so

mad, I said: "Mama, you wanna see me really spill some milk?" So I took the bottle and threw it against the door. I didn't throw it at her. That's just something she made up. I didn't throw it anywheres near her. Well, of course, alla milk went all over the floor. The whole twenny-four cents. Well, I was sorry right away, you know, but she ran outta the house.

*Pause.*

MOTHER. Well, I don't know what you want me to do, Virginia. If you want me, I'll go talk to her tonight.

*Thomas and Virginia suddenly frown and look down at their hands as if of one mind.*

THOMAS. Well, I'll tell you, Aunt Theresa . . .

VIRGINIA. Lemme tell it, Tommy.

THOMAS. Okay.

VIRGINIA (*leaning forward to the*

*mother*). We want you to do a very big favor for us, Aunt Theresa.

MOTHER. Sure.

VIRGINIA. Aunt Theresa, you got this big house here. You got four bedrooms upstairs. I mean, you got this big house just for you and Marty. All your other kids are married and got their own homes. And I thought maybe Tommy's mother could come here and live with you and Marty.

MOTHER. Well . . .

VIRGINIA. She's miserable living with Tommy and me, and you're the only one that gets along with her. Because I called up Tommy's brother, Joe, and I said: "Joe, she's driving me crazy. Why don't you take her for a couple of years?" And he said: "Oh, no!" I know I sound like a terrible woman . . .

MOTHER. No, Virginia, I know how you feel. My husband, may God bless his memory, his mother, she lived with us for a long time, and I know how you feel.

VIRGINIA (*practically on the verge of tears*). I just can't stand it no more! Every minute of the day! Do this! Do that! I don't have ten minutes alone with my husband! We can't even have a fight! We don't have no privacy! Everybody's miserable in our house!

THOMAS. All right, Ginnie, don't get so excited.

MOTHER. She's right. She's right. Young husband and wife, they should have their own home. And my sister, Catherine, she's my sister, but I gotta admit, she's an old goat. And plenny-a times in my life I feel like throwing the milk bottle at her myself. And I tell you now, as far as I'm concerned, if Catherine wantsa come live here with me and Marty, it's all right with me.

*Virginia promptly bursts into tears.*

THOMAS (*not far from tears himself, lowers his face*). That's very nice-a you, Aunt Theresa.

MOTHER. We gotta ask Marty, of course, because this is his house too. But he's gonna come home any minute now.

VIRGINIA (*having mastered her tears*). That's very nice-a you, Aunt Theresa.

MOTHER (*rising*). Now, you just sit here. I'm just gonna turn onna small fire under the food.

*She exits into the kitchen.*

VIRGINIA (*calling after her*). We gotta go right away because I promised the baby sitter we'd be home by six, and it's after six now . . .

*She kind of fades out. A moment of silence. Thomas takes out a cigarette and lights it.*

THOMAS (*calling to his aunt in the kitchen*). How's Marty been lately, Aunt Theresa?

MOTHER (*off in kitchen*). Oh, he's fine. You know a nice girl he can marry?

*She comes back into the dining room, wiping her hands on a kitchen towel.*

I'm worried about him, you know? He's thirty-six years old, gonna be thirty-seven in January.

THOMAS. Oh, he'll get married, don't worry, Aunt Theresa.

MOTHER (*sitting down again*). Well, I don't know. You know a place where he can go where he can find a bride?

THOMAS. The Waverly Ballroom. That's a good place to meet girls, Aunt Theresa. That's a kind of big dance hall, Aunt Theresa. Every Saturday night, it's just loaded with girls. It's a nice place to go. You pay seventy-seven cents. It used to be seventy-seven cents. It must be about a buck and a half now. And you go in and you ask some girl to dance. That's how I met Virginia. Nice, respectable place to meet girls. You tell Marty, Aunt Theresa, you tell him: "Go to the Waverly Ballroom. It's loaded with tomatoes."

MOTHER (*committing the line to memory*). The Waverly Ballroom. It's loaded with tomatoes.

THOMAS. Right.

VIRGINIA. You tell him, go to the Waverly Ballroom.

*There is the sound of a door being un-latched off through the kitchen. The mother promptly rises.*

MOTHER. He's here.

*She hurries into the kitchen. At the porch entrance to the kitchen, Marty has just come in. He is clos-ing the door behind him. He car-ries his butcher's apron in a bundle under his arm.*

MARTY. Hello, Ma.

*She comes up to him, lowers her voice to a whisper.*

MOTHER (*whispers*). Marty, Thomas and Virginia are here. They had an-other big fight with your Aunt Cather-ine. So they ask me, would it be all right if Catherine come to live with us. So I said, all right with me, but we have to ask you. Marty, she's a lonely old lady. Nobody wants her. Everybody's throwing her outta their house. . . .

MARTY. Sure, Ma, it's okay with me.

*The mother's face breaks into a fond smile. She reaches up and pats his cheek with genuine affection.*

MOTHER. You gotta good heart. (*Turning and leading the way back to the dining room. Thomas has risen.*) He says okay, it's all right Catherine comes here.

THOMAS. Oh, Marty, thanks a lot. That really takes a load offa my mind.

MARTY. Oh, we got plenny-a room here.

MOTHER. Sure! Sure! It's gonna be nice! It's gonna be nice! I'll come over tonight to your house, and I talk to Catherine, and you see, everything is gonna work out all right.

THOMAS. I just wanna thank you peo-ple again because the situation was just becoming impossible.

MOTHER. Siddown, Thomas, sid-down. All right, Marty, siddown. . . .

*She exits into the kitchen.*

*Marty has taken his seat at the head of the table and is waiting to be served. Thomas takes a seat around the corner of the table from him and leans across to him.*

THOMAS. You see, Marty, the kinda thing that's been happening in our house is Virginia was inna kitchen mak-ing some food for the baby. Well, my mother comes in, and she gets Virginia so nervous, she spills a couple-a drops . . .

VIRGINIA (*tugging at her husband*). Tommy, we gotta go. I promise the baby sitter six o'clock.

THOMAS (*rising without interrupting his narrative*). So she starts yelling at Virginia, waddaya spilling the milk for. So Virginia gets mad . . .

*His wife is slowly pulling him to the kitchen door.*

She says, "You wanna really see me spill milk?" So Virginia takes the bottle and she throws it against the wall. She's got a real Italian temper, my wife, you know that . . .

*He has been tugged to the kitchen door by now.*

VIRGINIA. Marty, I don't have to tell you how much we appreciate what your mother and you are doing for us.

THOMAS. All right, Marty, I'll see you some other time . . . I'll tell you all about it.

MARTY. I'll see you, Tommy.

*Thomas disappears into the kitchen after his wife.*

VIRGINIA (*off, calling*). Good-by, Marty!

*Close in on Marty, sitting at table.*

MARTY. Good-by, Virginia! See you soon!

*He folds his hands on the table before him and waits to be served.*

*The mother enters from the kitchen. She sets the meat plate down in front of him and herself takes a chair around the corner of the table from him. Marty without a word takes up his knife and fork and attacks the mountain of food in front of him. His mother sits quietly, her hands a little nervous on the table before her, watching him eat. Then . . .*

MOTHER. So what are you gonna do tonight, Marty?

MARTY. I don't know, Ma. I'm all knocked out. I may just hang arounna house.

*The mother nods a couple of times. There is a moment of silence. Then . . .*

MOTHER. Why don't you go to the Waverly Ballroom?

*This gives Marty pause. He looks up.*

MARTY. What?

MOTHER. I say, why don't you go to the Waverly Ballroom? It's loaded with tomatoes.

*Marty regards his mother for a moment.*

MARTY. It's loaded with what?

MOTHER. Tomatoes.

MARTY (*snorts*). Ha! Who told you about the Waverly Ballroom?

MOTHER. Thomas, he told me it was a very nice place.

MARTY. Oh, Thomas. Ma, it's just a big dance hall, and that's all it is. I been there a hundred times. Loaded with tomatoes. Boy, you're funny, Ma.

MOTHER. Marty, I don't want you hang arounna house tonight. I want you to go take a shave and go out and dance.

MARTY. Ma, when are you gonna give up? You gotta bachelor on your hands. I ain't never gonna get married.

MOTHER. You gonna get married.

MARTY. Sooner or later, there comes a point in a man's life when he gotta face some facts, and one fact I gotta face is that whatever it is that women like, I ain't got it. I chased enough girls in my life. I went to enough dances. I got hurt enough. I don't wanna get hurt no more. I just called a girl this afternoon, and I got a real brush-off, boy. I figured I was past the point of being hurt, but that hurt. Some stupid woman who I didn't even wanna call up. She gave me the brush. That's the history of my life. I don't wanna go to the Waverly Ballroom because all that ever happened to me there was girls made me feel like I was a bug. I got feelings, you know. I had enough pain. No, thank you.

MOTHER. Marty . . .

MARTY. Ma, I'm gonna stay home and watch Sid Caesar.

MOTHER. You gonna die without a son.

MARTY. So I'll die without a son.

MOTHER. Put on your blue suit . . .

MARTY. Blue suit, gray suit, I'm still a fat little man. A fat little ugly man.

MOTHER. You not ugly.

MARTY (*his voice rising*). I'm ugly . . . I'm ugly! . . . I'm UGLY!

MOTHER. Marty . . .

MARTY (*crying aloud, more in anguish than in anger*). Ma! Leave me alone! . . .

*He stands abruptly, his face pained and drawn. He makes half-formed gestures to his mother, but he can't find words at the moment. He turns and marches a few paces away, turns to his mother again.*

MARTY. Ma, waddaya want from me?! Waddaya want from me?! I'm miserable enough as it is! Leave me alone! I'll go to the Waverly Ballroom! I'll put onna blue suit and I'll go! And you know what I'm gonna get for my trouble? Heartache! A big night of heartache!

*He sullenly marches back to his seat, sits down, picks up his fork, plunges it into the lasagna, and stuffs a mouthful into his mouth; he chews vigorously for a moment. It is impossible to remain angry for long. After a while he is shaking his head and muttering.*

MARTY. Loaded with tomatoes . . . boy, that's rich . . .

*He plunges his fork in again. Camera pulls slowly away from him and his mother, who is seated—watching him.*

FADE OUT.

## ACT II

FADE IN: *Exterior, three-story building. Pan up to second floor . . . bright neon lights reading "Waverly Ballroom" . . . The large, dirty windows are open; and the sound of a fair-to-middling swing band whooping it up comes out.*

DISSOLVE TO: *Interior, Waverly Ballroom—large dance floor crowded with jitterbugging couples, eight-piece combination hitting a loud kick. Ballroom is vaguely dark, made so by papier-mâché over the chandeliers to create alleged romantic effect. The walls are lined with stags and waiting girls, singly and in small murmuring groups. Noise and mumble and drone.*

DISSOLVE TO: *Live shot—a row of stags along a wall. Camera is looking lengthwise down the row. Camera dollies slowly past each face, each staring out at the dance floor, watching in his own manner of hungry eagerness. Short, fat, tall, thin stags. Some pretend diffidence. Some exhibit patent hunger.*

*Near the end of the line, we find Marty and Angie, freshly shaved and groomed. They are leaning against the wall, smoking, watching their more fortunate brethren out on the floor.*

ANGIE. Not a bad crowd tonight, you know?

MARTY. There was one nice-looking one there in a black dress and beads, but she was a little tall for me.

ANGIE (*looking down past Marty along the wall right into the camera*). There's a nice-looking little short one for you right now.

MARTY (*following his gaze*). Where?

ANGIE. Down there. That little one there.

195

FROM UNITED ARTISTS CORPORATION PRODUCTION MARTY

*The camera cuts about eight faces down, to where the girls are now standing. Two are against the wall. One is facing them, with her back to the dance floor. This last is the one Angie has in mind. She is a cute little kid, about twenty, and she has a bright smile on—as if the other two girls are just amusing her to death.*

MARTY. Yeah, she looks all right from here.

ANGIE. Well, go on over and ask her. You don't hurry up, somebody else'll grab her.

*Marty scowls, shrugs.*

MARTY. Okay, let's go.

*They slouch along past the eight stags, a picture of nonchalant unconcern. The three girls, aware of their approach, stiffen, and their chatter comes to a halt. Angie advances to one of the girls along the wall.*

ANGIE. Waddaya say, you wanna dance?

*The girl looks surprised—as if this were an extraordinary invitation to receive in this place—looks confounded at her two friends, shrugs, detaches herself from the group, moves to the outer fringe of the pack of dancers, raises her hand languidly to dancing position, and awaits Angie with ineffable boredom. Marty, smiling shyly, addresses the short girl.*

MARTY. Excuse me, would you care for this dance?

*The short girl gives Marty a quick glance of appraisal, then looks quickly at her remaining friend.*

SHORT GIRL (*not unpleasantly*). Sorry. I just don't feel like dancing just yet.

MARTY. Sure.

*He turns and moves back past the eight stags, all of whom have covertly watched his attempt. He finds his old niche by the wall, leans there. A moment later he looks guardedly down to where the short girl and her friend are. A young, dapper boy is approaching the short girl. He asks her to dance. The short girl smiles, excuses herself to her friend, and follows the boy out onto the floor. Marty turns back to watching the dancers bleakly. A moment later he is aware that someone on his right is talking to him. . . . He turns his head. It is a young man of about twenty-eight.*

MARTY. You say something to me?

YOUNG MAN. Yeah. I was just asking you if you was here stag or with a girl.

MARTY. I'm stag.

YOUNG MAN. Well, I'll tell you. I got stuck onna blind date with a dog, and I just picked up a nice chick, and I was wondering how I'm gonna get ridda the dog. Somebody to take her home, you know what I mean? I be glad to pay you five bucks if you take the dog home for me.

MARTY (*a little confused*). What?

YOUNG MAN. I'll take you over, and I'll introduce you as an old army buddy of mine, and then I'll cut out. Because I got this chick waiting for me out by the hatcheck, and I'll pay you five bucks.

MARTY (*stares at the young man*). Are you kidding?

YOUNG MAN. No, I'm not kidding.

MARTY. You can't just walk off onna girl like that.

*The young man grimaces impatiently and moves down the line of stags. . . . Marty watches him, still a little shocked at the proposition. About two stags down, the young man broaches his plan to another stag. This stag, frowning and pursing his lips, seems more receptive to the idea. . . . The young man takes out a wallet and gives the stag a five-dollar bill. The stag detaches himself from the wall and, a little ill at ease, follows the young man back past Marty and into the lounge. Marty pauses a moment and then, concerned, walks to the archway that separates the lounge from the ballroom and looks in.*

*The lounge is a narrow room with a bar and booths. In contrast to the ballroom, it is brightly lighted—causing Marty to squint.*

*In the second booth from the archway sits a girl, about twenty-eight. Despite the careful grooming that she has put into her cosmetics, she is blatantly plain. The young man and the stag are standing, talking to her. She is looking up at the young man, her hands nervously gripping her Coca-Cola glass.*

*We cannot hear what the young man is saying, but it is apparent that he is introducing his new-found army buddy and is going through some cock-and-bull story about being called away on an emergency. The stag is presented as her escort-to-be, who will see to it that she gets home safely. The girl apparently is not taken in at all by this, though she is trying hard not to seem affected.*

*She politely rejects the stag's company and will get home by herself, thanks for asking anyway. The young man makes a few mild protestations, and then he*

FROM UNITED ARTISTS CORPORATION PRODUCTION MARTY

*and the stag leave the booth and come back to the archway from where Marty has been watching the scene. As they pass Marty, we overhear a snatch of dialogue.*

YOUNG MAN. . . . In that case, as long as she's going home alone, give me the five bucks back. . . .

STAG. . . . Look, Mac, you paid me five bucks. I was willing. It's my five bucks. . . .

*They pass on. Marty returns his attention to the girl. She is still sitting as she was, gripping and ungripping the glass of Coca-Cola in front of her. Her eyes are closed. Then, with a little nervous shake of her head, she gets out of the booth and stands—momentarily at a loss for what to do next. The open fire doors leading out onto the large fire escape catch her eye. She crosses*

*to the fire escape, nervous, frowning, and disappears outside.*

*Marty stares after her, then slowly shuffles to the open fire-escape doorway. It is a large fire escape, almost the size of a small balcony. The girl is standing by the railing, her back to the doorway, her head slunk down on her bosom. For a moment Marty is unaware that she is crying. Then he notices the shivering tremors running through her body and the quivering shoulders. He moves a step onto the fire escape. He tries to think of something to say.*

MARTY. Excuse me, Miss. Would you care to dance?

*The girl slowly turns to him, her face streaked with tears, her lip trembling. Then, in one of those peculiar moments of simultaneous impulse, she lurches to Marty with*

198

*a sob, and Marty takes her to him. For a moment they stand in an awkward embrace, Marty a little embarrassed, looking out through the doors to the lounge, wondering if anybody is seeing them. Reaching back with one hand, he closes the fire doors, and then, replacing the hand around her shoulder, he stands stiffly, allowing her to cry on his chest.*

DISSOLVE TO: *Exterior, apartment door. The mother is standing, in a black coat and a hat with a little feather, waiting for her ring to be answered. The door opens. Virginia stands framed in the doorway.*

VIRGINIA. Hello, Aunt Theresa, come in.

*The mother goes into the small foyer. Virginia closes the door.*

MOTHER (*in a low voice, as she pulls her coat off*). Is Catherine here?

VIRGINIA (*helps her off with coat, nods—also in a low voice*). We didn't tell her nothing yet. We thought we'd leave it to you. We thought you'd put it like how you were lonely, and why don't she come to live with you. Because that way it looks like she's doing you a favor, insteada we're throwing her out, and it won't be so cruel on her. Thomas is downstairs with the neighbors . . . I'll go call him.

MOTHER. You go downstairs to the neighbors and stay there with Thomas.

VIRGINIA. Wouldn't it be better if we were here?

MOTHER. You go downstairs. I talk to Catherine alone. Otherwise, she's gonna start a fight with you.

*A shrill, imperious woman's voice from an off-stage room suddenly*

*breaks into the muttered conference in the foyer.*

AUNT (*off*). Who's there?! Who's there?!

*The mother heads up the foyer to the living room, followed by Virginia, holding the mother's coat.*

MOTHER (*calls back*). It's me, Catherine! How you feel?

*At the end of the foyer, the two sisters meet. The aunt is a spare, gaunt woman with a face carved out of granite. Tough, embittered, deeply hurt type face.*

AUNT. Hey! What are you doing here?

MOTHER. I came to see you. (*The two sisters quickly embrace and release each other*). How you feel?

AUNT. I gotta pain in my left side and my leg throbs like a drum.

MOTHER. I been getting pains in my shoulder.

AUNT. I got pains in my shoulder, too. I have a pain in my hip, and my right arm aches so much I can't sleep. It's a curse to be old. How you feel?

MOTHER. I feel fine.

AUNT. That's nice.

*Now that the standard greetings are over, Aunt Catherine abruptly turns and goes back to her chair. It is obviously her chair. It is an old heavy oaken chair with thick armrests. The rest of the apartment is furnished in what is known as "modern"—a piece from* House Beautiful *here, a piece from* Better Homes and Gardens *there. Aunt Catherine sits, erect and forbidding, in her chair. The mother seats herself with a sigh in a neighbor-*

*ing chair. Virginia, having hung the mother's coat, now turns to the two older women. A pause.*

VIRGINIA. I'm going downstairs to the Cappacini's. I'll be up inna little while.

*Aunt Catherine nods expressionlessly. Virginia looks at her for a moment, then impulsively crosses to her mother-in-law.*

VIRGINIA. You feel all right?

*The old lady looks up warily, suspicious of this sudden solicitude.*

AUNT. I'm all right.

*Virginia nods and goes off to the foyer. The two old sisters sit, unmoving, waiting for the door to close behind Virginia. Then the mother addresses herself to Aunt Catherine.*

MOTHER. We gotta post card from my son, Nickie, and his bride this morning. They're in Florida inna big hotel. Everything is very nice.

AUNT. That's nice.

MOTHER. Catherine, I want you come live with me in my house with Marty and me. In my house, you have your own room. You don't have to sleep onna couch inna living room like here.

*The aunt looks slowly and directly at the mother.*

Catherine, your son is married. He got his own home. Leave him in peace. He wants to be alone with his wife. They don't want no old lady sitting inna balcony. Come and live with me. We will cook in the kitchen and talk like when we were girls. You are dear to me, and you are dear to Marty. We are pleased for you to come.

AUNT. Did they come to see you?

MOTHER. Yes.

AUNT. Did my son Thomas come with her?

MOTHER. Your son Thomas was there.

AUNT. Did he also say he wishes to cast his mother from his house?

MOTHER. Catherine, don't make an opera outta this. The three-a you anna baby live in three skinny rooms. You are an old goat, and she has an Italian temper. She is a good girl, but you drive her crazy. Leave them alone. They have their own life.

*The old aunt turns her head slowly and looks her sister square in the face. Then she rises slowly from her chair.*

AUNT (coldly). Get outta here. This is my son's house. This is where I live. I am not to be cast out inna street like a newspaper.

*The mother likewise rises. The two old women face each other directly.*

MOTHER. Catherine, you are very dear to me. We have cried many times together. When my husband died, I would have gone insane if it were not for you. I ask you to come to my house because I can make you happy. Please come to my house.

*The two sisters regard each other. Then Aunt Catherine sits again in her oaken chair, and the mother returns to her seat. The hardened muscles in the old aunt's face suddenly slacken, and she turns to her sister.*

AUNT. Theresa, what shall become of me?

MOTHER. Catherine . . .

AUNT. It's gonna happen to you. Mark it well. These terrible years. I'm afraida look inna mirror. I'm afraid I'm gonna see an old lady with white hair, like the old ladies inna park, little bundles inna black shawl, waiting for the coffin. I'm fifty-six years old. What am I to do with myself? I have strength in my hands. I wanna cook. I wanna clean. I wanna make dinner for my children. I wanna be of use to somebody. Am I an old dog to lie in fronta the fire till my eyes close? These are terrible years, Theresa! Terrible years!

MOTHER. Catherine, my sister . . .

*The old aunt stares, distraught, at the mother.*

AUNT. It's gonna happen to you! It's gonna happen to you! What will you do if Marty gets married?! What will you cook?! What happen to alla children tumbling in alla rooms?! Where is the noise?! It is a curse to be a widow! A curse! What will you do if Marty gets married?! What will you do?!

*She stares at the mother—her deep, gaunt eyes haggard and pained. The mother stares back for a moment, then her own eyes close. The aunt has hit home. The aunt sinks back onto her chair, sitting stiffly, her arms on the thick arm-rests. The mother sits hunched a little forward, her hands nervously folded in her lap.*

AUNT (*quietly*). I will put my clothes inna bag and I will come to you tomorrow.

*The camera slowly dollies back from the two somber sisters.*

SLOW FADE-OUT.

CUT TO: *Close-up, intimate, Marty and the girl dancing cheek to cheek. Occasionally the heads of other couples slowly waft across the camera view, temporarily blocking out view of Marty and the girl. Camera stays with them as the slow dance carries them around the floor. Tender scene.*

GIRL. . . . The last time I was here the same sort of thing happened.

MARTY. Yeah?

GIRL. Well, not exactly the same thing. The last time I was up here was about four months ago. Do you see that girl in the gray dress sitting over there?

MARTY. Yeah.

GIRL. That's where I sat. I sat there for an hour and a half without moving a muscle. Now and then, some fellow would sort of walk up to me and then change his mind. I just sat there, my hands in my lap. Well, about ten o'clock, a bunch of kids came in swaggering. They weren't more than seventeen, eighteen years old. Well, they swaggered down along the wall, leering at all the girls. I thought they were kind of cute . . . and as they passed me, I smiled at them. One of the kids looked at me and said: "Forget it, ugly, you ain't gotta chance." I burst out crying. I'm a big crier, you know.

MARTY. So am I.

GIRL. And another time when I was in college . . .

MARTY. I cry alla time. Any little thing. I can recognize pain a mile away. My brothers, my brother-in-laws, they're always telling me what a good-hearted guy I am. Well, you don't get goodhearted by accident. You get kicked around long enough you get to be a real professor of pain. I know exactly how you feel. And I also want you to know I'm having a very good time with you now and really enjoying myself. So you see, you're not such a dog as you think you are.

GIRL. I'm having a very good time too.

MARTY. So there you are. So I guess I'm not such a dog as I think I am.

GIRL. You're a very nice guy, and I don't know why some girl hasn't grabbed you off long ago.

MARTY. I don't know either. I think I'm a very nice guy. I also think I'm a pretty smart guy in my own way.

GIRL. I think you are.

MARTY. I'll tell you some of my wisdom which I thunk up on those nights when I got stood up, and nights like that, and you walk home thinking: "Watsa matter with me? I can't be that ugly." Well, I figure, two people get married, and they gonna live together forty, fifty years. So it's just gotta be more than whether they're good-looking or not. My father was a real ugly man, but my mother adored him. She told me that she used to get so miserable sometimes, like everybody, you know? And she says my father always tried to understand. I used to see them sometimes when I was a kid, sitting in the living room, talking and talking, and I used to adore my old man because he was so kind. That's one of the most beautiful things I have in my life, the way my father and my mother were. And my father was a real ugly man. So it don't matter if you look like a gorilla. So you see, dogs like us, we ain't such dogs as we think we are.

*They dance silently for a moment, cheeks pressed against each other. Close-ups of each face.*

GIRL. I'm twenty-nine years old. How old are you?

MARTY. Thirty-six.

*They dance silently, closely. Occasionally the heads of other couples*

*sway in front of the camera, blocking our view of Marty and the girl. Slow, sweet dissolve.*

DISSOLVE TO: *Interior, kitchen, Marty's home. Later that night. It is dark. Nobody is home. The rear porch door now opens, and the silhouettes of Marty and the girl appear—blocking up the doorway.*

MARTY. Wait a minute. Lemme find the light.

*He finds the light. The kitchen is suddenly brightly lit. The two of them stand squinting to adjust to the sudden glare.*

MARTY. I guess my mother ain't home yet. I figure my cousin Thomas and Virginia musta gone to the movies, so they won't get back till one o'clock, at least.

*The girl has advanced into the kitchen, a little ill at ease, and is looking around. Marty closes the porch door.*

MARTY. This is the kitchen.

GIRL. Yes, I know.

*Marty leads the way into the dining room.*

MARTY. Come on inna dining room. (*He turns on the light in there as he goes. The girl follows him in.*) Siddown, take off your coat. You want something to eat? We gotta whole halfa chicken left over from yesterday.

GIRL (*perching tentatively on the edge of a chair*). No, thank you. I don't think I should stay very long.

MARTY. Sure. Just take off your coat a minute.

*He helps her off with her coat and stands for a moment behind her, looking down at her. Conscious of his scrutiny, she sits uncomfortably, her breasts rising and falling unevenly. Marty takes her coat into the dark living room. The girl sits patiently, nervously. Marty comes back, sits down on another chair. Awkward silence.*

MARTY. So I was telling you, my kid brother Nickie got married last Sunday . . . That was a very nice affair. And they had this statue of some woman, and they had whisky spouting outta her mouth. I never saw anything so grand in my life. [*The silence falls between them again.*] And watta meal. I'm a butcher, so I know a good hunka steak when I see one. That was choice filet, right off the toppa the chuck. A buck-eighty a pound. Of course, if you wanna cheaper cut, get rib steak. That gotta lotta waste on it, but it comes to about a buck and a quarter a pound, if it's trimmed. Listen, Clara, make yourself comfortable. You're all tense.

GIRL. Oh, I'm fine.

MARTY. You want me to take you home, I'll take you home.

GIRL. Maybe that would be a good idea.

*She stands. He stands, frowning, a little angry—turns sullenly and goes back into the living room for her coat. She stands unhappily. He comes back and wordlessly starts to help her into her coat. He stands behind her, his hands on her shoulders. He suddenly seizes her, begins kissing her on the neck. Camera comes up quickly to intensely intimate close-up, nothing but the heads. The dialogue drops to quick, hushed whispers.*

GIRL. No, Marty, please . . .

MARTY. I like you, I like you, I been telling you all night I like you . . .

GIRL. Marty . . .

MARTY. I just wanna kiss, that's all . . .

*He tries to turn her face to him. She resists.*

GIRL. No . . .

MARTY. Please . . .

GIRL. No . . .

MARTY. Please . . .

GIRL. Marty . . .

*He suddenly releases her, turns away violently.*

MARTY (*crying out*). All right! I'll take you home! All right! (*He marches a few angry paces away, deeply disturbed. Turns to her. All I wanted was a lousy kiss! What am I, a leper or something?!*

*He turns and goes off into the living room to hide the flush of hot tears threatening to fill his eyes. The girl stands, herself on the verge of tears.*

GIRL (*mutters, more to herself than to him*). I just didn't feel like it, that's all.

*She moves slowly to the archway leading to the living room. Marty is sitting on the couch, hands in his lap, looking straight ahead. The room is dark except for the overcast of the dining-room light reaching in. The girl goes to the couch, perches on the edge beside him. He doesn't look at her.*

MARTY. Well, that's the history of my life. I'm a little, short, fat, ugly guy. Comes New Year's Eve, everybody starts arranging parties, I'm the guy they gotta dig up a date for. I'm old enough to know better. Let me get a packa cigarettes, and I'll take you home.

*He starts to rise, but doesn't . . . sinks back onto the couch, looking straight ahead. The girl looks at him, her face peculiarly soft and compassionate.*

GIRL. I'd like to see you again, very much. The reason I didn't let you kiss me was because I just didn't know how to handle the situation. You're the kindest man I ever met. The reason I tell you this is because I want to see you again very much. Maybe, I'm just so desperate to fall in love that I'm trying too hard. But I know that when you take me home, I'm going to just lie on my bed and think about you. I want very much to see you again.

*Marty stares down at his hands in his lap.*

MARTY (*without looking at her*). Waddaya doing tomorrow night?
GIRL. Nothing.
MARTY. I'll call you up tomorrow morning. Maybe we'll go see a movie.
GIRL. I'd like that very much.
MARTY. The reason I can't be definite about it now is my Aunt Catherine is probably coming over tomorrow, and I may have to help out.
GIRL. I'll wait for your call.
MARTY. We better get started to your house because the buses only run about one an hour now.
GIRL. All right.

*She stands.*

MARTY. I'll just get a packa cigarettes.

*He goes into his bedroom. We can see him through the doorway, opening his bureau drawer and extracting a pack of cigarettes. He comes out again and looks at the girl for the first time. They start to walk to the dining room. In the archway, Marty pauses, turns to the girl.*

MARTY. Waddaya doing New Year's Eve?
GIRL. Nothing.

*They quietly slip into each other's arms and kiss. Slowly their faces part, and Marty's head sinks down upon her shoulder. He is crying. His shoulders shake slightly. The girl presses her cheek against the back of his head. They stand . . . there is the sound of the rear porch door being unlatched. They both start from their embrace. A moment later the mother's voice is heard off in the kitchen.*

MOTHER. Hallo! Hallo, Marty? (*She comes into the dining room, stops at the sight of the girl.*) Hallo, Marty, when you come home?
MARTY. We just got here about fifteen minutes ago, Ma. Ma, I want you to meet Miss Clara Davis. She's a graduate of New York University. She teaches history in Benjamin Franklin High School.

*This seems to impress the mother.*

MOTHER. Siddown, siddown. You want some chicken? We got some chicken in the icebox.
GIRL. No, Mrs. Pilletti, we were just going home. Thank you very much anyway.
MOTHER. Well, siddown a minute. I just come inna house. I'll take off my coat. Siddown a minute.

*She pulls her coat off.*

MARTY. How'd you come home, Ma? Thomas give you a ride?

*The mother nods.*

MOTHER. Oh, it's a sad business, a sad business.

*She sits down on a dining room chair, holding her coat in her lap. She turns to the girl, who likewise sits.*

MOTHER. My sister Catherine, she don't get along with her daughter-in-law, so she's gonna come live with us.

MARTY. Oh, she's coming, eh, Ma?

MOTHER. Oh, sure. (*to the girl*) It's a very sad thing. A woman, fifty-six years old, all her life, she had her own home. Now, she's just an old lady, sleeping on her daughter-in-law's couch. It's a curse to be a mother, I tell you. Your children grow up and then what is left for you to do? What is a mother's life but her children? It is a very cruel thing when your son has no place for you in his home.

GIRL. Couldn't she find some sort of hobby to fill out her time?

MOTHER. Hobby! What can she do? She cooks and she cleans. You gotta have a house to clean. You gotta have children to cook for. These are the terrible years for a woman, the terrible years.

GIRL. You mustn't feel too harshly against her daughter-in-law. She also wants to have a house to clean and a family to cook for.

*The mother darts a quick, sharp look at the girl—then looks back to her hands, which are beginning to twist nervously.*

MOTHER. You don't think my sister Catherine should live in her daughter-in-law's house?

GIRL. Well, I don't know the people, of course, but, as a rule, I don't think a mother-in-law should live with a young couple.

MOTHER. Where do you think a mother-in-law should go?

GIRL. I don't think a mother should depend so much upon her children for her rewards in life.

MOTHER. That's what it says in the book in New York University. You wait till you are a mother. It don't work out that way.

GIRL. Well, it's silly for me to argue about it. I don't know the people involved.

MARTY. Ma, I'm gonna take her home now. It's getting late, and the buses only run about one an hour.

MOTHER (*standing*). Sure.

*The girl stands.*

GIRL. It was very nice meeting you, Mrs. Pilletti. I hope I'll see you again.

MOTHER. Sure.

*Marty and the girl move to the kitchen.*

MARTY. All right, Ma. I'll be back in about an hour.

MOTHER. Sure.

GIRL. Good night, Mrs. Pilletti.

MOTHER. Good night.

*Marty and the girl exit into the kitchen. The mother stands, expressionless, by her chair watching them go. She remains standing rigidly even after the porch door can be heard being opened and shut. The camera moves up to a close-up of the mother. Her eyes are wide. She is staring straight ahead. There is fear in her eyes.*

FADE OUT.

## ACT III

FADE IN: *Film—close-up of church bells clanging away. Pan down church to see typical Sunday morning, people going up the steps of a church and entering. It is a beautiful June morning.*

DISSOLVE TO: *Interior, Marty's bedroom —sun fairly streaming through the curtains. Marty is standing in front of his bureau, slipping his arms into a clean white shirt. He is freshly shaved and groomed. Through the doorway of his bedroom we can see the mother in the dining room, in coat and hat, all set to go to Mass, taking the last breakfast plates away and carrying them into the kitchen. The camera moves across the living room into the dining room. The mother comes out of the kitchen with a paper napkin and begins crumbing the table.*

*There is a knock on the rear porch door. The mother leaves her crumbing and goes into the kitchen. Camera goes with her. She opens the rear door to admit Aunt Catherine, holding a worn old European carpetbag. The aunt starts to go deeper into the kitchen, but the mother stays her with her hand.*

MOTHER (*in low, conspiratorial voice*). Hey, I come home from your house last night, Marty was here with a girl.
AUNT. Who?
MOTHER. Marty.
AUNT. Your son Marty?
MOTHER. Well, what Marty you think is gonna be here in this house with a girl?
AUNT. Were the lights on?
MOTHER. Oh, sure. (*Frowns suddenly at her sister*) The girl is a college graduate.
AUNT. They're the worst. College girls are one step from the streets. They smoke like men inna saloon.

*The aunt puts her carpetbag down and sits on one of the wooden kitchen chairs. The mother sits on another.*

MOTHER. That's the first time Marty ever brought a girl to this house. She seems like a nice girl. I think he has a feeling for this girl.

*At this moment a burst of spirited whistling emanates from Marty's bedroom.*

CUT TO: *Marty's bedroom—Marty standing in front of his mirror, buttoning his shirt or adjusting his tie, whistling a gay tune.*

CUT BACK TO: *The two sisters, both their faces turned in the direction of the whistling. The whistling abruptly stops. The two sisters look at each other. The aunt shrugs.*

MOTHER. He been whistling like that all morning.

*The aunt nods bleakly.*

AUNT. He is bewitched. You will see. Today, tomorrow, inna week, he's gonna say to you: "Hey, Ma, it's no good being a single man. I'm tired running around." Then he's gonna say: "Hey, Ma, wadda we need this old house? Why don't we sell this old house, move into a nicer parta town? A nice little apartment?"
MOTHER. I don't sell this house, I tell you that. This is my husband's house, and I had six children in this house.
AUNT. You will see. A couple-a months, you gonna be an old lady, sleeping onna couch in your daughter-in-law's house.
MOTHER. Catherine, you are a blanket of gloom. Wherever you go, the rain follows. Some day, you gonna smile, and we gonna declare a holiday.

*Another burst of spirited whistling comes from Marty, off. It comes closer, and Marty now enters in splendid spirits, whistling away. He is slipping into his jacket.*

MARTY (*ebulliently*). Hello, Aunt Catherine! How are you? You going to Mass with us?

AUNT. I was at Mass two hours ago.

MARTY. Well, make yourself at home. The refrigerator is loaded with food. Go upstairs, take any room you want. It's beautiful outside, ain't it?

AUNT. There's a chill. Watch out, you catch a good cold and pneumonia.

MOTHER. My sister Catherine, she can't even admit it's a beautiful day.

*Marty—now at the sink, getting himself a glass of water—is examining a piece of plaster that has fallen from the ceiling.*

MARTY (*examining the chunk of plaster in his palm*). Boy, this place is really coming to pieces. (*Turns to mother*) You know, Ma, I think, sometime we oughtta sell this place. The plumbing is rusty—everything. I'm gonna have to replaster that whole ceiling now. I think we oughtta get a little apartment somewheres in a nicer parta town. . . . You all set, Ma?

MOTHER. I'm all set.

*She starts for the porch door. She slowly turns and looks at Marty, and then at Aunt Catherine—who returns her look. Mother and Marty exit.*

DISSOLVE TO: *Church. The mother comes out of the doors and down a few steps to where Marty is standing, enjoying the clearness of the June morning.*

MOTHER. In a couple-a minutes nine o'clock Mass is gonna start—in a couple-a minutes . . . (*to passers-by off*) hallo, hallo . . . (*to Marty*) Well, that was a nice girl last night, Marty. That was a nice girl.

MARTY. Yeah.

MOTHER. She wasn't a very good-looking girl, but she look like a nice girl. I said, she wasn't a very good-looking girl, not very pretty.

MARTY. I heard you, Ma.

MOTHER. She look a little old for you, about thirty-five, forty years old?

MARTY. She's twenty-nine, Ma.

MOTHER. She's more than twenny-nine years old, Marty. That's what she tells you. She looks thirty-five, forty. She didn't look Italian to me. I said, is she an Italian girl?

MARTY. I don't know. I don't think so.

MOTHER. She don't look like Italian to me. What kinda family she come from? There was something about her I don't like. It seems funny, the first time you meet her she comes to your empty house alone. These college girls, they all one step from the streets.

*Marty turns, frowning, to his mother.*

MARTY. What are you talkin' about? She's a nice girl.

MOTHER. I don't like her.

MARTY. You don't like her? You only met her for two minutes.

MOTHER. Don't bring her to the house no more.

MARTY. What didn't you like about her?

MOTHER. I don't know! She don't look like Italian to me, plenty nice Italian girls around.

MARTY. Well, let's not get into a fight about it, Ma. I just met the girl. I probably won't see her again.

*Marty leaves frame.*

MOTHER. Eh, I'm no better than my sister Catherine.

DISSOLVE TO: *Interior, the bar . . .*

*about an hour later. The after-Mass crowd is there, about six men ranging from twenty to forty. A couple of women in the booths. One woman is holding a glass of beer in one hand and is gently rocking a baby carriage with the other.*

*Sitting in the booth of Act I are Angie and three other fellows, ages twenty, thirty-two, and forty. One of the fellows, aged thirty-two, is giving a critical résumé of a recent work of literature by Mickey Spillane.*

CRITIC.  . . . So the whole book winds up, Mike Hammer, he's inna room there with this doll. So he says: "You rat, you are the murderer." So she begins to con him, you know? She tells him how she loves him. And then Bam! He shoots her in the stomach. So she's laying there, gasping for breath, and she says: "How could you do that?" And he says: "It was easy."

TWENTY-YEAR-OLD. Boy, that Mickey Spillane. Boy, he can write.

ANGIE (*leaning out of the booth and looking down the length of the bar, says with some irritation*). What's keeping Marty?

CRITIC. What I like about Mickey Spillane is he knows how to handle women. In one book, he picks up a tomato who gets hit with a car, and she throws a pass at him. And then he meets two beautiful twins, and they throw passes at him. And then he meets some beautiful society leader, and she throws a pass at him, and . . .

TWENTY-YEAR-OLD. Boy, that Mickey Spillane, he sure can write . . .

ANGIE (*looking out, down the bar again*). I don't know watsa matter with Marty.

FORTY-YEAR-OLD. Boy, Angie, what would you do if Marty ever died? You'd die right with him. A couple-a old bachelors hanging to each other like barnacles. There's Marty now.

*Angie leans out of the booth.*

ANGIE (*calling out*). Hello, Marty, where you been?

CUT TO: *Front end of the bar. Marty has just come in. He waves back to Angie, acknowledges another hello from a man by the bar, goes over to the bar, and gets the bartender's attention.*

MARTY. Hello, Lou, gimme change of a half and put a dime in it for a telephone call.

*The bartender takes the half dollar, reaches into his apron pocket for the change.*

BARTENDER. I hear you was at the Waverly Ballroom last night.

MARTY. Yeah. Angie tell you?

BARTENDER (*picking out change from palm full of silver*). Yeah, I hear you really got stuck with a dog.

*Marty looks at him.*

MARTY. She wasn't so bad.

BARTENDER (*extending the change*). Angie says she was a real scrawny-looking thing. Well, you can't have good luck alla time.

*Marty takes the change slowly and frowns down at it. He moves down the bar and would make for the telephone booth, but Angie hails him from the booth.*

ANGIE. Who you gonna call, Marty?

MARTY. I was gonna call that girl from last night, take her to a movie tonight.

ANGIE. Are you kidding?

FROM UNITED ARTISTS CORPORATION PRODUCTION MARTY

MARTY. She was a nice girl. I kinda liked her.

ANGIE (*indicating the spot in the booth vacated by the forty-year-old*). Siddown. You can call her later.

*Marty pauses, frowning, and then shuffles to the booth where Angie and the other two sit. The critic moves over for Marty. There is an exchange of hellos.*

TWENTY-YEAR-OLD. I gotta girl, she's always asking me to marry her. So I look at that face, and I say to myself: "Could I stand looking at that face for the resta my life?"

CRITIC. Hey, Marty, you ever read a book called *I, the Jury*, by Mickey Spillane?

MARTY. No.

ANGIE. Listen, Marty, I gotta good place for us to go tonight. The kid here, he says, he was downna bazaar at Our Lady of Angels last night and . . .

MARTY. I don't feel like going to the bazaar, Angie. I thought I'd take this girl to a movie.

ANGIE. Boy, you really musta made out good last night.

MARTY. We just talked.

ANGIE. Boy, she must be some talker. She musta been about fifty years old.

CRITIC. I always figger a guy oughtta marry a girl who's twenny years younger than he is, so that when he's forty, his wife is a real nice-looking doll.

TWENTY-YEAR-OLD. That means he'd have to marry the girl when she was one year old.

CRITIC. I never thoughta that.

MARTY. I didn't think she was so bad-looking.

ANGIE. She musta kept you inna shadows all night.

CRITIC. Marty, you don't wanna hang around with dogs. It gives you a bad reputation.

ANGIE. Marty, let's go downna bazaar.

MARTY. I told this dog I was gonna call her today.

ANGIE. Brush her.

*Marty looks questioningly at Angie.*

MARTY. You didn't like her at all?

ANGIE. A nothing. A real nothing.

*Marty looks down at the dime he has been nervously turning between two fingers and then, frowning, he slips it into his jacket pocket. He lowers his face and looks down, scowling at his thoughts. Around him, the voices clip along.*

CRITIC. What's playing on Fordham Road? I think there's a good picture in the Loew's Paradise.

ANGIE. Let go down to Forty-second Street and walk around. We're sure to wind up with something.

*Slowly Marty begins to look up again. He looks from face to face as each speaks.*

CRITIC. I'll never forgive La Guardia for cutting burlesque outta New York City.

TWENTY-YEAR-OLD. There's burlesque over in Union City. Let's go to Union City. . . .

ANGIE. Ah, they're always crowded on Sunday night.

CRITIC. So wadda you figure on doing tonight, Angie?

ANGIE. I don't know. Wadda you figure on doing?

CRITIC. I don't know. (*Turns to the twenty-year-old.*) Wadda you figure on doing?

*The twenty-year-old shrugs.*

*Suddenly Marty brings his fist down on the booth table with a crash. The others turn, startled, toward him. Marty rises in his seat.*

MARTY. "What are you doing tonight?" "I don't know, what are you doing?" Burlesque! Loew's Paradise! Miserable and lonely! Miserable and lonely and stupid! What am I, crazy or something?! I got something good! What am I hanging around with you guys for?!

*He has said this in tones so loud that it attracts the attention of everyone in the bar. A little embarrassed, Marty turns and moves quickly to the phone booth, pausing outside the door to find his dime again. Angie is out of his seat immediately and hurries after him.*

ANGIE (*a little shocked at Marty's outburst*). Watsa matter with you?

MARTY (*in a low, intense voice*). You don't like her. My mother don't like her. She's a dog, and I'm a fat, ugly little man. All I know is I had a good time last night. I'm gonna have a good time tonight. If we have enough good times together, I'm going down on my knees and beg that girl to marry me. If we make a party again this New Year's, I gotta date for the party. You don't like her, that's too bad. (*He moves into the booth, sits, turns again to Angie, smiles.*) When you gonna get married, Angie? You're thirty-four years old. All your kid brothers are married. You oughta be ashamed of yourself.

*Still smiling at his private joke, he puts the dime into the slot and then —with a determined finger—he begins to dial.*

FADE OUT.

## FOR DISCUSSION

1. In all drama, even television drama, our first impressions capture the attention; the last impressions are what we remember most. How does *Marty* capture our attention at the beginning? What is the final impression we take away?

2. *Marty* has a happy, as well as a different ending. Why didn't the playwright in the final scene show Marty and Clara coming from church after being married? Would this have made a better ending, a happier ending, or perhaps a more satisfying ending? Are you satisfied with the ending of *Marty?* Or would you like to see more of Marty Piletti and his friends?

3. a) If you were directing *Marty* for a T-V production, describe the type person you would want for the leading role.

b) From your knowledge of actors on T-V and in the movies, who is the most perfect actor to play the role of Marty? Why?

c) In the Hollywood version of *Marty*, did a big-name star play the leading role? Would it have been better if, say Clark Gable or Burt Lancaster or Ray Milland played Marty?

4. What type person is Angie? Could it be said that in the beginning of the drama that Marty and Angie are portrayed as two fellows who grew up together, but remained boys at heart all their lives? Are they different types? Explain.

5. There is selfishness and generosity in everybody, but generally one or another of these qualities will be predominant in an individual. Tell which quality is predominant in each of the following:
a) Clara  b) Angie  c) Mother
d) Marty  e) Aunt

## STUDYING THE T-V PLAY

1. By the end of the first act, the audience should have sufficient knowledge of the main character, the other characters, the situation, the locale, etc., so as to follow the play clearly as it progresses. What does each of the following scenes in Act One of *Marty* add as regards this knowledge: a) scene one in the butcher shop; b) scene two in the bar; c) scene three in Marty's home?

2. The basic part of all drama is conflict in the main character, and to a more or less marked degree in that of the other characters. Conflict involves: 1) opening state of equilibrium or balance—no conflict; 2) progress and change in the situation bringing on conflict; and 3) a new state of equilibrium brought about by solving the conflict. Write a brief composition on the conflict in *Marty*. Show the conflict in the character of Marty Piletti, and the conflict that is portrayed in the minor characters.

3. Some dramas have what is called a "social twist" to them, that is, some dramas portray racial prejudice, religious prejudice, labor problems. *On the Waterfront* had a definite "social twist" to it. The whole conflict was based on this "social twist." Is there a "social twist" anywhere in the play *Marty?* If so, where? Is it connected with the conflict?

4. What is a "fade out" and a "fade in" as given in the stage directions? What purpose do they serve? How would this be handled on the stage in a theater?

5. The popular camera close-up in television drama serves a definite purpose. Why does the script call for close-ups at the following times in *Marty?*

a) at the end of Act One, scene one, in the butcher shop: close-up of Marty.

b) at the beginning of Act One, scene three, in the bar: close-up of the clock.

c) at the beginning of Act Two in the "Waverly Ballroom": close-up of the faces of the members of the stag line.

d) at the opening of Act Two, scene three, in the "Waverly Ballroom": close-up of Marty and Clara dancing.

e) at the opening of Act Three, the close-up of the church bells.

# THE GREEN PASTURES

## MARC CONNELLY

"This play is the divine comedy of the modern theater," wrote J. Brooks Atkinson in the NEW YORK TIMES, after he had seen Marc Connelly's drama. "Connelly has produced a fable of the Lord walking on the earth, a play of great emotional depth and spiritual exaltation." What was the author's purpose in writing a play from this strange viewpoint? "THE GREEN PASTURES," says Connelly, "is an attempt to present certain aspects of a living religion in the terms of its believers. The religion is that of thousands of Negroes in the Deep South." These uneducated Christians love their Bible with an intense love, and they have translated its contents into the workaday world of their everyday lives. ". . . they accept the Old Testament as a chronicle of wonders which happened to people like themselves in vague but actual places, and of rules of conduct, true acceptance of which will lead them to a tangible, three-dimensional Heaven. In this Heaven, if one has been born in a district where fish frys are popular, the angels do have magnificent fish frys through an eternity somewhat resembling a series of earthly holidays. The Lord Jehovah may look like a just but compassionate patriarch, like the Reverend Mr. Dubois, as our Sunday-school teacher speculates in the play. In any event, His face will be familiar to the one who has come for his reward."

Mr. Connelly's play was inspired by the novel, OL' MAN ADAM AND HIS CHILLUN, written by Roark Bradford. When the play was first produced in 1930 and won the Pulitzer prize, it was greeted with "rave" reviews. Read it now, not from the standpoint of a critic, but with the intent to enjoy an amusing, touching phantasy of American folklore.

# THE GREEN PASTURES

## CHARACTERS

| | |
|---|---|
| MR. DESHEE, THE PREACHER | WOMEN CLEANERS |
| SUNDAY SCHOOL CLASS | ABRAHAM |
| CUSTARD MAKER | ISAAC |
| ANGELS AT A FISH FRY | JACOB |
| GABRIEL | MOSES AND AARON |
| GOD | ZIPPORAH |
| CHOIR LEADER | PHARAOH |
| ADAM | WIZARDS AND MAGICIANS |
| EVE | JOSHUA |
| CAIN | MASTER OF CEREMONIES |
| CAIN'S GIRL | KING OF BABYLON |
| ZEBA | PROPHET |
| CAIN THE SIXTH | HIGH PRIEST |
| GROUP OF GAMBLERS | SCOUT |
| NOAH | SOLDIERS |
| NOAH'S WIFE AND SONS | HEZDREL |
| SINNERS WATCHING THE ARK | CHOIR |

## PART ONE

### SCENE I

*A corner in a Negro church.*

*Ten children and an elderly preacher. The costumes are those that might be seen in any lower Louisiana town at Sunday-school time. As the curtain rises,* MR. DESHEE, *the preacher, is reading from a Bible. The* CHILDREN *are listening with varied degrees of interest. Three or four are wide-eyed in their attention. Two or three are obviously puzzled, but interested, and the smallest ones are engaged in more physical concerns. One is playing with a little doll, and another runs his finger on all the angles of his chair.*

*Deshee.* "An' Adam lived a hundred and thirty years, an' begat a son in his own likeness, after his image; an' called his name Seth. An' de days of Adam, after he had begotten Seth, were eight hundred years; an' he begat sons an' daughters; an' all de days dat Adam lived were nine hundred an' thirty years; an' he died. An' Seth lived a hundred an' five years an' begat Enos; an' Seth lived after he begat Enos eight hund'ed an' seven years and begat sons and daughters. An' all de days of Seth were nine hund'ed and twelve years; an' he died." An' it go on like dat till we come to Enoch an' de book say: "An' Enoch lived sixty an' five years and begat Methuselah." Den it say: "An' all de days of Methuselah were nine hund'ed an' sixty an' nine years an' he died." An' dat was de oldest man dat ever was. Dat's why we call ol' Mr. Gurney's mammy ol' Mrs. Methuselah, caize she's so ol'. Den a little later it tell about another member of de fam'ly. His name was Noah. Maybe some of you know about him already. I'm gonter tell you all about him next Sunday. Anyway dat's de meat an' substance of de first five chapters of Genesis. Now, how you think you gonter like de Bible?

*Myrtle.* I think it's jest wonderful, Mr. Deshee. I cain't understand any of it.

---

213

*First Boy.* Why did dey live so long, Mr. Deshee?

*Deshee.* Why? Caize dat was de way God felt.

*Second Boy.* Dat made Adam a way back.

*Deshee.* Yes, he certainly 'way back by de time Noah come along. Want to ask me any mo' questions?

*Second Boy.* What de worl' look like when de Lawd begin, Mr. Deshee?

*Deshee.* How yo' mean what it look like?

*Myrtle.* Carlisle mean who was in N'Orleans den.

*Deshee.* Dey wasn't nobody in N'Orleans on 'count dey wasn't any N'Orleans. Dat's de whole idea I tol' yo' at de end of de first Chapter. Yo' got to git yo' minds fixed. Dey wasn't any Rampart Street. Dey wasn't any Canal Street. Dey wasn't any Louisiana. Dey wasn't nothin' on de earth at all caize fo' de reason dey wasn't any earth.

*Myrtle.* Yes, but what Carlisle wanter know is—

*Deshee* (*interrupting and addressing little boy who has been playing with his chair and paying no attention*). Now Randolph, if you don't listen, how yo' gonter grow up and be a good man? Yo' wanter grow up an' be a transgressor?

*Little Boy* (*frightened*). No.

*Deshee.* You tell yo' mammy yo' sister got to come wid you next time. She kin git de things done in time to bring you to de school. You content yo'self. [*The little boy straightens up in his chair.*] Now, what do Carlisle want to know?

*Carlisle.* How he decide he want de worl' to be right yere and how he git de idea he wanted it?

*Myrtle.* Caize de Book say, don't it, Mr. Deshee?

*Deshee.* De Book say, but at de same time dat's a good question. I remember when I was a little boy de same thing recurred to me. An' ol' Mr. Dubois, he was a wonderful preacher at New Hope Chapel over in East Gretna, he said: "De answer is dat de Book ain't got time to go into all de details." And he was right. You know sometimes I think de Lawd expects us to figure out a few things for ourselves. We know dat at one time dey wasn't anything except Heaven, we don't know jest where it was but we know it was dere. Maybe it was everywhere. Den one day de Lawd got de idea he'd like to make some places. He made de sun an' de moon, de stars. An' he made de earth.

*Myrtle.* Who was aroun' den, nothin' but angels?

*Deshee.* I suppose so.

*First Boy.* What was de angels doin' up dere?

*Deshee.* I suppose dey jest flew aroun' and had a good time. Dey wasn't no sin, so dey musta had a good time.

*First Boy.* Did dey have picnics?

*Deshee.* Sho, dey had the nicest kind of picnics. Dey probably had fish frys, wid b'iled custard and ten cent seegars for de adults. God gives us humans lotsa ideas about havin' good times. Maybe dey were things he'd seen de angels do. Yes, sir, I bet dey had a fish fry every week.

*Myrtle.* Did dey have Sunday School, too?

*Deshee.* Yes, dey musta had Sunday School for de cherubs.

*Myrtle.* What did God look like, Mr. Deshee?

*Deshee.* Well, nobody knows exactly what God looked like. But when I was a little boy I used to imagine dat he looked like de Reverend Dubois. He was de finest looking ol' man I ever knew. Yes, I used to bet de Lawd looked exactly like Mr. Dubois in de days when he walked de earth in de shape of a natchel man.

*Myrtle.* When was dat, Mr. Deshee?

*Deshee.* Why, when he was gettin' things started down heah. When he talked to Adam and Eve and Noah and Moses and all dem. He made mighty men in dem days. But aldo they was awful mighty dey always knew dat he was beyond dem all. Pretty near one o'clock, time fo' you chillun to go home to dinner, but before I let you go I wan' you to go over wid me de main facts of de first lesson. What's de name of de book?

*Children.* Genesis.

*Deshee.* Dat's right. And what's de other name?

*Children.* First Book of Moses.

*Deshee.* Dat's right. And dis yere's Chapter One. [*The lights begin to dim.*] "In the beginnin' God created de heaven an' de earth. An' de earth was widout form an' void. An' de darkness was upon de face of de deep."

### SCENE II

*In the darkness many voices are heard singing "Rise, Shine, Give God The Glory." They sing it gayly and rapidly. The lights go up as the second verse ends. The chorus is being sung diminuendo by a mixed company of angels. That is they are angels in that they wear brightly colored robes and have wings protruding from their backs. Otherwise they look and act like a company of happy Negroes at a fish fry. The scene itself is a pre-Creation Heaven with compromises. In the distance is an unbroken stretch of blue sky. Companionable varicolored clouds billow down to the floor of the stage and roll overhead to the branches of a live oak tree which is up left. The tree is leafy and dripping with Spanish moss, and with the clouds makes a frame for the scene. In the cool shade of the tree are the usual appurtenances of a fish fry; a large kettle of hot fat set on two small parallel logs, with a fire going underneath, and a large rustic table formed by driving four stakes into the ground and placing planks on top of the small connecting boards. On the table are piles of biscuits and corn bread and the cooked fish in dish pans. There are one or two fairly large cedar or crock "churns" containing boiled custard, which looks like milk. There is a gourd dipper beside the churns and several glasses and cups of various sizes and shapes from which the custard is drunk.*

*The principal singers are marching two by two in a small area at the R. of the stage. Two MAMMY ANGELS are attending to the frying beside the kettle. Behind the table a MAN ANGEL is skinning fish and passing them to the cooks. Another is ladling out the custard. A MAMMY ANGEL is putting fish on bread for a brood of cherubs, and during the first scene they seat themselves on a grassy bank upstage. Another MAMMY ANGEL is clapping her hands disapprovingly and beckoning a laughing BOY CHERUB down from a cloud a little out of her reach. Another MAMMY ANGEL is solicitously slapping the back of a GIRL CHERUB who has a large fish sandwich in her hand and a bone in her throat. There is much movement about the table, and during the first few minutes several individuals go up to the table to help themselves to the food and drink. Many of the women angels wear hats and a few of the men are smoking cigars. A large boxful is on the table. There is much laughter and chatter as the music*

THE GREEN PASTURES © COPYRIGHT 1936 BY WARNER BROS. PICTURES, INC.

*softens, but continues, during the early part of the action. The following short scenes are played almost simultaneously.*

*First Cook (at kettle calling off).* Hurry up, Cajey. Dis yere fat's cryin' fo' mo' feesh.

*A Voice (off stage).* We comin', fas' we kin. Dey got to be ketched, ain't dey? We cain't say, "C'm'on little fish. C'm'on an' git fried," kin we?

*Second Cook (at table).* De trouble is de mens is all worm fishin'.

*First Man Angel (at table).* What dif'runce do it make? Yo' all de time got to make out like somebody's doin' somethin' de wrong way.

*Second Cook (near table).* I s'pose you got de per'fec' way fo' makin' bait.

*First Man Angel.* I ain't sayin' dat. I is sayin' whut's wrong wid worm fishin'.

*Second Cook.* Whut's wrong wid worm fishin'? Ever'thing, dat's all. Dey's only one good way fo' catfishin', an' dat's minny fishin'. Anybody know dat.

*First Man Angel.* Well, it jest so happen dat minny fishin' is de doggondest fool way of fishin' dey is. You kin try minny fishin' to de cows come home an' all you catch'll be de backache. De trouble wid you, sister, is you jest got minny fishin' on de brain.

*Second Cook.* Go right on, loud mouf. You tell me de news. My, my! You jest de wisest person in de worl'. First you, den de Lawd God.

*First Man Angel (to the custard ladler).* You cain't tell dem nothin'. (*Walks away to the custard churn.*) Does you try to 'splain some simple fac' dey git man-deaf.

*First Mammy Angel (to CHERUB on

*the cloud*). Now, you heerd me. [*The* CHERUB *assumes several mocking poses, as she speaks.*] You fly down yere. You wanter be put down in de sin book? (*She goes to the table, gets a drink for herself and points out the cherub to one of the men behind the table.*) Dat baby must got imp blood in him he so vexin'. (*She returns to her position under the cloud.*) You want me to fly up dere an' slap you down? Now, I tol' you. [*The* CHERUB *starts to come down.*]

*Stout Angel* (*to the* CHERUB *with a bone in her throat*). I tol' you you was too little fo' catfish. What you wanter git a bone in yo' froat fo'? (*She slaps the* CHERUB'S *back.*)

*Slender Angel* (*leisurely eating a sandwich as she watches the back-slapping*). What de trouble wid Leonetta?

*Stout Angel.* She got a catfish bone down her froat. (*To the* CHERUB.) Doggone, I tol' you to eat grinnel instead.

*Slender Angel.* Ef'n she do git all dat et, she gonter have de bellyache.

*Stout Angel.* Ain't I tol' her dat? (*To* CHERUB.) Come on now; let go dat bone. [*She slaps* CHERUB'S *back again. The bone is dislodged and the* CHERUB *grins her relief.*] Dat's good.

*Slender Angel* (*comfortingly*). Now she all right.

*Stout Angel.* Go on an' play wid yo' cousins. [*The* CHERUB *joins the Cherubs sitting on the embankment. The concurrency of scenes ends here.*] I ain't see you lately, Lily. How you been?

*Slender Angel.* Me, I'm fine. I been visitin' my mammy. She waitin' on de welcome table over by de throne of grace.

*Stout Angel.* She always was pretty holy.

*Slender Angel.* Yes, ma'am. She like it dere. I guess de Lawd's took quite a fancy to her.

*Stout Angel.* Well, dat's natural. I declare yo' mammy one of de finest lady angels I know.

*Slender Angel.* She claim you de best one she know.

*Stout Angel.* Well, when you come right down to it, I suppose we is all pretty near perfec'.

*Slender Angel.* Yes, ma'am. Why is dat, Mis' Jenny?

*Stout Angel.* I s'pose it's caize de Lawd he don' 'low us 'sociatin' wid de devil any mo' so dat dey cain' be no mo' sinnin'.

*Slender Angel.* Po' ol' Satan. Whutevah become of him?

*Stout Angel.* De Lawd put him some place I s'pose.

*Slender Angel.* But dey ain't any place but Heaven, is dey?

*Stout Angel.* De Lawd could make a place, couldn't he?

*Slender Angel.* Dat's de truth. Dey's one thing confuses me though.

*Stout Angel.* What's dat?

*Slender Angel.* I do a great deal of travelin' an' I ain't never come across any place but Heaven anywhere. So if de Lawd kick Satan out of Heaven jest whereat did he go? Dat's my question.

*Stout Angel.* You bettah let de Lawd keep his own secrets, Lily. De way things is goin' now dey ain't been no sinnin' since dey give dat scamp a kick in de pants. Nowadays Heaven's free of sin an' if a lady wants a little constitutional she kin fly 'til she wing-weary widout gittin' insulted.

*Slender Angel.* I was jest a baby when Satan lef'. I don't even 'member what he look like.

*Stout Angel.* He was jest right fo' a

devil. [*An* ARCHANGEL *enters. He is older than the others and wears a white beard. His clothing is much darker than that of the others and his wings a trifle more imposing.*] Good mo'nin', Archangel.

[*Others say good morning.*]

*Archangel.* Good mo'nin', folks. I wonder kin I interrup' de fish fry an' give out de Sunday school cyards? [*Cries of "Suttingly!" "Mah goodness, yes"—etc. The marching* CHOIR *stops.*] You kin keep singin' if you want to. Why don' you sing "When de Saints Come Marchin' In?" Seem to me I ain' heard dat lately. [*The* CHOIR *begins "When the Saints Come Marching In," rather softly, but does not resume marching. The* ARCHANGEL *looks off left.*] All right, bring 'em yere. [*A prim looking* WOMAN TEACHER-ANGEL *enters, shepherding ten* BOY *and* GIRL CHER-UBS. *The* TEACHER *carries ten beribboned diplomas, which she gives to the* ARCHANGEL. *The cherubs are dressed in stiffly starched white suits and dresses, the little girls having enormous ribbons at the backs of their dresses and smaller ones in their hair and on the tips of their wings. They line up in front of the archangel and receive the attention of the rest of the company. The* CHOIR *sings through the ceremony.*] Now den cherubs, why is you yere?

*Children.* Because we so good.

*Archangel.* Dat's right. Now who de big boss?

*Children.* Our dear Lawd.

*Archangel.* Dat's right. When you all grow up what you gonter be?

*Children.* Holy angels at de throne of grace.

*Archangel.* Dat's right. Now, you passed yo' 'xaminations and it gives me great pleasure to hand out de cyards for de whole class. Gineeva Chaproe.

[*The* FIRST GIRL CHERUB *goes to him and gets her diploma. The* CHOIR *sings loudly and resumes marching, as the* ARCHANGEL *calls out another name—and presents diplomas.*] Corey Moulter. [SECOND GIRL CHERUB *gets her diploma.*] Nootzie Winebush. [THIRD GIRL CHERUB.] Harriet Prancy. [FOURTH GIRL CHERUB.] I guess you is Brozain Stew't. [*He gives the* FIFTH GIRL CHERUB *the paper. Each of the presentations has been accompanied by handclapping from the bystanders.*] Now you boys know yo' own names. Suppose you come yere and help me git dese 'sorted right?

[BOY CHERUBS *gather about him and receive their diplomas. The little* GIRLS *have scattered about the stage, joining groups of the adult angels. The angel* GABRIEL *enters. He is bigger and more elaborately winged than even the Archangel, but he is also much younger and beardless. His costume is less conventional than that of the other men, resembling more the Gabriel of the Doré drawings. His appearance causes a flutter among the others. They stop their chattering with the children. The* CHOIR *stops as three or four audible whispers of "Gabriel!" are heard. In a moment the heavenly company is all attention.*]

*Gabriel* (*lifting his hand*). Gangway! Gangway for de Lawd God Jehovah!

[*There is a reverent hush and* GOD *enters. He is the tallest and biggest of them all. He wears a white shirt with a white bow tie, a long Prince Albert coat of black alpaca, black trousers and congress gaiters. He looks at the assemblage. There is a pause. He speaks in a rich, bass voice.*]

*God.* Is you been baptized?

*Others* (*chanting*). Certainly, Lawd.

THE GREEN PASTURES © COPYRIGHT 1936 BY WARNER BROS. PICTURES, INC.

*God.* Is you been baptized?
*Others.* Certainly, Lawd.
*God (with the beginning of musical notation).* Is you been baptized?
*Others (now half-singing).* Certainly, Lawd. Certainly, certainly, certainly, Lawd. (*They sing the last two verses with equivalent part division.*)

Is you been redeemed?
Certainly, Lawd.
Is you been redeemed?
Certainly, Lawd.
Is you been redeemed?
Certainly, Lawd. Certainly, certainly, certainly, Lawd.

Do you bow mighty low?
Certainly, Lawd.
Do you bow mighty low?
Certainly, Lawd.

Do you bow mighty low?
Certainly, Lawd. Certainly, certainly, certainly, Lawd.

[*As the last response ends all heads are bowed.* GOD *looks at them for a moment; then lifts His hand.*]
God. Let de fish fry proceed.
[*Everyone rises. The* ANGELS *relax and resume their inaudible conversations. The activity behind the table and about the cauldron is resumed. Some of the choir members cross to the table and get sandwiches and cups of the boiled custard. Three or four of the children in the Sunday School class and the little girl who had the bone in her throat affectionately group themselves about God as he speaks with the Archangel. He pats their heads, they hang to his coattails, etc.*]

219

*Archangel.* Good mo'nin', Lawd.

*God.* Good mo'nin', Deacon. You lookin' pretty spry.

*Archangel.* I cain' complain. We just been givin' our cyards to de chillun.

God. Dat's good.

[*A small Cherub, his feet braced against one of God's shoes is using God's coattail as a trapeze. One of the* COOKS *offers a fish sandwich which* GOD *politely declines.*]

*First Mammy Angel.* Now, you leave go de Lawd's coat, Herman. You heah me?

*God.* Dat's all right, sister. He jest playin'.

*First Mammy Angel.* He playin' too rough.

[GOD *picks up the cherub and spanks him good-naturedly. The* CHERUB *squeals with delight and runs to his mother.* GABRIEL *advances to* GOD *with a glass of the custard.*]

*Gabriel.* Little b'iled custud, Lawd?

*God.* Thank you very kindly. Dis looks nice.

*Custard Maker (offering a box).* Ten cent seegar, Lawd?

*God (taking it).* Thank you, thank you. How de fish fry goin'? [*Ad lib. cries of "O. K. Lawd," "Fine an' dandy, Lawd," "De best one yit, Lawd," etc. To the choir.*] How you shouters gittin' on?

*Choir Leader.* We been marchin' and singin' de whole mo'nin'.

*God.* I heerd you. You gittin' better all de time. You gittin' as good as de one at de throne. Why don' you give us one dem 'ol time jump-ups?

*Choir Leader.* Anythin' you say, Lawd. (*To the others.*) "So High!"

[*The* CHOIR *begins to sing "So High You Can't Get Over It." They sing softly, but do not march. An* ANGEL *offers his cigar to* GOD *from which He can light His own.*]

*God.* No, thanks. I'm gonter save dis a bit. (*He puts the cigar in his pocket and listens to the singers a moment. Then he sips his custard. After the second sip, a look of displeasure comes on his face.*)

*Gabriel.* What's de matter, Lawd?

*God (sipping again).* I ain't jest sure, yit. Dey's something 'bout dis custahd. (*Takes another sip.*)

*Custard Maker.* Ain't it all right, Lawd?

*God.* It don't seem seasoned jest right. You make it?

*Custard Maker.* Yes, Lawd. I put everythin' in it like I allus do. It's supposed to be perfec'.

*God.* Yeah. I kin taste de eggs and de cream and de sugar. (*Suddenly.*) I know what it is. It needs jest a little bit mo' firmament.

*Custard Maker.* Dey's firmament in it, Lawd.

*God.* Maybe, but it ain' enough.

*Custard Maker.* It's all we had, Lawd. Dey ain't a drap in de jug.

*God.* Dat's all right. I'll jest r'ar back an' pass a miracle. [CHOIR *stops singing.*] Let it be some firmament! An' when I say let it be some firmament, I don't want jest a little bitty dab o' firmament caize I'm sick an' tired of runnin' out of it when we need it. Let it be a whole mess of firmament! [*The stage has become misty until* GOD *and the heavenly company are obscured. As he finishes the speech there is a burst of thunder. As the stage grows darker.*] Dat's de way I like it.

[*Murmurs from the others; "Dat's a lot of firmament." "My dat is firmament!" "Look to me like he's created rain," etc.*]

*First Mammy Angel* (*when the stage is dark*). Now, look Lawd, dat's too much firmament. De cherubs is gettin' all wet.

*Second Mammy Angel.* Look at my Carlotta, Lawd. She's soaked to de skin. Dat's *plenty* too much firmament.

*God.* Well, 'co'se we don't want de chillun to ketch cold. Can't you dreen it off?

*Gabriel.* Dey's no place to dreen it, Lawd.

*First Mammy Angel.* Why don't we jest take de babies home, Lawd?

*God.* No, I don' wanta bust up de fish fry. You angels keep quiet an' I'll pass another miracle. Dat's always de trouble wid miracles. When you pass one you always gotta r'ar back an' pass another. [*There is a hush.*] Let dere be a place to dreen off dis firmament. Let dere be mountains and valleys an' let dere be oceans an' lakes. An' let dere be rivers and bayous to dreen it off in, too. As a matter of fac' let dere be de earth. An' when dat's done let dere be de sun, an' let it come out and dry my cherubs' wings.

[*The lights go up until the stage is bathed in sunlight. On the embankment upstage there is now a waist-high wrought iron railing such as one sees on the galleries of houses in the French quarter of New Orleans. The* CHERUBS *are being examined by their parents and there is an ad lib. murmur of,* "You all right, honey?" "You feel better now, Albert?" "Now you all dry, Vangy?" *until the* ARCHANGEL, *who has been gazing in awe at the railing, drowns them out.*]

*Archangel.* Look yere!

[*There is a rush to the embankment accompanied by exclamations,* "My goodness!" "What's dis?" "I declah!" *etc.* GABRIEL *towers above the group on*

the middle of the embankment. GOD *is wrapped in thought, facing the audience. The* CHOIR *resumes singing* "So High You Can't Get Over It" *softly. The babbling at the balustrade dies away as the people lean over the railing.* GABRIEL *turns and faces* GOD *indicating the earth below the railing with his left hand.*]

*Gabriel.* Do you see it, Lawd?

*God* (*quietly, without turning his head upstage*). Yes, Gabriel.

*Gabriel.* Looks mighty nice, Lawd.

*God.* Yes.

[GABRIEL *turns and looks over the railing.*]

*Gabriel* (*gazing down*). Yes, suh. Dat'd make mighty nice farming country. Jest look at dat south forty over dere. You ain't going to let dat go to waste is you, Lawd? Dat would be a pity an' a shame.

*God* (*not turning*). It's a good earth. [GOD *turns, room is made for him beside* GABRIEL *on the embankment.*] Yes. I ought to have somebody to enjoy it. [*He turns, facing the audience. The others, save for the choir who are lined up in two rows of six on an angle up right, continue to look over the embankment.*] Gabriel! [GOD *steps down from the embankment two paces.*]

*Gabriel* (*joining him*). Yes, Lawd.

*God.* Gabriel, I'm goin' down dere.

*Gabriel.* Yes, Lawd.

*God.* I want you to be my working boss yere while I'm gone.

*Gabriel.* Yes, Lawd.

*God.* You know dat matter of dem two stars?

*Gabriel.* Yes, Lawd.

*God.* Git dat fixed up! You know dat sparrow dat fell a little while ago? 'Tend to dat, too.

*Gabriel.* Yes, Lawd.

*God.* I guess dat's about all. I'll be

back Saddy. (*To the* CHOIR.) Quiet, angels. [*The* CHOIR *stops singing. Those on the embankment circle down stage.* GOD *goes to embankment. Turns and faces the company.*] I'm gonter pass one more miracle. You all gonter help me an' not make a soun' caize it's one of de most impo'tant miracles of all. [*Nobody moves.* GOD *turns, facing the sky and raises his arms above his head.*] Let there be man.

[*There is growing roll of thunder as stage grows dark. The* CHOIR *bursts into "Hallelujah," and continues until the lights go up on the next scene.*]

### SCENE III

*Enclosing the stage is a heterogeneous cluster of cottonwood, camphor, live oak and sycamore trees, youpon and turkey berry bushes, with their purple and red berries, sprays of fern-like indigo fiera and splashes of various Louisiana flowers. In the middle of the stage, disclosed when the mistiness at rise grows into warm sunlight, stands* ADAM. *He is a puzzled man of 30, of medium height, dressed in the clothing of the average field hand. He is bare-headed. In the distance can be heard the choir continuing, "Bright Mansions Above." A bird begins to sing.* ADAM *smiles and turns to look at the source of this novel sound. He senses his strength and raises his forearms, his fists clenched. With his left hand he carefully touches the muscles of his upper right arm. He smiles again, realizing his power. He looks at his feet which are stretched wide apart. He stamps once or twice and now almost laughs in his enjoyment. Other birds begin trilling and* ADAM *glances up joyfully toward the foliage.* GOD *enters.*

*God.* Good mo'nin', Son.
*Adam* (*with a little awe*). Good mo'nin', Lawd.
*God.* What's yo' name, Son?
*Adam.* Adam.
*God.* Adam which?
*Adam* (*frankly, after a moment's puzzled groping*). Jest Adam, Lawd.
*God.* Well, Adam, how dey treatin' you? How things goin'?
*Adam.* Well, Lawd, you know it's kind of a new line of wukk.
*God.* You'll soon get de hang of it. You know yo' kind of a new style with me.
*Adam.* Oh, I guess I'm gonter make out all right soon as I learn de ropes.
*God.* Yes, I guess you will. Yo' a nice job.
*Adam.* Yes, Lawd.
*God.* Dey's jest one little thing de matter with you. Did you notice it?
*Adam.* Well, now you mentioned it, Lawd, I kind of thought dey was somethin' wrong.
*God.* Yes suh, you ain't quite right. Adam, you need a family. De reason for dat is in yo' heart you is a family man. (*Flicking the ash off his cigar.*) I'd say dat was de main trouble at de moment.
*Adam* (*smiling*). Yes sir. (*His smile fades and he is puzzled again.*) At de same time—dey's one thing puzzlin' me, Lawd. Could I ask you a question?
*God.* Why, certainly, Adam.
*Adam.* Lawd, jest what *is* a family?
*God.* I'm gonter show you. (*Indicates a spot.*) Jest lie down dere, Adam. Make out like you was goin' to slumber.
*Adam* (*gently*). Yes, Lawd.
[*He lies down.* GOD *stands beside him and as he raises his arms above his head the lights go down. In the darkness* GOD *speaks.*]

*God.* Eve. [*Lights go up.* EVE *is standing beside* ADAM. *She is about twenty-six, and quite pretty. She is dressed like a country girl. Her gingham dress is quite new and clean.* GOD *is now at the other side of the stage, looking at them critically.* EVE *looks at* ADAM *in timid wonder and slowly turns her head until she meets the glance of* GOD. ADAM *stands beside* EVE. *They gaze at each other for a moment.* GOD *smiles.*] Now you all right, Eve. [ADAM *and* EVE *face him.*] Now I'll tell you what I'm gonter do. I'm gonter put you in charge here. I'm gonter give you de run of dis whole garden. Eve, you take care of dis man an' Adam you take care of dis woman. You belong to each other. I don' want you to try to do too much caize yo' both kind of experiment wid me an' I ain't sho' whether you could make it. You two jest enjoy yo'self. Drink de water from de little brooks an' de wine from de grapes an' de berries, an' eat de food dat's hangin' for you in de trees. (*He pauses, startled by a painful thought.*) Dat is, in all but one tree. (*He pauses. Then, not looking at them.*) You know what I mean, my children?

*Adam and Eve.* Yes, Lawd. (*They slowly turn their heads left, toward the branches of an offstage tree. Then they look back at* GOD.)

*Adam.* Thank you, Lawd.

*Eve.* Thank you, Lawd.

*God.* I gotter be gittin' along now. I got a hund'ed thousan' things to do' fo' you take yo' nex' breath. Enjoy yo'-selves—

[GOD *exits.*]

[ADAM *and* EVE *stand looking after Him for a moment, then each looks down and watches their hands meet and clasp.*]

[*After a moment they lift their heads slowly until they are again gazing at the tree.*]

*Eve.* Adam.

*Adam* (*looking at the tree, almost in terror*). What?

*Eve* (*softly as she too continues to look at the tree*). Adam.

[*The* CHOIR *begins singing "Turn You Round" and as the lights go down the* CHOIR *continues until there is blackness. The* CHOIR *suddenly stops. The following scene is played in the darkness.*]

*Mr. Deshee's Voice.* Now, I s'pose you chillun know what happened after God made Adam 'n' Eve. Do you?

*First Girl's Voice.* I know, Mr. Deshee.

*Mr. Deshee's Voice.* Jest a minute, Randolph. Didn't I tell you you gotta tell yo' mammy let yo' sister bring you. Carlisle, take way dat truck he's eatin'. You sit by him, see kin you keep him quiet. Now, den, Myrtle what happened?

*First Girl's Voice.* Why den dey ate de fo'bidden fruit and den dey got driv' out de garden.

*Mr. Deshee's Voice.* An' den what happened?

*First Girl's Voice.* Den dey felt ver' bad.

*Mr. Deshee's Voice.* I don' mean how dey feel, I mean how dey do. Do dey have any children or anything like dat?

*First Girl's Voice.* Oh, yes, suh, dey have Cain 'n' Abel.

*Mr. Deshee's Voice.* Dat's right, dey have Cain an' Abel.

*Boy's Voice.* Dat was a long time after dey got married, wasn't it, Mr. Deshee? My mammy say it was a hund'ed years.

*Mr. Deshee's Voice.* Well, nobody kin be so sure. As I tol' you befo' dey was jest beginnin' to be able to tell de time an' nobody was any too sure 'bout anythin' even den. So de bes' thing to do is jest realize dat de thing happened an' don't bother 'bout how many years it was. Jest remember what I told you about it gittin' dark when you go to sleep an' it bein' light when you wake up. Dat's de way time went by in dem days. One thing we do know an' dat was dis boy Cain was a mean rascal.

[*The lights go up on the next scene.*]

### SCENE IV

*A roadside.*

CAIN, *a husky young Negro, stands over the body of the dead* ABEL. *Both are dressed as laborers.* CAIN *is looking at the body in awe, a rock in his right hand.* GOD *enters.*

*God.* Cain, look what you done to Abel.

*Cain.* Lawd, I was min'in' my own business and he come monkeyin' aroun' wit' me. I was wukkin' in de fiel' an' he was sittin' in de shade of de tree. He say "Me, I'd be skeered to git out in dis hot sun. I be 'fraid my brains git cooked. Co'se you ain't got no brains so you ain' in no danger." An' so I up and flang de rock. If it miss 'im all right, an' if it hit 'im, all right. Dat's de way I feel.

*God.* All right, but I'm yere to tell you dat's called a crime. When de new Judge is done talkin' to you you'll be draggin' a ball and chain de rest of yo' life.

*Cain.* Well, what'd he want to come monkeyin' aroun' me fo' den? I was jest plowin', min'in' my own business, and not payin' him no min', and yere he come makin' me de fool. I'd bust anybody what make me de fool.

*God.* Well, I ain't sayin' you right an' I ain't sayin' you wrong. But I do say was I you I'd jest git myself down de road 'til I was clean out of de county. An' you better take an' git married an' settle down an' raise some chillun. Dey ain't nothin' to make a man fo'git his troubles like raisin' a family. Now, you better git.

*Cain.* Yessuh.

[CAIN *walks off.*]

[GOD *watches him from the forestage and as the lights begin to dim looks off. The* CHOIR *begins "Run, Sinner, Run."*]

*God.* Adam an' Eve you better try again. You better have Seth an' a lot mo' chillun.

[*There is darkness. The* CHOIR *continues until the lights go up on the next scene.*]

### SCENE V

CAIN *is discovered walking on an unseen treadmill. A middle distance of trees, hillsides and shrubbery passes him on an upper treadmill. Behind is the blue sky. He stops under the branches of a tree to look at a sign on a fence railing. Only half the tree is visible on the stage. The sign reads,* "NOD PARISH. COUNTY LINE." [1]

*Cain* (*sitting down with a sigh of relief under the tree*). At las'! Phew! (*Wipes his forehead with a handkerchief.*) Feels like I been walkin' fo'ty years. (*He looks back.*) Well, dey cain' git me now. Now I kin raise a fam'ly. (*An idea occurs to him, and suddenly he begins looking right and left.*) Well, I'll be hit by a mule! Knock me down for a trustin' baby! Where I gonter git dat fam'ly? Dat preacher fooled me. (*He is quite dejected.*) Doggone!

[1] NOD PARISH—Nod is the land to which Cain fled after slaying Abel (Genesis 4:16). In Louisiana the term parish is used instead of the more common term, county.

*Cain's Girl (off stage).* Hello, Country Boy!

[CAIN *glances up to the offstage branches of the tree.*]

*Cain.* Hey-ho, Good Lookin'! Which way is it to town?

*Cain's Girl (off stage).* What you tryin' to do? You tryin' to mash me? I be doggone if it ain't gittin' so a gal cain't hardly leave de house 'out some of dese fast men ain' passin' remarks at her.

*Cain.* I ain' passin' remarks.

*Cain's Girl (off stage).* If I thought you was tryin' to mash me, I'd call de police an' git you tooken to de first precinct.

*Cain.* Look yere, gal, I ast you a question, an' if you don' answer me I'm gonter bend you 'cross my pants an' burn you up.

*Cain's Girl (off stage).* I'm comin' down.

[CAIN *takes his eyes from the tree.*]

*Cain.* Yes, an' you better hurry.

[CAIN'S GIRL *enters. She is as large as* CAIN, *wickedly pretty, and somewhat flashily dressed. She smiles at* CAIN.]

*Cain's Girl.* I bet you kin handle a gal mean wid dem big stout arms of your'n. I sho' would hate to git you mad at me, Country Boy.

*Cain (smiling).* Come yere. [*She goes a little closer to him.*] Don't be 'fraid, I ain' so mean.

*Cain's Girl.* You got two bad lookin' eyes. I bet yo' hot coffee 'mong de women folks.

*Cain.* I ain' never find out. What was you doin' in dat tree?

*Cain's Girl.* Jest coolin' myself in de element.

*Cain.* Is you a Nod Parish gal?

*Cain's Girl.* Bo'n an' bred.

*Cain.* You know yo' kinda pretty.

*Cain's Girl.* Who tol' you dat?

*Cain.* Dese yere two bad eyes of mine.

*Cain's Girl.* I bet you say dat to everybody all de way down de road.

*Cain.* Comin' down dat road I didn't talk to nobody.

*Cain's Girl.* Where you boun' for, Beautiful?

*Cain.* I'm jest seein' de country. I thought I might settle down yere fo' a spell. You live wit' yo' people?

*Cain's Girl.* Co'se I does.

*Cain.* 'Spose dey'd like to take in a boarder?

*Cain's Girl.* Be nice if dey would, wouldn' it?

*Cain.* I think so. You got a beau?

*Cain's Girl.* Huh-uh!

*Cain (smiling).* You has *now*.

*Cain's Girl.* I guess—I guess if you wanted to kiss me an' I tried to stop you, you could pretty nearly crush me wit' dem stout arms.

*Cain.* You wouldn't try too much, would you?

*Cain's Girl.* Maybe for a little while.

*Cain.* An' den what?

*Cain's Girl.* Why don' we wait an' see?

*Cain.* When would dat be?

*Cain's Girl.* Tonight. After supper. Think you kin walk a little further now, City Boy?

*Cain.* Yeh, I ain't so weary now.

[*She takes his hand.*]

*Cain's Girl.* What yo' name? (*Takes his arm.*)

*Cain.* Cain.

*Cain's Girl.* Then I'm Cain's gal. Come on, honey, an' meet de folks.

[*They exit.*]

[*The choir is heard singing "You Better Mind," as* GOD *enters.* GOD *watches the vanished* CAIN *and his girl.*]

*God (after shaking his head).* Bad

225

business. I don' like de way things is goin' atall.

[*The stage is darkened.*]

[*The* CHOIR *continues singing until the lights go up on the next scene.*]

SCENE VI

GOD's *private office in Heaven. It is a small room, framed by tableau curtains. A large window up center looks out on the sky. There is a battered roll-top desk. On the wall next to the window is a framed religious oleograph with a calendar attached to it underneath. A door is at the left. A hat rack is on the wall above the door. There are two or three cheap pine chairs beside the window, and beyond the door. In front of the desk is an old swivel armchair which creaks every time* GOD *leans back in it. The desk is open and various papers are stuck in the pigeonholes. Writing implements, etc. are on the desk. On a shelf above the desk is a row of law books. A cuspidor is near the desk, and a waste basket by it. The general atmosphere is that of the office of a Negro lawyer in a Louisiana town. As the lights go up* GOD *takes a fresh cigar from a box on the desk and begins puffing it without bothering to light it. There is no comment on this minor miracle from* GABRIEL *who is sitting in one of the chairs with a pencil and several papers in his hand. The singing becomes pianissimo.*

*Gabriel* (*looking at the papers*). Well, I guess dat's about all de impo'tant business this mornin', Lawd.

*God.* How 'bout dat cherub over to Archangel Montgomery's house?

*Gabriel.* Where do dey live, Lawd?

[*The singing stops.*]

*God.* Dat little two story gold house, over by de pearly gates.

*Gabriel.* Oh, *dat* Montgomery. I thought you was referrin' to de ol' gentleman. Oh, yeh. (*He sorts through the papers and finds one he is looking for.*) Yere it 'tis. (*Reads.*) "Cherub Christina Montgomery; wings is moltin' out of season an' nobody know what to do."

*God.* Well, now, take keer of dat. You gotter be more careful, Gabe.

*Gabriel.* Yes, Lawd.

[*Folds the papers and puts them in a pocket.* GOD *turns to his desk, takes another puff or two of the cigar, and with a pencil, begins checking off items on a sheet of paper before him. His back is turned toward* GABRIEL. GABRIEL *takes his trumpet from the hat rack and burnishes it with his robe. He then wets his lips and puts the mouthpiece to his mouth.*]

*God* (*without turning around*). Now, watch yo'self, Gabriel.

*Gabriel.* I wasn't goin' to blow, Lawd. I jest do dat every now an' den so I can keep de feel of it.

[*He leans trumpet against the wall.* GOD *picks up the papers and swings his chair around toward* GABRIEL.]

*God.* What's dis yere about de moon?

*Gabriel* (*suddenly remembering*). Oh! De moon people say it's beginnin' to melt a little, on 'count caize de sun's so hot.

*God.* It's goin' 'roun' 'cordin' to schedule, ain't it?

*Gabriel.* Yes, Lawd.

*God.* Well, tell 'em to stop groanin'. Dere's nothin' de matter wid dat moon. Trouble is so many angels is flyin' over dere on Saddy night. Dey git to beatin' dere wings when dey dancin' an' dat makes de heat. Tell dem dat from now on dancin' 'roun' de moon is sinnin'. Dey got to stop it. Dat'll cool off de

moon. (*He swings back and puts the paper on the desk. He leans back in the chair comfortably, his hands clasped behind his head.*) Is dere anythin' else you ought to remin' me of?

*Gabriel.* De prayers, Lawd.

*God* (*puzzled, slowly swinging chair around again*). De prayers?

*Gabriel.* From mankind. You know, down on de earth.

*God.* Oh, yeh, de poor little earth. Bless my soul, I almos' forgot about dat. Mus' be three or four hund'ed years since I been down dere. I wasn't any too pleased wid dat job.

*Gabriel* (*laughing*). You know you don' make mistakes, Lawd.

*God* (*soberly, with introspective detachment*). So dey tell me. (*He looks at* GABRIEL, *then through the window again.*) So dey tell me. I fin' I kin be displeased though, an' I was displeased wid de mankind I las' seen. Maybe I

ought to go down dere agin—I need a little holiday.

*Gabriel.* Might do you good, Lawd.

*God.* I think I will. I'll go down an' walk de earth agin an' see how dem poor humans is makin' out. What time is it, by de sun an' de stars?

*Gabriel* (*glancing out of the window*). Jest exactly half-past, Lawd.

[GOD *is taking his hat and stick from the hat rack.*]

*God* (*opening the door*). Well, take keer o' yo'self. I'll be back Saddy. (*He exits.*)

[*The stage is darkened. The* CHOIR *begins "Dere's no Hidin' Place," and continues until the lights go up on the next scene.*]

### SCENE VII

GOD *is walking along a country road. He stops to listen. Church bells are heard in the distance.*

*God.* Dat's nice. Nice an' quiet. Dat's de way I like Sunday to be. [*The sound is broken by a shrill voice of a girl. It is* ZEBA [2] *singing a "blues."*] Now, dat ain't so good. [GOD *resumes his walk and the upper treadmill brings on a tree stump on which* ZEBA *is sitting. She is accompanying her song with a ukulele.* GOD *and the treadmills stop. When the stump reaches the center of the stage, it is seen that* ZEBA *is a rouged and extremely flashily dressed chippy of about eighteen.*] Stop dat!

*Zeba.* What's de matter wid you, Country Boy? Pull up yo' pants. (*She resumes singing.*)

*God.* Stop dat!

*Zeba* (*stops again*). Say, listen to me, Banjo Eyes. What right you got to stop a lady enjoyin' herself?

*God.* Don't you know dis is de Sabbath? Da's no kin' o' song to sing on de Lawd's day.

*Zeba.* Who care 'bout de Lawd's day, anymo'? People jest use Sunday now to git over Saddy.

*God.* You a awful sassy little girl.

*Zeba.* I come fum sassy people! We even speak mean of de dead.

*God.* What's yo' name?

*Zeba* (*flirtatiously*). "What's my name?" Ain't you de ol'-time gal hunter! Fust, "What's my name?" den I s'pose, what would it be like if you tried to kiss me? You preachers is de debbils.

*God.* I ain't aimin' to touch you, daughter. [*A sudden sternness frightens* ZEBA. *She looks at him sharply.*] What is yo' name?

*Zeba.* Zeba.

*God.* Who's yo' fam'ly?

*Zeba.* I'm de great-great gran' daughter of Seth.

*God.* Of Seth? But Seth was a good man.

*Zeba.* Yeh, he too good, he die of holiness.

*God.* An' yere's his little gran' daughter reekin' wid cologne. Ain't nobody ever tol' you yo' on de road to Hell?

*Zeba* (*smiling*). Sho' dat's what de preacher say. Exceptin' of course, I happens to know dat I'm on de road to de picnic groun's, an' at de present time I'm waitin' to keep a engagement wid my sweet papa. He don' like people talkin' to me.

[CAIN THE SIXTH *enters. He is a swaggering young buck, wearing a "box" coat and the other flashy garments of a Rampart Street swell.*]

*Cain the Sixth.* Hello, sugah! (*He crosses in front of* GOD *and faces* ZEBA.) Hello, mamma! Sorry I'm late, baby, but de gals in de barrel-house jest wouldn't let me go. Doggone, one little wirehead swore she'd tear me down.

[ZEBA *smiles and takes his hand.*]

*God.* What's yo' name, son?

*Cain the Sixth* (*contemptuously; without turning*). Soap'n water, Country Boy.

*God* (*sternly*). What's yo' name, son?

[CAIN *slowly turns and for a moment his manner is civil.*]

*Cain the Sixth.* Cain the Sixth.

*God.* I was afraid so.

*Cain the Sixth* (*his impudence returning*). You a new preacher?

*God.* Where you live?

*Cain the Sixth.* Me, I live mos' any place.

*God.* Yes, an' you gonter see dem all. Is de udder young men all like you?

---

[2] ZEBA—The characters Zeba, Hezdrel, and many others in the play are the brain-children of the author, and are not to be thought of as actual people in the Bible.

*Cain the Sixth (smiling).* De gals don' think so.

[*He turns towards* ZEBA *again, picks her up and sits on the stump with the laughing* ZEBA *on his lap.*]

*Zeba.* Dey ain't nobody in de worl' like my honey-cake.

[CAIN *kisses her and she resumes her song.*]

[GOD *watches them.* ZEBA *finishes a verse of the song and begins another softly.* CAIN THE SIXTH's *eyes have been closed during the singing.*]

*Cain the Sixth (his eyes closed).* Is de preacher gone?

[ZEBA *looks quickly at* GOD *without seeing him, and then looks off. She stops the song.*]

*Zeba.* Yeh, I guess he walks fast.

[CAIN *pushes her off his lap and rises.*]

*Cain the Sixth (with acid sweetness).* Dey tell me las' night you was talkin' to a creeper man, baby.

*Zeba.* Why, you know dey ain't no-body in de world fo' me but you.

*Cain the Sixth (smiling).* I know dey ain't. I even got dat guaranteed. (*He takes a revolver from his pocket.*) See dat, baby?

*Zeba.* Sho' I see it, honey.

*Cain the Sixth.* Dat jest makes me positive. (*Puts the gun back.*)

*Zeba (pushing him back on the stump).* You don' wanter believe dem stories, papa.

*Cain the Sixth (with sinister light-ness).* No, I didn't believe dem, baby. Co'se dat big gorilla, Flatfoot, from de other side of de river *is* in town ag'in.

*Zeba.* Dat don' mean nothin'. Flat-foot ain't nothin' to me.

*Cain the Sixth (sitting again).* Co'se he ain't. Go 'head, sing some mo', baby.

[ZEBA *resumes singing.*]

*God.* Bad business. [*The treadmills*

start *turning.* GOD *resumes his walk.* ZEBA, *still singing, and* CAIN THE SIXTH *recede with the landscape.* GOD *is again alone on the country road. There is a twitter of birds.* GOD *looks up and smiles.*] De birds is goin' 'bout dere business, all right. [*A patch of flowers goes by, black-eyed Susans, conspicu-ously.*] How you flowers makin' out? [*Children's voices answer,* "We O.K., Lawd."] Yes, an' you looks very pretty. [*Children's voices:* "Thank you, Lawd." *The flowers pass out of sight.*] It's only de human bein's makes me down-hearted. Yere's as nice a Sunday as dey is turnin' out anywhere, an' nobody makin' de right use of it. [*Something ahead of him attracts his attention. His face brightens.*] Well, now dis is mo' like it. Now dat's nice to see people prayin'. It's a wonder dey don' do it in de church. But I fin' I don' min' it if dey do it outdoors.

[*A group of five adult Negroes and a boy on their knees in a semicircle, ap-pears. The treadmills stop. The* BOY, *his head bent, swings his hands rhyth-mically up to his head three or four times. There is a hush.*]

*Gambler.* Oh, Lawd, de smoke-house is empty. Oh, Lawd, lemme git dem groceries. Oh, Lawd, lemme see dat lit-tle six. (*He casts the dice.*) Wham! Dere she is, frien's.

[*Exclamations from the others:* "Well damn my eyes!" "Doggone, dat's de eighth pass he make." *The* BOY *is picking up the money.*]

*God.* Gamblin'! (*Looks over the group's shoulders.*) An' wid frozen[3] dice!

*Boy Gambler.* Dey's a dolla' 'n' a half talkin' fo' me. How much you want of it, Riney?

---

[3] FROZEN DICE—Loaded dice.

THE GREEN PASTURES © COPYRIGHT 1936 BY WARNER BROS. PICTURES, INC

*First Gambler.* I take fo' bits. Wait a minute. Mebbe I take a little mo'. (*He counts some money in his hand.*)

*Second Gambler* (*glancing up at* GOD). Hello, Liver Lips. (*To the others.*) Looka ol' Liver Lips.

[*The others look up and laugh goodnaturedly, repeating "Liver Lips."*]

*First Gambler.* Ain't his pockets high from de groun'? Ol' High-Pockets.

[*The others keep saying "Ole Liver Lips." "Ol' Liver Lips don't like to see people dicin'." "Dats a good name, 'High Pockets.'"*]

*Boy Gambler* (*to others*). Come on, you gonter fade me or not?

[GOD *seizes the boy's ears and drags him to his feet. The others do not move, but watch, amused.*]

*God.* Come yere, son. Why, yo' jest a little boy. Gamblin' an' sinnin'.

(GOD *looks at the boy's face.*) You been chewin' tobacco, too, like you was yo' daddy. (GOD *sniffs.*) An' you been drinkin' sonny-kick-mammy-wine. You oughta be 'shamed. (*To the others.*) An' you gamblers oughta be 'shamed, leadin' dis boy to sin.

*First Gambler.* He de bes' crap shooter in town, mister.

*God.* I'm gonter tell his mammy. I bet she don' know 'bout dis.

*First Gambler.* No, she don' know. [*The others laugh.*] She don' know anythin'.

*Second Gambler.* Das de God's truth.

*First Gambler.* See kin you beat 'im, High Pockets. Dey's a dolla' open yere.

*God.* I ain't gonter beat 'im. I'm gonter teach 'im. I may have to teach you all.

[*He starts walking from them. The*

BOY *sticks out his tongue the moment* GOD's *back is turned.*]

*Boy Gambler.* If you fin' my mammy you do mo'n I kin. Come on, gamblers, see kin you gimme a little action. Who wants any part of dat dollar?

[*The treadmill carries them off. The* FIRST GAMBLER *is heard saying: "I'll take anoder two bits," and the others, "Gimme a dime's wo'th," "I ain't only got fifteen cents left," etc. as they disappear.*]

*God* (*walking*). Where's dat little boy's home? [*The front of a shanty appears and* GOD *stops in front of the door.*] Yere's de place. It ain't any too clean, either. (*Knocks on the door with his cane.*)

*Voice in Shanty.* Who dar?

*God.* Never you min' who's yere. Open de door.

*Voice in Shanty.* You gotta search warrant?

*God.* I don' need one.

*Voice in Shanty.* Who you wanter see?

*God.* I wanter see de mammy of de little gamblin' boy.

*Voice in Shanty.* You mean little Johnny Rucker?

*God.* Dat may be his name.

*Voice in Shanty.* Well, Mrs. Rucker ain't home.

*God.* Where's she at?

*Voice in Shanty.* Who, Mrs. Rucker?

*God.* You heerd me.

*Voice in Shanty.* Oh, she run away las' night wid a railroad man. She's eloped.

*God.* Where's Rucker?

*Voice in Shanty.* He's flat under de table. He so drunk he cain't move.

*God.* Who are you?

*Voice in Shanty.* I'se jest a fren' an' neighbor. I come in las' night to de party, an' everybody in yere's dead drunk but me. De only reason I kin talk is I drank some new white mule I made myself, an' it burn my throat so I can't drink no mo'. You got any mo' questions?

*God.* Not for you.

[*The shanty begins to move off as* GOD *starts walking again.*]

*Voice in Shanty.* Good riddance, I say.

[*Shanty disappears.*]

*God.* Dis ain't gittin' me nowheres. All I gotta say dis yere mankind I been peoplin' my earth wid sho' ain't much. (*He stops and looks back.*) I got good min' to wipe 'em all off an' people de earth wid angels. No. Angels is all right, singin' an' playin' an' flyin' around, but dey ain't much on workin' de crops and building de levees. No, suh, mankind's jest right for my earth, if he wasn't so doggone sinful. I'd rather have my earth peopled wit' a bunch of channel catfish, dan I would mankin' an' his sin. I jest cain't stan' sin.

[*He is about to resume his walk when* NOAH *enters.* NOAH *is dressed like a country preacher. His coat is of the "hammer-tail" variety. He carries a prayer book under his arm.*]

*Noah.* Mo'nin', brother.

*God.* Mo'nin', brother. I declare you look like a good man.

*Noah.* I try to be, brother. I'm de preacher yere. I don't think I seen you to de meetin'.

[*They resume walking.*]

*God.* I jest come to town a little while ago an' I been pretty busy.

*Noah.* Yeh, mos' everybody say dey's pretty busy dese days. Dey so busy dey cain't come to meetin'. It seem like de mo' I preaches de mo' people ain't got time to come to church. I ain't hardly got enough members to fill up de choir. I gotta do de preachin' an' de bassin' too.

*God.* Is dat a fac'?

*Noah.* Yes, suh, brother. Everybody is mighty busy, gamblin', good-timin', an' goin' on. You jest wait, though. When Gabriel blow de horn you gonter fin' dey got plenty of time to punch chunks down in Hell. Yes, suh.

*God.* Seems a pity. Dey all perfec'ly healthy?

*Noah.* Oh, dey healthy, all right. Dey jest all lazy, and mean, and full of sin. You look like a preacher, too, brother.

*God.* Well, I am, in a way.

*Noah.* You jest passin' through de neighborhood?

*God.* Yes. I wanted to see how things was goin' in yo' part of de country, an' I been feelin' jest 'bout de way you do. It's enough to discourage you.

*Noah.* Yes, but I gotta keep wres'lin' wid 'em. Where you boun' for right now, brother?

*God.* I was jest walkin' along. I thought I might stroll on to de nex' town.

*Noah.* Well, dat's a pretty good distance. I live right yere. (*He stops walking.*) Why don' you stop an' give us de pleasure of yo' comp'ny for dinner? I believe my ol' woman has kilt a chicken.

*God.* Why, dat's mighty nice of you, brother. I don' believe I caught yo' name.

*Noah.* Noah, jest brother Noah. Dis is my home, brother. Come right in.

[GOD *and* NOAH *start walking towards Noah's house which is just coming into view on the treadmill.*]

[*The stage darkens, the* CHOIR *sings*

"*Feastin' Table," and when the lights go up again, the next scene is disclosed.*]

*Interior of Noah's house. The ensemble suggests the combination living-dining room in a fairly prosperous Negro's cabin. Clean white curtains hang at the window. A table and chairs are in the center of the room. There is a cheerful checked tablecloth on the table, and on the wall, a framed, highly colored picture reading "God Bless Our Home."*

NOAH'S WIFE, *an elderly Negress, simply and neatly dressed,* GOD *and* NOAH *are discovered grouped about the table.*

*Noah.* Company, darlin'. [*Noah's wife takes Noah's and God's hats.*] Dis gemman's a preacher, too. He's jest passin' through de country.

*God.* Good mo'nin', sister.

*Noah's Wife.* Good mo'nin'. You jest ketch me when I'm gittin' dinner ready. You gonter stay with us?

*God.* If I ain't intrudin'. Brother Noah suggested—

*Noah's Wife.* You set right down yere. I got a chicken in de pot an' it'll be ready in 'bout five minutes. I'll go out de back an' call Shem, Ham, 'n' Japheth. (*To* GOD.) Dey's our sons. Dey live right acrost de way but always have Sunday dinner wid us. You mens make yo'selves comf'table.

*God.* Thank you, thank you very kindly.

*Noah.* You run along, we all right. [GOD *and* NOAH *seat themselves.* NOAH'S WIFE *exits.*]

*God.* You got a fine wife, Brother Noah.

*Noah.* She pretty good woman.

*God.* Yes, suh, an' you got a nice little home. Have a ten cent seegar? (GOD *offers him one.*)

*Noah.* Thank you, much obliged.

[*Both men lean back restfully in their chairs.*]

*God.* Jest what seems to be de main trouble 'mong mankind, Noah?

*Noah.* Well, it seems to me de main trouble is dat de whol' distric' is wide open. Now you know dat makes fo' loose livin'. Men folks spen's all dere time fightin', loafin' an' gamblin', an' makin' bad likker.

*God.* What about de women?

*Noah.* De women is worse dan de men. If dey ain't makin' love powder dey out beg, borrow an' stealin' money for policy tickets. Doggone, I come in de church Sunday 'fo' las' 'bout an' hour befo' de meetin' was to start, and dere was a woman stealin' de altar cloth. She was goin' to hock it. Dey ain't got no moral sense. Now you take dat case las' month, over in East Putney. Case of dat young Willy Roback.

*God.* What about him?

*Noah.* Dere is a boy sebenteen years old. Doggone, if he didn't elope with a growed woman. Now, you know, dat kin' of goin' on is bad fo' a neighborhood.

*God.* Terrible, terrible.

*Noah.* Yes, suh. Dis use' to be a nice, decent community. I been doin' my best to preach de Word, but seems like every time I preach de place jest goes a little mo' to de dogs. De good Lawd only knows what's gonter happen.

*God.* Dat is de truth.

[*There is a pause. Each puffs his cigar. Suddenly* NOAH *grasps his knee, as if it were paining him, and twists his foot.*]

*Noah.* Huh!

*God.* What's de matter?

*Noah.* I jest got a twitch. My buck-

aguer I guess. Every now and den I gets a twitch in de knee. Might be a sign of rain.

*God.* That's just what it is. Noah, what's de mos' rain you ever had 'round dese parts?

*Noah.* Well, de water come down fo' six days steady last April an' de ribber got so swole it bust down de levee up 'bove Freeport. Raise cain all de way down to de delta.

*God.* What would you say was it to rain for forty days and forty nights?

*Noah.* I'd say dat was a *complete* rain!

*God.* Noah, you don't know who I is, do you?

*Noah* (*puzzled*). Yo' face looks easy, but I don' think I recall de name. [GOD *rises slowly, and as he reaches his full height there is a crash of lightning, a moment's darkness, and a roll of thunder. It grows light again.* NOAH *is on his knees in front of* GOD.] I should have known you. I should have seen de glory.

*God.* Dat's all right, Noah. You didn' know who I was.

*Noah.* I'm jes' ol' preacher Noah, Lawd, an' I'm yo' servant. I ain' very much, but I'se all I got.

*God.* Sit down, Noah. Don' let me hear you shamin' yo'se'f, caize yo' a good man. [*Timidly* NOAH *waits until* GOD *is seated, and then sits, himself.*] I jest wanted to fin' out if you was good, Noah. Dat's why I'm walkin' de earth in de shape of a natchel man. I wish dey was mo' people like you. But, far as I kin see you and yo' fam'ly is de only respectable people in de worl'.

*Noah.* Dey jest all poor sinners, Lawd.

*God.* I know. I am your Lawd. I am a God of wrath and vengeance an' dat's why I'm gonter destroy dis worl'.

*Noah (almost in a whisper; drawing back).* Jest as you say, Lawd.

*God.* I ain't gonter destroy you, Noah. You and yo' fam'ly, yo' sheep an' cattle, an' all de udder things dat ain't human I'm gonter preserve. But de rest is gotta go. *(Takes a pencil and a sheet of paper from his pocket.)* Look yere, Noah. [NOAH *comes over and looks over his shoulder.*] I want you to build me a boat. I want you to call it de "Ark," and I want it to look like dis. *(He is drawing on the paper. Continues to write as he speaks.)* I want you to take two of every kind of animal and bird dat's in de country. I want you to take seeds an' sprouts an' everythin' like dat an' put dem on dat Ark, because dere is gonter be all dat rain. Dey's gonter to be a deluge, Noah, an' dey's goin' to be a flood. De levees is gonter bust an' everything dat's fastened down is comin' loose, but it ain't gonter float long, caize I'm gonter make a storm dat'll sink everythin' from a hencoop to a barn. Dey ain't a ship on de sea dat'll be able to fight dat tempest. Dey all got to go. Everythin'. Everythin' in dis pretty worl' I made, except one thing, Noah. You an' yo' fam'ly an' de things I said are going to ride dat storm in de Ark. Yere's de way it's to be. [*He hands* NOAH *the paper.* NOAH *takes it and reads.*]

*Noah (pause; looks at paper again).* Yes, suh, dis seems to be complete. Now 'bout the animals, Lawd, you say you want everythin'?

*God.* Two of everythin'.

*Noah.* Dat would include jayraffes an' hippopotamusses?

*God.* Everythin' dat is.

*Noah.* Dey was a circus in town las' week. I guess I kin fin' dem. Co'se I kin git all de rabbits an' possums an' wil' turkeys easy. I'll sen' de boys out.

Hum, I'm jest wonderin'—

*God.* 'Bout what?

*Noah.* 'Bout snakes? Think you'd like snakes, too?

*God.* Certainly, I want snakes.

*Noah.* Oh, I kin git snakes, lots of 'em. Co'se, some of 'em's a little dangerous. Maybe I better take a kag of likker, too?

*God.* You kin have a kag of likker.

*Noah (musingly).* Yes, suh, dey's a awful lot of differ'nt kin's of snakes, come to think about it. Dey's water moccasins, cottonmoufs, rattlers—mus' be a hund'ed kin's of other snakes down in de swamps. Maybe I better take two kags of likker.

*God (mildly).* I think de one kag's enough.

*Noah.* No. I better take two kags. Besides I kin put one on each side of de boat, an' balance de ship wid dem as well as havin' dem fo' medicinal use.

*God.* You kin put one kag in de middle of de ship.

*Noah (buoyantly).* Jest as easy to take de two kags, Lawd.

*God.* I think one kag's enough.

*Noah.* Yes, Lawd, but you see forty days an' forty nights—

[*There is a distant roll of thunder.*]

*God (firmly).* One kag, Noah.

*Noah.* Yes, Lawd. One kag.

[*The door in the back opens and* NOAH'S WIFE *enters with a tray of dishes and food.*]

*Noah's Wife.* Now, den, gen'lemen, if you'll jest draw up cheers.

[*The stage is darkened. The* CHOIR *is heard singing "I Want to Be Ready." They continue in the darkness until the lights go up on the next scene.*]

SCENE IX

*In the middle of the stage is the Ark. On the hillside, below the Ark, a dozen or more men and women, townspeople, are watching* NOAH, SHEM, HAM, *and* JAPHETH *on the deck of the Ark. The three sons are busily nailing boards on the cabin.* NOAH *is smoking a pipe. He wears a silk hat, captain's uniform and a "slicker."*

*Noah* (*to* SHEM). You, Shem, tote up some ol' rough lumber, don' bring up any planed up lumber, caize dat ain't fo' de main deck.

*Shem.* Pretty near supper time, daddy.

*Noah.* Maybe 'tis, but I got de feelin' we ought to keep goin'.

*First Woman.* You gonter work all night, Noah, maybe, huh?

*Noah* (*without looking at her*). If de sperrit move me.

*Second Woman.* Look here, Noah, whyn't you give up all dis damn foolishness? Don' you know people sayin' yo' crazy? What you think you doin' anyway?

*Noah.* I'se buildin' a Ark. [*Other men and women join those in the foreground.*] Ham, you better stop for a while 'n see whether dey bringin' de animals up all right. (*He looks at his watch.*) Dey ought to be pretty near de foot o' de hill by dis time; if dey ain't you wait fo' dem and bring 'em yo'se'f.

[HAM *goes down a ladder at the side of the ship and exits during the following scene. The newcomers in group have been speaking to some of the early arrivals.*]

*Second Woman* (*to* THIRD WOMAN, *one of the newcomers*). No, you don't mean it!

*Third Woman.* I do so. Dat's what de talk is in de town.

*First Man.* You hear dat, Noah? Dey say yo' ol' lady is tellin' everybody it's gonter rain fo' fo'ty days and fo'ty

nights. You know people soon gonter git de idea you *all* crazy.

*Noah.* Lot I keer what you think. (*To* JAPHETH.) Straighten up dem boards down dere, Japheth. (*Indicates floor of deck.*)

*First Man* (*to* THIRD WOMAN). Was I you, I wouldn' go 'round with Mrs. Noah anymore, lady. Fust thing you know you'll be gittin' a hard name, too.

*Third Woman.* Don' I know?

*Second Woman.* A lady cain't be too partic'lar dese days.

[ZEBA *and* FLATFOOT, *a tall, black, wicked-looking buck, enter, their arms around each other's waist.*]

*Zeba.* Dere it is baby. Was I lyin'?

*Flatfoot.* Well, I'll be split in two!

*First Man.* What you think of it, Flatfoot?

*Flatfoot.* I must say! Look like a house wit' a warpin' cellar.

*Noah.* Dis yere vessel is a boat.

*Flatfoot.* When I was a little boy dey used to build boats down near de ribber, where de water was.

[*The others laugh.*]

*Noah.* Dis time it's been arranged to have de water come up to de boat. [JAPHETH *looks belligerently over the rail of the Ark at* FLATFOOT. *To* JAPHETH.] Keep yo' shirt on, son.

*Second Woman* (*to* THIRD WOMAN). Now, you see de whole fam'ly's crazy.

*Third Woman.* Listen, dey ain't gonter 'taminate me. It was me dat started resolvin' dem both out o' de buryin' society.

*Zeba.* When all dis water due up yere, Noah?

*Noah.* You won't know when it gits yere, daughter.

*Zeba.* Is she goin' to be a sidewheeler, like de Bessy-Belle?

*Flatfoot.* No! If she was a sidewheeler she'd get her wheels all clogged wid sharks. She gonter have jus' one great big stern wheel, like de Commodore. Den if dey ain't 'nuf water why de big wheel kin stir some up.

[*General laughter. Two or three of the* GAMBLERS *enter and join the group, followed by* CAIN THE SIXTH.]

*Cain the Sixth.* Dere's de fool an' his monument, jest like I said!

[*The* GAMBLERS *and* CAIN THE SIXTH *roar with laughter, slap their legs, etc., the members of the main group talk sotto voce to each other as* CAIN THE SIXTH *catches* ZEBA's *eye.* FLATFOOT *is on her right and is not aware of* CAIN THE SIXTH's *presence.*]

*Noah.* See how dey makin' out inside, son. (*Stops hammering.*)

[JAPHETH *exits into Ark.*]

[NOAH *turns and gazes towards the east.*]

*Cain the Sixth.* Hello, honey.

*Zeba* (*frightened but smiling*). Hello, sugah.

*Cain the Sixth* (*pleasantly*). Ain' dat my ol' frien' Flatfoot wid you?

*Zeba.* Why, so 'tis! [FLATFOOT *is now listening.*] (*To* FLATFOOT.) He's got a gun.

*Cain the Sixth.* No, I ain't.

[*He lifts his hands over his head.* ZEBA *quickly advances and runs her hands lightly over his pockets.*]

*Zeba* (*relieved*). I guess he ain't.

*Cain the Sixth.* No, I ain't got no gun for my ol' friend, Flatfoot. (*He walks up to him.*)

*Flatfoot* (*smiling*). Hi, Cain. How's de boy?

[CAIN *quickly presses his chest against* FLATFOOT's, *his downstage arm sweeps around* FLATFOOT's *body and his hand goes up to the small of* FLATFOOT's *back.*]

*Cain the Sixth* (*quietly, but triumphantly*). I got a little *knife* fo' him.

[FLATFOOT *falls dead.*]

[*The laughter of the others stops and they look at the scene.* ZEBA *for a moment is terrified, her clenched hand pressed to her mouth. She looks at* CAIN THE SIXTH, *who is smiling at her. He tosses the knife on the ground and holds his hands out to her. She goes to him, smiling.*]

*Zeba.* You sho' take keer of me, honey.

*Cain the Sixth.* Dat's caize I think yo' wo'th takin' keer of. (*To the others.*) It's all right, folks. I jest had to do a little cleanin' up.

*First Woman* (*smiling*). You is de quickes' scoundrel.

*First Gambler.* It was a nice quick killin'. Who was he?

*Second Woman* (*casually*). Dey called him Flatfoot. From over de river. He wa'nt any good. He owed me for washin' for over a year.

*Third Woman.* Used to peddle muggles. Said it had a kick like reg'lar snow.[4] Wasn't no good.

*Second Gambler.* Think we ought to bury him?

*First Man.* No, just leave him dere. Nobody comes up yere, 'cept ol' Manatee.[5] [*Indicates* NOAH. *Cries of "Ol' Manatee! Ol' Manatee, dat's good!"*]

*Noah* (*still looking off*). You bettah pray, you po' chillun.

[*They all laugh.*]

*First Woman.* We bettah pray? You bettah pray, Ol Manatee?

*Zeba.* You bettah pray for rain. [*Laughter again.*]

*Noah.* Dat's what I ain't doin', sinners. Shem! Japheth! [*To others, as*

---

[4] MUGGLES, SNOW—Slang terms for marihuana and opium, powerful narcotics.

[5] MANATEE—An aquatic animal which resembles a fleshy, ugly seal. The word is applied contemptuously to Noah who is about to become an "animal" of the sea.

*he points off. Patter of rain.*] Listen!

*Cain the Sixth* (*casually*). Doggone, I believe it *is* gonter shower a little.

*First Gambler.* It do looks like rain.

*First Woman.* I think I'll git on home. I got a new dress on.

*Zeba.* Me, too. I wants to keep lookin' nice fo' my sweet papa. [*She pats* CAIN THE SIXTH's *cheek.* CAIN THE SIXTH *hugs her.*]

*Noah* (*almost frantically*). Ham! Is de animals dere?

*Ham* (*off stage*). Yes, sir, dere yere. We're comin'.

*Noah.* Den bring 'em on.

[SHEM *and* JAPHETH *come on deck with their hammers. The stage begins to darken.*]

*Third Woman.* I guess we all might go home 'til de shower's over. Come on, papa.

*Second Gambler.* See you after supper, Noah. [*Crowd starts moving off* R.]

*Noah.* God's gittin' ready to start, my sons. Let's git dis plankin' done.

*Zeba.* Put a big Texas on it, Noah, an' we'll use it fo' excursions.

[*There is a distant roll of thunder, there are cries of "Good night, Admiral." "See you later." "So long, Manatee," as the crowd goes off. The thunder rumbles again. There is the sound of increasing rain. The hammers of* SHEM *and* JAPHETH *sound louder and are joined by the sounds of other hammerers. There is a flash of lightning. The* CHOIR *begins "Dey Ol' Ark's a-Movering," the sounds on the Ark become faster and louder. The rush of rain grows heavier.*]

*Noah.* Hurry! Hurry! Where are you, Ham?

*Ham* (*just off stage*). Yere, I am, father, wid de animals.

*Noah.* God's give us his sign. Send 'em up de gangplank.

[*An inclined plane is thrown against the Ark from the side of the stage by* HAM, *who cracks a whip.*]

*Ham.* Get on, dere.

[*The heads of two elephants are seen.*]

*Noah.* Bring 'em on board! De Lawd is strikin' down de worl'!

[*The singing and the noises reach fortissimo as* HAM *cracks his whip again, and the rain falls on the stage.*]

[*The stage is darkened. The* CHOIR *continues singing in the darkness.*]

### SCENE X

*When the lights go up on scene, the Ark is at sea. Stationary waves run in front of it. The hillside has disappeared. The Ark is in the only lighted area.*

SHEM *is smoking a pipe on the deck, leaning on the rail. A steamboat whistle blows three short and one long blast.* SHEM *is surprised. In a moment* HAM *appears, also with a pipe, and joins* SHEM *at the rail.*

*Shem.* Who'd you think you was signallin'?

*Ham.* Dat wasn't me, dat was daddy.

*Shem.* He think he gonter git a reply?

*Ham.* I don' know. He's been gittin' a heap of comfort out of dat likker.

*Shem.* De kag's nearly empty, ain't it?

*Ham.* Pretty nearly almos'. [*They look over the rail. A pause.*] Seen anythin'?

*Shem.* Dis mornin' I seen somethin' over dere migh'a' been a fish.

*Ham.* Dat's de big news of de week.

*Shem.* How long you think dis trip's gonter las'?

*Ham.* I don' know! Rain fo'ty days 'n' fo'ty nights an' when dat stop' I thought sho' we'd come up ag'inst a san' bar o' somethin'. Looks now like all dat rain was jest a little incident of de trip. [*The whistle blows again.*] Doggone! I wish he wouldn't do dat. Fust thing we know he'll wake up dem animals ag'in.

[JAPHETH *appears.*]

*Shem.* What de matter wit' de ol' man, Jape?

*Japheth.* Doggone, he say he had a dream dat we're nearly dere. Dat's why he pullin' de whistle cord. See kin he git a' answer. (*He looks over the rail.*) Look to me like de same ol' territory.

[MRS. NOAH *appears on deck.*]

*Noah's Wife.* You boys go stop yo' paw pullin' dat cord. He so full of likker he think he's in a race.

*Japheth.* He claim he know what he's doin'.

*Noah's Wife.* I claim he gittin' to be a perfec' nuisance. Me an' yo' wives cain't hardly heah ou'sel'es think. [NOAH *appears, his hat rakishly tilted on his head. He goes to the railing and looks out.*] You 'spectin' company?

*Noah.* Leave me be, woman. De watah don' look so rough today. De ol' boat's ridin' easier.

*Noah's Wife.* Ridin' like a ol' mule!

*Noah.* Yes, suh, de air don't feel so wet. Shem! 'Spose you sen' out 'nother dove. [SHEM *goes into the Ark.*] Ham, go git de soundin' line. Jape, keep yo' eye on de East.

[JAPHETH *goes to the end of the boat.*]

*Noah's Wife.* As fo' you, I s'pose you'll help things along by takin' a little drink.

*Noah.* Look yere, who's de pilot of dis vessel?

*Noah's Wife.* Ol' Mister Dumb Luck.

*Noah.* Well, see dat's where you don' know anythin'.

*Noah's Wife.* I s'pose you ain't drunk as a fool?

*Noah* (*cordially*). I feel congenial.

*Noah's Wife.* An' you look it. You look jest wonderful. I wonder if you'd feel so congenial if de Lawd was to show up?

*Noah.* De Lawd knows what I'm doin', don' you worry 'bout dat.

*Noah's Wife.* I wouldn't say anythin' ag'inst de Lawd. He suttinly let us know dey'd be a change in de weather. But I bet even de Lawd wonders sometimes why he ever put you in charge.

*Noah.* Well, you let de Lawd worry 'bout dat.

[SHEM *appears with the dove.*]

*Shem.* Will I leave her go, Paw?

*Noah.* Leave 'er go. [*There is a loud chorus of "Good Luck, Dove," from the group as the dove flies off stage.* HAM *appears with the sounding line.*] Throw 'er over, Boy. [HAM *proceeds to do so.*]

*Noah's Wife.* An' another thing—

*Ham.* Hey!

*Noah* (*rushing to his side*). What is it?

*Ham.* Only 'bout a inch! Look! [*They lean over.*]

*Japheth.* It 's gettin' light in de East.

[*As* HAM *works the cord up and down,* NOAH *and* NOAH'S WIFE *turn toward* JAPHETH. *The* CHOIR *begins "My Soul Is a Witness for the Lord."*]

*Noah.* Praise de Lawd, so it is.

*Noah's Wife.* Oh, dat's pretty.

*Noah* (*to* HAM). An' de boat's stopped. We've landed. Shem, go down n' drag de fires an' dreen de boiler. Yo go help 'im, Ham.

*Japheth.* Look, Paw.

[*The dove wings back to the Ark with an olive branch in its mouth.*]

*Noah.* 'N' yere's de little dove wid greenery in its mouth! Take 'er down,

Jape, so she kin tell de animals. [JA-PHETH *exits after* SHEM *and* HAM *carrying the dove. To* MRS. NOAH.] Now, maybe you feel little different.

*Noah's Wife (contritely).* It was jes' gittin' to be so tiresome. I'm sorry, Noah.

*Noah.* Dat's all right, ol' woman. [NOAH'S WIFE *exits.* NOAH *looks about him. The lights have changed and the water piece is gone and the ark is again on the hillside. Two mountains can be seen in the distance and a rainbow slowly appears over the Ark. The singing has grown louder.*] Thank you, Lawd, thank you very much indeed. Amen.

[*The singing stops with the "Amen."* GOD *appears on the deck.*]

*God.* Yo' welcome, Noah.

[NOAH *turns and sees him.*]

*Noah.* O, Lawd, it's wonderful.

*God (looking about him).* I sort of like it. I like de way you handled de ship, too, Noah.

*Noah.* Was you watchin', Lawd?

*God.* Every minute. (*He smiles.*) Didn't de ol' lady light into you?

*Noah (apologetically).* She was kinda restless.

*God.* That's all right. I ain't blamin' nobody. I don' even min' you' cussin' an drinkin'. I figure a steamboat cap'n on a long trip like you had has a right to a little redeye, jest so he don' go crazy.

*Noah.* Thank you, Lawd. What's de orders now?

*God.* All de animals safe?

*Noah.* Dey all fin'n' dandy, Lawd.

*God.* Den I want you to open dat starboard door, an' leave 'em all out. Let 'em go down de hill. Den you an' de family take all de seeds 'n de sprouts an' begin plantin' ag'in. I'm startin' all over, Noah.

[NOAH *exits.* GOD *looks around.*]

*God.* Well, now we'll see what happens. [GOD *listens with a smile, as noises accompanying the debarking of the animals are heard. There are the cracks of whips, the voices of the men on the Ark, shouting: "Git along dere." "Whoa, take it easy." "Duck yo' head." "Keep in line dere," etc. Over the Ark there is a burst of centrifugal shadows, and the sound of a myriad of wings.* GOD *smiles at the shadows.*] Dat's right, birds, fin' yo' new homes. [*Bird twitters are heard again.* GOD *listens a moment and rests an arm on the railing. He speaks softly.*] Gabriel, kin you spare a minute?"

[GABRIEL *appears.*]

*Gabriel.* Yes, Lawd?

[*The sounds from the other side of the Ark are by now almost hushed. The* LORD *indicates the new world with a wave of the hand.*]

*God.* Well, it's did.

*Gabriel (respectfully, but with no enthusiasm).* So I take notice.

*God.* Yes, suh, startin' all over again.

*Gabriel.* So I see.

*God (looking at him suddenly).* Don' seem to set you up much.

*Gabriel.* Well, Lawd, you see— (*He hesitates.*) 'Tain't none of my business.

*God.* What?

*Gabriel.* I say, I don' know very much about it.

*God.* I know you don'. I jest wanted you to see it. (*A thought strikes him.*) Co'se, it ain' yo' business, Gabe. It's my business. 'Twas my idea. De whole thing was my idea. An' every bit of it's my business 'n nobody else's. De whole thing rests on my shoulders. I declare, I guess *dat's* why I feel so solemn an' serious, at dis particklar time. You know *dis* thing's turned into quite a proposition.

Gabriel (*tenderly*). But, it's all right, Lawd, as you say, it's did.

God. Yes, suh, it's did. (*Sighs deeply. Looks slowly to the right and the left. Then softly.*) I only hope it's goin' to work out all right.

*Curtain*

## PART TWO

### SCENE I

*God's office again.*

*Somewhere the* CHOIR *is singing:* "A City Called Heaven." *In the office are* TWO WOMEN CLEANERS. *One is scrubbing the floor, the other dusting the furniture. The one dusting stops and looks out the window. There is a whirr and a distant faint Boom. The* CHOIR *stops.*

First Cleaner. Dat was a long way off.

Second Cleaner (*at window*). Yes, ma'am. An' dat must a' been a big one. Doggone, de Lawd mus' be mad fo' sho', dis mo'nin'. Dat's de fo'ty-six' thunde'-bolt since breakfast.

First Cleaner. I wonder where at he's pitchin' dem.

Second Cleaner. My goodness, don' you know?

First Cleaner (*a little hurt*). Did I know I wouldn't ask de question.

Second Cleaner. Every one of dem's bound fo' de earth.

First Cleaner. De earth? You mean dat little ol' dreenin' place?

Second Cleaner. Dat's de planet. [*Another faint whirr and boom.*] Dere goes another.

First Cleaner. Well, bless me. I didn't know de was thunde'-bolts.

Second Cleaner. Wha'd you think dey was?

First Cleaner (*above desk*). I wasn't sho', but I thought maybe He might be whittlin' a new star o' two, an' de noise was jest de chips fallin'.

Second Cleaner. Carrie, where you been? Don' you know de earth is de new scandal? Ever'body's talkin' 'bout it.

First Cleaner. Dey kep' it from me.

Second Cleaner. Ain't you noticed de Lawd's been unhappy lately?

First Cleaner (*thoughtfully*). Yeah, he ain't been his old self.

Second Cleaner. What did you think was de matteh? Lumbago?

First Cleaner (*petulantly*). I didn't know. I didn't think it was fo' me t'inquieh.

Second Cleaner. Well, it jest so happens dat de Lawd is riled as kin be by dat measly little earth. Or I should say de scum dat's on it.

First Cleaner. Dat's mankind down dere.

Second Cleaner. Dey mus' be scum, too, to git de Lawd so wukked up.

First Cleaner. I s'pose so. [*Another whirr and boom.*] Looks like he's lettin' dem feel de wrath. Ain' dat a shame to plague de Lawd dat way?

Second Cleaner. From what I hear dey been beggin' fo' what dey're gittin'. My brother flew down to bring up a saint de other day and he say from what he see mos' of de population down dere has made de debbil king an' dey wukkin' in three shifts fo' him.

First Cleaner. You cain't blame de Lawd.

Second Cleaner. Co'se you cain't. Dem human bein's 'd make anybody bile oveh. Ev'rytime de Lawd try to do sompin' fo' dem, doggone if dey don't staht some new ruckus.

*First Cleaner.* I take notice he's been wukkin' in yere mo' dan usual.

*Second Cleaner.* I wish he'd let us ladies fix it up. Wouldn't take a minute to make dis desk gold-plated.

*First Cleaner.* I 'spose he likes it dis way. De Lawd's kind o' ol' fashioned in some ways. I s'pose he keeps dis office plain an' simple on purpose.

*Second Cleaner (finishing her work).* I don' see why.

*First Cleaner (looking off).* Well, it's kind of a nice place to come to when he's studyin' somethin' impo'tant. 'Most evahthin' else in heaven's so fin' 'n' gran', maybe ev'ry now an den he jest gits sick an' tired of de glory. (*She is also collecting her utensils.*)

*Second Cleaner.* Maybe so. Jest de same I'd like to have a free hand wid dis place for a while, so's I could gold it up.

[GOD *appears in the doorway.*]

*God.* Good mo'nin', daughters.

*First and Second Cleaners.* Good mo'nin', Lawd. We was jest finishin'.

*God.* Go ahead den, daughters. (*Goes to the window.*)

*First and Second Cleaners.* Yes, Lawd. (*They exeunt. Off stage.*) Good mo'nin', Gabriel.

[*Off stage* GABRIEL *says, "Good mo'nin', sisters," and enters immediately. He stands in the doorway for a moment watching* GOD—*a notebook and pencil in his hand.*]

*God.* What's de total?

*Gabriel (consulting the book).* Eighteen thousand nine hund'ed an' sixty for de mo'nin'. Dat's includin' de village wid de fo'tune tellers. Dey certainly kin breed fast.

*God (solemnly).* Dey displease me. Dey displease me greatly.

*Gabriel.* Want some more bolts, Lawd?

*God (looking through window).* Look at 'em dere. Squirmin' an' fightin' an' bearin' false witness. Listen to dat liar, dere. He don' intend to marry dat little gal. He don' even love her. What did you say?

*Gabriel.* Should I git mo' bolts?

*God.* Wait a minute. (*He carefully points his finger down through the window.*) I'm goin' to git dat wicked man myself. [*From a great distance comes an agonized cry: "Oh, Lawd!"* GOD *turns from the window.*] No use gittin' mo' thunde'bolts. Dey don' do de trick. (*He goes to the swivel chair and sits.*) It's got to be somethin' else.

*Gabriel.* How would it be if you was to doom 'em all ag'in, like dat time you sent down de flood? I bet dat would make dem mind.

*God.* You see how much good de flood did. Dere dey is, jest as bad as ever.

*Gabriel.* How about cleanin' up de whole mess of 'em and sta'tin' all over ag'in wid some new kind of animal?

*God.* An' admit I'm licked?

*Gabriel (ashamedly).* No, of co'se not, Lawd.

*God.* No, suh. No, suh. Man is a kind of pet of mine and it ain't right fo' me to give up tryin' to do somethin' wid him. Doggone, mankin' *mus'* be all right at de core or else why did I ever bother wid him in de first place? (*Sits at desk.*)

*Gabriel.* It's jest dat I hates to see you worryin' about it, Lawd.

*God.* Gabe, dere ain't anythin' worth while anywheres dat didn't 'cause somebody some worryin'. I ain't never tol' you de trouble I had gittin' things started up yere. Dat's a story in itself. No, suh, de more I keep on bein' de Lawd de more I know I got to keep improvin' things. An' dat takes time and worry. De main trouble wid mankin' is

he takes up so much of my time. He ought to be able to help hisself a little. (*He stops suddenly and cogitates.*) Hey, dere! I think I got it!

*Gabriel* (*eagerly*). What's de news?

*God* (*still cogitating*). Yes, suh, dat seems like an awful good idea.

*Gabriel.* Tell me, Lawd.

*God.* Gabriel, have you noticed dat every now an' den, mankin' turns out some pretty good specimens?

*Gabriel.* Dat's de truth.

*God.* Yes, suh. Dey's ol' Abraham and Isaac an' Jacob an' all dat family.

*Gabriel.* Dat's so, Lawd.

*God.* An' everyone of dem boys was a hard wukker an' a good citizen. We got to admit dat.

*Gabriel.* Dey wouldn't be up yere flyin' wid us if dey hadn't been.

*God.* No, suh. An' I don' know but what de answer to de whole trouble is right dere.

*Gabriel.* How you mean, Lawd?

*God.* Why, doggone it, de good man is de man dat keeps busy. I mean I been goin' along on de principle dat he was something like you angels—dat you ought to be able to give him somethin' an' den jest let him sit back an' enjoy it. Dat ain't so. Now dat I recollec' I put de first one down dere to take keer o' dat garden an' den I let him go ahead an' do nothin' but git into mischief. (*He rises.*) Sure, *dat's* it. He ain't *built* jest to fool 'roun' an' not do nothin'. Gabe, I'm gonter try a new scheme.

*Gabriel* (*eagerly*). What's de scheme, Lawd?

*God.* I'll tell you later. Send in Abraham, Isaac an' Jacob. [*A voice outside calls:* "Right away, Lawd."] You go tell dem to put dem bolts back in de boxes. I ain' gonter use dem ag'in a while.

242

*Gabriel.* O. K., Lawd.

*God.* Was you goin' anywhere near de Big Pit?

*Gabriel.* I could go.

*God.* Lean over de brink and tell Satan he's jest a plain fool if he thinks he kin beat anybody as big as me.

*Gabriel.* Yes, suh, Lawd. Den I'll spit right in his eye. (GABRIEL *exits.*)

[GOD *looks down through the window again to the earth below.*]

*God.* Dat new polish on de sun makes it powerful hot. (*He* "*r'ar back.*") Let it be jest a little bit cooler. (*He feels the air.*) Dat's nice. (*Goes to His desk. A knock on the door.*) Come in.

[ABRAHAM, ISAAC *and* JACOB *enter. All are very old men, but the beard of* ABRAHAM *is the longest and the whitest, and they suggest their three generations. They have wings that are not quite so big as those of the native angels.*]

*Isaac.* Sorry we so long comin', Lawd. But Pappy and me had to take de boy (*Pointing to* JACOB.) over to git him a can of wing ointment.

*God.* What was de matter, son?

*Jacob.* Dey was chafin' me a little. Dey fine now, thank you, Lawd.

*God.* Dat's good. Sit down an' make yo'selves comf'table. [*The three sit.* MEN: "*Thank you, Lawd.*"] Men, I'm goin' to talk about a little scheme I got. It's one dat's goin' to affec' yo' fam'lies an' dat's why I 'cided I'd talk it over wid you, 'fo' it goes into ee-fect. I don' know whether you boys know it or not, but you is about de three best men of one fam'ly dat's come up yere since I made little apples. Now I tell you what I'm gonter do. Seein' dat you human bein's cain't 'preciate anythin' lessen you fust wukk to git it and den keep strug-glin' to hold it, why I'm gonter turn over a very valuable piece of property to yo'

fam'ly, and den see what kin dey do with it. De rest of de worl' kin go jump in de river fo' all I keer. I'm gonter be lookin' out fo' yo' descendents only. Now den, seein' dat you boys know de country pretty tho'ly, where at does you think is de choice piece of property in de whole worl'? Think it over for a minute. I'm gonter let you make de s'lection.

*Abraham.* If you was to ask me, Lawd, I don't think dey come any better dan de Land of Canaan.

*God* (*to* ISAAC *and* JACOB). What's yo' feelin' in de matter?

*Jacob* (*after a nod from* ISAAC). Pappy an' me think do we get a pick, dat would be it.

*God* (*goes to window again; looks out*). De Land of Canaan. Yes, I guess dat's a likely neighborhood. It's all run over wid Philistines and things right now, but we kin clean dat up. (*He turns from the window and resumes his seat.*) All right. Now who do you boys think is de best of yo' men to put in charge down dere? You see I ain't been payin' much attention to anybody in partic'lar lately.

*Isaac.* Does you want de brainiest or de holiest, Lawd? [MEN *look up.*]

*God.* I want de holiest. I'll make him brainy. [MEN *appreciate the miracle.*]

*Isaac* (*as* ABRAHAM *and* JACOB *nod to him*). Well, if you want A Number One, goodness, Lawd, I don't know where you'll git more satisfaction dan in a great-great-great-great grandson of mine.

*God.* Where's he at?

*Isaac.* At de moment I b'lieve he's in de sheep business over in Midian County. He got in a little trouble down in Egypt, but t'wan't his doin'. He killed a man dat was abusin' one of our boys in de brick works. Of co'se you know old King Pharaoh's got all our people in bondage.

*God.* I heard of it. (*With some ire.*) Who did you think put them dere? [*The visitors lower their heads.*] It's all right, boys. [*All rise.*] I'm gonter take dem out of it. An' I'm gonter turn over de whole Land of Canaan to dem. An' do you know whose gonter lead dem dere? Yo' great, great, great, great grandson. Moses, ain't it?

*Isaac.* Yes, Lawd.

*God* (*smiling*). Yes. I been noticin' him.

*Abraham.* It's quite a favor fo' de fam'ly, Lawd.

*God.* Dat's why I tol' you. You see, it so happens I love yo' fam'ly, an' I delight to honor it. Dat's all, gen'le-men. [*The three others rise and cross to the door, murmuring, "Yes, Lawd," "Thank you, Lawd," "Much obliged, Lawd." etc. The* CHOIR *begins, "My Lord's A-Writin' All De Time" pianis-simo.* GOD *stands watching the men leave.*] Enjoy yo' selves. [*He goes to the window. The singing grows softer. He speaks through the window to the earth.*] I'm comin' down to see you, Moses, an' dis time my scheme's got to wukk.

[*The stage is darkened. The singing grows louder and continues until the lights go up on the next scene.*]

### SCENE II

*The tableau curtains frame the opening of a cave, which is dimly lighted. A large turkey-berry bush is somewhere near the foreground.* MOSES *is seated on the grass eating his lunch from a basket in his lap.* ZIPPORAH, *his wife, stands watching him. He is about forty,* ZIP-PORAH *somewhat younger. They are dressed inconspicuously.* MOSES *stutters slightly when he speaks. He looks up to see* ZIPPORAH *smiling.*

*Moses.* What you smilin' at, Zip-porah?

*Zipporah.* Caize you enjoyin' yo'self.

*Moses.* You is a good wife, Zipporah.

*Zipporah.* You is a good husband, Moses. [MOSES *wipes his mouth with a handkerchief and begins putting into the basket the various implements of the meal which had been on the ground about him.*] Why you suppose it's so dark yere today? Dey's no rain in de air.

*Moses.* Seems like it's jest aroun' dis cave. Yo' father's house is got de sun on it. (*He looks in another direction.*) Looks all clear down toward Egypt.

*Zipporah.* Co'se it *would* be fine weather in Egypt. De sky looks all right. Maybe it's gonter rain jest right yere. Why don't you move de sheep over to de other pasture?

*Moses* (*a bit puzzled*). I don' know. It got dark like dis befo' you come along wid de dinner an' I was gonter stop you on de top of de hill. Den somethin' kep' me yere.

*Zipporah.* S'pose it could be de Lawd warnin' you dat dey's 'Gyptians hangin' 'roun'?

*Moses.* Dey may have fo'gotten all about dat killin' by now. Dey got a new Pharaoh down dere.

*Zipporah.* An' I hear he's jest as mean to yo' people as his pappy was. I wouldn't put it pas' him to send sol-jahs all the way up yere fo' you.

*Moses.* Dat's all right. De Lawd's looked after me so far, I don't 'spect him to fall down on me now. You better be gittin' home.

*Zipporah* (*taking the basket*). I'll be worryin' about you.

*Moses* (*kissing her and then smiling*). 'Parently de Lawd ain't. He knows I'm safe as kin be. Lemme see you feel dat way.

*Zipporah.* You is a good man, Moses.

*Moses.* I's a lucky man. [ZIPPORAH *exits with the basket.* MOSES *looks up at the sky.*] Dat's funny. De sun seems to be shinin' everyplace but right yere. It's shinin' on de sheep. Why ain't dey no cloud dere?

*God* (*off stage*). Caize I want it to be like dat, Moses.

*Moses* (*looking about him*). Who's dat?

*God* (*off stage again*). I'm de Lawd, Moses.

*Moses* (*smiling*). Dat's what you say. Dis yere shadow may be de Lawd's wukk, but dat voice soun' pretty much to me like my ol' brother Aaron.

*God* (*off stage*). Den keep yo' eyes open, son. [*The turkey-berry bush begins to glow and then turns completely red.* MOSES *looks at it fascinated.*] Maybe you notice de bush ain't burnin' up.

*Moses.* Dat's de truth. (MOSES *is full of awe but not frightened.*)

*God* (*off stage*). Now you believe me?

*Moses.* Co'se I does. It's wonderful. [*The light in the bush dies and* GOD *appears from behind it.*]

*God.* No, it ain't, Moses. It was jest a trick.

*Moses.* 'Scuse me doubtin' you, Lawd. I always had de feelin' you wuz takin' keer of me, but I never 'spected you'd fin' de time to talk wid me pussunly. (*He laughs.*) Dat was a good trick, Lawd. I'se seen some good ones, but dat was de beatenest.

*God.* Yo' gonter see lots bigger tricks dan dat, Moses. In fac', yo' gonter perfo'm dem.

*Moses* (*incredulously*). Me? I'm gonter be a tricker?

*God.* Yes, suh.

*Moses.* An' do magic? Lawd, my mouth ain't got de quick talk to go wid it.

*God.* It'll come to you now.

*Moses* (*now cured of stuttering*). Is I goin' wid a circus?

*God* (*slowly and solemnly*). Yo' is goin' down into Egypt, Moses, and lead my people out of bondage. To do dat I'm gonter make you de bes' tricker in de worl'.

*Moses* (*a little frightened*). Egypt! You know I killed a man dere, Lawd. Won't dey kill me?

*God.* Not when dey see yo' tricks. You ain't skeered, is you?

*Moses* (*simply and bravely*). No, suh, Lawd.

*God.* Den yere's what I'm gonter do. Yo' people is my chillun, Moses. I'm sick and tired o' de way ol' King Pharaoh is treatin' dem, so I'se gonter take dem away, and yo' gonter lead dem. You gonter lead 'em out of Egypt an' across de river Jordan. It's gonter take a long time, and you ain't goin' on no excursion train. Yo' gonter wukk awful hard for somethin' yo' goin' to fin' when de trip's over.

*Moses.* What's dat, Lawd?

*God.* It's de Land of Canaan. It's de bes' land I got. I've promised it to yo' people, an' I'm gonter give it to dem.

*Moses.* Co'se, ol' King Pharaoh will do everything he kin to stop it.

*God.* Yes, an' dat's where de tricks come in. Dey tell me he's awful fond of tricks.

*Moses.* I hear dat's *all* he's fon' of. Dey say if you can't take a rabbit out of a hat you can't even git in to see him.

*God.* Wait'll you see de tricks you an' me's goin' to show him.

*Moses* (*delightedly*).    Doggone! Huh, Lawd?

*God.* Yes, suh. Now de first trick— (GOD *is lifting a stick which he carries.*)

*Moses.* Jest a minute, Lawd. [GOD *halts the demonstration.*] I'm gonter learn de tricks and do just like you tell me, but I *know* it's gonter take me a little time to learn all dat quick talkin'. Cain't I have my brother Aaron go wid me? He's a good man.

*God.* I was gonter have him help you wid de Exodus. I guess he can watch, too.

*Moses.* I'll call 'im. (*He turns as if to shout.*)

*God.* Wait. [MOSES *turns and looks at* GOD.] I'll *bring* him. (*Softly.*) Aaron!

[AARON *appears between* GOD *and* MOSES *in the mouth of the cave. He is a little taller than* MOSES *and slightly older. He, too, is dressed like a field hand.*]

*Aaron* (*blankly*).    Hey!

[MOSES *goes to him, takes his hand and leads him, bewildered, down to where* MOSES *had been standing alone.* AARON *then sees* GOD.]

*Moses* (*almost in a whisper*).    It's all right.

*God.* Don't worry, son, I'm jest showin' some tricks. Bringin' you yere was one of dem. [AARON *stares at* GOD *as if hypnotized.*] Now den, you see dis yere rod? Looks like a ordinary walking stick, don' it?

*Moses.* Yes, Lawd.

*God.* Well, it ain't no ordinary walkin' stick, caize look. [MOSES *leans forward.*] When I lays it down on de groun'—

[*The stage is darkened. The* CHOIR *begins, "Go Down, Moses," and con-*tinues until the lights go up on the next scene.*]

## SCENE III

*The throne room of* PHARAOH. *It suggests a Negro lodge room. The plain board walls are colored by several large parade banners of varying sizes, colors and materials, bordered with gold fringe tassels on them. Some of the inscriptions on them read:*

SUBLIME ORDER OF PRINCES OF THE HOUSE OF PHARAOH HOME CHAPTER

MYSTIC BROTHERS OF THE EGYPTIAN HOME GUARD LADIES AUXILIARY, No. 1

SUPREME MAGICIANS AND WIZARDS OF THE UNIVERSE

PRIVATE FLAG OF HIS HONOR OLD KING PHARAOH

ROYAL YOUNG PEOPLE'S PLEASURE CLUB

ENCHANTED AND INVISIBLE CADETS OF EGYPT BOYS' BRIGADE

*There is one door up right and a window. The throne, an ordinary armchair with a drapery over its back, is on a dais.* PHARAOH *is seated on the throne. His crown and garments might be those worn by a high officer in a Negro lodge during a ritual. About the throne itself are high officials, several of them with plumed hats, clothing that suggests military uniforms, and rather elaborate sword belts, swords and scabbards. A few soldiers carrying spears are also in his neighborhood and one or two bearded ancients in brightly colored robes with the word "Wizard" on their conical hats. In the general group of men and women scattered elsewhere in the room Sunday finery is noticeable everywhere. Most of the civilians have bright "parade" ribbons and wear medals. In a cleared space immediately before the throne a* CANDIDATE MAGICIAN *is performing a sleight-of-hand trick with cards.* PHARAOH *watches him apathetically. He is receiving earnest attention from a few of the others, but the majority of the men and women are talking quietly among themselves. Beside the* CANDIDATE MAGICIAN *are several paraphernalia of previously demonstrated tricks.*

*Candidate Magician (holding up some cards).* Now den, ol' King Pharaoh, watch dis. [*He completes a trick. There is a murmur of "Not Bad," "Pretty Good," etc. from a few of the watchers.* PHARAOH *makes no comment.*] Now, I believe de cyard I ast you to keep sittin' on was de trey of diamonds, wasn't it?

*Pharaoh.* Yeah.

*Candidate Magician.* Den kin I trouble you to take a look at it now? [PHARAOH *half rises to pick up a card he has been sitting on, and looks at it.*] I believe you'll now notice dat it's de King of Clubs? [PHARAOH *nods and shows the card to those nearest him. The* CANDIDATE MAGICIAN *waits for an audible approval and gets practically none.*] An' dat, ol' King Pharaoh, completes de puffohmance.

[*An elderly man in a uniform steps forward.*]

*General.* On behalf of my nephew I beg Yo' Honor to let him jine de ranks of de royal trickers and magicians.

*Pharaoh (to the two* WIZARDS*).* What do de committee think? [*The* WIZARDS *shake their heads.*] Dat's what I thought. He ain't good enough. I'd like to help you out, General, but you know a man's got to be a awful good tricker to git in de royal society dese days. You better go back an' steddy some mo', son. (*He lifts his voice and directs two soldiers guarding the door.*) Is de head magician reached de royal waitin' room yit? [*One of the soldiers opens the door to look out.*] If he is, send him in.

[*The soldier beckons to some one off stage, throws the door open, and announces to the court.*]

*Soldier.* De Head Magician of de land of Egypt.

[*A very old and villainous man enters. His costume is covered with cabalistic and zodiacal signs. He advances to the King, the other magician and his uncle making way for him. He bows curtly to* PHARAOH.]

*Head Magician.* Good mo'nin', ol' King Pharaoh.

*Pharaoh.* Mo'nin', Professor. What's de news?

*Head Magician.* Evahthing's bein' carried out like you said.

*Pharaoh.* How's de killin' of de babies 'mongst de Hebrews comin' 'long?

*Head Magician.* Jes' like you ordered.

*Pharaoh (genially).* Dey killed all of 'em, huh?

*Head Magician.* Do dey see one, dey kill 'im. You teachin' 'em a great lesson. Dey don' like it a-tall.

*Pharaoh (smiling).* What do dey say?

*Head Magician (pawing the air inarticulately).* I hates to tell in front of de ladies.

*Pharaoh.* Dey feels pretty bad, huh?

*Head Magician.* Dat's jest de beginnin' of it. Betwixt de poleece and de soljahs we killed about a thousan' of 'em las' night. Dat's purty good.

*Pharaoh (thoughtfully).* Yeh, it's

fair. I guess you boys is doin' all you kin. But I fin' I ain't satisfied, though.

*Head Magician.* How you mean, Yo' Honor?

*Pharaoh.* I mean I'd like to make dose Hebrew chillun realize dat I kin be even mo' of a pest. I mean I hates dem chillun. An' I'm gonter think of a way of makin' 'em even mo' mizzable.

*Head Magician.* But dey ain't anythin' meaner dan killin' de babies, King.

*Pharaoh.* Dey must be sump'n. Doggone, you is my head tricker, you put yo' brains on it. (*To the others.*) Quiet, whilst de Head Magician go into de silence.

*Head Magician* (*after turning completely around twice, and a moment's cogitation*). I tell you what I kin do. All de Hebrews dat ain't out to de buryin' grounds or in de hospitals is laborin' in de brick wukks.

*Pharaoh.* Yeh?

*Head Magician* (*after a cackling laugh*). How would it be to take de straw away from 'em and tell 'em dey's got to turn out jest as many bricks as usual? Ain't dat nasty?

*Pharaoh.* Purty triflin', but I s'pose it'll have to do for de time bein'. Where's de extreme inner guard? [*One of the military attendants comes forward.*] Go on out an' tell de sup'intendent to put dat into ee-ffect. [*The attendant bows and starts for the door. He stops as* PHARAOH *calls to him.*] Wait a minute! Tell 'im to chop off de hands of anybody dat say he cain't make de bricks dat way. [*The attendant salutes and exits, the door being opened and closed by one of the soldiers.*] Now what's de news in de magic line?

*Head Magician.* I ain't got very many novelties today, King, I bin wukkin' too hard on de killin's. I'm so tired I don' believe I could lift a wand.

[*There are murmurs of protest from the assemblage.*]

*Pharaoh.* Doggone, you was to 'a been de chief feature o' de meetin' dis mawnin'. Look at de turn-out you got account of me tellin' 'em you was comin'.

*Head Magician.* Well, dat's de way it is, King. Why don' you git de wizards to do some spell castin'?

*Pharaoh.* Dey say it's in de cyards dat dey cain't wukk till high noon. (*He glances at the* WIZARDS.) Think mebbe you kin cheat a little?

*First Wizard.* Oh dat cain't be done, King.

*Pharaoh.* Well, we might as well adjourn, den. Looks to me like de whole program's shot to pieces. [*He starts to rise, when there is a furious banging on the door.*] What's de idea, dere? See who dat is. [*The soldiers open the door.* MOSES *and* AARON *enter, pushing the two soldiers aside and coming down in front of* PHARAOH. *The soldiers are bewildered and* PHARAOH *is angry.*] Say, who tol' you two baboons you could come in yere?

*Moses.* Is you ol' King Pharaoh?

*Pharaoh.* Dat's me. Did you heah what I asked you?

*Moses.* My name is Moses, and dis is my brother Aaron.

[*Murmur of "Hebrews" spreads through the room.*]

*Pharaoh* (*in a rage*). Is you Hebrews?

*Moses.* Yes, suh.

*Pharaoh* (*almost screaming*). Put 'em to de sword!

[*As the courtiers approach,* AARON *suddenly discloses the rod, which he swings once over his head. The courtiers draw back as if their hands had been stung. Cries of "Hey!" "Lookout," etc.*]

*Moses.* Keep outside dat circle.

[*The courtiers nearest* MOSES *and* AARON *look at each other, exclaiming ad lib.,* "*Did you feel dat?*" "*What is dat?*" "*What's goin' on, heah?*" "*My hands is stingin'!*" *etc.*]

*Pharaoh* (*puzzled but threatening*). What's de idea yere?

*Moses.* We is magicians, ol' King Pharaoh.

*Pharaoh* (*to the* HEAD MAGICIAN). Put a spell on 'em. [*The* HEAD MAGICIAN *stands looking at them bewildered. To* MOSES.] I got some magicians, too. We'll see who's got de bes' magic. [MOSES *and* AARON *laugh. Most of the courtiers are cowering. To the* HEAD MAGICIAN.] Go ahead, give 'em gri-gri.

*Moses.* Sure, go ahead.

*Pharaoh.* Hurry up, dey's laughin' at you. What's de matter?

*Head Magician.* I cain't think of de right spell.

*Pharaoh* (*now frightened himself*). You mean dey got even *you* whupped?

*Head Magician.* Dey's got a new kind of magic.

*Pharaoh* (*gazes at* HEAD MAGICIAN *a moment, bewildered. To the* WIZARDS). I s'pose if de Professor cain't, you cain't.

*First Wizard.* Dat's a new trick, King.

*Head Magician* (*rubbing his fingers along his palms*). It's got 'lectricity in it!

*Pharaoh.* Hm, well dat may make it a little diff'rent. So you boys is magicians, too?

*Moses.* Yes, suh.

*Pharaoh.* Well, we's always glad to see some new trickers in de co't, dat is if dey good. (*He glances about him.*) You look like you is O.K.

*Moses.* Dat's what we claims, ol' King Pharaoh. We think we's de best in de worl'.

*Pharaoh.* You certainly kin talk big. Jest what is it you boys would like?

*Moses.* We came to show you some tricks. Den we's goin' to ask you to do somethin' for us.

*Pharaoh.* Well, I s'pose you know I'm a fool for conjurin'. If a man kin show me some tricks I ain't seen, I goes out of my way to do him a favor.

*Moses.* Dat's good. Want to see de first trick?

*Pharaoh.* It ain't goin' to hurt nobody?

*Moses.* Dis one won't.

*Pharaoh.* Go ahead.

*Moses.* Dis yere rod my brother has looks jes' like a walkin' stick, don't it?

[*The courtiers now join the King in interest.*]

*Pharaoh.* Uh huh. Le's see.

[AARON *hands him the rod, which* PHARAOH *inspects and returns.*]

*Moses.* Well, look what happens when he lays it on de groun'.

[AARON *places the rod on the second step of the throne. It turns into a life-like snake. There are exclamations from the assemblage.*]

*Pharaoh.* Dat's a good trick! Now turn it back into a walkin' stick again. [AARON *picks it up and it is again a rod. Exclamations of* "*Purty good!*" "*Dat's all right!*" "*What do you think of that!*" *etc.*] Say, you is good trickers!

*Moses.* You ain't never seen de beat of us. Now I'm goin' to ask de favor.

*Pharaoh.* Sure, what is it?

*Moses* (*solemnly*). Let de Hebrew chillun go!

*Pharaoh.* [*Rises and stares at them. There is a murmur of* "*Listen to 'im!*" "*He's got nerve!*" "*I never in my life!*" "*My goodness!*" *etc.*] What did you say?

*Moses.* Let de Hebrew chillun go.

[PHARAOH *seats himself again.*]

*Pharaoh* (*slowly*). Don' you know de Hebrews is my slaves?

*Moses.* Yes, suh.

*Pharaoh.* Yes, suh, my slaves. [*There is a distant groaning.*] Listen, and you kin hear 'em bein' treated like slaves. (*He calls toward the window.*) What was dey doin' den?

*Man near the window.* Dey's jest gettin' de news down in de brick-yard.

*Pharaoh.* I won't let them go. (*He snorts contemptuously.*) Let's see another trick.

*Moses.* Yes, suh, yere's a better one. (*He lowers his head.*) Let's have a plague of de flies.

[AARON *raises the rod. The room grows dark and a great buzzing of flies is heard. The courtiers break out in cries of "Get away fum me!" "Take 'em away!" "De place is filled with flies!" "Dis is terrible!" "Do sump'n, Pharaoh!"*]

*Pharaoh* (*topping the others*). All right—stop de trick!

*Moses.* Will you let de Hebrews go?

*Pharaoh.* Sho' I will. Go ahead stop it!

*Moses* (*also above the others*). Begone!

[*The buzzing stops and the room is filled with light again, as* AARON *lowers the rod. All except* MOSES AND AARON *are brushing the flies from their persons.*]

*Pharaoh* (*laughing*). Doggone, dat was a good trick! [*The others, seeing they are uninjured, join in the laughter, with exclamations of "Doggone!" "You all right?" "Sho' I'm all right." "Didn' hurt me," etc.*] You is good trickers.

*Moses.* Will you let de Hebrew chillun go?

*Pharaoh* (*sitting down again*). Well, I'll tell you, boys. I'll tell you sump'n you didn' know. You take me. *I'm a*

pretty good tricker, an' I jest outtricked you. So, bein' de bes' tricker, I don' think I will let 'em go. You got any mo' tricks yo'self?

*Moses.* Yes, suh. Dis is a little harder one. [AARON *lifts the rod.*] Gnats in de mill pon', gnats in de clover, gnats in de tater patch, stingin' all over.

[*The stage grows dark again. There is the humming of gnats and the slapping of hands against faces and arms, and the same protests as were heard with the flies, but with more feeling, "I'm gittin' stung to death!" "I'm all stung!" "Dey're like hornets!" "Dey's on my face!" etc.*]

*Pharaoh.* Take 'em away, Moses!

*Moses* (*his voice drowning the others*). If I do, will you let 'em go?

*Pharaoh.* Sho' I will, dis time.

*Moses.* Do you mean it?

*Pharaoh.* Co'se I mean it! Doggone, one just stang me on de nose.

*Moses.* Begone! [*Lights come up as* AARON *lowers the rod. There is a moment of general recovery again.* PHARAOH *rubs his nose, looks at his hands, etc., as do the others.*] Now, how about it?

*Pharaoh* (*smiling*). Well, I'll tell you, Moses. Now dat de trick's over—

[MOSES *takes a step toward* PHARAOH.]

*Moses.* Listen, Pharaoh. You been lyin' to me, and I'm gittin' tired of it.

*Pharaoh.* I ain't lyin', I'm trickin', too. You been trickin' me and I been trickin' you.

*Moses.* I see. Well, I got one mo' trick up my sleeve which I didn't aim to wukk unless I had to. Caize when I does it, I cain't undo it.

*Pharaoh.* Wukk it an' I'll trick you right back. I don' say you ain't a good tricker, Moses. You is one of de best I ever seen. But I kin outtrick you. Dat's all.

*Moses.* It ain't only me dat's goin' to wukk dis trick. It's me an' de Lawd.

*Pharaoh.* Who?

*Moses.* De Lawd God of Israel.

*Pharaoh.* I kin outtrick you an' de Lawd too!

*Moses (angrily).* Now you done it, ol' King Pharaoh. You been mean to de Lawd's people, and de Lawd's been easy on you caize you didn' know no better. You been givin' me a lot of say-so and no do-so, and I didn' min' dat. But now you've got to braggin' dat you's better dan de Lawd, and dat's too many.

*Pharaoh.* You talk like a preacher, an' I never did like to hear preachers talk.

*Moses.* You ain't goin' to like it any better, when I strikes down de oldes' boy in every one of yo' people's houses.

*Pharaoh.* Now you've given up trickin' and is jest lyin'. (*He rises.*) Listen, I'm Pharaoh. I do de strikin' down yere. I strike down my enemies, and dere's no one in all Egypt kin kill who he wants to, 'ceptin' me.

*Moses.* I'm sorry, Pharaoh. Will you let de Hebrews go?

*Pharaoh.* You heard my word. [AARON *is lifting his rod again at a signal from* MOSES.] Now, no more tricks or I'll—

*Moses.* Oh, Lawd, you'll have to do it, I guess. Aaron, lift de rod.

[*There is a thunderclap, darkness and screams. The lights go up. Several of the younger men on the stage have fallen to the ground or are being held in the arms of the horrified elders.*]

*Pharaoh.* What have you done yere? Where's my boy?

[*Through the door come four men bearing a young man's body.*]

*First of the Four Men.* King Pharaoh.

[PHARAOH *drops into his chair, stunned, as the dead boy is brought to the throne.*]

*Pharaoh (grief-stricken).* Oh, my son, my fine son.

[*The courtiers look at him with mute appeal.*]

*Moses.* I'm sorry, Pharaoh, but you cain't fight de Lawd. Will you let his people go?

*Pharaoh.* Let them go.

[*The lights go out. The* CHOIR *begins, "Mary Don't You Weep," and continues until it is broken by the strains of "I'm Noways Weary and I'm Noways Tired." The latter is sung by many more voices than the former, and the cacophony ends as the latter grows in volume and the lights go up on the next scene.*]

SCENE IV

The CHILDREN OF ISRAEL *are marching on the treadmill and now singing fortissimo. They are of all ages and most of them are ragged. The men have packs on their shoulders, one or two have hand carts. The line stretches across the stage. It is nearing twilight, and the faces of the assemblage are illumined by the rays of the late afternoon sun. The upper treadmill carries a gradually rising and falling middle distance past the marchers. The foot of a mountain appears; a trumpet call is heard as the foot of the mountain reaches stage center. The marchers halt. The picture now shows the mountain running up out of sight off right. The singing stops. A babel of "What's de matter?" "Why do we stop?" "Tain't sundown yet!" "What's happened?" "What's goin' on?" "What are they blowin' for?" etc. Those look-*

*ing ahead begin to murmur, "It's Moses." "Moses." "What's happened to him?" The others take up the repetition of "Moses," and* MOSES *enters, on the arm of* AARON. *He is now an old man, as is his brother, and he totters toward the center of the stage. Cries of "What's de matter, Moses?" "You ain't hurt, is you?" "Ain't that too bad?" etc. He slowly seats himself on the rock at the foot of the mountain.*

*Aaron.* How you feelin' now, brother?

*Moses.* I'm so weary, Aaron. Seems like I was took all of a sudden.

*Aaron.* Do we camp yere?

*Moses (pathetically).* No, you got to keep goin'.

*Aaron.* But you cain't go no further tonight, brother.

*Moses.* Dis never happened to me befo'.

A *Young Woman.* But you's a ol' man, now, Father Moses. You cain't expect to go as fas' as we kin.

*Moses.* But de Lawd said I'd do it. He said I was to show you de Promised Land. Fo'ty years, I bin leadin' you. I led you out o' Egypt. I led you past Sinai, and through de wilderness. Oh, I cain't fall down on you now!

*Aaron.* Le's res' yere fo' de night. Den we'll see how you feel in de mo'nin'.

*Moses.* We tol' de scouts we'd meet 'em three miles furder on. I hate fo' 'em to come back all dis way to report. 'Tis gettin' a little dark, ain't it?

*Aaron.* It ain't dark, Brother.

*Moses.* No, it's my eyes.

*Aaron.* Maybe it's de dust.

*Moses.* No, I jest cain't seem to see. Oh, Lawd, dey cain't have a blind man

leadin' 'em! Where is you, Aaron?

*Aaron.* I'se right yere, Moses.

*Moses.* Do you think— *(Pause.)* Oh! Do you think it's de time He said?

*Aaron.* How you mean, Moses?

*[Crowd look from one to another in wonder.]*

*Moses.* He said I could lead 'em to de Jordan, dat I'd *see* de Promised Land, and dat's all de further I could go, on account I broke de laws. Little while back I thought I *did* see a river ahead, and a pretty land on de other side. *[Distant shouts "Hooray!" "Yere dey are!" "Dey traveled quick." etc.]* Where's de young leader of de troops? Where's Joshua?

*[The call "Joshua" is taken up by those on the right of the stage, followed almost immediately by "Yere he is!" "Moses wants you!" etc.]*

*[*JOSHUA *enters. He is a fine looking Negro of about thirty.]*

*Joshua (going to* MOSES' *side).* Yes, suh.

*Moses.* What's de shoutin' 'bout, Joshua?

*Joshua.* De scouts is back wid de news. De Jordan is right ahead of us, and Jericho is jest on de other side. Moses, we're dere! *[There are cries of "Hallelujah!" "De Lawd be praised!" "Hooray!" "De Kingdom's comin'!" etc. With a considerable stir among the marchers, several new arrivals crowd in from right, shouting "Moses, we're dere!"* JOSHUA *seeing the newcomers.]* Yere's de scouts!

*[Three very ragged and dusty young men advance to* MOSES.]

*Moses (as the shouting dies).* So it's de River Jordan?

*First Scout.* Yes, suh.

*Moses.* All we got to take is de city of Jericho.

*First Scout.* Yes, suh.

*Moses.* Joshua, you got to take charge of de fightin' men, an' Aaron's gotta stay by de priests.

*Joshua.* What about you?

*Moses.* You are leavin' me behind. Joshua, you gonter get de fightin' men together and take dat city befo' sundown.

*Joshua.* It's a big city, Moses, wid walls all 'round it. We ain't got enough men.

*Moses.* You'll take it, Joshua.

*Joshua.* Yes, suh, but how?

*Moses.* Move up to de walls wid our people. Tell de priests to go wid you with de rams' horns. You start marchin' 'roun' dem walls, and den—

*Joshua.* Yes, suh.

*Moses.* De Lawd'll take charge, jest as he's took charge ev'y time I've led you against a city. He ain't never failed, has he?

*Several Voices.* No, Moses. (*All raise their heads.*)

*Moses.* And he ain't goin' to fail us now. (*He prays. All bow.*) Oh, Lawd, I'm turnin' over our brave young men to you, caize I know you don' want me to lead 'em any further. (*Rises.*) Jest like you said, I've got to de Jordan but I cain't git over it. An' yere dey goin' now to take de city of Jericho. In a little while dey'll be marchin' 'roun' it. An' would you please be so good as to tell 'em what to do? Amen. (*To* JOSHUA.) Go ahead. Ev'ybody follows Joshua now. Give de signal to move on wid e'vything. [*A trumpet is heard.*] You camp fo' de night in de City of Jericho. (MOSES *seats himself on the rock.*)

*Joshua.* Cain't we help you, Moses?

*Moses.* You go ahead. De Lawd's got his plans fo' me. Soun' de signal to march. [*Another trumpet call is heard. The company starts marching off.* AARON *lingers a moment.*] Take care of de Ark of de Covenant, Aaron.

*Aaron.* Yes, Brother. Good-bye.

*Moses.* Good-bye, Aaron. [*The singing is resumed softly and dies away. The last of the marchers has disappeared.*] Yere I is, Lawd. De chillun is goin' into de Promised Land. [GOD *enters from behind the hill. He walks to* MOSES, *puts his hands on his shoulders.*] You's with me, ain't you, Lawd?

*God.* Co'se I is.

*Moses.* Guess I'm through, Lawd. Jest like you said I'd be, when I broke de tablets of de law. De ol' machine's broke down.

*God.* Jest what was it I said to you, Moses? Do you remember?

*Moses.* You said I couldn't go into de Promised Land.

*God.* Dat's so. But dat ain't all dey was to it.

*Moses.* How you mean, Lawd?

*God.* Moses, you been a good man. You been a good leader of my people. You got me angry once, dat's true. And when you anger me I'm a God of Wrath. But I never meant you wasn't gonter have what was comin' to you. An' I ain't goin' to do you out of it, Moses. It's jest de country acrost de river dat you ain't gonter enter. You gonter have a Promised Land. I been gettin' it ready fo' you, fo' a long time. Kin you stand up?

*Moses* (*rising, with* GOD'S *help*). Yes, suh, Lawd.

*God.* Come on, I'm goin' to show it to you. We goin' up dis hill to see it. Moses, it's a million times nicer dan de Land of Canaan. [*They start up the hill.*]

*Moses.* I cain't hardly see.

*God.* Don't worry. Dat's jest caize you so old.

[*They take a step or two up the hill, when* MOSES *stops suddenly.*]

*Moses.* Oh!

*God.* What's de matter?

*Moses.* We cain't be doin' dis!

*God.* Co'se we kin!

*Moses.* But I fo'got! I fo'got about Joshua and de fightin' men!

*God.* How about 'em?

*Moses.* Dey're marchin' on Jericho. I tol' 'em to march aroun' de walls and den de Lawd would be dere to tell 'em what to do.

*God.* Dat's all right. He's dere.

*Moses.* Den who's dis helpin' me up de hill?

*God.* Yo' faith, yo' God.

*Moses.* And is you over dere helpin' them too, Lawd? Is you goin' to tell dem poor chillun what to do?

*God.* Co'se I is. Listen, Moses. I'll show you how I'm helpin' dem.

[*From the distance comes the blast of the rams' horns, the sound of crumbling walls, a roar, and a moment's silence. The* CHOIR *begins "Joshua Fit De Battle of Jericho" and continues through the rest of the scene.*]

*Moses.* You did it, Lawd! You've tooken it! Listen to de chillun'—dey's in de Land of Canaan at last! You's de only God dey ever was, ain't you, Lawd?

*God* (*quietly*). Come on, ol' man. [*They continue up the hill.*]

[*The stage is darkened.*]

*Mr. Deshee* (*in the dark*). But even dat scheme didn' work. Caize after dey got into the Land of Canaan dey went to de dogs again. And dey went into bondage again. Only dis time it was in de City of Babylon.

[*The* CHOIR, *which has been singing "Cain't Stay Away," stops as the next scene begins.*]

SCENE V

*Under a low ceiling is a room vaguely resembling a Negro night club in New Orleans. Two or three long tables run across the room, and on the left is a table on a dais with a gaudy canopy above it. The table bears a card marked "Reserved for King and guests."*

*Flashy young men and women are seated at the tables. About a dozen couples are dancing in the foreground to the tune of a jazz orchestra. The costumes are what would be worn at a Negro masquerade to represent the debauchees of Babylon.*

*First Man.* When did yuh git to Babylon?

*Second Man.* I jes' got in yesterday.

*Third Man* (*dancing*). How do you like dis baby, Joe?

*Fourth Man.* Hot damn! She could be de King's pet!

*A Woman.* Anybody seen my papa?

*Third Man.* Don' fo'git de dance at de High Priest's house tomorrow.

[*The dance stops as a bugle call is heard. Enter* MASTER OF CEREMONIES.]

*Master of Ceremonies.* Stop! To-night's guest of honor, de King of Babylon an' party of five.

[*Enter the* KING *and five girls. The* KING *has on an imitation ermine cloak over his conventional evening clothes and wears a diamond tiara. All rise as the* KING *enters, and sing, "Hail, de King of Bab—Bab—Babylon."*]

*King.* Wait till you see de swell table I got. [*He crosses the stage to his table. The girls are jabbering.*] Remind me to send you a peck of rubies in de mo'nin'.

*Master of Ceremonies.* Ev'nin', King!

*King.* Good ev'nin'. How's de party goin'?

*Master of Ceremonies.* Bes' one we ever had in Babylon, King.

*King.* Any Jew boys yere?

*Master of Ceremonies (indicating some of the others).* Lot o' dem yere. I kin go git mo' if you want 'em.

*King.* I was really referrin' to de High Priest. He's a 'ticlar frien' o' mine an' he might drop in. You know what he look like?

*Master of Ceremonies.* No, suh, but I'll be on de look-out fo' him.

*King.* O.K. Now le's have a li'l good time.

*Master of Ceremonies.* Yes, suh. *(To the orchestra.)* Let 'er go, boys.

*[The music begins, waiters appear with food and great urns painted gold and silver, from which they pour out wine for the guests. The* MASTER OF CEREMONIES *exits. The* KING's *dancing-girls go to the middle of the floor, and start to dance. The* KING *puts his arms about the waists of two girls, and draws them to him.]*

*King.* Hot damn! Da's de way! Let de Jew boys see our gals kin dance better'n dere's. *[There is an ad lib. babel of "Da's de truth, King!" "I don' know —we got some good gals, too!" etc.]* Dey ain' nobody in de worl' like de Babylon gals.

*[The dancing grows faster, the watchers keep time with handclaps. The door at the left opens suddenly, and the* PROPHET, *a patriarchal, ragged figure enters. He looks belligerently about the room, and is followed almost immediately by the* MASTER OF CEREMONIES.]*

*Prophet.* Stop! *[The music and the dancers halt.]*

*King.* What's the idea, bustin' up my party?

*Master of Ceremonies.* He said he was expected, King. I thought mebbe he was de—

*King.* Did you think he was de High Priest of de Hebrews? Why, he's jest an ol' bum! De High Priest is a fashion plate. T'row dis ole bum out o' yere!

*Prophet.* Stop!

*[Those who have been advancing to seize him stop, somewhat amused.]*

*King.* Wait a minute. Don't throw him out. Let's see what he has to say.

*Prophet.* Listen to me, King of Babylon! I've been sent yere by de Lawd God Jehovah. Don't you dare lay a hand on de Prophet!

*King.* Oh, you're a prophet, is yuh? Well, you know we don' keer much fo' prophets in dis part of de country.

*Prophet.* Listen to me, sons and daughters of Babylon! Listen, you children of Israel dat's given yo'selves over to de evil ways of yo' oppressors! You're all wallowin' like hogs in sin, an' de wrath of Gawd ain' goin' to be held back much longer. I'm tellin' you, repent befo' it's too late. Repent befo' Jehovah casts down de same fire dat burned up Sodom and Gomorrah. Repent befo' de— *[Yells increase as the* PROPHET *continues.]*

*[The* HIGH PRIEST *enters Left. He is a fat voluptuary, elaborately clothed in brightly colored robes. He walks in hand in hand with a gaudily dressed "chippy."]*

*High Priest.* *[Noise stops.]* Whoa, dere! What you botherin' the King fo'?

*Prophet (wheeling).* And you, de High Priest of all Israel, walkin' de town wid a dirty li'l tramp.

*King.* Seems to be a frien' o' yours, Jake.

*High Priest (crossing to the* KING *with his girl).* Aw, he's one of dem wild men, like Jeremiah and Isaiah. Don' let him bother you none. *(Pushes* PROPHET *aside and goes to* KING's *table.)*

*Prophet.* You consort with harlots,

an' yo' is pollution in the sight of de Lawd. De Lawd God's goin' to smite you down, jest as he's goin' to smite down all dis wicked world! (*Grabs* HIGH PRIEST *and turns him around.*)

*King* (*angrily against the last part of the preceding speech*). Wait a minute. I'm getting tired of this. Don' throw him out. Jest kill him! [*There is the sound of a shot. The* PROPHET *falls.*]

*Prophet.* Smite 'em down, Lawd, like you said. Dey ain't a decent person left in de whole world.

[*He dies.* MASTER OF CEREMONIES, *revolver in hand, looks down at the* PROPHET.]

*Master of Ceremonies.* He's dead, King.

*King.* Some of you boys take him out.

[*A couple of young men come from the background and walk off with the body.*]

*High Priest.* Don' know whether you should'a done that, King.

*King.* Why not?

*High Priest.* I don' know whether de Lawd would like it.

*King.* Now, listen, Jake. You know yo' Lawd ain't payin' much attention to dis man's town. Except fo' you boys, it's tho'ly protected by de Gods o' Babylon.

*High Priest.* I know, but jest de same—

*King.* Look yere, s'pose I give you a couple hund'ed pieces of silver. Don' you s'pose you kin arrange to persuade yo' Gawd to keep his hands off?

*High Priest* (*oilily*). Well of co'se we could try. I dunno how well it would work.

[*As the* HIGH PRIEST *speaks, the* KING *claps his hands.* MASTER OF CEREMONIES *enters with bag of money.*]

*King.* Yere it is.

*High Priest* (*smiling*). I guess we kin square things up. (*He prays—whiningly.*) Oh Lawd, please forgive my po' frien' de King o' Babylon. He didn't know what he was doin' an'—

[*There is a clap of thunder, darkness for a second. The lights go up and* GOD *is standing in the center of the room.*]

*God* (*in a voice of doom*). Dat's about enough. [*The guests are horrified.*] I's stood all I kin from you. I tried to make dis a good earth. I helped Adam, I helped Noah, I helped Moses, an' I helped David. What's de grain dat grew out of de seed? Sin! Nothin' but sin throughout de whole world. I've given you ev'y chance. I sent you warriors and prophets. I've given you laws and commandments, an' you betrayed my trust. Ev'ything I've given you, you've defiled. Ev'y time I've fo'given you, you've mocked me. An' now de High Priest of Israel tries to trifle wid my name. Listen, you chillun of darkness, yo' Lawd is tired. I'm tired of de struggle to make you worthy of de breath I gave you. I put you in bondage ag'in to cure you an' yo' worse dan you was amongst de flesh pots of Egypt. So I renounce you. Listen to the words of yo' lawd God Jehovah, for dey is de last words yo' ever hear from me. I repent of dese people dat I have made and I will deliver dem no more.

[*There is darkness and cries of* "Mercy!" "Have pity, Lawd!" "We didn' mean it, Lawd!" "Forgive us, Lawd!" *etc. The* CHOIR *sings* "Death's Gwinter Lay His Cold Icy Hands on Me" *until the lights go up on the next scene.*]

SCENE VI

GOD *is writing at his desk. Outside, past the door, goes* HOSEA, *a dignified old man, with wings like* JACOB'S. GOD, *sensing his presence, looks up from the paper he is examining, and follows him out of the corner of his eye. Angrily he resumes his work as soon as* HOSEA *is out of sight. There is a knock on the door.*

God. Who is it?

[GABRIEL *enters.*]

Gabriel. It's de delegation, Lawd.

God (*wearily*). Tell 'em to come in.

[ABRAHAM, ISAAC, JACOB, *and* MOSES *enter.*] Good mo'nin', gen'lemen.

The Visitors. Good mo'nin', Lawd.

God. What kin I do for you?

Moses. You know, Lawd. Go back to our people.

God (*shaking his head*). Ev'ry day fo' hund'eds of years you boys have come in to ask dat same thing. De answer is still de same. I repented of de people I made. I said I would deliver dem no more. Good mo'nin', gen'lemen. [*The four visitors rise and exeunt.* GABRIEL *remains.*] Gabe, why do dey do it?

Gabriel. I 'spect dey think you gonter change yo' mind.

God (*sadly*). Dey don' know me.

[HOSEA *again passes the door. His shadow shows on wall.* GABRIEL *is perplexed, as he watches.* GOD *again looks surreptitiously over His shoulder at the passing figure.*] I don' like dat, either.

Gabriel. What, Lawd?

God. Dat man.

Gabriel. He's jest a prophet, Lawd. Dat's jest old Hosea. He jest come up the other day.

God. I know. He's one of de few dat's come up yere since I was on de earth last time.

Gabriel. Ain' been annoyin' you, has he?

God. I don' like him walkin' past de door.

Gabriel. All you got to do is tell him to stop, Lawd.

God. Yes, I know. I don' want to tell him. He's got a right up yere or he wouldn' be yere.

Gabriel. You needn' be bothered by him hangin' aroun' de office all de time. I'll tell 'im. Who's he think—

God. No, Gabe. I find it ain't in me to stop him. I sometimes jest wonder why he don' come in and say hello.

Gabriel. You want him to do dat? (*He moves as if to go to the door.*)

God. He never has spoke to me, and if he don' wanta come in, I ain't gonter make him. But dat ain't de worst of it, Gabriel.

Gabriel. What is, Lawd?

God. Ev'y time he goes past de door I hears a voice.

Gabriel. One of de angels?

God (*shaking his head*). It's from de earth. It's a man.

Gabriel. You mean he's prayin'?

God. No, he ain't exactly prayin'. He's jest talkin' in such a way dat I got to lissen. His name is Hezdrel.

Gabriel. Is he on de books?

God. No, not yet. But ev'y time dat Hosea goes past I hear dat voice.

Gabriel. Den tell it to stop.

God. I find I don' want to do that, either. Dey's gettin' ready to take Jerusalem down dere. Dat was my big fine city. Dis Hezdrel, he's jest one of de defenders. (*Suddenly and passionately, almost wildly.*) I ain't comin' down. You hear me? I ain't comin' down. (*He looks at* GABRIEL.) Go ahead, Gabriel. 'Tend to yo' chores. I'm gonter keep wukkin' yere.

Gabriel. I hates to see you feelin' like dis, Lawd.

God. Dat's all right. Even bein' Gawd ain't a bed of roses. [GABRIEL *exits.* HOSEA'S *shadow is on the wall.*

*For a second* HOSEA *hesitates.* GOD *looks at the wall. Goes to window.*] I hear you. I know yo' fightin' bravely, but I ain't comin' down. Oh, why don' you leave me alone? You know you ain't talkin' to me. *Is you talkin' to me?* I cain't stand yo' talkin' dat way. I kin only hear part of what you' sayin', and it puzzles me. Don' you know you cain't puzzle God? (*A pause. Then, tenderly.*) Do you want me to come down dere ve'y much? You know I said I wouldn't come down? (*Fiercely.*) Why don' he answer me a little? (*With clenched fists, looks down through the window.*) Listen! I'll tell you what I'll do. I ain't goin' to promise you anythin', and I ain't goin' to do nothin' to help you. I'm jest feelin' a little low, an' I'm only comin' down to make myself feel a little better, dat's all.

[*The stage is darkened.* CHOIR *begins* "A Blind Man Stood In De Middle of De Road," *and continues until the lights go up on the next scene.*]

### SCENE VII

*It is a shadowed corner beside the walls of the temple in Jerusalem. The light of camp fires flickers on the figure of* HEZDREL, *who was* ADAM *in Part I. He stands in the same position* ADAM *held when first discovered but in his right hand is a sword, and his left is in a sling. Around him are several prostrate bodies. Pistol and cannon shots, then a trumpet call. Six young men enter from left in command of a* CORPORAL. *They are all armed.*

*Corporal.* De fightin's stopped fo' de night, Hezdrel.

*Hezdrel.* Yes?

*Corporal.* Dey're goin' to begin ag'in at cockcrow. [*Man enters, crosses the stage and exits.*] Herod say he's goin' to take de temple tomorrow, burn de books and de Ark of de Covenant, and put us all to de sword.

*Hezdrel.* Yo' ready, ain't you?

*Everybody.* Yes, Hezdrel.

*Hezdrel.* Did de food get in through de hole in de city wall?

[*Two soldiers enter, cross the stage and exit.*]

*Corporal.* Yessuh, we's goin' back to pass it out now.

*Hezdrel.* Good. Any mo' of our people escape today?

*Corporal.* Ol' Herod's got de ol' hole covered up now, but fifteen of our people got out a new one we made.

[*Other soldiers enter, cross the stage and exit.*]

*Hezdrel.* Good. Take dese yere wounded men back and git 'em took care of.

*Corporal.* Yes, suh.

[*They pick up the bodies on the ground and carry them offstage as* HEZDREL *speaks.*]

*Hezdrel.* So dey gonter take de temple in de mo'nin'? We'll be waitin' for 'em. Jest remember, boys, when dey kill us we leap out of our skins, right into de lap of God.

[*The men disappear with the wounded; from the deep shadow upstage comes* GOD.]

*God.* Hello, Hezdrel—Adam.

*Hezdrel* (*rubbing his forehead*). Who is you?

*God.* Me? I'm jest an ol' preacher, from back in de hills.

*Hezdrel.* What you doin' yere?

*God.* I heard you boys was fightin'. I jest wanted to see how it was goin'.

*Hezdrel.* Well, it ain't goin' so well.

*God.* Dey got you skeered, huh?

*Hezdrel.* Look yere, who is you, a spy in my brain?

*God.* Cain't you see I's one of yo' people?

*Hezdrel.* Listen, Preacher, we ain't skeered. We's gonter be killed, but we ain't skeered.

*God.* I's glad to hear dat. Kin I ask you a question, Hezdrel?

*Hezdrel.* What is it?

*God.* How is it you is so brave?

*Hezdrel.* Caize we got faith, dat's why!

*God.* Faith? In who?

*Hezdrel.* In our dear Lawd God.

*God.* But God say he abandoned ev' one down yere.

*Hezdrel.* Who say dat? Who dare say dat of de Lawd God of Hosea?

*God.* De God of Hosea?

*Hezdrel.* You heard me. Look yere, you *is* a spy in my brain!

*God.* No, I ain't, Hezdrel. I'm jest puzzled. You ought to know dat.

*Hezdrel.* How come you so puzzled 'bout de God of Hosea?

*God.* I don' know. Maybe I jest don' hear things. You see, I live 'way back in de hills.

*Hezdrel.* What you wanter find out?

*God.* Ain't de God of Hosea de same Jehovah dat was de God of Moses?

*Hezdrel* (*contemptuously*). No. Dat ol' God of wrath and vengeance? We have de God dat Hosea preached to us. He's de one God.

*God.* Who's he?

*Hezdrel* (*reverently*). De God of mercy.

*God.* Hezdrel, don' you think dey must be de same God?

*Hezdrel.* I don' know. I ain't bothered to think much about it. Maybe dey is. Maybe our God is de same ol' God. I guess we jest got tired of his appearance dat ol' way.

*God.* What you mean, Hezdrel?

*Hezdrel.* Oh, dat ol' God dat walked de earth in de shape of a man. I guess he lived wid man so much dat all he seen was de sins in man. Dat's what made him de God of wrath and vengeance. Co'se he made Hosea. An' Hosea never would a found what mercy was unless dere was a little of it in God, too. Anyway, he ain't a fearsome God no mo'. Hosea showed us dat.

*God.* How you s'pose Hosea found dat mercy?

*Hezdrel.* De only way he could find it. De only way I found it. De only way anyone kin find it.

*God.* How's dat?

*Hezdrel.* Through sufferin'.

*God* (*after a pause*). What if dey kill you in de mo'nin', Hezdrel.

*Hezdrel.* If dey do, dey do. Dat's all.

*God.* Herod say he's goin' to burn de temple—

*Hezdrel.* So he say.

*God.* And burn de Ark an' de books. Den dat's de end of de books, ain't it?

*Hezdrel* (*buoyantly*). What you mean? If he burns dem things in dere? Naw. Dem's jest copies.

*God.* Where is de others?

*Hezdrel* (*tapping his head*). Dey's a set in yere. Fifteen got out through de hole in the city wall today. A hundred and fifty got out durin' de week. Each of em is a set of de books. Dey's scattered safe all over de countryside now, jest waitin' to git pen and paper fo' to put 'em down again.

*God* (*proudly*). Dey cain't lick you, kin dey Hezdrel?

*Hezdrel* (*smiling*). I know dey cain't. [*Trumpet.*] You better get out o' yere, Preacher, if you wanter carry de news to yo' people. It'll soon be daylight.

*God.* I'm goin'. (*He takes a step*

THE GREEN PASTURES © COPYRIGHT 1936 BY WARNER BROS. PICTURES, INC.

*upstage and stops.*) Want me to take any message?

*Hezdrel.* Tell de people in de hills dey ain't nobody like de Lawd God of Hosea.

*God.* I will. If dey kill you tomorrow I'll bet dat God of Hosea'll be waitin' for you.

*Hezdrel.* I *know* he will.

*God (quietly).* Thank you, Hezdrel.

*Hezdrel.* Fo' what?

*God.* Fo' tellin' me so much. You see I been so far away, I guess I was jest way behin' de times.

[*He exits. Pause, then trumpet sounds.*]

[HEZDREL *paces back and forth once or twice. Another young soldier appears. Other men enter and stand grouped about* HEZDREL.]

*Second Officer (excitedly).* De cock's jest crowed, Hezdrel. Dey started de fightin' ag'in.

*Hezdrel.* We's ready for 'em. Come on, boys. [*From the darkness upstage comes another group of soldiers.*] Dis is de day dey say dey'll git us. Le's fight till de last man goes. What d'you say?

*Corporal.* Le's go, Hezdrel!

*Hezdrel (calling left).* Give 'em ev'ything, boys!

[*There is a movement toward the left, a bugle call and the sound of distant battle. The lights go out. The* CHOIR *is heard singing, "March On," triumphantly. They continue to sing after the lights go up on the next scene.*]

SCENE VIII

It is the same setting as the Fish Fry Scene in Part I. The same angels are present but the CHOIR, instead of marching, is standing in a double row on an angle upstage right. GOD is seated in an armchair near center. He faces the audience. As the CHOIR continues to sing, GABRIEL enters, unnoticed by the chattering angels. He looks at GOD who is staring thoughtfully toward the audience.

Gabriel. You look a little pensive, Lawd. [GOD nods his head.] Have a seegar, Lawd?

God. No thanks, Gabriel.

[GABRIEL goes to the table, accepts a cup of custard; chats with the angel behind the table for a moment as he sips, puts the cup down and returns to the side of GOD.]

Gabriel. You look awful pensive, Lawd. You been sittin' yere, lookin' dis way, an awful long time. Is it somethin' serious, Lawd?

God. Very serious, Gabriel.

Gabriel (awed by His tone). Lawd, is de time come for me to blow?

God. Not yet, Gabriel. I'm just thinkin'.

Gabriel. What about, Lawd? [Puts up hand. Singing stops.]

God. 'Bout somethin' de boy tol' me. Somethin' 'bout Hosea, and himself. How dey foun' somethin'.

Gabriel. What, Lawd?

God. Mercy. (A pause.) Through sufferin', he said.

Gabriel. Yes, Lawd.

God. I'm tryin' to find it, too. It's awful impo'tant. It's awful impo'tant to all de people on my earth. Did he mean dat even God must suffer?

[GOD continues to look out over the audience for a moment and then a look of surprise comes into his face. He sighs. In the distance a voice cries.]

The Voice. Oh, look at him! Oh, look, dey goin' to make him carry it up dat high hill! Dey goin' to nail him to it! Oh, dat's a terrible burden for one man to carry!

[GOD rises and murmurs "Yes!" as if in recognition. The heavenly beings have been watching him closely, and now, seeing him smile gently, draw back, relieved. All the angels burst into "Hallelujah, King Jesus." GOD continues to smile as the lights fade away. The singing becomes fortissimo.]

*Curtain*

◇◇◇◇◇◇◇◇◇◇◇◇◇◇◇◇◇◇◇◇◇◇◇◇◇◇◇

FOR DISCUSSION

PART I

SCENE I:

1. The first scene in any play usually gives the setting, indicates the plot, and introduces some of the main characters. In what way does Scene one fulfill these requirements? Why does the play begin on earth and later switch to heaven? List some of the words which give us the atmosphere of a little Negro town in Louisiana.

2. The method used in your Catechism class is that of question and answer. Is there any similarity here in the presentation of Scene one? Comment on the statement: "Dey wasn't no sin, so dey [the angels] musta had a good time."

SCENE II:

1. What actions or events in Scene two had already been mentioned in Scene one as probably happening in heaven? What does the author mean by calling this scene "a pre-Creation Heaven with compromises?" Is it a fault in the play to have scenery, which could only be found on earth, existing in heaven before the earth was created? List some of the angels' joys in heaven.

2. How does the author explain that Satan is no longer an angel? What does the Stout Angel mean when she says, ". . . if a lady wants a little constitutional she kin fly 'til she's wing-weary widout gittin' insulted"?

261

3. An important scene in the play is the first appearance of the Lawd. What did the author gain by introducing Him through a semi-religious chant-song, instead of having Him stride in and begin speaking? What added effect derives from the first direct words which God speaks, "Let de fish fry proceed"? What other things happen which show how kind He is? List some words and phrases used by de Lawd and Gabriel which are characteristically Negro. How does the singing of the choir in the background add atmosphere to the play? Discuss.

4. Describe the event which leads up to the creation of the world. What great virtue of God is shown as He creates a giant sun "to dry my cherubs' wings"? What is the most powerful event in Scene two?

SCENE III:

1. In Scene three describe the two main events which take place in Adam's life. How does the author indicate that Eve will bring about Adam's fall?

2. What is the purpose of introducing Mr. Deshee and his class again at the end of Scene three? Explain how many years are passed over, how new characters are introduced, and how swift transitions are made.

SCENE IV:

1. Scene four opens with Cain standing over the dead Abel. Since the creation of the world and man this is the first time Cain had ever seen what new strange thing?

2. What are de Lawd's instructions to Cain? What reason did Cain give for killing Abel? What reason does the Bible give for Cain's killing Abel? What is the significance of the song which the choir sings as Cain leaves God's presence?

SCENE V:

1. What staging technique is made use of in presenting the opening part of Scene five? Explain how you think it works.

What is the significance of the sign "Nod Parish. County Line"?

2. How does the author intimate that the people of Nod Parish are rather sinful? What is the meaning behind Cain's Girl's sudden shifting from "Country Boy" to "City Boy"? Explain the significance of the choir's song and God's brief entrance at the close of Scene five.

SCENE VI:

1. Throughout this play the author is presenting what he thinks heaven would look like to the uneducated Negro mind. Do you think his description of God's Office is rich enough? Should the office be more ornate, filled with signs of wealth? Why, or why not?

2. Scene six is seemingly an unimportant scene, yet it serves what definite purpose in the scheme of the play? List some of the "duties" which God has to attend to, even though they are Gabriel's tasks. What two things do we learn about "de poor little earth" from God's conversation with Gabriel?

SCENE VII:

1. What various types of sin are symbolized in Scene seven? What charming scene breaks up the depressing picture of sin as God walks along? Explain the irony in de Lawd's statement, "Now dat's nice to see people prayin'."

2. Re-read de Lawd's speech just before He meets Noah. Do you see any foreshadowing here of things to come? What virtues does Noah seem to possess?

SCENE VIII:

1. In what tone of voice do you think Noah says the words: "I should have known you. I should have seen de glory"? What does he mean when he says, "I ain' very much, but I'se all I got"? How does this idea apply to us all?

2. Describe the scene in which God gives instructions for building the Ark, and what Noah should take into it. What humorous event takes place? What is the

significance of the song the choir sings as the scene closes?

SCENE IX:

1. In what ways does the early part of Scene nine agree with what we actually read in the Bible about Noah's preparations? Do you think there is any connection suggested between this final crime of murder and the coming of the rain? What casual remarks of the bystanders take on a foreboding significance as they move away to shelter from the oncoming rain?

SCENE X:

1. Is the author's point one of humor only when he portrays Noah as feeling "congenial" after finishing the keg of liquor? Does the scene of the Ark's grounding agree substantially with the account given in the Bible? Explain.

2. How does the appearance of God on the Ark help to bring the whole of Scene ten and Part I to a satisfactory conclusion? What foreboding statements do Gabriel and God make as the scene ends? How does this help prepare for what follows?

PART TWO

SCENE I:

1. It is a part of dramatic technique to have two minor characters exchange views on what action has been going on off stage in order to acquaint the audience with the latest developments. What recent events are made known to the audience by the two cleaning women in scene one? What reason is given for God's having such a plain office? Does Gabriel's number of "eighteen thousand nine hund'ed and sixty" refer to sinners killed, or to thunderbolts thrown by the Lawd? Explain.

2. What is de Lawd's new scheme to save mankind? What do we find out about Moses before we see him? What are his qualifications for his new task of leading the Jews into the Land of Canaan? Who are the Philistines who have to be driven out?

SCENE II:

1. What virtues and characteristics of Moses are shown in the beginning of Scene two? Who did Moses think was trying to fool him when God spoke? Why was Moses cured of stuttering? Zipporah seems to be one of the few good women we have seen in the play. With what other female characters does she contrast?

2. What new power is given to Moses? Is he just a "tricker" or has God given him the power to work miracles? What is the difference between a miracle and a magician's trick? What is the significance of the song "Go Down, Moses" at the end of the scene? Read the words of this song in the Folk Literature section near the end of this book before answering.

SCENE III:

1. What indications of the simple Negro's love of display make this opening of Scene three convincing? Briefly describe the scene in which Moses shows his supremacy over the Head Magician. What two instances, before Moses's arrival, show us what an evil man the Head Magician is?

2. What favor does Moses ask of Pharaoh, and what is the ruler's first reaction to it? Enumerate the "tricks" Moses is forced to perform before Pharaoh gives in. How does Pharaoh try to trick Moses? During this episode, Moses seems to have used a bad means to achieve a good end. Is he justified? Explain and discuss.

SCENE IV:

1. Why wasn't Moses allowed to enter the Promised Land? How does the city of Jericho fall into the hands of Aaron and his people? To what Promised Land does God personally escort Moses? What device does the author use to tell us that the Jews could not stand the prosperity of Canaan?

SCENE V:

1. How is the sinful city of Babylon symbolized as Scene five opens? What two types of people are contrasted in this

scene? What sinful act causes God to appear in the midst of the sinners? What are de Lawd's final words to his sinful people?

2. Can you think of any instances during the past two or three hundred years in which Christ has appeared, or sent someone else, on earth to warn sinners that they must do penance or lose their souls? Discuss.

## SCENE VI:

1. What causes de Lawd's remark, "Even being Gawd ain' a bed of roses"? What emotions does this simple statement arouse in you? What are the various emotions which seem to tear at de Lawd's heart as He gives His speech to the silent Hosea?

2. In this scene we see an example of perseverance in prayer. What characters give us this example? Do you think it true to say that only the prayers of a comparative few keep God from destroying our modern world because of its sins? Discuss.

## SCENE VII:

1. What do we learn of Hezdrel from his early conversation with his corporal? How does this man's character grow in our estimation although all he does is talk? Hezdrel seems to be the most clear-sighted character of all the men we have seen in the play. Show how this is true. Discuss.

2. What is Hezdrel's new idea about God? What are the two most important words spoken by Hezdrel in this scene? Explain and discuss. What plan did Hezdrel concoct in order to save the books of the Temple? What is the significance of the song "March On" as the scene ends?

3. Hezdrel says that the God of Moses was a God of wrath. What reasons did God have for being angry with the people? Do you think that Hezdrel's statement is entirely true? What scenes in the play show that God is also loving, tender, and kind? Does God always punish men here on earth for their sins? Why is He always merciful even when He punishes?

## SCENE VIII:

1. What changes have taken place in God since we first saw Him at an earlier fish fry? What is the new plan God sees He must carry out if mankind is to be saved and redeemed? Is the ending of the play satisfactory? Show how it synopsizes all the important events which have taken place.

## MISCELLANEOUS:

1. Is this play a drama in the strict sense? or is it more a dramatic pageant? Explain. In your estimation what was the most powerful scene in the play? the most humorous? the most emotional? Discuss.

2. Re-read the play and find motives for (a) the creation of the world; (b) the flood; (c) the leading of the Jews out of Egypt; (d) the crucifixion of Christ.

3. God is, we know, a pure spirit. It is a mistake, then, to think of Him as feeling and behaving as mere men do. Still, since men are creatures of sense and imagination, they do commonly speak of God and even to Him in familiar human terms. So long as they realize that this is only a manner of speaking, there is no harm in it. Bearing all this in mind, how appropriate do you find the picture of God given in the play? Discuss. Did you detect any bits of blasphemy (i.e., mocking speeches against God) in the play? If so, point them out. Were these remarks always made by evil people? Could a pagan enjoy this play?

4. Generally speaking, our suffering is the result of our sinful or imprudent actions or of those of other people; or, suffering is often due to natural causes beyond our control. God allows His established laws to run their course. He is not happy when we act contrary to His laws and suffer the consequences. Point out natural and evil results of some particular sins: e.g., drunkenness, murder, stealing.

5. God does not take delight in our pains and troubles, but He blesses us if our minds and wills see and adopt the right attitude toward whatever happens to us.

What should this attitude be? Is it consistent in one who has this attitude to groan and moan about the pain he endures? Why or why not?

PROJECTS

1. Take the Bible and read the actual account of each of the scenes presented in the play. Compare the two versions.

2. Select an event from the Bible, e.g., Daniel in the lion's den, and write it in the dramatic style of Marc Connelly in this play. Present it for the class.

3. Go to the library and read the critics' reviews of this play in various magazines and newspapers of 1930. Not all the critics were favorable. Prepare a report on these reviews, adding a criticism of your own.

4. If possible, obtain Roark Bradford's *Ol' Man Adam and His Chillun*, the book which inspired this play, and read sections to the class.

5. At the library read a book describing what the Miracle and Morality Cycle Plays of English literature are. Then compare *The Green Pastures* with these medieval dramas which resemble it so much.

# MODERN NONFICTION

## BIOGRAPHY

Do you remember Humpty Dumpty? How all the king's horses and all the king's men could never put him together again? It must seem to the biographer sometimes that he is attempting just as hopeless a task. For he is trying to put together a life—in print. It is not easy to do.

If the biographer is too close to his subject, it is hard to keep an unprejudiced viewpoint; if he is too far removed in time, it is hard to get trustworthy information. The autobiographer has an especially hard time; for since he is writing about himself, he must avoid the two unpleasant extremes of boastfulness and false modesty. However, the excellent biographical writings of the last few years prove that such difficulties can be overcome. One successful method seems to be to use the objective approach—that is, to tell what the subject of the account did, what he said, how he felt, what he accomplished. With this method, whether the author writes of himself or of someone else, he is letting the life tell its own story. If he is a good reporter, he makes it possible for the reader to make his own estimates of the character and personality portrayed.

Biography is not a new art; in fact it is one of the oldest literary forms. It is really personalized history. Some of the great biographies of all times are to be found in the Bible. And a Greek historian of the first century, Plutarch, wrote biographies so interesting that they served as the basis of some of Shakespeare's finest plays.

Since the days of Plutarch, biography has swung through many changes in treatment. The famous Greek had included trivial events, a word, a joke, because he realized that such trifles may be as revealing of character as campaigns and battles. Then came a time when biography was stiff and dignified, when it concerned itself only with heroes, and chiefly with their virtues. Not many years ago, we passed through an unpleasant "debunking" period, when the author in an attempt to avoid sentimentalism, went to the other extreme of overdrawing faults and failures. Some writers seemed to delight in dragging a good name through the mire. Fortunately the public has tired of sensational muckraking, just as it had tired of the sentimentalized portrait painting that preceded it. The reader has a right to expect in a biography information as accurate as may be obtained, enlivened by sidelights of human interest. Modern biography is providing just that—authentic records of men and women, almost as readable as fiction because the author has presented his subjects as persons like ourselves.

Good biography has a humanizing effect. It is a powerful antidote to provincialism and narrow-mindedness. Do you find yourself prejudiced against any class? Try living its life—through an autobiography. Do you need inspiration and encouragement? Associate for a few hours with the records of men and women who have enshrined themselves in the hearts and hopes of humanity. You will find your own sympathies and generous resolves quickening to life. Know the heroism of Joan of Arc and of Abraham Lincoln. If you are puzzled about choosing a vocation, there are books to help you sample different callings. Ride with "Country Doctor" on his rounds, or with some social worker on her visits. Read Katherine Burton's vivid accounts of the nursing sisters and their work. Who knows how many a doctor, nurse, mother, musician, farmer, actor has been inspired to a life of service through admiration of a heroic personality unfolded in the pages of a book? A love for human souls glows in a work like John Farrow's *Damien the Leper* and in Father Talbot's *Saint Among Savages*. It flames anew in Theodore Maynard's record of the globe-trotting Francis Xavier, who disputes with bonzes,[1] rebukes corrupt merchants, and lures with song the furtive little children of the Spice Islands to teach them a rhyming catechism. The study of such lives sharpens the desire that rises, like hunger in the soul, to serve God and man whole-heartedly.

[1] BONZES—Buddhist monks.

The lives of critical, appreciative immigrants and the chronicles of converts teach us to value deeply two familiar blessings—our country and our faith. Newcomers and converts find this land and our faith precious possessions. One little Russian girl sitting on the steps of the Boston Library put her thoughts about America into words: "This is my latest home, and it invites me to a glad new life. . . . I am the youngest of America's children and into my hands is given all her priceless heritage, to the last white star espied through the telescope, to the last great thought of the philosopher. Mine is the whole majestic past; mine is the shining future." And these are the words with which a former agnostic closes the story of his conversion: "Yet I have sometimes wondered whether such favored Catholics ever know the rapture of the homeless waif, to whom the splendors of his Father's house are suddenly revealed; the consolation of the mariner, whose storm-tossed vessel finally attains the sheltered port; the gratitude of the lonely wanderer, long lost in cold and darkness, who shares at last, however undeservedly, the warmth and light of God's great spiritual *home!*"

Truly, sympathetic authentic biography is potent literary art.

## THE TWENTIETH-CENTURY ESSAY

It is not easy to define an essay. Perhaps the closest one can come to the truth is to say that it is an attempt to put on paper some ideas on a chosen subject that interests the writer and that he hopes will interest the reader. The essayist may be in earnest, or he may be joking. He may take us into his confidence like an old friend, or he may assume an impersonal aloofness. All that one expects of an essayist is that he follow a train of thought to something like a conclusion, and that he point out to us some new ideas along the way.

It has been the custom to classify essays as *formal* or as *familiar*. In the formal essay, the author takes his subject seriously. He is trying to instruct the reader or to convince him on some matter. His style is therefore dignified and perhaps impersonal. Essays of criticism, like Poe's "Philosophy of Composition," are formal. Such essays today usually appear as articles in the literary magazines and in the scholarly reviews and quarterlies.

The informal or familiar essay is lighter in subject and manner. It may range all the way from the out-and-out nonsense of Stephen Leacock or Robert Benchley to the pleasant story-telling style of David Grayson with its interwoven thread of sober thought. The familiar essay is usually personal in style, with the author chatting with the reader or playing with his own thinking. Consciously or unconsciously it reveals a good deal of the personality of the writer.

The easy conversational type of the informal essay reached its peak during the nineteenth century. The first twenty years of the present century also produced some essayists of delightful style. But since 1940 the trend has been away from the leisurely-paced personal essay. The present-day humorous essay is brief and unreserved—streamlined so that he who rides the subway may read. And the more dignified informal discussion has been shouldered off the pages of popular magazines by racy commentaries on men and news or by serious feature articles. Having experienced two world-wide conflicts and a great depression, becoming more and more aware of existing social evils, Americans today want to know what is happening and why. They are acutely curious about economics, politics, public personalities, current trends and policies. And so the informative article has largely replaced the informal literary essay.

Among the essayists of today and yesterday whose works are still enjoyed, one may list the exquisitely delightful Agnes Repplier, the fastidious Logan Pearsall Smith, and the whimsical columnist "F.P.A.," Franklin P. Adams. Nature-loving Americans can forget briefly their concern for man and his problems by exploring jungle or ocean floor with William Beebe, getting close to our own birds and trees and flowers with Donald Culross Peattie and John Kieran, or tracking through woods and up mountains with Stewart Edward White. And we still smile at the antics of our funmakers: at Robert Benchley's involvements with the complexities of modern living, at Frank Colby's ironic observations of his neighbors, at Clarence Day's recollections of a hectic life with father, and at James Thurber's sketches and self-depreciative reminiscences. Men like E. B. White with their light and lucid writing suggest that not every idea walks heavy-footed. There are nuggets of sense in tangy New England wit and in soft-voiced Southern drawl.

Other writers are trying to meet the need for information on matters of science, history, economics, current affairs as well as to provide leadership in appraising matters of principle and opinion. One of the leaders in the field is the prolific, balanced Carlton J. Hayes. There are, moreover, the vigorously intellectual, emotional columns of Father James M. Gillis; and there are essays in appreciation by Brother Leo, Michael Williams, and James J. Daly. Such men lend us their eyes and understanding hearts, fostering awareness of what is fine and true.

## MODERN ORATORY

Nineteen hundred years ago the wise old Roman Quintilian declared, "Oratory is the greatest gift of the gods to men." It is still true that a man with a brilliant tongue can bend the world to his will. At least for a time!

An *oration*, in its strictest sense, is a formal address, elevated in tone and usually delivered on some notable occasion. We may think of this sort of oration as belonging to the past; however, it has its counterparts today. Oral communication belongs to all of us, and modern life has multiplied the opportunities for public speaking.

According to Daniel Webster—one of the powerful orators of the past—three things are needed for a great address: the man, the subject, and the occasion. In appraising any speech one must consider the three factors, but most of all the man.

The man who would influence others must have an active, versatile mind; he must be sensitive in judging reactions in others and quick to modify his words to fit those reactions. He must understand people and the forces that move them to act. He must be skillful with words. He needs a sense of rhythm in language, a sense of fitness in figures of speech, and a fund of apt illustrations. And he must have an emotional nature, carefully controlled perhaps, but deep seated. No man can sway the feelings of others unless he feels deeply himself. He must, moreover, be able to direct the feelings of his audience. For the main purpose of oratory is not merely to stir the emotions; it is rather to rouse others to *action*. The orator must win the trust of his hearers. He must at least seem honest. And to be a great orator, he must *be* honest. These, then, are the qualities that mark the great speaker: intelligent understanding, deep feeling, impressive style, genuine sincerity.

Because a democracy is based on the principle of the rule of the majority, a democratic government allows the art of oratory to flourish. Public speaking reaches its highest development under democratic rule. The orator is a "popularizer"; and the appeal in a democracy is always to the people.

Today radio, television, and talking pictures bring national problems directly to the masses. More than ever before the spoken word wields influence, because it is almost universally heard. An address given in New York, London, or Rome can be heard simultaneously in every country of the world. And so, although public speaking is no longer pompous and florid, it is vastly important. The voice of the upright leader from the rostrum or over the radio opens gates of understanding to bewildered men.

A resurrected Patrick Henry or Webster might rub his eyes in amazement at the number of twentieth-century speakers and at the vastness of their audience. He would have heard Charles Eliot and Robert M. Hutchins discourse on education; Thomas E. Dewey on "rackets"; Nicholas Murray Butler on international relations; Carl W. Ackerman on the press; and John L. Lewis on labor. In the field of politics there have been the voices of Theodore Roosevelt, Woodrow Wilson, Wendell Willkie, Robert LaFollette, Franklin D. Roosevelt, and Adlai Stevenson, to name only a few.

The outstanding clerical speaker of the twentieth century is Bishop Fulton Sheen. *Time* magazine said he is "perhaps the most famous preacher in the United States, certainly America's best known Roman Catholic priest." Another periodical considers him the "most influential voice in Christendom next to that of Pius XII."

His style is brilliant in imagery, clever in paradox, clear and precise. His delivery is restrained but carries a strong steady undercurrent of emotion. As a background for his oratory there is a splendid foundation of scholarship and achievement. He holds twelve college degrees, has taken honors abroad in philosophy, has written over forty books—both technical and popular—works eighteen hours a day, and lives a deeply religious life. His is truly a happy combination of scholarship and eloquence.

# TEEN-AGERS

*FULTON J. SHEEN*

*Forty years ago a college debate coach bluntly told one of his debaters, "Sheen, you're absolutely the worst speaker I ever heard." Today an estimated twenty million television viewers listen weekly to the soft resonant voice of that same speaker, Bishop Fulton Sheen.*

*When Bishop Sheen first attempted to appear on television, he was refused by two of the three major networks. They feared that no one would care to listen to a bishop who would just talk for a half an hour. People want action. Bishop Sheen reasoned otherwise. He knew that an action in which the listener himself takes part is far more engrossing than the action of any performer. He realized that an internal action demanded of the listener's mind in following an important thought from point to point can be more interesting than any external action. Accepting this challenge, Bishop Sheen has convincingly proven his point by receiving the highest rating ever recorded for anyone on television. He has shown professional entertainers some new ideas.*

*Neither memorizing nor writing out his talks beforehand, he extemporizes on nondogmatic themes that so perfectly blend common sense with Christian doctrine that the talks appeal to people of all faiths. His topics deal with serious problems but do not lack a lightness of touch. Many a comedian envies his spontaneous humor, as when he remarked at the beginning of his new season after the summer, "Long time no Sheen." But the Bishop's captivating power is not due solely to his thoughts and humor. Underlying these, a deep genuine ring of sincerity convinces people that the Bishop considers every listener of great importance because that person possesses an immortal soul, no matter what his race, color, nationality, or position in life.*

*The following television talk does not have the polish that a carefully written talk might have, and it suffers from the fact that it was intended to be heard and not read; but it still retains much power in its analysis of the modern teen-ager and his problems.*

---

The best definition of an adult that was ever given is one who has stopped growing at both ends and has begun to grow in the middle. But no one has ever given a good definition of a teen-ager.

George Bernard Shaw once said, "It is a pity that youth has been wasted on the young." The contrary is true. It is no secret at all that the Good Lord knew that it was better to put the illusions of life at the beginning in order that as we grew closer to eternity, we might the better see the purpose of living.

Since we cannot think of a good definition of a teen-ager, possibly it would be interesting to discuss the psychology of the teen-ager. The psychology of teen-agers may be reduced to three dominant characteristics: self-consciousness, imitativeness, and restlessness.

The difference between a child and a teen-ager is that a child wants to be loved, a teen-ager wants to love. The affections of free choice are preferred to the natural affections in the family.

When a teen-ager emerges, he discovers his own personality and begins to affirm his ego. A teen-ager is like a chick just breaking the shell in which he has been confined—the shell of the family—and beginning to find himself in a great, broad, world. Identification bracelets begin to appear: "It's me!" Up to this point, his life has been merged very much in the family. If the parents say, "We are going to visit Aunt Jane today," the child has to go. But the teen-ager puts up an argument; he refuses to be a part of an anonymous group. His personality asserts itself, saying, "I don't want to go." This is the age when the boy begins to carry a comb, and the girl wins the battle of lipstick. The only world in which they feel at home is with fellow teen-agers. Hence they have a language of their own. Only in their own milieu do they feel they are understood. They are rather proud of it when nobody understands them. Ordinary words have little "exchange value," particularly with adults. There is much they would have to say if they could find words. Fear of being misunderstood drives them to silence or else to "bebop talk," which only the initiated can understand.

In addition to that, they love to wear clothes that attract attention. They feel that there is a kind of conspiracy against their own ego which they resist by overasserting themselves. The boys wear socks that are so "loud" their feet can never go to sleep. Girls do their hair a thousand different ways to express various personalities. There is a fondness for writing names on fences, driving hot rods, making loud noises on street corners and in buses, in order that people may be conscious that here, at last, a personality is beginning to emerge.

Gestures are quick, gauche, and awkward. Sloppiness is cultivated to attract attention; feelings are easily hurt. But all these are signs that a personality is being born into the adult world, and democracy is founded on personalities. Be not too hard on them.

The second characteristic of a teen-ager is imitation. The ego must emerge from its inferiority. It may do it in one of two ways, either by *creation* or by *imitation*. If the teen-ager is keen on developing his own character, being himself and not someone else, then he creates; he assumes responsibility; he has a sense of value, and he discovers the purpose of life and concentrates on the development of his character in a constructive way. He is willing to say "No" to certain things; he resists the crowd and the mob, knowing that the crowd and the mob are often wrong. There are not many, however, who are creative, even among adults. The creative group in society is always the minority.

Release from inferiority most often comes through imitation. Imitation is an escape from responsibility, the ignoring of character building, a flight from true self-expression, and the avoidance of originality. Imitation enables the ego to assert without being committed to moral values or self-restraint. The teen-ager then becomes very sensitive to outside influences and is afraid of ever doing anything which is not "the thing." A teen-ager in such a case never really becomes *himself* or *herself*, but *like* others. He imitates to escape choosing in such a way as to develop personal responsibility. Imitation without moral standards is loss of personality or the spoiling of character. This kind of mimicry develops a mass civilization which is the raw material of Communism.

Imitation is seen in boys who want to be like the "old man"; so they smoke. Some of them even inhale! Some boys even smoke pipes to look like authors! They are the more "studious" kind. Girls wear high heels and, whenever possible, Mother's mink. Father still owes eight hundred dollars on it, but they want it. Ever notice, when a high school empties, that almost all the girls are dressed alike? A few dress a certain way, and almost everyone follows.

Because this is the age when personality is not able to stand by itself, it loves to merge into groups and fan clubs; there is even a kind of mass courtship, in which a group of boys will meet a group of girls—they find it difficult to present their own personalities to each other. Hardly strong enough to stand on his own amorous feet, a youth has to lean on somebody else. Hero worship is very strong; very often the hero is a player of the drums, or a celluloid phantom, or a moaning singer. The nobler the hero, the nobler the character which will unfold in later life.

Sometimes the teen-ager revolts against the parents, because he feels that this personality of his should not be submerged in another. He forgets very often that the parents were once teen-agers and hence know the strength and weakness of those difficult years. Parents have greater vision and are capable of better guidance than youth suspects.

The third characteristic of a teen-ager is restlessness. The teen-ager is like mercury, which can be dispersed in several directions. The restlessness is due in part to the discovery of vital and biological impulses stirring within. The body-imperative is more immediate than the soul-imperative. Hence the teen-ager finds perseverance difficult and long attention to the same subject almost impossible. It is this fidgety quality which most tries the patience of adults. He discovers less the laws than the illusions of life. This tremendous physical energy is ready to spend itself on a tackling dummy or "jitterbugging" but almost completely disappears when Mother wants the screens put up in the springtime. "Puppy love," "crushes," and infatuations are common. There are no friendships that seem closer than the friendships of teen-agers, and yet there are hardly any friendships that are quite as volatile. Adults must remember, however, that this urge for affection, for love, for friendship, for society, is good and right. God put it in them, and it is not to be crushed, but developed along right lines.

There are various kinds of music: there is *head* music, such as the music of Bach; there is *heart* music, like Schubert's; and then there is what might be called *visceral* music, that is, music which stirs legs, arms, and the body in general. Teen-agers generally love that kind of music. It is a music in which there is the suggestion of movement, but since the notes are not carried through, the listener is induced to complete the motion. That is why it comes out in violent antics, giving a release to the tremendous biological pressure within. Swooning often accompanies it as the consummation of an emotion. "Swooning" is a vicarious, erotic experience, a desire to live out to the utmost the emotions generated within. General MacArthur said that old soldiers never die, they just fade away; so do teen-agers fade away.

The great advantage of mercurial restlessness is the fact that the young are able to exhaust many of the possible vocations that there are in life. In this time of life, the teen-ager decides for himself whether he will be a lawyer, a doctor, a farmer, or a professor. In his drive from one task to another he often finds his life career.

We have noted three characteristics of teen-agers. The first two are physical, and the third, which is biological, deserves further stress. Here we shall speak of a virtue which is hardly ever held up to teen-agers, a virtue which is the key to their future happiness and good social relations, the virtue of purity.

Too often, it is thought that this virtue is negative, the denial of self-expression, the extinction of personality, the suppression of vital urges. It is none of these things; it is something very positive. Pure water is more than the absence of dirt; a pure diamond is more than the absence of carbon; purity has its own content.

What is purity? *Purity is reverence for mystery.* Mystery like a sacrament, is made up of two elements; one is visible, and the other is invisible; one is material, and the other ethereal. A handshake is a mystery or sacrament; there is something visible about it, namely the clasping of hands; there is something invisible and spiritual too, namely, the communication of friendship. A word is mystery. There is something material about it, namely, the auditory stimuli or the sound. The horse hears a joke as much as you do, but the horse does not give a horse-laugh, and you do. Why? Because the horse does not have the capacity and the power to understand the invisible spiritual element, namely, the meaning of words. A kiss is a mystery. There is something visible or material, such as the touching of lips; the invisible, spiritual element is the communication of affection. When the spiritual element is wanting, it becomes an insult.

Purity is a reverence for mystery. What mystery? The mystery of sex. Sex has two elements. One is material —everyone is male or female. The other is spiritual, namely, the power of creativeness that has been given to man and woman. Almighty God has prolonged His great creative power to man and woman. It is this urge for creativeness that drives man and woman to marry and then stirs them to bring forth the mutual incarnation of their love, or the raw material for the King- dom of Heaven.

So sacred has been this consciousness of the power of creativity, that all peo- ple, Jewish, Christian, and pagan, have always surrounded marriage with reli- gious, sacred, liturgical rites in order to indicate that here is the communica- tion of a great God-given power.

*Purity is reverence for the mystery of creation.* Why is it no one is ever scan- dalized at seeing people eat in public? There are some who do not mind eating in the front window of Child's on Fifth Avenue in New York. Most people in Paris eat outside. But why is it that we are scandalized by seeing people make love in public? Is a manifesta- tion of affection wrong? Certainly not! Why then are we shocked? We are shocked because there is something so personal, so intimate, so sacred and mysterious about love that we do not want to see it vulgarized, profaned, and made common.

Obscenity is the turning of mystery into a jest. It is the making of some- thing holy, unholy, and something per- sonal, vulgar. Vulgar comes from the Latin word *vulgus*, meaning "crowd." Purity is the sacristan of love, a tribute to the mystery, the giving of the pri- macy to the spiritual over the carnal. Impurity is the using of a person as a means to satisfy one's ego. But purity never allows a material sign to be robbed of its spiritual content. If a youth is pure, he keeps his vital urges controlled until the Divinely appointed time when both God and society sanc- tion their use.

Mozart, the great musician, wrote in this vein to his father, on December 15, 1781: "Nature speaks in me as loudly as in any one else, and I believe with greater force than in the uncultured and the gross. Nevertheless, I refuse to regulate my conduct on the same basis as some young men of my age. On the one side, I have a spirit sincerely reli- gious; I have too much honor and too much love of my neighbor, to deceive any innocent creature. On the other hand, my health is infinitely too pre- cious to hazard in any passing fancy. I can swear before God, that I can re- proach myself with no failure."

Victor Hugo penned the same senti- ments to his fiancée in 1820: "It is my desire to be worthy of you, that has made me so severe on myself. If I am constantly preserved from those ex- cesses, it is not because I have not had a chance to sin; but rather it is that the thought of you constantly preserves me. Thus I have kept intact, thanks to you, the sole treasure I can offer you on the day of marriage; a pure body and a vir- ginal heart."

It is this consciousness of mystery which produces chivalry in the teen- ager, though he does not know its meaning, nor could he explain it. Even the awkwardness of a teen-ager boy be- fore a girl is a sign of awe before a mystery. The timidity of the girl, too, is a sign that there is the guarding of a secret from a too precocious revelation. Whence shame in the young? It is the veil which God has drawn over that mystery until the Divinely appointed time when it may be used as God in- tended that it should be used. The dis- gust that follows from the profanation of the mystery is a summons to return to reverence for mystery; it is also a re- alization that in vain will he snare the music of love who breaks the lute.

The mystery that surrounds the vital impulse is something like the mystery of a flag. The flag of this great country is materially just a piece of cloth. That is what is visible and material about it, but there is something invisible and spiritual about the flag, namely, the tradition and the institutions and the land for which it stands. Americans want to see the flag over their heads, not under anyone's feet. The way we treat our flag is the way youth should treat its energy.

Youth has only one arrow in its quiver; it may be shot but once—that is the arrow of youth. Be sure that it hits the target—the Divinely appointed target—love of God, love of country, love of neighbor.

<><><><><><><><><><><><><><><><><><><>

## FOR DISCUSSION

1. Do you think Bishop Sheen really understands the teen-agers? With what ideas do you especially agree or disagree?

2. What does Shaw mean by his statement, "It is a pity that youth has been wasted on the young"?

3. Why does the boy start carrying a comb and the girl lipstick?

4. What is the difference between "creation" and "imitation"? Mention several ways a person can prove that he has a "creative" character? Why will a person who has a "creative" character have a better personality than someone with an imitative character?

5. Several statements in the talk caused a good deal of laughter from the audience who were present at this particular television program. Point out at least three statements that, when spoken, would draw laughter.

6. Explain the sentence, "The nobler the hero, the nobler the character which will unfold in later life."

7. Do you agree with the statement that "parents have greater vision and are capable of better guidance than youth suspects"? Explain.

8. Is "puppy love" the same thing as infatuation? What is the difference between "puppy love" and true love?

9. In what way is purity something "positive," not "negative"?

10. Explain the spiritual element in a kiss. Why is a kiss an insult when the spiritual element is missing?

11. Do you think the modern world would esteem or ridicule great men like Mozart and Victor Hugo for their purity? Give reasons for your answer.

## WORDS

1. *Anonymous* is derived from the Greek words: *an*, a negative, and *onyma* meaning *name*. What would be meant by an *anonymous* author?

2. *Milieu* and *gauche* are two French words meaning *center* or *middle* and *left handed*. What do they usually mean in English?

3. V*olatile* is derived from the Latin word *volo* meaning *to fly*. Explain how *volatile* probably developed into its present meaning.

4. We speak of the pope as being the Vicar of Christ. *Vicarious* is the adjective of the same word. What does it mean in the text?

## PROJECTS

1. Watch one of Bishop Sheen's television programs and hand in a written report on it, evaluating his thoughts, voice, gestures, humor, choice of words, *etc.*

2. Compare "Teen-Agers" with a written article in this book and show how the style of a talk differs from that of a written article.

3. Work out a television program in your class and see if you can have it televised on one of the television educational programs in your city.

## RELATED READING

A series of Bishop Sheen's television talks has been published in the book, *Life Is Worth Living*. This book covers a variety of topics from a serious treatment of the philosophy of communism to a humorous explanation of the Irish.

# THE STORY OF ABRAHAM

*FULTON OURSLER*

In 1943 the well known writer, Fulton Oursler, after having been a skeptic for nearly thirty-five years, became a Catholic. Like the conversion of Cardinal Newman a century earlier, Fulton Oursler's conversion resulted from an intense study of the Church Fathers and the development of Christianity. This study, which included reading more than a thousand books dealing with Christianity and ten years of research, gave him the background material for his three great books on the Bible, THE GREATEST BOOK EVER WRITTEN, THE GREATEST STORY EVER TOLD, and THE GREATEST FAITH EVER KNOWN.

Rarely have the stories of the Old Testament ever been retold so simply, beautifully, and interestingly as they are in THE GREATEST BOOK EVER WRITTEN. The following selection tells of an incident in the life of Abraham. Although it happened thousands of years ago, people today still find it very similar to trials that they experience in their own lives, trials in which they also feel like crying out against Providence. Abraham's example proves to them that God eventually works out all things for the good of those who trust Him and obey His commands.

God had promised Abraham that he was to be the father of the Hebrew race. Naturally, Abraham took it for granted that it would be through Isaac, his only son, that this new nation would spring, and . . .

He found in that laughing, tender child new life, new joy, a fullness of purpose and a reason for living. The old man's heart was set on Isaac to the exclusion of all other thoughts. Their companionship was constant and each delighted in the other. Abraham told his son the great tales of the past, so that the boy could have drawn a

map of the Garden of Eden; could repeat what Adam and Eve and the Serpent had said; trace with a twig in the dust the profile of the ark and the façade of the abandoned Tower of Babel.

In his father Isaac beheld a man with whom he identified himself, wanting only to be like him, and Abraham saw in the beloved youth the reality of long-denied dreams and disappointed hopes, ultimate proof of God's tender care for His own. Isaac's growing years were full of placid happiness, which seemed as if it would never end. And with all at peace, Abraham, too, contentedly assumed that all would continue to go well with him and his family. Why not? Did he not sacrifice yearling lambs to the Lord, the altars of fieldstone running with blood as the smoke rose from burning faggots? Regularly Abraham thanked God for His goodness and implored His continued blessings. What, then, had he to fear?

Thus the patriarch was taken by surprise one windy afternoon as he trudged alone across a brown and fallow field and suddenly heard the Voice of the Lord God speaking for the first time since Isaac's weaning feast:

"Abraham!"

The old man halted in the wind-swept field, exclaiming:

"Behold, here I am."

"Abraham! Take Isaac, your beloved son, to a mountain which I shall show you in the land of Moriah. And there offer him for a burnt offering."

What were these words the old man heard? Oh, Voice of Almighty God— You cannot mean what I have heard? My son? My Isaac? My dearly beloved against whom I have never once lifted my hand—Isaac to be burnt like a beast on the altar! I am having a nightmare.

The command was no illusion; Jehovah, the Creator, the one God, the true God, the only God, had spoken to His most obedient servant Abraham. Now, having learned to love his little boy with a love deeper than the springs of the desert, Abraham must ask himself a question:

Do I love God more than anything else in the world? Or do I love Isaac more than I love God? Old Abraham, more than any of his forebears, more

than faithful old Noah, even, had seemed to love his Creator perfectly. But now he was being tested as no mortal, before or since. His long wait for his son to be conceived and born was a part of that test; his separation from Ishmael doubled its sharpness; the happy years of his growing up increased the force of his love. Now, would he obey?

For the rest of that day and night,

frowning Abraham brooded and walked alone. At dusk he waved away his bowl of milk and his wheaten loaves, pacing in the darkness outside his tent. But when the night was blackest he shouted his orders:

"Up by dawn! Isaac and two men-servants—we go to a distant place."

They loaded a pile of faggots on the back of a young gray ass and set out. Three days they traveled across the ripening golden plain of Mamre and on and up into the thickly wooded hills. In all that time there was no talk between father and son. Abraham's browned face was like a mask of stone and the deep gleam in his eyes was like a fire in the depth of a cave.

At last the boy Isaac dared to break the silence.

"If we are going to worship," he remarked, "behold the wood—but where is the lamb?"

Abraham closed his eyes and groaned as he answered:

"God will provide a lamb for a burnt offering."

The boy said nothing else. No reason had been given to him for this sudden departure to a new and distant altar. Nor could it have entered into the boy's head to suppose that these faggots were being fetched to burn under his own body or that his father carried in his sleeve a knife with which to cut his throat.

At a clearing near the mountaintop, when a natural plateau stretched right and left for quite a distance, Abraham bade his servants remain. Then Isaac loosened the thongs of the asses and loaded the firewood on his own back, as he trudged after his father, still higher until they reached the bald, deserted patch of level land on the very peak of Mount Moriah. Both were panting and out of breath, but Abraham did not dare to rest for fear that all his terrible resolution would forsake him; even now he wanted to scream out against this fiery and bloody sacrifice.

His palsied hands could hardly lift the stones with which to fashion the altar, but Isaac helped him. Why must he give up his healthy son, his good and decent son? Abraham and Isaac, alone together, were the first to be tormented with this dreadful requirement; first but not the last; countless millions since have shared Abraham's agony, making ready for the dearly beloved to be sacrificed on another altar, raised to war, whose commands must also be obeyed.

Isaac saw how his father was quaking. Something was wrong; his question flew back again; where was the sacrificial lamb? The broken heart of Abraham was reflected in his helpless eyes; one glance was Isaac's answer. The boy's cheeks turned white, his eyes rolled back; then, obedient son of obedient father, he held out his hands. His wrists were tied with strips of pliable leather, feet and ankles bound, and still not a word between them. The boy was a prisoner, bound fast beyond the hope of escape, and now the old man lifted the young body, so warm, so yielding, and laid him on the mound of faggots piled on the altar. A jerk of the arm, a clutch of fingers around a flashing blade, and there it is, quivering high in the air, the knife in Abraham's hand.

It was then the Voice spoke:

"Abraham! Abraham!"

"Lord, here am I," faltered the old man.

"Lay not your hand upon the lad, neither do you anything unto him; for now I know that you fear God, seeing you have not withheld your only son from me."

Abraham heard no more. Through eyes streaming with tears, he beheld a ram caught by the horns in a thicket just beyond the pile of stones. The beast for the burnt offering was waiting for him there.

Shaken and yet uplifted, the two men descended from the mountaintop together, the smoke of the sacrifice rising from the altar behind them high toward the morning sun. They knew then, as never before, that if a man gave all to God he received God in return, and that is all in all.

❖❖❖❖❖❖❖❖❖❖❖❖❖❖❖❖❖❖❖❖❖❖❖

## FOR DISCUSSION

1. Why did Abraham think that God could not mean what He had said? What great decision was Abraham forced to make? Do you think this story is a good example of Christ's words, "He that loveth son or daughter more than me is not worthy of me."? Explain.

2. The author says that "countless millions since have shared Abraham's agony, making ready for the dearly beloved to be sacrificed on another altar, raised to war, whose commands must also be obeyed." Would parents who have lost a son in war be comforted or angered by this story about Abraham? Explain.

3. People think that if they live good lives, God will not permit any misfortunes to happen to them. Is this true? Using this article as an example, explain your answer.

4. Explain what the author means by the last sentence in the article. Do you think that the author may have personally experienced the truth of this statement? Explain.

## PROJECTS

1. Read some incident in the Old Testament such as the story of Job, Samson, David and Goliath, and retell it in your own words in a modern popular style.

2. An idea is conveyed not only by what is said but also by the way it is said. The author uses leisurely flowing sentences until the section in which Isaac becomes suspicious. Then the sentences are short and abrupt; e.g., "Something was wrong; his question flew back again; where was the sacrificial lamb?" What effect does this sudden change in style have? Find another article in this book in which the author uses a similar technique, and compare the two.

## WORDS FROM THE LATIN

1. *Patriarch* comes from the Latin words *patria*, race, and *archo*, rule. From this, what do you think would be the difference between a patriarch and a patriot?

2. *Illusion* comes from the Latin words *in*, on, and *ludo*, play. What is an illusion? How do you think it developed its present meaning? What is the difference between an *illusion* and an *allusion*?

3. Everyone knows what a pair of pliers is. Since the word *pliable* comes from the same Latin word, what do you think *pliable* would mean?

4. *Placid* comes from the Latin verb *placere*, to please. How might the English word have developed its present meaning?

5. The modern English word *implore* comes from the Latin words *im*, in, and *plorare*, to cry aloud. What connection do you see between the meanings of the English and the Latin words?

## RELATED READING

Besides his trilogy on the Bible, Fulton Oursler has written novels, biographies, and plays. You would enjoy any of his detective stories, published under his pen name of Anthony Abbot. Some other books that he has written are *Modern Parables*, *Why I Know There Is a God*, and *Father Flanagan of Boy's Town*.

# THE FIFTH FREEDOM

## SEYMOUR ST. JOHN

*Today the value of many modern educational programs is being seriously questioned. Returning from military service, a soldier recently complained to one of his old college professors that his education had failed to teach him how to live. After hearing his arguments, the professor also began to question the "traditional skepticism of collegiate thinking," and said that, "that rotting lumber will build no bright new house for humanity." The professor was even forced to admit that the armed services seemed to be training youth better than most secular colleges for at least the armed services "commission no chaplains for irreligion." Because of this present interest in our educational curricula, the following article was "one of the most widely-read, widely-discussed pieces of the year."*

More than three centuries ago a handful of pioneers crossed the ocean to Jamestown and Plymouth in search of freedoms they were unable to find in their own countries, the freedoms we still cherish today: freedom from want, freedom from fear, freedom of speech, freedom of religion. Today the descendants of the early settlers, and those who have joined them since, are fighting to protect these freedoms at home and throughout the world.

And yet there is a fifth freedom—basic to those four—that we are in danger of losing: *the freedom to be one's best.* St. Exupéry describes a ragged, sensitive-faced Arab child, haunting the streets of a North African town, as a lost Mozart: he would never be trained or developed. Was he free? "No one grasped you by the shoulder, while there was still time; and nought will awaken in you the sleeping poet or musician or astronomer that possibly inhabited you from the beginning." The freedom to be one's best is the chance for the development of each person to his highest power.

How is it that we in America have begun to lose this freedom, and how can we regain it for our nation's youth? I believe it has started slipping away from us because of three great misunderstandings.

First, the misunderstanding of the meaning of democracy. The principal of a great Philadelphia high school is driven to cry for help in combating the notion that it is undemocratic to run a special program of studies for outstanding boys and girls. Again, when a good independent school in Memphis re-

"The Fifth Freedom" by Seymour St. John, from the October 10, 1953 issue of *The Saturday Review.* Reprinted by permission of Seymour St. John and *The Saturday Review.*

cently closed some thoughtful citizens urged that it be taken over by the public-school system and used for boys and girls of high ability; that it have entrance requirements and give an advanced program of studies to superior students who were interested and able to take it. The proposal was rejected because it was undemocratic! Out of this misunderstanding comes the middle-muddle. Courses are geared to the middle of the class. The good student is unchallenged, bored. The loafer receives his passing grade. And the lack of an outstanding course for the outstanding student, the lack of a standard which a boy or girl must meet, passes for democracy.

The second misunderstanding concerns what makes for happiness. The aims of our present-day culture are avowedly ease and material well-being: shorter hours; a shorter week; more return for less accomplishment; more soft-soap excuses and fewer honest, realistic demands. In our schools this is reflected by the vanishing hickory stick and the emerging psychiatrist. The hickory stick had its faults, and the psychiatrist has his strengths. But the trend is clear: *Tout comprendre c'est tout pardonner*.[1] Do we really believe that our softening standards bring happiness? Is it our sound and considered judgment that the tougher subjects of the classics and mathematics should be thrown aside, as suggested by some educators, for doll-playing? Small wonder that Charles Malik, Lebanese delegate at the U.N., writes: "There is in the West"—in the United States—"a general weakening of moral fiber. (Our) leadership does not seem to be adequate to the unprecedented challenges of the age."

The last misunderstanding is in the area of values. Here are some of the most influential tenets of teacher education over the past fifty years: there is no eternal truth; there is no absolute moral law; there is no God. Yet all of history has taught us that the denial of these ultimates, the placement of man or state at the core of the universe, results in a paralyzing mass selfishness; and the first signs of it are already frighteningly evident.

Arnold Toynbee has said that all progress, all development come from challenge and a consequent response. Without challenge there is no response, no development, no freedom. So first we owe to our children the most demanding, challenging curriculum that is within their capabilities. Michelangelo did not learn to paint by spending his time doodling. Mozart was not an accomplished pianist at the age of eight as a result of spending his days in front of a television set. Like Eve Curie, like Helen Keller, they responded to the challenge of their lives by a disciplined training: and they gained a new freedom.

The second opportunity we can give our boys and girls is the right to failure. "Freedom is not only a privilege, it is a test," writes De Nöuy. What kind of a test is it, what kind of freedom where no one can fail? The day is passed when the United States can afford to give high-school diplomas to all who sit through four years of instruction, regardless of whether any visible results can be discerned. We live in a narrowed world where we must be alert, awake to realism: and realism demands a standard which either must be met or result in failure. These are hard words,

[1] *Tout comprendre . . . tout pardonner* —Complete understanding begets complete pardon.

but they are brutally true. If we deprive our children of the right to fail we deprive them of the knowledge of the world as it is.

Finally, we can expose our children to the best values we have found. By relating our lives to the evidences of the ages, by judging our philosophy in the light of values that history has proven truest, perhaps we shall be able to produce that "ringing message, full of content and truth, satisfying the mind, appealing to the heart, firing the will, a message on which one can stake his whole life." This is the message that could mean joy and strength and leadership—freedom as opposed to serfdom.

◇◇◇◇◇◇◇◇◇◇◇◇◇◇◇◇◇◇◇◇◇◇◇◇◇◇◇

## FOR DISCUSSION

1. Describe in a short paragraph what is "The Fifth Freedom."

2. What was the tragedy of the Arab child described by St. Exupéry? Do you think that most American children have the advantage of this fifth freedom? Give concrete reasons for your answer.

3. How has education in the United States suffered because of a false understanding of democracy? What solution does the author suggest? Do you agree with him? Explain.

4. The second misunderstanding is the belief "that softening standards bring happiness." By what examples does the author prove that this false standard exists today in the lives of students as well as adults? What solution does the author suggest? Do you agree with him? Explain your answer in terms of your own school experiences and those of your friends and classmates.

5. Mark each of these statements true or false and explain your reason:

a) The education of teachers over the last fifty years has included many false ideas.

b) The ideas of modern education have been derived from the lessons of history.

c) Denial of the existence of God results in mass selfishness.

d) Freedom implies the right to fail as well as the right to succeed.

6. Why must education provide a challenge? How do most people feel about doing work which does not challenge their capabilities or their talents?

7. What good is derived from failure in school?

8. In the last paragraph the author says that we must judge our philosophy or sense of values in the light of what history has proved true. What does this mean? What do you think is the "message on which one can stake his whole life"?

9. How will false spiritual and moral values deprive a person of his fifth freedom?

## WORDS TO KNOW

1. *Inhabit* means to live or dwell in, occupy as a home. Explain what the word means as used in the article.

2. Many words that seem difficult to understand are frequently built from very simple words. The basic word in *avowedly* is *vow*. What do you think *avowedly* means? Can you use avowedly correctly in a sentence?

3. *Ultimate* means beyond which there is no other. It comes from the Latin *ultimatus* meaning last. To what does the word *ultimates* refer in this article?

## A PROJECT

A closer study of the style of this article will be profitable. Pick out the topic sentence of each paragraph and outline the whole article. Explain how the orderly development is maintained throughout the article. Does the article have a fitting conclusion? Why or why not? If you do not think it does, write an ending which you feel is fitting.

# AN AMERICAN MARTYR

FRANCIS X. TALBOT

Over three hundred years ago, on April 8, 1636, Father Isaac Jogues and seven other Jesuit Blackrobes sailed from the France of Richelieu for the New France across the seas. They sought neither riches nor adventure, only the spiritual welfare of the Indians. Yet adventures they had, adventures which culminated for two of that band of eight, Fathers Jogues and Garnier, in cruel martyrdom.

After sharing for six years the crude life of the natives, Jogues and a little band of his fellow laborers were ambushed and captured by the fierce Mohawks. A year of torture and enslavement followed for Jogues before he, the only one of the captives to survive, made his escape with the help of Dutch officials at New Amsterdam and returned to France.

There, to his great discomfort, he was hailed by all as a hero from the Front; his gaunt body and mangled hands were his medals of distinction. These honors weighed heavily upon him; he was eager for nothing but to return to New France and his Indians. Before his return could he perhaps obtain permission to offer the Holy Sacrifice of the Mass in spite of the loss of his left thumb and the crippled condition of other fingers? The Holy Father's answer to his petition is celebrated: "INDIGNUM ESSET CHRISTI MARTYREM CHRISTI NON BIBERE SANGUINEM." "It would be a shame not to allow a martyr of Christ to drink the blood of Christ."

In this chapter from Father Talbot's SAINT AMONG SAVAGES we find Father Jogues, less than a year after his escape, at Three Rivers, south of Quebec, preparing to return to the treacherous Mohawks who but lately had treated him with the utmost barbarism.

A cold dawn spread over Three Rivers on Monday, September twenty-fourth. It was a blue lingering of the night rather than a flushed break of the day.

Father Jogues gave communion to young Jean de la Lande and finished his Mass in the Chapel de la Conception. They gulped down their breakfast hurriedly, and, accompanied by one or two of the Fathers who then happened to be at the residence, walked briskly down the road along the hillside to the strand of the river. Scarcely any of the French were about. Governor Montmagny, Father Lalemant, and all the important personages had departed a few days previously for Quebec. Sieur de la Poterie, the Commandant, had not yet emerged from his residence. Most of the people still slept, or were occupied in beginning the week's work. A knot of Hurons stood and haunched about the canoes.

All was hushed and silent, save the lapping of the waters and the muted voices which sounded hollow in the mist. The Hurons were ready to start. Joques bundled his black cassock up about his waist, cleaned the sand and mire from his feet, and climbed into the canoe. Jean de la Lande raised himself carefully over the rim and took his place. Otrihouré and another Huron jumped in skillfully, and the Hurons in the other canoe settled themselves and held the paddles poised for the stroke. A third canoe was filled with Mohawks who were returning home for the winter. The Hurons standing about the shore uttered their guttural farewells. The Fathers raised their arms in benediction. The canoes glided into the fog.

On the second evening, Father Jogues' band turned the lip of land that banked the Richelieu River. They ascended the hill and encamped near the ruins of Fort Richelieu. The garrison had been withdrawn that summer, both because in wartime the fort had been ineffective as a barrier to the Iroquois and because peace with the Iroquois was now a certainty. The fort always had been regarded with especial hate by the Mohawks, and on its abandonment they had reduced it to a charred mound.

That night, among the ruins of the old fort, Jogues and the Hurons talked tersely. He realized fully how precari-ous was the situation. On the one side, the peace seemed to be firmly pledged. The Mohawk nation professed to be dealing honestly; it had faithfully fulfilled all the requirements of the code of statecraft sacred among the natives. As far as he could see, there was no ground for suspicion, no cause for alarm. And yet, there was some subtle, some intangible something that was disturbing and unsettling. As for himself and De la Lande, they were resolved to go forward and to dare what might be.

Not so with the Huron ambassadors. Neither they nor their chiefs had put such implicit trust in the Mohawk promises and fair words. They wanted peace, and they were willing to work for the peace under the moral suasion of the French; but their instincts told them to beware. Now, in the camp at Richelieu, when they were about to paddle down to and be swallowed up in the Mohawk territory, the Huron envoys were seized with dread. Their observations, which could not be expressed in words,—their intuitions, warned them against continuing the journey. They were convinced that somehow, somewhere, was a trap which would close in and destroy them.

Ondessonk [1] argued with them and tried to quiet their trepidation. Otrihouré also strove to hearten them. But their courage was gone. The Huron ambassadors decided they would postpone their journey to the Mohawk villages. Pointing their canoe across the St. Lawrence, they wildly scurried back to their own people. Otrihouré, who had a special, personal claim of protection from the Mohawks, was alone resolute enough to continue with Jogues and De la Lande. About this time there

[1] ONDESSONK—The Indian name, "Bird of Prey," given to Father Jogues by the Hurons.

was an added cause for suspicion. The Mohawks deserted and drove their canoe off on a scouting expedition.

The three voyageurs struck out the next morning against the rippling flow of the Richelieu River. They were in the vast wilderness of the narrow river which cut its way between the close banks of the forests. They paddled for hours in the utter stillness, clambered over the rocks along the rapids and trudged across the portages. Their progress was slow, their labors were exhausting. After several days of struggle they reached the Lake of Champlain. They had expected, before this, to be meeting with stray bands of Mohawks. But not a living soul was passing up or down along the route, not a sound of anything human was anywhere heard. The quiet was strange and foreboding.

September had now turned into October. Autumn cooled the summer heats and sapped the green from the leaves and the grass. The hillsides along Lake Champlain were faded into brown and russet, and many of the trees showed their naked branches. The far elevations of the mountains were dull and depressing. All the land seemed to be desolated and so rugged as to be menacing. An ominous quiet seemed to be brooding over all the earth and the waters. Ceaselessly the three travelers pulled the canoes through the heavy calm, past the slow succession of banks until, about the middle of the second week of October, they twisted up the little stream to the rapids that poured the Lake of the Blessed Sacrament [2] into Lake Champlain.

They climbed the trail through the woods, with the canoe over their heads,

and debouched on the smaller lake. Even yet they encountered no Mohawks. They found no signs of parties who had recently passed along the way. There was nothing but the impenetrable mystery of the forests and lakes. A few days of paddling through the stupendous heights that hemmed in the Lake of the Blessed Sacrament brought them to the circular inclosure of Andiatarocté. It was about the twentieth day since they had left Three Rivers. They had journeyed safely along the water route; there remained but three or four days along the trail through the mountains. Then they would be arriving at Ossernenon.[3]

The three of them were worn out by now, and their store of food was sparse. Young Jean de la Lande had proved himself to be a lad of worth and mettle. He was more agile than René Goupil, more experienced in the ways of the wilderness, and far more venturesome. He had, too, the dogged fidelity of René and much of his simple faith. He had not been molded in the savage life, as had Guillaume Coûture,[4] but he had the sharpness and intelligence of Guillaume. All through the laborious days he had borne up strongly under the physical and mental strain, and his courage still flamed. He had listened eagerly to Father Isaac's instructions as to how he must comport himself among the Mohawks. He was prepared for any emergency. He prayed in unison with

[3] OSSERNENON—A Mohawk village on the Mohawk River.

[4] RENÉ GOUPIL . . . GUILLAUME COÛTURE —Young men who like Jean de la Lande had come to New France in search of adventure, had attached themselves to the Fathers, and served them as guides, interpreters, catechists, and servants. Captured with Jogues the year before, Goupil had been martyred at Ossernenon; Coûture, like Jogues, had been enslaved.

[2] LAKE OF THE BLESSED SACRAMENT—Now Lake George, situated directly west of Lake Champlain in the state of New York.

Father Isaac, and often expressed his spiritual joy that he should have been chosen for this service of God in the Mission of the Martyrs. His young eyes glowed and his heart expanded under the inspired words that *mon père* spoke to him. Again and again, he protested that he was ready for life or death, through love of God.

It was October the fourteenth when they defiled along the leaf-strewn trail that led to Ossernenon. They were burdened down, all three of them, with the baggage of clothes and blankets and presents. They grew more apprehensive than ever when they were shrouded by the tree trunks and the overhanging branches. They mounted the rise of the path over the ridge of hills and dug their heels into it as they descended to the depression caused by the juncture of the Oiogué and Sacandaga rapids. A few days more and they would have the first welcome, friendly or hostile, at Ossernenon. It might be only a few hours, for most certainly there would be Mohawks along these well-traveled trails.

Father Jogues was exalted in spirit, now that he was coming back to the village he had dedicated to the Holy Trinity. He was at the ending of the journey that he had prayed for so insistently, that he had longed for amid such desolation. He was back with the beloved Mohawks, he would sit at their fires in their cabins and talk to them of God and the mysteries of the Faith. He would try to convert his "aunt" [5] and Honatteniate and other friendly ones; he would make these the corner stones for the Church, as he had helped for six

years despite all the assaults of the devil to build the Church among the Hurons. He hurried his steps along the trail, so that De la Lande and Otrihouré could scarcely keep pace with him. He was never so happy, never so expectant in all his life. He had the thought that he was coming to his own home. When he had traveled this trail before, in the first journey, his steps had lagged and he had begged Goupil and Coûture to escape, to die of starvation in the woods rather than face the tortures. Now he was encouraging young Jean to hurry along faster with him, and Jean, panting breathlessly, beamed with the ardor of an apostle.

A file of savages came toward them along the trail. Jogues halted, and called out a greeting. The savages melted away out of sight. He sharpened his eyes and peered anxiously through the trees. Again he shouted his welcome and announced that he was Ondessonk. The Mohawks emerged from the trees on all sides and closed in with blood-curdling war-whoops. Jogues stood fastened to the earth, shocked and amazed; Jean de la Lande froze beside him; Otrihouré was terrified. The Mohawks were streaked with crimson war paint. They swung their muskets before them, and held gleaming knives in their right hands. They howled and shrieked wildly, danced about Father Jogues menacingly, as if they were about to fall on him and tear him to pieces.

Father Jogues could not comprehend. He thought perhaps this was play-acting. He spoke to them in a friendly way and smiled but they drowned out his words with their screeches and glared at him fiercely. All of an instant the warriors leaped on him and De la Lande, bore them to the ground, pounded and rolled

---

[5] FATHER JOGUES' "AUNT"—Sister of the chief who owned Father Jogues during his captivity, and on more than one occasion, the one who saved his life.

them around, and with violent rage tore off the black robe and underclothes of Father Jogues, and stripped him naked. They ripped off the garments of Jean de la Lande, meanwhile beating him furiously.

Appalled, Jogues understood. This was a war party. The Mohawks had repudiated the peace. These warriors were taking the trail to the St. Lawrence, to surprise the Algonquins and Hurons, to take the French unawares. His soul sickened at the terror of the thought. All was ended. There was war again. He began to understand the howls of the savages. They hated the French. They were going to massacre all the French. They hated him. He was an evil sorcerer. He had plotted their ruin and death. They intended to cut him to pieces, to burn him at the stake, to split open his head, to eat his flesh.

Meanwhile, they were dragging him and De la Lande and Otrihouré along the path with them, triumphantly, to their village. They held their arch-enemy, Ondessonk. They would revenge themselves on him. This time he would not escape them. Runners sped along the path as fast as their legs could carry them to announce that Ondessonk was captured and was being led into the village.

Father Jogues groaned in the abyss of his soul. He had dared death and he did not fear it. He was heartbroken for young Jean whom he had led with him; he would secure the release of the lad if he possibly could. He feared the havoc that would be wrought along the St. Lawrence; hundreds of Algonquins would be caught during the autumn and winter hunts; miserably the Hurons would perish. He was in terror when he thought of possible sudden, ruthless on-slaughts on Montreal, even on Three Rivers. There would be no warning given. There was no help, now, save in the good God.

Driven madly along, he was prodded up the series of hills till he reached the ridge above the valley and river of the Mohawks. He padded down the incline with his persecutors to the flats by the bank of the river and the ford where he had first been caressed by the villagers. They mobbed about the place in a terrifying turmoil. They were struggling with one another, Jogues could see, arguing among themselves, threatening and imprecating. He and De la Lande were hurled into the midst of the throng. Some threatened him and lifted their arms as if to strike him. Others warded off the blows and pressed in to guard him. It was an angry, aroused crowd that rioted about him and split his ears with their cries. He and Jean, finally, were extricated, were hurried up the roadway to the summit of the hill, dragged through the gate of the stockade, and pushed violently into a cabin.

For the time being they were safe. They had been rescued by the Wolf and Turtle clans from the old enemies, the Bears. They were in the Wolfs' lodge, and no one of the Mohawks, however lawless, would dare to invade this sanctuary. Father Jogues' "aunt," her grandson Honatteniate, and some few friendly persons sat them on the mat and put food in their hands. They explained what had happened to change the minds of the people since his last visit. Part of the story was well known to him. Kiotseaeton, supported by the Wolf and Turtle and some less powerful clans, had advocated the peace with the French and their allies in good faith and with all sincerity. They had overcome the resistance of the strong union of the Bear families who raged violently, in and out of the national councils, against carrying on any peace negotiations. The Bears had aroused their kinsmen among the Upper Iroquois, the Oneidas, the Onondagas, the Senecas, the Cayugas,[6] to support them, while the Mohawk Wolfs could not persuade their clansmen among these nations to follow their leadership. And so, after their temporary victory in pledging the Mohawks to the peace, the Wolfs were being worsted. That had been the state of affairs since June when Ondessonk had visited them as ambassador.

Not many weeks after he had left them, the friendly Wolfs related, a few of the people had fallen sick. They were not disturbed much. But then others had contracted the disease. It had spread from cabin to cabin. It had appeared in Andagaron, then in Tionontoguen. They had invoked the sorcerers, they had watched their dreams, they had fulfilled the commands of their okis, they had offered sacrifices to the demons, and made feasts; they had danced and chanted and played games; they had held sweats; but to no avail. The sickness had become more prevalent during August. Many of the warriors and squaws and children had died. By the beginning of September, the people had been frantic. It looked as though they were being ruined by another epidemic.

There had been some adopted Hurons who offered an explanation. They remembered how six or seven years before, their peoples had been similarly afflicted; they had blamed the disease on Ondessonk and the Blackrobes, and had been on the point of murdering them time and time again. These Blackrobes were evil sorcerers, and Ondessonk was the worst of them. He and Echon[7] and the other Blackrobes wrought frightful witchery. They wished to destroy all the native peoples so that they would have the land to themselves. They brought disease and pestilence and destruction wherever they went. They and the French were not truly seeking for peace; they were trying to annihilate the Iroquois. The sickness had been brought on by Ondessonk, they asserted. Many of the Mohawks had accepted their words.

In September, the corn in the fields down by the river had begun to wither, just when it should have been fattening for the harvest. The stalks shriveled, and the ears of corn were destroyed by worms. There would be no corn for the winter, and without corn there would be starvation. Under this new affliction, the Mohawks had grown more frenzied. Some demon was persecuting them. Again they had consulted their sorcerers and wizards. Pitifully they had employed their superstitions. But again to no avail. The crop had been ruined.

Then they had remembered the chest which Ondessonk had left in the cabin of his "aunt." The sorcerers had pronounced their infallible judgment. Ondessonk had left an evil spirit locked up in this black box. They had accused him of this before he left, but he had denied it. True, he had opened the box in their presence and had shown them the articles inclosed in it. But he had fastened it in such a manner that no one of them could open it without smashing it. Why had he done this if he did not wish to conceal something

---

[6] UPPER IROQUOIS . . . CAYUGAS—All tribes of the Iroquois nation.

[7] ECHON—The Indian name for Jean de Brébeuf, given to him by the Hurons.

from them? Ondessonk was a wicked magician, he was in league with the devil. He had left his demon, over which he had control, in this firmly fastened box. It was this demon which was killing the people and destroying the corn.

The suspicion had not taken long to become a firm conviction in the minds of many of the Mohawks. Ondessonk had preached a strange doctrine when he was among them. He had told them of a Deity who would punish them for their wrongdoings, of a place where they would burn forever after they died; he had reprimanded them for certain of their actions and habits; he had always sought out those who were sick and dying, and made queer motions over them, pouring water on their heads and saying some words of a charm; he had made the sign which the Dutch told them was an abomination and for which they had killed the other Frenchman who came with Ondessonk. As an ambassador of the French, he had not worn his black robe, nor had he spoken openly to them of his beliefs, as he had done on his first visit. It was clear that he meant to deceive them and take them off their guard. He did not wish peace with them. He planned only to exterminate them. For that reason he had locked up the evil demon in the chest.

They must destroy that chest left by Ondessonk. They had come to the cabin where it was stored and demanded it. They would not listen to any assurances that the chest contained no evil spirit. They had asserted they had proved conclusively that there was a demon in the box. They dared not smash it open, nor pry the bands apart. For then the demon would escape and would find some other place where it could lurk and continue to do them

harm. Some of the more courageous among the sorcerers, those with powerful demons of their own who would protect them, had taken up the box left by Ondessonk and fearfully carried it out of the village and down the trail to the river. Some distance below, where the water was deep, they had lifted it carefully out of their canoe and let it sink down into the water. The demon was now trapped and could not escape, but would perish. However, Ondessonk still lived. He had plotted to kill and ruin them. They had destroyed his demon. They had only to capture and murder him. Then they would be free of their curse.

At the time when the chest of Father Jogues was being destroyed, about the middle of September, the Mohawks had held a council for the reopening of the discussions about peace. The Bear clan was stronger now, with the suspicion against Ondessonk and the French so clearly confirmed. Their orators pleaded with the assembly to remain loyal to the traditions of their nation and the doctrine of their ancestors. They pointed out the danger of the Mohawks' alienating themselves from the alliances which their forefathers had established with the other Iroquois nations, and of their breaking all the bonds of blood and marriage with these nations which were their brothers and their children. With vivid recitals they recalled the murder of the Mohawks perpetrated by their ancient enemies, the Algonquin nations, and by the Huron nation which they had sworn to subjugate.

The Bear chiefs swayed the minds of the people, now already unbalanced by the spread of the epidemic and the plague on the corn, and now quite firmly convinced that the French were contriv-

ing evil through witchcraft and the power of the evil spirit. Kiotseaeton and the peace advocates were repudiated. The council resolved to send presents and envoys to the Oneidas, the Onondagas, the Cayugas and the Sencas in order to reaffirm and consolidate the alliance and kinship of the Mohawks with them, and in order to indicate their willingness to join with them in their war expeditions against the French, the Hurons, and the Algonquins.

Father Jogues listened and understood. This was the end of all the peace efforts. The Mohawks had raised the bloody hatchet. They had raised it treacherously and were giving no warning that they were once more taking up the warpath. As for his own fate and that of De la Lande, he knew nothing. His friends told him that messengers had been sent through all the cabins

and villages, announcing that a great council would be held the next night in Tionontoguen. The chiefs and the elders would then decide upon their fate.

It was on Wednesday evening, October seventeenth, 1646, that Father Isaac Jogues and Jean de la Lande were brought captive into the village of Oneougiouré, formerly called Ossernenon. All that night their ears rang with threats and maledictions. "You will die tomorrow. Do not be surprised," one of the braves shrieked into Ondessonk's ear. Another, gloating, told him: "We will not torture you or burn you. Keep up your courage. We will strike you over the head with a hatchet. We will set your head on the points of the stockade, so that when we bring some of your brothers here as captives, they may still see you." Still another made as if to slash him with a

291

knife, saying: "Let us see if this white flesh is the flesh of a manitou or demon." Jogues answered calmly: "No, I am nothing more than a man like you. And understand, I have no fear either of your torments or of death. I do not know why you threaten to kill me. I have come into your country to help you to preserve the peace, and to level the earth, and to show you the road to heaven. And you treat me like a dog. God governs the French and the Iroquois; He knows well how to punish you."

All through that night Oneougiouré was noisy with disputes. The clans of the Wolf and the Bear were in violent altercation, the one demanding safety for Ondessonk and the Frenchman, the other swearing to kill the two of them. The chiefs were powerless to quell the rioting. They feared that the young braves, lusting for revenge and notoriety, under the impulse of dreams or their demons, would commit a deed that would be regretted. Both factions ranged through the cabin where Ondessonk lodged, and beset the doorways, some to tomahawk him if he emerged, others to obey their chiefs and guard him faithfully.

October eighteenth dawned. Emotions had quieted with the morning. Ondessonk and Jean were now accepted as public hostages. They were not to be troubled until the council was held and the elders had pronounced sentence. Jogues was warned by his friends that he must be most cautious, for there were many ready, on the slightest provocation, to strike him down. He was forbidden absolutely to venture out of the gates or to go beyond the stockade, unless with a strong guard about him. He was given back some of his clothes, so that he could appear in public without shame. He felt quite secure. The storm had played itself out, as usual, in the first violent gusts. Now the Mohawks would consider his presence more calmly, and with some logic reason out what had best be done. The moment of greatest peril was safely past.

During the morning he made opportunity to talk to the chiefs, not as the docile, silent slave of four years ago, but with the air and the dignity of the ambassador he had been in June, though he did not pretend to hold that same office now. He professed boldly that he had come to them this third time as a Blackrobe, to teach them the trail to heaven, to instruct them in true thoughts, to reveal to them the knowledge of God. Facing them defiantly, he accused them of the basest treachery in violating the peace without warning, and he threatened them with the terrible wrath of Onontio [8] and the French.

In regard to the little black box which he had left with them, he recalled how he opened it in their presence, how he showed them all the contents, how he had tried to make them see that no demon was shut up in it. He ridiculed their superstitions, and swore to them that he had had absolutely nothing to do with bringing the sickness and the blight on the corn. While he professed his sorrow for these afflictions, he begged them to rid themselves of their fancies and absurdities, to listen to the things he would tell them, to believe as he believed in the great God who ruled all men. They listened. Some approved while others flared out at him anew for being a sorcerer and a dealer in death.

That afternoon, the chiefs of all degrees, the elders of the families, all the

[8] ONONTIO—Indian name given to Charles Huault de Montmagny, Governor-General of New France.

responsible people of Ossernenon trailed out of the village and along the river path to Tionontoguen. They knew the arguments that would be presented on both sides. Kiotseaeton and the Wolfs would harangue for peace with the French and their allies. They would, failing in this, scarify those who were bringing dishonor on the nation by breaking out into war without signifying that resolution to Onontio. If they decided for war, let them release Ondessonk and his comrade, and send them back to their people to announce that the Mohawks had changed their mind and no longer were in favor of peace. Let them not commit an act of treachery that would disgrace them among all the nations, so that no one ever after would put faith in the word of a Mohawk.

The Bear orators would brush aside the thoughts of peace. They would appeal to the bonds of blood and alliances with the other Iroquois nations. They would point out that there was no need to truckle to the French for their trade, since they had the Dutch near by who would continue to supply them with guns and powder. They would point out the immemorial enmity with the Algonquins and cry for their extermination. They would demand that the Huron nations should be subdued and thus forced to form one people with them, as had been in the days of their fathers. The Mohawks had no need to placate Onontio, nor to give him warning of their change of policy, save by a sudden attack.

As for Ondessonk, he must be killed. He had wandered among them of his own free will, not as an envoy whose person must be protected. He was a Blackrobe in the employ of evil demons. Already he had committed hideous wrong by hiding his demon in his black box, by sending the disease, by destroying the corn. He would always practise his prayers and incantations and gestures. Arrogantly, he preached to them about his God; he was an offense to the gods and demons of the Mohawks. He must be sacrificed in order to placate Areskoui and their other friendly spirits.

Thus the orators would debate. Neither they nor any of the people could estimate the effect that their words would have. The nation was divided in opinion, as it had been for years. It had veered from war to peace, from peace to war. The people would listen to the speeches of the chiefs. In family groups they would weigh the arguments. In clans they would compare their findings. In the general council they would declare their decisions. Then only would the will of the nation be made manifest.

Oneougiouré was deserted and strangely quiet that Thursday afternoon. Jogues and De la Lande were in no way molested. Father Isaac spent these hours of peace in prayer with Jean, in raising the thoughts of the lad to God, in exhorting him to courage and confidence in the Providence of God. He explained the situation fully. It was possible that the council would condemn them to death, that they would both be murdered. It might be that he alone would be struck down, but that Jean would be held as a prisoner. Or else, both of them might be allowed to live but be forced to return to Three Rivers. This last, Jogues said, would probably happen. However, he instructed Jean what he should do in all emergencies.

About sundown, when the shadows were lengthening over the village, there came a young brave to the cabin. He sought out Ondessonk and invited him to visit another lodge where there were people who wished to eat and talk with him. Jogues recognized the man as belonging to the Bear clan, a man who had been somewhat hostile. To refuse this brave would be interpreted as an act of great discourtesy and would betray a suspicion that might breed greater ill-feeling. Spurning an invitation to eat in a cabin was an insult not easily forgiven. Besides, Jogues thought, to show fear of this brave would be cowardly.

He consulted with his "aunt" and the friends of his family. They were of two minds, as to whether it would be safe for him to venture out into the village or whether it would be more prudent to offer the proper excuses. Jogues was eager to make friends with the young brave and the Bears who had invited him. His "aunt" feared treachery. Nevertheless, she agreed that he should go. She sent Honatteniate, her grandson and the sworn brother of Ondessonk, to guard him. Jean was left in the lodge.

The smoky half-light of the October evening lingered over the cabins and the tang of autumn was cool in the air as Jogues emerged into the open. He and Honatteniate followed their guide silently through the subdued paths of the village till they arrived before the long house where their guide turned to pause. Jogues could discern in the dimness the rough carvings of the Bear signs on the doorpost. He looked quizzically at his guide, but the young brave gave back a stolid and expressionless stare. Jogues did not hesitate for long. Suspicion or fear, either one would give the Mohawk an advantage over him. Casually, then, he placed his hand against the stiff skin which hung down from the lintel and pushed it inward so that he might enter. Honatteniate followed closely after him. A blast of warm, smelly air assailed him. Through the heavy gloom and smoke he glimpsed the fires gleaming down the center of the long, narrow room, and saw the people dimly shadowed about them. He shoved with his shoulder against the shaggy skin and bent his head under the low doorway. He saw and knew no more.

Behind the doorpost a warrior stood, with a tomahawk poised ready to strike. The bowed head of Ondessonk came forward around the edge of the skin curtain. Honatteniate leaped into the entry, thrusting out his arm to ward off the blow he saw crashing down. The tomahawk slashed his forearm and thudded upon the head of Ondessonk. The guide sent Honatteniate reeling into a corner and with another blow the murderer smashed the skull of Ondessonk. Father Jogues lay as he fell, crumpled at the doorway of the lodge. The moment was still. No one spoke. The braves leaned over the bleeding head and the prostrate form. They whispered in awed tones that Ondessonk was dead.

Honatteniate roared curses on the murderers and rushed out of the cabin, shouting wildly. Aroused, the village came flocking to the cabin. The murderers and their friends dragged the body of Ondessonk out into the street. They set up a frenzied dance and chant of triumph. They had saved the nation. They had destroyed the great sorcerer, the Blackrobe Ondessonk. They had revenged themselves for all the evil he had brought on them. They had drowned his demon. They had split his head. They were free from his spells and charms. Into the mob, Ondessonk's "aunt" fought her way. She confronted the murderers. She raged against them: "You kill me!" she screamed shrilly in the darkness. "It is I myself whom you kill! He was my kinsman! He belonged to my family! You must pay the penalty! What will the two other villages say? You have not consulted them! You have not waited for the decision of the council! What will the others say about this murder, so unexpectedly, so rashly perpetrated?"

The people of the Bear pushed her aside. The braves bent over Ondessonk, scalped him, and with their long knives cut the head from the neck. They held it up, streaming with blood, and started down in procession through the dark lanes between the cabins, toward the corner of the stockade that faced to the north and the east. While some held flaring torches, others clambered up on the latticed scaffolding along the inner side of the palisades. They lifted up the head of Ondessonk. One of them jammed it down on the sharpened point of a pole at the angle of the walls. The face of Father Jogues looked across the valley of the Mohawks, over toward the trail which descended from the hills beyond, northward toward the St. Lawrence. With boasts and imprecations the Mohawks shrieked their defiance against the French and warned that all French palefaces would be slaughtered. Look at Ondessonk!

Another Frenchman still lived. He was concealed in the village. He must be found and killed. The mob spread out from the corner of the stockade and streamed through the lanes. Everywhere they searched for the young paleface named Jean. He was in the cabin of the Wolfs. He was under their protection. The leaders of the crowd would not dare to invade that cabin, for it would be a grievous offense to the families who lodged there and to all their kinsmen throughout the five Iroquois nations. They must force the Wolf family to surrender the Frenchman to them, or they must trick the Frenchman out into the open night.

Braves stood about the cabin, and in the darkness bellowed their threats and curses. They had killed Ondessonk. They would kill his brother. This other Frenchman was also a sorcerer. He talked to himself, when no one was listening; he lifted his head and eyes to the sky; he bent his knees on the earth and held himself upright; he made the hateful sign on his forehead and shoulders and breast; he had little beads tied together and flat pieces of iron with marks on them; he wove incantations with Ondessonk and invited deadly demons to descend on the Mohawks and destroy them off the face of the earth. He was an evil witch. He must be destroyed out of their midst, that very night, before he could do any more harm. If he were allowed to live, he would wreak a terrible revenge and call on his gods to punish them for murdering Ondessonk.

Young Jean de la Lande remained quietly sitting by the fire of Father Isaac's "aunt." The old squaw, after she had raged against the killers of her "nephew," hurried back to protect the other Frenchman from his assailants. She related to Jean what had happened, and warned him to beware. He must not move one step from the circle of the fire, she told him. She and Honatteniate, whose arm was deeply gashed by the blow of the tomahawk, and others of her young men haunched about Jean, guarding him closely. Beyond the doors and the bark walls, the village was in tumult. The raucous cries and excited voices sounded menacingly.

Jean waited. Father Isaac was dead. His body was cast somewhere on the streets, his head was pinned on the palisades. Jean prayed. He was doomed to death. Nothing could save him. He felt the tremor pass through him. He was feverish. He looked into the burning embers of the fire and watched the weird shadows that flickered through the cabin and across the posts and walls. Father Isaac was dead. He alone remained, the only white man in all the Mohawk villages. He prayed to God for courage. He examined his conscience. That day he had confessed his sins and Father Isaac had spoken the words of absolution. He was ready to die, for he knew he was in the state of grace, that he should not dread meeting God. He had pledged himself to follow Father Isaac, in life and death, for God's greater glory and service. He had known from the beginning that he might be murdered. Father Jogues had told him often that he must be prepared.

While Jean prayed and waited in meditation, the turmoil of the village softened into silence. The crowds were no longer shouting about the cabin and pressing against the walls. The savages were evidently gone off to their huts to sleep. Those of the cabin felt reassured. Nothing more would happen that night, so they wrapped themselves in their blankets and skins and laid themselves on their beds of twigs about the warmth of the fires. The silence of night brooded over Ossernenon. The fires crackled, the soft winds ruffled the bark walls, the people breathed heavily and snored. Jean stretched himself on the earth, in the darkness. Father Isaac was beyond this silence, beyond this world. He was with God, a martyr of Christ. He had hoped for so much. He was so certain that God would soften the hearts of the Iroquois. He was so brave. He had known he might die, and yet he was not afraid. He was not afraid of anything. He was a saint.

Jean remembered the story Father Isaac had told him about René Goupil; of how they had murdered René and thrown his body in the ravine; of how he had sought for the body, everywhere, since René was a martyr and his bones sacred. Father Isaac had escaped then. He was not killed. He was kept a slave and then he managed to free himself. Guillaume Coûture had lived four years among the Mohawks. He was adopted by them, and became well liked and respected. Father Isaac's "aunt" was friendly and her family was powerful. They would probably protect him against the Bear clan. As he thought, he inclined to believe that he would not be put to death. At least, now that the village was quiet as the grave, he had nothing much to fear for the rest of the night. In the morning, the Mohawks of Ossernenon would be calmer and the chiefs holding council at Tionontoguen would make known their decision. The fires burned low. All were soundly asleep.

He grieved for his dear Father. Into his mind came the instructions Father Isaac had given him in case he survived. He must be faithful, he must have courage. The body of Father Isaac was outside, he believed, abandoned on the path not far from the cabin. Jean longed to see his Father. He wanted to recover some articles which Father Isaac carried with him. If he waited till the morning, he would not be allowed to venture out. Besides, the savages would have carried the body off and thrown it over the side of the ravine, as they had done to the corpse of René. Now was the chance. It was dark, past midnight, and all the cabin and all the village was asleep. This was the time. He had a duty. He must slip out before the dawn and find Father Isaac. He would save the relics and bring them back to Three Rivers, if he were released or if he escaped. He listened intently. There was no sound.

Stealthily, Jean lifted himself to his feet and stepped slowly and carefully toward the door. It was so dark that he could scarcely see. He strained his eyes to discover the posts and the cracks of the door. He crept forward on his toes and safely reached the doorway. Cautiously, lest the skin barring the outer door creak, he pushed it aside, and felt the tingle of the night air on his face and neck. The night was clear and fresh. He could see more clearly now. The yellow paths were light, the dark cabins were heavy against the deep-blue sky. The winds sighed faintly as they rustled the dried leaves of the trees and there sounded the whir of the night creatures. No dark figures or shadows moved. He thought he knew where the body of Father Isaac lay. He would steal from the dark shelter of cabin to cabin.

More noiseless than Jean, blacker than the shadows of the trees and cabins, were the savages who lay motionless by the wall of his cabin. They were on guard through the stillness of the night. They rose like specters out of the earth, and before he could utter a cry crashed down the tomahawk upon his head. The blow felled him. Another blow, and another cracked his skull. They had the Frenchman, the brother of Ondessonk, the other sorcerer. He and Ondessonk had come together, they had prayed together, they had only one mind, to ask their God to bring ruin on the Mohawk nation. The braves did not rouse the village, but they laughed and rejoiced quietly among themselves. Expertly, they cut off his scalplock, and with the strong strokes of their knives they severed the head from the trunk. They left the body where it was, in the roadway. The head they carried over to the angle of the palisades, and there they placed it on the point of a pole, next to the head of Ondessonk.

The night passed quietly in Oneougiouré. The villagers stirred. The old squaw and Honatteniate and their families looked about for their Frenchman. They found his dead body a few steps from their door. The cabins were awake, the buzz of voices rose to a roar. In the first gleams of the morning sun the people rushed to see with their own eyes the heads of the two Frenchmen perched on the poles of the palisades. All of the Bear clan exulted and chanted and danced in triumph. Those of the Wolf and Turtle families burst with anger and threats and curses. They demanded revenge. Almost they were tempted to strike down the jeering Bears. They knew that all was over now. They were powerless.

Scarcely had the sun risen over the hills above the valley when messengers raced up the trail from the river flats and burst through the west gate of the stockade. They came from Tionontoguen, bearing the decisions of the council that had been debating through the night. They spoke to no one, nor listened to anyone, as was their custom, until they had reached the cabin where the Frenchmen lodged and had eaten of the food placed before them. Then they announced their message. The great chiefs and the ancients of the

Mohawks had ordained: Ondessonk and his French brother were free; no harm must be done to them; they were ordered out of the Mohawk village and were to be escorted back to Three Rivers.

At first in silence, and then in an uproar, the villagers heard the judgment of the chiefs. It had happened as the Bear clan had feared. Slyly they rejoiced in that they had circumvented the Wolf, who had sought the release of the French. They had clamored for the death of Ondessonk four years before, but the Wolf and Turtle had always obstructed them. They had tried to prove from the beginning that he was an evil genius, a malicious sorcerer, a Blackrobe who preached an unheard-of doctrine, who prayed and made signs hateful in their eyes, who was in league with enemy demons. They feared him always, even when he pretended to be a harmless slave. He had escaped from them through the treachery of the Dutch, just when they were surely going to murder him. He had deceived the people when he came back dressed like other Frenchmen, calling himself an ambassador. But then he came back dressed in his black robe, after he had begun their ruin through the demon locked up in his black box. When they killed his demon by drowning it in the river, he was in their power. He was no longer protected. Still, as they had feared, the council even then sought to let him live, foolishly, since he was an enemy who would keep on striving to destroy them. Now they had destroyed him outright, and they had destroyed his brother. There was nothing more for the council to debate.

The messengers who had come to Oneougiouré ordering the release of Ondessonk, immediately turned back along the trail to announce his murder. The chiefs and sachems, still assembled at Tionontoguen, heard of the murders with amazement and consternation. Hurriedly they assembled in a new council. In a public session they all agreed in condemnation of the act. Even the chiefs of the Bear clan expressed regret and blamed the deed on the senseless, rash, unscrupulous young men of their tribe. The Wolf and the Turtle orators vehemently denounced the murderers and their accomplices. They cried woe on this treachery that wouuld forever shame and humiliate the Mohawks before all nations.

Above all others, the lordly Kiotseaeton bewailed the death of his brother, Ondessonk. Untold evils would descend upon the Mohawks, he prophesied, because of this mutinous, rebellious deed carried out by the young men of the Bears. Now there was no alternative but war. This war, he foretold as one seeing a vision, was to bring ruin upon his people. The more that the hatchets and the arms of the Iroquois were raised for war, so much the worse it would be for the nation, so much the greater would be the calamities that would befall his people.

No punishment could legally be inflicted upon the murderers of Ondessonk and the young French paleface. Nevertheless, Kiotseaeton and his colleagues still hoped to preserve good relations with Onontio and the French. They were jealous of the honor and faith of their nation, as they were sincerely outraged by the perfidy of their own warriors. They therefore commissioned the Huron, Otrihouré, who had been the comrade of Ondessonk, to assure Onontio that the Mohawks had no intention of breaking the peace and waging war against the French, that

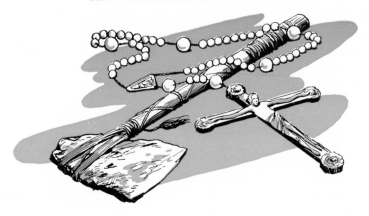

they were hostile only to the Algonquins. Furthermore, Otrihouré was instructed to announce to Onontio that the Mohawks would refrain from warlike acts until they had clearly announced their intention to repudiate the peace with the Algonquins. Finally, they commissioned the Huron to carry back presents which would speak to Onontio, saying that the Mohawks apologized for the killing of Ondessonk and his white brother, that Kiotseaeton and the chiefs were so indignant that they had difficulty in restraining their arms against the murderers, that they would like to kill and exterminate all the proud, uncontrollable madmen in their midst. But Otrihouré was also killed before ever he reached Three Rivers.

So grieved and humiliated were the chiefs that they counseled all the people to keep secret the vile deeds. Nevertheless, the news leaked from the mouths of some of them down at the Dutch village of Rensselaerswyck.[9] Arendt Van Corlaer, Dominie Megapolensis, Jean Labatie and the other burghers were horrified. They were fond of Isaac, priest and Jesuit though

he was. They made diligent inquiries as to the cause and the details of his death. They could learn but little, since the Mohawks were secretive. No one would admit that he witnessed the affair. Each one solemnly swore that he was not in Oneougiouré that night. All that they would admit they knew was that Ondessonk was struck down by young braves belonging to the Bear clan, and that their act was in disobedience to the desires of their elders.

Jean Labatie, the interpreter of the Dutch, collected the scant bits of information he could pry out of the savages and forwarded an account to New Amsterdam,[10] to his friend, Johannes La Montagne, a French Huguenot. In due time, Father Jogues' "aunt" came down to Rensselaerswyck and gave to Dominie Megapolensis all the goods of Ondessonk that she had been able to save from the rapacious hands of the Iroquois. His possessions were few, a pair of pantaloons, a small missal, a breviary, a ritual, and a few trinkets.

Long since, his body and that of Jean de la Lande had been dragged down the hill under the stockade and across the flats to the Mohawk River, where

---

[9] RENSSELAERSWYCK—Albany, New York.

[10] NEW AMSTERDAM—New York City.

they were carried off by the current. Through October, through November, through the bleak winter, on the point of the palisades overlooking the valley, remained impaled the withered heads of Jean de la Lande and Isaac Jogues.

## FOR DISCUSSION

1. From what you have learned in reading the selection, comment on Father Jogues' character—especially his courage, charity, and zeal.

2. Why were the Mohawks hostile to Father Jogues? Give examples of people who are guided by prejudices as unreasonable and violent as those of the Mohawks.

3. Comment on Indian law as it appears in the council and decision of the chiefs. Where did the Indians learn ideas of truthfulness, fidelity to treaties, justice for captives?

4. Do you think Jogues acted prudently in leaving his "aunt's" cabin to accompany the young brave from the Bear clan? Explain.

5. Why did the Indians not attack Jean openly instead of stealthily lying in wait for him? Would you say that Jean had sufficient reason for going out to look for the body of Jogues?

6. What became of Otrihouré? Why was it difficult to learn the truth about St. Isaac Jogues' martyrdom?

## PROJECTS

1. Re-enact the scene of the chiefs' council at Tionontoguen.

2. Trace on a map the journey of Jogues and De la Lande from Three Rivers (near Quebec) to the Mohawk village.

3. Report on Catholic missions to the American Indians in our own time.

## WORDS TO LEARN

1. You know the meaning of the term *tangent* as used in geometry. With this knowledge can you determine the meaning of *tangible?* of *intangible?*

2. The word *scar,* but not *scare,* will give you a clue to the meaning of *scarify.* What is the meaning of *scarify* as it is used by Father Talbot?

3. *Truckle* and *kowtow* are synonyms. Can you give their meaning? What is the connection between *truckle* and *truckle bed?*

## RELATED READING

For further reading about the Indians and early missionaries, choose *Saint Among Savages* by Francis X. Talbot, S.J.; *The Song of Tekakwitha,* by Robert E. Holland, S.J., a poetic life of the Lily of the Mohawks, written in the meter of Longfellow's *Song of Hiawatha;* or see their own stories in the volumes of *The Jesuit Relations.*

# ROSE HAWTHORNE
# LATHROP

## KATHERINE BURTON

*Katherine Burton, herself a convert to Catholicism, has done the reading public an invaluable service in chronicling the road that many outstanding American men and women have traveled on their way to the Catholic Church. She states that from her research into the lives of these converts it appears that "it was the harshness of the Puritan faith that drove men and women from it, out to something that had love and kindness and fellow feeling in it. Many of the best of their day—Emerson, Hawthorne, Longfellow, Thoreau—left the harsh sects for something better. Catholicism they did not consider as a living faith, for to them it was only something dead though still lovely in a faraway land. They could not see that it was living and that it was the necessity they lacked."*

*The following sketch of the life of Rose Hawthorne, Nathaniel Hawthorne's daughter, tells the story of one who did not stop at any halfway stage but went on until she found her true home in the Catholic Faith.*

*"Human beings owe a debt of love to one another."*

The inheritance which a father bequeaths to his daughter is not always merely money or houses or stocks. It is sometimes a mental, social, or spiritual inheritance.

To his youngest daughter, whom he affectionately called the Rose of all the Hawthornes, Nathaniel Hawthorne left various legacies. He left her the memory of a brave gentleman, a sensitive soul; he left her the memory of happy days spent with him in Italy—in Rome,

"Rose Hawthorne Lathrop" from *In No Strange Land* by Katherine Burton, reprinted by permission of Longmans, Green & Company, Inc.

where the seeds of faith were sown in her that later ripened to fruition. But, best of all, he left her his love of humankind, even the most wretched—and a sense of duty towards them, a feeling of service that must be rendered mentally or physically, with the pen or the voice or perhaps with the devotion of a lifetime.

Rose was a very small child when her father was appointed American consul at Liverpool. In England he was made much of, invited to great houses, hunted, as she put it in the charming book she wrote about him many years later, "to gorgeous dinners against his better instincts." For the Hawthornes never cared much for gorgeousness—unless it were that of a sunset or a great deed. In one of her [1] letters to her father in the United States, Mrs. Hawthorne wrote of the "hideous condition of the very poor—this most crying and worst of evils." That was the sort of thing that Hawthornes were most likely to notice.

Along with the grandeur of the stately homes to which Hawthorne was being continually invited, he saw also the terrible squalor and poverty of England's poor. One morning of a dark English February in 1856 he went with several friends to visit the West Derby workhouse. He was shown through the different rooms, and the bare poverty, the coldness of charity, and what he called the "atmosphere of the house of paupers" filled him with dismay.

To a woman walking beside him he said, " 'Tis a curious thing—this atmosphere. For no matter how fastidiously we breathe it in we are forced to inhale it into our inmost being. If even the Queen were here, I know not how she would escape the necessity." The woman who walked beside him looked in surprise at him as if she thought this American a bit odd.

Later in his notebooks Hawthorne recorded the incident which occurred on this visit to the workhouse and which so mightily moved him. "What an intimate brotherhood is this in which we dwell, do what we may to put an artificial remoteness between the high creature and the low. It is but an example of how by every moment in our lives the flow and reflux of a common humanity pervades us all. How superficial are the niceties of such as pretend to keep aloof. Let the whole world be

[1] HER—Mrs. Hawthorne, Rose's mother. The letter was to Rose's grandfather.

cleansed or not a man or woman of us can be clean."

He went into the children's ward, as unpleasant and unwholesome as was the rest of the establishment. In a corner where several grimy children were playing together, one detached itself from the group and came over to the visitor —a child of six, its face disfigured with something which the Governor of the workhouse who was their guide said was scurvy. The child came straight to Hawthorne, not even noticing the others, smiled up at him, took hold of his coat, followed him around as they went about the ward and then standing directly in front of him, lifted its arms with the confidence his own little Rose would have shown, and without any words plainly showed it wanted the visitor to pick it up. Hawthorne was a person with a great love of niceties and cleanliness and the soiled little mite below him clutching at his knees made him hesitate a moment, but only for a moment. There was such confidence in the small face that he stooped and gathered the soiled atom in his arms. "It was," he wrote later, "as if God had promised the child this favor in my behalf and I must needs fulfil the contract."

So he held the little thing for a while and, even after he had put it down again, it followed him about, held two of his fingers in its scrawny blotched hand, playing with them—"as if it were a child of his own," he thought. They went into another part of the wards, but after they came down there was the child again with its dim red eyes and the sickly smile on its defaced mouth— "I should never have forgiven myself had I repelled its advances," he told his wife that evening.

Later in the day he was taken to another house—this time a lovely English home, with great sloping lawns and carefully tended gardens. And that evening he wrote in his diary: "I wonder how many people live and die in the workhouse having no other home, because other people have a great deal more home than enough."

When the family left England they went to Rome to live for a while. This city Rose's father learned to love dearly and so did her mother. Here the New England Protestantism in them both grew dim sometimes as the brightness of Catholic realities began to shine before them. They all loved Rome—the parents, serious sixteen-year-old Una, Julian, the sturdy ten-year-old son of the house, and usually Rose the youngest also.

Rose, however, was not so moved by Rome as were the others. Years later she wrote in retrospect of the great impression made on her by the Holy Father on his balcony, but the strangeness of the Latin prayers chanted in the streets made her feel it was all a child's game, and no one explained them to her. During Lent she watched cakes being fried in oil and sold on the streets and tasted them. She wrote, "I found them to be indistinct in taste for all their pretty tint and the dexterous twist of the cook's wrist as he picked them up. If they had been appetizing I should have been sharply interested in the idea of becoming a Catholic, but their entire absence of relish convinced me that the Italians lacked mental grasp and salvation at a single swoop."

It was not until she was grown up and a Catholic herself that she realized how close both her parents had come to the Faith during their years in Rome. "They didn't believe that Italy was really under an incubus, and they felt the spiritual weight of Catholicism and of the Cross and half guessed its spiritual meaning."

Mrs. Hawthorne wrote home to her family about a visit to Saint Peter's. "There alone in Rome is perpetual summer. It would seem warmed by the ardent soul of Peter, or the breath of prayer from innumerable saints." Then, too, her dear friend, Anna Ward, had been recently received into the Church. Though both Nathaniel Hawthorne and his wife had Catholic spirits, they remained, so far as their outer faith went, purely Protestant. Yet Hawthorne could write about the Eternal City that "the desolation of its ruins does not prevent her from being more intimately our home than even the spot where we were born." And that spot was Puritan New England!

The Hawthornes went back home to their little house in Concord, with its pleasant outlook on the Lexington Road. And, after a few happy years there, Hawthorne died and was buried with Concord men in Sleepy Hollow burial ground. The rest of the family went to live in Europe and while in England Mrs. Hawthorne died. Una decided to stay there and to become a member of an Anglican sisterhood. Julian and Rose came home and not long after George Parsons Lathrop, whom they had met abroad, joined them and persuaded Rose to be his wife.

Then came news of the sudden death of Una in London, and Rose scarcely realized this loss when it was followed by another—that of her four-year-old son Francis, the Lathrops' only child. Shortly after this Rose and her husband were received into the Catholic Faith in the Paulist Church in New York City.

Of all her family only Julian was left

now, and her husband. But though she had striven with all her heart to make her married life a success she was not able to do so. It was not that she did not love George Lathrop, for she did and dearly. But there were inherent weaknesses in him and an instability that finally forced her to leave him. She went back to him several times, until at last she saw there was no use trying again.

Now her life was very empty. One day in an effort to forget her troubles, she decided to look up a dressmaker who used to work for her, and have some gowns made over. She learned that the woman had been a victim of cancer and had been taken to the City Home on Blackwell's Island.[2] She went to see her and found she had died and been buried before she reached the Island. But during her brief visit there she had seen the horror of what it meant to be one of the cancerous poor, shunted off to the City Home to die. A dear friend of hers, Emma Lazarus, had recently died of that disease and she had seen how much her friend had suffered, even though surrounded by every comfort and care. It seemed a terrible thing, she mused on her way home, to endure such pain and receive no comfort, no tending, merely because one was poor. Worst of all, at that time cancer was thought to be contagious and often the family itself drew away from the sufferer.

She came home to her empty rooms, sick at heart. Her own sadness was forgotten in the thought of the misery she had seen. She sat down and drew from her bookshelves one of her father's books, as she often did. Tonight especially she felt she must be a little in touch with someone who had loved her.

The volume she picked up was "Our Old Home," the sketches of his year in England and she read over paragraphs of his life there. She had herself been too young to remember much of it, but even so some of those days came back to her.

She turned the pages and her eye fell on his account of his visit to the workhouse—the diseased child who followed him—how he felt he was responsible for it and dared not let it go without comforting it. He wrote in the third person, as he often did about himself. "No doubt the child's mission was to remind him that he was responsible in his degree for all the sufferings and misdemeanors of the world in which he lived, and was not entitled to look upon a particle of its dark calamity as if it were none of his concern: the offspring of a brother's iniquity being his own blood-relation, and the guilt, likewise, a burden to him, unless he expiated it by better deeds. It might almost make a man doubt the existence of his own soul, to observe how nature has flung the little wretches into the street and left them there, so evidently regarding them as nothing worth, and how all mankind acquiesces in the great mother's estimate of her offspring. For if they have no immortality, what superior claims can I assert for mine? And how difficult to believe that anything so precious as a gem of immortal growth can have been buried under this dirt heap, plunged in this cesspool of misery and vice. Ah, what a mystery. Slowly, slowly, as after groping at the bottom of a deep, noisome, stagnant pool, my hope struggles upward to the surface, bearing the half drowned body of a child along with it and heaving it aloft for its life

[2] BLACKWELL'S ISLAND—Now known as Welfare Island, in East River, New York. City prison and hospitals.

and my life and all our lives. Unless these slime-clogged nostrils can be made capable of inhaling celestial air, I know not how the purest and most intellectual of us can reasonably expect to taste a breath of it. The whole question of eternity is staked here. If a single one of these helpless ones is lost, the world is lost."

It seemed to her that she was learning a lesson just as her father had taught her years ago. She turned to another page. "Human beings owe a debt of love to one another," he had written, "because there is no other method of paying the debt of love and care which all of us owe Providence which put me here among other things, in order that I may make amends for the inhospitality of my neighbors."

She knew now that there was something for her to do. The first thing was to take away, as much as was in her power, the look of horror and fear she had seen on the faces in the cancer ward at the Island. She enrolled for a course in cancer nursing, and found she had

indeed embarked on a hard work. When the nursing was finished, she rented, with money contributed by friends, a small two-room flat in lower New York and announced it would be a free home for incurable cancer patients. There would be only two rules to govern the venture: patients must be entirely without funds and there must be no hope of any cure. At first she could take only one or two women patients in the house itself, and the rest of the work was among patients who came to have their sores dressed.

When the *Times* learned that Mrs. George Parsons Lathrop, a member of New York's best social group, a woman who had books to her credit, whose father had been one of America's great geniuses, was devoting herself to work among the slum's cancerous outcasts, the paper sent a reporter to get details of such a remarkable story. When the people who had met her at parties and the opera read this they could not believe their eyes.

Not long afterwards the *Times* chronicled in a paragraph the death of G. P. Lathrop and stated, "Mrs. Lathrop was at his bedside when he died."

Her name through the years was often in the *Times* in the letters she wrote appealing for help for her work—letters that had literary value as well as heart value, for had Rose Lathrop chosen to follow a literary path, there is no doubt she would have become one of our remembered writers.

From here and there the money came —never much, but enough to keep the work going. The patients, hearing of this chance for help without having to go to the dreaded Island, came in numbers to the little flat and Mrs. Lathrop treated them as clinic patients. Only the worst and saddest she kept in her small space and cared for them day and night. When she was able to add two more rooms to her clinic she was a happy woman.

In the crowded little rooms she kept pain at bay and brought into the sad lives which entrusted themselves to her care as much respite from agony as she could, a certain hope that though this life was ebbing there was another, with pain no longer even a memory, near at hand for them. She had in her two qualities that bore her through the hardest times: love of God and a deep sense of joy.

She lived long enough to see the realization of her fondest wishes and unceasing prayers. The two poor little rooms in which she began her work grew into a big house on Cherry Street, still in use today as one of New York's best cancer hospitals. A great group of houses was built in Westchester to shelter her poor patients; her work and her group of workers became a part of the great Dominican Order, under the patronage of St. Rose of Lima.

She had chosen in religion the name "Alphonsa," after the saint who had been devoted to charity for the sick poor. She lived up to that name every day.

She lived to be nearly seventy and she never ceased being busy. On the day before she died she wrote a great pile of letters asking for help with the big new house just built, and laid them at the feet of St. Joseph in the chapel. Next morning they found she had died in her sleep during the night. It was obvious too that St. Joseph had indeed helped her, for not one of those letters went unanswered, and the answers were checks and money.

The spirit of Rose Hawthorne lives on in her homes. There is in them a sense of gaiety and joy that is not often seen in institutions of this tragic kind, houses where death is always as close as the next bed. Out of tragedy and sorrow, out of loss and death in her own heart and home, she had built beauty for God's unfortunates. When she was a little girl her mother had showed her God in the sunrise and the sunset and the small ways of the world, showed her paintings and statues wrought for love of God. And her father who had loved his fellowmen so much that he felt the greatest sin was to refuse to help the needy, showed her how she could help them. Between them her parents had given her a love of God and a love of man and she, an adopted daughter of the Faith, had put this service into action for Christ's poor.

Nathaniel Hawthorne had indeed given his Rose a precious inheritance, the realization of personal responsibility, so far as one person can have it, for the pain of the world. He was a gentle sensitive man who hated ugliness and disfigurement, but he took the workhouse child in his arms because it needed his love. And his daughter, who also hated the unclean, the hideous—the dainty girl who shrank from pain and ugliness, the woman who loved beauty and pleasant living—took that pain and ugliness into her arms as he had taken the disfigured baby.

There is one difference between them. She held the unclean and the hideously deformed and did not let them go again —at least not until God took them from the safety of her arms to the safety of His own. Her father had done the philosophizing about it. He had laid the groundwork for her later life, by his love for his own family and his sympathy and his understanding of the pain of the world. His great contribution was to help in words; his books were a plea for pity and understanding for the human soul. Her contribution, having, as he had not, the power of the Catholic Faith to sustain her, was to transmute her inheritance into deeds, to offer her human sorrow and love and the broken bodies that came to her for helping— to offer them all to God, to unite small human pity to the Everlasting Mercy.

◇◇◇◇◇◇◇◇◇◇◇◇◇◇◇◇◇◇◇◇◇◇◇◇◇◇◇

## FOR DISCUSSION

1. What legacies did Nathaniel Hawthorne leave to his daughter? Which of them do you consider the most precious? Why?

2. What sort of thing were the Hawthornes most likely to notice wherever they went? What did Nathaniel mean by his statement that we are forced to inhale the "atmosphere of the house of paupers" into our inmost being?

3. Explain what Nathaniel meant by this statement: "Let the whole world be cleansed or not a man or woman of us can be clean."

4. What did Nathaniel's treatment of the little girl in the poorhouse tell you about his character? In what way did he show that he had a sense of social justice?

5. What effect did Rose have on the Hawthornes? In this short sketch of Rose Hawthorne's life why does the author trouble to sketch the character of Nathaniel Hawthorne?

6. How did Rose react when she learned that her dressmaker had died from cancer untended?

7. How did the passage from "Our Old Home" affect Rose? What was it that Rose knew she had to do?

8. What two qualities carried Rose through the hardest times?

9. What differences does the author point out between Rose and her father?

## PROJECTS

1. Katherine Burton has written a complete account of Rose Hawthorne Lathrop's life in her book, *Sorrow Built a Bridge*. Choose this book for your next report. When you have read the book, explain the meaning of the title.

2. Make a list of outstanding Americans of the past hundred years who have come into the Church. How many of the authors represented in this book are converts? Write a short biographical sketch of one of these converts.

3. Katherine Burton is herself a convert. Write a short account of her life. What are some of the factors which influenced her conversion?

## WORDS TO EXPLAIN

1. *Retrospect* means to look back, to consider the past. What does *introspect* mean?

2. *Dexterous* comes from the Latin word *dexter*, meaning *right*. The English word *dexter* means *right hand*. Explain how *dexterous* comes to mean *expert, skillful, adroit*.

3. The word *noisome* has nothing to do with noisy unless you can speak of a noisy smell. Are *noisome* smells pleasant?

# LINCOLN SPEAKS AT GETTYSBURG

*CARL SANDBURG*

It is difficult to write a good short speech. Any good speaker will tell you that.

Lincoln's "Gettysburg Address" is a masterpiece, not because of his skill in the techniques of oratory, but because he spoke sincerely and simply from his great heart overburdened with national cares.

The following selection is an accurate history of how Lincoln wrote his immortal address and how it was received by the people.

A printed invitation came to Lincoln's hands notifying him that on Thursday, November 19, 1863, exercises would be held for the dedication of a National Soldiers' Cemetery at Gettysburg. The same circular invitation had been mailed to Senators, Congressmen, the governors of Northern States, members of the Cabinet, by the commission of Pennsylvanians who had organized a corporation through which Maine, New Hampshire, Vermont, Massachusetts, Rhode Island, Maryland, Connecticut, New York, New Jersey, Pennsylvania, Delaware, West Virginia, Ohio, Indiana, Illinois, Michigan, Wisconsin, and Minnesota were to share the cost of a decent burying-ground for the dust and bones of the Union and Confederate dead.

In the helpless onrush of the war, it was known, too many of the fallen had lain as neglected cadavers rotting in the open fields or thrust into so shallow a resting-place that a common farm plow caught in their bones. Now by order of Governor Curtin of Pennsylvania seventeen acres had been purchased on Cemetery Hill, where the Union center stood its colors on the second and third of July, and plots of soil had been allotted each State for its graves.

The sacred and delicate duties of orator of the day had fallen on Edward Everett. An eminent cultural figure, perhaps foremost of all distinguished American classical orators, he was born in 1794, had been United States Senator, Governor of Massachusetts, member of Congress, Secretary of State under Fillmore, Minister to Great Britain, Phi Beta Kappa poet at Harvard, professor of Greek at Harvard, president of Harvard. . . .

Serene, suave, handsomely venerable in his sixty-ninth year, a prominent specimen of Northern upper-class distinction, Everett was a natural choice of the Pennsylvania commissioners, who

"Lincoln Speaks at Gettysburg" from *Abraham Lincoln; The War Years*, by Carl Sandburg, copyright, 1939, by Harcourt, Brace and Company, Inc. and reprinted by their permission.

sought an orator for a solemn national occasion. When in September they notified him that the date of the occasion would be October 23, he replied that he would need more time for preparation, and the dedication was postponed till November 19.

Lincoln meanwhile, in reply to the printed circular invitation, sent word to the commissioners that he would be present at the ceremonies. This made it necessary for the commissioners to consider whether the President should be asked to deliver an address when present. Clark E. Carr of Galesburg, Illinois, representing his State on the Board of Commissioners, noted that the decision of the Board to invite Lincoln to speak was an afterthought. "The question was raised as to his ability to speak upon such a grave and solemn occasion. . . . Besides, it was said that, with his important duties and responsibilities, he could not possibly have the leisure to prepare an address. . . . In answer . . . it was urged that he himself, better than any one else, could determine as to these questions, and that, if he were invited to speak, he was sure to do what, under the circumstances, would be right and proper."

And so on November 2 David Wills of Gettysburg, as the special agent of Governor Curtin and also acting for the several States, by letter informed Lincoln that the several States having soldiers in the Army of the Potomac who were killed, or had since died at hospitals in the vicinity, had procured grounds for a cemetery and proper burial of their dead. "These grounds will be consecrated and set apart to this sacred purpose by appropriate ceremonies on Thursday, the 19th instant. I am authorized by the Governors of the various States to invite you to be present

and participate in these ceremonies, which will doubtless be very imposing and solemnly impressive. It is the desire that after the oration, you, as Chief Executive of the nation, formally set apart these grounds to their sacred use by a few appropriate remarks.". . .

Lamon [1] noted that Lincoln wrote part of his intended Gettysburg address at Washington, covered a sheet of foolscap paper with a memorandum of it, and before taking it out of his hat and reading it to Lamon he said that it was not at all satisfactory to him, that he was afraid he would not do himself credit nor come up to public expectation. He had been too busy to give it the time he would like to. . . .

Various definite motives besides vague intuitions may have guided Lincoln in his decision to attend and speak even though half his Cabinet had sent formal declinations in response to the printed circular invitations they had all received. Though the Gettysburg dedication was to be under interstate auspices, it had tremendous national significance for Lincoln because on the platform would be the State governors whose co-operation with him was of vast importance. Also a slander and a libel had been widely mouthed and printed that on his visit to the battlefield of Antietam nearly a year before he had laughed obscenely at his own funny stories and called on Lamon to sing a cheap comic song. Perhaps he might go to Gettysburg and let it be seen how he demeaned himself on a somber landscape of sacrifice. . . .

When Lincoln boarded the train for

[1] LAMON—Ward Hill Lamon, Lincoln's law partner in Springfield, Illinois. When Lincoln was elected president, Lamon became his private secretary. Later he wrote a book entitled *Recollections of Abraham Lincoln.*

Gettysburg on November 18, his best chum in the world, Tad, lay sick abed and the doctors not sure what ailed him. The mother still remembered Willie and was hysterical about Tad. But the President felt imperative duty called him to Gettysburg.

Provost Marshall General James B. Fry as a War Department escort came to the White House, but the President was late in getting into the carriage for the drive to the station. They had no time to lose, Fry remarked. Lincoln said he felt like an Illinois man who was going to be hanged and as the man passed along the road on the way to the gallows the crowds kept pushing into the way and blocking passage. The condemned man at last called out, "Boys, you needn't be in such a hurry to get ahead, there won't be any fun till I get there."

Flags and red-white-and-blue bunting decorated the four-car special train. Aboard were the three Cabinet members, Nicolay and Hay, army and navy representatives, newspapermen, the French and Italian Ministers and attaches.[2] The rear third of the last coach had a drawing-room, where from time to time the President talked with nearly everyone aboard as they came and went. Henry Clay Cochrane, lieutenant of the Marines, noted:

"I happened to have a *New York Herald* and offered it to Mr. Lincoln. He took it and thanked me, saying, 'I like to see what they say about us.' The news was about Burnside at Knoxville, Grant and Sherman at Chattanooga, and Meade on the Rapidan, all expecting trouble. He read for a little while and then began to laugh at some wild guesses of the paper about pending movements. It was pleasant to see his sad face lighted up. He was looking sallow, sunken-eyed, thin, care-worn, and very quiet. He returned the paper remarking among other things that when he had first passed over that road on his way to Congress in 1847 he noticed square-rigged vessels up the Patapsco river as far as the Relay House and now there seemed to be only small craft.

"At the Calvert Street Station Secretary Seward began to get uneasy as we approached Baltimore. Upon reaching the Calvert Street Station in Baltimore all was quiet, less than two hundred people assembled, among them women with children in arms. They called for the President. He took two or three of the babies up and kissed them which greatly pleased the mothers. General Schenck and staff joined us and soon after the President went forward in the car and seated himself with a party of choice spirits, among whom was Mayor Frederick W. Lincoln of Boston, not a kinsman. They told stories for an hour or so, Mr. Lincoln taking his turn and enjoying it. Approaching Hanover Junction, he arose and said, 'Gentlemen, this is all very pleasant, but the people will expect me to say something to them tomorrow, and I must give the matter some thought.' He then returned to the rear room of the car.". . .

At sundown the train pulled into Gettysburg and Lincoln was driven to the Wills residence, Seward to the Harper home fronting on the public square. A sleepy little country town of 3,500 was overflowing with human pulses again. Private homes were filled with notables and nondescripts. Hundreds slept on the floors of hotels. Military bands blared till late in the night serenading whomsoever. The weather was mild and the moon up for those

---

[2] ATTACHES (ăt′á·shā′z)—Members of diplomatic staffs; assistants to an ambassador.

who chose to go a-roaming. When serenaders called on the President for a speech, he made again one of those little addresses saying there was nothing to say. "In my position it is sometimes important that I should not say foolish things. (A voice: "If you can help it.") It very often happens that the only way to help it is to say nothing at all. Believing that is my present condition this evening, I must beg of you to excuse me from addressing you further."

The crowd didn't feel it was much of a speech. They went next door with the band and blared for Seward. He spoke so low that Hay could not hear him, but he opened the stopgaps of patriotic sentiment, saying in part, "I thank my God for the hope that this is the last fratricidal war which will fall upon the country which is vouchsafed to us by Heaven—the richest, the broadest, the most beautiful, the most magnificent, and capable of a greater destiny than has ever been given to any part of the human race." What more could a holiday crowd ask for on a fair night of moonlit November? Seward gave them more and closed: "Fellow citizens, good night." It was good night for him but not for them. They serenaded five other speakers. . . .

At dinner in the Wills home that evening Lincoln met Edward Everett, a guest under the same roof, and Governor Curtin and others. About ten o'clock he was in his room, with paper and pencil ready to write, when he sent a colored servant down for Judge Wills to come up. Still later, about eleven o'clock, he sent the colored servant down again for Judge Wills, who came up and heard Lincoln request to see Mr. Seward. Judge Wills offered to go and bring Seward from next door at the Harpers'. "No, I'll go and see him,"

said Lincoln, who gathered his sheets of paper and went for a half-hour with his Secretary of State.

Whether Seward made slight or material alterations in the text on the sheets was known only to Lincoln and Seward. It was midnight or later that Lincoln went to sleep, probably perfectly clear in his mind as to what his speech would be the next day. The one certainty was that his "few appropriate remarks," good or bad, would go to an immense audience. Also he slept better for having a telegram from Stanton reporting there was no real war news and "On inquiry Mrs. Lincoln informs me that your son is better this evening."

Fifteen thousand, some said 30,000 or 50,000, people were on Cemetery Hill for the exercises the next day when the procession from Gettysburg arrived afoot and horseback representing the United States Government, the army and navy, governors of States, mayors of cities, a regiment of troops, hospital corps, telegraph-company representatives, Knights Templar, Masonic Fraternity, Odd Fellows, and other benevolent associations, the press, fire departments, citizens of Pennsylvania and other States. They were scheduled to start at ten o'clock and at that hour of the clock Lincoln in a black suit, high silk hat, and white gloves came out of the Wills residence and mounted a horse. A crowd was on hand and he held a reception on horseback. At eleven the parade began to move. The President's horse seemed small for him, as some looked at it. Clark E. Carr, just behind the President, believed he noticed that the President sat erect and looked majestic to begin with and then got to thinking so that his body leaned forward, his arms hung limp, and his head bent far down. . . .

The march of the procession of military and civic bodies began. "Mr. Lincoln was mounted upon a young and beautiful chestnut horse, the largest in the Cumberland Valley," wrote Lieutenant Cochrane. This seemed the first occasion that anyone had looked at the President mounted with a feeling that just the right horse had been picked to match his physical length. "His towering figure surmounted by a high silk hat made the rest of us look small," thought Cochrane. . . .

The march was over in fifteen minutes. But Mr. Everett, the orator of the day, had not arrived. . . . Bands played till noon. Mr. Everett arrived. . . .

The United States House chaplain, the Reverend Thomas H. Stockton, offered a prayer while the thousand stood with uncovered heads. . . . Benjamin B. French, officer in charge of buildings in Washington, introduced the Honorable Edward Everett, orator of the day, who rose, bowed low to Lincoln, saying, "Mr. President." Lincoln responded, "Mr. Everett."

The orator of the day then stood in silence before a crowd that stretched to limits that would test his voice. Beyond and around were the wheat fields, the meadows, the peach orchards, long slopes of land, and five and seven miles farther the contemplative blue ridge of a low mountain range. His eyes could sweep them as he faced the audience. He had taken note of it in his prepared and rehearsed address. "Overlooking these broad fields now reposing from the labors of the waning year, the mighty Alleghenies dimly towering before us, the graves of our brethren beneath our feet, it is with hesitation that I raise my poor voice to break the eloquent silence of God and Nature. But the duty to which you have called me must be performed;—grant me, I pray you, your indulgence and your sympathy.". . .

Northern cities would have been trampled in conquest but for "those who sleep beneath our feet," said the orator. He gave an outline of how the war began, traversed decisive features of the three days' battles at Gettysburg, discussed the doctrine of State sovereignty and denounced it, drew parallels from European history, and came to his peroration [3] quoting Pericles on dead patriots: "The whole earth is the sepulcher of illustrious men." The men of nineteen sister States had stood side by side on the perilous ridges. "Seminary Ridge, the Peach-Orchard, Cemetery, Culp, and Wolf Hill, Round Top, Little Round Top, humble names, henceforward dear and famous,—no lapse of time, no distance of space, shall cause you to be forgotten." He had spoken for an hour and fifty-seven minutes, some said a trifle over two hours, repeating almost word for word an address that occupied nearly two newspaper pages, as he had written it and as it had gone in advance sheets to many newspapers.

Everett came to his closing sentence without a faltering voice: "Down to the latest period of recorded time, in the glorious annals of our common country there will be no brighter page than that which relates the battles of Gettysburg." It was the effort of his life and embodied the perfections of the school of oratory in which he had spent his career. His erect form and sturdy shoulders, his white hair and flung-back head at dramatic points, his voice, his poise, and chiefly some quality of inside good-

[3] PERORATION—The concluding part of a speech; the summing up of an argument.

heartedness, held most of his audience to him, though the people in the front rows had taken their seats three hours before his oration closed.

The Baltimore Glee Club sang an ode written for the occasion by Benjamin B. French, who had introduced Everett to the audience. The poets Longfellow, Bryant, Whittier, Lowell, George Boker, had been requested but none found time to respond with a piece to be set to music. . . .

Having read Everett's address, Lincoln knew when the moment drew near for him to speak. He took out his own manuscript from a coat pocket, put on his steel-bowed glasses, stirred in his chair, looked over the manuscript, and put it back in his pocket. The Baltimore Glee Club finished. The specially chosen Ward Hill Lamon rose and spoke the words "The President of the United States," who rose, and holding in one hand the two sheets of paper at which he occasionally glanced, delivered the address in his high-pitched and clear-carrying voice. The *Cincinnati Commercial* reporter wrote, "The President rises slowly, draws from his pocket a paper, and, when commotion subsides, in a sharp, unmusical treble voice, reads the brief and pithy remarks." Hay wrote in his diary, "The President, in a firm, free way, with more grace than is his wont, said his half dozen words of consecration." Charles Hale of the *Boston Advertiser*, also officially representing Governor Andrew of Massachusetts, had notebook and pencil in hand, took down the slow-spoken words of the President, as follows:

Fourscore and seven years ago, our fathers brought forth upon this continent a new nation, conceived in liberty and dedicated to the proposition that all men are created equal.

Now we are engaged in a great civil war, testing whether that nation—or any nation, so conceived and so dedicated—can long endure.

We are met on a great battle-field of that war. We are met to dedicate a portion of it as the final resting place of those who have given their lives that that nation might live.

It is altogether fitting and proper that we should do this.

But, in a larger sense, we cannot dedicate, we cannot consecrate, we cannot hallow, this ground. The brave men, living and dead, who struggled here, have consecrated it, far above our power to add or to detract.

The world will very little note nor long remember what we say here; but it can never forget what they did here.

It is for us, the living, rather, to be dedicated, here, to the unfinished work that they have thus far so nobly carried on. It is rather for us to be here dedicated to the great task remaining before us; that from these honored dead we take increased devotion to that cause for which they here gave the last full measure of devotion; that we here highly resolve that these dead shall not have died in vain; that the nation shall, under God, have a new birth of freedom, and that government of the people, by the people, for the people, shall not perish from the earth. . . .

The *New York Tribune* and many other newspapers indicated "(Applause.)" at five places in the address and "(Long continued applause.)" at the end. The applause, however, according to most of the responsible witnesses, was formal and perfunctory,[4] a tribute to the occasion, to the high office, to the array of important men of the nation on the platform, by persons who had sat as an audience for three hours. Ten sentences had been spoken in five minutes, and some were surprised that it should end before the orator had really begun to get his outdoor voice.

A photographer had made ready to record a great historic moment, had bustled about with his dry plates, his black box on a tripod, and before he had his head under the hood for an exposure, the President had said "by the people, for the people" and the nick of time was past for a photograph. . . .

According to Lamon, Lincoln himself felt that about all he had given the audience was ordinary garden-variety dedicatory remarks, for Lamon wrote that Lincoln told him just after delivering the speech that he had regret over not having prepared it with greater care. "Lamon, that speech won't *scour*. It is a flat failure and the people are disappointed." On the farms where Lincoln grew up as a boy when wet soil stuck to the mold board of a plow they said it didn't "scour."

The near-by *Patriot and Union* of Harrisburg took its fling: "The President succeeded on this occasion because

---

[4] PERFUNCTORY—Mechanical; without interest or enthusiasm.

he acted without sense and without constraint in a panorama that was gotten up more for the benefit of his party than for the glory of the nation and the honor of the dead. . . . We pass over the silly remarks of the President; for the credit of the nation we are willing that the veil of oblivion shall be dropped over them and that they shall no more be repeated or thought of.". . .

The *Philadelphia Evening Bulletin* said that thousands who would not read the elaborate oration of Mr. Everett would read the President's few words "and not many will do it without a moistening of the eye and a swelling of the heart." The *Detroit Advertiser and Tribune* said Mr. Everett had nobly told the story of the battle, "but he who wants to take in the very spirit of the day, catch the unstudied pathos that animates a sincere but simple-minded man, will turn from the stately periods of the professed orator to the brief speech of the President." The *Providence Journal* reminded readers of the saying that the hardest thing in the world is to make a good five-minute speech: "We know not where to look for a more admirable speech than the brief one which the President made at the close of Mr. Everett's oration. . . . Could the most elaborate and splendid oration be more beautiful, more touching, more inspiring, than those thrilling words of the President? They had in our humble judgment the charm and power of the very highest eloquence.". . .

Everett's opinion of the speech he heard Lincoln deliver was written in a note to Lincoln the next day and was more than mere courtesy: "I should be glad if I could flatter myself that I came as near to the central idea of the occasion in two hours as you did in two minutes." Lincoln's immediate reply was: "In our respective parts yesterday, you could not have been excused to make a short address, nor I a long one. I am pleased to know that, in your judgment, the little I did say was not entirely a failure.". . .

After the ceremonies at Gettysburg Lincoln lunched with Governor Curtin, Mr. Everett, and others at the Wills home, held a reception that had not been planned, handshaking nearly an hour, looking gloomy and listless but brightening sometimes as a small boy or girl came in line, and stopping one tall man for remarks as to just how high up he reached. At five o'clock he attended a patriotic meeting in the Presbyterian church, walking arm-in-arm with old John Burns, and listening to an address by Lieutenant Governor-elect Anderson of Ohio. At six-thirty he was on the departing Washington train. . . .

The ride to Washington took until midnight. Lincoln was weary, talked little, stretched out on one of the side seats in the drawing-room, and had a wet towel laid across his eyes and forehead.

He had stood that day, the world's foremost spokesman of popular government, saying that democracy was yet worth fighting for. He had spoken as one in mist who might head on deeper yet into mist. He incarnated[5] the assurances and pretenses of popular government, implied that it could and might perish from the earth. What he meant by "a new birth of freedom" for the nation could have a thousand interpretations. The taller riddles of democracy stood up out of the address. It had the dream touch of vast and furious events epitomized[6] for any foreteller to

---

[5] INCARNATED—Embodied in human form.
[6] EPITOMIZED—Abridged; summarized.

read what was to come. He did not assume that the drafted soldiers, substitutes, and bounty-paid privates had died willingly under Lee's shot and shell, in deliberate consecration of themselves to the Union cause. His cadences sang the ancient song that where there is freedom men have fought and sacrificed for it, and that freedom is worth men's dying for. For the first time since he became President he had on a dramatic occasion declaimed, howsoever it might be read, Jefferson's proposition which had been a slogan of the Revolutionary War—"All men are created equal"—leaving no other inference than that he regarded the Negro slave as a man. His outwardly smooth sentences were inside of them gnarled and tough with the enigmas [7] of the American experiment.

Back at Gettysburg the blue haze of the Cumberland Mountains had dimmed till it was a blur in a nocturne. The moon was up and fell with a bland golden benevolence on the new-made graves of soldiers, on the sepulchers of old settlers, on the horse carcasses of which the onrush of war had not yet permitted removal. The *New York Herald* man walked amid them and ended the story he sent his paper: "The air, the trees, the graves are silent. Even the relic hunters are gone now. And the soldiers here never wake to the sound of reveille."

In many a country cottage over the land, a tall old clock in a quiet corner told time in a tick-tock deliberation. Whether the orchard branches hung with pink-spray blossoms or icicles of sleet, whether the outside news was seedtime or harvest, rain or drouth, births or deaths, the swing of the pendulum was right and left and right and left in a tick-tock deliberation.

The face and dial of the clock had known the eyes of a boy who listened to its tick-tock and learned to read its minute and hour hands. And the boy had seen years measured off by the swinging pendulum, and grown to man size, had gone away. And the people in the cottage knew that the clock would stand there and the boy never again come into the room and look at the clock with the query, "What is the time?"

In a row of graves of the Unidentified the boy would sleep long in the dedicated final resting-place at Gettysburg. Why he had gone away and why he would never come back had roots in some mystery of flags and drums, of national fate in which individuals sink as in a deep sea, of men swallowed and vanished in a man-made storm of smoke and steel.

The mystery deepened and moved with ancient music and inviolable consolation because a solemn Man of Authority had stood at the graves of the Unidentified and spoken the words "we cannot consecrate—we cannot hallow—this ground. The brave men, living and dead, who struggled here, have consecrated it far above our poor power to add or detract. . . . From these honored dead we take increased devotion to that cause for which they gave the last full measure of devotion."

To the backward and forward pendulum swing of a tall old clock in a quiet corner they might read those cadenced words while outside the windows the first flurry of snow blew across the orchard and down over the meadow, the beginnings of winter in a gun-metal gloaming to be later arched with a star-flung sky.

---

[7] ENIGMAS (ê·nĭg′măz)—Obscure sayings; riddles; things difficult to explain.

## FOR DISCUSSION

1. Did the commissioners do better in choosing Everett rather than Lincoln to deliver the formal oration at Gettysburg? Why? Why would Lincoln feel relief that he was not asked?

2. What indications are there in this selection that Lincoln was not altogether popular as president?

3. Compare the style of Lincoln's speech with that of the few excerpts taken from Everett's. Is there any orator today to whom you think you would listen for two hours?

4. What human characteristics of Lincoln does Mr. Sandburg disclose in this sketch?

## WORDS

1. Try to determine the meaning of the italicized words from the sense of the sentences in which they are used.

   a. He *demeaned* himself with all the dignity of his age and high social position.

   b. He has the *suave* manner of the perfect polished gentleman.

   c. He *traversed* the country from ocean to ocean trying to sell his political ideals to the people.

   d. The *peroration* of his speech was greeted with a sigh of relief, but he spent as much time summing up his argument as he had in putting it forth.

   e. He *expatiated* on each statement, examining it from every possible angle until both his ideas and the audience were exhausted.

2. Study the difference between *imply* and *infer*.

## PROJECTS

1. Memorize the "Gettysburg Address."

2. Compare the text of the address printed here with the one generally used. Note the differences. Why did Sandburg use this one?

3. Read some speeches by prominent men of our day and compare them with Everett's address.

# Further Readings in Twentieth-Century Literature

## THE SHORT STORY

Note: Books marked with an asterisk (*) throughout this volume are books by Catholic authors.

BENÉT, STEPHEN VINCENT, *Selected Works*

CATHER, WILLA, *Youth and the Bright Medusa; Obscure Destinies*

CONNELL, RICHARD, *Apes and Angels*

* CONNOLLY, JAMES BRENDAN, *Gloucestermen*

EDMONDS, WALTER D., *Mostly Canallers*

FISHER, DOROTHY CANFIELD, *Hillsboro People*

* GABLE, SISTER MARIELLA, ed., *They Are People; Our Father's House*

GALE, ZONA, *Friendship Village*

* HURLEY, DORAN, *Old Parish*

JOHNSON, JOSEPHINE, *Winter Orchard and Other Stories*

JOHNSON, OWEN, *The Tennessee Shad*

KANTOR, MACKINLAY, *Author's Choice*

LA FARGE, OLIVER, *All the Young Men*

LARDNER, RING, *Round Up*

LEWIS, SINCLAIR, *Selected Short Stories of Sinclair Lewis*

LONDON, JACK, *Best Short Stories of Jack London*

PORTER, W. S. (O. HENRY), *The Four Million; Cabbages and Kings*

RINEHART, MARY ROBERTS, *The Amazing Adventures of Letitia Carberry*

RUNYON, DAMON, *The Best of Runyon*

SAROYAN, WILLIAM, *My Name Is Aram*

STEELE, W. D., *The Best Stories of Wilbur Daniel Steele*

STUART, JESSE, *Tales from the Plum Tree Hills*

SUCKOW, RUTH, *Iowa Interiors*

TARKINGTON, BOOTH, *The Fascinating Stranger and Other Stories*

THURBER, JAMES, *The Beast in Me and Other Animals*

WELTY, EUDORA, *A Curtain of Green; The Wide Net*

WEST, JESSAMYN, *The Friendly Persuasion*

WILLIAMS, BEN AMES, *Fraternity Village*

## POETRY

* BARRETT, ALFRED J., *Mint by Night*

BENÉT, STEPHEN VINCENT, *John Brown's Body*

FROST, ROBERT, *The Collected Poems of Robert Frost*

* KILMER, ALINE, *Selected Poems*

* KILMER, JOYCE, *Trees and Other Poems*

LINDSAY, VACHEL, *Selected Poems*

LOWELL, AMY, *Selected Poems*

* MADELEVA, SISTER MARY, *Selected Poems*

* MERTON, THOMAS, *Man in the Divided Sea*

* O'DONNELL, CHARLES L., *Rime of the Rood*

* POWERS, JESSICA, *The Lantern Burns*

ROBINSON, EDWIN ARLINGTON, *Collected Poems*

* WALSH, WILLIAM THOMAS, *Lyric Poems*

WYLIE, ELINOR, *Angels and Earthly Creatures*

## DRAMA

ANDERSON, MAXWELL, *Joan of Lorraine; Winterset*

* BARRY, PHILIP, *The Joyous Season*

HELLMAN, LILLIAN, *Watch on the Rhine*

KELLY, GEORGE, *The Show-Off*

* LAVERY, EMMET, *Second Spring; Theatre for Tomorrow*

* MURRAY, GERARD, *Career Angel*

MILLER, ARTHUR, *All My Sons*

O'NEILL, EUGENE, *Emperor Jones; The Hairy Ape*

SHERWOOD, ROBERT, *Abe Lincoln in Illinois*

WILDER, THORNTON, *Our Town; The Skin of Our Teeth*

## NONFICTION PROSE: BIOGRAPHY

ADAMS, ELIZABETH LAURA, *Dark Symphony*

BOWEN, CATHERINE DRINKER, *Yankee from Olympus*

* BURTON, KATHERINE, *Sorrow Built a Bridge; His Dear Persuasion*

CHASE, MARY ELLEN, *A Goodly Heritage*

* DAY, DOROTHY, *From Union Square to Rome*

* DOHERTY, EDDIE, *Gall and Honey*

* JORDAN, ELIZABETH, *Three Rousing Cheers*

* KELLEY, FRANCIS CLEMENT, *The Bishop Jots It Down*

* MAGARET, HELENE, *Father De Smet*

* MAYNARD, THEODORE, *Too Small a World; The Odyssey of Francis Xavier*

* MERTON, THOMAS, *The Seven-Storey Mountain*

* SARGENT, DANIEL, *Mitri; All the Day Long*

* TALBOT, FRANCIS X., *Saint Among Savages*

## NONFICTION PROSE: THE ESSAY

BENCHLEY, ROBERT, *Inside Benchley*

* DALY, JAMES J., *The Cheerful Ascetic and Other Essays*

DAY, CLARENCE, *Life with Father*

LEACOCK, STEPHEN, *Laugh Parade*

MORLEY, CHRISTOPHER, *Mince Pie*

* REILLY, JOSEPH J., *Of Books and Men*

* REPPLIER, AGNES, *In Our Convent Days; Essays in Miniature*

## NONFICTION PROSE: JOURNALISM AND ORATORY

* BROUN, HEYWOOD, *Collected Works* (journalism)

* GANNON, ROBERT, *After Black Coffee* (oratory)

* GILLIS, JAMES M., *This Our Day* (journalism)

HERSEY, JOHN, *Hiroshima* (journalism)

PYLE, ERNIE, *Brave Men* (journalism)

* SHEEN, FULTON J., *The Divine Romance* (oratory)

* SPELLMAN, FRANCIS J., *Action This Day* (journalism)

WHITE, E. B., *One Man's Meat* (journalism)

STEVENSON, ADLAI, *The Campaign Speeches of Adlai Stevenson* (oratory)

# THE COLONIAL PERIOD

1 6 0 7 - 1 7 6 5

It is almost incredible that modern complex America is a flowering of little more than three centuries of growth. Yet the year 1607 marks the establishment of the first permanent English colony in what is now the United States. For nearly two hundred years thereafter, America was a strip of seacoast communities lying between the Appalachian Mountains and the Atlantic Ocean. It was an America of Cavalier and Puritan, of adventurer and zealot.

To the southern colonies came venturous gentlemen seeking wealth and pleasant living. And with them, in much larger numbers, came the unfortunates of England's slums and prisons—debtors, criminals, bondslaves. To them America offered a very literal kind of freedom—life itself and the chance to develop with a new land. The settlers of Virginia and Georgia found life not too difficult. Though the country was not quite the paradise pictured by the romantic-minded John Smith, yet the climate was affable and the land productive. Large plantations sprang up, and an easy way of living was the fashion. Gentlemen's sons were sent back to England to be educated. They returned, bringing the fashions of London and Paris, importing books and art and culture to the new world from the old.

Quite different were the colonies of the North. For one thing, the colonists themselves were of a sterner pattern. Plymouth in 1620 and Massachusetts Bay ten years later were founded by religious dissenters. These people crossed the ocean intent on establishing communities safe from the persistent and harassing efforts of the English Crown to compel absolute conformity to all the prescriptions of the Church of England. "In short," says Beard, "Puritans came to Massachusetts to develop, among other things, religious liberty for themselves, not to establish an idea of toleration for all religions . . ." (*Basic History of United States*, page 20). Only after many, many years would the idea of religious freedom as now understood in the United States find general acceptance. For the time being the Puritans were seeking a haven from religious persecution. At the same time they, like the rest of the emigrants from England, had faith in the material future of the American continent. In that land of promise, more securely than in Europe, they would establish their homes, rear their families, and find their fortunes. The cost in hardships and austere living would come high. They were ready to pay the price.

Naturally our best knowledge and understanding of these early colonists comes from a study of their writings. However, were we to classify colonial writings as real literature, we should be making a concession rather than expressing a sound critical judgment. The colonials wrote theological treatises, histories, travelogues, and diaries. When we consider the toilsome nature of their life, we marvel that there was time at all for writing. Their chief concern was bread, not reading material. The wildness of the land and danger from the Indians kept colonial fingers on the trigger and colonial hands on the plow and ax. The farmer raising grain was of more importance than the artist creating beauty. It was a long while before the colonists could find leisure to devote to the finer aspects of life.

But some writing there was even from the very beginning. For one thing, the Puritan settlers, conscious of the fact that as pioneers they were doing a momentous thing, felt that it was their duty to leave records of the enterprise; and so we see Bradford and Winthrop writing in the cabins of the ships that brought them westward, or laboring with stiff pens in the candlelight of their cabins. The clergymen, usually leaders in each community, were educated men and tireless workers. They preached and labored and wrote incessantly.

Colonial America, however, was Protestant, with a harsh, cold doctrine that afforded little inspiration for creative writing. Despite the religious motive that had brought many colonists to America—freedom to practice their own religion without hindrance—few were ready to extend that same freedom to religious groups, whether Protestant or Catholic, that differed from their own. Puritans, Baptists, Anglicans, and other sects had little love for each other, little tolerance of other religious faiths. As for Catholics—even in Maryland, founded by Catholics, they soon had few liberties or privileges. Only among the gentle Quakers of Pennsylvania could Catholics feel any degree of security. Little wonder, then, that in such circumstances and in a land where priests were few and the population scattered, anything like a Catholic culture was impossible.

Material prosperity and religion, then, were the dominant interests in the colonies. In the South, Captain John Smith had been a "promoter." He and others who were interested in "selling America" to prospective colonists wrote romantic accounts of adventure to lure settlers to the new land. In New England the zeal of the Puritans produced a great bulk of religious writings. By 1640, Massachusetts had the first colonial press printing hymnbooks, prayer books, sermons, and controversial writings.

Curiously outstanding among a host of minister-authors was Cotton Mather, who put forth nearly four hundred separate works. Bound by a rigorous conscience, Mather was for a time the incarnation of intolerance and bigotry. His *Wonders of the Invisible World* tells the story of the infamous witchcraft trials at Salem in 1692, in which he played an important part. But to think of the man as a fanatical persecutor of unfortunate Salemites is to see only one phase of a many-sided personality. His diary discloses, in addition to his activities, his personal sorrows and the sorrows of his parish. In the fall of 1702, for example, Boston suffered another epidemic of smallpox; and Mather's account of his visits to the scores of sick families reveals him in sharp contrast to the man who urged the execution of his fellow men.

Another representative clergyman was Jonathan Edwards, called the greatest of the Puritan theologians. Though a pleasant and gentle man outside the pulpit, Edwards held fiercely to the harsh theories of Calvinism. His treatise on *The Freedom of the Will* (1754) denies free will. His sermon, "Sinners in the Hands of an Angry God" (1741) tries to make men love God by inspiring a terrible fear of Hell. The religious views of the Puritans show how thoroughly the Protestant Revolt had shut England off from the great Catholic tradition of sixteen centuries. Some sects, like the Anglicans, had chosen to retain some Catholic doctrine; others, like the Calvinists, little. Puritan Calvinism "purified" the church of all ritual and ceremony, abandoned the priesthood and sacrifice, and rejected the sacramental system which consecrates to God every phase of our lives and the material world around us. The richness of early Christian and medieval life was cast aside for a cold, bleak doctrine that robbed life of its essential beauty and joy.

More entertaining than these religious treatises are William Bradford's *History of Plimouth Plantation* and the journals of John Winthrop. When one first glances over these selections by early colonial writers, his eye catches the surface curiosities of style—the strange spellings and the long, uncertain sentences. The manner seems crude, almost childish. Yet as the reader makes a closer study—when he begins to read these day-by-day jottings—he discovers that, in one sense, here are true histories. The very artlessness of the records makes them valuable. They sound real. And they are certainly complete. Most of the incidents would never have found their way into a formal chronicle; but read one after the other, they revive with remarkable clarity the life of that early period. Note the three following items from John Winthrop's diary of 1631:

*January.* A house at Dorchester was burnt down.

*February 11.* Mr. Freeman's house at Watertown was burned down, but, being in the daytime, his goods were saved.

*March 16.* About noon the chimney of Mr. Sharp's house in Boston took fire, (the splinters not being clayed at the top) and taking the thatch burnt it down, and the wind being N. W., drove the fire to Mr. Colburn's house, and burnt that down also, yet they saved most of their goods.

We have read in later histories of the "hardships and privations" of the settlers; but here in concrete form they come to life—wooden buildings, thatched roofs, open fireplaces, lack of water—a combination that spells the loss and hazard of fire.

Just as the diaries detail the physical features of colonial life, so too they reflect the opinions of the time. We know that the colonists were religious; that a desire to please God was uppermost in their minds; that their distinctions between right and wrong were arbitrary and often narrow and misguided. But we know, too, that as persons they were affectionate and tender. History has pictured Miles Standish as a good soldier. Bradford's *Journal* shows him tending the sick, "washing their loathesome clothes . . . and doing all the homely and necessary offices for them." And this was in time of pestilence. Here was courage of a different sort than was needed to fight the Indians.

The virtue of the diary, then, lies in its completeness of detail and in the sincerity of its writer. We trust its story because the author makes no "alibis"; he does not shield himself nor his neighbor. The good and the bad are put down side by side. One responsibility rests with the reader—to choose some truly representative readings. Most of the journals cover long periods of time, anywhere from twenty to fifty years. As opinions change during the lifetime, we find often very different views in the opening and closing pages of a diary.

As the second and third generations of Americans came along, life assumed a more natural pace. Indeed, Cotton Mather as an old man in 1725 is lamenting the looseness of "these modern times." Mather must have looked with disapproval at the sprightly Madam Knight undertaking a long horseback journey without a suitable companion, even writing up her adventures with "unseemly levity." Sarah Knight knew that there is pleasure in reliving one's experiences; that in recollection, even past discomforts may appear amusing. And so each day at her journey's end she "noted" incidents and impressions in good-natured fashion. She was writing only for entertainment, not with any attempt to educate or "to do good." At times she slips in a bit of verse. She describes a pleasant garden or expresses her delight in the full moon. Her journal, thus, shows a conscious effort toward literary style.

Very similar to Sarah Knight's writings were those of Samuel Sewall who kept a *Diary* from 1673 to 1729. In him we also discover a more amiable and humane Puritan than we ordinarily meet in the pages of literature.

Very little needs to be said about early American verse. For one thing, not much of it was written. For another, what did appear was not outstanding. Either statement is not really surprising. As has been pointed out, the settlers had other matters to fill their lives. Poetry in particular must wait upon leisure. For the first four or five generations, our ancestors expressed their love of beauty in the building of homes and gardens, schools, churches, and cities.

Some religious verse appeared fairly early. There was the *Bay Psalm Book*, which was published in 1640. It contained paraphrases of the Psalms to be used in religious worship. But the meters and rhymes were flat and forced. The result was certainly less poetic than the original Scriptures. So-called poems on religious themes contained more dogma and more sensationalism than poetry. What Anne Bradstreet, author of *The Tenth Muse Lately Sprung Up in America*, accomplished in religious and nature poetry was good in comparison with any other verse of the time, with the exception of that of Edward Taylor. Michael Wigglesworth wrote the most popular poem of his times—"The Day of Doom," a description of the Last Judgment and the tortures of the damned.

Such is the extent of our earliest literature. Though we may have little sympathy with the harshness and intolerance that often marked the religion of the first Americans, we must pay tribute to their intellectual alertness and their heroic industry in trying circumstances. They realized the superior worth of mind and spirit over body and strove energetically to preserve the heritage they had received. In so doing, they left us records of extraordinary endeavors which are the beginnings of our traditions.

# GOD GAVE THEM PLENTIE

## WILLIAM BRADFORD

*To the Pilgrims God sent many trials and blessings. Governor Brad-ford's history of their landing and settlement gives testimony of their struggle for existence. Bradford led the first exploring party from the "Mayflower." In this mysterious, savage land, no one knew what to ex-pect. Every move the settlers made was cautious. In their fear, their eyes were keen, their ears sharp.*

So they made a barricado with logs, stakes, and thick pine boughs, the height of a man, leaving it open to lee-ward, partly to shelter them from the cold and wind (making their fire in the middle, and lying round about it) and partly to defend them from any sudden assaults of the savages, if they should surround them. So, being very weary, they betooke them to rest. . . . Pres-ently, all on the sudain, they heard a great and strange crie, and one of their company being abroad came runing in, and cried, "Men! Indeans, Indeans!" and withal,[1] their arrows came flying in amongst them. . . . The crie of the Indeans was dreadful, especially when they saw (our) men run out of the ran-devoue towards the shalop,[2] to recover their armes, the Indians wheeling about upon them. But some, running out with coats of maile on, and cutlasses in their hands, soone got their armes and let flye amongst them, and quickly stopped their violence. Yet ther was a lustie man, and no less valiante, stood behind a tree within halfe a musket shot, and let his arrows flie at them. He stood three shot of a musket, till one,

¹ WITHAL—Immediately; together with this.
² SHALOP—A light open boat with oars or sails or both.

taking full aime at him, made the barke of splinters of the tree fly about his ears, after which he gave an extraordinary shriek, and away they went, all of them. They left some to keep the shalop, and followed them about a quarter of a mile, and shouted once or twice, and shot off two or three pieces, and so re-turned. This they did, that they might conceive that they were not afraid of them, or any way discouraged. . . . Afterwards they gave God solemn thanks and praise for their deliverance, and gathered up a bundle of their ar-rows, and sente them into England aft-erwards by the master of the ship, and called that place the First Encounter.

[*The first winter called not merely for courage but for a show of Christian vir-tues. When pestilence struck the set-tlement, the charity of the Pilgrims was tested and not found wanting.*]

And in the time of most distress there were about six or seven sound persons . . . who spared no pains night or day, but with abundance of toil and hazard of their owne health fetched them woode, made them fires, drest them meat, made their beds, washed their loathsome clothes . . . in a word, did all the homely and necessarie offices for

them which dainty and quesie stomachs cannot endure to hear named; and all this willingly and cheerfully without any grudging in the least, shewing herein their true love unto their friends and bretheren. A rare example and worthy to be remembered.

[*The golden promise of the socialist experiment, encouraged, no doubt, by the feeling of brotherhood, led the Pilgrims to live for three years on the common-labor, common-storehouse basis. For three years a grimly grinning Famine stalked the colony. Then Bradford resolved to return to the principle of private property.*]

So they begane to thinke how they might obtaine a better crope . . . and thus not languish in miserie. At length, after much debate, the governor (with the advice of the cheefest among them) gave way that they should set corne every man for his own particuler, and in that regard trust to themselves, . . . and so assigned to every family a parcel of land, according to the proportion of their number. This had very good success, for it made all hands very industrious, so as much more corne was planted, and saved the governor a great deal of trouble, and gave far better contents. The women now went willingly into the field, and took their little ones with them to set corne, which before would alledge weakness and inability; whom to have compelled would have been thought great tyranie and oppression.

The experience that was had in this commone course and condition, tried sundrie[3] years, and that amongst godly and sober men, may well evince the vanitie of that conceit[4] of Plato's (applauded by some of later times) that the taking away of propertie and bringing in community into a commone wealth, would make them happy and flourishing. For this communitie was found to breed much confusion and discontente, and retard much imployment that would have been to their benefite and

[3] SUNDRIE—Sundry: various, several.
[4] CONCEIT—Thought, opinion.

comforte. . . . Let none object, this is men's corruption and nothing in the course itself. I answer, seeing all men have this corruption in them, God in his wisdome saw another course fitter for them. . . .

By this time harvest was come, and instead of famine, now God gave them plentie. And the face of things was changed, to the rejoysing of the hearts of many, for which they blessed God. And the effect of their particuler planting was well seen; for all had, one way and another, pretty well to bring the year about; and some of the abler and more industrious sorte had to spare and to sell to others. So as any general want or famine hath not been amongst them to this day.

FOR DISCUSSION

1. Do these selections show the Pilgrims to have been men of sound practical sense as well as of firm religious convictions? How?

2. In which incident do they show most courage? What reason can you give for your judgment?

3. What statement gives you a clue to the fact that Bradford was an educated man?

4. Why is any experiment in communism a failure?

PROJECTS

1. Make a comparison between the start of the Jamestown colony and that of the Plymouth colony.

2. Compare the experiment of Robert Owen, English Socialist, between 1824 and 1828 in New Harmony, Indiana, with that of the Pilgrims.

3. Rewrite the passages, changing them only as much as is necessary to make them clear. Pay special attention to the vague antecedents, and be sure to correct Bradford's archaic spelling.

RELATED READING

For an idealized account of the Puritans read "The Landing of the Pilgrim Fathers in New England," a poem by Mrs. Felicia Hemans, or Longfellow's narrative poem, "The Courtship of Miles Standish." Hawthorne, on the other hand, pictures the fanatical furrows in the faces of the Pilgrims in his short story telling of a famous incident—"The Maypole of Merry Mount." In *Saints and Strangers* George Willison gives us the straight facts about the Pilgrims and shows that many of our ideas about them have their origin in obscure legends and myths. In 1952 Samuel Eliot Morison published a modernized version of Bradford's *Of Plimoth Plantation*, the book from which this selection was taken, which is easy and interesting reading, and which gives you a picture of colonial life you cannot get in history books.

# LETTER TO THE
# REV. MR. TIMOTHY EDWARDS

*JONATHAN EDWARDS*

*Today we are apt to think of life in colonial New England as having been completely grim, austere, and sober. In this letter from Jonathan Edwards to his father, however, we see that the students at Yale College in 1721 were no more staid or dignified than college students are today.*

Yale College: March 1st, 1721

Honoured Sir:

It was not with a little Joy and satisfaction that I received your letter of the 21st of February by Mr. Grant,[1] and with a great deal of thankfulness from the Bottom of My Heart for your wholesome advice and counsel and the Abundance of Father-like tenderness therein expressed.

As concerning the complaint of the scholars about their Commons,[2] the manner of it I believe was no less surprising to me than to you. It was on this wise: Every Undergraduate, one and all, that had anything to do with Colledge Commons, all on a sudden, before Mr. Cutler or (I believe) anybody knew that they were discontented, entered into a Bond of 15 shillings[3] never to have any more Commons of the steward.[4]

Whereupon they all forwarned him never to provide more for them, telling him If he did they would not pay him for it.

Mr. Brown, notwithstanding, ordered commons to be provided and set upon the table as it used to be, and accordingly it was. But there was nobody to eat it. Mr. Cutler[5] as soon as he was apprised of this Cabal[6] sent on the same day for Mr. Andrew and Mr. Russel[7] who came on the next, and with the Rector ordered all to appear before them. The Rector manifested himself exceedingly vexed and displeased at the Act which so affrighted the scholars that they unanimously agreed to come into Commons again. I believe the scholars that were in this agreement have so lost Mr. Cutler's favour that they scarce ever will regain it.

Stiles[8] (to my Grief and I believe much more to his) was one that set his hand to this Bond. He did it by the strong instigation of Others who per-

[1] LETTER . . . BY MR. GRANT—The letter was delivered by Mr. Grant. Public mail service was not begun in the American colonies until 1746.

[2] COMMONS—The commons were the meals prepared for and served to the students of the college.

[3] BOND OF 15 SHILLINGS—The students made an agreement not to eat the college commons. Those who broke the agreement were to forfeit the sum of 15 shillings.

[4] STEWARD—The man (here Mr. Brown) who was responsible for the commons.

[5] MR. CUTLER—The rector (president) of the college.

[6] CABAL—A conspiracy.

[7] MR. ANDREW AND MR. RUSSEL—Founders and trustees of Yale College.

[8] STILES—Isaac Stiles of Windsor, Connecticut, Edward's home town. He was at this time a junior at Yale.

swaded him to it; neither had he a minute's time to consider before his hand was down. As soon as I understood him to be one of them, I told him that I thought he had done exceeding unadvisedly, and I told him also what I thought the ill consequences of it would be, and quickly made him sorry that he did not take advice in this matter. I am apt to think that this thing will be the greatest Obstacle of any to Stiles's being Butler.[9]

I must needs say for my own part, that although the commons at sometimes have not been sufficient as to quality, yet I think there has been very little Occasion for Such an Insurrection as this.

Although these Disturbances were so speedyly quashed, yet they are succeeded by Much Worse and Greater, and I believe Greater than ever were in the Colledge before. They are occasioned by the Discovery of some Monstrous impieties and Acts of Immorality lately committed in the Colledge, particularly stealing of Hens, Geese, turkies, piggs, meat, wood, etc.—, unseasonable nightwalking, Breaking People's windows, playing at Cards, cursing, swearing, and Damning, and using all manner of Ill Language, which never were at such a pitch in the Colledge as they now are. The Rector has called a meeting of the trustees on this Occasion. They are expected here today. 'Tis thought the upshot will be the Expulsion of some and the Publick Admonition of Others.

Through the goodness of God I am perfectly free of all their janglings. My condition att the Colledge at present is in every way comfortable. I live in very Good Amity And Agreement with my

[9] BUTLER—An undergraduate officer who collected board bills and oversaw the kitchen and dormitory rooms. This position, which had been held by Edwards, was considered something of an honor.

Chambermate. There has been no new quarrels broke out betwixt me and the scholars, though they still persist in their former Combination.[10] But I am not without Hopes that it will be abolished by this meeting of the Trustees.

I have not as yet wrote to Uncle Mix [11] because I heard he was coming down, but he delaying his coming I shall do it speedily. I am at present in perfect health, and it is a time of health throughout the Colledge and Town. I am about taking the remainder of my lignum vitae.[12] I am much reformed with respect to visiting of friends, and intend to do more att it for the future than in time past. I think I shall not have Occasion for the Coat you mentioned in your letter till I come home. I received a letter from my sister Mary the week before last and have heard of her welfare this week by a Man that came directly from thence. I pray you in your next letter please to give My humble Duty to my Mother, hearty love to sister, and still to be mindfull before the throne of Grace of me, who am,

Honoured sir
your
most Dutyfull
son
Jonathan E:

[10] COMBINATION—Edwards was probably teaching some courses at this time, and had apparently been having some difficulty with his students.
[11] UNCLE MIX—The Reverend Mr. Stephen Mix of Wethersfield, Connecticut.
[12] LIGNUM VITAE—The wood of a tropical American tree, once thought to have medicinal properties. It was considered especially useful in the treatment of rheumatism.

◇◇◇◇◇◇◇◇◇◇◇◇◇◇◇◇◇◇◇◇◇◇◇◇◇◇◇◇

FOR DISCUSSION

1. Edwards was not yet eighteen when he wrote this letter. Do you think he

shows more than average maturity in his attitude toward life? Give reasons for your answer.

2. Judging from the antics which Edwards describes the students as performing, do you think that young men of the 1720's were very much like young men today? Have the basic qualities of people changed, or are people today much as they have always been? Explain.

A PROJECT

Read the first few chapters of *Northwest Passage* by Kenneth Roberts; there is a description here of an occurrence at the Harvard College commons much like the one which Edwards describes in his letter. Then write your own description of the commons dispute at Yale. Fill in the details which Edwards leaves out; show exactly why the students revolted.

◇◇◇◇◇

# EXCERPTS FROM A JOURNAL

## JOHN WINTHROP

Winthrop's JOURNAL, *which he kept for nineteen years, is wealthy with anecdotes and details. It reads like a combination history and morning newspaper. The wild, chaotic items include such topics as pigeons, phantom ships, Indians, ministers, stray pigs, the "cornering" of the wheat market and scandalously high prices, cows and goats overeating, heresy, and the Providence of God. Here are two typical items. The first one shows that the effect of the Bible on the Puritan disposition was not always happy. In one case, however, a Bible-look and the simplicity of an Indian averted a minor catastrophe.*

At Kennebeck the Indians, wanting food, and there being a store in the Plimoth trading house, they conspired to kill the English there for their provisions; and some Indians coming into the house, Mr. Willet, the master, being reading in the Bible, his countenance was more solemn than at other times, so as he did not look cheerfully upon them, as he was wont to do; whereupon they went out and told their fellows that their purpose was discovered. They

asked them how it could be. The others told them that they knew it by Mr. Willet's countenance, and that he had discovered it by a book that he was reading. Whereupon they gave over their design.

[*Women authors were not much in favor in the New England colonies. If Mrs. Hopkins had been content with trying to see her face in her pots and pans instead of trying to put her mind on paper, she might have kept her wits —so thought the men of Boston and Massachusetts Bay!*]

Mr. Hopkins, the governor of Hartford on Connecticut, came to Boston and brought his wife with him (a godly young woman, and of special parts) who was fallen into a sad infirmity, the loss of her understanding and reason, which had been growing upon her divers years by occasion of her giving herself wholly to reading and writing, and had written many books. Her husband, being very loving and tender of her, was loath to grieve her; but he saw his error when it was too late. For if she had attended to household affairs, and such things as belong to women, and not gone out of her way calling to meddle in such things as are proper for men, whose minds are stronger, etc., she had kept her wits, and might have improved them usefully and honorably in the place God had set

her. He brought her to Boston . . . to try what means might be had here for her. But no help could be had.

◇◇◇◇◇◇◇◇◇◇◇◇◇◇◇◇◇◇◇◇◇◇◇◇◇◇◇◇◇

FOR DISCUSSION

1. Why should Mr. Willet's countenance be solemn while he was reading the Bible? Is solemnity the natural effect of such reading? Discuss.
2. How would you defend your own religion against the accusation that it too is a gloomy one? Do you know people whose personalities are soured or oversobered by religion? Why do they not have the right attitude toward the relations between God and man?
3. Is Winthrop's idea on the place of women in society an old-fashioned one today? What hint of good sense do you find in his words?
4. How many prominent women authors can you name? Do you think that women are as good writers as men?

◇◇◇◇◇

# TUESDAY, OCTOBER YE THIRD

## SARAH KEMBLE KNIGHT

*Maybe it required the courage of a St. Joan of Arc for a woman to travel the 270 miles of semiwilderness between Boston and New York in 1704. Madam Knight, however, displays no false heroics. In her JOURNAL she tells us plainly of the terrors that gripped her feminine heart. Despite the dangers, though, she kept her high sense of humor.*

About Three, afternoon, went on with my Third Guide, who Rode very hard; and having crossed Providence Ferry, we came to a River which they Generally Ride thro'. But I dare not venture; so the Post [1] got a Ladd and Cannoo to carry me to tother side, and he rode

[1] POST—The postman who was her guide.

thro' and Led my horse. The Cannoo was very small and shallow, so that when we were in she seem'd ready to take in water, which greatly terrified me, and caused me to be very circumspect, sitting with my hands fast on each side, my eyes steady, not daring so much as to lodge my tongue a hair's breadth more on one side of my mouth than tother, nor so much as think on Lott's wife, for a wry thought would have oversett our wherry: [2] But was soon put out of this pain, by feeling the Cannoo on shore, which I as soon almost saluted with my feet; and Rewarding my sculler, again mounted and made the best of our way forwards. The Road here was very even and y^e day pleasant, it being now near Sunsett. But the Post told me we had near 14 miles to Ride to the next Stage (where we were to Lodge). I askt him of the rest of the Road, fore-seeing we must travel in the night. He told me there was a bad River we were to Ride thro', which was so very fierce a horse could sometimes hardly stem it: But it was but narrow, and we should soon be over. I cannot express the concern of mind this relation set me in: no thoughts but those of the dangerous River could entertain my Imagination, and they were as formidable as various, still Tormenting me with blackest Ideas of my Approaching fate—sometimes seeing my self drowning, otherwhiles drowned, and at the best like a holy Sister Just come out of a Spiritual Bath in dripping Garments.[3]

Now was the Glorious Luminary, with his swift Courses arrived at his Stage,[4] leaving poor me with the rest of this part of the lower world in darkness, with which we were soon Surrounded. The only Glimmering we now had was from the spangled Skies, Whose Imperfect Reflections rendered every Object formidable. Each lifeless Trunk, with its shatter'd Limbs, appear'd an Armed Enymie; and every little stump like a Ravenous devourer. Nor could I so much as discern my Guide, when at any distance, which added to the terror.

Thus, absolutely lost in Thought, and dying with the very thoughts of drowning, I come up with the Post, who I did not see till even with his Horse: he told me he stopt for me; and we Rode on Very deliberately a few paces, when we entered a Thicket of Trees and Shrubs, and I perceived by the Horse's going, we were on the descent of a Hill, which, as we come nearer the bottom, 'twas totally dark with the Trees that surrounded it. But I knew by the Going of the Horse we had entered the water, which my Guide told me was the hazzardous River he had told me of; and he, Riding up close to my Side, Bid me not fear—we should be over Immediately. I now rallied all the Courage I was mistress of, Knowing that I must either Venture my fate of drowning, or be left like y^e Children in the wood. So, as the Post bid me, I gave Reins to my Nag; and sitting as Steady as Just before in the Cannoo, in a few minutes got safe to the other side, which he told me was the Narragansett country. . . .

Being come to Mr. Havens', I was very civilly Received, and courteously entertained, in a clean comfortable House; and the Good woman was very active in helping off my Riding clothes, and then ask't what I would eat. I told her I had some Chocolett, if she would prepare it; which with the help of some

[2] WHERRY—A light rowboat.

[3] HOLY SISTER . . . GARMENTS—The Baptists baptize by dipping a person completely under water.

[4] GLORIOUS LUMINARY . . . STAGE—Apollo, god of the sun, rode a chariot across the skies. What is Madam Knight saying here?

Milk, and a little clean brass Kettle, she soon effected to my satisfaction.

I then betook me to my Apartment, which was a little Room parted from the Kitchen by a single board partition; where, after I had noted the Occurrences of the past day, I went to bed, which, tho' pretty hard, Yet neat and handsome. But I could get no sleep, because of the Clamor of some of the Town tope-ers in next Room, Who were entered into a strong debate concerning yᵉ Signification of the name of their Country, (viz) Narraganset. One said is was named so by yᵉ Indians, because there grew a Briar there, of a prodigious Height and bigness, the like hardly ever known, called by the Indians Narragansett; And quotes an Indian of so Barbarous a name for his Author, that I could not write it.

His Antagonist Replied no—It was from a Spring it had its name, which he well knew where it was, which was extreme cold in summer, and as Hot as could be imagined in the winter, which was much resorted to by the natives, and by them called Narragansett, (Hot and Cold,) and that was the original of their place's name—with a thousand Impertinences not worth notice, which He utter'd with such a Roaring voice and Thundering blows with the fist of wickedness on the Table, that it pierced my very head. I heartily fretted, and wish't 'um tongue tied; but with as little success as a friend of mine once, who was (as she said) kept a whole night awake, on a Journey, by a country Left.[5] and a Sergeant, Ensign and a Deacon, contriving how to bring a triangle into a Square. They kept calling for tother Gill, which while they were swallowing, was some Intermission; But presently,

[5] LEFT—Abbreviation of the English pronunciation of Lieutenant: leftenant.

like Oil to fire, increased the flame.

I set my Candle on a Chest by the bed side, and sitting up, fell to my old way of composing my Resentments, in the following manner:

I ask thy Aid, O Potent Rum!
To Charm these wrangling Topers
    Dumb.
Thou hast their Giddy Brains possest—
The man confounded with the Beast—
And I, poor I, can get no rest.
Intoxicate them with thy fumes;
O still their Tongues till morning comes!

And I know not but my wishes took effect; for the dispute soon ended with 'tother Dram; and so Good Night!

◇◇◇◇◇◇◇◇◇◇◇◇◇◇◇◇◇◇◇◇◇◇◇◇◇◇◇◇

## FOR DISCUSSION

1. Point out instances of Madam Knight's humor; of her vivid imagination.

2. Why is her reference to Lot's wife appropriate? Explain her reference to the children in the wood.

3. What personal qualities do you like in her?

## A PROJECT

Madam Knight's grammar and spelling are inconsistent and not up to modern standards. Make a corrected list of the words she misspelled and rewrite the sentences where you find errors in grammar.

## RELATED READING

If you have found this selection pleasing, you will enjoy Madam Knight's other adventures. The latest edition appeared in 1935. You will find another kind of story, more gruesome and heart-rending, in A Narrative of the Captivity and Restoration of Mrs. Mary Rowlandson, told by the captive herself after eleven weeks spent as prisoner of King Philip's warriors.

# The Ebb and Flow

## EDWARD TAYLOR

*You and I see a portable metal box; in it, some highly inflammable sub-
stance—charred linen, perhaps—and some flint and steel to ignite the
tinder.  The poet, full of thoughts of God, sees it, too, and his ingenious
mind at once seizes upon a comparison.*

When first thou on me, Lord, wroughtst thy sweet print,
 My heart was made thy tinder box.
 My 'ffections were thy tinder in't:
  Where fell thy sparks by drops.
Those holy sparks of heavenly fire that came,       5
Did ever catch and often out would flame.

But now my heart is made thy censer trim,
 Full of thy golden altar's fire,
 To offer up sweet incense in
  Unto thyself entire:           10
I find my tinder scarce thy sparks can feel
That drop out from thy holy flint and steel.

Hence doubts out bud for fear thy fire in me
 'S a mocking Ignis Fatuus,
 Or lest thine altar's fire out be,        15
  It's hid in ashes thus.
Yet when the bellows of thy Spirit blow
Away mine ashes, then thy fire doth glow.

14. IGNIS FATUUS—A delusion, a false guiding hope.  Translated literally from Latin, the expression means a foolish or baseless fire.  The name is given to a phosphorescent light seen hover-
ing or flitting over marshy ground and is supposed to be due to spontaneous combustion of a gas
derived from decaying matter.  It recedes, vanishes, appears in another direction.  The notion
arose that it was the work of a mischievous spirit trying to lead unwary travelers astray.

FOR DISCUSSION

1. To what does the first line refer: to
the poet's birth, his baptism, or the first
time he "felt" that God had elected him
to salvation?

2. What is peculiar about a Puritan's
comparing his heart to a *censer?* About
his speaking of a *golden* altar and about
*incense?*

3. Can a person love God even though
he does not *feel* the emotional warmth
in his heart?  Explain.

4. What lines show that the Puritan is,
after all, not too sure of his salvation?
How is it that we can doubt whether God
loves us?

5. Show how all the images in the poem
are consistent with one another.

# Further Readings About the Colonial Period

## COLONIAL WRITERS

BRADFORD, WILLIAM, *Of Plimouth Plantation*

BRADSTREET, ANNE, *The Tenth Muse*

BYRD, WILLIAM, *A History of the Dividing Line; The Secret Diary of William Byrd of Westover 1709–1712*

JOHNSON, EDWARD, *History of New England*

KENYON, EDNA (ed.), *The Jesuit Relations*

KNIGHT, SARAH KEMBLE, *Journal*

MATHER, COTTON, *The Wonders of the Invisible World*

MORTON, NATHANIEL, *New England's Memoriall*

MORTON, THOMAS, *New English Canaan*

ROWLANDSON, MARY, *The Captivity and Restoration*

SEWALL, SAMUEL, *Diary*

SMITH, JOHN, *A Description of New England; A True Relation*

TAYLOR, EDWARD, *The Poetical Works of Edward Taylor*

WINTHROP, JOHN, *Journal*

## MODERN WRITERS

AUSTIN, J. G., *Standish of Standish*

BOYD, THOMAS, *Shadow of the Long Knives*

BROKUNIER, S. H., *The Irrepressible Democrat, Roger Williams*

CATHER, WILLA, *Shadows on the Rock*

CHAMBERS, ROBERT, *The Man They Hanged*

FLETCHER, INGLIS, *Roanoke Hundred*

JOHNSTON, MARY, *To Have and to Hold; Croatan*

KNOWLTON, D. C. and GILL, C. M., *When We Were Colonies*

LONGFELLOW, HENRY W., *The Courtship of Miles Standish* (poetry)

MORISON, S. E., *Builders of the Bay Colony*

* PHELAN, THOMAS, *Catholics in Colonial Days*

ROBERTS, KENNETH, *Northwest Passage*

WHITTIER, JOHN G., "The Double-Headed Snake of Newbury" (poetry)

WILLISON, GEORGE, *Saints and Strangers*

WRIGHT, L. B., *Atlantic Frontier*

# THE REVOLUTIONARY

# PERIOD

## 1 7 6 5 – 1 8 0 0

When ships in increasing numbers docked in American ports, stevedores lugged out not only tea and spices and manufactured goods, but also newspapers, magazines, and books from Britain. Off the gangplanks stepped young American men, returning from their education in England and from the fashionable "grand tour" of continental Europe. America was doing its best to keep up with the civilized world.

English literature and thought were taking new twists, and the colonists tried to keep up with the times. Home-produced newspapers, magazines, and almanacs, all in imitation of the British, appeared in the cities. At first, newssheets held little more than essays on manners and morals; magazines were secondhand collections of materials gathered from various sources. Early writing lacked any distinctive American tang. It was Benjamin Franklin who first adapted literary styles to portraying American life and who gave our literature its first bit of genuine Yankee flavoring. *Poor Richard's Almanac* and the *Pennsylvania Gazette* (later the *Saturday Evening Post*) were the *Life* and *Time* of the day.

Religion, though still a force in life, was losing some pre-eminence to philosophy and politics. In face of the new thinkers, the Rationalists and the Deists, Protestantism began to fidget uneasily and to modify her doctrines. New England resisted longest but yielded in part to more liberal views. Sects quarreled and split into more sects. Religious revivalism, with its climax in The Great Awakening, 1745–1759, shocked many by degrading exhibitions of uncontrolled emotionalism in worship.

The Age of Reason and Enlightenment was dawning in America. With great advances in astronomy, mathematics, and physics, there were many who conceived of the world as a great machine with perfectly co-ordinated parts kept in motion by regular laws of nature. God had made the universe, had pushed the button to start it, and now sat back watching. There was no need for His interfering.

Man, the new philosophers were saying, was as perfect as the universe. By taking thought, he *could* "add a cubit to his stature." Reason could explain all things; there was no need for the revelations of God. Supernatural religion?—a fanciful dream. Original sin?—an ugly nightmare. Man was a naturally good creature; a free creature with God-given rights, capable of self-rule.

A sort of universal Society for the Prevention of Cruelty to Human Beings seemed to be the aim of the thinkers. The universal brotherhood of man (an orphan idea without the Fatherhood of God) was the chief doctrine. Benevolence, good will, was the highest virtue. But a man should follow his self-interest to achieve the good of society. He should be allowed to profess any religion he chose. Belief in God was an individual's concern, not the state's. The state was an earth-bound institution that lifted its head to the heavens only to admire or to study the stars. These were the theories of men like Locke and Paine, who profoundly influenced American thought.

Yet however diverse the religious views of early Americans may have been, there was a strong uniting force in the desire for liberty. Life in the wilderness had developed in the Americans an actual freedom unknown in Europe. Class distinctions were less strictly drawn; any man had opportunity to own land. A man was his own master, and the free air he breathed induced him to expand his chest and demand a voice in the government. *Letters from an American Farmer* by St. Jean de Crèvecoeur, a French Catholic who settled in New York, idealized this new man of history.

As the quarrels with England grew louder, the newspapers set off firecracker articles, and cannon-ball orations made noise about the situation. Pamphlets, ballads, and satires spilled off the presses. Patrick Henry sounded the call to arms; Thomas Paine's *Common Sense* cried out for rebellion. And then, a nation aroused to defend its liberties boldly and clearly pronounced in a *Declaration of Independence* that political creed which was to become the rock-foundation of our nation.

From what sources our Founding Fathers derived their political ideals is still a debatable question. The basic freedom and dignity of man and his natural right to choose his own government had been taught, explained, and expanded by St. Thomas Aquinas and by the Jesuits, St. Robert Bellarmine and Francis Suarez. American statesmen may have based their doctrines directly on Catholic philosophy. They may have received them in diluted form from the Englishman, John Locke. Or, they may have accepted the conclusions of the Rationalists, for it is sometimes possible to get the right answers, even though one works the problem out in the wrong way. At any rate, Catholics in America gave their whole-hearted support to the Revolution, for they believed and held as their own the truths for which Americans fought.

During the time of battle, pens and voices were as busy as the artillery. Like a captured gun, "Yankee Doodle" was wrested from the mocking British and turned against them. In every town a ballad-maker and in every newspaper a poets' corner celebrated in song the most recent events on land and sea. The best of the lot were "Hale in the Bush" and Francis Hopkinson's "Battle of the Kegs." Philip Freneau's vinegar and vitriol verse satirized the British cause. The most popular and widely quoted poem was "M'Fingal," a mock-epic burlesque about a Tory squire, written by John Trumbull.

During Washington's 1776 retreat across New Jersey, when the cause seemed lost, the pen of Paine, racing along with the author while he dodged the British, made an heroic effort to bolster American morale. The call to sacrificial courage raised in *The Crisis* inspired the nation even in its darkest days of pessimism and defeat.

The prose of the American Revolution speaks for itself, eloquently. Classification is not easy. Most of it was nonfiction, comprising impromptu speeches, formal addresses, letters, papers of state, essays, and at least one autobiography.

Most of the orations were extempore—sparks struck out in the heat of the times. Patrick Henry, for example, had no written copy of his address before the Virginia House of Burgesses. The phrases were born of the moment, and have an unstudied terseness and fervor. The speech as it now stands was written later from memory by one of those who heard it. That these extempore addresses should be so well expressed speaks to the the credit of the general education of our ancestors. These are not uncouth utterances. They are clear, exact, and polished. When words were needed, there were words to use. Modern America, with all her schooling, can well look to her dictionaries when reading the prose of her fathers.

In contrast with the sharp, clear-cut speeches of the extempore orators may be placed Washington's "Farewell Address," which was not delivered at all but was printed in Claypoole's *American Daily Advertiser* for September 19, 1796. This was not a speech intended to arouse action. It was an explanation of a policy, and it invited deliberation. The corresponding difference in style is apparent. Notice the long sentences, the careful phrasing. Here is not fire, but judgment and deep, considered meaning.

The papers of state show this same deliberateness. Though they all contain phrases that were passing from lips to lips—the ringing slogans of the day—each current word was smoothly fitted into place and cemented with logic that would bear the scrutiny of the years. Again we admire the keenness of the minds which wrought these works, and the perfection of expression. A skeptical Old World was brought to attention. The American Declaration of Independence and the American Constitution have affected the thought and—to some extent—the destiny of peoples around the globe.

With independence won, the nation settled down to the business of governing itself. Little was done to establish a purely American literature except by the political writers who won the admiration even of the English. Alexander Hamilton's contributions to *The Federalist Papers* are the outstanding writings. But the time for American independence in the field of pure literature was not yet ripe.

Matthew Carey, an Irish Catholic, became the leading publisher of the new country, and his establishment helped make Philadelphia the literary center. The Quaker City produced, also, the first American to adopt literature as a profession, Charles Brockden Brown, whose novels of American life first showed a trend away from British themes and blazed the way for Cooper. In the poet Freneau—his bitterness mellowed with victory—we have another man with an eye for the American scene. In some of his lyrics, we find our country's native beauty discovered and revealed.

The speech of Bishop John Carroll on George Washington brings a fitting close to the century. It expresses the reverence and esteem of the nation for the courageous and selfless man who best embodies the national idea. To Washington especially we owe our national heritage. His life is an example to all who profess the American political credo.

# SPEECH IN THE VIRGINIA CONVENTION

*PATRICK HENRY*

The Virginia House of Burgesses had been dissolved by the royal governor. In March, 1775, however, a Provincial Convention met in the "Old Church" at Richmond, Virginia. Patrick Henry proposed the establishment of a colonial militia which would make English troops or mercenary forces unnecessary and which would protect the rights and liberties of the Virginians. He further resolved: "That this colony be immediately put into a posture of defense."

There was considerable opposition to his resolutions. Some thought Henry had gone too far. When the opponents had finished their contra-arguments, there occurred the following scene, recorded in Tyler's LIFE OF PATRICK HENRY:

"Henry rose with an unearthly fire burning in his eye. He commenced somewhat calmly, but the smothered excitement began more and more to play upon his features and thrill in the tones of his voice. The tendons of his neck stood out white and rigid like whipcords. His voice rose louder and louder, until the walls of the building, and all within them, seemed to shake and rock in its tremendous vibrations. Finally his pale face and glaring eyes became terrible to look upon. Men leaned forward and their eyes glared like the speaker's. His last exclamation, 'Give me liberty or give me death!' was like the shout of the leader which turns back the rout of battle."

Mr. President:

No man thinks more highly than I do of the patriotism, as well as abilities, of the very worthy gentlemen [1] who have just addressed the house. But different men often see the same subject in different lights; and, therefore, I hope it will not be thought disrespectful to those gentlemen, if, entertaining as I do opinions of a character very opposite to theirs, I shall speak forth my sentiments freely, and without reserve. This is no time for ceremony. The question before the house is one of awful mo-

[1] WORTHY GENTLEMEN—The gentlemen who had opposed Henry's resolution.

ment[2] to this country. For my own part, I consider it as nothing less than a question of freedom or slavery. And in proportion to the magnitude of the subject ought to be the freedom of the debate. It is only in this way that we can hope to arrive at truth, and fulfill the great responsibility which we hold to God and our country. Should I keep back my opinions at such a time, through fear of giving offense, I should consider myself as guilty of treason toward my country, and of an act of disloyalty toward the Majesty of Heaven, which I revere above all earthly kings.

Mr. President, it is natural to man to indulge in the illusions of hope. We are apt to shut our eyes against a painful truth, and listen to the song of that siren[3] till she transforms us into beasts. Is this the part of wise men, engaged in a great and arduous struggle for liberty? Are we disposed to be of the number of those who having eyes see not, and having ears hear not, the things which so nearly concern their temporal salvation? For my part, whatever anguish of spirit it may cost, I am willing to know the whole truth; to know the worst and to provide for it.

I have but one lamp by which my feet are guided, and that is the lamp of experience. I know of no way of judging of the future but by the past. And judging by the past, I wish to know what there has been in the conduct of the British ministry for the last ten years, to justify those hopes with which gentlemen have been pleased to solace themselves and the house. Is it that insidious[4] smile with which our petition has been lately received. Trust it not, sir: it will prove a snare to your feet. Suffer not yourselves to be be-

[2] AWFUL MOMENT—The speaker thought, with others, that war could not be avoided.

[3] SIREN—Henry confuses the sirens with Circe, a powerful enchantress who turned men into beasts. The sirens, monsters with faces of beautiful women, lured sailors to their island by their singing and then devoured them.

[4] INSIDIOUS—Treacherous and deceitful.

trayed with a kiss.[5] Ask yourselves how this gracious reception of our petition comports with those warlike preparations[6] which cover our waters and darken our land. Are fleets and armies necessary to a work of love and reconciliation? Have we shown ourselves so unwilling to be reconciled that force must be called in to win back our love? Let us not deceive ourselves, sir. These are the implements of war and subjugation—the last arguments to which kings resort. I ask, sir, what means this martial array, if its purpose be not to force us to submission? Can gentlemen assign any other possible motive for it? Has Great Britain any enemy in this quarter of the world, to call for all this accumulation of navies and armies? No, sir, she has none. They are meant for us: they can be meant for no other. They are sent over to bind and rivet upon us those chains which the British ministry have been so long forging. And what have we to oppose to them? Shall we try argument? Sir, we have been trying that for the last ten years.[7] Have we anything new to offer upon the subject? Nothing. We have held the subject up in every light of which it is capable; but it has been all in vain. Shall we resort to entreaty and humble supplication? What terms shall we find which have not been already exhausted? Let us not, I beseech you, sir, deceive ourselves longer.

Sir, we have done everything that could be done to avert the storm which is now coming on. We have petitioned; we have remonstrated; we have supplicated; we have prostrated ourselves before the throne, and have implored its interposition to arrest the tyrannical hands of the ministry and Parliament. Our petitions have been slighted; our remonstrances have produced additional violence and insult; our supplications have been disregarded; and we have been spurned with contempt from the foot of the throne![8] In vain, after these things, may we indulge the fond hope of peace and reconciliation. There is no longer any room for hope. If we wish to be free, if we mean to preserve inviolate those inestimable privileges for which we have been so long contending, if we mean not basely to abandon the noble struggle in which we have been so long engaged, and which we have pledged ourselves never to abandon until the glorious object of our contest

[7] FOR THE LAST TEN YEARS—The French and Indian Wars ended with the Treaty of Paris in 1763. As early as 1660 England had begun to regulate the commerce of the colonies to her own advantage by a series of Navigation Acts whereby she forbade the colonists to trade with any other nation. As years passed, these acts became more and more detrimental to the colonists and were increasingly resented. Smuggling increased to escape the restrictions of the Navigation Acts. In 1763, George Grenville, prime minister to George III, attempted to enforce these laws more vigorously. Writs of Assistance were issued, which permitted officers to search the homes of the colonists for smuggled goods. This enforcement of the Navigation Acts, together with the maintenance of a standing army of English soldiers in the colonies, and the taxes introduced by Grenville, were the causes of the Revolutionary War. During this whole time the colonists had tried by petition and by argument to gain the freedom they desired.

[5] BETRAYED WITH A KISS—As Jesus was betrayed by Judas in a show of friendship.

[6] WARLIKE PREPARATIONS—After the French and Indian Wars, British troops remained in the colonies, much against the wishes of the colonists. In 1768 the fifty-gun frigate *Romney* had been sent to Boston Harbor. Later, two regiments of soldiers were quartered in Boston.

[8] SPURNED . . . FROM THE FOOT OF THE THRONE—The speaker here refers to the various petitions sent to the king by the colonies. For example, Samuel Adams petitioned the king for the Massachusetts Assembly in a sincere and humble letter which the king received with silent contempt. The First Continental Congress sent the king a humble petition begging him to redress their wrongs.

shall be obtained—we must fight! I repeat it, sir, we must fight! An appeal to arms and to the God of Hosts is all that is left us!

They tell us, sir, that we are weak—unable to cope with so formidable an adversary. But when shall we be stronger? Will it be the next week, or the next year? Will it be when we are totally disarmed, and when a British guard shall be stationed in every house? Shall we gather strength by irresolution and inaction? Shall we acquire the means of effectual resistance by lying supinely on our backs, and hugging the delusive phantom of hope until our enemies shall have bound us hand and foot? Sir, we are not weak, if we make the proper use of those means which the God of nature hath placed in our power. Three millions of people, armed in the holy cause of liberty, and in such a country as that which we possess, are invincible by any force which our enemy can send against us. Besides, sir, we shall not fight our battles alone. There is a just God who presides over the destinies of nations, and who will raise up friends to fight our battles for us.[9] The battle, sir, is not to the strong alone; it is to the vigilant, the active, the brave. Besides, sir, we have no election.[10] If we were base enough to desire it, it is now too late to retire from the contest. There is no retreat but in submission and slavery! Our chains are forged! their clanking may be heard on the plains of Boston![11] The war is inevita-ble—and let it come! I repeat, sir, let it come!

It is in vain, sir, to extenuate the matters. Gentlemen may cry, Peace, Peace —but there is no peace. The war is actually begun! The next gale that sweeps from the north will bring to our ears the clash of resounding arms![12] Our brethren are already in the field! Why stand we here idle? What is it that gentlemen wish? What would they have? Is life so dear, or peace so sweet, as to be purchased at the price of chains and slavery? Forbid it, Almighty God! I know not what course others may take; but as for me, give me liberty or give me death!

[9] FRIENDS TO FIGHT OUR BATTLES FOR US—France did join the colonies against England.

[10] ELECTION—Choice.

[11] ON THE PLAINS OF BOSTON—All the colonies might expect the treatment given Massachusetts, where the Intolerable Acts had deprived the colony of its charter; closed the harbor; quartered troops more insistently; provided that British officers and soldiers be tried for crimes in England rather than in America.

[12] RESOUNDING ARMS—The speech was delivered in March, 1775. In April, the battles of Lexington and Concord were fought; and in June, the battle of Bunker Hill.

## FOR DISCUSSION

1. Is the purpose of this speech to pass the resolution or to prove that "we must fight"? Why does Henry not state his purpose in the very beginning of the speech?

2. What arguments does Henry use to show that war is inevitable?

3. How does he answer the objection that the colonies are too weak to fight England?

4. Do you think Henry's use of the question is effective? Does he overdo it?

5. An orator should convince our intellects and stir our feelings. Does Henry do both? Can you point out passages in which he does both at the same time? Where does he show the strongest feeling?

6. Who were the "friends" that God raised up to "fight our battles for us"? To what "chains" does Henry refer when he says, "their clanking may be heard on the plains of Boston"?

## TYPE STUDY

1. Did this speech of Patrick Henry's strike you on first reading as being "extempore"? Why or why not?

2. At what point in the speech does Henry's rising emotion or "natural fire" begin to show itself? With which sentence does the climax of the speech begin?

3. Although this speech has been worked over by later men, do you think it is as polished as one that Washington might have delivered? Why or why not?

4. Show both from the speech itself and from the historical occasion of its delivery how Henry "drew inspiration from his audience" for this oration.

## WORDS WITH LATIN PREFIXES

Latin prefixes often give a clue to the meanings of words. Study the following words taken from Henry's speech and discuss the meaning of each prefix. Show how the meaning of the word is formed by joining the root of the word and the prefix: resounding, reconciliation; inviolate, invincible, inestimable; irresolution; avert; subjugation, submission.

Make a list of words you know that contain the prefixes ir, in, im, a, sub.

◇◇◇◇◇

# Hale in the Bush

## OLD BALLAD

One September dawn in 1776, the sun rose to witness a hanging. With the death of darkness died a spy; with the birth of day, a new hero was born. Nathan Hale lost his one life, but his spirit sprang alive in the breast of every true American.

An unknown poet of the Revolution has given us this ballad version of the well-known story of an American patriot.

The breezes went steadily through the tall pines,
    A-saying "Oh! hu-ush!" a-saying "Oh! hu-ush!"
As stilly stole by a bold legion of horse,
    For Hale in the bush, for Hale in the bush.

"Keep still!" said the thrush, as she nestled her young          5
    In a nest by the road, in a nest by the road;
"For the tyrants are near, and with them appear
    What bodes us no good, what bodes us no good."

The brave captain heard it, and thought of his home
    In a cot by the brook, in a cot by the brook;          10
With mother and sister and memories dear,
    He so gaily forsook, he so gaily forsook.

10. cot—Cottage.

Cooling shades of the night were coming apace,
  The tatoo had beat, the tatoo had beat;
The noble one sprang from his dark lurking-place      15
  To make his retreat, to make his retreat.

He warily trod on the dry rustling leaves
  As he passed through the wood, as he passed through the wood,
And silently gained his rude launch on the shore,
  As she played with the flood, as she played with the flood.    20

The guards of the camp on that dark dreary night,
  Had a murderous will, had a murderous will;
They took him and bore him afar from the shore,
  To a hut on the hill, to a hut on the hill.

No mother was there, nor a friend who would cheer,      25
  In that little stone cell, in that little stone cell;
But he trusted in love from his Father above—
  In his heart all was well, in his heart all was well.

An ominous owl with his solemn bass voice
  Sat moaning hard by, sat moaning hard by:      30
"The tyrant's proud minions most gladly rejoice,
  For he must soon die, for he must soon die."

The brave fellow told them, no thing he restrained,—
   The cruel gen'ral; the cruel gen'ral!
His errand from camp, of the ends to be gained,      35
   And said that was all, and said that was all.

They took him and bound him and bore him away,
   Down the hill's grassy side, down the hill's grassy side.
'Twas there the base hirelings, in royal array,
   His cause did deride, his cause did deride.      40

Five minutes were given, short moments, no more,
   For him to repent, for him to repent.
He prayed for his mother—he asked not another,—
   To heaven he went, to heaven he went.

The faith of a martyr the tragedy showed,      45
   As he trod the last stage, as he trod the last stage.
And Britons still shudder at gallant Hale's blood,
   As his words do presage, as his words do presage:

"Thou pale king of terrors, thou life's gloomy foe,
   Go frighten the slave, go frighten the slave;      50
Tell tyrants, to you their allegiance they owe—
   No fears for the brave, no fears for the brave!"

48. PRESAGE—Foretell; predict.

◆◇◆◇◆◇◆◇◆◇◆◇◆◇◆◇◆◇◆◇◆◇◆◇◆◇◆◇◆◇◆◇◆◇◆◇◆◇◆◇◆◇◆◇◆◇◆◇◆◇◆◇◆◇◆◇◆

## FOR DISCUSSION

1. How is nature itself shown to be in sympathy with Hale?

2. What is the meaning of the words in stanza 4: "The tatoo had beat"?

3. What is the poet's attitude toward the British? How does he express it throughout the poem?

4. Why do the "Britons still shudder at gallant Hale's blood"?

5. Was Hale hanged unjustly? What do you think about the execution of Major André who was captured behind American lines?

6. Compare the story in this ballad with the historical event. What details are added or omitted? Can you tell why?

## WORDS TO EXPLAIN

Explain the meaning of the following italicized words: what *bodes* us no good; an *ominous* owl; the tyrant's proud *minions*; in royal *array*; gained his *rude* launch on the shore.

## RELATED READING

You will find many an exciting and interesting account of spies in *The Secret History of the American Revolution* by Carl Van Doren. The author takes his accounts of the conspiracies of Benedict Arnold and others from the Secret Service papers of the British Headquarters in North America.

# POOR RICHARD SAYS

*BENJAMIN FRANKLIN*

*Throughout the calendars and weather predictions of his almanac,* POOR RICHARD *scattered a wealth of wise sayings, anecdotes, and moral maxims, which soon became familiar to the lips of the American colonists.*

1. If you'd lose a troublesome Visitor, lend him money.

2. It is ill manners to silence a Fool, and Cruelty to let him go on.

3. We are not so sensible[1] of the greatest Health as of the least Sickness.

4. A Mob's a Monster; Heads enough but no Brains.

5. Love your Enemies, for they tell you your Faults.

6. Vice knows she's ugly, so puts on her Mask.

7. Most people return small Favours, acknowledge middling ones, and repay great ones with Ingratitude.

8. Being ignorant is not so much a Shame, as being unwilling to learn.

9. Today is Yesterday's pupil.

10. Hide not your Talents, they for Use were made. What's a Sun-Dial in the shade?

11. A slip of the foot you may soon recover,
    A slip of the tongue you may never get over.

12. The good or ill hap[2] of a good or ill life, is the good or ill choice of a good or ill wife.

13. Many complain of their memory, few of their judgment.

14. He that spills the Rum, loses that only; He that drinks it, often loses both that and himself.

15. The Sting of a Reproach is the Truth of it.

16. As honest Hodge the Farmer sow'd his Field,
    Chear'd with the Hope of future Gain 'twould yield,
    Two upstart Jacks in Office, proud and vain,
    Come riding by, and thus insult the Swain:[3]
    *You drudge and sweat and labour here, Old Boy,*
    *But we the Fruit of your hard Toil enjoy.*
    Belike you may, *quoth Hodge,* and but your Due,
    For, Gentlemen, 'tis HEMP I'm sowing now.

17. He is not well bred, that cannot bear Ill-Breeding in others.

18. Those who in quarrels interpose,
    Must often wipe a bloody nose.

19. Good sense is a thing all need, few have, and none think they want.[4]

20. Where yet was ever found the mother,
    Who'd change her booby for another?

21. Anger is never without a Reason, but seldom with a good One.

22. He that is of Opinion Money will

---

[1] SENSIBLE—Aware.
[2] HAP—Luck, chance.

[3] SWAIN—Peasant, country fellow.
[4] WANT—Lack, need.

do every Thing may well be suspected of doing every Thing for Money.

23. To bear other people's afflictions, every one has courage and enough to spare.

24. Fond Pride of Dress is sure an
    empty Curse;
    Ere Fancy you consult, consult
    your Purse.

25. Here comes Glib-Tongue: who can out-flatter a Dedication; and lie, like ten Epitaphs.

26. Sal laughs at everything you say. Why? Because she has fine teeth.

27. Nothing brings more pain than too much pleasure.

28. Three may keep a secret, if two of them are dead.

29. A false Friend and a Shadow attend only while the Sun shines.

30. He that falls in love with himself, will have no rivals.

31. Blessed is he that expects nothing, for he shall never be disappointed.

32. Epitaph on a Scolding Wife by her Husband. Here my poor Bridget's Corpse doth lie, she is at rest,—and so am I.

33. If a man could have half his Wishes, he would double his Troubles.

34. There is no Man so bad but he secretly respects the Good.

## FOR DISCUSSION

1. Discuss the meaning of the more difficult maxims.

2. Are there any statements with which you disagree? Are there any judgments that deal too harshly with human nature?

3. Which saying do you like best? Why?

## PROJECTS

1. Write a short story or an essay, exemplifying one of the sayings or explaining it at greater length.

2. Draw a cartoon illustrating the thought of one of the maxims.

3. Bring a modern almanac to school. See if your library has a copy of "Poor Richard." Compare Franklin's almanac with the modern one in make-up and material.

## RELATED READINGS

Franklin believed that virtue helped one to achieve material prosperity. His *Autobiography* tells of his personal success. This self-portrait shows the practical self-made man, ever ready to please men and God. He appears clear, simple, and unhypocritical; but even the sayings of his almanac show how worldly he was in his views and how lacking in inspiration for the higher things in life.

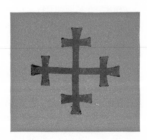

# A BORN LEADER

## BENJAMIN FRANKLIN

*Benjamin Franklin was not only a successful statesman, scientist, and businessman, he also was a great writer. His autobiography is one of the best in American literature. The following selection from it is a good example of his ability to combine humor, interest, facts, and wisdom.*

At ten years old, I was taken to help my father in his business of a tallow-chandler and soap-boiler, a business to which he was not bred, but had assumed on his arrival in New England, because he found that his dyeing trade, being in little request, would not maintain his family. Accordingly, I was employed in cutting the wick for the candles, filling the molds for cast candles, attending the shop, going of errands, &c.

I disliked the trade, and had a strong inclination to go to sea, but my father declared against it; but residing near the water, I was much in and on it. I learnt to swim well, and to manage boats; and when embarked with other boys, I was commonly allowed to govern,[1] especially in any case of difficulty; and upon other occasions, I was generally the leader among the boys, and sometimes led them into scrapes, of which I will mention an instance, as it shews [2] an early projecting public spirit, though not then justly conducted.

There was a salt marsh which bounded part of the mill-pond, on the edge of which at high water we used to stand to fish for minnows; by much trampling we had made it a mere quagmire.[3] My proposal was to build a wharf there for us to stand upon, and I shewed my comrades a large heap of stones, which were intended for a new house near the marsh, and which would very well suit our purpose. Accordingly, in the evening, when the workmen were gone home, I assembled a number of my playfellows, and we worked diligently like so many emmets,[4] sometimes two or three to a stone, till we had brought them all to make our little wharf. The next morning the workmen were surprised, on missing the stones which formed our wharf; inquiry was made after the authors of this transfer, we were discovered, complained of, and corrected by our fathers; and though I demonstrated the utility of our work, mine convinced me that, *that which was not truly honest could not be truly useful.*

[4] EMMETS—Ants.

[1] GOVERN—Steer; lead.
[2] SHEWS—Shows.
[3] QUAGMIRE—Soft, wet, swampy land.

◇◇◇◇◇◇◇◇◇◇◇◇◇◇◇◇◇◇◇◇◇◇◇◇◇◇◇◇◇◇◇

### FOR DISCUSSION

1. Mention some of the qualities manifested in this article that indicated that Franklin would be a leader later in his life.

2. What does he mean when he says that this incident showed "an early projecting public spirit?"

3. How do you think his father "convinced" him that "that which was not truly honest could not be truly useful?" What does this mean?

# The Indian Burying Ground

## PHILIP FRENEAU

*It was the custom of the North American Indians to bury their dead in a sitting position. In the grave were also placed the bow, arrows, pottery, and trinkets which were thought necessary for the journey into the "Happy Hunting Ground."*

In spite of all the learned have said,
 I still my old opinion keep;
The posture that we give the dead
 Points out the soul's eternal sleep.

Not so the ancients of these lands;—   5
 The Indian, when from life released,
Again is seated with his friends,
 And shares again the joyous feast.

His imaged birds, and painted bowl,
 And venison, for a journey dressed,
Bespeak the nature of the soul,   11
 Activity, that wants no rest.

His bow for action ready bent,
 And arrows with a head of stone,
Can only mean that life is spent,   15
 And not the old ideas are gone.

Thou, stranger, that shalt come this way,
 No fraud upon the dead commit,—
Observe the swelling turf, and say,
 They do not lie, but here they sit.   20

Here still a lofty rock remains,
 On which a curious eye may trace
(Now wasted half by wearing rains)
 The fancies of a ruder race.

Here still an aged elm aspires,   25
 Beneath whose far-projecting shade
(And which the shepherd still admires)
 The children of the forest played.

There oft a restless Indian queen   29
 (Pale Shebah with her braided hair)
And many a barbarous form is seen
 To chide the man that lingers here.

By midnight moons, o'er moistening dews,
 In habit for the chase arrayed,
The hunter still the deer pursues,   35
 The hunter and the deer—a shade!

And long shall timorous Fancy see
 The painted chief, and pointed spear,
And Reason's self shall bow the knee
 To shadows and delusions here.   40

30. SHEBAH—A queen of ancient times.

<hr>

## FOR DISCUSSION

1. Who are the "learned" referred to in line 1? In this poem does Freneau show a belief in life after death as we Catholics believe? What lines prove your opinion?

2. Who are the "ancients of these lands"? Compare the burying posture of the Indians with that of the white man. What does each signify? What is the Indian idea of the hereafter?

3. Explain the following phrases: *swelling turf; fancies of a ruder race; children of the forest; in habit for the chase arrayed; a shade; no fraud upon the dead commit; timorous Fancy.*

4. Discuss the meaning of the last stanza.

# THE CRISIS

*THOMAS PAINE*

*Even the leaders of the American Revolution were beginning to feel disheartened during the early winter of 1776. Then on December 19 there appeared in the* PENNSYLVANIA JOURNAL *an article to bolster men's courage. It was "The Crisis, No. I," the first of a series which appeared during the war. The author was Thomas Paine, a Quaker rather recently come from England. He had a fiery faith in the principles of democracy, and he became one of the active forces in the fight for American Independence.*

*At Washington's request, "The Crisis" was read aloud to his troops before they crossed the Delaware to win the victory of Trenton.*

These are the times that try men's souls. The summer soldier and the sunshine patriot will, in this crisis, shrink from the service of their country; but he that stands it *now*, deserves the love and thanks of man and woman. Tyranny, like hell, is not easily conquered; yet we have this consolation with us, that the harder the conflict, the more glorious the triumph. What we obtain too cheap, we esteem too lightly: it is dearness only that gives everything its value. Heaven knows how to put a proper price upon its goods; and it would be strange indeed, if so celestial an article as FREEDOM should not be highly rated. Britain with an army to enforce her tyranny, has declared that she has a right (*not only to* TAX) but "to BIND us in ALL CASES WHATSOEVER," and if being *bound in that manner*, is not slavery, then is there not such a thing as slavery upon earth. Even the expression is impious; for so unlimited a power can belong only to God.

Whether the independence of the continent was declared too soon, or delayed too long, I will not now enter into as an argument; my own simple opinion is, that had it been eight months earlier, it would have been much better. We did not make a proper use of last winter, neither could we, while we were in a dependent state. However, the fault, if it were one, was all our own; we have none to blame but ourselves. But no great deal is lost yet. All that Howe has been doing for this month past, is rather a ravage [1] than a conquest, which the spirit of the Jerseys, a year ago, would have quickly repulsed, and which time and a little resolution will soon recover.

I have as little superstition in me as any man living, but my secret opinion has ever been, and still is, that God Almighty will not give up a people to military destruction, or leave them un-

[1] RAVAGE—A pillaging or plundering policy, a sort of guerrilla warfare.

supportedly to perish, who have so earnestly and so repeatedly sought to avoid the calamities of war, by every decent method which wisdom could invent. Neither have I so much of the infidel in me, as to suppose that He has relinquished the government of the world, and given us up to the care of devils: and as I do not, I cannot see on what grounds the King of Britain can look up to heaven for help against us: a common murderer, a highwayman, or a house-breaker, has as good a pretence as he.

'Tis surprising to see how rapidly a panic will sometimes run through a country. All nations and ages have been subject to them: Britain has trembled like an ague at the report of a French fleet of flat bottomed boats; and in the fourteenth century the whole English army, after ravaging the kingdom of France, was driven back like men petrified with fear; and this brave exploit was performed by a few broken forces collected and headed by a woman, Joan of Arc. Would that heaven might inspire some Jersey maid to spirit up her countrymen, and save her fair fellow sufferers! Yet panics, in some cases, have their uses; they produce as much good as hurt. Their duration is always short; the mind soon grows through them, and acquires a firmer habit than before. But their peculiar advantage is, that they are the touchstones of sincerity and hypocrisy, and bring things and men to light, which might otherwise have lain forever undiscovered. In fact, they have the same effect on secret traitors, which an imaginary apparition would have upon a private murderer. They sift out the hidden thoughts of man, and hold them up in public to the world. Many a disguised Tory has lately shown his head, that shall penitentially solemnize

with curses the day on which Howe arrived upon the Delaware. . . .

I once felt all that kind of anger, which a man ought to feel, against the mean principles that are held by the Tories: a noted one, who kept a tavern at Amboy, was standing at his door, with as pretty a child in his hand, about eight or nine years old, as I ever saw, and after speaking his mind as freely as he thought was prudent, finished with this unfatherly expression, *"Well! give me peace in my day."* Not a man lives on the continent but fully believes that a separation must some time or other finally take place, and a generous parent should have said *"If there must be trouble, let it be in my day, that my child may have peace"*; and this single reflection, well applied, is sufficient to awaken every man to duty. Not a place upon earth might be so happy as America. Her situation is remote from all the wrangling world, and she has nothing to do, but to trade with them. A man can distinguish himself between temper and principle, and I am as confident, as I am that God governs the world, that America will never be happy till she gets clear of foreign dominion. Wars, without ceasing, will break out till that period arrives, and the continent must in the end be conqueror; for though the flame of liberty may sometimes cease to shine, the coal can never expire.

◇◇◇◇◇◇◇◇◇◇◇◇◇◇◇◇◇◇◇◇◇◇◇◇◇◇◇

## FOR DISCUSSION

1. Review briefly the history of the first year of the Revolutionary War. Why was December of 1776 a particularly discouraging time for the colonists?

2. What chiefly determines the value of man's possessions? Cite, from your own experience or observation, two or three illustrations of this truth.

3. Why did Paine feel that the colonies deserved a victory in the war?

4. What good does Paine say may be accomplished by a panic?

5. Explain why it was an unfatherly wish for the tavern-keeper to say, "Well! give me peace in my day."

6. In 1776 Paine wrote, "Not a place on earth might be so happy as America." Has time verified his statement? Discuss.

## WORDS TO STUDY

1. Discuss the meaning of the italicized words. Why are they effective?

a. The *summer* soldier and the *sunshine* patriot. (How do you describe friends who fail to show up in your time of trouble?)

b. Panics are the *touchstone* of sincerity and hypocrisy.

c. A man can distinguish himself between *temper* and *principle*.

2. What difficulties does your imagination encounter in picturing an "army . . . driven back like men *petrified* with fear"?

3. Look up the pronunciation of *ague* and *impious*. What do the words mean?

## PROJECTS

1. Write an essay or short story illustrating either of these statements: "What we obtain too cheap, we esteem too lightly"; "It is dearness that gives everything its value."

2. Read "Prelude to Part First," lines 21–32, of *The Vision of Sir Launfal*, by Lowell, and come to class prepared to compare the ideas in Paine's fourth and fifth sentences in "The Crisis" with those of the poet. Is there a conflict in their opinions or not? If so, where? If not, how are they reconciled?

◇◇◇◇◇

# FAREWELL ADDRESS

## GEORGE WASHINGTON

*After eight years as president, Washington decided to retire into private life. In his "Farewell Address" he wished to give the nation some heartfelt warnings about the dangers that lay ahead in the path of its progress. His knowledge of the threats to the welfare of the country came from actual experience; therefore, the advice is, above all, very practical. Indeed, after a century and a half, it is still worth our consideration.*

*Because the address is long and dwells in considerable detail on matters of especial interest in 1796, we present here a condensation. Washington did not deliver this address orally. It was printed, as he desired, in Claypoole's* AMERICAN DAILY ADVERTISER *for September 19, 1796.*

I

[In the first part of the address, Washington declines to run a third time for the office of president. It is not a lessening of his zeal nor a lack of gratitude that leads him to retire. Indeed, it is a sense of duty that had kept him from withdrawing earlier. Now that the na-

*tion has passed her first tests and is firmly established, he does not think it unpatriotic to leave public life.*

*As he is about to give up his post, he gratefully acknowledges the honors, the confidence, the constant support his countrymen have given him. He prays that the nation will continue in the bonds of union and brotherly affection and that the constitutional liberties will always be preserved in such a way as to be a blessing and glory to America and an admirable example to all the world.]*

## II

Here, perhaps, I ought to stop. But a solicitude for your welfare, which cannot end but with my life, and the apprehension of danger natural to that solicitude, urge me, on an occasion like the present, to offer to your solemn contemplation, and to recommend to your frequent review, some sentiments which are the result of much reflection, of no inconsiderable observation, and which appear to me all-important to the permanency of your felicity [1] as a people.

Interwoven as is the love of liberty with every ligament [2] of your hearts, no recommendation of mine is necessary to fortify or confirm the attachment.

The unity of government, which constitutes you one people, is also dear to you.[3] It is justly so; for it is a main pil-

[1] FELICITY—Happiness.

[2] LIGAMENT—Tie, bond. Compare the expression "heart strings."

[3] UNITY . . . ALSO DEAR TO YOU—In 1792 Jefferson wrote Washington: "The confidence of the whole Union is centered in you. Your being at the helm will be more than an answer to every argument, which can be used to alarm and lead the people in any quarter into violence or secession. North and South will hang together, if they have you to hang on." By 1796 the strong feeling of local patriotism which had threatened the complete adoption of the Constitution had considerably diminished.

lar in the edifice of your real independence, the support of your tranquility at home, your peace abroad; of your safety; of your prosperity; of that very liberty which you so highly prize. But as it is easy to foresee that from different causes and from different quarters much pains will be taken, many artifices [4] employed, to weaken in your minds the conviction of this truth; it is of infinite moment [5] that you should cherish a cordial, habitual, and immovable attachment to it; accustoming yourselves to think and speak of it as of the palladium [6] of your political safety and prosperity; watching for its preservation with jealous anxiety; discountenancing [7] whatever may suggest even a suspicion that it can in any event be abandoned; and indignantly frowning upon the first dawning of every attempt to alienate any portion of our country from the rest, or to enfeeble the sacred ties which now link together the various parts.

For this you have every inducement of sympathy and interest. Citizens, by birth or choice, of a common country, that country has a right to concentrate your affections.[8] The name of America, which belongs to you, in your national capacity, must always exalt the just pride of patriotism, more than any appellation [9] derived from local discriminations. With slight shades of difference,

[4] ARTIFICES—Devices, stratagems, wiles.

[5] MOMENT—Consequence, importance.

[6] PALLADIUM—Safeguard. In classical mythology, the palladium was a statue of Pallas Athene in the citadel of ancient Troy. It was believed that the safety of Troy depended upon this statue.

[7] DISCOUNTENANCING—Disapproving; refusing to look favorably on.

[8] TO CONCENTRATE YOUR AFFECTIONS—That is, to demand that your affections be centered upon it.

[9] APPELLATION—Name. Washington alludes to the pride which some of his contemporaries took in being called Virginians or New Yorkers.

you have the same religion, manners, habits, and political principles. You have in a common cause fought and triumphed together; the independence and liberty you possess are the work of joint counsels and joint efforts, of common dangers, sufferings and successes.

[*Washington here emphasizes the reasons for maintaining unity in government. Each part of the country, he points out, benefits from its friendly intercourse and association with the other parts. In union, each part finds greater security against dangers abroad and wars between themselves. In particular, he warns against the formation of party systems which do not have the interests of the whole country at heart.*]

In contemplating the causes which may disturb our Union, it occurs as a matter of serious concern, that any ground should have been furnished for characterizing parties by geographical discriminations Northern and Southern, Atlantic and Western; whence designing men may endeavor to excite a belief that there is a real difference of local interests and views. One of the expedients of party to acquire influence, within particular districts, is to misrepresent the opinions and aims of other districts. You cannot shield yourselves too much against the jealousies and heart-burnings which spring from these misrepresentations; they tend to render alien to each other those who ought to be bound together by fraternal affection.

[*Here Washington further warns against parties based on geographical divisions; enlarges on the necessity of union; urges respect for existing laws; declares that any attempt to act contrary to existing laws is destructive of government; and pleads against the "spirit of innovation."*]

### III

I have already intimated to you the danger of parties in the State, with particular reference to the founding of them on geographical discrimination. Let me now take a more comprehensive view, and warn you in the most solemn manner against the baneful effects of the spirit of party,[1] generally.

This spirit, unfortunately, is inseparable from our nature, having its root in the strongest passions of the human mind. It exists under different shapes in all governments, more or less stifled, controlled, or repressed; but in those of the popular form it is seen in its greatest rankness, and is truly their worst enemy.

The alternate domination of one faction over another, sharpened by the spirit of revenge, natural to party dissension, which in different ages and countries has perpetrated the most horrid enormities,[2] is itself a frightful despotism. But this leads at length to a more formal and permanent despotism. The disorders and miseries which result, gradually incline the minds of men to seek security and repose in the absolute

[1] BANEFUL EFFECTS OF THE SPIRIT OF PARTY—Washington himself suffered much from what he called the "baneful effects of party." According to Bassett, he was charged by the Republicans with "betraying the pledge given to France, and taking more salary than was allotted to him. His mail was even tampered with, in the hope of finding political matters of advantage to his opponents, and a most shameful forgery of letters in 1777 was searched out and reprinted as genuine. He was sensitively devoted to official integrity, and all these attacks cut him to the quick."

[2] MOST HORRID ENORMITIES—Washington had in mind very likely the excesses to which party rivalry led in the French Revolution, and also proscriptions in Rome under Marius and Sulla.

power of an individual;[3] and sooner or later the chief of some prevailing faction, more able or more fortunate than his competitors, turns this disposition to the purposes of his own elevation, on the ruins of public liberty.

It [the spirit of party] serves always to distract the public councils, and enfeeble the public administration. It agitates the community with ill-founded jealousies and false alarms; kindles the animosity of one part against another, foments occasionally riot and insurrection. It opens the doors to foreign influence and corruption, which find a facilitated access to the government itself through the channels of party passions. Thus the policy and the will of one country are subjected to the policy and will of another.

There is an opinion, that parties in free countries are useful checks upon the administration of the government, and serve to keep alive the spirit of liberty. This within certain limits is probably true, and in governments of a monarchical cast, patriotism may look with indulgence, if not with favor, upon the spirit of party. But in those of the popular character, in governments purely elective, it is a spirit not to be encouraged. From their natural tendency, it is certain there will always be enough of that spirit for every salutary purpose. And there being constant danger of excess, the effort ought to be, by force of public opinion to mitigate and assuage it. A fire not to be quenched, it demands a uniform vigilance to prevent its bursting into a flame, lest, instead of warming, it should consume.

[3] THE DISORDERS . . . INDIVIDUAL—The rise of Napoleon is a good illustration of this statement, but it is to be questioned if Washington had Napoleon in mind. It is more likely that he was thinking of such men as Marius, Sulla, and Julius Cæsar.

IV

It is important, likewise, that the habits of thinking in a free country should inspire caution, in those intrusted with its administration, to confine themselves within their respective constitutional spheres, avoiding in the exercise of the powers of one department to encroach upon another.[1] The spirit of encroachment tends to consolidate the powers of all the departments in one, and thus to create, whatever the form of government, a real despotism. A just estimate of that love of power, and proneness to abuse it, which predominates in the human heart, is sufficient to satisfy us of the truth of this position. The necessity of reciprocal checks[2] in the exercise of political power, by dividing and distributing it into different depositories and constituting each the guardian of the public weal against invasions by the others, has been evinced by experiments ancient and modern, some of them in our country and under our own eyes.[3]

[1] TO CONFINE . . . ENCROACH UPON ANOTHER—Washington here alludes, of course, to the danger which would follow upon permitting one department of the government, say for example, the executive, to usurp the powers of the legislative and judicial branches. In the course of our history Congress has shown itself very jealous of its privileges. Possibly Washington himself had in mind a resolution of the House of Representatives passed in March, 1796, requesting him to lay before the House "a copy of the instructions to the minister of the United States, who negotiated the treaty with the King of Great Britain, together with the correspondence and other documents relative to that treaty."

[2] RECIPROCAL CHECKS—Washington here refers to such constitutional checks as the following: (1) the President may make no appointments to office without the advice and consent of the Senate; (2) the laws made by Congress may be declared unconstitutional by the Supreme Court; (3) the President is given the power of veto.

[3] IN OUR OWN COUNTRY AND UNDER OUR OWN EYES—As a matter of fact, those things in our Constitution which have worked well had been in operation in colonial governments.

To preserve them must be as necessary as to institute them. If, in the opinion of the people, the distribution or modification of the constitutional powers be in any particular wrong, let it be corrected by an amendment in the way which the Constitution designates. But let there be no change by usurpation; for, though this, in one instance, may be the instrument of good, it is the customary weapon by which free governments are destroyed. The precedent must always greatly overbalance in permanent evil any partial or transient benefit which the use can at any time yield.

v

Of all the dispositions and habits which lead to political prosperity, religion and morality are indispensable supports. In vain would that man claim the tribute of patriotism, who should labor to subvert these great pillars of human happiness, these firmest props of the duties of men and citizens. The mere politician equally with the pious man ought to respect and to cherish them. A volume could not trace all their connections with private and public felicity. Let it simply be asked, Where is the security for property, for reputation, for life, if the sense of religious obligation desert the oaths, which are the instruments of investigation in courts of justice? And let us with caution indulge the supposition, that morality can be maintained without religion. Whatever may be conceded to the influence of refined education on minds of peculiar structure, reason and experience [1] both forbid us to expect, that na-

[1] EXPERIENCE—Washington no doubt had in mind the attempt made by the French Revolutionists to abolish both God and religion and to set up a rule of reason. We have seen a similar thing attempted in our day in revolutionary Russia.

tional morality can prevail in exclusion of religious principle.

As a very important source of strength and security, cherish public credit. One method of preserving it is to use it as sparingly as possible; avoiding occasions of expense by cultivating peace, but remembering also that timely disbursements to prepare for danger frequently prevent much greater disbursements to repel it; avoiding likewise the accumulation of debt, not only by shunning occasions of expense, but by vigorous exertion in time of peace to discharge the debts, which unavoidable wars may have occasioned, but ungenerously throwing upon posterity the burden which we ourselves ought to bear. The execution of these maxims belongs to your representatives, but it is necessary that public opinion should coöperate. To facilitate to them the performance of their duty it is essential that you should practically bear in mind, that towards the payment of debts there must be revenue; that to have revenue there must be taxes; that no taxes can be devised which are not more or less inconvenient and unpleasant.

## VI

Observe good faith and justice towards all nations; cultivate peace and harmony with all. Religion and morality enjoin this conduct; and can it be, that good policy does not equally enjoin it? It will be worthy of a free, enlightened, and at no distant period a great nation, to give to mankind the magnanimous and too novel example of a people always guided by an exalted justice and benevolence.

In the execution of such a plan, nothing is more essential than that permanent, inveterate antipathies[1] against

[1] INVETERATE ANTIPATHIES—Deeply rooted dislikes or feelings of hostility.

particular nations, and passionate attachments[2] for others, should be excluded; and that, in place of them, just and amicable feelings towards all should be cultivated. The nation which indulges towards another an habitual hatred, or an habitual fondness, is in some degree a slave. It is a slave to its animosity or to its affection, either of which is sufficient to lead it astray from its duty and its interest. Antipathy in one nation against another disposes each more readily to offer insult and injury, to lay hold of slight causes of umbrage,[3] and to be haughty and intractable[4] when accidental or trifling occasions of dispute occur. Hence, frequent collisions, obstinate, envenomed, and bloody contests.

So likewise, a passionate attachment of one nation for another produces a variety of evils. Sympathy for the favorite nation, facilitating the illusion of an imaginary common interest in cases where no real common interest exists, and infusing into one the enmities of the other, betrays the former, into a participation in the quarrels and wars of the latter, without adequate inducement or justification. It leads also to concessions to the favorite nation of privileges denied to others, which is apt doubly to injure the nation making the concessions, by unnecessarily parting with what ought to have been retained, and by exciting jealousy, ill-will, and a disposition to retaliate, in the parties from whom equal privileges are withheld. And it gives to ambitious, corrupted, or deluded citizens (who devote themselves

[2] ATTACHMENTS—Washington here alludes to the pro-British sympathies of the Federalists and the pro-French sympathies of the Republicans which had heightened the bitter party strife of his two administrations.

[3] UMBRAGE—Offense, resentment.

[4] INTRACTABLE—Obstinate, unmanageable.

to the favorite nation), facility to betray or sacrifice the interests of their own country, without odium, sometimes even with popularity.

Against the insidious wiles of foreign influence (I conjure you to believe me, fellow citizens), the jealousy of a free people ought to be constantly awake, since history and experience prove that foreign influence is one of the most baneful foes of republican government. But that jealousy, to be useful, must be impartial; else it becomes the instrument of the very influence to be avoided, instead of a defense against it. Excessive partiality for one foreign nation, and excessive dislike for another, cause those whom they actuate [5] to see danger only on one side, and serve to veil and even second the arts of influence on the other. Real patriots, who may resist the intrigues of the favorite, are liable to become suspected and odious; while its tools and dupes usurp the applause and confidence of the people, to surrender their interests.

The great rule of conduct for us, in regard to foreign nations, is, in extending our commercial relations, to have with them as little political connection as possible. So far as we have already formed engagements, let them be fulfilled with perfect good faith. Here let us stop.

Europe has a set of primary interests, which to us have none, or a very remote relation. Hence she must be engaged in frequent controversies, the causes of which are essentially foreign to our concerns. Hence, therefore, it must be unwise in us to implicate ourselves, by artificial ties, in the ordinary vicissitudes [6] of her politics, or the ordinary combinations and collisions of her friendships or enmities.

[5] ACTUATE—Influence.
[6] VICISSITUDES—Changes.

Our detached and distant situation invites and enables us to pursue a different course. If we remain one people, under an efficient government, the period is not far off when we may defy material injury from external annoyance; when we may take such an attitude as will cause the neutrality, we may at any time resolve upon, to be scrupulously respected; when belligerent nations, under the impossibility of making acquisitions upon us, will not lightly hazard the giving us provocation; when we may choose peace or war, as our interest, guided by justice, shall counsel.

It is our true policy to steer clear of permanent alliances with any portion of the foreign world; so far, I mean, as we are now at liberty to do it; for let me not be understood as capable of patronizing infidelity to existing engagements. I hold the maxim no less applicable to public than to private affairs, that honesty is always the best policy. I repeat it, therefore, let those engagements be observed in their genuine sense. But, in my opinion, it is unnecessary and would be unwise to extend them.

Taking care always to keep ourselves, by suitable establishments, on a respectable defensive posture, we may safely trust to temporary alliances for extraordinary emergencies.

Harmony, liberal intercourse with all nations, are recommended by policy, humanity, and interest. But even our commercial policy should hold an equal and impartial hand; neither seeking nor granting exclusive favors or preferences; consulting the natural course of things; diffusing and diversifying by gentle means the streams of commerce, but forcing nothing; establishing with powers so disposed, in order to give trade a stable course, to define the rights of our merchants, and to enable the government to support them, conventional rules of intercourse, the best that present circumstances and mutual opinion will permit, but temporary, and liable to be from time to time abandoned or varied, as experience and circumstances shall dictate; constantly keeping in view, that it is folly in one nation to look for disinterested favors from another; that it must pay with a portion of its independence for whatever it may accept under that character; that, by such acceptance, it may place itself in the condition of having given equivalents for nominal favors,[7] and yet of being reproached with ingratitude for not giving more. There can be no greater error than to expect or calculate upon real favors from nation to nation. It is an illusion, which experience must cure, which a just pride ought to discard.

### VII

In offering to you, my countrymen, these counsels of an old and affectionate friend, I dare not hope they will make the strong and lasting impression I could wish; that they will control the usual current of the passions, or prevent our nation from running the course which has hitherto marked the destiny of nations. But, if I may even flatter myself that they may be productive of some partial benefit, some occasional good; that they may now and then recur to moderate the fury of party spirit, to warn against the mischiefs of foreign intrigue, to guard against the impostures of pretended patriotism; this hope will be a full recompense for the solicitude for your welfare, by which they have been dictated.

How far in the discharge of my official duties I have been guided by the principles which have been delineated,[1]

[7] NOMINAL FAVORS—So small or slight as hardly worth the name.

[1] DELINEATED—Set forth.

the public records and other evidences of my conduct must witness to you and to the world. To myself, the assurance of my own conscience is, that I have at least believed myself to be guided by them.

Though, in reviewing the incidents of my administration, I am unconscious of intentional error, I am nevertheless too sensible of my defects not to think it probable that I may have committed many errors. Whatever they may be, I fervently beseech the Almighty to avert or mitigate the evils to which they may tend. I shall also carry with me the hope that my country will never cease to view them with indulgence; and that, after forty-five years of my life dedicated to its service with an upright zeal, the faults of incompetent abilities will be consigned to oblivion, as myself must soon be to the mansions of rest.

Relying on its kindness in this as in other things, and actuated by that fervent love towards it, which is so natural to a man who views in it the native soil of himself and his progenitors [2] for several generations, I anticipate with pleasing expectation that retreat, in which I promise myself to realize, without alloy,[3] the sweet enjoyment of partaking, in the midst of my fellow citizens, the benign influence of good laws under a free government, the ever favorite object of my heart, and the happy reward, as I trust, of our mutual cares, labors, and dangers.

[2] PROGENITORS—Forefathers. John Washington, the great-grandfather of the President, emigrated to Virginia and settled in Westmoreland County in 1658.

[3] WITHOUT ALLOY—That is, wholly.

### FOR DISCUSSION

1. Is there any conflict of interests between sections or classes of society today that threatens to destroy our national

unity? Any that threatens to weaken it? What is there in human nature that causes these conflicts? What virtues are needed to settle such disputes peacefully? Compare our national unity and the spirit of patriotism with those of other nations; with our own in Washington's day.

2. How could the domination of one political party destroy the liberties of our nation? Discuss the good and evil of the political party system.

3. How does the party system open "the doors to foreign influence and corruption"? Is the party system safer in a monarchy than it is in a republic? Why?

4. Why is it that most men love power? Do those who exercise power tend to abuse it? Why or why not?

5. Is the reciprocal-checks system efficient in time of war? Would you give the president powers of a dictator in time of war? How would you safeguard democracy if you did?

6. Why are religion and morality indispensable supports to political prosperity? Are they indispensable in business life? in social life? Has any nation which disregarded religion and morality prospered for great lengths of time? Would Washington break a treaty with another nation if the terms of the contract were no longer of benefit to the United States? Would he act justly if he did?

7. In modern times have we seen any examples of the "insidious wiles of foreign influence"? Can you show from history how citizens of one nation, favorable to another, have betrayed the interests of their own country? What accounts for such betrayals?

8. Is it still true that Europe has a set of primary interests that have little or no relation to us? What would Washington's attitude be toward the United Nations organization?

## PROJECTS

1. Outline the chief points of Washington's address. Note which warnings are still timely today because of politics or because human nature is what it is.

2. Draw a cartoon or a series of cartoons illustrating any conflicts that may exist between sections or classes of society in our country, and show how their struggle weakens our national unity.

3. Write an essay or short story showing how a man or woman, stirred by ambition, acquires power and then abuses it.

4. Make a list of well-known men and women who have abused political power. Make another list of those who have used power well and justly. Note the length of each list.

## WORDS TO USE CORRECTLY

Which of the two words in parentheses is the correct word to use in the sentence?

1. The party spirit (*foments, ferments*) jealousy and hatred.

2. If you lend your help, we can (*felicitate, facilitate*) the passage of this law.

3. The witness (*explicated, implicated*) George in the crime.

4. You may now (*condign, consign*) the liberties of the country to this man without fear.

5. He (*mitigated, castigated*) the vicious criminal and refused to (*mitigate, castigate*) the prison sentence.

# FIRST INAUGURAL ADDRESS

*THOMAS JEFFERSON*

*On March 4, 1801 Thomas Jefferson was sworn in for his first term as President of the United States. In the following excerpt from the address he gave on this occasion Jefferson sets forth the principles on which he believes the country's policies should be founded.*

During the contest of opinion [1] through which we have passed, the animation [2] of discussion and of exertions has sometimes worn an aspect which might impose on [3] strangers unused to think freely and to speak and to write what they think; but this being now decided by the voice of the nation, announced according to the rules of the constitution, all will, of course, arrange themselves under the will of the law, and unite in common efforts for the common good. All, too, will bear in mind this sacred principle, that though the will of the majority is in all cases to prevail, that will, to be rightful, must be reasonable; that the minority possess their equal rights, which equal laws must protect, and to violate which would be oppression. Let us, then, fellow-citizens, unite with one heart and one mind. Let us restore to social intercourse that harmony and affection without which liberty and even life itself are but dreary things. And let us reflect that having banished from our land that religious intolerance under which mankind so long bled and suffered, we have yet gained little if we countenance a political intolerance as despotic, as wicked, and capable of as bitter and bloody persecutions. During the throes and convulsions of the ancient world, during the agonizing spasms of infuriated man, seeking through blood and slaughter his long-lost liberty, [4] it was not wonderful [5] that the agitation of the billows should reach even this distant and peaceful shore; that this should be more felt and feared by some and less by others; that this should divide opinions as to measures of safety. [6] But every

---

[1] CONTEST OF OPINION—The election of 1800, hotly contested between the Federalists, whose candidate was John Adams, and the Republicans supporting Jefferson. (Note: The Republican party of today is not the same party which supported Jefferson. The present party was formed in 1854.)

[2] ANIMATION—Spirit, ardor, liveliness.

[3] IMPOSE ON—Deceive. That is, the passion with which opposing views have been put forth might lead "strangers unused to think freely and to speak and write as they please" to believe that the country is so decisively split that there is no possibility of the two parties working together harmoniously. Jefferson goes on to point out that this is not so.

[4] THROES AND CONVULSIONS . . . LIBERTY —A reference to the French Revolution.

[5] NOT WONDERFUL—Not to be wondered at.

[6] MEASURES OF SAFETY—The Alien and Sedition Acts passed under the Federalist administration. The passage of these laws was stimulated by the fear that the bloody excesses of the French Revolution might be re-enacted in America.

difference of opinion is not a difference of principle. We have called by different names brethren of the same principle. We are all republicans—we are all federalists.[7] If there be any among us who would wish to dissolve this Union or to change its republican form, let them stand undisturbed as monuments of the safety with which error of opinion may be tolerated where reason is left free to combat it. I know, indeed, that some honest men fear that a republican government cannot be strong; that this government is not strong enough. But would the honest patriot, in the full tide of successful experiment, abandon a government which has so far kept us free and firm, on the theoretic and visionary fear that this government, the world's best hope, may by possibility want energy to preserve itself? I trust not. I believe this, on the contrary, the strongest government on earth, I believe it is the only one where every man, at the call of the laws, would fly to the standard of the law, and would meet invasions of the public order as his own personal concern. Sometimes it is said that man cannot be trusted with government of himself. Can he, then, be trusted with the government of others? Or have we found angels in the forms of kings to govern him? Let history answer this question.

Let us, then, with courage and confidence pursue our own federal and republican principles, our attachment to our union and representative government. Kindly separated by nature and a wide ocean from the exterminating havoc of one quarter of the globe; too high-minded to endure the degradations of the others;[8] possessing a chosen country, with room enough for our descendants to the hundredth and thousandth generation; entertaining a due sense of our equal right to the use of our own faculties, to the acquisitions of our industry, to honor and confidence from our fellow citizens, resulting not from birth but from our actions and their sense of them; enlightened by a benign religion, professed, indeed, and practiced in various forms, yet all of them including honesty, truth, temperence, gratitude, and the love of man: acknowledging and adoring an overruling Providence, which by all its dispensations proves that it delights in the happiness of man here and his greater happiness hereafter; with all these blessings, what more is necessary to make us a happy and prosperous people? Still one thing more, fellow citizens—a wise and frugal government, which shall restrain men from injuring one another, which shall leave them otherwise free to regulate their own pursuits of industry and improvement, and shall not take from the mouth of labor the bread it has earned. This is the sum of good government, and this is necessary to close the circle of our felicities.

About to enter, fellow citizens, on the exercise of duties which comprehend[9] everything dear and valuable to you, it is proper that you should understand what I deem the essential principles of our government, and consequently those which ought to shape its administration. I will compress them within the narrowest compass they will bear, stating the

---

[7] REPUBLICANS . . . FEDERALISTS—Jefferson means that all Americans believe in a republican form of government and in a strong federal government.

[8] EXTERMINATING HAVOC OF ONE QUARTER . . . DEGRADATIONS OF THE OTHERS—The first quarter of the globe to which Jefferson refers is Europe; the "exterminating havoc" is the continual wars there. "The degradations of the others" (the other quarters) refers to the miserable standard of living in Asia and Africa.

[9] COMPREHEND—Encompass, include.

general principle, but not all its limitations. Equal and exact justice to all men, of whatever state or persuasion, religious or political; peace, commerce, and honest friendship with all nations—entangling alliances with none; the support of the State governments in all their rights, as the most competent administrations for our domestic concerns and the surest bulwarks against anti-republican tendencies; the preservation of the general government in its whole constitutional vigor, as the sheet anchor of our peace at home and safety abroad; a jealous care of the right of election by the people—a mild and safe corrective of abuses which are lopped by the sword of the revolution where peaceable remedies are unprovided; absolute acquiescence in the decisions of the majority—the vital principle of republics, from which there is no appeal but to force, the vital principle and immediate parent of despotism; a well-disciplined militia—our best reliance in peace and for the first moments of war, till regulars may relieve them; the supremacy of the civil over the military authority; economy in the public expense, that labor may be lightly burdened; the honest payment of our debts and sacred preservation of the public faith; encouragement of agriculture, and of commerce as its hand maid; the diffusion of information and the arraignment of all abuses at the bar of public reason; freedom of religion; freedom of the press; freedom of persons under the protection of the *habeas corpus*; and trial by juries impartially selected—these principles form the bright constellation which has gone before us, and guided our steps through an age of revolution and reformation. The wisdom of our sages and the blood of our heroes have been devoted to their attainment. They should be the creed

of our political faith—the text of civil instruction—the touchstone [10] by which to try the services of those we trust; and should we wander from them in moments of error or alarm, let us hasten to retrace our steps and to regain the road which alone leads to peace, liberty, and safety.

[10]TOUCHSTONE—A test; a criterion or standard by which to judge.

◇◇◇◇◇◇◇◇◇◇◇◇◇◇◇◇◇◇◇◇◇◇◇◇◇◇◇◇◇◇◇

## FOR DISCUSSION

1. In the first paragraph of this selection Jefferson says, "All, too, will bear in mind this sacred principle, that though the will of the majority is in all cases to prevail, that will, to be rightful, must be reasonable; that the minority possess their equal rights, which equal laws must protect, and to violate which would be oppression." Explain in your own words what this passage means. How can a course of action to which a sizeable minority is unalterably opposed be justified? On what questions of national importance today would this statement bear?

2. Jefferson refers to "That religious intolerance under which mankind so long bled and suffered." From what you know of colonial America and of England during the seventeenth and eighteenth centuries, can you tell specifically what he is speaking of? Do you agree or disagree with Jefferson's statement that "every difference of opinion is not a difference of principle?" Cite several examples from current politics or from history to support your position.

3. The Alien Acts were presumably passed to prevent the spread of radical ideas from France and to provide a ready means of deporting foreigners who upheld these ideas. The Sedition Act, however, was aimed more specifically at American citizens, and, in effect, made political opposition to the administration a crime. One man, for example, was convicted and sent to prison for calling President John

Adams incompetent. Jefferson did not agree with these laws. He says that "error of opinion may be tolerated where reason is left free to combat it." Do you believe there should be no restraints at all on free speech, or do you feel that people should be prevented by law from saying some things—from urging the overthrow of the government, for example. Give arguments to support your belief.

# Further Readings About Revolutionary Times

## WRITERS OF REVOLUTIONARY TIMES

BARLOW, JOEL, *The Hasty Pudding* (poetry)

BRACKENRIDGE, HUGH HENRY, *Modern Chivalry*

BROWN, CHARLES BROCKDEN, *Wieland; Ormond*

* CARROLL, JOHN, *An Address to the Roman Catholics of the United States*

* DE CREVECOEUR, HECTOR ST. JEAN, *Letters from an American Farmer*

DICKINSON, JOHN, *Letters of a Farmer in Pennsylvania*

FRANKLIN, BENJAMIN, *Autobiography*

FRENEAU, PHILIP, "To the Memory of Brave Americans"; "Captain Barney's Victory" (poetry)

HAMILTON, ALEXANDER, *The Federalist* (selections)

HOPKINSON, FRANCIS, *A Pretty Story*

JEFFERSON, THOMAS, *Autobiography; Notes on Virginia;* "The Declaration of Independence"

OTIS, JAMES, *In Opposition to the Writs of Assistance*

TRUMBULL, JOHN, *M'Fingal* (poetry)

WISTER, SALLY, *Journal*

## MODERN WRITERS

ADAMS, JAMES TRUSLOW, *The Adams Family*

ATHERTON, GERTRUDE, *The Conqueror*

BOWEN, CATHERINE DRINKER, *John Adams and the American Revolution*

BOWERS, CLAUDE G., *Young Jefferson; Jefferson and Hamilton; Jefferson in Power*

BOYD, JAMES, *Drums*

CHURCHILL, WINSTON, *Richard Carvel*

DARROW, JANE, *Nathan Hale, A Story of Loyalties*

EDMONDS, WALTER D., *Drums Along the Mohawk*

FORD, PAUL LEICESTER, *Janice Meredith*

* GURN, JOSEPH, *Commodore John Barry*

MITCHELL, S. WIER, *Hugh Wynn*

NICOLAY, HELEN, *The Boys' Life of Benjamin Franklin*

ROBERTS, KENNETH, *Arundel; Rabble in Arms; Oliver Wiswell*

SAFFORD, HENRY B., *That Bennington Mob*

VAN DOREN, CARL, *Benjamin Franklin*

VAN DOREN, DOROTHY (ed.), *The Lost Art: Letters of Seven Famous Women*

# THE NATIONAL PERIOD

## 1 8 0 0 – 1 8 6 5

If America had just begun to stretch in the later eighteenth century, the nineteenth century found her shooting up through adolescence into mighty manhood. No other nation ever grew so large so fast. When Jefferson was elected president in 1800, the United States was an eastern band of fifteen states. There were few roads. Transportation was laborsome. The vastness of the unexplored West was deceptive. In his inaugural address, Jefferson recounted the blessings of the nation, naming among them—"room enough for our descendants to the hundredth and thousandth generation."

But immigrants swarmed to our shores. Open land beckoned westward. Roads were built. By 1830, both steamboat and railroad had been invented to speed the opening-up of the interior. Jefferson himself had negotiated the Louisiana Purchase and started Lewis and Clark on a cross-country expedition that brought them to another ocean. California and Oregon offered promise that the Union would some day stretch from coast to coast.

Such growth was not without its pains. There were troubles at home. The difficult problem of states' rights, problems of tariffs, of slave trade, and slave labor complicated the domestic situation. Abroad, England and France waited to gloat over the eventual "crack-up." Sure that the Republic could not survive, they bullied our seamen, disregarded our protests, and nagged us into a second war with England. Again patriotism flared high. Two years of fighting saw America vindicated. This country could hold up its head among the nations of the world.

Then came real prosperity. The administration of Monroe from 1817 to 1825 was known as the "Era of Good Feeling." Trade and industry flourished; expansion and development were phenomenal. In spite of domestic problems, life was good.

## THE RISE OF ROMANTICISM

And now came an outpouring of national literature. America had been born and was coming of age when the new spirit of freedom known as *romanticism* was sweeping over Europe. America not only shared in it, but contributed to it. There was a kinship between the American spirit of nationalism and the spirit of romanticism. Both believed that there is divinity in the common man; both exalted the individual. Both spoke for liberty in a revolt against institutions—religious or political—which would press men into molds that stifled personality.

The romanticist worshiped nature passionately, sometimes to the exclusion of God. He craved freedom. He wanted to develop his imagination and emotions; to express his own feeling and fancies. He reveled in the picturesque, the sensuous, the mysterious, the preternatural. He interpreted nature according to his moods—now dark and melancholy, now cheerful and optimistic. In revolt against the present, he sought his themes in distant lands or in ages past. Or, he preached a gospel of reform that would bring greater freedom. He dreamed of an ideal world where he could roam unfettered. He scolded and ranted against the realities of life that made him a responsible creature and against the circumstances that made men tyrants with gold; or slaves of it, or slaves for it. In literature the romanticist sought naturalness in expression. He simplified poetic forms; he enlivened his diction. He perfected and popularized the short story and the novel, for in fiction he could create fresh moods and characters as well as propagate his ideas.

The new era had promised Catholics an opportunity to add their positive note to our culture. Unhappily, the effects of the Cinderella role they had been forced to play did not wear off easily. A few Catholics like the Carrolls and Matthew Carey had won recognized places in the American scene. The greatest number, deprived of schools under colonial laws, had little or no education. Schools for Catholics were slow in being built, for the Catholics were not rich and teachers were scarce. The first care of the bishops was seminaries. Priests were sorely needed.

Nor must we assume that the Constitution of the United States had done away completely with religious prejudice. Some eastern states still had anti-Catholic laws. Protestant presses still protested against Catholic doctrine and warned men against the dark shadow of the Pope. Catholics were on the defensive.

The bishops and the clergy took the lead in establishing Catholic presses in the cities. Articles defending the faith were the most important contributions. But the editors did not fail to foster an interest in literature, and they encouraged the efforts of aspiring Catholic authors. These efforts did not outlive their day; yet they enheartened the Catholics and kept alive the Catholic voice.

## THE TRIUMPH OF ROMANTICISM

For the next thirty years, from 1830 to 1860, struggles between the North and South over the issues of states' rights, slavery, and the tariff dominated public life. But until the conflict broke out into actual war, the spirit of national power and romantic hopefulness rode high. The winning of Texas and California and the acquisition of the great Northwest territories had stimulated the physical and spiritual expansion of the young nation.

The surge of nationalism, however, brought more trouble for the Catholics. Waves of prejudice mounted high after 1829, breaking violently in the Nativist movement. Immigrants from Catholic countries, especially from Ireland, were swarming over the land. The cheapening of labor and the rise of the newcomers in political and social life brought problems accompanied by strong feeling against the foreigners. Some native Americans, confusing nationalities with religion, raised arms as well as voice against "agents employed by the Pope." An age-old artillery of charges was again brought to bear against all Catholics. Some zealots, hearing the thunder of verbal cannons from press and pulpit intensified the attack by burning a few churches and convents. The Church had not yet attained the peace for which she yearned.

The literary voices of the time came mostly from New England. A new philosophy called "transcendentalism" led the field. Its effect was to intensify the glorification of romantic ideals. Transcendentalism is not an easy movement to define. It concerns itself with abstract thought. Transcendentalists taught that our knowledge does not come from the experience of our senses and the use of reason. It goes beyond, or "transcends" experience. It is inborn in us. The world is all One. The one reality is the Over-Soul, or God, which dwells in each part of the universe however small. Each part contains the meaning and the laws of the whole. Each person is identical with the Soul of the world—literally, with God—and contains, in a hidden way, all that the Soul contains. And so—to the transcendentalist—life is a continual expansion, unfolding the divine in us. God did not become incarnate in Jesus Christ, says the philosopher; He took the form of the material universe. Therefore the individual, by studying the beauty, truth, and goodness in nature, comes in contact with and takes on the spirit and being of God.

The members of the transcendentalist cult had their divergent theories, which each propagated in his own way. The writers contributed their ideas to *The Dial*, a magazine edited first by Margaret Fuller, then by Emerson. Besides writing, Emerson lectured, going as far west as Wisconsin to preach his doctrine of self-reliance. Thoreau put the theory of rugged individualism into practice by playing the hermit at Walden. Bronson Alcott, the father of Louisa May, nearly starved his family to death in a similar back-to-nature experiment at "Fruitlands," a farm in Harvard, Massachusetts. George Ripley led a group—including, for a short time, Nathaniel Hawthorne—in an attempt at a community life of "plain living and high thinking" on Brook Farm, at Roxbury, just outside Boston. Men and women shared in the common work of plowing, milking, and baking. Between chores they gathered for intellectual discussions. But there were no experienced farmers in the group; the soil was poor; the socialistic system just wouldn't work; and finally a disastrous fire brought the enterprise to an end in 1846, after five years of trial.

There were other voices besides those of the transcendentalists in Boston, Concord, Salem, and Cambridge. These Liberals spoke out with the same dogmatic note of authority which they deplored in the Pope. They held romantic ideas about religion, democracy, the common man, slavery, science, and human progress. They were all liberal thinkers, but of such independent minds that co-operation was impossible.

From these ranks stepped the leonine figure of Orestes Augustus Brownson (1803–1876). He had roared in turn for socialism, for deism, for transcendentalism. He had preached as a Presbyterian, as a Universalist, and as a Unitarian. At last he found his meat in the Catholic Church. He was converted and used his vigorous voice and violent pen in defense of the faith. Brownson remained as individualistic as the intellectuals he had separated from; the authority of the Church guided, but did not silence him. *Brownson's Quarterly Review* became a forceful influence in the thought of the times.

Most intellectuals of the period disdained Calvinism and its dogma; Unitarianism had become the fashionable religion in New England. It was much like transcendentalism and had prepared the New England mind for that philosophy. Its doctrines made life seem pleasant and thought less anxious. Yet in spite of the death of Puritan dogma, the influence of Puritan morality lived on. It dressed literature with artificial situations and pious reflections. In reaction against the romantic tendency toward paganism, Catholic authors, too, were led into the error of over-emphasizing the didactic or teaching element. The tendency was especially noticeable in fiction. Catholics filled their short stories and novels with explanations of doctrine and refutations of heresy in order to offset the effects of anti-Catholic writers.

Though romantic doctrines were upsetting to religious thought, the movement made certain wholesome contributions to literature. The romanticists were agreed upon the importance of feeling in art. It is true that the less gifted writers opened flood-gates of sentimentality and that even men like Longfellow and Whittier and Lowell had difficulty keeping emotions strong and deep. Yet more surely than ever before, American poetry was reflecting quiet, intense feeling.

The romanticists also led men to a fresh appreciation of the beauty of life, especially of the beauties of nature; and literature was filled with delightful images drawn from the woods and mountains and sea and shore.

Moreover, they encouraged the use of the imagination and an open and unfolding mind. They took delight in the lore of olden times and foreign lands. Longfellow wrote about the early Indians, and about the fair land of Acadia. Like Hawthorne and Whittier, he retold the legends of early New England. Like Lowell he found beauty in the Catholic Middle Ages and in the earlier and later culture of Western Europe. William Prescott and Francis Parkman captured the romance of the past in glowing histories. True, they occasionally showed prejudice against Catholicism, which they never came to understand; still Prescott won his fame with his histories of Catholic Spain in the Old and New World. Parkman seized upon his own country's history, and filled his volumes with the exciting stories of French-English and Indian Wars in the American wilderness.

The imagination turned, too, to the mysterious and preternatural. As Poe had turned to the unreal out of sheer delight, so did Fitz-James O'Brien—an Irish-born Catholic who wrote stories uncanny and weird. This tendency was especially apparent in the short stories and in some of the poetry of the period.

Only in the South did men seem to miss the kindling spirit of the times. In the years before the war, Southern literature lagged far behind the production of cotton and tobacco. Plantations covered the land. Plantation owners led an almost feudal life with slaves to do their bidding. Hunting, horse racing, cockfighting, and barbecues engrossed their leisure. Culture these gentlemen had, but their interests at the moment were not literary. They were interested in politics, and public speaking flourished. The Southerner had a ready, fluent tongue, and he used it to debate the burning issues of the day. Henry Clay, John Calhoun, Robert Hayne—these men were idolized in Dixie as was Daniel Webster in the North.

# THE FIRST AMERICAN NOVELS

The first American novel had been written as the Revolutionary period was draw-ing to a close. Its author, Charles Brockden Brown, was a talented but moody young man who had been born four years before the signing of the Declaration of Independence and who died two years before the beginning of the War of 1812. His writing was hampered by ill health; but he produced four full-length novels that pointed the way to the novelists who were to follow—Cooper, Simms, and Hawthorne. Brown used American scenes and characters; he created situations of mystery and horror; and he enjoyed analyzing the feelings of his characters. The best of his novels was his first—*Wieland*. But in it, as in the others, there were weaknesses. His works are forgotten today, except by the special student.

Such has not been the case with the novelists who followed him. The works of James Fenimore Cooper are still read, and with reason. They have a backwoods setting that is convincingly realistic. They have for their characters American trap-pers and Indians. Many of the events are from history. In truth, Cooper did for America what Sir Walter Scott was doing for Great Britain; he demonstrated the fact that history is one of the best sources for the materials of fiction. The appear-ance of *The Spy* in 1821 announced to the world that the American novel was ready to take its place on the shelves of lasting literature. Another Revolutionary tale, *The Pilot*, is equally good. Then came the Leatherstocking series, comprising five novels: *The Deerslayer*, *The Last of the Mohicans*, *The Pathfinder*, *The Pioneers*, and *The Prairie*.

Cooper's lead in the historical romance was followed by the gifted South Caro-linian, William Gilmore Simms. Simms wrote over thirty novels, most of them on Colonial and Revolutionary themes. His best known work is *The Yemassee*, a story of the conflicts between the Southern colonists and the Indians. But Simms did not limit himself to the Southern scene. His stories of exploration, pioneering, and Indian fighting ranged up and down the continent.

And then, to prove that the American novel need not depend upon history for its theme, Hawthorne produced *The Scarlet Letter*. The setting, it is true, is his-torical—a small town in one of the Northern colonies; but the characters are not the men and women of recorded fame, nor are the events such as determined the growth of a nation. The characters are a young wife, a mysterious absent husband, and a young minister. The material of the story is partly the incidents that en-tangle the three lives and even more largely the effects of those incidents upon the personalities of the characters. In other words, it is a psychological novel of re-markable power—one of the greatest in our literature. Two other novels show a similar treatment, *The House of the Seven Gables* and *The Marble Faun*. In these longer works as in his short stories, Hawthorne is concerned with developing a defi-nite theme; he is interested primarily in the souls of men; and he uses external de-vices—a letter, a house, a veil—as symbols of spiritual incidents. These longer works of Hawthorne are not always happy; but they are strong, and true at least to some phases of life. They still rank among the best of our novels.

# THE BIRTH OF THE AMERICAN SHORT STORY

The Puritan belief that life was "real" and "earnest" had laid a restricting hand on fiction. Literature for pure pleasure had been frowned down. But by the early 1800's Puritan influence was a tradition—hardly more.

When Washington Irving began experimenting with literature as a profession, it was with the idea that he could entertain himself and others as he earned his living. So he began spinning leisurely yarns and sketching tranquil, often sentimental, scenes. Probably quite by accident the short story emerged. Irving's method had been to retell in semihumorous style the more entertaining legends of the Dutch settlers of New York State. But he became particularly interested in one— the story of a man who slept for twenty years—and in telling the tale, he developed a unity of effect which marked the work as something more than a retold legend. The same thing happened when he wrote "The Legend of Sleepy Hollow," "The Devil and Tom Walker," and "The Specter Bridegroom."

We know today that these four bits of fiction are short stories. Each has a concise, well-developed plot; a singleness of impression derived from a blend of character and place; and a skillful manipulation of material to shape a satisfying climax and conclusion. One other tale is kept from the list only by its length—"Woolfert Webber, or Golden Dreams," which is really a delightful novelette. Most of Irving's short prose shows a vagueness of form that places it in the classification of the short essay or the less pretentious "sketch." But "Rip Van Winkle" and the other titles named above won for Irving his distinction as "the father of the American short story." His settings were definite localities, peopled with real persons or with the whimsies of their own fancies—the headless horseman of a credulous countryside or a specter bridegroom who turned out to be more bridegroom than ghost. And knowing human nature, he added humor to his characters and situations. His stories are rich in descriptive material—scenery, people, manners, dress—but are lacking in rapid movement and realistic dialogue. Nevertheless, they still have a strong appeal and are models of beautiful English prose.

Hawthorne and Poe took up the new form and perfected some definite techniques. Hawthorne's Puritanical background and his brooding, meditative spirit would not let him write a story for the story's sake. He seems to have begun each story with a theme—a clear-cut thought about some element of human life—around which he built his structure. The unity of his fiction lies in a oneness of thought or idea. Yet so artistically did Hawthorne work, that there is no obvious moralizing. He does not preach; he suggests a thought. His studies are psychological, rather than merely ethical or moral. He has a stern, prophetic tone and his stories are somber and moody, but not horrible or gruesome.

Poe stands apart in our early American literature—mysterious, erratic, and abnormal. Unlike many of the New England writers, he had no political ax to grind. Writing to him was an art. He worked out his own philosophy of beauty: literature must express the beautiful, not preach sermons, not hammer philosophic or economic theories. Unfortunately, his wretched life and morbid temperament turned his great gift of musical expression to moody and grotesque tones which, while they may thrill us, also depress us with a sense of his own despair.

To step from one of Irving's tales, like "Rip Van Winkle" to Poe's "The Cask of Amontillado" is like stepping from one world into another. Where Irving played with the ghostly and legendary, Poe was a somber artist fascinated by the weird and macabre. Irving's phantoms were all in fun. Poe trafficked in horror and grimness and terror. Poe's stories are tense and dramatic. It was Poe's contention that the short story must be so compact that no single episode could be taken out without tearing the fabric of the whole. Poe worked for atmosphere, and dexterously selected and arranged details to produce each predestined effect. His singular handling of plot, character, and setting is the basis of modern technique in the short story. In his stories, as in his poems, *mood* is most important. Instead of developing an idea, he creates an emotional impression. He does it deliberately. As Hawthorne began with a theme, Poe began with a feeling. "The Pit and the Pendulum," "The Descent into the Maelstrom," "The Masque of the Red Death," "The Fall of the House of Usher"—each is a study in building up a situation to inspire terror, compressed fear, maudlin dissolution, or utter and weird depression. Whether or not the story is plausible is a matter of no concern. Meaning is subordinated to impression and feeling. Poe is the writer most often imitated by young people because his technique is so obvious and his mood so dramatic.

Poe added one important new type to the short story repertory—the detective story. When in 1841 his "The Murders in the Rue Morgue" appeared, the public applauded what was to become the model for the "Sherlock Holmes" type of story and for almost all detective fiction since.

In the works of the three story writers, there is reflected one characteristic of the romanticism which was dominating the literature of the time: the flair for the mysterious and occult. This particular romantic quality appears in one way or another in the works of all three men.

In Irving's works, it is an amused acceptance of the superstitions of others—especially of the New York Dutch. In every one of his stories there is a ghost or a goblin, which—however—the author obviously does not expect us to take seriously.

With Hawthorne, the preternatural is used deliberately as an aid to developing the theme of the story. There is usually just a touch of it: a drink which deludes four old people into thinking themselves young again, although a mirror still shows them wrinkled and haggard; or a heart of lime left among the ashes of a cruel man, indicating that his heart had been of marble instead of flesh and blood. The reader understands that these touches are symbolic—devices employed to represent an idea.

With Poe, it is a conscious piling up of weird or grotesque details to achieve a certain artistic effect. True, it is a distorted kind of art—like that of the impressionistic or surrealistic painter. But the popularity of Poe's works indicates that there is a kind of fascination in the horror story. The author's method appears at its best in "The Cask of Amontillado" and in the longer, strangely gruesome "The Fall of the House of Usher."

◇◇◇◇◇

# THE LEGEND OF THE
# MOOR'S LEGACY

## WASHINGTON IRVING

*For generations after the Moors withdrew from Spain, their once magnificent fortress-palace, the Alhambra, at Granada remained shrouded in mystery. Weird, misty legends drifted about it. Spanish peasants, rich only in imagination, whispered many a tale of buried treasure. Their poverty-pinched fingers itched at the thought of fabulous hidden wealth, but their knees knocked at the prospect of entering the shadowy place.*

*By 1829, some of the awful mystery had vanished; and Washington Irving was able to live for several months within the palace itself. One result of his visit was his collection of prose tales and sketches called* THE ALHAMBRA. *Especially entertaining is its "Legend of the Moor's Legacy" —a typical blending of Irving's wit, his delight in the legendary, and his mellow humor. The story tells how an act of charity, a nagging wife, and the loss of a donkey contrived to send a poor water carrier into the forbidding Alhambra. A magic parchment and taper were the "open sesame" for this latter-day Ali Baba and his Mohammedan partner; and they had not forty thieves, but three, to outwit in the venture—quite enough for heroes cut down to modern size. Did they find a treasure? Well, in the answer to that question lies the heart of the story.*

Just within the fortress of the Alhambra, in front of the royal palace, is a broad open esplanade,[1] called the place or square of the cisterns, so called from being undermined by reservoirs of water, hidden from sight, and which have existed from the time of the Moors. At one corner of this esplanade is a Moorish well, cut through the living rock to a great depth, the water of which is cold as ice and clear as crystal. The wells made by the Moors are always in repute, for it is well known what pains they took to penetrate to the purest and sweetest springs and fountains. The one of which we now speak is famous throughout Granada, insomuch that water carriers, some bearing great water jars on their shoulders, others driving asses before them, laden with earthen vessels, are ascending and descending the steep woody avenues of the Alhambra from early dawn until a late hour of the night.

Fountains and wells, ever since the Scriptural days, have been noted gossiping places in hot climates, and at the well in question there is a kind of perpetual club kept up during the livelong day, by the invalids, old women, and other curious, do-nothing folk of the fortress, who sit here on the stone benches under an awning spread over the well to shelter the tollgatherer from the sun, and dawdle over the gossip of the fortress, and question every water carrier that arrives about the news of the city, and make long comments on everything they hear and see. Not an hour of the day but loitering housewives and idle maidservants may be seen, lingering with pitcher on head or in hand, to hear the last of the endless tattle of these worthies.

Among the water carriers who once resorted to this well there was a sturdy,

[1] ESPLANADE—A level open space before a fortress or along a waterside, used for taking walks.

strong-backed, bandy-legged [2] little fellow, named Pedro Gil, but called Peregil for shortness. Being a water carrier, he was a Gallego, or native of Gallicia, of course. Nature seems to have formed races of men as she has of animals for different kinds of drudgery. In France the shoeblacks are all Savoyards,[3] the porters of hotels all Swiss, and in the days of hoops and hair powder in England, no man could give the regular swing to a sedan chair, but a bog-trotting Irishman. So in Spain the carriers of water and bearers of burdens are all sturdy little natives of Gallicia. No man says, "Get me a porter," but, "Call a Gallego."

To return from this digression. Peregil the Gallego had begun business with merely a great earthen jar, which he carried upon his shoulder; by degrees he rose in the world, and was enabled to purchase an assistant of a correspondent class of animals, being a stout shaggy-haired donkey. On each side of this long-eared aid-de-camp, in a kind of pannier,[4] were slung his water jars covered with fig leaves to protect them from the sun. There was not a more industrious water carrier in all Granada, nor one more merry withal. The streets rang with his cheerful voice as he trudged after his donkey, singing forth the usual summer note that resounds through the Spanish towns: "Who wants water—water colder than snow—who wants water from the well of the Alhambra—cold as ice and clear as crystal?" When he served a customer with a sparkling glass, it was always with a pleasant word that caused a smile, and if, perchance, it was a comely dame, or dimpling damsel,

it was always with a sly leer and a compliment to her beauty that was irresistible. Thus Peregil the Gallego was noted throughout all Granada for being one of the civilest, pleasantest, and happiest of mortals. Yet it is not he who sings loudest and jokes most that has the lightest heart. Under all this air of merriment, honest Peregil had his cares and troubles. He had a large family of ragged children to support, who were hungry and clamorous as a nest of young swallows, and beset him with their outcries for food whenever he came home of an evening. He had a helpmate, too, who was anything but a help to him. She had been a village beauty before marriage, noted for her skill at dancing the bolero and rattling the castanets, and she still retained her early propensities, spending the hard earnings of honest Peregil in frippery, and laying the very donkey under requisition for junketing [5] parties into the country on Sundays, and saints' days, and those innumerable holidays which are rather more numerous in Spain than the days of the week. With all this she was a little of a slattern,[6] something more of a lie-a-bed, and, above all, a gossip of the first water; neglecting house, household, and everything else, to loiter slipshod in the houses of her gossip neighbors.

He, however, who tempers the wind to the shorn lamb, accommodates the yoke of matrimony to the submissive neck. Peregil bore all the heavy dispensations of wife and children with as meek a spirit as his donkey bore the water jars; and, however he might shake his ears in private, never ventured to question the household virtues of his slattern spouse.

He loved his children too, even as an

[2] BANDY-LEGGED—Bow-legged.

[3] SAVOYARDS—Natives of Savoy, in the southeastern part of France.

[4] PANNIER (păn'yĕr)—A basket for carrying a load on the back.

[5] JUNKETING—Picknicking.

[6] SLATTERN—A negligent or untidy woman.

owl loves its owlets, seeing in them his own image multiplied and perpetuated, for they were a sturdy, long-backed, bandy-legged little brood. The great pleasure of honest Peregil was, whenever he could afford himself a scanty holiday and had a handful of maravedis [7] to spare, to take the whole litter forth with him, some in his arms, some tugging at his skirts, and some trudging at his heels, and to treat them to a gambol among the orchards of the vega,[8] while his wife was dancing with her holiday friends in the *angosturas* of the Darro.[9]

It was a late hour one summer night, and most of the water carriers had desisted from their toils. The day had been uncommonly sultry; the night was one of those delicious moonlights, which tempt the inhabitants of southern climes to indemnify themselves for the heat and inaction of the day, by lingering in the open air and enjoying its tempered sweetness until after midnight. Customers for water were therefore still abroad. Peregil, like a considerate, painstaking father, thought of his hungry children. "One more journey to the well," said he to himself, "to earn a Sunday's *puchero* [10] for the little ones." So saying, he trudged manfully up the steep avenue of the Alhambra, singing as he went, and now and then bestowing a hearty thwack with a cudgel on the flanks of his donkey, either by way of cadence to the song, or refreshment to

[7] MARAVEDIS (măr′a·vā′dĭs)—A former Spanish coin worth about two-fifths of a cent.
[8] VEGA—The extensive and fertile plain south and west of the city.
[9] ANGOSTURAS OF THE DARRO (ăng′gŏs·tū′-räs)—The Darro is a stream that enters Granada on the east, flows west for about a mile and then turns sharply south to join the Xenil (see note 14). An angostura is a gorge or ravine near which would be a level place used for picnicking.
[10] *Puchero* (pōō·chär′o)—Porridge; thick broth or stew.

the animal: for dry blows serve in lieu of provender in Spain, for all beasts of burden.

When arrived at the well, he found it deserted by everyone except a solitary stranger in Moorish garb, seated on a stone bench in the moonlight. Peregil paused at first, and regarded him with surprise, not unmixed with awe, but the Moor feebly beckoned him to approach.

"I am faint and ill," said he; "aid me to return to the city, and I will pay thee double what thou couldst gain by thy jars of water."

The honest heart of the little water carrier was touched with compassion at the appeal of the stranger. "God forbid," said he, "that I should ask fee or reward for doing a common act of humanity."

He accordingly helped the Moor on his donkey, and set off slowly for Granada, the poor Moslem being so weak that it was necessary to hold him on the animal to keep him from falling to the earth.

When they entered the city, the water carrier demanded whither he should conduct him. "Alas!" said the Moor, faintly, "I have neither home nor habitation. I am a stranger in the land. Suffer me to lay my head this night beneath thy roof, and thou shalt be amply repaid."

Honest Peregil thus saw himself unexpectedly saddled with an infidel guest, but he was too humane to refuse a night's shelter to a fellow-being in so forlorn a plight; so he conducted the Moor to his dwelling. The children, who had sallied forth, openmouthed as usual, on hearing the tramp of the donkey, ran back with affright, when they beheld the turbaned stranger, and hid themselves behind their mother. The latter stepped forth intrepidly, like a ruffling hen before her brood, when a vagrant dog approaches.

"What infidel companion," cried she, "is this you have brought home at this late hour, to draw upon us the eyes of the Inquisition?" [11]

"Be quiet, wife," replied the Gallego, "here is a poor sick stranger, without friend or home: wouldst thou turn him forth to perish in the streets?"

The wife would still have remonstrated, for although she lived in a hovel, she was a furious stickler for the credit of her house; the little water carrier, however, for once was stiff-necked, and refused to bend beneath the yoke. He assisted the poor Moslem to alight, and spread a mat and a sheepskin for him, on the ground, in the coolest part of the house; being the only kind of bed that his poverty afforded.

In a little while the Moor was seized with violent convulsions, which defied all the ministering skill of the simple water carrier. The eye of the poor patient acknowledged his kindness. During an interval of his fits he called him to his side, and addressing him in a low voice; "My end," said he, "I fear is at hand. If I die I bequeath you this box as a reward for your charity." So saying, he opened his cloak, and showed a small box of sandalwood,[12] strapped round his body.

"God grant, my friend," replied the worthy little Gallego, "that you may live many years to enjoy your treasure, whatever it may be."

The Moor shook his head; he laid his hand upon the box, and would have said something more concerning it, but his convulsions returned with increased violence, and in a little while he expired.

The water carrier's wife was now as one distracted. "This comes," said she, "of your foolish good nature, always running into scrapes to oblige others. What will become of us when this corpse is found in our house? We shall be sent to prison as murderers; and if we escape with our lives, shall be ruined by notaries and alguazils." [13]

Poor Peregil was in equal tribulation, and almost repented himself of having done a good deed. At length a thought struck him. "It is not yet day," said he. "I can convey the dead body out of the city and bury it in the sands on the banks of the Xenil.[14] No one saw the Moor enter our dwelling, and no one will know anything of his death." So said, so done. The wife aided him. They rolled the body of the unfortunate Moslem in the mat on which he had expired, laid it across the ass, and Peregil set out with it for the banks of the river.

As ill luck would have it, there lived opposite to the water carrier a barber, named Pedrillo Pedrugo, one of the most prying, tattling, mischief-making, of his gossipy tribe. He was a weasel-faced, spider-legged varlet, supple [15] and insinuating; [16] the famous Barber of

---

[11] INQUISITION—The ecclesiastical court that tried suspected heretics and handed the guilty over to the state for punishment. Mohammedans and Jews were highly distrusted in Spain since not a few of them pretended to be converted. Some of the hypocritical converts even became bishops.

[12] SANDALWOOD—The fragrant wood of an East Indian tree.

[13] NOTARIES AND ALGUAZILS (ăl'gwȧ·zēlz′) —A notary is an officer with power to administer oaths, take testimony, and draw up legal papers. An alguazil is a constable or policeman.

[14] XENIL (ksĕn·ĭl′)—The westward flowing river which forms the southern boundary of the city.

[15] SUPPLE—Easily bent or influenced, flexible, pliant.

[16] INSINUATING—Here, one who worms his way into another's confidence or favor by artful, indirect means.

Seville [17] could not surpass him for his universal knowledge of the affairs of others, and he had no more power of retention than a sieve. It was said that he slept but with one eye at a time, and kept one ear uncovered, so that, even in his sleep, he might see and hear all that was going on. Certain it is, he was a sort of scandalous chronicle for the quidnuncs [18] of Granada, and had more customers than all the rest of the fraternity.

This meddlesome barber heard Peregil arrive at an unusual hour at night, and the exclamations of his wife and children. His head was instantly popped out of a little window which served him as a lookout, and he saw his neighbor assist a man in Moorish garb into his dwelling. This was so strange an occurrence that Pedrillo Pedrugo slept not a wink that night—every five minutes he was at his loophole, watching the lights that gleamed through the chinks of his neighbor's door, and before daylight he beheld Peregil sally forth with his donkey unusually laden.

The inquisitive barber was in a fidget; he slipped on his clothes, and, stealing forth silently, followed the water carrier at a distance, until he saw him dig a hole in the sandy bank of the Xenil, and bury something that had the appearance of a dead body.

The barber hied him home and fidgeted about his shop, setting everything upside down, until sunrise. He then took a basin under his arm, and sallied forth to the house of his daily customer, the Alcalde.[19]

[17] BARBER OF SEVILLE—The Frenchman Beaumarchais wrote a drama, *The Barber of Seville* (1775). The barber, Figaro, is a typically clever, daring, and cunning rascal.

[18] QUIDNUNC (kwĭd'nŭngk)—From the Latin: *quid nunc?*: What now? What's the news? Therefore, a busybody or gossip.

[19] ALCALDE (äl·käl'då)—Chief magistrate; mayor.

The Alcalde was just risen. Pedrillo Pedrugo seated him in a chair, threw a napkin round his neck, put a basin of hot water under his chin, and began to mollify his beard with his fingers.

"Strange doings," said Pedrugo, who played barber and newsmonger at the same time. "Strange doings! Robbery, and murder, and burial, all in one night!"

"Hey? How? What is that you say?" cried the Alcalde.

"I say," replied the barber, rubbing a piece of soap over the nose and mouth of the dignitary, for a Spanish barber disdains to employ a brush; "I say that Peregil the Gallego has robbed and murdered a Moorish Mussulman, and buried him this blessed night,—accursed be the night for the same!"

"But how do you know all this?" demanded the Alcalde.

"Be patient, Señor, and you shall hear all about it," replied Pedrillo, taking him by the nose and sliding a razor over his cheek. He then recounted all that he had seen, going through both operations at the same time, shaving his beard, washing his chin, and wiping him dry with a dirty napkin, while he was robbing, murdering, and burying the Moslem.

Now it so happened that this Alcalde was one of the most overbearing, and at the same time most griping and corrupt curmudgeons [20] in all Granada. It could not be denied, however, that he set a high value upon justice, for he sold it at its weight in gold. He presumed the case in point to be one of murder and robbery; doubtless there must be rich spoil; how was it to be secured into the legitimate hands of the law? for as to merely entrapping the delinquent—that

[20] CURMUDGEONS (kẽr·mŭj'ŭnz)—Miserly, rude, ungracious persons.

would be feeding the gallows; but entrapping the booty—that would be enriching the judge; and such, according to his creed, was the great end of justice. So thinking, he summoned to his presence his trustiest alguazil; a gaunt, hungry-looking varlet, clad, according to the custom of his order, in the ancient Spanish garb—a broad black beaver, turned up at its sides; a quaint ruff, a small black cloak dangling from his shoulders; rusty black underclothes that set off his spare wiry frame; while in his hand he bore a slender white wand, the dreaded insignia of his office. Such was the legal bloodhound of the ancient Spanish breed, that he put upon the traces of the unlucky water carrier; and such was his speed and certainty that he was upon the haunches of poor Peregil before he had returned to his dwelling, and brought both him and his donkey before the dispenser of justice.

The Alcalde bent upon him one of the most terrific frowns. "Hark ye, culprit," roared he in a voice that made the knees of the little Gallego smite together,—"Hark, ye culprit! there is no need of denying thy guilt: everything is known to me. A gallows is the proper reward for the crime thou hast committed, but I am merciful, and readily listen to reason. The man that has been murdered in thy house was a Moor, an infidel, the enemy of our faith. It was doubtless in a fit of religious zeal that thou hast slain him. I will be indulgent, therefore; render up the property of which thou hast robbed him, and we will hush the matter up."

The poor water carrier called upon all the saints to witness his innocence; alas! not one of them appeared, and if they had, the Alcalde would have disbelieved the whole calendar. The water carrier related the whole story of the dying Moor with the straightforward simplicity of truth, but it was all in vain; "Wilt thou persist in saying," demanded the judge, "that this Moslem had neither gold nor jewels, which were the object of thy cupidity?"

"As I hoped to be saved, your worship," replied the water carrier, "he had nothing but a small box of sandalwood, which he bequeathed to me in reward for my services."

"A box of sandalwood! a box of sandalwood!" exclaimed the Alcalde, his eyes sparkling at the idea of precious jewels, "and where is this box? where have you concealed it?"

"An [21] it please your grace," replied the water carrier, "it is in one of the panniers of my mule, and heartily at the service of your worship."

He had hardly spoken the words when the keen alguazil darted off and reappeared in an instant with the mysterious box of sandalwood. The Alcalde opened it with an eager and trembling hand; all pressed forward to gaze upon the treasure it was expected to contain; when, to their disappointment, nothing appeared within but a parchment scroll, covered with Arabic characters, and an end of a waxen taper!

When there is nothing to be gained by the conviction of a prisoner, justice, even in Spain is apt to be impartial. The Alcalde, having recovered from his disappointment and found that there was really no booty in the case, now listened dispassionately to the explanation of the water carrier, which was corroborated by the testimony of his wife. Being convinced, therefore, of his innocence, he discharged him from arrest; nay more, he permitted him to carry off the Moor's legacy, the box of sandalwood and its contents, as the well-

[21] AN—Archaic for *and if*, or *if*.

merited reward of his humanity; but he retained his donkey in payment of cost and charges.

Behold the unfortunate little Gallego reduced once more to the necessity of being his own water carrier, and trudging up to the well of the Alhambra with a great earthen jar upon his shoulder. As he toiled up the hill in the heat of a summer noon his usual good humor forsook him. "Dog of an Alcalde!" would he cry, "to rob a poor man of the means of his subsistence—of the best friend he had in the world!" And then, at the remembrance of the beloved companion of his labors, all the kindness of his nature would break forth. "Ah, donkey of my heart!" would he exclaim, resting his burden on a stone, and wiping the sweat from his brow, "Ah, donkey of my heart! I warrant thee thou thinkest of thy old master! I warrant me thou missest the water jars—poor beast!"

To add to his afflictions his wife received him, on his return home, with whimperings and repinings; she had clearly the vantage ground of him, having warned him not to commit the egregious act of hospitality which had brought on him all these misfortunes, and like a knowing woman, she took every occasion to throw her superior sagacity in his teeth. If her children lacked food, or needed a new garment, she could answer with a sneer, "Go to your father; he is heir to king Chico of the Alhambra. Ask him to help you out of the Moor's strong box."

Was ever poor mortal so soundly punished, for having done a good action! The unlucky Peregil was grieved in flesh and spirit, but still he bore meekly with the railings of his spouse. At length one evening, when, after a hot day's toil, she taunted him in the usual manner, he lost all patience. He did not venture to retort upon her, but his eye rested upon the box of sandalwood, which lay on a shelf with lid half open, as if laughing in mockery at his vexation. Seizing it up he dashed it with indignation to the floor. "Unlucky was the day that I ever set eyes on thee," he cried, "or sheltered thy master beneath my roof."

As the box struck the floor the lid flew wide open, and the parchment scroll rolled forth. Peregil sat regarding the scroll for some time in moody silence. At length rallying his ideas, "Who knows," thought he, "but this writing may be of some importance, as the Moor seems to have guarded it with such care." Picking it up, therefore, he put it in his bosom, and the next morning, as he was crying water through the streets, he stopped at the shop of a Moor, a native of Tangiers, who sold trinkets and perfumery in the Zacatin,[22] and asked him to explain the contents.

The Moor read the scroll attentively, then stroked his beard and smiled. "This manuscript," said he, "is a form of incantation for the recovery of hidden treasure that is under the power of enchantment. It is said to have such virtue that the strongest bolts and bars, nay the adamantine[23] rock itself will yield before it."

"Bah!" cried the little Gallego, "what is all that to me? I am no enchanter, and know nothing of buried treasure." So saying he shouldered his water jar, left the scroll in the hands of the Moor, and trudged forward on his daily rounds.

That evening, however, as he rested himself about twilight at the well of the Alhambra, he found a number of gossips assembled at the place, and their conversation, as is not unusual at that

[22] ZACATIN (zä·kä·tēēn')—The market street in Granada.
[23] ADAMANTINE—Of impenetrable hardness.

shadowy hour, turned upon old tales and traditions of a supernatural nature. Being all poor as rats, they dwelt with peculiar fondness upon the popular theme of enchanted riches left by the Moors in various parts of the Alhambra. Above all, they concurred in the belief that there were great treasures buried deep in the earth under the tower of the Seven Floors.

These stories made an unusual impression on the mind of the honest Peregil, and they sank deeper and deeper into his thought as he returned alone down the darkling avenues. "If, after all, there should be treasure hid beneath that tower—and if the scroll I left with the Moor should enable me to get at it!" In the sudden ecstasy of the thought he had well nigh let fall his water jar.

That night he tumbled and tossed, and could scarcely get a wink of sleep for the thoughts that were bewildering his brain. Bright and early, he repaired to the shop of the Moor, and told him all that was passing in his mind. "You can read Arabic," said he, "suppose we go together to the tower and try the effect of the charm; if it fails we are no worse off than before, but if it succeeds we will share equally all the treasure we may discover."

"Hold," replied the Moslem, "this writing is not sufficient of itself; it must be read at midnight, by the light of a taper singularly compounded and prepared, the ingredients of which are not within my reach. Without such a taper the scroll is of no avail."

"Say no more!" cried the little Gallego. "I have such a taper at hand and will bring it here in a moment." So saying he hastened home, and soon returned with the end of yellow wax taper that he had found in the box of sandalwood.

The Moor felt it and smelt of it. "Here are rare and costly perfumes," said he, "combined with this yellow wax. This is the kind of taper specified in the scroll. While this burns, the strongest walls and most secret caverns will remain open; woe to him, however, who lingers within until it be extinguished. He will remain enchanted with the treasure."

It was now agreed between them to try the charm that very night. At a late hour, therefore, when nothing was stirring but bats and owls, they ascended the woody hill of the Alhambra, and approached that awful tower, shrouded by trees and rendered formidable by so many traditionary tales.

By the light of a lantern, they groped their way through bushes, and over fallen stones, to the door of a vault beneath the tower. With fear and trembling they descended a flight of steps cut into the rock. It led to an empty chamber, damp and drear, from which another flight of steps led to a deeper vault. In this way they descended four several flights, leading into as many vaults, one below the other, but the floor of the fourth was solid, and though, according to tradition, there remained three vaults still below, it was said to be impossible to penetrate farther, the residue being shut up by strong enchantment. The air of this vault was damp and chilly, and had an earthy smell, and the light scarce cast forth any rays. They paused here for a time in breathless suspense, until they faintly heard the clock of the watchtower strike midnight; upon this they lit the waxen taper, which diffused an odor of myrrh, and frankincense, and storax.[24]

The Moor began to read in a hurried voice. He had scarce finished, when

[24] STORAX—A gum with the odor of vanilla.

there was a noise as of subterraneous thunder. The earth shook, and the floor yawning open disclosed a flight of steps. Trembling with awe they descended, and by the light of the lantern found themselves in another vault, covered with Arabic inscriptions. In the center stood a great chest, secured with seven bands of steel, at each end of which sat an enchanted Moor in armor, but motionless as a statue, being controlled by the power of the incantation. Before the chest were several jars filled with gold and silver and precious stones. In the largest of these they thrust their arms up to the elbow, and at every dip hauled forth hands full of broad yellow pieces of Moorish gold, or bracelets and ornaments of the same precious metal, while occasionally a necklace of Oriental pearl would stick to their fingers. Still they trembled and breathed short while cramming their pockets with the spoils;

and cast many a fearful glance at the two enchanted Moors, who sat grim and motionless, glaring upon them with unwinking eyes. At length, struck with sudden panic at some fancied noise, they both rushed up the staircase, tumbled over one another into the upper apartment, overturned and extinguished the waxen taper, and the pavement again closed with a thundering sound.

Filled with dismay, they did not pause until they had groped their way out of the tower, and beheld the stars shining through the trees. Then seating themselves upon the grass, they divided the spoil, determining to content themselves for the present with this mere skimming of the jars, but to return on some future night and drain them to the bottom. To make sure of each other's good faith, also, they divided the talismans between them, one retaining the scroll and the other the taper;

this done, they set off with light hearts and well-lined pockets for Granada.

As they wended their way down the hill, the shrewd Moor whispered a word of counsel in the ear of the simple little water carrier.

"Friend Peregil," said he, "all this affair must be kept a profound secret until we have secured the treasure and conveyed it out of harm's way. If a whisper of it gets to the ear of the Alcalde we are undone!"

"Certainly!" replied the Gallego; "nothing can be more true."

"Friend Peregil," said the Moor, "you are a discreet man, and I make no doubt can keep a secret; but—you have a wife—"

"She shall not know a word of it!" replied the little water carrier sturdily.

"Enough," said the Moor, "I depend upon thy discretion and thy promise."

Never was promise more positive and sincere; but alas! what man can keep a secret from his wife? Certainly not such a one as Peregil the water carrier, who was one of the most loving and tractable of husbands. On his return home he found his wife moping in a corner.

"Mighty well!" cried she, as he entered; "you've come at last; after rambling about until this hour of the night. I wonder you have not brought home another Moor as a housemate." Then bursting into tears she began to wring her hands and smite her breast. "Unhappy woman that I am!" exclaimed she, "what will become of me! My house stripped and plundered by lawyers and alguazils; my husband a do-nogood that no longer brings home bread to his family, but goes rambling about, day and night, with infidel Moors. Oh, my children! my children! what will become of us; we shall all have to beg in the streets!"

Honest Peregil was so moved by the distress of his spouse, that he could not help whimpering also. His heart was as full as his pocket, and not to be restrained. Thrusting his hand into the latter he hauled forth three or four broad gold pieces and slipped them into her bosom. The poor woman stared with astonishment, and could not understand the meaning of this golden shower. Before she could recover her surprise, the little Gallego drew forth a chain of gold and dangled it before her, capering with exultation, his mouth distended from ear to ear.

"Holy Virgin protect us!" exclaimed the wife. "What hast thou been doing, Peregil? Surely thou hast not been committing murder and robbery!"

The idea scarce entered the brain of the poor woman than it became a certainty with her. She saw a prison and a gallows in the distance, and a little bandy-legged Gallego hanging pendent from it; and, overcome by the horrors conjured up by her imagination, fell into violent hysterics.

What could the poor man do? He had no other means of pacifying his wife and dispelling the phantoms of her fancy, than by relating the whole story of his good fortune. This, however, he did not do until he had exacted from her the most solemn promise to keep it a profound secret from every living being.

To describe her joy would be impossible. She flung her arms round the neck of her husband, and almost strangled him with her caresses. "Now, wife!" exclaimed the little man with honest exultation, "What say you now to the Moor's legacy? Henceforth never abuse me for helping a fellow creature in distress."

The honest Gallego retired to his

sheepskin mat, and slept as soundly as if on a bed of down. Not so his wife. She emptied the whole contents of his pockets upon the mat, and sat counting gold pieces of Arabic coin, trying on necklaces and earrings, and fancying the figure she should one day make when permitted to enjoy her riches.

On the following morning the honest Gallego took a broad golden coin, and repaired with it to a jeweller's shop in the Zacatin to offer it for sale; pretending to have found it among the ruins of the Alhambra. The jeweller saw that it had an Arabic inscription and was of the purest gold; he offered, however, but a third of its value, with which the water carrier was perfectly content. Peregil now bought new clothes for his little flock, and all kinds of toys, together with ample provisions for a hearty meal, and returning to his dwelling set all his children dancing around him, while he capered in the midst, the happiest of fathers.

The wife of the water carrier kept her promise of secrecy with surprising strictness. For a whole day and a half she went about with a look of mystery and a heart swelling almost to bursting, yet she held her peace, though surrounded by her gossips. It is true she could not help giving herself a few airs, apologized for her ragged dress, and talked of ordering a new basquiña [25] all trimmed with gold lace and bugles, [26] and a new lace mantilla. [27] She threw out hints of her husband's intention of leaving off his trade of water-carrying, as it did not altogether agree with his health. In fact she thought they should all retire to the country for the summer, that the children might have the benefit of the mountain air, for there was no living in the city in this sultry season.

The neighbors stared at each other, and thought the poor woman had lost her wits, and her airs and graces and elegant pretensions were the theme of universal scoffing and merriment among her friends, the moment her back was turned.

If she restrained herself abroad, however, she indemnified herself at home, and, putting a string of rich Oriental pearls round her neck, Moorish bracelets on her arms; an aigrette [28] of diamonds on her head, sailed backwards and forwards in her slattern rags about the room, now and then stopping to admire herself in a broken mirror. Nay, in the impulse of her single vanity, she could not resist on one occasion showing herself at the window, to enjoy the effect of her finery on the passers-by.

As the fates would have it, Pedrillo Pedrugo, the meddlesome barber, was at this moment sitting idly in his shop on the opposite side of the street, when his ever watchful eye caught the sparkle of a diamond. In an instant he was at his loophole, reconnoitring the slattern spouse of the water carrier, decorated with the splendor of an eastern bride. No sooner had he taken an accurate inventory of her ornaments than he posted off with all speed to the Alcalde. In a little while the hungry alguazil was again on the scent, and before the day was over, the unfortunate Peregil was once more dragged into the presence of the judge.

"How is this, villain!" cried the Alcalde in a furious voice. "You told me that the infidel who died in your house left nothing behind but an empty coffer,

---

[25] BASQUIÑA (bàs·kēēn′yà)—A rich outer petticoat worn by Spanish women.
[26] BUGLES—Tube-shaped glass beads.
[27] MANTILLA—A lace shawl worn as a head-covering.

[28] AIGRETTE (â·grĕt′)—A tuft of feathers or gems worn on a headdress.

and now I hear of your wife flaunting in her rags decked out with pearls and diamonds. Wretch that thou art! prepare to render up the spoils of thy miserable victim, and to swing on the gallows that is already tired of waiting for thee."

The terrified water carrier fell on his knees, and made a full relation of the marvellous manner in which he had gained his wealth. The Alcalde, the alguazil, and the inquisitive barber listened with greedy ears to the Arabian tale of enchanted treasure. The alguazil was despatched to bring the Moor who had assisted in the incantation. The Moslem entered half frightened out of his wits at finding himself in the hands of the harpies [29] of the law. When he beheld the water carrier standing with sheepish look and downcast countenance, he comprehended the whole matter. "Miserable animal," said he, as he passed near him, "did I not warn thee against babbling to thy wife?"

The story of the Moor coincided exactly with that of his colleague; but the Alcalde affected to be slow of belief, and threw out menaces of imprisonment and rigorous investigation.

"Softly, good Señor Alcalde," said the Mussulman, who by this time had recovered his usual shrewdness and self-possession. "Let us not mar fortune's favors in the scramble for them. Nobody knows anything of this matter but ourselves; let us keep the secret. There is wealth enough in the cave to enrich us all. Promise a fair division, and all shall be produced; refuse, and the cave shall remain forever closed."

The Alcalde consulted apart with the

[29] HARPIES—In Greek and Roman mythology, filthy, plundering, winged monsters, half-women and half-birds. Hence, any extortioner or plunderer.

alguazil. The latter was an old fox in his profession. "Promise anything," said he, "until you get possession of the treasure. You may then seize upon the whole, and if he or his accomplice dare to murmur, threaten them with the fagot and the stake as infidels and sorcerers."

The Alcalde relished the advice. Smoothing his brow and turning to the Moor,—"This is a strange story," said he, "and may be true, but I must have ocular proof of it. This very night you must repeat the incantation in my presence. If there really be such treasure, we shall share it amicably between us, and say nothing further of the matter; if ye have deceived me, expect no mercy at my hands. In the meantime you must remain in custody."

The Moor and the water carrier cheerfully agreed to these conditions, satisfied that the event would prove the truth of their words.

Towards midnight the Alcalde sallied forth secretly, attended by the alguazil and the meddlesome barber, all strongly armed. They conducted the Moor and the water carrier as prisoners, and were provided with the stout donkey of the latter, to bear off the expected treasure. They arrived at the tower without being observed, and tying the donkey to a fig tree, descended into the fourth vault of the tower.

The scroll was produced, the yellow waxen taper lighted, and the Moor read the form of incantation. The earth trembled as before, and the pavement opened with a thundering sound, disclosing the narrow flight of steps. The Alcade, the alguazil, and the barber were struck aghast, and could not summon courage to descend. The Moor and the water carrier entered the lower vault and found the two Moors seated as before, silent and motionless. They removed two of the great jars filled with golden coin and precious stones. The water carrier bore them up one by one upon his shoulders, but though a strong-backed little man, and accustomed to carry burdens, he staggered beneath their weight, and found, when slung on each side of his donkey, they were as much as the animal could bear.

"Let us be content for the present," said the Moor; "here is as much treasure as we can carry off without being perceived, and enough to make us all wealthy to our heart's desire."

"Is there more treasure remaining behind?" demanded the Alcalde.

"The greatest prize of all," said the Moor; "a huge coffer, bound with bands of steel, and filled with pearls and precious stones."

"Let us have up the coffer by all means," cried the grasping Alcalde.

"I will descend for no more," said the Moor, doggedly. "Enough is enough for a reasonable man; more is superfluous."

"And I," said the water carrier, "will bring up no further burden to break the back of my poor donkey."

Finding commands, threats, and entreaties equally vain, the Alcalde turned to his two adherents. "Aid me," said he, "to bring up the coffer, and its contents shall be divided between us." So

saying he descended the steps, followed, with trembling reluctance, by the alguazil and the barber.

No sooner did the Moor behold them fairly earthed than he extinguished the yellow taper: the pavement closed with its usual crash, and the three worthies remained buried in its womb.

He then hastened up the different flights of steps, nor stopped until in the open air. The little water carrier followed him as fast as his short legs would permit.

"What hast thou done?" cried Peregil, as soon as he could recover breath. "The Alcade and the other two are shut up in the vault!"

"It is the will of Allah!" said the Moor, devoutly.

"And you will not release them?" demanded the Gallego.

"Allah forbid!" replied the Moor, smoothing his beard. "It is written in the book of fate that they shall remain enchanted until some future adventurer arrive to break the charm. The will of God be done!" So saying he hurled the end of the waxen taper far among the gloomy thickets of the glen.

There was now no remedy; so the Moor and the water carrier proceeded with the richly-laden donkey towards the city; nor could honest Peregil refrain from hugging and kissing his long-eared fellow-laborer, thus restored to him

from the clutches of the law; and, in fact, it is doubtful which gave the simple-hearted little man most joy at the moment, the gaining of the treasure or the recovery of the donkey.

The two partners in good luck divided their spoil amicably and fairly, except that the Moor, who had a little taste for trinketry, made out to get into his heap the most of the pearls and precious stones, and other baubles, but then he always gave the water carrier in lieu magnificent jewels of massy gold of five times the size, with which the latter was heartily content. They took care not to linger within reach of accidents, but made off to enjoy their wealth undisturbed in other countries. The Moor returned to Africa, to his native city of Tangiers, and the Gallego, with his wife, his children, and his donkey, made the best of his way to Portugal. Here, under the admonition and tuition of his wife, he became a personage of some consequence, for she made the worthy little man array his long body and short legs in doublet and hose, with a feather in his hat and a sword by his side; and, laying aside his familiar appellation of Peregil, assume the more sonorous title of Don Pedro Gil. His progeny grew up a thriving and merry-hearted, though short and bandy-legged generation; while Señora Gil, be-fringed, be-laced, and be-tasselled from her head to her heels, with glittering rings on every finger, became a model of slattern fashion and finery.

As to the Alcalde, and his adjuncts, they remained shut up under the great tower of the Seven Floors, and there they remain spellbound at the present day. Whenever there shall be a lack in Spain of pimping[31] barbers, sharking alguazils, and corrupt Alcaldes, they

[31] PIMPING—Small, mean, petty.

may be sought after; but if they have to wait until such time for their deliverance, there is danger of their enchantment enduring until doomsday.

◇◇◇◇◇◇◇◇◇◇◇◇◇◇◇◇◇◇◇◇◇◇◇◇◇◇◇◇◇◇

## FOR DISCUSSION

1. Where today, in the country and in the city, can you find the favorite gossiping places of men and women? Discuss the good and bad effects of such gatherings.

2. Why does a Catholic country like Spain have more frequent holidays than a non-Catholic country? Do you think "innumerable holidays" are impractical in a busy industrial country like ours? What advantages besides that of pleasurable relaxation does the commemoration of the saints' days offer us?

3. What does "to temper the wind to the shorn lamb" mean?

4. In what respects were Peregil and his donkey alike?

5. Why do Irving's characters stand out clearly in your imagination? Describe with a few adjectives the following characters: Peregil, his wife, the barber, the Alcalde, the alguazil. What was the chief vice or virtue of each of them?

6. What circumstances, following the loss of his donkey, led Peregil to seek his fortune with the help of the Moor?

7. What hints does the wife give her neighbors of her good fortune? Why do they not "catch on"?

8. What is the primary purpose of this story: to teach a moral lesson or to amuse the reader? Give reasons for your answer.

9. What elements of romanticism can you point out in this story?

## WORDS

1. Authors frequently use comparisons to enliven their writing. A striking comparison is often borrowed by others and used till it becomes hackneyed, well worn with use. The result is that it loses its

force. Which of the following sound new and fresh to you? Try to express the same ideas by other comparisons of your own.

a. Water: *cold as ice and clear as crystal.*
b. Children: *as hungry and clamorous as a nest of young swallows.*
c. Peregil's wife: *like a ruffling hen before her brood when a vagrant dog approaches.*
d. Peregil's family: *poor as rats.*
e. A busybody who has learned something new: *no more power of retention than a sieve.*

2. Answer the following questions by giving a definition of the *italicized* words.

a. What is the difference between a *comely* and a *homely* person?
b. In private schools students pay *tuition* and teachers give *tuition.*
c. How can a man asleep and a donkey awake both be *sonorous*?
d. Peregil's wife threw her superior

*sagacity* in his teeth. Would that be enough to knock his teeth out?

e. What is the particular *virtue* of your favorite book?

PROJECTS

1. Write a paragraph or a composition on the topic: "It is not he who sings loudest and jokes most that has the lightest heart." Use the fourth paragraph of Irving's story as a model.

2. Make a list of the instances in which Irving uses humor to describe the characters or events of the story or to comment on them. What is the predominant device he uses to effect his humor?

RELATED READING

*The Alhambra* contains many other stories of mystery and romance. It is hard to select the best. All of them are well worth reading.

◇◇◇◇◇

# DR. HEIDEGGER'S EXPERIMENT

## NATHANIEL HAWTHORNE

*You have heard the story of Ponce de Leon's fruitless search for the Fountain of Youth. In this story Hawthorne imagines that the magic water has actually been found. He creates an atmosphere quaintly homelike, though musty, as a setting for the magic. And into it he brings four aged but exceedingly lively characters.*

That very singular man, old Dr. Heidegger, once invited four venerable friends to meet him in his study. There were three white-bearded gentlemen, Mr. Medbourne, Colonel Killigrew, and Mr. Gascoigne, and a withered gentlewoman, whose name was the Widow Wycherly. They were all melancholy old creatures, who had been unfortunate in life, and whose greatest misfortune it was that they were not long ago in their graves. Mr. Medbourne, in the vigor of his age, had been a prosperous merchant, and had lost his all by a frantic speculation, and was now little better than a mendicant. Colonel Killigrew had wasted his best years, and his health and substance, in the pursuit of sinful pleasures, which had given birth to a brood of pains, such as the gout [1] and divers other torments of soul and body. Mr. Gascoigne was a ruined politician, a man of evil fame, or at least had been so, till time had buried him from the knowledge of the present generation and made him obscure instead of infamous. As for the Widow Wycherly, tradition tells us that she was a great beauty in her day; but, for a long while past, she had lived in deep seclusion on account of certain scandalous stories, which had prejudiced the gentry of the town against her. It is a circumstance worth mentioning, that each of these three old gentlemen, Mr. Medbourne, Colonel Killigrew, and Mr. Gascoigne, were early lovers of the Widow Wycherly and had once been on the point of cutting each other's throats for her sake. And, before proceeding farther, I will merely hint that Dr. Heidegger and all his four guests were sometimes thought to be a little beside themselves; as is not unfrequently the case with old people, when worried either by present troubles or woeful recollections.

"My dear old friends," said Dr. Heidegger, motioning them to be seated, "I am desirous of your assistance in one of those little experiments with which I amuse myself here in my study."

If all stories were true, Dr. Heidegger's study must have been a very curious place. It was a dim, old-fashioned chamber, festooned with cobwebs and besprinkled with antique dust. Around the walls stood several oaken bookcases, the lower shelves of which were filled with rows of gigantic folios and black-letter quartos, and the upper with little parchment-covered duodecimos.[2] Over the central bookcase was a bronze bust of Hippocrates,[3] with which, according to some authorities, Dr. Heidegger was accustomed to hold consultations in all difficult cases of his practice. In the obscurest corner of the room stood a tall and narrow oaken closet, with its door ajar, within which doubtfully appeared a skeleton. Between two of the bookcases hung a looking-glass, presenting its high and dusty plate within a tarnished gilt frame. Among many wonderful stories related of this mirror, it was fabled that the spirits of all the doctor's deceased patients dwelt within its verge and would stare him in the face whenever he looked thitherward. The opposite side of the chamber was ornamented with the full-length portrait of a young lady, arrayed in the faded magnificence of silk, satin, and brocade, and with a visage as faded as her dress. Above half a century ago, Dr. Heidegger had been on the point of marriage with this young lady; but being affected with some slight disorder, she had swallowed one of her lover's prescriptions and died on the bridal evening. The greatest curiosity of the study remains to be mentioned; it was a ponderous folio volume, bound in black leather, with

[1] GOUT—A disease resulting from excessive eating and drinking, and manifested by swelling of joints.

[2] FOLIOS, QUARTOS, DUODECIMOS—Different sizes of books; the folio page is half of a very large sheet; the quarto, a fourth; the duodecimo, a twelfth.

[3] HIPPOCRATES (hĭ·pŏk′rȧ·tēz)—A Greek physician of the fourth century B.C.; known as the Father of Medicine.

massive silver clasps. There were no letters on the back, and nobody could tell the title of the book. But it was well known to be a book of magic; and once, when a chambermaid had lifted it, merely to brush away the dust, the skeleton had rattled in its closet, the picture of the young lady had stepped one foot upon the floor, and several ghastly faces had peeped forth from the mirror; while the brazen head of Hippocrates frowned and said, "Forbear!"

Such was Dr. Heidegger's study. On the summer afternoon of our tale, a small round table, as black as ebony,[4] stood in the center of the room, sustaining a cut-glass vase of beautiful form and elaborate workmanship. The sunshine came through the window between the heavy festoons of two faded damask curtains, and fell directly across this vase; so that a mild splendor was reflected from it on the ashen visages of the five old people who sat around. Four champagne glasses were also on the table.

"My dear old friends," repeated Dr. Heidegger, "may I reckon on your aid in performing an exceedingly curious experiment?"

Now Dr. Heidegger was a very strange old gentleman, whose eccentricity[5] had become the nucleus for a thousand fantastic stories. Some of these fables, to my shame be it spoken, might possibly be traced back to mine own veracious self; and if any passages of the present tale should startle the reader's faith, I must be content to bear the stigma of a fiction-monger.

When the doctor's four guests heard him talk of his proposed experiment, they anticipated nothing more wonderful than the murder of a mouse in an air-pump, or the examination of a cobweb by the microscope, or some similar nonsense, with which he was constantly in the habit of pestering his intimates. But without waiting for a reply, Dr. Heidegger hobbled across the chamber and returned with the same ponderous folio, bound in black leather, which common report affirmed to be a book of magic. Undoing the silver clasps, he opened the volume and took from among its black-letter pages a rose, or what was once a rose, though now the green leaves and crimson petals had assumed one brownish hue, and the ancient flower seemed ready to crumble to dust in the doctor's hands.

"This rose," said Dr. Heidegger, with a sigh, "this same withered and crumbling flower, blossomed five-and-fifty years ago. It was given me by Sylvia Ward, whose portrait hangs yonder; and I meant to wear it in my bosom at our wedding. Five-and-fifty years it has been treasured between the leaves of this old volume. Now, would you deem it possible that this rose of half a century could ever bloom again?"

"Nonsense!" said the Widow Wycherly, with a peevish toss of her head. "You might as well ask whether an old woman's wrinkled face could ever bloom again."

"See!" answered Dr. Heidegger.

He uncovered the vase and threw the faded rose into the water which it contained. At first it lay lightly on the surface of the fluid, appearing to imbibe none of its moisture. Soon, however, a singular change began to be visible. The crushed and dried petals stirred and assumed a deepening tinge of crimson, as if the flower were reviving from a death-like slumber; the slender stalk and twigs of foliage became green; and there was the rose of half a century, looking

4 EBONY—A hard, black wood.
5 ECCENTRICITY—Strangeness, oddity.

as fresh as when Sylvia Ward had first given it to her lover. It was scarcely full-blown; for some of its delicate red leaves curled modestly around its moist bosom, within which two or three dewdrops were sparkling.

"That is certainly a very pretty deception," said the doctor's friends, carelessly, however, for they had witnessed greater miracles at a conjuror's show; "pray how was it effected?"

"Did you never hear of the 'Fountain of Youth,'" asked Dr. Heidegger, "which Ponce de Leon, the Spanish adventurer, went in search of two or three centuries ago?"

"But did Ponce de Leon ever find it?" said the Widow Wycherly.

"No," answered Dr. Heidegger, "for he never sought it in the right place. The famous Fountain of Youth, if I am rightly informed, is situated in the southern part of the Floridian peninsula, not far from Lake Macaco. Its source is overshadowed by several gigantic magnolias, which, though numberless centuries old, have been kept as fresh as violets by the virtues of this wonderful water. An acquaintance of mine, knowing my curiosity in such matters, has sent me what you see in the vase."

"Ahem!" said Colonel Killigrew, who believed not a word of the doctor's story; "and what may be the effect of this fluid on the human frame?"

"You shall judge for yourself, my dear Colonel," replied Dr. Heidegger; "and all of you, my respected friends, are welcome to so much of this admirable fluid as may restore to you the bloom of youth. For my own part, having had much trouble in growing old, I am in no hurry to grow young again. With your permission, therefore, I will merely watch the progress of the experiment."

While he spoke, Dr. Heidegger had been filling the four champagne glasses with the water of the Fountain of

Youth. It was apparently impregnated [6] with an effervescent [7] gas, for little bubbles were continually ascending from the depths of the glasses and bursting in silvery spray at the surface. As the liquor diffused a pleasant perfume, the old people doubted not that it possessed cordial and comfortable properties; and, though utter skeptics as to its rejuvenescent [8] power, they were inclined to swallow it at once. But Dr. Heidegger besought them to stay a moment.

"Before you drink, my respectable old friends," said he, "it would be well that, with the experience of a lifetime to direct you, you should draw up a few general rules for your guidance in passing a second time through the perils of youth. Think what a sin and shame it would be, if, with your peculiar advantages, you should not become patterns of virtue and wisdom to all the young people of the age."

The doctor's four venerable friends made him no answer, except by a feeble and tremulous laugh, so very ridiculous was the idea, that, knowing how closely repentance treads behind the steps of error, they should ever go astray again.

"Drink, then," said the doctor, bowing. "I rejoice that I have so well selected the subjects of my experiment."

With palsied hands, they raised the glasses to their lips. The liquor, if it really possessed such virtues as Dr. Heidegger imputed to it, could not have been bestowed on four human beings who needed it more woefully. They looked as if they had never known what youth or pleasure was, but had been the offspring of Nature's dotage, and always the gray, decrepit, sapless, miserable

creatures who now sat stooping round the doctor's table, without life enough in their souls or bodies to be animated even by the prospect of growing young again. They drank off the water and replaced their glasses on the table.

Assuredly there was an almost immediate improvement in the aspect of the party, not unlike what might have been produced by a glass of generous wine, together with a sudden glow of cheerful sunshine, brightening over all their visages at once. There was a healthful suffusion on their cheeks, instead of the ashen hue that had made them look so corpse-like. They gazed at one another and fancied that some magic power had really begun to smooth away the deep and sad inscriptions which Father Time had been so long engraving on their brows. The Widow Wycherly adjusted her cap, for she felt almost like a woman again.

"Give us more of this wonderful water!" cried they, eagerly. "We are younger—but we are still too old! Quick—give us more!"

"Patience, patience!" quoth Dr. Heidegger, who sat watching the experiment with philosophic coolness. "You have been a long time growing old. Surely, you might be content to grow young in half an hour! But the water is at your service."

Again he filled their glasses with the liquor of youth, enough of which still remained in the vase to turn half the old people in the city to the age of their own grandchildren. While the bubbles were yet sparkling on the brim, the doctor's four guests snatched their glasses from the table, and swallowed the contents in a single gulp. Was it delusion? [9] Even while the draught was

[6] IMPREGNATED—Saturated, filled through and through.

[7] EFFERVESCENT—Pertaining to a liquid which continuously gives off bubbles of gas.

[8] REJUVENESCENT—Restoring youth.

[9] DELUSION—Something unreal, an intended deception.

passing down their throats, it seemed to have wrought a change on their whole systems. Their eyes grew clear and bright; a dark shade deepened among their silvery locks; they sat around the table, three gentlemen of middle age and a woman hardly beyond her buxom prime.

"My dear widow, you are charming!" cried Colonel Killigrew, whose eyes had been fixed upon her face while the shadows of age were flitting from it like darkness from the crimson daybreak.

The fair widow knew, of old, that Colonel Killigrew's compliments were not always measured by sober truth; so she started up and ran to the mirror, still dreading that the ugly visage of an old woman would meet her gaze. Meanwhile, the three gentlemen behaved in such a manner as proved that the water of the Fountain of Youth possessed some intoxicating qualities; unless, indeed, their exhilaration of spirits were merely a lightsome dizziness caused by the sudden removal of the weight of years. Mr. Gascoigne's mind seemed to run on political topics, but whether relating to the past, present, or future, could not easily be determined, since the same ideas and phrases have been in vogue these fifty years. Now he rattled forth full-throated sentences about patriotism, national glory, and the people's right; now he muttered some perilous stuff or other, in a sly and doubtful whisper, so cautiously that even his own conscience could scarcely catch the secret; and now, again, he spoke in measured accents and deeply deferential [10] tone, as if a royal ear were listening to his well-turned periods. Colonel Killigrew all this time had been trolling forth a jolly bottle-song and ringing his glass in symphony with the

chorus, while his eyes wandered toward the buxom figure of the Widow Wycherly. On the other side of the table, Mr. Medbourne was involved in a calculation of dollars and cents, with which was strangely intermingled a project for supplying the East Indies with ice by harnessing a team of whales to the polar icebergs.

As for the Widow Wycherly, she stood before the mirror curtsying and simpering to her own image and greeting it as the friend whom she loved better than all the world beside. She thrust her face close to the glass to see whether some long-remembered wrinkle or crow's-foot [11] had indeed vanished. She examined whether the snow had so entirely melted from her hair that the venerable cap could be safely thrown aside. At last, turning briskly away, she came with a sort of dancing step to the table.

"My dear old doctor," cried she, "pray favor me with another glass!"

"Certainly, my dear madam, certainly!" replied the complaisant doctor; "see! I have already filled the glasses."

There, in fact, stood the four glasses, brimful of this wonderful water, the delicate spray of which, as it effervesced from the surface, resembled the tremulous glitter of diamonds. It was now so nearly sunset that the chamber had grown duskier than ever; but a mild and moon-like splendor gleamed from within the vase and rested alike on the four guests and on the doctor's venerable figure. He sat in a high-backed, elaborately-carved oaken armchair, with a gray dignity of aspect that might have well befitted that very Father Time, whose power had never been disputed

[10] DEFERENTIAL—Respectful.

[11] CROW'S-FOOT—The wrinkles radiating from the outer corner of the eye, often noticed in aged people.

save by this fortunate company. Even while quaffing the third draught of the Fountain of Youth, they were almost awed by the expression of his mysterious visage.

But, the next moment, the exhilarating gush of young life shot through their veins. They were now in the happy prime of youth. Age, with its miserable train of cares and sorrows and diseases was remembered only as the trouble of a dream from which they had joyously awoke. The fresh gloss of the soul, so early lost, and without which the world's successive scenes had been but a gallery of faded pictures, again threw its enchantment over all their prospects. They felt like new-created beings in a new-created universe.

"We are young! We are young!" they cried exultingly. Youth, like the extremity of age, had effaced the strongly marked characteristics of middle life and mutually assimilated[12] them all. They were a group of merry youngsters, almost maddened with the exuberant frolicsomeness of their years. The most singular effect on their gaiety was an impulse to mock the infirmity and decrepitude of which they had so lately been the victims. They laughed loudly at their old-fashioned attire, the wide-skirted coats and flapped waistcoats of the young men, and the ancient cap and gown of the blooming girl. One limped across the floor like a gouty grandfather; one set a pair of spectacles astride of his nose and pretended to pore over the black-letter pages of the book of magic; a third seated himself in an armchair and strove to imitate the venerable dignity of Dr. Heidegger. Then all shouted mirthfully and leaped about the room. The Widow Wycherly—if so fresh a damsel could be called a widow—trip-

[12] ASSIMILATED—Made alike.

ping up to the doctor's chair, with a mischievous merriment in her rosy face.

"Doctor, you dear old soul," cried she, "get up and dance with me!" and then the four young people laughed louder than ever to think what a queer figure the poor old doctor would cut.

"Pray excuse me," answered the doctor, quietly. "I am old and rheumatic, and my dancing days were over long ago. But either of these gay young gentlemen will be glad of so pretty a partner."

"Dance with me, Clara!" cried Colonel Killigrew.

"No, no, I will be her partner!" shouted Mr. Gascoigne.

"She promised me her hand fifty years ago!" exclaimed Mr. Medbourne.

They all gathered round her. One caught both her hands in his passionate grasp—another threw his arm about her waist—the third buried his hand among the glossy curls that clustered beneath the widow's cap. Blushing, panting, struggling, chiding, laughing, her warm breath fanning each of their faces by turns, she strove to disengage herself, yet still remained in their triple embrace. Never was there a livelier picture of youthful rivalship, with bewitching beauty for the prize. Yet, by a strange deception, owing to the duskiness of the chamber and the antique dresses which they still wore, the tall mirror is said to have reflected the figures of the three old, gray, withered grandsires, ridiculously contending for the skinny ugliness of a shriveled grandam.

But they were young, their burning passions proved them so. Inflamed to madness by the coquetry of the girl-widow, who neither granted nor quite withheld her favors, the three rivals began to interchange threatening glances. Still keeping hold of the fair prize, they grappled fiercely at one another's throats. As they struggled to and fro, the table was overturned and the vase dashed into a thousand fragments. The precious Water of Youth flowed in a bright stream across the floor, moistening the wings of a butterfly, which, grown old in the decline of summer, had alighted there to die. The insect fluttered lightly through the chamber and settled on the snowy head of Dr. Heidegger.

"Come, come, gentlemen!—come, Madam Wycherly," exclaimed the doctor, "I really must protest against this riot."

They stood still and shivered; for it seemed as if gray Time were calling them back from their sunny youth, far down into the chill and darksome vale of years. They looked at old Dr. Heidegger, who sat in his carved armchair, holding the rose of half a century, which he had rescued from among the fragments of the shattered vase. At the motion of his hand, the four rioters resumed their seats, the more readily because their violent exertions had wearied them, youthful though they were.

"My poor Sylvia's rose!" ejaculated Dr. Heidegger, holding it in the light of the sunset clouds; "it appears to be fading again."

And so it was. Even while the party were looking at it, the flower continued to shrivel up till it became as dry and fragile as when the doctor had first thrown it into the vase. He shook off the few drops of moisture which clung to its petals.

"I love it as well thus, as in its dewy freshness," observed he, pressing the withered rose to his withered lips. While he spoke, the butterfly fluttered down from the doctor's snowy head and fell upon the floor.

His guests shivered again. A strange chillness, whether of the body or spirit they could not tell, was creeping gradually over them all. They gazed at one another and fancied that each fleeting moment snatched away a charm and left a deepening furrow where none had been before. Was it an illusion? [13] Had the changes of a lifetime been crowded into so brief a space, and were they now four aged people, sitting with their old friend, Dr. Heidegger?

"Are we grown old again, so soon!" cried they, dolefully.

In truth, they had. The Water of Youth possessed merely a virtue more transient than that of wine. The delirium which it created had effervesced away. Yes! they were old again. With a shuddering impulse that showed her a woman still, the widow clasped her skinny hands before her face and wished that the coffin-lid were over it, since it could be no longer beautiful.

"Yes, friends, ye are old again," said Dr. Heidegger; "and lo! the Water of Youth is all lavished on the ground. Well—I bemoan it not; for if the fountain gushed at my very doorstep I would not stoop to bathe my lips in it—no, though its delirium were for years instead of moments. Such is the lesson ye have taught me!"

But the doctor's four friends had taught no such lesson to themselves. They resolved forthwith to make a pilgrimage to Florida and quaff at morning, noon, and night from the Fountain of Youth.

[13] ILLUSION—A false, unreal appearance.

⸭⸭⸭⸭⸭⸭⸭⸭⸭⸭⸭⸭⸭⸭⸭⸭⸭⸭⸭⸭⸭⸭⸭⸭⸭⸭⸭

FOR DISCUSSION

1. Do you agree, or disagree, that most people, given a second life to live, would do no better the second time?

2. Do you think most old people that you know want to regain their lost youth, or do not want to? Discuss.

3. What is it that makes some old people seem much younger than their age, that makes some young or middle-aged people seem much older than their age?

4. What type of person is represented by each of Dr. Heidegger's four friends?

5. Why does the mirror reflect the Widow Wycherly and her three suitors as withered old people although they have apparently been rejuvenated?

6. Show how the incidents of the rejuvenated rose and of the butterfly make the story easier to believe.

7. Why would Dr. Heidegger not touch the Water of Youth even if it gushed at his very doorstep?

## WORDS—SHADES OF MEANING

1. Hawthorne uses the word *visage* four times in this story; the word *face*, six times. Synonyms are *countenance* and *physiognomy*. How are the four words distinguished? Try substituting the other three for *face* in the sentence: " 'My dear widow, you are charming!' cried Colonel Killigrew, whose eyes had been fixed upon her *face*."

2. "It was a *ponderous* folio volume." *Ponderous* (from the Latin *pondus* weight) means heavy in weight; or heavy in spirit, as a *ponderous* joke. What is the meaning in the sentence quoted? What is the difference among *ponderous, bulky, massive*?

3. "Blushing, panting, struggling, *chiding*, laughing . . . she strove to disengage herself." English is rich in words of reproval like *chiding*, good substitutes for the overworked "bawl out." What different shades of meaning do the following words suggest: *reprove; rebuke; reprimand; admonish; chide; upbraid; objurgate; scold; berate?*

## PROJECTS

1. Tell the story of Ponce de Leon's search for the Fountain of Youth, putting as much imagination into the account as you can.

2. In your own words describe Dr. Heidegger's study.

3. Compare the details of Hawthorne's restrained but effective atmosphere in this story with the unrestrained horror of "The Cask of Amontillado."

## RELATED READING

You will enjoy "The Minister's Black Veil" and "The Carbuncle" in *Twice-Told Tales*, by Nathaniel Hawthorne.

*Dear Brutus* is a play by James M. Barrie on the same theme as "Dr. Heidegger's Experiment."

# THE CASK OF
# AMONTILLADO

*EDGAR ALLAN POE*

You have heard of the Roman catacombs, underground rooms and passageways carved out of soft stone and commonly used as burial places. What a setting for a horror story!  Poe chooses the private catacombs under an Italian PALAZZO as the scene for most of this story.

The thousand injuries of Fortunato I had borne as best I could, but when he ventured upon insult, I vowed revenge. You, who so well know the nature of my soul, will not suppose, however, that I gave utterance to a threat. *At length* I would be avenged; this was a point definitely settled—but the very definitiveness with which it was resolved precluded the idea of risk. I must not only punish, but punish with impunity. A wrong is unredressed [2] when retribution [3] overtakes its redresser. It is equally unredressed when the avenger fails to make himself felt as such to him who has done the wrong.

It must be understood that neither by word nor deed had I given Fortunato cause to doubt my good will. I continued, as was my wont, to smile in his face; and he did not perceive that my smile *now* was at the thought of his immolation.[4]

He had a weak point—this Fortunato —although in other regards he was a man to be respected and even feared. He prided himself on his connoisseurship [5] in wine. Few Italians have the true virtuoso spirit.[6] For the most part their enthusiasm is adopted to suit the time and opportunity, to practice imposture upon the British and Austrian millionaires. In painting and gemmary, Fortunato, like his countrymen, was a quack; but in the matter of old wines he was sincere. In this respect I did not differ from him materially; I was skillful in the Italian vintages myself and bought largely whenever I could.

It was about dusk, one evening during the supreme madness of the carnival season,[7] that I encountered my friend. He accosted me with excessive warmth, for he had been drinking much. The man wore motley. He had on a tight-fitting parti-striped dress, and his head was surmounted by the conical cap and

Title—AMONTILLADO (*à·mŏn′tĭ·lä′dō*)—A rare kind of sherry wine.

[2] UNREDRESSED—Unrepaired.

[3] RETRIBUTION—Punishment.

[4] IMMOLATION—Death through sacrifice, here used in mockery.

[5] CONNOISSEURSHIP (kŏn·ĭ·sûr′shĭp)—Ability to judge accurately the excellence of food, wine, art, and the like.

[6] VIRTUOSO SPIRIT—Spirit of one greatly skilled in an art.

[7] CARNIVAL SEASON—The days of celebration before the beginning of the Lenten fast.

bells. I was so pleased to see him that I thought I should never have done wringing his hand.

I said to him, "My dear Fortunato, you are luckily met. How remarkably well you are looking today! But I have received a pipe [8] of what passes for amontillado, and I have my doubts."

"How?" said he. "Amontillado? A pipe? Impossible! And in the midst of the carnival!"

"I have my doubts," I replied; "and I was silly enough to pay the full amontillado price without consulting you in the matter. You were not to be found, and I was fearful of losing a bargain."

"Amontillado!"

"I have my doubts."

"Amontillado!"

"And I must satisfy them."

"Amontillado!"

"As you are engaged, I am on my way to Luchesi. If anyone has a critical turn, it is he. He will tell me—"

"Luchesi cannot tell amontillado from sherry."

"And yet some fools will have it that his taste is a match for your own."

"Come, let us go."

"Whither?"

"To your vaults."

"My friend, no; I will not impose upon your good nature. I perceive you have an engagement. Luchesi—"

"I have no engagement—come."

"My friend, no. It is not the engagement, but the severe cold with which I perceive you are afflicted. The vaults are insufferably damp. They are incrusted with niter."

"Let us go, nevertheless. The cold is merely nothing. Amontillado! You have been imposed upon. And as for Luchesi, he cannot distinguish sherry from amontillado."

[8] PIPE—A large cask used for wine.

Thus speaking, Fortunato possessed himself of my arm; and putting on a mask of black silk and drawing a roquelaure [9] closely about my person, I suffered him to hurry me to my *palazzo*.

There were no attendants at home; they had absconded to make merry in honor of the time. I had told them that I should not return until the morning and had given them explicit orders not to stir from the house. These orders were sufficient, I well knew, to insure their immediate disappearance, one and all, as soon as my back was turned.

I took from their sconces two flambeaux, [10] and giving one to Fortunato, bowed him through several suites of rooms to the archway that led into the vaults. I passed down a long and winding staircase, requesting him to be cautious as he followed. We came at length to the foot of the descent and stood together upon the damp ground of the catacombs of the Montresors.

The gait of my friend was unsteady, and the bells upon his cap jingled as he strode.

"The pipe," said he.

"It is farther on," said I; "but observe the white webwork which gleams from these cavern walls."

He turned towards me and looked into my eyes with two filmy orbs that distilled the rheum [11] of intoxication.

"Niter?" he asked at length.

"Niter," I replied. "How long have you had that cough?"

"Ugh! ugh! ugh!—ugh! ugh! ugh!—ugh! ugh! ugh!—ugh! ugh! ugh!—ugh! ugh!"

My poor friend found it impossible to reply for many minutes.

[9] ROQUELAURE (rŏk′ĕ·lōr)—A knee-length cloak.

[10] FLAMBEAUX (flăm′bōz)—Torches.

[11] RHEUM (rōōm)—A watery substance discharged from the eyes.

"It is nothing," he said at last.

"Come," I said with decision, "we will go back; your health is precious. You are rich, respected, admired, beloved; you are happy, as once I was. You are a man to be missed. For me it is no matter. We will go back; you will be ill, and I cannot be responsible. Besides, there is Luchesi—"

"Enough," he said; "the cough is a mere nothing; it will not kill me. I shall not die of a cough."

"True—true," I replied; "and, indeed, I had no intention of alarming you unnecessarily—but you should use all proper caution. A draught of this Medoc [12] will defend us from the damps."

Here I knocked off the neck of a bottle which I drew from a long row of its fellows that lay upon the mold.

"Drink," I said, presenting him the wine.

He raised it to his lips with a leer. He paused and nodded to me familiarly, while his bells jingled.

"I drink," he said, "to the buried that repose around us."

"And I to your long life."

He again took my arm, and we proceeded.

"These vaults," he said, "are extensive."

"The Montresors," I replied, "were a great and numerous family."

"I forget your arms."

"A huge human foot d'or, in a field azure; the foot crushes a serpent rampant [13] whose fangs are embedded in the heel."

"And the motto?"

"*Nemo me impune lacessit.*" [14]

[12] MEDOC—Wine from Medoc, France.
[13] FOOT D'OR . . . RAMPANT—A golden foot on a blue background, crushing a springing serpent.
[14] "*Nemo me impune lacessit*"—No one offends me without being punished.

"Good!" he said.

The wine sparkled in his eyes, and the bells jingled. My own fancy grew warm from the Medoc. We had passed through long walls of piled skeletons, with casks and puncheons intermingling, into the inmost recesses of the catacombs. I paused again, and this time I made bold to seize Fortunato by the arm above the elbow.

"The niter!" I said; "see, it increases. It hangs like moss upon the vaults. We are below the river's bed. The drops of moisture trickle among the bones. Come, we will go back ere it is too late. Your cough—"

"It is nothing," he said; "let us go on. But first, another draught of the Medoc."

I broke and reached him a flagon of De Grâve. [15] He emptied it at a breath. His eyes flashed with a fierce light. He laughed and threw the bottle upwards with a gesticulation I did not understand.

I looked at him in surprise. He repeated the movement—a grotesque one.

"You do not comprehend?" he said.

"Not I," I replied.

"Then you are not of the brotherhood."

"How?"

"You are not of the masons."

"Yes, yes," I said; "yes, yes."

"You? Impossible! A mason?"

"A mason," I replied.

"A sign," he said, "a sign."

"It is this," I answered, producing a trowel from beneath the folds of my roquelaure.

"You jest," he exclaimed, recoiling a few paces. "But let us proceed to the amontillado."

"Be it so," I said, replacing the tool beneath the cloak and again offering my

[15] DE GRÂVE—A dry white wine.

arm. He leaned upon it heavily. We continued our route in search of the amontillado. We passed through a range of low arches, descended, passed on, and descending again, arrived at a deep crypt, in which the foulness of the air caused our flambeaux rather to glow than flame.

At the most remote end of the crypt there appeared another, less spacious. Its walls had been lined with human remains, piled to the vault overhead in the fashion of the great catacombs of Paris. Three sides of this interior crypt were still ornamented in this manner. From the fourth side the bones had been thrown down and lay promiscuously upon the earth, forming at one point a mound of some size. Within the wall thus exposed by the displacing of the bones, we perceived a still interior crypt or recess, in depth about four feet, in width three, in height six or seven. It seemed to have been constructed for no especial use within itself but formed merely the interval between two of the colossal supports of the roof of the catacombs and was backed by one of their circumscribing walls of solid granite.

It was in vain that Fortunato, uplifting his dull torch, endeavored to pry into the depth of the recess. Its termination the feeble light did not enable us to see.

"Proceed," I said; "herein is the amontillado. As for Luchesi—"

"He is an ignoramus," interrupted my friend, as he stepped unsteadily forward, while I followed immediately at his heels. In an instant he had reached the extremity of the niche, and finding his progress arrested by the rock, stood stupidly bewildered. A moment more and I had fettered him to the granite. In its surface were two iron staples, distant from each other about two feet, horizontally. From one of these depended a short chain, from the other a padlock. Throwing the links about his waist, it was but the work of a few seconds to secure it. He was too much astounded to resist. Withdrawing the key, I stepped back from the recess.

"Pass your hand," I said, "over the wall; you cannot help feeling the niter. Indeed it is *very* damp. Once more let me *implore* you to return. No? Then I must positively leave you. But I must first render you all the little attentions in my power."

"The amontillado!" ejaculated my friend, not yet recovered from his astonishment.

"True," I replied; "the amontillado."

As I said these words, I busied myself amid the piles of bones of which I have before spoken. Throwing them aside, I soon uncovered a quantity of building stone and mortar. With these materials and with the aid of my trowel, I began vigorously to wall up the entrance of the niche.

I had scarcely laid the first tier of the masonry when I discovered that the intoxication of Fortunato had in a great measure worn off. The earliest indication I had of this was a low moaning cry from the depth of the recess. It was *not* the cry of a drunken man. There was then a long and obstinate silence. I laid the second tier, and the third, and the fourth; and then I heard the furious vibrations of the chain. The noise lasted for several minutes, during which, that I might hearken to it with the more satisfaction, I ceased my labors and sat down upon the bones. When at last the clanking subsided, I resumed the trowel and finished without interruption the fifth, the sixth, and the seventh tier. The wall was now nearly upon a level with my breast. I again paused and,

holding the flambeaux over the masonwork, threw a few feeble rays upon the figure within.

A succession of loud and shrill screams, bursting suddenly from the throat of the chained form, seemed to thrust me violently back. For a brief moment I hesitated—I trembled. Unsheathing my rapier, I began to grope with it about the recess; but the thought of an instant reassured me. I placed my hand upon the solid fabric of the catacombs and felt satisfied. I reapproached the wall; I replied to the yells of him who clamored. I re-echoed—I aided—I surpassed them in volume and in strength. I did this, and the clamorer grew still.

It was now midnight, and my task was drawing to a close. I had completed the eighth, the ninth, and the tenth tier. I had finished a portion of the last and the eleventh; there remained but a single stone to be fitted and plastered in. I struggled with its weight; I placed it partially in its destined position. But now there came from out the niche a low laugh that erected the hairs upon my head. It was succeeded by a sad voice, which I had difficulty in recognizing as that of the noble Fortunato. The voice said:

"Ha! ha! ha!—he! he! he!—a very good joke indeed—an excellent jest. We shall have many a rich laugh about it at the *palazzo*—he! he! he!—over our wine—he! he! he!"

"The amontillado!" I said.

"He! he! he!—he! he! he!—yes, the amontillado. But is it not getting late? Will they not be awaiting us at the *palazzo*, the Lady Fortunato and the rest? Let us be gone."

"Yes," I said, "let us be gone."

*"For the love of God, Montresor!"*

"Yes," I said, "for the love of God!"

But to these words I hearkened in vain for a reply. I grew impatient. I called aloud—

"Fortunato!"

No answer. I called again—"Fortunato!"

No answer still. I thrust a torch through the remaining aperture and let it fall within. There came forth in return only a jingling of the bells. My heart grew sick—it was the dampness of the catacombs that made it so. I hastened to make an end of my labor. I forced the last stone into its position; I plastered it up. Against the new masonry I re-erected the old rampart of bones. For the half of a century no mortal has disturbed them. *In pace requiescat!* [16]

[16] *In pace requiescat*—May he rest in peace.

◇◇◇◇◇◇◇◇◇◇◇◇◇◇◇◇◇◇◇◇◇◇◇◇◇◇

## FOR DISCUSSION

1. What are the two essential elements in Montresor's analysis of "perfect" vengeance? Have you anything to add?

2. How is Montresor's un-Christian thirst for vengeance different from the kind of revenge often hurled by the loser at the victor in a quarrel: "I'll get even with you"?

3. In what way does Montresor's analysis contribute to the horror of the story?

4. What fault of Fortunato makes him such an easy victim of Montresor's cruel plan? Why is Fortunato so anxious to continue through the catacombs?

5. Why did the author choose the carnival season as the time for the story?

6. Why does Montresor repeatedly call attention to the dampness and niter, once the pair is in the catacombs?

7. How does the brief conversation about the Montresor coat of arms and motto contribute to the atmosphere of the story?

8. What does Fortunato mean by the word *mason?* What does Montresor mean by it?

9. Discuss the thoroughness of the preparations made by Montresor for his revenge against Fortunato.

10. If you sensed a lack of plausibility as you were reading the story, what part of the action did you question? How does Poe try to make the implausible seem plausible?

## WORDS TO STUDY

1. A *pipe* of wine is the bait that draws Fortunato on. Discover and explain the other words used in the story for containers of wine.

2. *Habit, custom, usage, practise,* and *wont* mean about the same thing. Which synonym is closest to *wont?*

3. *Grotesque, fanciful, fantastic,* and *bizarre* are related in idea, though not in origin. Show that *grotesque* is the best of the four words to describe the action of Fortunato's throwing the empty bottle upwards.

## PROJECTS

1. Look up the words *carnival* and *vendetta,* and write a short paragraph in explanation of each.

2. Try your hand at writing a detective story leading to the discovery of Montresor's crime.

3. Point out passages where Poe appeals to the sense of touch, hearing, smelling, or seeing in order to increase the emotion of horror.

## RELATED READING

Other Poe favorites are "The Murders in the Rue Morgue," "The Pit and the Pendulum," and "The Fall of the House of Usher."

Another horror story by a later writer of the National Period is "The Turn of the Screw," by Henry James.

# THE POETRY OF THE NATIONAL
# PERIOD

Since the rise of national prosperity in the early 1800's, there had come both time and taste for original poetry.  In the preceding century, American verse had followed the fashions of English writers; and English poetry in the 1700's had been elaborate and artificial.  But just as European poetry had come to life in the romantic movement of the nineteenth century, so did American verse respond to the new spirit of freedom and originality.  Beginning with William Cullen Bryant, there appeared a line of poets truly American in inspiration and expression.  These men dealt with three themes which still dominate our literature: love of nature, love of home, and love of country.

The colonists had been surrounded by great tracts of land; they had grown up overcoming and using the forces of nature. Their life fostered a love of the out-of-doors which they bequeathed to their children. It was strong in our first poets. "Bryant," says one critic, "loved nature for her own sake"; Whittier "regarded nature as a background for life"; Emerson saw nature always as the handwriting of God. Like the English Wordsworth, he found poetic sermons in the trees, the birds, the fields, the hills, and the seas.

And then, perhaps because he had worked so hard to establish it, the early American loved his home. Home was the center of all social life. Before the fireplace women knitted and spun, fathers and uncles swapped stories, visitors were entertained, lessons were studied—and sometimes taught. Our most delightful pictures of this home-centered culture appear in the poems of Longfellow, Lowell, and Whittier.

An expression of national pride also appeared in the songs of the period. Notable among these were "The Star-Spangled Banner," written by Francis Scott Key in a critical moment of America's history; Samuel Francis Smith's beautiful hymn, "America"; "Home, Sweet Home!" by John Howard Payne; and the familiar, well-loved songs of Stephen Foster.

There was one other type of patriotic verse—the poems that were inspired by the controversial issues which caused the War Between the States. In the North, Whittier aligned himself openly with the Abolitionists, so that most of his work between the years 1833 and the end of the war is now a forgotten chapter. A few of his poems were vivid and appealing enough for us to find them still interesting, but most of them died with the days that bred them. Lowell, too, was concerned with the politics of the time, using his pen in political satire. The milder Emerson and Longfellow wrote poems about brave deeds of the past and exhorted men to hold fast. Among their poems we find, for example, "The Concord Hymn," "The Ride of Paul Revere," and "The Building of the Ship"—patriotic, but not controversial. There were to be poets, also, in the Southern field, but their writings appeared after the war. Lanier, Hayne, Ryan, and Timrod—all were soldiers in the Confederate Army and all, except Lanier, wrote poems for the South. Lanier—loyal as he was to his cause—nevertheless refused to use his poetry for any but universal themes. Poetry was to him an art above sectionalism and politics.

Most of the poets of this nineteenth century had inherited from their Puritan forefathers a serious moral outlook upon life. It was the fashion for a while for the poet not only to teach a lesson with his verses, but to point out the lesson in a special stanza, usually the last one. It was a fashion, we must confess, which lessened the artistic effect of their verse—not that we disagree with the message, but that we like to have the thought suggested rather than labeled. Lowell admits this fault in some of his own verse. He was talking about himself when he wrote,

> The top of the hill he will ne'er come nigh reaching
> Till he learns the distinction 'twixt singing and preaching.

## CHARACTERISTICS OF INDIVIDUAL POETS

We have reviewed briefly the general themes and elements that characterized the poetry of the national period. For the moment, now, let us consider the particular qualities that made the work of each poet individual and distinctive.

For the most part, Bryant's poetry has to do with nature, as the titles prove: "To a Waterfowl," "To a Fringed Gentian," "Green River," "A Forest Hymn," "The Prairies." One might go on indefinitely. And much of his verse is touched with melancholy. He wrote often of death, the most famous example being, of course, his "Thanatopsis." The sonorous lines of the poem make it seem almost impossible that a boy of eighteen could have written it, until we recall that this boy had been brought up on the Bible, Bunyan's *Pilgrim's Progress*, and Milton's *Paradise Lost*. One who has memorized chapters from Job and Ecclesiastes develops as a matter of course an ear for noble verse.

Remembering Poe's unique theories in regard to the short story, it is not surprising to find that his ideas about poetry differ greatly from those of his contemporaries. In the first place, there are elements usually present in great poetry which Poe disregarded. For instance, he considered *meaning* of no consequence. He believed that a poem must have two qualities—melody and mood. It need not speak a message; but it must produce an effect. There are lines in his verse which cannot be given a literal interpretation; nor do they have symbolic meaning. They merely lend tone or color. "The Bells" illustrates his point especially well, although in it he has suggested four different moods instead of the usual *one* of weird depression.

Poe was a master of metrical form. All his poems are delightful to hear. And they make that elusive claim upon fancy, which—as we have said before—is one of the first tests of poetic quality. As he suggests in "Israfel," a happier, more normal life might have lifted him to superlative heights.

Emerson's verse, like Bryant's, is thoughtful rather than emotional. His famous poem "Fable" expresses in abbreviated form the theme of his long essay, "Self-Reliance." "The Rhodora" is typical of his method of drawing from nature proof of a religious doctrine, sometimes of his own making.

Unlike Emerson and Bryant, Longfellow concerned himself chiefly with people. Nature is a secondary interest in his poems, his best descriptions serving merely as a background for thought or action. He excelled as a writer of story-telling verse, and has given immortality to the names of Paul Revere, Hiawatha, Minnehaha, and Evangeline. There are poems by Longfellow that everybody knows. There are other poems that should be better known, particularly his sonnets. He was the most widely known and best-beloved American poet of the nineteenth century.

Oliver Wendell Holmes complained that having once written a humorous poem, people thereafter expected everything that he wrote to be funny. He seldom disappointed them, for he had a light touch that lent itself well to whimsical verse. But he had his serious moments, as we know from reading poems like "The Chambered Nautilus" and "The Voiceless." And one of his best-known humorous poems, "The Wonderful One-Hoss Shay," demonstrates a serious idea. Indeed, like many a wit, he could slip a neat little sermon into a gay rhyme. Abraham Lincoln called "The Last Leaf" "inexpressibly touching" and knew it by heart. Like Lincoln, Holmes knew well that humor and pathos are often two phases of the same experience.

Lowell's serious poems center about themes of home, friends, and nature. In poems like "The First Snowfall," "She Came and Went," and "My Love," he mirrored the tragedies and joys of family life. His best descriptions of nature may be found in such poems as "To a Dandelion," "Indian Summer Reverie," and "The Birch Tree"; and in the introduction to "The Vision of Sir Launfal."

Like Whittier, Lowell became an Abolitionist; but instead of pathos and sentiment, Lowell used wit, poking fun at corrupt politicians and slipping in shrewd comments on current affairs. His humor found outlet also in a serio-humorous poem called "A Fable for Critics." It was published anonymously, and features keen but kindly criticisms of the writers of his day, including himself. The verse is flippantly careless, in marked contrast with the singing quality of his lyrics or with the dignity of the "Commemoration Ode." At his best, Lowell is one of our finest poets.

More than any of his contemporaries, Whittier is the poet of New England. He was always a lover of nature; and long hours of farm work stored his mind with details of rural landscape. "Snowbound," "In School Days," "The Barefoot Boy," "Telling the Bees"—these are simple poems made bright with bits of down-East countryside. Like Longfellow, Whittier did well with narrative verse, preserving in rhyme, legends and incidents from American history—as for example, in "Maud Muller" and "Barbara Frietchie."

In the South as in the North, the Civil War brought out enduring poetry. Henry Timrod, Paul Hayne, Father Abram Ryan, and Sidney Lanier served with the Confederate armies. Each returned after the war, broken in health, to meet the problem of rebuilding homes and lives. The writings of Timrod, Hayne, and Ryan reflect all the fortunes of the conflict. They had written songs to celebrate the victories. And they grieved when the cause was lost. Lanier wrote no war poems, saving his verse for more universal themes. But all four wrote lyrics that have a grace and languor not bred in Northern soil. Their birds are mockingbirds. Their landscapes show live oaks, orange trees, marshes, and Southern skies. As a group they reflect the culture and gentleness of the South.

A list of other Southern lyricists, not so well known today, includes such men as Richard Henry Wilde, Edward Coote Pinckney, Thomas Holley Chivers, Philip Pendleton Cooke, and Theodore O'Hara. The verses of these men, too, reflect the literary tradition of the South.

Sidney Lanier was the greatest of the Southern poets. He was a musician as well as a writer; and with the possible exception of Poe, he is the most melodious of all America's poets. It is not always possible to describe the patterns of his verse, but one is conscious of the lilt and flow of the lines. There is in them a kind of natural harmony drawn from the winds, trees, brooks, and seas.

# Thanatopsis

## WILLIAM CULLEN BRYANT

Bryant wrote this VIEW OF DEATH in 1812 when he was only eighteen. He left the paper in his desk and forgot it. Several years later, his father discovered the poem and excitedly sent it to THE NORTH AMERICAN REVIEW. The editors could not believe that a boy had written it, but they were finally persuaded to print it. In 1817, when the poem was printed in book form, Bryant added the first seventeen and the concluding nine lines.

That Bryant was a Puritan would be enough to account for the grim subject. Add to this, however, the fact that he was a near-victim of consumption and that he had read and studied the "Graveyard School" of English poetry, and you have reasons a-plenty for his mood. Yet, the poem has great merit and has been a universal favorite.

To him who in the love of Nature holds
Communion with her visible forms, she speaks
A various language; for his gayer hours
She has a voice of gladness, and a smile
And eloquence of beauty, and she glides
Into his darker musings, with a mild       6
And healing sympathy, that steals away
Their sharpness, ere he is aware. When thoughts
Of the last bitter hour come like a blight
Over thy spirit, and sad images       10
Of the stern agony, and shroud, and pall,
And breathless darkness, and the narrow house,
Make thee to shudder and grow sick at heart;—
Go forth, under the open sky, and list
To Nature's teachings, while from all around—       15
Earth and her waters, and the depths of air—

Comes a still voice.—
                              Yet a few days, and thee
The all-beholding sun shall see no more
In all his course; nor yet in the cold ground,
Where thy pale form was laid with many tears,       20
Nor in the embrace of ocean, shall exist
Thy image. Earth, that nourished thee, shall claim
Thy growth, to be resolved to earth again,
And, lost each human trace, surrendering up
Thine individual being, shalt thou go
To mix forever with the elements,   26
To be a brother to the insensible rock
And to the sluggish clod, which the rude swain
Turns with his share, and treads upon. The oak
Shall send his roots abroad, and pierce thy mold.       30

Yet not to thine eternal resting-place
Shalt thou retire alone, nor couldst thou
    wish
Couch more magnificent.  Thou shalt
    lie down
With patriarchs of the infant world—
    with kings,
The powerful of the earth—the wise, the
    good,                                        35
Fair forms, and hoary seers of ages past,
All in one mighty sepulcher.  The hills
Rock-ribbed and ancient as the sun—the
    vales
Stretching in pensive quietness between;
The venerable woods—rivers that move
In majesty, and the complaining brooks
That make the meadows green; and,
    poured round all,                          42
Old  Ocean's  gray  and  melancholy
    waste—
Are but the solemn decorations all
Of the great tomb of man.  The golden
    sun,                                        45
The planets, all the infinite host of
    heaven,
Are shining on the sad abodes of death
Through the still lapse of ages.  All that
    tread
The globe are but a handful to the tribes
That slumber in its bosom.—Take the
    wings                                       50
Of morning, pierce the Barcan wilder-
    ness,
Or lose thyself in the continuous woods
Where rolls the Oregon, and hears no
    sound,
Save his own dashings—yet the dead are
    there;
And millions in those solitudes, since
    first                                       55
The flight of years began, have laid them
    down

51.  BARCAN—Barca is a desert in northern
Africa.
    53.  OREGON—The  Columbia  River  was
formerly called the Oregon River.

In their last sleep—the dead reign there
    alone.
So shalt thou rest, and what if thou
    withdraw
In silence from the living, and no friend
Take note of thy departure?  All that
    breathe                                     60
Will share thy destiny.  The gay will
    laugh
When thou art gone, the solemn brood
    of care
Plod on, and each one as before will
    chase
His favorite phantom; yet all these shall
    leave
Their mirth and their employments, and
    shall come                                  65
And make their bed with thee.  As the
    long train
Of ages glides away, the sons of men,
The youth in life's green spring, and he
    who goes
In the full strength of years, matron and
    maid,
The speechless babe, and the gray-
    headed man—                                 70
Shall one by one be gathered to thy side,
By those who in their turn shall follow
    them.

    So live, that when thy summons
    comes to join
The innumerable caravan, which moves
To that mysterious realm, where each
    shall take                                  75
His chamber in the silent halls of death,
Thou go not, like the quarry-slave at
    night,
Scourged to his dungeon, but, sustained
    and soothed
By an unfaltering trust, approach thy
    grave,
Like one who wraps the drapery of his
    couch                                        80
About him, and lies down to pleasant
    dreams.

## FOR DISCUSSION

1. Does the poet give a complete and satisfying picture of death? A critic says that a noble pagan of republican Rome could have held the same ideas. Is there anything distinctly Christian about the poem?

2. Does the poet make you fear death? If so, is it a healthy fear of death, or one that depresses and dampens your spirits? What do you think is a proper attitude toward death?

3. Do all the details of the poem create in your imagination a unified picture; and in your senses, a single impression? Does any word or phrase spoil the unity of the effect?

4. Nature "speaks a various language." What does this phrase mean? Does nature really speak, or do men put their own moods into nature?

5. Explain the meaning and appropriateness of the following expressions—line 28: "sluggish clod"; line 41: "complaining brooks"; line 50: "Take the wings of morning"; line 63: "Each one as before will chase his favorite phantom."

## WORDS

Find synonyms for the following words: *pall* (line 11); narrow *house* (line 12); *pensive* (line 39); *hoary* (line 36).

## PROJECTS

1. Note the numerous full vowel sounds (especially the o sounds) which give the poem a slow, deliberate, solemn tone.

2. Write a cheerful essay on death, using a description of nature in a more pleasant mood.

3. Imagine nature at any season of the year. Write two contrasting paragraphs showing how the same scene can be joyful or sorrowful, according to the mood of the person viewing it.

## RELATED READING

Compare the ideas of death expressed in the following selections: R. W. Emerson, "Threnody"; Philip Freneau, "The Indian Burying Ground," "The Preface for the Mass of the Dead."

# To a Waterfowl

## WILLIAM CULLEN BRYANT

*Unable to continue his studies at Yale, Bryant turned to law, though his heart was bent on a literary career. Forlorn and desolate, he was walking from Cummington to Plainfield, Massachusetts, where he hoped to start his practice.*

*It was a winter's evening, but the western heavens were fired with warmth. The lone walker lifted his eyes—and was glad. For he felt a kinship with a solitary bird that was winging its homeward way across the pathless sky. Into his troubled breast there gradually settled a calm confidence in the providence of God.*

Whither, midst falling dew,
While glow the heavens with the last
   steps of day,
Far, through their rosy depths, dost thou
   pursue
  Thy solitary way?

Vainly the fowler's eye    5
Might mark thy distant flight to do thee
   wrong,
As, darkly seen against the crimson sky,
  Thy figure floats along.

Seek'st thou the plashy brink
Of weedy lake, or marge of river wide,
Or where the rocking billows rise and
   sink    11
  On the chafed ocean-side?

There is a Power whose care
Teaches thy way along that pathless
   coast—
The desert and illimitable air—   15
  Lone wandering, but not lost.

9. PLASHY BRINK—The shore, with waves splashing in.
10. MARGE—Edge, bank.

All day thy wings have fanned,
At that far height, the cold thin atmos-
   phere,
Yet stoop not, weary, to the welcome
   land,
  Though the dark night is near.   20

And soon that toil shall end;
Soon shalt thou find a summer home,
   and rest,
And scream among thy fellows; reeds
   shall bend
  Soon, o'er thy sheltered nest.

Thou'rt gone, the abyss of heaven  25
Hath swallowed up thy form; yet, on my
   heart
Deeply has sunk the lesson thou hast
   given
  And shall not soon depart.

He who, from zone to zone,
Guides through the boundless sky thy
   certain flight,   30
In the long way that I must tread alone,
  Will lead my steps aright.

## FOR DISCUSSION

1. What comparison does the poet make between his condition and that of the waterfowl?
2. How is God's providence toward the bird shown? Does God guide men and beasts in the same way?
3. Find lines in which the rhythm seems to imitate the bird's flight? What metric pattern is used in these lines?

## A PROJECT

Compare the central thought of this poem, as expressed in the last stanza, with the theme of Ralph Waldo Emerson's "The Rhodora" (page 416). What similarity is there between the two ideas? Which poem best expresses the idea? Write a brief essay answering these questions, explaining the reasons for your answers fully.

# To Helen

## EDGAR ALLAN POE

*"The first purely ideal love of my soul," said Poe of Mrs. Jane Stannard, mother of one of his early classmates. Her kindness, sympathy, and gracious manner had made a deep impression on his boyish heart. He was engaged, at the time, in classical studies. She loomed, therefore, in his brilliant imagination as an embodiment of all those classic traits of refined beauty that the ancient Greeks—and those who study them—love so well.*

Helen, thy beauty is to me
  Like those Nicaean barks of yore,
That gently, o'er a perfumed sea,
  The weary, way-worn wanderer bore
To his own native shore.     5

On desperate seas long wont to roam,
  Thy hyacinth hair, thy classic face,

Thy naiad airs have brought me home
  To the glory that was Greece,
And the grandeur that was Rome.   10

Lo! in yon brilliant window niche
  How statue-like I see thee stand,
  The agate lamp within thy hand!
Ah, Psyche, from the regions which
Are Holy Land!    15

2. NICAEAN BARKS, etc.—Nicaea was an ancient seaport of Asia Minor. If in line 4 by "weary . . . wanderer" Poe had in mind Odysseus, he should have used Phaeacian instead of Nicaean, for it was the Phaeacian king who sent Odysseus safely home.

7. HYACINTH HAIR—Curling hair, such as demanded by the Greek fashion.

8. NAIAD—The naiads were water nymphs, inexpressibly fair.

14. PSYCHE—Symbolizes the soul. Probably with the lamp, the idea is the light of knowledge.

15. HOLY LAND—Here, Greece.

◇◇◇◇◇◇◇◇◇◇◇◇◇◇◇◇◇◇◇◇◇◇◇◇◇◇◇◇◇◇◇◇◇◇◇◇◇◇◇◇◇◇◇◇◇◇◇◇◇◇◇◇◇◇

## FOR DISCUSSION

1. What famous Helen of history does the poem suggest? What was the "glory that was Greece"? the "grandeur that was Rome"? How could "Helen" bring him home to them?

2. Why does the poet compare Greece to the Holy Land?

3. What is the Christian ideal of perfect womanhood? What more, besides physical and intellectual beauty, must a person possess to be perfect?

## WORDS

When ancient Romans described a person as *classicus*, they meant he was of the highest or first rank in society. What slang word with the same root do we use to say that someone is perfect in a certain respect? What are the *classical* languages? What is a national *classic*?

## RELATED READING

Among the many poems which Edgar Allan Poe wrote to or about women, some real and some imaginary, you will enjoy these: "Lenore," "To One in Paradise," "Annabel Lee," and "Ulalume."

Another Southern poet, Thomas Holley Chivers, was a friend of Poe and wrote poetry much like his. Read his "To Allegra Florence in Heaven," "Lily Adair," "Rosalie Lee," or "Isadore."

# The Bells

EDGAR ALLAN POE

*"The Bells" is a sound poem to be read aloud if you would catch the full and ingenious magic of its music.*

Hear the sledges with the bells—
  Silver bells!
What a world of merriment their mel-
    ody foretells!
  How they tinkle, tinkle, tinkle,
    In the icy air of night!    5
While the stars that oversprinkle
All the heavens, seem to twinkle
  With a crystalline delight;
Keeping time, time, time,
  In a sort of Runic rhyme,    10
To the tintinnabulation that so musi-
    cally wells
  From the bells, bells, bells, bells,
    Bells, bells, bells—
From the jingling and the tinkling of the
    bells.

  Hear the mellow wedding bells—   15
    Golden bells!
What a world of happiness their har-
    mony foretells!
  Through the balmy air of night
How they ring out their delight!—
    From the molten-golden notes,   20
    And all in tune,
  What a liquid ditty floats
To the turtle-dove that listens, while she
    gloats
    On the moon!
Oh, from out the sounding cells,   25
What a gush of euphony voluminously
    wells!

  How it swells!
  How it dwells
    On the Future!—how it tells
    Of the rapture that impels    30
To the swinging and the ringing
    Of the bells, bells, bells—
Of the bells, bells, bells, bells,
    Bells, bells, bells—
To the rhyming and the chiming of the
    bells!    35

  Hear the loud alarum bells—
    Brazen bells!
What a tale of terror now their turbu-
    lency tells!
  In the startled ear of night
How they scream out their affright!
    Too much horrified to speak,   41
    They can only shriek, shriek,
    Out of tune.
In a clamorous appealing to the mercy
    of the fire,
In a mad expostulation with the deaf
    and frantic fire,    45
  Leaping higher, higher, higher,
  With a desperate desire,
And a resolute endeavor
Now—now to sit, or never,
By the side of the pale-faced moon.   50
  Oh, the bells, bells, bells!
  What a tale their terror tells
    Of Despair!

1. SLEDGES—Sleighs.
10. RUNIC—Secret, mysterious.
11. TINTINNABULATION—A    Poe-coined word, meaning a tinkling or jingling sound.

26. EUPHONY—Full, sweet sound.
26. VOLUMINOUSLY—With great volume or full, deep resonance.
36. ALARUM—Archaic for alarm.
45. EXPOSTULATION—Protest.

How they clang, and clash, and roar!
What a horror they outpour        55
On the bosom of the palpitating air!
    Yet the ear, it fully knows,
        By the twanging,
        And the clanging,
    How the danger ebbs and flows;   60
Yet the ear distinctly tells;
        In the jangling,
        And the wrangling,
    How the danger sinks and swells,
By the sinking or the swelling in the an-
        ger of the bells—        65
        Of the bells—
    Of the bells, bells, bells, bells,
        Bells, bells, bells,—
In the clamor and the clanging of the
        bells!

Hear the tolling of the bells—        70
        Iron bells!
What a world of solemn thought their
        monody compels!
    In the silence of the night
    How we shiver with affright
At the melancholy menace of their
        tone!        75
    For every sound that floats
    From the rust within their throats
        Is a groan.
    And the people,—ah, the people—
    They that dwell up in the steeple,

72. MONODY—Funeral song, dirge.

All alone,        81
And who, tolling, tolling, tolling,
    In that muffled monotone
Feel a glory in so rolling        85
    On the human heart a stone—
They are neither man nor woman,—
They are neither brute nor human—
    They are Ghouls:—
And their king it is who tolls:—
And he rolls, rolls, rolls,        90
    Rolls
    A paean from the bells!
And his merry bosom swells
    With the paean of the bells!
And he dances, and he yells;        95
    Keeping time, time, time,
    In a sort of Runic rhyme,
        To the paean of the bells:—
        Of the bells:
    Keeping time, time, time,        100
    In a sort of Runic rhyme,
        To the throbbing of the bells—
    Of the bells, bells, bells—
        To the sobbing of the bells:—
    Keeping time, time, time,        105
        As he knells, knells, knells,
    In a happy Runic rhyme,
    To the rolling of the bells—
Of the bells, bells, bells:—
        To the tolling of the bells—        110
Of the bells, bells, bells, bells,
        Bells, bells, bells—
To the moaning and the groaning of the
        bells.

## FOR DISCUSSION

1. What different moods are expressed in the four stanzas? Which mood is most typical of Poe?

2. Is there any other connection among the stanzas beside the fact that all are about bells? Could you reasonably suggest a better arrangement of the stanzas; for example, would you place the joyous stanzas at the end?

## PROJECTS

1. Make a list of the sounds that produce the impressions of sleigh bells. What consonants give the effect?

2. List the sounds that give the wedding bells' smooth, mellow tones in the second stanza.

3. The short *a*, especially when followed by an *r* or an *ng* is an unpleasantly harsh sound. List the words in the third

stanza in which *a* is the chief vowel. List, too, the words with harsh gutturals (*k*, hard *c*) and sibilants (*s, z, sh*).

4. List the words that give an idea of the solemnity and quiet of death. Underline the vowel and consonant sounds that appear most frequently.

5. Can you think of any other effect that bells might have on human life? Write a composition telling their significance, or write a stanza imitating Poe. Some examples: bells at Mass; bells on a buoy or on a ship; bells of traveling pedlars; school bells; doorbells.

◇◇◇◇◇

# The Concord Hymn

## RALPH WALDO EMERSON

*The first bullets that sang the fight for American independence came from the guns of farmers on Concord Bridge.*

*Sixty years later, in the quiet of peace, grateful human voices sang another song, one of tender remembrance for the brave who fell in battle that nineteenth day of April, 1775.*

By the rude bridge that arched the flood,
  Their flag to April's breeze unfurled,
Here once the embattled farmers stood,
  And fired the shot heard round the
    world.

The foe long since in silence slept;   5
  Alike the conqueror silent sleeps;
And Time the ruined bridge has swept
  Down the dark stream which seaward
    creeps.

On this green bank, by this soft stream,
  We set today a votive stone;   10
That memory may their deed redeem,
  When, like our sires, our sons are
    gone.

Spirit, that made those heroes dare
  To die, and leave their children free,
Bid Time and Nature gently spare   15
  The shaft we raise to them and thee.

10. VOTIVE—Consecrated by a vow.

◇◇◇◇◇◇◇◇◇◇◇◇◇◇◇◇◇◇◇◇◇◇◇◇◇◇◇◇◇◇◇◇◇◇◇◇◇◇◇◇◇◇◇◇◇◇◇◇

FOR DISCUSSION

1. Is the idea in line four an exaggeration? Explain its meaning.
2. What is the poem's central idea?
3. Note the quiet and reserved mood of the poem. In this case, why is such a mood preferable to an enthusiastic and fiery outcry?
4. What is the "Spirit" that the poet addresses in the fourth stanza?
5. Why do we erect monuments? Do they serve a practical purpose? What monuments are there in your city?

USING WORDS

*Rude* is from the Latin *rudis* meaning *rough*. From your understanding of *rude* as applied to persons, tell how it applies to a bridge.

THE POET'S CRAFT

In line 15 why are the words "Time" and "Nature" capitalized? What is this poetic device called? What is its effect in this poem?

415

# The Rhodora

## RALPH WALDO EMERSON

*To the practical-minded, who want to know a* USE *for everything, the world's beautiful things seem like unnecessary creations. Emerson tries to give a satisfactory reason for the existence of beauty.*

In May, when sea-winds pierced our solitudes,
I found the fresh Rhodora in the woods,
Spreading its leafless blooms in a damp nook,
To please the desert and the sluggish brook.
The purple petals, fallen in the pool,                    5
Made the black water with their beauty gay;
Here might the redbird come his plumes to cool,
And court the flower that cheapens his array.
Rhodora! if the sages ask thee why
This charm is wasted on the earth and sky,              10
Tell them, dear, that if eyes were made for seeing,
Then Beauty is its own excuse for being:
Why thou wert there, O rival of the rose!
I never thought to ask, I never knew:
But, in my simple ignorance, suppose                    15
The self-same Power that brought me there brought you.

Title—RHODORA—A low shrub, which, before its green leaves come out, bears large, purplish-pink flowers.

◇◇◇◇◇◇◇◇◇◇◇◇◇◇◇◇◇◇◇◇◇◇◇◇◇◇◇◇◇◇◇◇◇◇◇◇◇◇◇◇◇◇◇◇◇◇◇◇◇◇◇◇◇◇◇◇◇◇

## FOR DISCUSSION

1. Do you think Emerson answers fully the question of the sages? Read the Canticle of the Three Young Men who were cast into the fiery furnace (Daniel 3:57–88). In this song, all things created are called upon to praise and bless the Lord. How can flowers, birds, whales, ice, frost praise the Lord?

2. The fine arts produce beautiful things that are not intended for practical purposes. Do artists, in a way, imitate God? How? When you have praised the work of art and the artist, can you go beyond them in your praise? Why?

3. What colors does Emerson use to paint the scenery of the poem? What contrasts does he use to make the flower even more beautiful?

4. Note the rhyme scheme of the poem. Is there any imperfect rhyme? Are there proportion and orderliness in the arrangement of the rhyme scheme?

5. Can you discover the most quoted line in the poem and tell why it is often cited?

6. Why does the rhodora "cheapen" the array of the redbird? What does the word "cheapen" mean here?

## A PROJECT

Bring a poem about a flower to class and tell what ideas inspired the poet.

# The Day Is Done

## HENRY WADSWORTH LONGFELLOW

*"These lines have been justly admired for the delicacy of their expression. Some of the images are very effective. . . . The poem, on the whole, however, is chiefly to be admired for the graceful . . . metre, so well in accordance with the character of the sentiments, and especially for the* EASE *of the general manner." So said Edgar Allan Poe in his essay, "The Poetic Principle."*

*Longfellow wrote this poem as an introduction to* THE WAIF, *a collection of the work of minor poets which he had edited.*

The day is done, and the darkness,
  Falls from the wings of Night,
As a feather is wafted downward
  From an eagle in his flight.

I see the lights of the village    5
  Gleam through the rain and the mist,
And a feeling of sadness comes o'er me,
  That my soul cannot resist;

A feeling of sadness and longing
  That is not akin to pain,    10
And resembles sorrow only
  As the mist resembles the rain.

Come, read to me some poem,
  Some simple and heartfelt lay,
That shall soothe this restless feeling,
  And banish the thoughts of day.   16

Not from the grand old masters,
  Not from the bards sublime,
Whose distant footsteps echo
  Through the corridors of Time.   20

For, like strains of martial music,
  Their mighty thoughts suggest
Life's endless toil and endeavor;
  And tonight I long for rest.

Read from some humbler poet,   25
  Whose songs gushed from his heart,
As showers from the clouds of summer,
  Or tears from the eyelids start;

Who, through long days of labor,
  And nights devoid of ease,   30
Still heard in his soul the music
  Of wonderful melodies.

Such songs have power to quiet
  The restless pulse of care,
And come like the benediction   35
  That follows after prayer.

Then read from the treasured volume
  The poem of thy choice,
And lend to the rhyme of the poet
  The beauty of thy voice.   40

And the night shall be filled with music,
  And the cares that infest the day,
Shall fold their tents, like the Arabs,
  And as silently steal away.

---

417

## FOR DISCUSSION

1. What is the general mood of the poem? Is it a pleasant or a depressing one?

2. Why would the grand old masters and the bards sublime be unsuitable at nightfall under the circumstances given in the poem? Can you think of times when their martial music and mighty thoughts would be proper?

3. When you are tired at the end of a long day, do you prefer lively and stirring music to the sweet and quiet? Can you see advantages in both types?

4. What picture do you get from the first stanza? What is the figure of speech there? What figures of speech are in the last stanza?

## THE POET'S WORDS

1. *Lay,* derived from the French *lai,* means a song or a short narrative poem.

Scott's *Lay of the Last Minstrel* and Macaulay's *Lays of Ancient Rome* are famous narrative poems in English literature. Why are poems frequently referred to as songs? Do the folk songs you have read or heard give you any clue?

2. *Bard* is another literary term you will meet frequently. It comes from a Welsh noun referring to the poets of old who composed verses glorifying the deeds of heroes. They sang their poems to the accompaniment of a musical instrument, usually the harp. A *minstrel* was a musical entertainer or traveling poet of the later Middle Ages. Minstrels catered to all classes. Some of them sang at courts, others in the market place or in taverns. In France, minstrels were called *troubadors* (from the Old French, *troubar,* to "find" or "invent") because they improvised their songs to meet all occasions. In Germany, they were called *minnesingers* because they restricted themselves to love songs.

◇◇◇◇◇

# Two Sonnets for the Divina Commedia

## HENRY WADSWORTH LONGFELLOW

The DIVINA COMMEDIA, an epic poem written by the Italian, Dante, in the fourteenth century, is regarded even by non-Catholics as a "medieval miracle in song." It was to this great poem that Longfellow went for comfort and distraction after the tragic accident in which his second wife was burned in 1861. His translation was published in 1867.

A Longfellow sonnet precedes and follows each of the three major divisions of the DIVINE COMEDY: the INFERNO, PURGATORIO, and PARADISO. The first sonnet compares Dante's work to a cathedral where the poet can pray and find refuge. The figure of speech is carried into the fifth sonnet wherein we see the climactic splendor of the poem.

## SONNET I

Oft have I seen at some cathedral door
A laborer, pausing in the dust and heat,
Lay down his burden, and with reverent
feet
Enter and cross himself, and on the floor
Kneel to repeat his paternoster o'er;  5
Far off the noises of the world retreat;
The loud vociferations of the street
Become an undistinguishable roar.
So, as I enter here from day to day
And leave my burden at this minster
gate,  10
Kneeling in prayer and not ashamed to
pray,
The tumult of the time disconsolate
To inarticulate murmurs dies away,
While the eternal ages watch and wait.

## SONNET V

I lift mine eyes, and all the windows
blaze
With forms of Saints and holy men who
died,

5. PATERNOSTER—The Our Father.
7. VOCIFERATIONS—Loud cries.
10. MINSTER GATE—Door of the cathedral.
12. TIME DISCONSOLATE—This sonnet was
written in 1864.

Here martyred and hereafter glorified;
And the great Rose upon its leaves dis-
plays
Christ's Triumph, and the angelic roun-
delays,  5
With splendor upon splendor multi-
plied;
And Beatrice again at Dante's side
No more rebukes, but smiles her words
of praise.
And then the organ sounds, and unseen
choirs
Sing the old Latin hymns of peace and
love  10
And benedictions of the Holy Ghost;
And the melodious bells among the
spires
O'er all the house-tops and through
heaven above
Proclaim the elevation of the Host.

5. ROUNDELAYS—Melodies, songs.
7. BEATRICE—The central figure of the
poem. Beatrice was a beautiful woman of
Dante's native city Florence. The poet loved
her and wrote many songs in her honor. In
the *Commedia* she symbolizes Faith and Theology. She conducts Dante through Paradise.
8. NO MORE REBUKES—In the *Purgatorio*,
Beatrice appears to Dante and rebukes him for
the error of his ways: for setting so much store
in philosophy and neglecting the Church and
Faith.

---

## FOR DISCUSSION

1. What is the double comparison in
the first sonnet? Do you know of any
books that would have an effect similar to
that of the *Divina Commedia* on Longfellow?

2. Do you think that it is merely religious sentimentality that brings comfort
to people in church? How do you account for the consolation and strength
people get from prayer or from reading
great works of literature? Why should
you prefer prayer to literature in time of
trouble? What kind of literature could
be termed "prayerful"?

4. Name some saints and martyrs whose
pictures would appear in the stained glass
windows of Dante's "cathedral."

5. What is the climax of all the splendor of sight and sound in the cathedral?

6. Compare the emotions in the sonnets. Which poem do you like better?
Why?

7. Judging by these sonnets, do you
think Longfellow would read the *Commedia* while in the mood of his poem,
"The Day is Done"?

## A PROJECT

Write out the rhyme schemes of both
sonnets; compare the scheme of the sestets.

# Sail On, O Ship of State

## HENRY WADSWORTH LONGFELLOW

This final stanza from the poem, "The Building of the Ship," has been recited many times on public occasions and printed in hundreds of newspapers. A favorite with Lincoln, this symbolic ode was often recited by him with deep emotion. During the Second World War before the United States entered it, President Roosevelt sent this stanza to Winston Churchill, the Prime Minister of England, and said that this "applies to your people as it does to us."

Thou, too, sail on, O Ship of State!
Sail on, O Union, strong and great!
Humanity with all its fears,
With all its hopes of future years,
Is hanging breathless on thy fate!  5
We know what Master laid thy keel,
What Workmen wrought thy ribs of steel,
Who made each mast, and sail, and rope,
What anvils rang, what hammers beat,
In what a forge and what a heat  10
Were shaped the anchors of thy hope!
Fear not each sudden sound and shock,
'Tis of the wave and not the rock;
'Tis but the flapping of the sail,
And not a rent made by the gale!  15
In spite of rock and tempest's roar,
In spite of false lights on the shore,
Sail on, nor fear to breast the sea!
Our hearts, our hopes, are all with thee.
Our hearts, our hopes, our prayers, our tears,  20
Our faith triumphant o'er our fears,
Are all with thee—are all with thee!

---

FOR DISCUSSION

1. Who are the "Workmen" and the "Master" who made this ship?

2. What would be some of the "false lights on the shore" and the "rock and tempest roar"?

420

# The Ballad of the Oysterman

## OLIVER WENDELL HOLMES

It was a tall young oysterman lived by the river-side,
His shop was just upon the bank, his boat was on the tide;
The daughter of a fisherman, that was so straight and slim,
Lived over on the other bank, right opposite to him.

It was the pensive oysterman that saw a lovely maid,                    5
Upon a moonlight evening, a-sitting in the shade;
He saw her wave her handkerchief, as much as if to say,
"I'm wide awake, young oysterman, and all the folks away."

Then up arose the oysterman, and to himself said he,
"I guess I'll leave the skiff at home, for fear that folks should see;   10
I read it in the story-book, that, for to kiss his dear,
Leander swam the Hellespont,—and I will swim this here."

And he has leaped into the waves, and crossed the shining stream,
And he has clambered up the bank, all in the moonlight gleam;
Oh there were kisses sweet as dew, and words as soft as rain,—          15
But they have heard her father's step, and in he leaps again!

Out spoke the ancient fisherman,—"Oh, what was that, my daughter?"
" 'Twas nothing but a pebble, sir, I threw into the water."
"And what is that, pray tell me, love, that paddles off so fast?"
"It's nothing but a porpoise, sir, that's been a-swimming past."        20

Out spoke the ancient fisherman,—"Now bring me my harpoon!
I'll get into my fishing-boat, and fix the fellow soon."
Down fell that pretty innocent, as falls a snow-white lamb,
Her hair drooped round her pallid cheeks, like seaweed on a clam.

Alas for those two loving ones! she waked not from her swound,          25
And he was taken with a cramp, and in the waves was drowned;
But Fate has metamorphosed them, in pity of their woe,
And now they keep an oyster-shop for mermaids down below.

12. LEANDER—Leander swam the Hellespont nightly to visit Hero, a priestess of Aphrodite. One night he was drowned. In her grief, Hero cast herself into the sea.
27. METAMORPHOSED (mĕt′à·môr′fōzd)—Changed, transformed.

## FOR DISCUSSION

1. What words, phrases, rhymes, does the poet use to achieve comic effect?
2. What legend of ancient Greece does he parody?

## WORDS FROM FOREIGN TONGUES

1. *Penser* is a French word meaning to think, reflect. Describe the face of a person in a *pensive* mood.
2. *Meta* is a Greek preposition meaning "over"; *morphē* is Greek for "form." What English word do we derive from joining the two?

## RELATED READING

For more fun in rhyme read John Godfrey Saxe's "Pyramus and Thisbe" and "Echo." Or, try Holmes's "The Deacon's Masterpiece."

✧✧✧✧✧

# The Vision of Sir Launfal

### JAMES RUSSELL LOWELL

The Holy Grail disappeared when one of the descendants of Joseph of Arimathea, who had brought the Last Supper cup to England, violated the vow of chastity which all had to take who safeguarded the relic. Of all King Arthur's Round Table, only the stainless Sir Galahad could find and recover it.

The story of the search for the Grail has been retold often by writers, many of whom use it as a symbol of the pursuit of high ideals. So it is with Lowell, who has added brotherly love and humility as conditions for success in the quest.

Proud Sir Launfal resolves to go on the quest. As he sleeps on the eve of his departure, a vision comes to him. In his dream, all his life, through all the world, he searches fruitlessly. On his return, beaten with disappointment and suffering, he finds at his very doorstep, where he had spurned it before, the object of his search.

### Prelude to Part First

Over his keys the musing organist,
  Beginning doubtfully and far away,
First lets his fingers wander as they list,

3. LIST—Wish, please.

And builds a bridge from Dreamland for his lay.
Then, as the touch of his loved instrument     5
  Gives hope and fervor, nearer draws his theme,

First guessed by faint auroral flushes
    sent
    Along the wavering vista of his dream.

Not only around our infancy     9
Doth heaven with all its splendors lie:
Daily, with souls that cringe and plot,
We Sinais climb and know it not.

Over our manhood bend the skies;
    Against our fallen and traitor lives
The great winds utter prophecies;   15
    With our faint hearts the mountain
    strives;
Its arms outstretched, the Druid wood
    Waits with its benedicite;
And to our age's drowsy blood
    Still shouts the inspiring sea.    20

Earth gets its price for what earth
    gives us;
    The beggar is taxed for a corner to
    die in,
The priest hath his fee who comes and
    shrives us,
We bargain for the graves we lie in;
At the devil's booth are all things sold,
Each ounce of dross costs its ounce of
    gold;    26
    For a cap and bells our lives we pay,

8. VISTA—A long view or prospect; a mental view or prospect extending over a series of events.

9–10. NOT ONLY . . . SPLENDORS LIE—Lowell disagrees with Wordsworth's line: "Heaven lies about us in our infancy." See "Ode on the Intimations of Immortality," line 87.

17. DRUID WOOD—A metaphor. Druids were priests in ancient Gaul, Britain, and Ireland to whom the oak tree was sacred. They worshiped in forests.

18. BENEDICITE—A noun meaning blessing.

23. SHRIVES—Hears confession and gives absolution. There are non-Catholics even today who believe that penitents have to pay the priests for absolution from sin.

26. DROSS—Scum; anything worthless.

27. CAP AND BELLS—The medieval court jester wore them as symbols of his foolishness.

Bubbles we buy with a whole soul's
    tasking;
    'Tis Heaven alone that is given away,
    'Tis only God may be had for the ask-
    ing;    30
    No price is set on the lavish summer,
June may be had by the poorest comer.

And what is so rare as a day in June?
    Then, if ever, come perfect days;   34
Then Heaven tries earth if it be in tune,
    And over it softly her warm ear lays;
Whether we look, or whether we listen,
We hear life murmur, or see it glisten;
Every clod feels a stir of might,
    An instinct within it that reaches and
    towers,    40
And, groping blindly above it for light,
    Climbs to a soul in grass and flowers;
The flush of life may well be seen
    Thrilling back over hills and valleys;
The cowslip startles in meadows green,
    The buttercup catches the sun in its
    chalice,    46
And there's never a leaf nor a blade too
    mean
    To be some happy creature's palace;
The little bird sits at his door in the sun,
    Atilt like a blossom among the leaves,
And lets his illumined being o'errun   51
    With the deluge of summer it re-
    ceives;
His mate feels the eggs beneath her
    wings,
    And the heart in her dumb breast flut-
    ters and sings;
He sings to the wide world, and she to
    her nest,—    55
    In the nice ear of Nature which song
    is the best?

Now is the high tide of the year,
    And whatever of life hath ebbed away
Comes flooding back with a ripply cheer
    Into every bare inlet and creek and
    bay;    60

56. NICE—Discriminating; refined.

Now the heart is so full that a drop over-
   fills it,
We are happy now because God wills it.
No matter how barren the past may
   have been,
'Tis enough for us now that the leaves
   are green;
We sit in the warm shade and feel right
   well            65
How the sap creeps up and the blossoms
   swell;
We may shut our eyes, but we cannot
   help knowing
That skies are clear and grass is growing;
The breeze comes whispering in our ear,
That dandelions are blossoming near,
   That maize has sprouted, the streams
     are flowing,          71
That the river is bluer than the sky,
That the robin is plastering his house
   hard by;
And if the breeze kept the good news
   back,            74
For other couriers we should not lack;
   We could guess it all by yon heifer's
    lowing,—
And hark! how clear bold chanticleer,
Warmed with the new wine of the year,
   Tells all in his lusty crowing!

Joy comes, grief goes, we know not how;
Everything is happy now,       81
   Everything is upward striving;
'Tis as easy now for the heart to be true
As for grass to be green or skies to be
   blue,—
   'Tis the natural way of living.   85
Who knows whither the clouds have
   fled?
   In the unscarred heaven they leave no
    wake,
And the eyes forget the tears they have
   shed,
   The heart forgets its sorrow and ache;
The soul partakes the season's youth,

And the sulphurous rifts of passion
   and woe         91
Lie deep 'neath a silence pure and
   smooth,
   Like burnt-out craters healed with
    snow.
What wonder if Sir Launfal now   94
Remembered the keeping of his vow?

## PART FIRST

### I

"My golden spurs now bring to me,
   And bring to me my richest mail,
For tomorrow I go over land and sea
   In search of the Holy Grail;
Shall never a bed for me be spread,   100
Nor shall a pillow be under my head,
Till I begin my vow to keep;
Here on the rushes will I sleep,
And perchance there may come a vision
   true
Ere day create the world anew."   105
   Slowly Sir Launfal's eyes grew dim,
   Slumber fell like a cloud on him,
And into his soul the vision flew.

### II

The crows flapped over by twos and
   threes,
In the pool drowsed the cattle up to
   their knees,     110
   The little birds sang as if it were
   The one day of summer in all the
    year,
And the very leaves seemed to sing on
   the trees.
The castle alone in the landscape lay
Like an outpost of winter, dull and gray;
'Twas the proudest hall in the North
   Countree,     116
And never its gates might opened be,
Save to lord or lady of high degree;
Summer besieged it on every side,
But the churlish stone her assaults de-
   fied;     120

She could not scale the chilly wall,
Though around it for leagues her pavil-
 ions tall
Stretched left and right,
Over the hills and out of sight;    124
 Green and broad was every tent,
 And out of each a murmur went
Till the breeze fell off at night.

### III

The drawbridge dropped with a surly
 clang,
And through the dark arch a charger
 sprang,    129
Bearing Sir Launfal, the maiden knight,
In his gilded mail, that flamed so bright
It seemed the dark castle had gathered
 all
Those shafts the fierce sun had shot over
 its wall
 In his siege of three hundred summers
 long,

And, binding them all in one blazing
 sheaf,    135
 Had cast them forth; so, young and
 strong,
And lightsome as a locust leaf,
Sir Launfal flashed forth in his unscarred
 mail,
To seek in all climes for the Holy Grail.

### IV

It was morning on hill and stream and
 tree,    140
 And morning in the young knight's
 heart;
Only the castle moodily
Rebuffed the gifts of the sunshine free,
 And gloomed by itself apart;    144
The season brimmed all other things up
Full as the rain fills the pitcher plant's
 cup.

146. PITCHER PLANT—Any plant with
pitcher-shaped leaves.

V

As Sir Launfal made morn through the darksome gate,
He was 'ware of a leper, crouched by the same,
Who begged with his hand and moaned as he sate;
And a loathing over Sir Launfal came.
The sunshine went out of his soul with a thrill,    151
The flesh 'neath his armor 'gan shrink and crawl,
And midway its leap his heart stood still
Like a frozen waterfall,
For this man, so foul, and bent of stature,    155
Rasped harshly against his dainty nature,
And seemed the one blot on the summer morn,—
So he tossed him a piece of gold in scorn.

VI

The leper raised not the gold from the dust:    159
"Better to me the poor man's crust,
Better the blessing of the poor,
Though I turn me empty from his door;
That is no true alms which the hand can hold;
He gives nothing but worthless gold
    Who gives from a sense of duty;    165
But he who gives but a slender mite,
And gives to that which is out of sight,
    That thread of the all-sustaining Beauty
Which runs through all and doth all unite,—
The hand cannot clasp the whole of his alms,    170
The heart outstretches its eager palms,
For a god goes with it and makes it store
To the soul that was starving in darkness before."

*Prelude to Part Second*

Down swept the chill wind from the mountain peak,
    From the snow five thousand summers old;    175
On open wold and hilltop bleak
    It had gathered all the cold,
And whirled it like sleet on the wanderer's cheek.
It carried a shiver everywhere
From the unleafed boughs and pastures bare;    180
The little brook heard it and built a roof
'Neath which he could house him, winter-proof;
All night by the white stars' frosty gleams
He groined his arches and matched his beams;    184
Slender and clear were his crystal spars
As the lashes of light that trim the stars;
He sculptured every summer delight
In his halls and chambers out of sight;
Sometimes his tinkling waters slipped
Down through a frost-leaved forest crypt,    190
Long, sparkling aisles of steel-stemmed trees
Bending to counterfeit a breeze;
Sometimes the roof no fretwork knew
But silvery mosses that downward grew;
Sometimes it was carved in sharp relief    195
With quaint arabesques of ice-fern leaf;
Sometimes it was simply smooth and clear
For the gladness of heaven to shine through, and here
He had caught the nodding bulrush-tops
And hung them thickly with diamond drops,    200
That crystaled the beams of moon and sun,

172. STORE—Food.

And made a star of every one.
No mortal builder's most rare device
Could match this winter-palace of ice;
'Twas as if every image that mirrored
    lay                205
In his depths serene through the sum-
    mer day,
Each fleeting shadow of earth and sky,
  Lest the happy model should be lost,
Had been mimicked in fairy masonry
  By the elfin builders of the frost.   210
Within the hall are song and laughter,
  The cheeks of Christmas glow red and
    jolly,
And sprouting is every corbel and rafter
  With lightsome green of ivy and
    holly;
Through the deep gulf of the chimney
  wide                215
Wallows the Yule-log's roaring tide;
The broad flame-pennons droop and flap
  And belly and tug as a flag in the
    wind;
Like a locust shrills the imprisoned
  sap,                219
  Hunted to death in its galleries blind;
And swift little troops of silent sparks,
  Now pausing, now scattering away as
    in fear,
Go threading the soot-forest's tangled
  darks
  Like herds of startled deer.

But the wind without was eager and
  sharp;              225
Of Sir Launfal's gray hair it makes a
  harp,
  And rattles and wrings
  The icy strings,
Singing, in dreary monotone,
A Christmas carol of its own,    230
Whose burden still, as he might guess,

213. CORBEL—A projection from the face of
a wall, supporting a weight; a bracket.
231. BURDEN—The prevailing idea or tone;
the refrain.

Was—"Shelterless, shelterless, shelter-
  less!"
The voice of the seneschal flared like a
  torch
As he shouted the wanderer away from
  the porch,
And he sat in the gateway and saw all
  night             235
  The great hall-fire, so cheery and bold,
  Through the window-slits of the castle
    old,
Build out its piers of ruddy light
  Against the drift of the cold.

PART SECOND

I

There was never a leaf on bush or
  tree,              240
The bare boughs rattled shudderingly;
The river was dumb and could not
  speak,
  For the weaver Winter its shroud had
    spun;
A single crow on the tree-top bleak
  From his shining feathers shed off the
    cold sun;          245
Again it was morning, but shrunk and
  cold,
As if her veins were sapless and old,
And she rose up decrepitly
For a last dim look at earth and sea.

II

Sir Launfal turned from his own hard
  gate,            250
For another heir in his earldom sate;
An old, bent man, worn out and frail,
He came back from seeking the Holy
  Grail.
Little he recked of his earldom's loss,
No more on his surcoat was blazoned
  the cross,          255
But deep in his soul the sign he wore,
The badge of the suffering and the poor.

233. SENESCHAL—A steward.

### III

Sir Launfal's raiment thin and spare
Was idle mail 'gainst the barbèd air,
For it was just at the Christmas time.
So he mused, as he sat, of a sunnier
    clime,        261
And sought for a shelter from cold and
    snow
In the light and warmth of long ago;
He sees the snake-like caravan crawl
O'er the edge of the desert, black and
    small,        265
Then nearer and nearer, till, one by one,
He can count the camels in the sun,
As over the red-hot sands they pass
To where, in its slender necklace of
    grass,
The little spring laughed and leaped in
    the shade,        270
And with its own self like an infant
    played,
And waved its signal of palms.

### IV

"For Christ's sweet sake, I beg an
    alms"—
The happy camels may reach the spring,
But Sir Launfal sees only the gruesome
    thing,        275
The leper, lank as the rain-blanched
    bone,
That cowers beside him, a thing as lone
And white as the ice-isles of Northern
    seas
In the desolate horror of his disease.

### V

And Sir Launfal said,—"I behold in
    thee        280
An Image of Him who died on the tree;
Thou also hast had thy crown of
    thorns,—
Thou also hast had the world's buffets
    and scorns,—
And to thy life were not denied

The wounds in the hands and feet and
    side.        285
Mild Mary's Son, acknowledge me;
Behold, through him, I give to Thee!"

### VI

Then the soul of the leper stood up in
    his eyes
    And looked at Sir Launfal, and
        straightway he        289
Remembered in what a haughtier guise
    He had flung an alms to leprosie,
When he girt his young life up in gilded
    mail
And set forth in search of the Holy
    Grail.
The heart within him was ashes and
    dust,
He parted in twain his single crust,    295
He broke the ice on the streamlet's
    brink,
And gave the leper to eat and drink;
'Twas a moldy crust of coarse brown
    bread,
    'Twas water out of a wooden bowl,—
Yet with fine wheaten bread was the
    leper fed,        300
    And 'twas red wine he drank with his
        thirsty soul.

### VII

As Sir Launfal mused with a downcast
    face,
A light shone round about the place;
The leper no longer crouched at his side,
But stood before him glorified,    305
Shining and tall and fair and straight
As the pillar that stood by the Beautiful
    Gate—
Himself the Gate whereby men can
Enter the temple of God in Man.

### VIII

His words were shed softer than leaves
    from the pine    310

And they fell on Sir Launfal as snow on
    the brine,
That mingle their softness and quiet in
    one
With the shaggy unrest they float down
    upon;
And the voice that was calmer than
    silence said,
  "Lo, it is I, be not afraid!     315
In many climes, without avail,
Thou has spent thy life for the Holy
    Grail;
Behold, it is here—this cup which thou
Didst fill at the streamlet for Me but
    now;     319
This crust is My body broken for thee,
This water His blood that died on the
    tree;
The Holy Supper is kept, indeed,
In whatso we share with another's need;
Not what we give, but what we share,
For the gift without the giver is bare;
Who gives himself with his alms feeds
    three—     326
Himself, his hungering neighbor, and
    Me."

IX

Sir Launfal awoke as from a swound;
"The Grail in my castle here is found!

Hang my idle armor up on the wall,   330
Let it be the spider's banquet-hall;
He must be fenced with stronger mail
Who would seek and find the Holy
    Grail."

X

The castle gate stands open now,
  And the wanderer is welcome to the
    hall     335
As the hangbird is to the elm-tree
    bough;
  No longer scowl the turrets tall,
The summer's long siege at last is o'er;
When the first poor outcast went in at
    the door,
She entered with him in disguise,   340
And mastered the fortress by surprise;
There is no spot she loves so well on
    ground,
She lingers and smiles there the whole
    year round,
The meanest serf on Sir Launfal's land
Has hall and bower at his command;
And there's no poor man in the North
    Countree    346
But is lord of the earldom as much as he.

336. HANGBIRD—The oriole, which builds a
hanging nest.

---

## FOR DISCUSSION

### PRELUDE TO PART FIRST

1. In line 7, to what does the poet compare the coming of his inspiration? Where is the general theme of the poem first struck? What is the attitude of nature toward our cringing souls? How does the sea inspire us to greatness?

2. In lines 27 and 28, what do "cap and bells" suggest? Why are bubbles a good representation of worthless things which fascinate and attract us? Why are lines 81–84 true?

3. Explain the thought or idea that holds together the many subjects Lowell touches in his "Prelude to Part First."

### PART FIRST

1. What hardship does Sir Launfal resolve to undergo until he finds the Holy Grail? In view of the moral of the story, why was this bodily penance not enough to enable him to succeed?

2. Why was it natural for the knight to start on his quest in the spring? How does the description of the castle give you the key to Sir Launfal's character?

3. Explain line 141: "(It was) morning in the young knight's heart"; line 147: "As Sir Launfal made morn through the darksome gate."

4. What mistake does Sir Launfal make at the very start of his quest? In giving to others, what intention should we have in heart and mind? What is that "true alms" (line 163) which the hand cannot hold?

#### PRELUDE TO PART SECOND

Compare the description of winter with that of spring in the first prelude. Which do you personally prefer? Why?

#### PART SECOND

1. In line 256, what was the badge of the suffering and the poor that Sir Launfal wore in his soul? Where had he worn this badge before? What lesson does this transfer of the badge suggest to you?

2. In line 294 ashes and dust are the symbols of penance and death. What is the meaning of the line?

3. In lines 300–301, was there a real transformation of the bread and water, or did the spirit in which they were given make them seem other than they were? Give reasons for your answer.

4. How does Sir Launfal find the Holy Grail? What lessons did he learn in his dream? What is the meaning of line 325, "The gift without the giver is bare"?

### WORDS TO STUDY

1. Make a list of words that appeal to the senses: words representing color, taste, sound, smell, shape.

2. Find the meanings of the italicized words and discuss the appropriateness of their use: line 91, *sulphurous* rifts of passion; line 120, *churlish* stones her assaults defied; line 128, *surly* clang; line 130, *maiden* knights; line 248, (morning) rose up *decrepitly*.

### PROJECTS

1. Make a list of the various contrasts and balances of scene, mood, and action in the poem.

2. Note down the instances where Lowell makes use of direct or indirect reference to Holy Scripture.

3. Go through the descriptive passages and list the American birds, insects, flowers, and grains of which Lowell makes use.

✧✧✧✧✧

# Barbara Frietchie

## JOHN GREENLEAF WHITTIER

*A gray-haired old woman defies the Southern troops and keeps her country's flag flying.*

Up from the meadows rich with corn,
Clear in the cool September morn,

The clustered spires of Frederick stand
Green-walled by the hills of Maryland.

Round about them orchards sweep, 5
Apple and peach tree fruited deep,

Fair as the garden of the Lord
To the eyes of the famished rebel horde,

On that pleasant morn of the early fall
When Lee marched over the mountain
  wall;        10

Over the mountains winding down,
Horse and foot, into Frederick town.

Forty flags with their silver stars,
Forty flags with their crimson bars, 14

Flapped in the morning wind; the sun
Of noon looked down, and saw not one.

Up rose old Barbara Frietchie then,
Bowed with her fourscore years and ten;

Bravest of all in Frederick town,
She took up the flag the men hauled
  down;        20

In her attic window the staff she set,
To show that one heart was loyal yet.

Up the street came the rebel tread,
Stonewall Jackson riding ahead.    24

Under his slouched hat left and right
He glanced; the old flag met his sight.

"Halt!"—the dust-brown ranks stood
  fast.
"Fire!"—out blazed the rifle blast.

It shivered the window, pane and sash;
It rent the banner with seam and
  gash.        30

Quick, as it fell, from the broken staff
Dame Barbara snatched the silken scarf.

She leaned far out on the window sill,
And shook it forth with a royal will.

"Shoot, if you must, this old gray head,
But spare your country's flag," she
  said.        36

A shade of sadness, a blush of shame,
Over the face of the leader came;

The nobler nature within him stirred
To life at that woman's deed and
  word;        40

"Who touches a hair of yon gray head
Dies like a dog! March on!" he said.

All day long through Frederick street
Sounded the tread of marching feet:

All day long that free flag tost    45
Over the heads of the rebel host.

Ever its torn folds rose and fell
On the loyal winds that loved it well;

And through the hill gaps sunset light
Shone over it with a warm good-night.

Barbara Frietchie's work is o'er,    51
And the Rebel rides on his raids no
  more.

Honor to her! and let a tear
Fall, for her sake, on Stonewall's bier.

Over Barbara Frietchie's grave    55
Flag of Freedom and Union, wave!

Peace and order and beauty draw
Round thy symbol of light and law;

And ever the stars above look down  59
On thy stars below in Frederick town!

◇◇◇◇◇◇◇◇◇◇◇◇◇◇◇◇◇◇◇◇◇◇◇◇◇◇◇◇◇◇◇◇◇◇◇◇◇◇◇◇◇◇◇◇◇◇◇◇◇◇◇◇◇◇◇◇

FOR DISCUSSION

1. In lines 15–16, why couldn't the sun
see any of the forty flags?

2. How is Stonewall Jackson's regard
for Barbara typical of the Southern character? Would he have reacted the same

way if a younger woman had defied the troops? an old man? a young man?

3. Why would the author have a tear fall, for Barbara Frietchie's sake, on Stonewall's grave? Can you suggest more than one reason?

4. Do you think the poem would be better without the last five stanzas? Why or why not?

5. Can you find any imperfect rhymes? Are they excusable?

## THE POET'S WORDS

A *transferred epithet* is an adjective applied to a noun which it does not logically modify, though the relationship is so close that the meaning is clear. In line 23, Whittier speaks of *rebel tread*. We usually speak of the soldiers as being rebellious and not their marching. The transferred epithet is used by poets for greater effectiveness. Find and name some others.

❖❖❖❖❖

# *Ode to the Confederate Dead*

## HENRY TIMROD

*This ode, with its sweet music, is one of the many beautiful tributes written to commemorate the bravery of the Southern soldiers. It was sung on Memorial Day, 1867, at Magnolia Cemetery, Charleston, South Carolina.*

Sleep sweetly in your humble graves,
  Sleep, martyrs of a fallen cause;
Though yet no marble column craves
  The pilgrim here to pause.

In seeds of laurel in the earth          5
  The blossom of your fame is blown,
And somewhere, waiting for its birth,
  The shaft is in the stone!

Meanwhile, behalf the tardy years
  Which keep in trust your storied
    tombs,                              10

Behold! your sisters bring their tears,
  And these memorial blooms.

Small tributes! but your shades will
    smile
  More proudly on these wreaths today,
Than when some cannon-moulded pile
  Shall overlook this bay.             16

Stoop, angels, hither from the skies!
  There is no holier spot of ground
Than where defeated valor lies,
  By mourning beauty crowned.          20

3. MARBLE COLUMN—Later, a granite monument surmounted by a bronze figure of a color-bearer was erected.
9. BEHALF—In behalf of.

15. CANNON-MOULDED—Melted cannon are frequently used in making monuments to soldiers.

FOR DISCUSSION

1. What memorials must, on this occasion, substitute for a stone or metal monument? Are they more appropriate?

2. Compare this ode with Emerson's "Concord Hymn." Which occasion do you think is more moving? Why?

3. Explain the meaning of the following phrases: *storied tombs; defeated valor.*

◇◇◇◇◇

# Song of the Mystic

## ABRAM J. RYAN

*In Father Ryan's use of the word, a mystic is one to whom God has disclosed Himself and whom God teaches, in the silence of his heart, the spiritual meaning of life while the soul lives in intimate union with Him. The soul's search for happiness is a long and hard search. Earth offers nothing that is unmixed with disappointment and sin. Only in the "Valley of Silence" can the poet find refuge and peace.*

I walk down the Valley of Silence—
  Down the dim, voiceless valley—
    alone!
And I hear not the fall of a footstep
  Around me, save God's and my own;
And the hush of my heart is as holy   5
  As hovers where angels have flown!

Long ago was I weary of voices
  Whose music my heart could not win;
Long ago was I weary of noises
  That fretted my soul with their din;
Long ago was I weary of places   11
  Where I met but the human—and
    sin.

I walked in the world with the worldly;
  I craved what the world never gave;
And I said: "In the world each
    Ideal,   15
  That shines like a star on life's wave,
Is wrecked on the shores of the Real,
  And sleeps like a dream in a grave."

And still did I pine for the Perfect,
  And still found the False with the
    True;   20
I sought 'mid the Human for Heaven,
  But caught a mere glimpse of its Blue:
And I wept when the clouds of the Mortal
  Veiled even that glimpse from my
    view.

And I toiled on, heart-tired of the Human,   25
  And I moaned 'mid the mazes of
    men,

1. VALLEY OF SILENCE—The spirit of quiet and untroubled concentration on God and the things of God; the spirit that is necessary for union with God.

6. HOVERS—Hover, a shelter or retreat. Or, using *hovers* as a verb, the line could be explained thus—The hush of my heart is as holy as (the holiness that) hovers (over places) where angels have flown.

"Song of the Mystic" from *Eulogy on George Washington* by John Carroll, reprinted by permission of P. J. Kenedy & Sons.

Till I knelt, long ago, at an altar
  And I heard a voice call me. Since
    then
I walk down the Valley of Silence
  That lies far beyond mortal ken.  30

Do you ask what I found in the Valley?
  'Tis my Trysting Place with the Di-
    vine.
And I fell at the feet of the Holy,
  And above me a voice said: "Be
    Mine."
And there arose from the depths of my
    spirit     35
  An echo—"My heart shall be Thine."

Do you ask how I live in the Valley?
  I weep—and I dream—and I pray.
But my tears are as sweet as the dew-
    drops
  That fall on the roses in May;  40
And my prayer, like a perfume from
    censers,
  Ascendeth to God night and day.

In the hush of the Valley of Silence
  I dream all the songs that I sing;
And the music floats down the dim Val-
    ley,     45
  Till each finds a word for a wing,

That to hearts, like the Dove of the
    Deluge,
  A message of Peace they may bring.

But far on the deep there are billows
  That never shall break on the
    beach;     50
And I have heard songs in the Silence
  That never shall float into speech;
And I have had dreams in the Valley
  Too lofty for language to reach.

And I have seen Thoughts in the Val-
    ley—     55
  Ah me! how my spirit was stirred!
And they wear holy veils on their faces,
  Their footsteps can scarcely be heard;
They pass through the Valley like Vir-
    gins,
  Too pure for the touch of a word!  60

Do you ask me the place of the Valley,
  Ye hearts that are harrowed by Care?
It lieth afar between mountains,
  And God and His angels are there:
And one is the dark mount of Sor-
    row,     65
And one the bright mountain of
    Prayer.

57. HOLY VEILS—The poet glimpses divine mysteries but he does not see their fully exposed beauty.
58. FOOTSTEPS—The thoughts come to him almost unawares.

30. KEN—Range of sight; understanding.
32. TRYSTING PLACE—Appointed place of meeting; rendezvous.

<hr />

## FOR DISCUSSION

1. When you reflect on our purpose in life, why is it that the soul can be weary in this world? Is it true that our ideals can be easily wrecked? Why? Suggest reasons why nothing on earth—riches, pleasures, honors, friendship, nature, learning—can give us perfect happiness.

2. Is there such a thing as a sweet sorrow? Explain.

3. What is there in common between a mystic and a poet?

4. Have you ever had thoughts or feelings so deep and penetrating that words could not express them? How does Father Ryan express this condition of the soul?

5. Is the first part of the poem pessimistic? Discuss.

6. Father Ryan was a busy man all his life. How could a busy man working in the world reach the Valley of Silence?

# The Sword of Robert Lee

## ABRAM J. RYAN

PURE . . . BRIGHT . . . STAINLESS *describe both the reputation and character of a great American soldier.*

Forth from its scabbard, pure and bright,
　Flashed the sword of Lee!
Far in the front of the deadly fight,
High o'er the brave in the cause of
　　Right,
Its stainless sheen, like a beacon light,
　Led us to victory.　　　　　　6

Out of its scabbard, where full long
　It slumbered peacefully,
Roused from its rest by the battle's
　　song,　　　　　　　　　9
Shielding the feeble, smiting the strong,
Guarding the right, avenging the wrong,
　Gleamed the sword of Lee.

Forth from its scabbard, high in air
　Beneath Virginia's sky—　　　14
And they who saw it gleaming there,
And knew who bore it, knelt to swear
That where that sword led they would
　　dare
　To follow and to die.

Out of its scabbard! Never hand
　Waved sword from stain as free;　20
Nor purer sword led braver band,
Nor braver bled for a brighter land,
Nor brighter land had a cause as grand,
　Nor cause a chief like Lee!

Forth from its scabbard! How we
　　prayed　　　　　　　　25
　That sword might victor be;
And when our triumph was delayed,
And many a heart grew sore afraid,
We still hoped on while gleamed the
　　blade
　Of noble Robert Lee.　　　　30

Forth from its scabbard all in vain
　Bright flashed the sword of Lee;
'Tis shrouded now in its sheath again,
It sleeps the sleep of our noble slain,
Defeated, yet without a stain,　　35
　Proudly and peacefully.

"The Sword of Robert Lee" from *Eulogy on George Washington* by John Carroll, reprinted by permission of P. J. Kennedy & Sons.

FOR DISCUSSION
　1. How many great leaders would be worthy of such sentiments?
　2. With what feelings did Lee's leadership inspire the South? What was the cause for which the South fought? In what lines is Father Ryan's most passionate love for the South expressed?

# A Ballad of Trees and the Master

### SIDNEY LANIER

*Forsaken by friends, Christ found comfort under the trees of the Garden of Gethsemane.*

Into the woods my Master went,
Clean forspent, forspent.
Into the woods my Master came,
Forspent with love and shame.
But the olives they were not blind to
  Him,     5
The little gray leaves were kind to Him:
The thorn-tree had a mind to Him
When into the woods He came.

Out of the woods my Master went,
And He was well content.    10
Out of the woods my Master came,
Content with death and shame.
When Death and Shame would woo
  Him last,
From under the trees they drew Him
  last:
'Twas on a tree they slew Him—last  15
When out of the woods He came.

"A Ballad of Trees and the Master" by Sidney Lanier, reprinted by permission of Charles Scribners' Sons.

◇◇◇◇◇◇◇◇◇◇◇◇◇◇◇◇◇◇◇◇◇◇◇◇◇◇◇◇◇◇◇◇◇◇◇◇◇◇◇◇◇◇◇◇◇◇◇◇◇◇

## FOR DISCUSSION

1. What effect did the trees have on Christ?

2. Why are death and shame capitalized in line 13?

3. Is there irony (in the sense of a turn of events the reverse of what is to be expected) in the last two lines of the poem?

4. Triple rhyme is usually used in humorous verse. Does its use here spoil or help the poem?

# The Revenge of Hamish

SIDNEY LANIER

*"I will kill a red deer," quoth Maclean, "in the sight of the wife and the child." But Hamish, his servant, was slow. Tyrannical Maclean lost his temper. Hamish, stripped and striped, lost his senses. And the hunter, not the deer, suffered tragically.*

It was three slim does and a ten-tined buck in the bracken lay;
    And all of a sudden the sinister smell of man,
    Awaft on a wind-shift, wavered and ran,
Down the hillside and sifted along through the bracken and passed that way.

Then Nan got a-tremble at nostril; she was the daintiest doe;       5
    In the print of her velvet flank on the velvet fern
    She reared, and rounded her ears in turn.
Then the buck leapt up, and his head as a king's to a crown did go

Full high in the breeze, and he stood as if Death had the form of a deer;
    And the two slim does long lazily stretching arose,       10
    For their daydream slowlier came to a close,
Till they woke and were still, breath-bound with waiting and wonder and fear.

Then Alan the huntsman sprang over the hillock, the hounds shot by,
    The does and the ten-tined buck made a marvelous bound,
    The hounds swept after with never a sound,       15
But Alan loud winded his horn in sign that the quarry was nigh.

For at dawn of that day proud Maclean of Lochbuy to the hunt had waxed wild,
    And he cursed at old Alan till Alan fared off with the hounds
    For to drive him the deer to the lower glen-grounds:
"I will kill a red deer," quoth Maclean, "in the sight of the wife and the child."   20

So gayly he paced with the wife and the child to his chosen stand;
    But he hurried tall Hamish the henchman ahead: "Go turn,"—
    Cried Maclean,—"if the deer seek to cross to the burn,
Do thou turn them to me: nor fail, lest thy back be red as thy hand."

  1. TINED—Tine: a prong, as of an antler.
  1. BRACKEN—A thick growth of fern.
 16. QUARRY—Prey; the game.
 19. GLEN—A narrow, secluded valley.
 23. BURN—Brook, rivulet.

"The Revenge of Hamish" by Sidney Lanier, reprinted by permission of Charles Scribners' Sons.

Now hard-fortuned Hamish, half blown of his breath with the height of the
 hill,      25
 Was white in the face when the ten-tined buck and the does
 Drew leaping to burn-ward; huskily rose
His shouts, and his nether lip twitched, and his legs were o'erweak for his will.

So the deer darted lightly by Hamish and bounded away to the burn.
 But Maclean never bating his watch tarried waiting below;   30
 Still Hamish hung heavy with fear for to go
All the space of an hour; then he went, and his face was greenish and stern,

And his eye sat back in the socket, and shrunken the eyeballs shone,
 As withdrawn from a vision of deeds it were shame to see.
 "Now, now, grim henchman, what is 't with thee?"   35
Brake Maclean, and his wrath rose red as a beacon the wind hath upblown.

"Three does and a ten-tined buck made out," spoke Hamish, full mild,
 "And I ran for to turn, but my breath it was blown; and they passed;
 I was weak, for ye called ere I broke me my fast."
Cried Maclean: "Now a ten-tined buck in the sight of the wife and the child 40

I had killed if the gluttonous kern had not wrought me a snail's own wrong!"
 Then he sounded, and down came kinsmen and clansmen all:
 "Ten blows, for ten tine, on his back let fall,
And reckon no stroke if the blood follow not at the bite of thong!"

So Hamish made bare, and took him his strokes; at the last he smiled,  45
 "Now I'll to the burn," quoth Maclean, "for it still may be,
 If a slimmer-paunched henchman will hurry with me,
I shall kill me the ten-tined buck for a gift to the wife and the child."

Then the clansmen departed, by this path and that; and over the hill
 Sped Maclean with an outward wrath for an inward shame;   50
 And that place of the lashing full quiet became;
And the wife and the child stood sad; and bloody-backed Hamish sat still.

But look! red Hamish has risen; quick about and about turns he.
 "There is none betwixt me and the craig-top!" he screams under breath.
 Then livid as Lazarus lately from death,   55
He snatches the child from the mother, and clambers the craig toward the sea.

Now the mother drops breath; she is dumb, and her heart goes dead for a space,
 Till the motherhood, mistress of death, shrieks, shrieks through the glen,
 And that place of the lashing is live with men,
And Maclean, and the gillie that told him, dash up in a desperate race. 60

  28. NETHER—Lower; under.
  36. BRAKE—Archaic past tense of *break*: to burst forth violently in speech.
  41. KERN—Rude peasant; boor.
  60. GILLIE—Servant; attendant at a hunt.

Not a breath's time for asking; an eye-glance reveals all the tale untold.
  They follow mad Hamish afar up the crag toward the sea,
    And the lady cries: "Clansmen, run for a fee!
Yon castle and lands to the two first hands that shall hook him and hold

"Fast Hamish back from the brink!"—and ever she flies up the steep,      65
  And the clansmen pant, and they sweat, and they jostle and strain.
    But, mother, 'tis vain; but, father, 'tis vain;
Stern Hamish stands bold on the brink, and dangles the child o'er the deep.

Now a faintness falls on the men that run, and they all stand still.
  And the wife prays Hamish as if he were God, on her knees,      70
    Crying: "Hamish, O Hamish! but please, but please
For to spare him!" and Hamish still dangles the child, with a wavering will.

On a sudden he turns; with a sea-hawk scream, and a gibe, and a song,
  Cries: "So; I will spare ye the child if, in sight of ye all,
    Ten blows on Maclean's bare back shall fall,      75
And ye reckon no stroke if the blood follow not at the bite of the thong!"

Then Maclean he set hardly his tooth to his lip that his tooth was red,
  Breathed short for a space, said: "Nay, but it never shall be!
    Let me hurl off the damnable hound in the sea!"
But the wife: "Can Hamish go fish us the child from the sea, if dead?      80

"Say yea!—Let them lash *me*, Hamish?"—"Nay!"—"Husband, the lashing will
    heal;

But, oh, who will heal me the bonny sweet bairn in his grave?
Could ye cure me my heart with the death of a knave?
Quick! Love! I will bare thee—so—kneel!" Then Maclean 'gan slowly to kneel

With never a word, till presently downward he jerked to the earth,                85
Then the henchman—he that smote Hamish—would tremble and lag;
"Strike, hard!" quoth Hamish, full stern, from the crag;
Then he struck him, and "One!" sang Hamish, and danced with the child in his
    mirth.

And no man spake beside Hamish, he counted each stroke with a song.
When the last stroke fell, then he moved him a pace down the height,                90
And he held forth the child in the heartaching sight
Of the mother, and looked all pitiful grave, as repenting a wrong.

And there as the motherly arms stretched out with the thanksgiving prayer—
And there as the mother crept up with a fearful swift pace,
Till her finger nigh felt of the bairnie's face—                                    95
In a flash fierce Hamish turned round and lifted the child in the air,

And sprang with the child in his arms from the horrible height in the sea,
Shrill screeching, "Revenge!" in the wind-rush; and pallid Maclean,
Age-feeble with anger and impotent pain,
Crawled up on the crag, and lay flat, and locked hold of dead roots of a
    tree—                                                                           100

And gazed hungrily o'er, and the blood from his back drip-dripped in the brine,
And a sea-hawk flung down a skeleton fish as he flew,
And the mother stared white on the waste of blue,
And the wind drove a cloud to seaward, and the sun began to shine.

---

## FOR DISCUSSION

1. Was Hamish insane? Can you point out some actions that support your judgment?

2. How would you describe the character of Maclean? Do you have any sympathy for him at the end of the poem? What character deserves most pity?

3. Explain the following expressions: line 3, "awaft on a wind-shift"; line 9, "he stood as if Death had the form of a deer"; line 12, "breath-bound with waiting"; line 25, "Hamish, half blown of his breath with the height of the hill"; line 41, "if the gluttonous kern had not wrought me a snail's own wrong"; line 50, "with an outward wrath for an inward shame"; line 55, "livid as Lazarus lately from death"; line 57, "the mother drops breath"; line 98, "shrill screeching 'Revenge' in the wind-rush."

4. Point out what you think are the two most striking scenes in the poem.

5. Look up the meaning of the word "melodrama." Would you describe this poem as melodramatic? Discuss.

## RELATED READING

If you like the rhythm of Lanier's poetry, you will get great pleasure from his "Song of the Chattahoochee."

# NONFICTION PROSE

## THE ESSAY

As the new nation turned into the nineteenth century, she paused to draw breath. We have seen how prosperity followed on the heels of an established government. With prosperity had come leisure, and with leisure—the development of the essay.

Again it was Washington Irving who began it. The comfortable circumstances of his family paralleled the growing wealth and ease of the nation. He could afford to read, to browse, to travel, and to write. He could make of writing an art and a diversion, two certain marks of the essayist. He was only nineteen when he began submitting sketches in imitation of Addison and Steele's *Spectator* essays to his brother's newspaper. Two years later he continued the experiment with the *Salmagundi Papers,* which he and his brother published as a literary periodical. *Salmagundi* lived only fifteen months, but Irving kept on writing. Most of the selections in his *Sketch Book* and *Bracebridge Hall* are of the essay type—meditations on manners and morals and places and persons, sometimes with a sentimental, sometimes with an ironic or whimsical twist.

While Irving was still busy writing, other essayists began to appear. Irving's later contributions had gone to *Knickerbocker Magazine* in New York. But by the middle of the century there was a strong literary group in and about Concord, Massachusetts, and the nurture of the American essay was largely in its hands. This Concord group was a literary aristocracy. Men were admitted if they had wealth of ideas. Money did not matter. Henry Thoreau who could and did live for six months on twenty-five dollars was no less welcome than Longfellow or Lowell. The circle included poets, scientists, lecturers, journalists. Most of them were closely attached to Harvard College as alumni or professors. All were idealists interested in philosophy and culture. Their influence gave a sober tone to most of the essays of the middle century.

Linked with the phenomenal growth of our nineteenth-century literature were the establishment and prospering of the American literary magazine. Magazines, it is true, had appeared in colonial times. Benjamin Franklin in 1741 published the *General Magazine or Historical Chronical,* but it lasted for only six numbers. Other attempts followed, almost equally short-lived. Indeed it was fifty-nine years before a really enduring magazine was born. The *Boston Anthology* arrived with the new century. When, after ten volumes, it merged with the *North American Review*, the magazine was established as an influence in American letters. The *Review* itself became an important publication; and other similar periodicals began to appear. It was the *North American Review* that printed Bryant's "Thanatopsis"; it was *Graham's* that had Poe as editor, that printed his stories, and gave him an opportunity to write his brilliant critical essays. It was for the *Atlantic Monthly* that Holmes, over a period of twenty-five years, wrote his "Breakfast Table" essays and Lowell his scholarly literary criticisms. It was *Scribner's* that introduced to the North the works of the brilliant Southern writers—Sidney Lanier, Paul Hamilton Hayne, George Washington Cable, Thomas Nelson Page, and Joel Chandler Harris. The Southern magazines had not survived the war, and *Scribner's* proved a life line to writers like Lanier and Hayne.

The magazines were especially receptive to the essay. There were, of course, discussions of politics and policies, but even these current topics were given a more scholarly treatment than they receive in the informal "article" of our modern magazines. Literary subjects, problems in ethics and philosophy were especially acceptable. And there was always room for a good bit of whimsy and fun. To look over the indexes to nineteenth century magazines is to call the roll of our foremost writers—Irving, Bryant, Emerson, Hawthorne, Holmes, Thoreau, Poe, Lanier—one can continue at length. And although outlet was provided for poetry and fiction, it was the welcome given to short non-fiction prose that gave the essay its eminent position in literature of the period.

## ORATORY OF THE NATIONAL PERIOD

The oratory of the national period must not be overlooked, for it reflects the fervor of soldier and statesman, influential figures of the times. The list of selections could be long; but orations depend much upon matters of the moment for their effectiveness. At the time of delivery, great speeches glow with the fire of a great occasion or a great personality. Reading the words cold from a printed page, one misses their original force. John Calhoun and Daniel Webster were men of commanding presence and magnificent voice. "Godlike" was the term used to describe Webster at the height of his power. Today we can still admire the logic and a certain brilliance of style in the speeches of both men. But the live eloquence died with the speakers and the issues they argued.

Only rarely does there appear a man like Lincoln whose spoken words are "not for an age, but for all time." Lincoln was not an orator. His appearance did not command attention. He was homely, shambling, a little awkward, very human. But when he talked, he had a message. His sentences were pronounced simply; and they were so fitting, so *right* that men did not always realize that here was deathless language. But he had the rare, rare power to set free in words the uttermost nobility of human heart and soul. In cold, carved granite his words still live to fill men's eyes with tears.

## HISTORIES AND BIOGRAPHIES

One of the early novelists—Simms—had written also some excellent histories and biographies. He made a careful study of his native state and produced two books, *The History of South Carolina* and *South Carolina in the Revolution*. Moreover, he wrote excellent readable biographies of many of the Southern war heroes—of men like Francis Marion and General Greene. Two other historians wrote books authentic in all details but so filled with adventure and so vividly told that they read like fiction. There was William Hickling Prescott who told the lurid stories of *The Conquest of Mexico* and *The Conquest of Peru*; and there was Francis Parkman who recorded in eight readable volumes the early wars of the French, the English, and the Indians. Because those wars were really a struggle for the domination of the continent of North America, Parkman's work has great historical significance. It is, besides, a masterpiece of prose writing. He is most widely known, however, for a different study—*The California and Oregon Trail*, an account of his own journey over the historic trail while it still led through a wilderness and while the Indian still walked erect, lord of the plain and prairie. For their work in recording brilliantly significant episodes in the pageant of America, both Prescott and Parkman have won a permanent place in the field of our literature.

◇◇◇◇◇

# WOUTER VAN TWILLER

## WASHINGTON IRVING

In 1809 the newspapers of New York and Philadelphia carried advertisements describing and asking information about a certain Diedrich Knickerbocker. He had left the Columbian Hotel in New York without paying *his bill. Among the things he had left behind was a manuscript titled,* A History of New York from the Beginning of the World to the End of the Dutch Dynasty. *The manager wanted some word from his defaulting lodger before he sold the literary work to pay the author's debt. No word came. The book was printed.*

*The sophisticated Dutch-ancestried New Yorkers sniffed the publicity-fanned air. Here, they thought, was a book glorifying their very own forefathers. To the Stuyvesants, the Vanderbilts, the Van Rensselaers, the books were like hot cakes. They bought and bit.*

*The grand title had given them no hint that the two volumes were packed with good-humored fun poked at their noble ancestors. When the New Yorkers discovered the trick and the author—a young lawyer named Washington Irving—most of them laughed with him at their family pride. Some, however, found it difficult though not impossible to forgive. In time the Dutch-blooded even began priding themselves on being "genuine Knickerbockers."*

*Imagine how eagerly Madame Van Twiller's eyes peered through her lorgnette as her chubby hands hastily paged to Book III, Chapter I, for the account of her husband's great-great-great grandfather, Wouter, one-time governor of New Netherlands.*

The renowned Wouter (or Walter) Van [1] Twiller was descended from a long line of Dutch burgomasters, who had successively dozed away their lives and grown fat upon the bench of magistracy in Rotterdam, and who had comported themselves with such singular wisdom and propriety that they were never either heard or talked of—which, next to being universally applauded, should be the object of ambition of all magistrates and rulers. There are two opposite ways by which some men make a figure in the world: one, by talking faster than they think, and the other by holding their tongues and not thinking at all. By the first, many a smatterer acquires the reputation of a man of quick parts; by the other, many a dunderpate, like the owl, the stupidest of birds, comes to be considered the very type of wisdom. This, by the way, is a casual remark, which I would not for the universe have it thought I apply to Governor Van Twiller. It is true he was a man shut up within himself, like an oyster, and rarely spoke except in monosyllables; but then it was allowed he seldom said a foolish thing. So invincible was his gravity that he was never known to laugh or even to smile through the whole course of a long and prosperous life. Nay, if a joke were uttered in his presence that set light-minded hear-

[1] van—Like the Von in German names and De in French, meaning "of" or "from." The name that followed denoted the family or estate from which a man came; hence it indicated a person of prominence.

ers in a roar, it was observed to throw him into a state of perplexity. Sometimes he would deign to inquire into the matter, and when, after much explanation, the joke was made as plain as a pike-staff, he would continue to smoke his pipe in silence, and at length, knocking out the ashes, would exclaim: "Well! I see nothing in all that to laugh about."

With all his reflective habits, he never made up his mind on a subject. His adherents accounted for this by the astonishing magnitude of his ideas. He conceived every subject on so grand a scale that he had not room in his head to turn it over and examine both sides of it. Certain it is, that, if any matter were propounded to him on which ordinary mortals would rashly determine at first glance, he would put on a vague, mysterious look, shake his capacious head, smoke some time in profound silence, and at length observe that he "had his doubts about the matter"; which gained him the reputation of a man slow of belief and not easily imposed upon. What is more, it gained him a lasting name, for to this habit of mind has been attributed his surname of Twiller, which is said to be a corruption of [2] the original Twijfler, or, in plain English, *Doubter*.

The person of this illustrious old gentleman was formed and proportioned, as though it had been molded by the hands of some cunning Dutch statuary, as a model of majesty and lordly grandeur. He was exactly five feet six inches in height and six feet five inches in circumference. His head was a perfect sphere, and of such stupendous dimensions that Dame Nature, with all her sex's ingenuity, would have been puzzled to construct a neck capable of supporting

[2] CORRUPTION OF—A less accurate form of.

it; wherefore she wisely declined the attempt, and settled it firmly on the top of his backbone, just between the shoulders. His body was oblong and particularly capacious at bottom; which was wisely ordered by Providence, seeing that he was a man of sedentary habits and very averse to the idle labor of walking. His legs were short, but sturdy in proportion to the weight they had to sustain, so that when erect he had not a little the appearance of a beer-barrel on skids. His face, that infallible index of the mind, presented a vast expanse, unfurrowed by any of those lines and angles which disfigure the human countenance with what is termed expression. Two small gray eyes twinkled feebly in the midst, like two stars of lesser magnitude in a hazy firmament, and his full-fed cheeks, which seemed to have taken toll of everything that went into his mouth, were curiously mottled and streaked with dusky red, like a Spitzenberg apple.

His habits were as regular as his person. He daily took his four stated meals, appropriating exactly an hour to each; he smoked and doubted eight hours, and he slept the remaining twelve of the four-and-twenty. Such was the renowned Wouter Van Twiller—a true philosopher, for his mind was either elevated above, or tranquilly settled below, the cares and perplexities of this world. He had lived in it for years without feeling the least curiosity to know whether the sun revolved round it or it round the sun; and he had watched for at least half a century the smoke curling from his pipe to the ceiling, without troubling his head with any of those numerous theories by which a philosopher would have perplexed his brain in accounting for its rising above the surrounding atmosphere.

In his council he presided with great state and solemnity. He sat in a huge chair of solid oak, hewn in the celebrated forest of the Hague, fabricated by an experienced timmerman [3] of Amsterdam, and curiously carved about the arms and feet into exact imitations of gigantic eagle's claws. Instead of a sceptre he swayed a long Turkish pipe, wrought with jasmin and amber, which had been presented to a stadtholder [4] of Holland at the conclusion of a treaty with one of the petty Barbary powers. In this stately chair would he sit and this magnificent pipe would he smoke, shaking his right knee with a constant motion, and fixing his eye for hours together upon a little print of Amsterdam which hung in a black frame against the opposite wall of the council chamber. Nay, it has ever been said that when any deliberation [5] of extraordinary length and intricacy was on the carpet,[6] the renowned Wouter would shut his eyes for full two hours at a time, that he might not be disturbed by external objects; and at such times the internal commotion of his mind was evinced by certain regular guttural sounds, which his admirers declared were merely the noise of conflict made by his contending doubts and opinions.

---

[3] TIMMERMAN—A carpenter or cabinet-maker. Compare with the German *Zimmermann*.

[4] STADTHOLDER—The chief executive officer of the United Provinces of the Netherlands. The title was discontinued in 1802.

[5] DELIBERATION—Matter for consideration.

[6] ON THE CARPET—A figurative expression meaning "brought before a magistrate to be decided."

◇◇◇◇◇◇◇◇◇◇◇◇◇◇◇◇◇◇◇◇◇◇◇◇◇◇◇◇

## FOR DISCUSSION

1. What is the first hint that the essay is not from a serious history of New York?

2. *Irony* is the art of saying one thing and meaning the opposite. It is a gentle art and is handled smoothly and without bitterness by the true artist. How many instances of irony can you find in the description of Wouter Van Twiller? Is Irving's irony biting or smooth?

3. A *simile* is a figure of speech in which two objects unlike in nature are compared. How many can you find? Do they give you a clear picture of Wouter?

4. The humorous author sometimes uses *hyperbole*, or intentional exaggeration, to caricature his characters. What instances of hyperbole can you find?

5. Do you think Wouter's characteristics are true to human nature? Have you noticed any of his peculiarities, partially at least, in other human beings? Discuss.

## WORDS

Re-write the sentences in which the following words appear, substituting synonyms (a word or a phrase) for them. Read your sentences in class; emphasize the synonyms you have inserted. Have the class give the word used by the author.

| | |
|---|---|
| comport | appropriating |
| deign | fabricated |
| adherents | mottled |
| ingenuity | intricacy |
| sedentary | evince |
| toll | guttural |

## PROJECTS

1. Now and then everyone meets an odd or unusual person. Using Irving's essay as a model, write a character study of one of them.

2. Write a caricature of yourself.

## RELATED READING

The last chapter, Book III, of *The Knickerbocker History* tells of a crisis in New Amsterdam, of a famous ride, and of how Wouter's reign ended with his last puff of breath and smoke.

# EXORDIUM IN THE KNAPP MURDER CASE

## DANIEL WEBSTER

Salem was excited and scared, and the whole country was aroused by the murder of Joseph White. It was a cool, deliberate, bold crime, executed in the most populous and central part of town. After the discovery of the body, carpenters were busy fixing door bolts and fastening windows. Cutlasses, firearms, and watchdogs became popular overnight. Large rewards were offered and the law went into action. By the twenty-sixth of May, the culprits were under arrest. On request, Daniel Webster appeared as counsel to the prosecutor.

HISTORY OF THE CASE: *Joseph J. Knapp knew that Mr. White had made his will, leaving Mrs. Beckford (White's niece-housekeeper and Knapp's mother-in-law) fifteen thousand dollars. If White died without leaving a will, Knapp expected she would get nearly two hundred thousand dollars. Joseph told his brother, John Francis (Frank), his intention to destroy the will and kill White. Frank hired an assassin, Richard Crowninshield, Jr.*

*Joseph had free access to the house. He stole the will and arranged to unbar and unfasten the back window. On the sixth of April, Joseph persuaded Mrs. Beckford to spend the night with her daughter at Wenham.*

*All preparations were complete. Crowninshield and Frank met about ten o'clock on the evening of the sixth, in Brown Street, which passes the rear of Mr. White's garden, and stood there some time observing the movements in the house. They waited till White and his two servants went to bed. Then Crowninshield told Frank to go home. Frank went, but soon returned and awaited the killer's return to learn that the deed was done.*

*The suspects were rounded up through a series of mistakes they had committed. Crowninshield hanged himself in jail. Frank Knapp was indicted for murder as a principal, and Joseph as an accessory.*

Title—EXORDIUM—The introductory part of a speech.

*Frank was put on trial first, since an accessory could not be tried until a principal had been convicted. To convict the prisoner, it was necessary for the government to prove that he was* PRESENT, *actually or as an aider or abettor in the murder. The jury was convinced that Frank was present on Brown Street ready to give help if necessary. He was convicted. So was Joseph. Both were executed.*

Gentlemen, it is a most extraordinary case. In some respects, it has hardly a precedent anywhere; certainly none in our New England history. This bloody drama exhibited no suddenly excited ungovernable rage. The actors in it were not surprised by any lion-like temptation springing upon their virtue, and overcoming it, before resistance could begin. Nor did they do the deed to glut savage vengeance, or satiate [2] long-settled and deadly hate. It was a cool, calculating, money-making murder. It was all "hire and salary, not revenge." It was the weighing of money against life; and the counting out of so many pieces of silver, against so many ounces of blood.

An aged man, without an enemy in the world, in his own house and in his own bed, is made the victim of a butcherly murder, for mere pay. Truly, here is a new lesson for painters and poets. Whoever shall hereafter draw the portrait of murder, if he will show it as it has been exhibited in an example, where such example was last to have been looked for, in the very bosom of our New England society, let him not give it the grim visage of Moloch,[3] the brow knitted by revenge, the face black with settled hate, and the bloodshot eye emitting livid fires of malice. Let him

draw, rather, a decorous,[4] smoothfaced, bloodless demon; a picture in repose, rather than in action; not so much an example of human nature in its depravity and in its paroxysms of crime, as an infernal nature, a fiend, in the ordinary display and development of his character.

The deed was executed with a degree of self-possession and steadiness equal to the wickedness with which it was planned. The circumstances, now clearly in evidence, spread out the whole scene before us. Deep sleep had fallen on the destined victim and on all beneath his roof. A healthful old man, to whom sleep was sweet, the first sound slumbers of the night held him in their soft but strong embrace. The assassin enters, through the window already prepared, into an unoccupied apartment. With noiseless foot he paces the lonely hall, half lighted by the moon; he winds up the ascent of the stairs and reaches the door of the chamber. Of this, he moves the lock, by soft and continued pressure, till it turns on its hinges without noise; and he enters and beholds his victim before him. The room was uncommonly open to the admission of light. The face of the innocent sleeper was turned from the murderer, and the beams of the moon, resting on the gray locks of his aged temple, showed him where to strike. The fatal blow is given! and the victim passes, without a struggle or a motion, from the repose of sleep to the repose of death! It is the

[2] SATIATE—To satisfy fully an appetite or desire; glut.

[3] MOLOCH (mō′lŏk)—A Phoenician god to whom human lives were offered as sacrifices.

[4] DECOROUS (dē·kō′rŭs or dĕk′ô·rŭs)—Proper, becoming, suitable.

assassin's purpose to make sure work; and he yet plies the dagger, though it was obvious that life had been destroyed by the blow of the bludgeon. He even raises the aged arm, that he may not fail in his aim at the heart, and replaces it again over the wounds of the poniard! To finish the picture, he explores the wrist for the pulse! He feels for it and ascertains that it beats no longer! It is accomplished. The deed is done. He retreats, retraces his steps to the window, passes out through it as he came in, and escapes. He has done the murder—no eye has seen him, no ear has heard him. The secret is his own, and it is safe!

Ah! gentlemen, that was a dreadful mistake. Such a secret can be safe nowhere. The whole creation of God has neither nook nor corner where the guilty can bestow it and say it is safe. Not to speak of that eye which glances through all disguises and beholds everything as in the splendor of noon—such secrets of guilt are never safe from detection, even by men. True it is, generally speaking, that "murder will out." True it is, that Providence hath so ordained and doth so govern things that those who break the great law of heaven by shedding man's blood seldom succeed in avoiding discovery. Especially, in a case exciting so much attention as this, discovery must come and will come sooner or later. A thousand eyes turn at once to explore every man, every thing, every circumstance connected with the time and place; a thousand ears catch every whisper; a thousand excited minds intently dwell on the scene, shedding all their light and ready to kindle the slightest circumstance into a blaze of discovery. Meantime, the guilty soul cannot keep its own secret. It is false to itself; or rather it feels an irresistible impulse of conscience to be true to itself. It labors under its guilty possession and knows not what to do with it. The human heart was not made for the residence of such an inhabitant. It finds itself preyed on by a torment which it dares not acknowledge to God nor man.

449

A vulture is devouring it, and it can ask no sympathy or assistance, either from heaven or earth. The secret which the murderer possesses soon comes to possess him; and, like the evil spirits of which we read, it overcomes him and leads him whithersoever it will. He feels it beating at his heart, rising to his throat, and demanding disclosure. He thinks the whole world sees it in his face, reads it in his eyes, and almost hears its workings in the very silence of his thoughts. It has become his master. It betrays his discretion, it breaks down his courage, it conquers his prudence. When suspicions from without begin to embarrass him, and the net of circumstance to entangle him, the fatal secret struggles with still greater violence to burst forth. It must be confessed; it will be confessed; there is no refuge from confession but suicide, and suicide is confession.

◇◇◇◇◇◇◇◇◇◇◇◇◇◇◇◇◇◇◇◇◇◇◇◇◇◇◇◇◇

## FOR DISCUSSION

1. Do you think that a lawyer would use the same style of language in court today as Webster used? Why or why not?

2. In his description of the murder what emotion does the orator try to arouse? Why?

3. Does the orator give a true picture of a murderer after the commission of the crime? Does he exaggerate? Would his description fit a person who had committed even a lesser crime that weighs on his conscience? Would it fit a hardened criminal?

## WORDS TO STUDY

1. You know what *precede* means. The noun *precedent* (accent on the first syllable) should give you little difficulty then; use it in a sentence.

2. You know what a *glutton* is. What does he do when he *gluts* himself?

3. People in pain sometimes suffer violent fits or convulsions. They are beside (Greek, *para*) themselves with the sharpness (Greek, *oxus*) of the pain. What English word do we derive from the two Greek words?

## PROJECTS

1. Write a description of a crime with the purpose of inspiring pity for the victim and horror for the deed.

2. Plan and stage a murder trial in class, or have several students study the entire speech by Webster, arrange cross-examinations, and have a jury decide the case.

## RELATED READING

Read Webster's "Oration on Adams and Jefferson," especially that part which deals with Adams' speech on the Declaration of Independence. Webster composes and puts into the mouth of Adams the famous lines beginning "Sink or swim, live or die, survive or perish, I give my hand and my heart to this vote."

# LE JEUNE AND THE HUNTERS

*FRANCIS PARKMAN*

In 1633, Father Paul Le Jeune, S.J., Superior of the Residence of Quebec, had been hardly more than a year away from civilized France when he decided to accept an invitation of the Montagnais, a tribe of Algonquins, to go on a winter hunting trip in the forests along the lower St. Lawrence.

He knew the dangers and the hardships. Just a year before, Father Anne de Noué had tried the experience. After three weeks, he had returned, sick, famished, and half dead from exhaustion. Here was a chance, though, for Le Jeune to master the Indian language, for the French fur traders, hostile to the Jesuits, had refused to help. Moreover, he hoped he might win a few souls to Christ.

It was no special love for the priest that earned him the invitation. The Indians had their minds on the plentiful provisions he would bring along. There were twenty Montagnais in the group: men, women, children. In the early stages of the march they were joined by two other bands that increased their numbers to forty-five. The chief personages in the party were three brothers: a skillful hunter, Mestigoit; the "medicineman"; and Pierre, an apostate.

Winter had set in, and already dead Nature was sheeted in funereal white. Lakes and ponds were frozen, rivulets sealed up, torrents encased with stalactites of ice; the black rocks and the black trunks of the pine trees were beplastered with snow, and its heavy masses crushed the dull green boughs into the drifts beneath. The forest was silent as the grave.

Through this desolation the long file of Indians made its way, all on snow-shoes, each man, woman, and child bending under a heavy load, or dragging a sledge, narrow, of prodigious length. They carried their whole wealth with them, on their backs or on their sledges —kettles, axes, bales of meat, if such they had, and huge rolls of birch-bark for covering their wigwams. The Jesuit was loaded like the rest. The dogs alone floundered through the drifts unburdened. There was neither path nor level ground. Descending, climbing, stooping beneath half-fallen trees, clambering over piles of prostrate trunks, struggling through matted cedar swamps, threading chill ravines, and crossing streams no longer visible, they toiled on till the day began to decline, then stopped to encamp. Burdens were thrown down, and sledges unladen. The squaws, with knives and hatchets, cut long poles of birch and spruce saplings; while the men, with snowshoes for shovels, cleared a round or square space in the snow, which formed an upright wall three or four feet high, enclosing the area of the wigwam. On one side, a passage was cut for an entrance, and the poles were planted around the top of the wall of snow, sloping and converging. On these poles were spread the sheets of birch-bark; a bearskin was hung in the passageway for a door; the bare ground within and the surrounding snow were covered with spruce boughs; and the work was done.

This usually occupied about three hours, during which Le Jeune, spent with travel and weakened by the precarious and unaccustomed fare, had the choice of shivering idleness, or taking part in a labor which fatigued, without warming, his exhausted frame. The sorcerer's wife was in far worse case. Though in the extremity of a mortal sickness, they left her lying in the snow till the wigwam was made—without a word, on her part, of remonstrance or complaint. Le Jeune, to the great ire of her husband, sometimes spent the interval in trying to convert her; but she proved intractable, and soon died unbaptized.

Thus lodged, they remained so long as game could be found within a circuit of ten or twelve miles, and then, subsistence failing, removed to another spot. Early in the winter, they hunted the beaver and the Canada porcupine; and, later, in the season of the deep snows, chased the moose and the caribou.

Put aside the bearskin, and enter the hut. Here, in a space some thirteen feet square, were packed nineteen savages, men, women, and children, with their dogs, crouched, squatted, coiled like hedgehogs, or lying on their backs, with knees drawn up perpendicularly to keep their feet out of the fire. Le Jeune, always methodical, arranges the grievances inseparable from these rough quarters under four chief heads—Cold, Heat, Smoke, and Dogs. The bark covering was full of crevices, through which the icy blasts streamed in upon him from all sides; and the hole above, at once window and chimney, was so large, that, as he lay, he could watch the stars as well as in the open air. While the fire in the midst, fed with fat pine knots, scorched him on one side, on the other he had much ado to keep himself from freezing. At times, however, the crowded hut seemed heated to the temperature of an oven. But these evils were light, when compared with the intolerable plague of smoke. During a snowstorm, and often at other times, the wigwam was filled with fumes so dense, stifling, and acrid, that all its inmates were forced to lie flat on their faces, breathing through mouths in contact with the cold earth. Their throats and nostrils felt as if on fire; their scorched eyes streamed with tears; and when Le Jeune tried to read, the letters of his breviary seemed printed in blood. The dogs were not an unmixed evil, for, by sleeping on and around him, they kept him warm at night; but, as an offset to this good service, they walked, ran, and jumped over him as he lay, snatched the food from his birchen dish, or, in a mad rush at some bone or discarded morsel, now and then upset both dish and missionary.

Sometimes of an evening he would leave the filthy den, to read his breviary in peace by the light of the moon. In the forest around sounded but the sharp crack of frost-riven trees;[1] and from the horizon to the zenith[2] shot up the silent meteors of the northern lights, in whose fitful flashing the awe-struck Indians beheld the dancing of the spirits of the dead. The cold gnawed him to the bone; and, his devotions over, he turned back shivering. The illumined hut, from many a chink and crevice, shot forth into the gloom long streams of light athwart the twisted boughs. He stooped and entered. All within glowed red and fiery around the blazing pine knots, where, like brutes in their kennel, were gathered the savage crew. He stepped to his place, over recumbent bodies and leggined and moccasined limbs, and seated himself on the carpet of spruce boughs. Here a tribulation awaited him, the crowning misery of his winter quarters—worse, as he declares, than cold, heat, and dogs.

Of the three brothers who had invited him to join the party, one, we have seen, was the hunter, Mestigoit; another, the sorcerer; and the third, Pierre, whom, by reason of his falling away from the Faith, Le Jeune always mentions as the Apostate. He was a weak-minded young Indian, wholly under the influence of his brother, the sorcerer, who, if not more vicious, was far more resolute and wily. From the antagonism of their respective professions, the sorcerer hated the priest, who lost no opportunity of denouncing his incanta-

tions, and he ridiculed his perpetual singing and drumming as puerility[3] and folly. The former, being an indifferent hunter, and disabled by a disease which he had contracted, depended for subsistence on his credit as a magician; and in undermining it Le Jeune not only outraged his pride, but threatened his daily bread. He used every device to retort ridicule upon his rival. At the outset, he had proffered his aid to Le Jeune in his study of the Algonquin; and, like the Indian practical jokers of Acadia in the case of Father Biard,[4] palmed off upon him the foulest words in the language as the equivalent of things spiritual. Thus it happened, that, while the missionary sought to explain to the assembled wigwam some point of Christian doctrine, he was interrupted by peals of laughter from men, children, and squaws. And now, as Le Jeune took his place in the circle, the sorcerer bent upon him his malignant eyes, and began that course of rude bantering which filled to overflowing the cup of the Jesuit's woes. All took their cue from him, and made their afflicted guest the butt of their inane[5] witticisms. "Look at him! His face is like a dog's!" —"His head is like a pumpkin!"—"He has a beard like a rabbit's." The missionary bore in silence these and countless similar attacks; indeed, so sorely was he harassed, that, lest he should exasperate his tormentor, he sometimes passed whole days without uttering a word.

[3] PUERILITY (pū·ĕr·ĭl'ĭ·tĭ)—Childishness, foolishness.

[4] FATHER BIARD—Pierre Biard, S.J. (1567–1622). His mission in Acadia (Nova Scotia), 1611–13, was unsuccessful. He had hardly started another mission when he was captured by Samuel Argall, a marauding Virginian. He was carried to Jamestown and later to England in a series of exciting adventures.

[5] INANE—Stupid, empty.

[1] FROST-RIVEN TREES—Trees with branches torn apart or split by the frost.

[2] ZENITH—The point in the heavens vertically above one; the top, highest point.

household was a model of harmony. True, they showed no tenderness or consideration towards the sick and disabled; but for the rest, each shared with all in weal or woe: the famine of one was the famine of the whole, and the smallest portion of food was distributed in fair and equal partition. Upbraidings and complaints were unheard; they bore each other's foibles with wonderous equanimity;[8] and while persecuting Le Jeune with constant importunity[9] for tobacco, and for everything else he had, they never begged among themselves.

When the fire burned well and food was abundant, their conversation, such as it was, was incessant. They used no oaths, for their language supplied none —doubtless because their mythology had no beings sufficiently distinct to swear by. Their expletives were foul words, of which they had a super-abundance, and which men, women, and children alike used with a frequency and hardihood that amazed and scandalized the priest. . . .

Prone to believe in the immediate presence of the nether powers, Le Jeune watched the sorcerer with an eye prepared to discover in his conjurations the signs of a genuine diabolic agency. His observations, however, led him to a different result; and he could detect in his rival nothing but a vile compound of impostor and dupe. The sorcerer believed in the efficacy of his own magic, and was continually singing and beating his drum to cure the disease from which he was suffering. Towards the close of the winter Le Jeune fell sick, and in his pain and weakness nearly succumbed

Le Jeune, a man of excellent observation, already knew his red associates well enough to understand that their rudeness did not of necessity imply ill-will. The rest of the party, in their turn, fared no better. They rallied and bantered each other incessantly, with as little forbearance and as little malice as a troop of unbridled schoolboys. No one took offense. To have done so would have been to bring upon one's self genuine contumely.[6] This motley[7]

[6] CONTUMELY—Contempt, scorn.

[7] MOTLEY—Mixed; composed of various parts of people, especially in queer or ridiculous combinations.

[8] EQUANIMITY—Calmness, composure.

[9] IMPORTUNITY—Troublesome, annoying perseverance.

under the nocturnal uproar of the sorcerer, who hour after hour sang and drummed without mercy, sometimes yelling at the top of his throat, then hissing like a serpent, then striking his drum on the ground as if in a frenzy,[10] then leaping up, raving about the wigwam, and calling on the women and children to join him in singing. Now ensued a hideous din; for every throat was trained to the utmost, and all were beating with sticks or fists on the bark of the hut to increase the noise, with the charitable object of aiding the sorcerer to conjure down his malady, or drive away the evil spirit that caused it.

He had an enemy, a rival sorcerer, whom he charged with having caused by charms the disease that afflicted him. He therefore announced that he should kill him. As the rival dwelt at Gaspé, a hundred leagues off, the present execution of the threat might appear difficult; but distance was no bar to the vengeance of the sorcerer. Ordering all the children and all but one of the women to leave the wigwam, he seated himself, with the woman who remained, on the ground in the center, while the men of the party, together with those from other wigwams in the neighborhood, sat in a ring around. Mestigoit, the sorcerer's brother, then brought in the charm, consisting of a few small pieces of wood, some arrowheads, a broken knife, and an iron hook, which he wrapped in a piece of hide. The woman next rose, and walked around the hut, behind the company. Mestigoit and the sorcerer now dug a large hole with two pointed stakes, the whole assembly singing, drumming, and howling meanwhile with a deafening uproar. The hole made, the charm, wrapped in the hide, was thrown into it. Pierre, the

Apostate, then brought a sword and a knife to the sorcerer, who, seizing them, leaped into the hole, and with furious gesticulation hacked and stabbed at the charm, yelling with the whole force of his lungs. At length he ceased, displayed the knife and sword stained with blood, proclaimed that he had mortally wounded his enemy, and demanded if none present had heard his death-cry. The assembly, more occupied in making noises than in listening for them, gave no reply, till at length two young men declared that they had heard a faint scream, as if from a great distance; whereat a shout of gratulation and triumph rose from all the company.

There was a young prophet, or diviner, in one of the neighboring huts, of whom the sorcerer took counsel as to the prospect of his restoration to health. The divining-lodge was formed, in this instance, of five or six upright posts planted in a circle and covered with a blanket. The prophet ensconced[11] himself within; and after a long interval of singing, the spirits declared their presence by their usual squeaking utterances from the recesses of the mystic tabernacle. Their responses were not unfavorable; and the sorcerer drew much consolation from the invocations of his brother impostor.

Besides his incessant endeavors to annoy Le Jeune, the sorcerer now and then tried to frighten him. On one occasion, when a period of starvation had been followed by a successful hunt, the whole party assembled for one of the gluttonous feasts usual with them at such times. While the guests sat expectant, and the squaws were about to ladle out the banquet, the sorcerer suddenly leaped up, exclaiming that he had lost

[10] FRENZY—Madness, delirium.

[11] ENSCONCED—Hid or sheltered; settled comfortably.

his senses, and that knives and hatchets must be kept out of his way, as he had a mind to kill somebody. Then rolling his eyes towards Le Jeune, he began a series of frantic gestures and outcries, then stopped abruptly and stared into vacancy, silent and motionless, then resumed his former clamor, raged in and out of the hut, and, seizing some of its supporting poles, broke them, as if in an uncontrollable frenzy. The missionary, though alarmed, sat reading his breviary as before. When, however, on the next morning, the sorcerer began again to play the maniac, the thought occurred to him that some stroke of fever might in truth have touched his brain. Accordingly, he approached him and felt his pulse, which he found, in his own words, "as cool as a fish." The pretended madman looked at him with astonishment, and, giving over the attempt to frighten him, presently returned to his senses.

Le Jeune, robbed of his sleep by the ceaseless thumping of the sorcerer's drum and the monotonous cadence of his medicine-songs, improved the time in attempts to convert him. "I began," he says, "by evincing a great love for him, and by praises, which I threw to him as a bait whereby I might catch him in a net of truth." But the Indian, though pleased with the Father's flatteries was neither caught nor conciliated.

Nowhere was his magic in more requisition than in procuring a successful chase to the hunters—a point of vital interest, since on it hung the lives of the whole party. They often, however, returned empty-handed; and for one, two, or three successive days no other food could be had than the bark of trees or scraps of leather. So long as tobacco lasted, they found solace in their pipes, which seldom left their lips. "Unhappy infidels," writes Le Jeune, "who spend their lives in smoke, and their eternity in flames!"

As Christmas approached, their condition grew desperate. Beavers and porcupines were scarce, and the snow was not deep enough for hunting the moose. Night and day the medicine-drums resounded from the wigwams, mingled with the wail of starving children. The hunters grew weak and emaciated; and as after a forlorn march the wanderers encamped once more in the lifeless forest, the priest remembered that it was the eve of Christmas. "The Lord gave us for our supper a porcupine, large as a suckling pig, and also a rabbit. It was not much, it is true, for eighteen or nineteen persons; but the Holy Virgin and St. Joseph, her glorious spouse, were not so well treated, on this very day, in the stable of Bethlehem."

On Christmas Day, the despairing hunters, again unsuccessful, came to pray succor from Le Jeune. Even the Apostate had become tractable, and the famished sorcerer was ready to try the efficacy of an appeal to the deity of his rival. A bright hope possessed the missionary. He composed two prayers, which, with the aid of the repentant Pierre, he translated into Algonquin. Then he hung against the side of the hut a napkin which he had brought with him, and against the napkin a crucifix and a reliquary, and, this done, caused all the Indians to kneel before them with hands raised and clasped. He now read one of the prayers, and required the Indians to repeat the other after him, promising to renounce their superstitions and obey Christ, whose image they saw before them, if he would give them food and save them from perishing. The pledge given, he dismissed the hunters with a benediction.

At night they returned with game enough to relieve the immediate necessity. All was hilarity. The kettles were slung, and the feasters assembled. Le Jeune rose to speak, when Pierre, who having killed nothing was in ill humor, said, with a laugh, that the crucifix and the prayer had nothing to do with their good luck; while the sorcerer, his jealousy reviving as he saw his hunger about to be appeased, called out to the missionary, "Hold your tongue! You have no sense!" As usual, all took their cue from him. They fell to their repast with ravenous jubilation, and the disappointed priest sat dejected and silent.

Repeatedly, before the spring, they were thus threatened with starvation. Nor was their case exceptional. It was the ordinary winter life of all those Northern tribes who did not till the soil, but lived by hunting and fishing alone. The desertion or killing of the aged, sick, and disabled, occasional cannibalism, and frequent death from famine were natural incidents of an existence which during half the year was but a desperate pursuit of the mere necessaries of life under the worst conditions of hardship, suffering, and debasement.

At the beginning of April, after roaming for five months among forests and mountains, the party made their last march, regained the bank of the St. Lawrence, and waded to the island where they had hidden their canoes. Le Jeune was exhausted and sick, and Mestigoit offered to carry him in his canoe to Quebec. This Indian was by far the best of the three brothers, and both Pierre and the sorcerer looked to him for support. He was strong, active, and daring, a skillful hunter and a dexterous canoeman. Le Jeune gladly accepted his offer, embarked with him and Pierre on the dreary and tempestuous

river, and, after a voyage full of hardship, during which the canoe narrowly escaped being ground to atoms among the floating ice, landed on the Island of Orleans, six miles from Quebec. The afternoon was stormy and dark, and the river was covered with ice, sweeping by with the tide. They were forced to encamp. At midnight the moon had risen, the river was comparatively unencumbered, and they embarked once more. The wind increased, and the waves tossed furiously. Nothing saved them but the skill and courage of Mestigoit. At length they could see the rock of Quebec towering through the gloom, but piles of ice lined the shore, while floating masses were drifting down on the angry current. The Indian watched his moment, shot his canoe through them, gained the fixed ice, leaped out, and shouted to his companions to follow. Pierre scrambled up, but the ice was six feet out of the water, and Le Jeune's agility failed him. He saved himself by clutching the ankle of Mestigoit, by whose aid he gained a firm foothold at the top, and, for a moment, the three voyagers, aghast at the narrowness of their escape, stood gazing at each other in the silence.

It was three o'clock in the morning when Le Jeune knocked at the door of his rude little convent on the St. Charles; and the Fathers, springing in joyful haste from their slumbers, embraced their long-absent superior with ejaculations of praise and benediction.

❖❖❖❖❖❖❖❖❖❖❖❖❖❖❖❖❖❖❖❖❖❖❖❖

FOR DISCUSSION

1. What are stalactites of ice?
2. Why did the people in the wigwam lie flat on their faces when the smoke became dense and stifling?

3. What are the "northern lights"? If you have ever seen them, describe your impressions.

4. Under the circumstances, why was the Indians' banter at first so difficult to bear?

5. By contrast, what equipment would a modern hunter use in the wilds of Canada? How would his discomforts compare with Le Jeune's? Le Jeune went with the Indians to promote the greater honor and glory of God. How well did he succeed? Does Parkman have any sympathy with Le Jeune's missionary work?

6. Why did the sorcerer hate the priest? Do you think Le Jeune was hypocritical when, as he reported, he showed great love for the sorcerer in his attempts to convert him?

7. What were some of the characteristics of the Indians? Did they have any good points?

8. In what respect does the result of the Christmas hunt remind you of the Israelites in the desert? Why do men willingly forget the favors of God? Can you draw any conclusions from that fact about suffering in the world?

## WORDS FROM THE LATIN

1. When you are in doubt or fear about something, you pray: *precor, precari.* What, then, is a *precarious* situation? Why does Parkman call the fare, that is, the food, *precarious* for Le Jeune?

2. There are two words spelt the same way: *c-o-n-j-u-r-e.* One is accented on the first syllable; the other, on the second. How would you pronounce the word if you were binding somebody by a solemn oath? if you were talking about the *conjurations* of a magician or spiritualist?

3. In the following, you will be given a Latin word and its meaning; then, an English word derived from the Latin, and a phrase in which the derivative is used. Try to figure out the meaning of the derived word.

    *a. Cado:* fall—cadence—the monotonous *cadence* of his medicine songs.

    *b. Efficio:* to bring to pass, fulfill, effect—efficacy—the sorcerer believed in the *efficacy* of his own magic.

    *c. Macies:* thinness, leanness—emaciated—the hunters grew *emaciated.*

    *d. Prodigium:* a miraculous or strange sign; anything strange or unnatural—prodigious—a sledge of *prodigious* length.

## A PROJECT

Write a short account of some hunting trip, real or imaginary, in which you suffer great hardships. You need not make it serious. Your hunting need not be restricted to wild game and the forests.

## RELATED READING

You will find many other interesting accounts in Parkman's *Jesuits in North America.* This selection is taken from Chapter IV. *Saint Among Savages* is the story of St. Isaac Jogues and his companions told by F. X. Talbot, S.J. Agnes Repplier's *Junipero Serra* is the story of a famous Franciscan missionary among the Indians of the West Coast.

# TATTOOING

## HERMAN MELVILLE

*In 1841, at the age of twenty-two, Melville shipped as a sailor on a whaling vessel. Because of the hardships of the work and the brutality of the captain, he and Toby, another sailor, deserted at the Marquesas Islands in the South Pacific. There they were captured by the Typees. Although the Typees were cannibals, they treated Melville and Toby kindly. This selection from the novel* TYPEE *describes one of the most interesting customs of these island savages—tattooing.*

In one of my strolls with Kory-Kory,[1] in passing along the border of a thick growth of bushes, my attention was arrested by a singular noise. On entering the thicket I witnessed for the first time the operation of tattooing as performed by these islanders.

I beheld a man extended flat upon his back on the ground, and, despite the forced composure of his countenance, it was evident that he was suffering agony. His tormentor bent over him, working away for all the world like a stone-cutter with mallet and chisel. In one hand he held a short, slender stick, pointed with a shark's tooth, on the upright end of which he tapped with a small hammer-like piece of wood, thus puncturing the skin and charging it with the coloring matter in which the instrument was dipped. A coconut shell containing this fluid was placed upon the ground. It is prepared by mixing with a vegetable juice the ashes of the "armor," or candle-nut,[2] always preserved for the purpose. Beside the savage, and spread out upon a piece of soiled tappa,[3] were a great number of curious, black-looking little implements of bone and wood, used in the various divisions of his art. A few terminated in a single fine point, and, like very delicate pencils, were employed in giving the finishing touches or in operating upon the more sensitive portions of the body, as was the case in the present instance. Others presented several points distributed in a line, somewhat resembling the teeth of a saw. These were employed in the coarser parts of the work, and particularly in pricking in straight marks. Some presented their points disposed in small figures, and being placed upon the body, were, by a single blow of the hammer, made to leave their indelible impression. I observed a few the handles of which were mysteriously curved, as if intended to be introduced into the orifice[4] of the ear, with a view perhaps of beating the tattoo upon the tympa-

---

[1] KORY-KORY—The savage who was Melville's attendant and bodyguard.

[2] CANDLE-NUT—A very oily nut which was burned as a candle.

[3] TAPPA—Native cloth made from the bark of trees.

[4] ORIFICE—A relatively small opening.

num.[5] Altogether the sight of these strange instruments recalled to mind that display of cruel-looking mother-of-pearl-handled things which one sees in their velvet-lined cases at the elbow of a dentist.

The artist was not at this time engaged on an original sketch, his subject being a venerable savage whose tattooing had become somewhat faded with age and needed a few repairs, and accordingly he was merely employed in touching up the works of some of the old masters of the Typee school, as delineated upon the human canvas before him. The parts operated upon were the eyelids, where a longitudinal streak, like the one which adorned Kory-Kory, crossed the countenance of the victim.

In spite of all the efforts of the poor old man, sundry[6] twitchings and screwings of the muscles of the face denoted the exquisite sensibility of these shutters to the windows of his soul which he was now having repainted. But the artist, with a heart as callous as that of any army surgeon, continued his performance, enlivening his labors with a wild chant, tapping away the while as merrily as a woodpecker.

So deeply engaged was he in his work that he had not observed our approach until, after having enjoyed an unmolested view of the operation, I chose to attract his attention. As soon as he perceived me, supposing that I sought him in his professional capacity, he seized hold of me in a paroxysm[7] of delight, and was all eagerness to begin the work. When, however, I gave him to understand that he had altogether mistaken my views, nothing could exceed his grief and disappointment. But, recovering from this, he seemed determined not to credit my assertion, and, grasping his implements, he flourished them about in fearful vicinity to my face, going through an imaginary performance of his art, and every moment bursting into some admiring exclamation at the beauty of his designs.

Horrified at the bare thought of being rendered hideous for life if the wretch were to execute his purpose upon me, I struggled to get away from him, while Kory-Kory, turning traitor, stood by and besought me to comply with the outrageous request. On my reiterated[8] refusals the excited artist got half beside himself, and was overwhelmed with sorrow at losing so noble an opportunity of distinguishing himself in his profession.

The idea of engrafting his tattooing upon my white skin filled him with all a painter's enthusiasm; again and again he gazed into my countenance, and every fresh glimpse seemed to add to the vehemence of his ambition. Not knowing to what extremities he might proceed, and shuddering at the ruin he might inflict upon my figurehead, I now endeavored to draw off his attention from it, and holding out my arm in a fit of desperation, signed to him to commence operations. But he rejected the compromise indignantly, and still continued his attack on my face, as though nothing short of that would satisfy him. When his forefinger swept across my features, in laying out the borders of those parallel bands which were to encircle my countenance, the flesh fairly crawled upon my bones. At last, half wild with terror and indignation, I suc-

[5] TYMPANUM—A pun on beating the tattoo upon the drum and beating the tattoo upon the tympanum, or eardrum.
[6] SUNDRY—Various, several.
[7] PAROXYSM—Sudden violent action or emotion; a fit.

[8] REITERATED—Repeated.

ceeded in breaking away from the three savages and fled towards old Marheyo's [9] house, pursued by the indomitable [10] artist, who ran after me, implements in hand. Kory-Kory, however, at last interfered and drew him off from the chase.

This incident opened my eyes to a new danger; and I now felt convinced that, in some luckless hour I should be disfigured in such a manner as never more to have the *face* to return to my country-men, even should an opportunity offer.

These apprehensions were greatly increased by the desire which King Mehevi [11] and several of the inferior chiefs now manifested that I should be tattooed. The pleasure of the king was first signified to me some three days after my casual encounter with Karky

[9] MARHEYO—The father of Kory-Kory, at whose house Melville and Toby stayed.

[10] INDOMITABLE—Unconquerable; not to be subdued.

[11] MEHEVI—King of the Typees.

the artist. Heavens! What imprecations I showered upon that Karky! Doubtless he had plotted a conspiracy against me and my countenance, and would never rest until his diabolical purpose was accomplished. Several times I met him in various parts of the valley, and invariably, whenever he descried me, he came running after me with his mallet and chisel, flourishing them about my face as if he longed to begin. What an object he would have made of me!

When the king first expressed his wish to me, I made known to him my utter abhorrence of the measure, and worked myself into such a state of excitement that he absolutely stared at me in amazement. It evidently surpassed his majesty's comprehension how any sober-minded and sensible individual could entertain the least possible objection to so beautifying an operation.

Soon afterwards he repeated his suggestion, and meeting with a like repulse, showed some symptoms of displeasure at my obduracy.[12] On his a third time renewing his request, I plainly perceived that something must be done, or my visage was ruined forever; I therefore screwed up my courage to the sticking point, and declared my willingness to have both arms tattooed from just above the wrist to the shoulder. His majesty was greatly pleased at the proposition, and I was congratulating myself with having thus compromised the matter, when he intimated that as a thing of course my face was first to undergo the operation. I was fairly driven to despair; nothing but the utter ruin of my "face divine," as the poets call it, would, I perceived, satisfy the inexorable[13] Mehevi and his chiefs, or rather that infernal Karky, for he was at the bottom of it all.

The only consolation afforded me was a choice of patterns: I was at perfect liberty to have my face spanned by three horizontal bars, after the fashion of my serving-man's[14] or to have as many oblique stripes slanting across it; or if, like a true courtier, I chose to model my style on that of royalty, I might wear a sort of freemason badge upon my countenance in the shape of a mystic triangle. However, I would have none of these, though the king most earnestly impressed upon my mind that my choice was wholly unrestricted. At last, seeing my unconquerable repugnance, he ceased to importune me.

But not so some other of the savages. Hardly a day passed but I was subjected to their annoying requests, until at last my existence became a burden to me; the pleasures I had previously enjoyed no longer afforded me delight, and all my former desire to escape from the valley now revived with additional force.

A fact which I soon afterwards learned augmented[15] my apprehension. The whole system of tattooing was, I found, connected with their religion, and it was evident, therefore, that they were resolved to make a convert of me.

In the decoration of the chiefs it seems to be necessary to exercise the most elaborate penciling, while some of the inferior natives looked as if they had been daubed over indiscriminately with a house-painter's brush. I remember one fellow who prided himself hugely upon a great oblong patch, placed high upon his back, and who always reminded me of a man with blister of Spanish flies[16] stuck between his shoulders. Another whom I frequently met had the hollow of his eyes tattooed in two regular squares, and his visual organs being remarkably brilliant, they gleamed forth from out this setting like a couple of diamonds inserted in ebony.

[15] AUGMENTED—Increased.
[16] SPANISH FLIES—A kind of small beetle which, when dried and powdered, is used to raise a blister.

◇◇◇◇◇◇◇◇◇◇◇◇◇◇◇◇◇◇◇◇◇◇◇◇◇◇◇◇◇

## FOR DISCUSSION

1. In your own words describe the tools used for tattooing.

2. Point out one of the figures of speech that the author uses. Why do they make the article more enjoyable? What are "the shutters to the windows of his soul"?

3. A pun is a play on words of the same sound but different meanings or on different applications of a word for the witty effect. One pun has already been pointed out in this article. Find another one and explain it.

[12] OBDURACY—Refusal to yield.
[13] INEXORABLE—Cannot be persuaded.
[14] SERVING-MAN'S—Kory-Kory's.

4. Do you think all this actually happened to Melville? Point out phrases or sentences that make you tend to believe that he is exaggerating.

## WORDS TO USE

Give the meaning of the following words and use them in a sentence: *terminate, delineate, callous, unmolested, visage, intimate, repugnance, importune, oblong.*

Melville is noted for his tremendous vocabulary. Go through the article and pick out ten other words whose meanings you do not know and look them up.

## PROJECTS

1. Compare this account of tattooing with one given by the encyclopedia or some other source.

2. Make a report on the religious custom of tattooing by these natives. It is explained immediately after this selection in Melville's novel, *Typee.*

◇◇◇◇◇

FROM # WALDEN

## HENRY DAVID THOREAU

WALDEN, OR LIFE IN THE WOODS *was published in 1854 and its success made Thoreau known throughout the English speaking world. The book tells of the simple life he had lived in the one-room hut built by himself near Walden Pond. He supported himself during this time by raising a garden and doing various small jobs around the neighborhood. But these two years were not wasted. The following two selections show that during this time his power of observing and understanding both human and animal life was keenly developed.*

### THE BATTLE OF THE WOOD-PILE

One day when I went out to my wood-pile, or rather my pile of stumps, I observed two large ants, the one red, the other much larger, nearly half an inch long, and black, fiercely contending with one another. Having once got hold they never let go, but struggled and wrestled and rolled on the chips incessantly. Looking farther, I was surprised to find that the chips were covered with such combatants, that it was not a *duellum*,[1] but a *bellum*,[2] a war between two races of ants, the red always pitted against the black, and frequently two red ones to one black. The legions of these Myrmidons[3] covered all the hills and vales in my wood-yard, and the ground was already strewn with the dead and dying, both red and black. It

[1] *Duellum*—A duel between two.
[2] *Bellum*—A war.
[3] MYRMIDONS—Achilles' troops in the Trojan Wars. Then the word meant "ant-men."

was the only battle which I have ever witnessed, the only battlefield I ever trod while the battle was raging; internecine [4] war; the red republicans on the one hand, and the black imperialists on the other. On every side they were engaged in deadly combat, yet without any noise that I could hear, and human soldiers never fought so resolutely. I watched a couple that were fast locked in each other's embraces, in a little sunny valley amid the chips, now at noonday prepared to fight till the sun went down or life went out. The smaller red champion had fastened himself like a vice to his adversary's front, and through all the tumblings on that field never for an instant ceased to gnaw at one of his feelers near the root, having already caused the other to go by the board; while the stronger black one dashed him from side to side, and, as I saw on looking nearer, had already divested him of several of his members.[5] They fought with more pertinacity than bulldogs. Neither manifested the least disposition to retreat. It was evident that their battle cry was "Conquer or die." In the meanwhile there came along a single red ant on the hillside of this valley, evidently full of excitement, who either had dispatched his foe or had not yet taken part in the battle; probably the latter, for he had lost none of his limbs; whose mother had charged him to return with his shield or upon it.[6] Or perchance he was some Achilles, who had nourished his wrath apart and had now come to avenge or rescue his Patroclus.[7] He saw this unequal combat from afar—for the blacks were nearly twice the size of the red—he drew near with rapid pace till he stood on his guard within half an inch of the combatants; then, watching his opportunity, he sprang upon the black warrior and commenced his operations near the root of his right fore leg, leaving the foe to select among his own members; and so there were three united for life, as if a new kind of attraction had been invented which put all other locks and cements to shame. I should not have wondered by this time to find that they had their respective musical bands stationed on some eminent chip, and playing their national airs the while, to excite the slow and cheer the dying combatants. I was myself excited somewhat even as if they had been men. The more you think of it, the less the difference. And certainly there is not the fight recorded in Concord history, at least, if in the history of America, that will bear a moment's comparison with this, whether for the numbers engaged in it, or for the patriotism and heroism displayed. For numbers and for courage it was an Austerlitz or Dresden.[8] . . . There was not one hireling there. I have no doubt that it was a principle they fought for, as much as our ancestors, and not to avoid a threepenny tax on their tea; and the results of this battle will be as important and memorable to those whom it concerns as those of the battle of Bunker Hill, at least.

[4] INTERNECINE—Mutually slaughterous or destructive of life.

[5] DIVESTED . . . MEMBERS—Torn off parts of the red ant's body.

[6] WHOSE MOTHER . . . UPON IT—According to legend, Spartan mothers said this to their sons as they left for battle. It means to return victorious or to die in battle.

[7] PATROCLUS—Achilles, the Greek leader, refused to fight because he had been insulted by his commander. When his closest friend Patroclus was killed, however, he returned to the battle to avenge his death.

[8] AUSTERLITZ . . . DRESDEN—Battles in the Napoleonic wars.

I took up the chip on which the three I have particularly described were struggling, carried it into my house, and placed it under a tumbler on my window sill, in order to see the issue. Holding a microscope to the first-mentioned red ant, I saw that, though he was assiduously gnawing at the near fore leg of his enemy, having severed his remaining feeler, his own breast was all torn away, exposing what vitals he had there to the jaws of the black warrior, whose breastplate was apparently too thick for him to pierce; and the dark carbuncles [9] of the sufferer's eyes shone with a ferocity such as war only could excite. They struggled half an hour longer under the tumbler, and when I looked again the black soldier had severed the heads of his foes from their bodies, and the still living heads were hanging on either side of him like ghastly trophies at his saddlebow, still apparently as firmly fastened as ever, and he was endeavoring with feeble struggles, being without feelers and with only the remnant of a leg, and I know not how many other wounds, to divest himself of them;

which at length, after half an hour more, he accomplished. I raised the glass, and he went off over the window sill in that crippled state. Whether he finally survived that combat and spent the remainder of his days in some Hotel des Invalides,[10] I do not know; but I thought that his industry would not be worth much thereafter. I never learned which party was victorious, nor the cause of the war; but I felt for the rest of that day as if I had had my feelings excited and harrowed [11] by witnessing the struggle, the ferocity and carnage, of a human battle before my door.

## CONCLUSION TO *WALDEN*

I left the woods for as good a reason as I went there. Perhaps it seemed to me that I had several more lives to live and could not spare any more time for that one. It is remarkable how easily and insensibly we fall into a particular route and make a beaten track for ourselves. I had not lived there a week before my feet wore a path from my door to the pond-side; and though it is five or six years since I trod it, it is still quite

[9] CARBUNCLES—At one time it meant any one of several red precious stones.

[10] HOTEL DES INVALIDES—A veterans hospital in Paris.
[11] HARROWED—Tormented; vexed.

distinct. It is true, I fear, that others may have fallen into it, and so helped to keep it open. The surface of the earth is soft and impressible by the feet of men; and so with the paths which the mind travels. How worn and dusty, then, must be the highways of the world, how deep the ruts of tradition and conformity! I did not wish to take a cabin passage, but rather to go before the mast and on the deck of the world, for there I could best see the moonlight amid the mountains. I do not wish to go below now.

I learned this, at least, by my experiment; that if one advances confidently in the direction of his dreams and endeavors to live the life which he has imagined, he will meet with a success unexpected in common hours. He will put some things behind, will pass an invisible boundary; new, universal, and more liberal laws will begin to establish themselves around and within him; or the old laws be expanded and interpreted in his favor in a more liberal sense, and he will live with the license [1] of a higher order of beings. In proportion as he simplifies his life, the laws of the universe will appear less complex, and solitude will not be solitude, nor poverty poverty, nor weakness weakness. If you have built castles in the air, your work need not be lost; that is where they should be. Now put the foundations under them.

[1] LICENSE—Freedom.

◇◇◇◇◇◇◇◇◇◇◇◇◇◇◇◇◇◇◇◇◇◇◇◇◇

## FOR DISCUSSION

1. Does the author make it seem as though it is a battle between human beings? How does he achieve this effect? Point out different words or phrases that help in this respect.

2. Does the author say that there were actually "musical bands . . . playing their national airs"? If not, why does the author suggest it?

3. The author says, "I was myself excited somewhat as if they had been men. The more you think of it, the less the difference." What does he mean by this last sentence? Do you agree with him? Later he says, "I have no doubt that it was a principle they fought for." Do you think the author seriously means this? Can insects or animals fight for a principle? What big distinction would we make that Thoreau seems to overlook?

4. Explain the meaning of the following sentences from the conclusion:

a) "I do not wish to take a cabin passage, but rather to go before the mast and on the deck of the world. . . ."

b) ". . . if one advances confidently in the direction of his dreams and endeavors to live the life which he has imagined, he will meet with a success unexpected in common hours."

c) "If you have built castles in the air, your work need not be lost; that is where they should be. Now put the foundations under them."

## WORDS FROM THE LATIN

1. If *vestio* in Latin means *to cover* or *to clothe*, what would you expect *divested* to mean?

2. *Pertinacity* means *obstinacy* or *persistency*. What other synonyms can you add to these?

3. The Latin *assiduus*, derived from *sedere*—*to sit*, first meant *sitting in a place constantly* and then simply *constant* or *unceasing*. What then do you think *assiduously* would mean?

4. *Carnage*, meaning *great destruction of life*, comes from the Latin *carno, carnis* meaning *flesh*. Where in the last gospel of the Mass is the word *caro* used?

# SECOND INAUGURAL ADDRESS

## ABRAHAM LINCOLN

*Between Lincoln's first and second inaugurals stretch four fateful years—
four years of war. In this speech we see the perfection of Lincoln's style,
the simplicity which is the highest art, the unerring feeling for rhythm, the
wealth of emotional appeal. Perhaps it was worth the years of suffering to
have given us such orations as this one and his "Gettysburg Address."*

Fellow-countrymen:

At this second appearing to take the
oath of the presidential office,[1] there is
less occasion for an extended address
than there was at first. Then a statement, somewhat in detail, of a course to
be pursued, seemed fitting and proper.
Now, at the expiration of four years,
during which public declarations have
been constantly called forth on every
point and phase of the great contest
which still absorbs the attention and
engrosses the energies of the nation, little that is new could be presented. The
progress of our arms, upon which all else
chiefly depends, is as well known to the
public as to myself; and it is, I trust, reasonably satisfactory and encouraging to
all.[2] With high hopes for the future,
no prediction in regard to it is ventured.

On the occasion corresponding to this
four years ago, all thoughts were anxiously directed to an impending civil
war. All dreaded it—all sought to avoid
it. While the inaugural address was being delivered from this place, devoted altogether to saving the Union without
war, insurgent agents were in the city
seeking to destroy it without war—seeking to dissolve the Union, and divide
effects, by negotiation.[3] Both parties
deprecated war; but one of them would
make war rather than let the nation survive; and the other would accept war
rather than let it perish. And the
war came.

One-eighth of the whole population
were colored slaves, not distributed generally over the Union, but localized in
the southern part of it. These slaves
constituted a peculiar and powerful interest. All knew that this interest was

[1] AT THIS SECOND APPEARING, etc.—This
speech was given on March 4, 1865.

[2] THE PROGRESS OF OUR ARMS, etc.—In
August, 1864, Admiral Farragut had taken
Mobile. In September, Sherman had reached
Atlanta and started on his march to the sea,
which ended with the capture of Savannah in
December. The North was winning on every
front. Just after this speech was made the
Army of the Potomac began a new drive on
Richmond. April 3, 1865, the Union forces
entered the city. Lee surrendered April 9,
1865.

[3] INSURGENT AGENTS WERE IN THE CITY,
etc.—"Three agents of the confederate government were in Washington to negotiate for the
recognition of independence, the surrender of
the forts, and an adjustment of monetary
losses to the federal government through the
surrender of federal property in the South."
Bassett, *Short History of the United States.*

the object for which the insurgents would rend the Union, even by war; while the government claimed no right to do more than to restrict the territorial enlargement of it.[4]

Neither party expected for the war the magnitude or the duration which it has already attained. Neither anticipated that the cause of the conflict[5] might cease with, or even before, the conflict itself should cease. Each looked for an easier triumph and a result less fundamental and astounding. Both read the same Bible, and pray to the same God; and each invokes His aid against the other. It may seem strange that any men should dare to ask a just God's assistance in wringing their bread from the sweat of other men's faces; but let us judge not, that we be not judged. The prayers of both could not be answered—that of neither has been answered fully.

The Almighty has his own purposes. "Woe unto the world because of of-

[4] THE GOVERNMENT CLAIMED NO RIGHT, etc.—See Lincoln's *First Inaugural Address*. He reiterates his belief that he has no right "to interfere with the institution of slavery in the states where it exists."

[5] CAUSE OF THE CONFLICT—Slavery was the real cause. The Emancipation Proclamation was January 1, 1863.

fenses! for it must needs be that offenses come; but woe to that man by whom the offense cometh."[6] If we shall suppose that American slavery is one of those offenses which in the providence of God, must needs come, but which, having continued through his appointed time, He now wills to remove, and that He gives to both North and South this terrible war, as the woe due to those by whom the offense came, shall we discern therein any departure from those divine attributes which the believers in a living God always ascribe to Him? Fondly do we hope—fervently do we pray—that this mighty scourge of war may speedily pass away. Yet, if God wills that it continue until all the wealth piled by the bondman's two hundred and fifty years of unrequited toil shall be sunk, and until every drop of blood drawn with the lash shall be paid by another drawn with the sword, as was said three thousand years ago, still it must be said, "The judgments of the Lord are true and righteous altogether."[7]

With malice toward none; with charity for all; with firmness in the right, as

[6] WOE UNTO THE WORLD, etc.—See *Matthew*, xviii:7.

[7] THE JUDGMENTS OF THE LORD, etc.—See Psalms 19:9. In 1862 Lincoln had written in his personal papers for his own comfort: "The will of God prevails. In great contests each party claims to act in accordance with the will of God. Both may be, and one must be wrong. God can not be for and against the same thing at the same time. In the present civil war it is quite possible that God's purpose is something different from the purpose of either party; and yet the human instrumentalities, working just as they do, are of the best adaptation to effect His purpose. I am almost ready to say that this is probably true; that God wills this contest, and wills that it shall not end yet. By his mere great power on the minds of the now contestants, He could have either saved or destroyed the Union without a human contest. Yet the contest began. And, having begun, He could give the final victory to either side any day. Yet the contest proceeds."

God gives us to see the right, let us strive on to finish the work we are in; to bind up the nation's wounds; to care for him who shall have borne the battle, and for his widow and his orphan—to do all which may achieve and cherish a just and lasting peace among ourselves, and with all nations.

◇◇◇◇◇◇◇◇◇◇◇◇◇◇◇◇◇◇◇◇◇◇◇◇◇◇◇◇◇◇

## FOR DISCUSSION

1. Why is the speech so short? Is the tone of this speech fearful or confident?

2. Point out sentences that show that Lincoln had suffered since he became president.

3. In Lincoln's sentences there is a perfect blending of thought, feeling, and words. Pick out sentences that you think stand out above the rest for their harmony of sound and thought.

## WORDS—SHADES OF MEANING

What are the differences in meaning of the following pairs of words: *imprecate—deprecate; inspiration—expiration; impend—expend; insurgent—resurgent?*

## RELATED READING

Read "Anne Rutledge" in *Spoon River Anthology*, by Edgar Lee Masters. The poem contains an echo of the last paragraph of this speech.

◇◇◇◇◇

# TO MRS. LYDIA BIXBY

### ABRAHAM LINCOLN

Executive Mansion
Washington, Nov. 21, 1864

To Mrs. Bixby, Boston, Mass.

Dear Madam,

I have been shown in the files of the War Department a statement of the Adjutant General of Massachusetts that you are the mother of five sons who died gloriously on the field of battle. I feel how weak and fruitless must be any word of mine which should attempt to beguile you from the grief of a loss so overwhelming. But I cannot refrain from tendering you the consolation that may be found in the thanks of the republic they died to save. I pray that our Heavenly Father may assuage the anguish of your bereavement, and leave you only the cherished memory of the loved and lost, and the solemn pride that must be yours to have laid so costly a sacrifice upon the altar of freedom.

Yours very sincerely and respectfully,
A. Lincoln

◇◇◇◇◇◇◇◇◇◇◇◇◇◇◇◇◇◇◇◇◇◇◇◇◇◇◇◇◇◇

## FOR DISCUSSION

1. In whose behalf does Lincoln express appreciation to Mrs. Bixby? Does the letter sound stiff and formal, or warmly personal?

2. What consolations does he offer to Mrs. Bixby? Do you think that the mother must have found some comfort in the letter? Discuss.

# Further Readings in Literature of the National Period

## WRITERS OF THE NATIONAL PERIOD—FICTION

BALDWIN, JOSEPH G., *The Flush Times of Alabama and Mississippi*

COOPER, JAMES F., *The Spy; The Deerslayer; The Pathfinder; The Last of the Mohicans; The Pilot; Satanstoe*

DANA, RICHARD HENRY, *Two Years Before the Mast*

HALE, EDWARD EVERETT, "The Man Without a Country"

HAWTHORNE, NATHANIEL, *Twice-Told Tales; The Marble Faun; The House of Seven Gables; Mosses from an Old Manse*

IRVING, WASHINGTON, *The Alhambra; The Conquest of Granada; Bracebridge Hall; Tales of a Traveller*

KENNEDY, JOHN PENDLETON, *Horse-Shoe Robinson; Swallow Barn*

LONGSTREET, AUGUSTUS BALDWIN, *Georgia Times*

MELVILLE, HERMAN, *Moby Dick; Billy Budd, Foretopman*

* O'BRIEN, FITZ-JAMES, "What Was It?"; "The Diamond Lens"

POE, EDGAR ALLAN, *Tales of the Grotesque and Arabesque*

SIMMS, WILLIAM GILMORE, *The Yemassee; The Forayers; Woodcraft*

STOWE, HARRIET BEECHER, *Uncle Tom's Cabin*

## WRITERS OF THE NATIONAL PERIOD—POETRY

BRYANT, WILLIAM CULLEN, *Collected Poems*

EMERSON, RALPH WALDO, *Poems; Mayday*

HALLECK, FITZ-GREENE, "Marco Bozzaris"; "On the Death of Joseph Rodman Drake"

* HARNEY, JOHN M., "The Echo and the Lover"

HAYNE, PAUL, *Collected Poems*

HOLMES, OLIVER WENDELL, *Complete Poetical Works*

LANIER, SIDNEY, *Poems*

LONGFELLOW, HENRY WADSWORTH, *Complete Poetical Works*

LOWELL, JAMES RUSSELL, *The Vision of Sir Launfal; Heartsease and Rue*

POE, EDGAR ALLAN, *Poems*

* RYAN, ABRAM J., *Poems*

TIMROD, HENRY, *Complete Poems*

WHITTIER, JOHN GREENLEAF, *Collected Poems*

## WRITERS OF THE NATIONAL PERIOD—NONFICTION

AUDUBON, JOHN J., *Birds of America*

* BROWNSON, ORESTES, *The Convert*

CALHOUN, JOHN, *Speech on the Slavery Question*

CLAY, HENRY, *Emancipation of the South; On the Compromise of 1850*

CROCKETT, DAVID, *Autobiography*

DOUGLAS, STEPHEN A., *The Lincoln-Douglas Debates*

EMERSON, RALPH WALDO, *Essays*

* ENGLAND, BISHOP JOHN, *American Citizenship*

* FAIRBANKS, C. B. (AQUECHEEK), *My Unknown Chum*

GREELEY, HORACE, *Autobiography*

HAYNE, ROBERT, "The Doctrine of States' Rights" (oration)

HOLMES, OLIVER WENDELL, *The Autocrat of the Breakfast Table*

* HUGHES, BISHOP JOHN, "The Civil War in America" (oration)

IRVING, WASHINGTON, *The Sketch Book; Diedrich Knickerbocker's History of New York*

LINCOLN, ABRAHAM, "Farewell Address at Springfield"; "A House Divided"

LOWELL, JAMES RUSSELL, *My Study Windows; Among My Books*

PARKMAN, FRANCIS S., *The Conspiracy of Pontiac; The Oregon Trail*

THOREAU, HENRY DAVID, *Walden; A Week on the Concord and Merrimac Rivers*

WEBSTER, DANIEL, "Speech on the Constitution and the Union"; "Bunker Hill Oration"

## MODERN WRITERS—FICTION

CHURCHILL, WINSTON, *The Crossing; The Crisis*

EDMONDS, WALTER, *Erie Water; Rome Haul; Chad Hanna*

ROBERTS, KENNETH, *Captain Caution; The Lively Lady*

## MODERN WRITERS—NONFICTION

ARVIN, NEWTON, *Hawthorne*

BENNETT, WHITMAN, *Whittier, Bard of Freedom*

BOYNTON, H. W., *James Fenimore Cooper*

* BURTON, KATHERINE, *His Dear Persuasion* (Mother Seton)

BROOKS, VAN WYCK, *The World of Washington Irving; The Flowering of New England; The Times of Melville and Whitman; The Life of Emerson*

CANBY, H. S., *Thoreau*

CATTON, BRUCE, *Glory Road; Mr. Lincoln's Army; Surrender at Appomattox*

* ERSKINE, MARJORY, *Mother Philippine Duchesne*

FREEMAN, DOUGLAS SOUTHALL, *R. E. Lee*

HAWTHORNE, HILDEGARDE, *The Happy Autocrat; The Romantic Rebel*

* MAYNARD, THEODORE, *The Reed and the Rock* (Bishop Simon Bruté)

MUMFORD, LEWIS, *Herman Melville*

* O'BRIEN, JOSEPH, *John England—Bishop of Charleston*

PEATTIE, DONALD CULROSS, *Singing in the Wilderness; Forward the Nation*

ROURKE, CONSTANCE, *Audubon; Davy Crockett*

SANDBURG, CARL, *Abraham Lincoln, the Prairie Years; Abraham Lincoln, the War Years*

THARP, LOUISE HALL, *The Peabody Sisters of Salem*

* WHALEN, DOREN, *Granite for God's House* (Orestes Brownson)

WHITE, STEWART, *Daniel Boone, Wilderness Scout*

# THE TRANSITION PERIOD

## 1 8 6 5 – 1 9 0 0

Early in the nineteenth century, a multitude of eager, daring young men accepted the challenge, "Go West, young man, go West." They set out in covered wagons with a few household goods, a trusty flintlock, a yoke of oxen, and kept going until a likely stretch of farm land invited them to settle down and make their homes and fortunes. Throughout the nineteenth century, the frontier leaped westward. In 1849, the lure of gold in California attracted untold thousands to undertake the hazardous journey over Indian trails to the western boundary of the continent. It was a vigorous type of man that set out from the Eastern states and even from Europe to conquer the vast stretches of the West. Weaker men did not survive. The men who formed the pioneer army were rugged, self-reliant men. For the most part they were uneducated, but they were not unintelligent. With great ingenuity they cleared the wilderness, built homes, protected themselves against the Indians, and provided food by hunting, fishing, and farming. After the long, hard day they gathered about the campfires and told of their adventures in picturesque, ungrammatical language. Long and hearty laughs over tall tales brought relief from the hardships of pioneer life.

Obviously, such an atmosphere offered fertile grounds for literature—not for the conventional type written by Holmes, Emerson, and Lowell back in the East, but for a new, vigorous record of men and women who were building a great nation. All that was needed was some gifted individual to put down what he saw and heard among the pioneers.

The literary genius who arose to meet the need was Samuel Langhorne Clemens, known to all Americans as Mark Twain. The greatness of Mark Twain consists in the fact that he wrote of real life and real people. *Tom Sawyer* and *Huckleberry Finn* are largely autobiographical. Works like *Roughing It* and *Innocents Abroad* grew out of Mark Twain's own travels and his shrewd observations of the doings of men. The close contact which Mark Twain had with his material gave his writing the quality that is called realistic in contrast to romantic. It is for this reason that Mark Twain heads the list of transition authors. He began the swing of the pendulum, the *transition*, from the romantic writing of an earlier day to the realistic writing of the twentieth century.

It is almost unnecessary to add that Mark Twain also heads the list of American humorists. What American has not laughed at the antics of Tom Sawyer and Huck Finn? The same vein of broad humor keeps the reader chuckling through practically all of Mark Twain's works. In his unending flow of humor, Mark Twain far surpassed such earlier humorists as Josh Billings and Artemus Ward; and he set the pace for later ones like Will Rogers and Irvin S. Cobb.

# TRANSITION PROSE

## THE GROWTH OF THE AMERICAN NOVEL

After the Civil War was over, novelists responded to the new trends with floods of books. One of the first men to show the entertaining possibilities of realistic fiction—particularly when it had real adventure for its material—was Herman Melville. His experiences on a sailing vessel in the Pacific resulted in two novels—*Typee* and *Omoo*, the first of our present store of literature of the South Seas. His masterpiece is a third novel, *Moby Dick*, the story of the pursuit of a white whale by the half-mad Captain Ahab.

Another writer who met the demand for fiction that would reflect the present in terms of the real and not the artificial was William Dean Howells. Howells' novels deal frankly with the life of his period. His best, *The Rise of Silas Lapham*, is said to be the first American novel to have a businessman for its chief character.

There were other novelists in great number. With few exceptions, their best books are those which give the most faithful pictures of contemporary life. Among them may be named *The Hoosier Schoolmaster* by Edward Eggleston, *Colonel Carter of Cartersville* by Francis Hopkinson Smith, *The Awakening of Helena Ritchie* by Margaret Deland, and *The Grandissimes* by George Washington Cable. A group of excellent historical novels of the period are: *Ben-Hur* by Lew Wallace, *Ramona* by Helen Hunt Jackson, *Red Rock* by Thomas Nelson Page, and *Richard Carvel* and *The Crisis* by Winston Churchill.

## THE LOCAL COLOR SHORT STORY

Shortly after Mark Twain became famous, another transition author came into the literary spotlight. This time it was an Easterner who had gone to California in the gold-rush days. Francis Bret Harte had hoped for a literary career from his boyhood, but it was not until he hit upon the idea of telling about life in the California mining camps that he won popular acclaim. Bret Harte had lived in California for ten years before he wrote "The Luck of Roaring Camp" in 1868. In it he set the pattern for "Tennessee's Partner," "The Outcasts of Poker Flat," and other stories on which his fame rests. His settings show us the strange grandeur of California scenery. His characters are the rough, undisciplined miners whom he knew so well. His plots concern the adventures of these Western bad men.

The importance of Bret Harte lies in the fact that he made the *local-color* story popular. He showed the world that story material is where you find it. Do you want a character or a setting? Look around you. If your home happens to be a mining camp, well and good. But a New England farming center will do, too.

Local-colorists all over the country quickly discovered that very fact. Among the best of them were those who began to tell the nation about the charm of life in the South. George Washington Cable found his story material in the colorful, half-foreign manners of the French and Spanish people who had settled New

Orleans. Kate Chopin wrote about the country folk of Louisiana with a sympathy and insight that reflected her Catholic background. Joel Chandler Harris has long been a favorite with children and adults for his Uncle Remus stories—tales told by an old Georgia Negro to a young white lad. In these stories the dialogue and the atmosphere of plantation life are reproduced so accurately that the reader can almost hear old Uncle Remus' pleasant voice. Other sections of the South were made known by Mary Noailles Murfree (Charles Egbert Craddock) in stories about the unique people of the Tennessee mountains, and by Thomas Nelson Page, who gives us more romantic tales of Virginia aristocracy.

The New England group of local-color writers reflected the strong individualism and Puritan traits of that region. Sarah Orne Jewett wrote of the simple farm people of Maine, but she tends to gloss over the less pleasant side of their life. In *Deephaven* and in *The Country of the Pointed Firs*, as well as in several other volumes, she gives us a sympathetic picture of her native state. Mary E. Wilkins Freeman, in volumes entitled *A New England Nun and Other Stories* and *A Humble Romance and Other Stories*, gives a fairly realistic record of life in her own state of Massachusetts.

It is obvious that the local-color stories have been a great contribution to American life and letters. Coming in the period of expansion after the Civil War, they served to inform a growing nation about itself in times when travel and communication were much more difficult than they are now. More important, they injected into American literature the element of realism. Although the local-colorists often cast a romantic hue over the localities of which they wrote, still their close observation of life led to the strength and vitality of twentieth-century realism.

## TRANSITION PERIOD ORATORY

In the difficult period of reconstruction after the Civil War, there was occasion for great oratory. Two Southerners were important in healing the rift between the North and the South. One was Henry Woodfin Grady. He won fame with his after-dinner speech, "The New South," which still serves as a model for students of oratory. The other was Henry Watterson, founder of the Louisville *Courier-Journal*, a brilliant speaker and writer, and a leader in the Democratic party.

Political oratory was well served by Grover Cleveland and by Ulysses S. Grant. Among those who attained eminence as lecturers and occasional orators were Chauncey M. Depew, Thomas Nelson Page, Edward Everett Hale, and Phillips Brooks.

Several Catholic bishops of the period are still remembered for their pulpit oratory. Patrick John Ryan, Archbishop of Philadelphia, was perhaps the greatest Catholic preacher of his day. He commanded large and distinguished audiences, Protestant as well as Catholic. Martin John Spalding, Archbishop of Baltimore, was a noted journalist, author, controversialist, and lecturer. James Cardinal Gibbons, America's first cardinal, was one of the greatest prelates the country has produced. His famous works, *The Faith of Our Fathers* and *Our Christian Heritage*, are still widely read. His oratorical ability was equal to his literary talents.

# SCIENCE VS. LUCK

*MARK TWAIN*

*Typical of American humor is the tall story—an exaggerated joke told with complete solemnity. Mark Twain is famous as one of the artists in this type of fiction. In the following unusual episode he settles the argument as to whether science or luck determines the winner in card playing.*

At that time, in Kentucky (said the Honorable Mr. K——), the law was very strict against what is termed "games of chance." About a dozen of the boys were detected playing "seven-up" or "old sledge" for money, and the grand jury [1] found a true bill [2] against them. Jim Sturgis was retained to defend them when the case came up, of course. The more he studied over the matter and looked into the evidence, the plainer it was that he must lose a case at last—there was no getting around that painful fact. Those boys had certainly been betting money on a game of chance. Even public sympathy was roused in behalf of Sturgis. People said it was a pity to see him mar his successful career with a big prominent case like this, which must go against him.

But after several restless nights an inspired idea flashed upon Sturgis, and he sprang out of bed delighted. He thought he saw his way through. The next day he whispered around a little among his clients and a few friends, and then when the case came up in court he acknowledged the seven-up and the betting, and, as his sole defense, had the astounding effrontery to put in the plea that old sledge was not a game of chance! There was the broadest sort of a smile all over the faces of that sophisticated audience. The judge smiled with the rest. But Sturgis maintained a countenance whose earnestness was even severe. The opposite counsel tried to ridicule him out of his position, and did not succeed. The judge jested in a ponderous judicial way about the thing, but did not move him. The matter was becoming grave. The judge lost a little of his patience and said the joke had gone far enough. Jim Sturgis said he knew of no joke in the matter—his clients could not be punished for indulging in what some people chose to consider a game of chance until it was *proven* that it was a game of chance. Judge and counsel said that would be an easy matter, and forthwith called Deacons Job, Peters, Burke, and Johnson, and Dominies [3] Wirt and Miggles, to testify; and they unanimously and with strong feeling put down the legal quibble of Sturgis by pronouncing that old sledge *was* a game of chance.

"What do you call it *now?*" said the judge.

[1] GRAND JURY—A jury that examines evidence against accused persons and returns indictments if the evidence is sufficient.

[2] TRUE BILL—A bill of indictment returned by the grand jury.

[3] DOMINIES—Ministers.

"I call it a game of science!" retorted Sturgis; "and I'll prove it, too!"

They saw his little game.

He brought in a cloud of witnesses, and produced an over-whelming mass of testimony, to show that old sledge was not a game of chance but a game of science.

Instead of being the simplest case in the world, it had somehow turned out to be an excessively knotty one. The judge scratched his head over it awhile, and said there was no way of coming to a determination, because just as many men could be brought into court who would testify on one side as could be found to testify on the other. But he said he was willing to do the fair thing by all parties, and would act upon any suggestion Mr. Sturgis would make for the solution of the difficulty.

Mr. Sturgis was on his feet in a second.

"Impanel a jury of six of each, Luck *versus* Science. Give them candles and a couple of decks of cards. Send them into the jury-room, and just abide by the result!"

There was no disputing the fairness of the proposition. The four deacons and the two dominies were sworn in as the "chance" jurymen, and six inveterate old seven-up professors were chose to represent the "science" side of the issue. They retired to the jury-room.

In about two hours Deacon Peters sent into court to borrow three dollars from a friend. (Sensation.) In about two hours more Dominie Miggles sent into court to borrow a "stake" from a friend. (Sensation.) During the next three or four hours the other dominie and the other deacons sent into court for small loans. And still the packed audience waited, for it was a prodigious occasion in Bull's Corners, and one in which every father of a family was necessarily interested.

The rest of the story can be told briefly. About daylight the jury came in, and Deacon Job, the foreman, read the following verdict.

"We, the jury in the case of the Commonwealth of Kentucky *vs.* John Wheeler *et al.*,[4] have carefully considered the points of the case, and tested the merits of the several theories advanced, and do hereby unanimously decide that the game commonly known as old sledge or seven-up is eminently a game of science and not of chance. In demonstration whereof it is hereby and herein stated, iterated, reiterated, set forth, and made manifest that, during the entire night, the 'chance' men never won a game or turned a jack, although both feats were common and frequent to the opposition; and furthermore, in support of this our verdict, we call attention to the significant fact that the 'chance' men are all busted, and the 'science' men have got the money. It is the deliberate opinion of this jury, that the 'chance' theory concerning seven-up is a pernicious doctrine, and calculated to inflict untold suffering and pecuniary loss upon any community that takes stock in it."

"That is the way that seven-up came to be set apart and particularized in the statute-books of Kentucky as being a game not of chance but of science, and therefore not punishable under the law," said Mr. K——. "That verdict is on record, and holds good to this day."

[4] *Et al.—Et alii*, and others.

◇◇◇◇◇◇◇◇◇◇◇◇◇◇◇◇◇◇◇◇◇◇◇◇◇◇◇◇◇◇

FOR DISCUSSION

1. What was the grave charge brought against "the boys"; namely, John Wheeler *et al.?*

2. What was Sturgis' "inspired idea" for the defense?

3. What character, if any, stands out? How do you come to know him—through description or through action?

4. Point out three or four places where mock seriousness is employed.

5. Humor results from putting together things which are out of proportion to one another—for example, Mutt and Jeff. Discuss how this idea of humor is verified in "Science vs. Luck." Give several instances.

6. By its verdict did the jury approve of gambling?

7. Is gambling always morally wrong? Why do most cities have stringent laws against gambling?

## TYPE STUDY—THE SHORT STORY

1. The first paragraph gives the background for the story by simple narration. Is this the best way to begin a short story? Discuss.

2. At what point does the action of the story begin? Where would you say the climax occurs?

## WORDS TO KNOW AND USE

1. What are three good synonyms for effrontery?

2. The deacons and dominies considered Sturgis to be quibbling. What precisely is the meaning of quibble?

3. Four synonyms for prodigious are monstrous, tremendous, stupendous, and colossal. Which of these might replace prodigious in the following sentence:

". . . it was a prodigious occasion in Bull's Corners."

4. The Latin adverb iterum means again. What, then, does the English verb to iterate mean? to reiterate?

5. Would the substitution of financial or monetary significantly change the meaning of the phrase pecuniary loss?

## PROJECTS

1. Rewrite the story as a radio script. You will want to develop the comedy that went on in the jury room through the night.

2. In Hoyle's The Official Rules of Card Games, learn how to play seven-up; and be prepared to explain the game to the class. Explain also the meaning of the expression: "That's not according to Hoyle."

3. From a lawyer acquaintance get a copy of a jury verdict in a real court case and compare the language with that used by the Bull's Corners jury.

## RELATED READING

No one should miss "The Celebrated Jumping Frog of Calaveras County." It was this story which made Mark Twain famous.

You will also want to sample the work of other well-known American humorists. Charles Farrar Browne, better known as Artemus Ward, has an entertaining sketch entitled "Interview with President Lincoln." Finley Peter Dunne, a Catholic writer of the late nineteenth century, is famous for the character of Mr. Dooley. Read Mr. Dooley in War and Peace.

# JEAN-AH POQUELIN

## GEORGE WASHINGTON CABLE

*A "haunted" house is usually dwelt in only by ghosts. In the following
story the haunted house is occupied by two men and, apparently, by a real
live ghost. Woven in with the suspense of the plot are many details of
local color from the old Creole settlement of New Orleans. The reader
should note how all these details contribute to the development of the plot.*

I

In the first decade of the present century,[1] when the newly established American Government was the most hateful
thing in Louisiana—when the Creoles [2]
were still kicking at such vile innova-
tions as the trial by jury, American
dances, anti-smuggling laws, and the
printing of the Governor's proclamation
in English—when the Anglo-American
flood [3] that was presently to burst in a
crevasse of immigration upon the delta
had thus far been felt only as slippery
seepage which made the Creole tremble
for his footing—there stood, a short distance above what is now Canal Street,[4]
and considerably back from the line of
villas which fringed the river-bank on
Tchoupitoulas Road, an old colonial
plantation-house half in ruin.

It stood aloof from civilization, the
tracts that had once been its indigo [5]
fields given over to their first noxious
wildness, and grown up into one of the
horridest marshes within a circuit of fifty
miles.

The house was of heavy cypress, lifted
up on pillars, grim, solid, and spiritless,
its massive build a strong reminder of
days still earlier, when every man had
been his own peace officer and the insurrection of the blacks a daily contingency. Its dark, weather-beaten roof
and sides were hoisted up above the
jungly plain in a distracted way, like a
gigantic ammunition wagon stuck in the
mud and abandoned by some retreating
army. Around it was a dense growth of
low water willows, with half a hundred
sorts of thorny or fetid bushes, savage
strangers alike to the "language of flowers" and to the botanist's Greek. They
were hung with countless strands of discolored and prickly smilax, and the im-
passable mud below bristled with *chevaux de frise* [6] of the dwarf palmetto.[7]

[1] FIRST DECADE OF THE PRESENT CENTURY
—1800–1810.
[2] CREOLES—A population in Louisiana,
part French and part Spanish.
[3] ANGLO-AMERICAN FLOOD—As opposed to
the Latin-American population.
[4] CANAL STREET—The main street in New
Orleans.

[5] INDIGO—A plant whose leaves yield a
blue dyestuff.
[6] *Chevaux de frise* (shä·vō′ dà frēz′)—Obstructions in shallow water made by the roots,
which projected in all directions, resembling a
medieval defensive barrier of this name.
[7] PALMETTO—Palm tree with simple, fan-
shaped leaves.

"Jean-Ah Poquelin" from *Ole Creole Days* by
George Washington Cable, reprinted by permission
of Charles Scribners' Sons.

Two lone forest-trees, dead cypresses, stood in the center of the marsh, dotted with roosting vultures. The shallow strips of water were hid by myriads of aquatic plants, under whose coarse and spiritless flowers, could one have seen it, was a harbor of reptiles, great and small, to make one shudder to the end of his days.

The house was on a slightly raised spot, the levee of a draining canal. The waters of this canal did not run; they crawled, and were full of big, ravening fish and alligators, that held it against all comers.

Such was the home of old Jean Marie Poquelin, once an opulent indigo planter, standing high in the esteem of his small, proud circle of exclusively male acquaintances in the old city; now a hermit, alike shunned by and shunning all who had ever known him. "The last of his line," said the gossips. His father lies under the floor of the St. Louis Cathedral, with the wife of his youth on one side, and the wife of his old age on the other. Old Jean visits the spot daily. His half brother—alas! there was a mystery; no one knew what had become of the gentle, young half brother, more than thirty years his junior, whom once he seemed so fondly to love, but who, seven years ago, had disappeared suddenly and left no clew of his fate.

They had seemed to live so happily in each other's love. No father, mother, wife to either, no kindred upon earth. The elder a bold, frank, impetuous, chivalric adventurer; the younger a gentle, studious, book-loving recluse; they lived upon the ancestral estate like mated birds, one always on the wing, the other always in the nest.

There was no trait in Jean Marie Poquelin, said the old gossips, for which he was so well known among his few friends as his apparent fondness for his "little brother." "Jacques said this," and "Jacques was good," or "wise," or "just," or "farsighted," as the nature of the case required; and "he should ask Jacques as soon as he got home," since Jacques was never elsewhere to be seen.

It was between the roving character of the elder brother, and the bookishness of the younger, that the estate fell into decay. Jean Marie, generous gentleman, gambled the slaves away one by one, until none was left, man or woman, but one old African mute.[8]

The indigo fields and vats of Louisiana had been generally abandoned as unremunerative. Certain enterprising men had substituted the culture of sugar; but while the recluse was too apathetic to take so active a course, the other saw larger, and, at that time, equally respectable profits, first in smuggling, and later in the African slave trade. What harm could he see in it? The whole people said it was vitally necessary, and to minister to a vital public necessity,—good enough, certainly, and so he laid up many a doubloon,[9] that made him none the worse in the public regard.

One day old Jean Marie was about to start upon a voyage that was to be longer, much longer, than any he had yet made. Jacques had begged him hard for many days not to go, but he laughed him off, and finally said, kissing him:

"*Adieu, 'tit frère.*"[10]

"No," said Jacques, "I shall go with you."

They left the old hulk of a house in the sole care of the African mute, and went away to the Guinea coast together.

[8] MUTE—One who cannot speak.
[9] DOUBLOON—A Spanish coin worth about eight dollars.
[10] *Adieu, 'tit frère* (à·dü′ tē frär′)—Goodby, little brother.

## II

Two years after, old Poquelin came home without his vessel. He must have arrived at his house by night. No one saw him come. No one saw "his little brother"; rumor whispered that he, too, had returned, but he had never been seen again.

A dark suspicion fell upon the old slave-trader. No matter that the few kept the many reminded of the tenderness that had ever marked his bearing to the missing man. The many shook their heads. "You know he has a quick and fearful temper"; and "Why does he cover his loss with mystery?" "Grief would out with the truth."

"But," said the charitable few, "look in his face; see that expression of true humanity." The many did look in his face, and, as he looked in theirs, he read the silent question: "Where is thy brother Abel?" [11] The few were silenced, his former friends died off, and the name of Jean Marie Poquelin became a symbol of witchery, devilish crime, and hideous nursery fictions.

The man and his house were alike shunned. The snipe and duck hunters forsook the marsh, and the woodcutters abandoned the canal. Sometimes the hardier boys who ventured out there snake-shooting heard a slow thumping of oarlocks on the canal. They would look at each other for a moment half in consternation, half in glee, then rush from their sport in wanton haste to assail with their gibes the unoffending, withered old man who, in rusty attire, sat in the stern of a skiff, rowed homeward by his white-headed African mute.

"O Jean-ah Poquelin! O Jean-ah! Jean-ah Poquelin!"

It was not necessary to utter more

than that. No hint of wickedness, deformity, or any physical or moral demerit; merely the name and tone of mockery: "Oh, Jean-ah Poquelin!" and while they tumbled one over another in their needless haste to fly, he would rise carefully from his seat, while the aged mute, with downcast face, went on rowing, and rolling up his brown fist, and extending it toward the urchins, would pour forth such an unholy broadside of French imprecation and invective as would all but craze them with delight.

Among both blacks and whites the house was the object of a thousand superstitions. Every midnight, they affirmed, the *feu follet* [12] came out of the marsh and ran in and out of the rooms, flashing from window to window. The story of some lads, whose words in ordinary statements were worthless, was generally credited, that the night they camped in the woods, rather than pass the place after dark, they saw, about sunset, every window blood-red, and on each of the four chimneys an owl sitting, which turned his head three times round, and moaned and laughed with a human voice. There was a bottomless well, everybody professed to know, beneath the sill of the big front door under the rotten veranda; whoever set his foot upon that threshold disappeared forever in the depth below.

What wonder the marsh grew as wild as Africa! Take all the Faubourg Ste Marie, [13] and half the ancient city, you would not find one graceless dare-devil reckless enough to pass within a hundred yards of the house after nightfall.

The alien races pouring into old New Orleans began to find the few streets

[11] ABEL—An illusion to the Biblical story of Abel who was slain by his brother Cain.

[12] *Feu follet* (fù fŏ·là')—The phosphorescent light which comes from decaying vegetable matter.

[13] FAUBOURG STE MARIE (fō·bür sănt mȧ·rè')—A suburb of New Orleans.

named for the Bourbon princes too strait for them. The wheel of fortune, beginning to whirl, threw them off beyond the ancient corporation lines, and sowed civilization and even trade upon the lands of the Graviers and Girods.[14] Fields became roads, roads streets. Everywhere the leveller [15] was peering through his glass, rodsmen were whacking their way through willow-brakes and rose-hedges, and the sweating Irishmen tossed the blue clay up with their long-handled shovels.

"Ha! that is all very well," quoth Jean-Baptistes, feeling the reproach of an enterprise that asked neither cooperation nor advice of them, "but wait till they come yonder to Jean Poquelin's marsh; ha! ha! ha!" The supposed predicament so delighted them, that they put on a mock terror and whirled about in an assumed stampede, then caught their clasped hands between their knees in excess of mirth, and laughed till the tears ran; for whether the street-makers mired in the marsh, or contrived to cut through old "Jean-ah's" property, either event would be joyful. Meantime a line of tiny rods, with bits of white paper in their split tops, gradually extended its way straight through the haunted ground, and across the canal diagonally.

"We shall fill that ditch," said the men in mud-boots, and brushed close along the chained and padlocked gate of the haunted mansion. Ah, Jean-ah Poquelin, those were not Creole boys, to be stampeded with a little hard swearing.

He went to the Governor. That official scanned the odd figure with no slight interest. Jean Poquelin was of short, broad frame, with a bronzed, leo-nine face. His brow was ample and deeply furrowed. His eye, large and black, was bold and open like that of a war-horse, and his jaws shut together with the firmness of iron. He was dressed in a suit of Attakapas cotton-ade,[16] and his shirt unbuttoned and thrown back from the throat and bosom, sailor-wise, showed a herculean breast, hard and grizzled. There was no fierceness or defiance in his look, no harsh ungentleness, no symptom of his unlawful life or violent temper; but rather a peaceful and peaceable fearlessness. Across the whole face, not marked in one or another feature, but as it were laid softly upon the countenance like an almost imperceptible veil, was the imprint of some great grief. A careless eye might easily overlook it, but, once seen, there it hung —faint but unmistakable.

The Governor bowed.

"*Parlez-vous francais?*" [17] asked the figure.

"I would rather talk English, if you can do so," said the Governor.

"My name, Jean Poquelin."

"How can I serve you, Mr. Poquelin?"

"My 'ouse is yond'; *dans le marais là-bas.*" [18]

The Governor bowed.

"Dat *marais* billong to me."

"Yes, sir."

"To me; Jean Poquelin; I hown 'im meself."

"Well, sir?"

"He don't billong to you; I get him from me father."

"That is perfectly true, Mr. Poquelin, as far as I am aware."

[16] ATTAKAPAS COTTONADE—A coarse cotton cloth made by a tribe of Indians inhabiting the southwestern part of Louisiana.

[17] *Parlez-vous francais?* (pàr·lā·vōō′ frän-sā′)—Do you speak French?

[18] *Dans le marais là-bas* (dàn là mà·rā là·bà′)—In the swamp yonder.

[14] GRAVIERS AND GIRODS—Prominent families of New Orleans.

[15] LEVELLER—Surveyor.

"You want to make strit pass yond'?"

"I do not know, sir; it is quite probable; but the city will indemnify you for any loss you may suffer—you will get paid, you understand."

"Strit can't pass dare."

"You will have to see the municipal authorities about that, Mr. Poquelin."

A bitter smile came upon the old man's face:

"*Pardon, Monsieur,* you is not *le Gouverneur?*"

"Yes."

"*Mais,*[19] yes. You har *le Gouverneur* —yes. Veh—well, I come to you. I tell you strit can't pass at me 'ouse."

"But you will have to see—"

"I come to you. You is *le Gouverneur.* I know not the new laws. I ham a Fr-r-rench-a-man! Fr-r-rench-a-man have something *aller au contraire* [20]—he come at his *Gouverneur.* I come to you. If me had not been bought from me king like *bossals* [21] in the hold time, de king gof—France would-a-show *Monsieur le Gouverneur* to take care his men to make strit in right places. *Mais,* I know; we billong to *Monsieur le Président.* I want you do somesin for me, eh?"

"What is it?" asked the patient Governor.

"I want you tell *Monsier le Président* strit—can't—pass—at me—'ouse."

"Have a chair, Mr. Poquelin"; but the old man did not stir. The Governor took a quill and wrote a line to a city official, introducing Mr. Poquelin, and asking for him every possible courtesy. He handed it to him, instructing him where to present it.

"Mr. Poquelin," he said with a con-ciliatory smile, "tell me, is it your house that our Creole citizens tell such odd stories about?"

The old man glared sternly upon the speaker, and with immovable features said:

"You don't see me trade some Guinea nigga'?"

"Oh, no."

"You don't see me make some smugglin'?"

"No, sir; not at all."

"But, I am Jean Marie Poquelin. I mine me hown bizniss. Dat all right? *Adieu.*"

He put his hat on and withdrew. By and by he stood, letter in hand, before the person to whom it was addressed.

This person employed an interpreter.

"He says," said the interpreter to the officer, "he come to make you the fair warning how you muz not make the street pas' at his 'ouse."

The officer remarked that "such impudence was refreshing"; but the experienced interpreter translated freely.

"He says: 'Why don't want?' " said the interpreter.

The old slave-trader answered at some length.

"He says," said the interpreter, again turning to the officer, "the marass is a too unhealth' for peopl' to live."

"But we expect to drain his old marsh; it's not going to be a marsh."

"*Il dit* [22]—" The interpreter explained in French.

The old man answered tersely.

"He says the canal is private property," said the interpreter.

"Oh! *that* old ditch; that's to be filled up. Tell the old man we're going to fix him up nicely."

Translation being duly made, the man

---

[19] *Mais* (mā)—But.

[20] *Aller au contraire* (ȧ·lā ō cŏn·trär')—Go wrong.

[21] *Bossals* (bŏ·sȧl')—Vassals, slaves.

[22] *Il dit* (ēl dē')—He says.

in power was amused to see a thunder-cloud gathering on the old man's face.

"Tell him," he added, "by the time we finish, there'll not be a ghost left in his shanty."

The interpreter began to translate, but—

"*J'comprehends*,[23] *j'comprehends*," said the old man, with an impatient gesture, and burst forth, pouring curses upon the United States, the President, the Territory of Orleans, Congress, the Governor and all his subordinates, striding out of the apartment as he cursed, while the object of his maledictions roared with merriment and rammed the floor with his foot.

"Why, it will make his old place worth ten dollars to one," said the official to the interpreter.

" 'Tis not for de worse of de property," said the interpreter.

"I should guess not," said the other, whittling his chair,—"seems to me as if some of these old Creoles would liever live in a crawfish hole than to have a neighbor."

"You know what make old Jean Poquelin ack like that? I will tell you. You know—"

The interpreter was rolling a cigarette, and paused to light his tender; then, as the smoke poured in a thick double stream from his nostrils, he said, in a solemn whisper:

"He is a witch."

"Ho, ho, ho!" laughed the other.

"You don't believe it? What you want to bet?" cried the interpreter, jerking himself half up and thrusting out one arm while he bared it of his coat sleeve with the hand of the other. "What do you want to bet?"

"How do you know?" asked the official.

"Das what I goin' to tell you. You know, one evening I was shooting some *grosbec*.[24] I killed three; but I had trouble to find them, it was becoming so dark. When I have them I start' to come home; then I got to pas' at Jean Poquelin's house."

"Ho, ho, ho!" laughed the other, throwing his leg over the arm of the chair.

"Wait," said the interpreter. "I come along slow, not making some noises; still, still—"

"And scared," said the smiling one.

"*Mais*, wait. I get all pas' the 'ouse. 'Ah!' I say; 'all right!' Then I see two thing' before! Hah! I get as cold and humide,[25] and shake like a leaf. You think it was nothing? There I see, so plain as can be (though it was making nearly dark) I see Jean-Marie-Po-que-lin walkin' right in front, and right there beside of him was something like a man —but not a man—white like paint!—I dropp' on the grass from scared—they pass'; so sure as I live 'twas the ghos' of Jacques Poquelin, his brother!"

"Pooh!" said the listener.

"I'll put my han' in the fire," said the interpreter.

"But did you never think," asked the other, "that that might be Jack Poquelin, as you call him, alive and well, and for some cause hid away by his brother?"

"But there har' no cause!" said the other, and the entrance of third parties changed the subject.

### III

Some months passed and the street was opened. A canal was first dug

---

[23] *J'comprehends* (jă côm·prahăn′)—I understand.

[24] *Grosbec* (grō·běk′)—Grosbeak—a bird with a stout conical bill.
[25] HUMIDE—Clammy.

484

through the marsh, the small one which passed so close to Jean Poquelin's house was filled, and the street, or rather a sunny road, just touched a corner of the old mansion's dooryard. The morass ran dry. Its venomous denizens slipped away through the bulrushes, the cattle roaming freely upon its hardened surface trampled the super-abundant undergrowth. The bellowing frogs croaked to westward. Lilies and the flower-de-luce sprang up in the place of reeds; smilax and poison-oak gave way to the purple-plumed ironweed and pink spiderwort; the bindweeds ran everywhere blooming as they ran, and on one of the dead cypresses a giant creeper hung its green burden of foliage and lifted its scarlet trumpets. Sparrows and redbirds flitted through the bushes, and dewberries grew ripe beneath. Over all these came a sweet, dry smell of salubrity which the place had not known since the sediments of the Mississippi first lifted it from the sea.

But its owner did not build. Over the willow-brakes, and down the vista of the open street, bright new houses, some singly, some by ranks, were prying in on the old man's privacy. They even settled down toward his southern side. First a woodcutter's hut or two, and all at once the faubourg had flanked and half surrounded him and his dried-up marsh.

Ah! then the common people began to hate him. "The old tyrant!" "You don't mean an old *tyrant?*" "Well, then, why don't he build when the public need demands it? What does he live in that unneighborly way for?" "The old pirate!" "The old kidnapper!" How easily even the most ultra Louisianians put on the imported virtues of the North when they could be brought to bear against the hermit. "There he

goes, with the boys after him! Ah! ha! ha! Jean-ah Poquelin! Ah! Jean-ah! Aha! aha! Jean-ah Marie! Jean-ah Poquelin! The old villain!" How merrily the swarming Américains echo the spirit of persecution! "The old fraud," they say—"pretends to live in a haunted house, does he? We'll tar and feather him some day. Guess we can fix him."

He cannot be rowed home along the old canal now; he walks. He has broken sadly of late, and the street urchins are ever at his heels. It is like the days when they cried: "Go up, thou baldhead," and the old man now and then turns and delivers ineffectual curses.

To the Creoles—to the incoming lower class of superstitious Germans, Irish, Sicilians, and others—he became an omen and embodiment of public and private ill-fortune. Upon him all the vagaries of their superstitions gathered and grew. If a house caught fire, it was imputed to his machinations. Did a woman go off in a fit, he had bewitched her. Did a child stray off for an hour, the mother shivered with the apprehension that Jean Poquelin had offered him to strange gods. The house was the subject of every bad boy's invention who loved to contrive ghostly lies. "As long as that house stands we shall have bad luck. Do you not see our peas and beans dying, our cabbages and lettuce going to seed and our gardens turning to dust, while every day you can see it raining in the woods? The rain will never pass old Poquelin's house. He keeps a fetich.[26] He has conjured the whole Faubourg Ste Marie. And why, the old wretch? Simply because our playful and innocent children call after him as he passes."

A "Building and Improvement Company," which had not yet got its charter,

[26] FETICH—A charm.

"but was going to," and which had not, indeed, any tangible capital yet, but "was going to have some," joined the "Jean-ah Poquelin" war. The haunted property would be such a capital site for a market-house! They sent a deputation to the old mansion to ask its occupant to sell. The deputation never got beyond the chained gate and a very barren interview with the African mute. The President of the Board was then empowered (for he had studied French in Pennsylvania and was considered qualified) to call and persuade M. Poquelin to subscribe to the company's stock; but—

"Fact is, gentlemen," he said at the next meeting, "it would take us at least twelve months to make Mr. Pokaleen understand the original features of our system, and he wouldn't subscribe when we'd done; besides, the only way to see him is to stop him on the street."

There was a great laugh from the Board; they couldn't help it. "Better meet a bear robbed of her whelps," said one.

"You're mistaken as to that," said the President. "I did meet him, and stopped him, and found him quite polite. But I could get no satisfaction from him: the fellow wouldn't talk in French, and when I spoke in English he hoisted his old shoulders up, and gave the same answer to everything I said."

"And that was—?" asked one or two, impatient of the pause.

"That it 'don't worse w'ile.'"

One of the Board said: "Mr. President, this market-house project, as I take it, is not altogether a selfish one; the community is to be benefited by it. We may feel that we are working in the public interest (the Board smiled knowingly), if we employ all possible means to oust this old nuisance from among us. You may know that at the time the street was cut through, this old Poquelann did all he could to prevent it. It was owing to a certain connection which I had with that affair that I heard a ghost story (smiles, followed by a sudden dignified check)—ghost story, which, of course, I am not going to relate; but I *may* say that my profound conviction, arising from a prolonged study of that story, is that this old villain, John Poquelann, has his brother locked up in that old house. Now, if this is so, and we can fix it on him, I merely *suggest* that we can make the matter highly useful. I don't know," he added, beginning to sit down, "but that it is an action we owe to the community —hem!"

"How do you propose to handle the subject?" asked the President.

"I was thinking," said the speaker, "that, as a Board of Directors, it would be unadvisable for us to authorize any action involving trespass; but if you, for instance, Mr. President, should, as it were, for mere curiosity, *request* someone, as, for instance, our excellent Secretary, simply as a personal favor, to look into the matter—this is merely a suggestion."

The Secretary smiled sufficiently to be understood that, while he certainly did not consider such preposterous service a part of his duties as secretary, he might, not withstanding, accede to the President's request; and the Board adjourned.

Little White, as the Secretary was called, was a mild, kind-hearted little man, who, nevertheless, had no fear of anything, unless it was the fear of being unkind.

"I tell you frankly," he privately said to the President, "I go into this purely for reasons of my own."

The next day, a little after nightfall, one might have descried this little man slipping along the rear fence of the Poquelin place, preparatory to vaulting over into the rank, grass-grown yard, and bearing himself altogether more after the manner of a collector of rare chickens than according to the usage of secretaries.

The picture presented to his eye was not calculated to enliven his mind. The old mansion stood out against the western sky, black and silent. One long, lurid pencil-stroke along a sky of slate was all that was left of daylight. No sign of life was apparent; no light at any window, unless it might have been on the side of the house hidden from view. No owls were on the chimneys, no dogs were in the yard.

He entered the place, and ventured up behind a small cabin which stood apart from the house. Through one of its many crannies he easily detected the African mute crouched before a flickering pine-knot, his head on his knees, fast asleep.

He concluded to enter the mansion, and, with that view, stood and scanned it. The broad rear steps of the veranda would not serve him; he might meet someone midway. He was measuring, with his eye, the proportions of one of the pillars which supported it, and estimating the practicability of climbing it, when he heard a footstep. Someone had dragged a chair out toward the railing, then seemed to change his mind and began to pace the veranda, his footfalls resounding on the dry boards with singular loudness. Little White drew a step backward, got the figure between himself and the sky, and at once recognized the short, broad-shouldered form of old Jean Poquelin.

He sat down upon a billet of wood, and, to escape the stings of a whining cloud of mosquitoes, shrouded his face and neck in his handkerchief, leaving his eyes uncovered.

He had sat there but a moment when he noticed a strange, sickening odor, faint, as if coming from a distance, but loathsome and horrid.

Whence could it come? Not from the cabin; not from the marsh, for it was as dry as powder. It was not in the air; it seemed to come from the ground.

Rising up, he noticed, for the first time, a few steps before him a narrow footpath leading toward the house. He glanced down it—ha! right there was someone coming—ghostly white!

Quick as thought, and as noiselessly, he lay down at full length against the cabin. It was bold strategy, and yet, there was no denying it, little White felt that he was frightened. "It is not a ghost," he said to himself. "I *know* it cannot be a ghost"; but the perspiration burst out at every pore, and the air seemed to thicken with heat. "It is a living man," he said in his thoughts. "I hear his footstep, and I hear old Poquelin's footsteps, too, separately, over on the veranda. I am not discovered; the thing has passed; there is that odor again; what a smell of death! Is it coming back? Yes. It stops at the door of the cabin. Is it peering in at the sleeping mute? It moves away. It is in the path again. Now it is gone." He shuddered. "Now, if I dare venture, the mystery is solved." He rose cautiously, close against the cabin, and peered along the path.

The figure of a man, a presence if not a body—but whether clad in some white stuff or naked the darkness would not allow him to determine—had turned, and now, with a seeming painful gait, moved slowly from him. "Great Heaven! Can it be that the dead do walk?" He withdrew again the hands which had gone to his eyes. The dreadful object passed between two pillars and under the house. He listened. There was a faint sound as of feet upon a staircase, then all was still except the measured tread of Jean Poquelin walking on the veranda, and the heavy respirations of the mute slumbering in the cabin.

The little Secretary was about to retreat; but as he looked once more toward the haunted house a dim light appeared in the crack of a closed window, and presently old Jean Poquelin came, dragging his chair, and sat down close against the shining cranny. He spoke in a low, tender tone in the French tongue, making some inquiry. An answer came from within. Was it the voice of a human? So unnatural was it—so hollow, so discordant, so unearthly—that the stealthy listener shuddered again from head to foot, and when something stirred in some bushes near by—though it may have been nothing more than a rat—and came scuttling through the grass, the little Secretary actually turned and fled. As he left the enclosure he moved with bolder leisure through the bushes; yet now and then he spoke aloud: "Oh, oh! I see, I understand!" and shut his eyes in his hands.

IV

How strange that henceforth little White was the champion of Jean Poquelin! In season and out of season—wherever a word was uttered against him—the Secretary, with a quiet, aggressive force that instantly arrested gossip, demanded upon what authority the statement or conjecture was made; but as he did not condescend to explain his own remarkable attitude, it was not long before the disrelish and suspicion which had followed Jean Poquelin so many years fell also upon him.

It was only the next evening but one after his adventure that he made himself a source of sullen amazement to one hundred and fifty boys, by ordering them to desist from their wanton hallooing. Old Jean Poquelin, standing and shaking his cane, rolling out his long-drawn maledictions, paused and stared, then gave the Secretary a courteous bow and started on. The boys, save one, from pure astonishment, ceased, but a ruffianly little Irish lad, more daring than any had yet been, threw a big hurtling clod, that struck old Poquelin between the shoulders and burst like a shell. The enraged old man wheeled with uplifted staff to give chase to the scampering vagabond; and—he may have tripped, or he may not, but he fell full length. Little White hastened to help him up, but he waved him off with a fierce imprecation and staggering to his feet resumed his way homeward. His lips were reddened with blood.

Little White was on his way to the meeting of the Board. He would have given all he dared spend to have stayed away, for he felt both too fierce and too tremulous to brook the criticisms that were likely to be made.

"I can't help it, gentlemen; I can't help to make a case against the old man, and I'm not going to."

"We did not expect this disappointment, Mr. White."

"I can't help that, sir. No, sir; you had better not appoint any more investigations. Somebody'll investigate himself into trouble. No, sir; it isn't a threat, it is only my advice, but I warn you that whoever takes the task in hand will rue it to his dying day—which may be hastened, too."

The President expressed himself "surprised."

"I don't care a rush," answered little White, wildly and foolishly, "I don't care a rush if you are, sir. No, my nerves are not disordered; my head's as clear as a bell. No, I'm *not* excited."

A Director remarked that the Secretary looked as though he had waked from a nightmare.

"Well, sir, if you want to know the fact, I have; and if you choose to cultivate old Poquelin's society you can have one, too."

"White," called a facetious member, but White did not notice. "White," he called again.

"What?" demanded White, with a scowl.

"Did you see a ghost?"

"Yes, sir; I did," cried White, hitting the table, and handing the President a paper which brought the Board to other business.

The story got among the gossips that somebody (they were afraid to say little White) had been to the Poquelin mansion by night and beheld something appalling. The rumor was but a shadow of the truth, magnified and distorted as is the manner of shadows. He had seen skeletons walking, and had barely escaped the clutches of one by making the sign of the cross.

Some madcap boys with an appetite for the horrible plucked up courage to venture through the dried marsh by the cattle path, and come before the house at the spectral hour when the air was full of bats. Something which they but half saw—half a sight was enough—sent them tearing back through the willow-brakes and acacia bushes to their homes, where they fairly dropped down, and cried:

"Was it white?" "No—yes—nearly so—we can't tell—but we saw it." And one could hardly doubt, to look at their ashen faces, that they had, whatever it was.

"If that old rascal lived in the country we come from," said certain Américains, "he'd have been tarred and feathered before now, wouldn't he, Sanders?"

"Well, now he just would."

"And we'd have rid him on a rail, wouldn't we?"

"That's what I allow."

"Tell you what you *could* do." They were talking to some rollicking Creoles who had assumed an absolute necessity for doing *something*. "What is it you call this thing where an old man marries a young girl, and you come out with horns, and—"

"*Charivari?*" [27] asked the Creoles.

"Yes, that's it. Why don't you shivaree him?" Felicitous suggestion.

Little White, with his wife beside him, was sitting on their doorstep on the sidewalk, as Creole custom had taught them, looking toward the sunset. They had moved into the lately opened street. The view was not attractive on the score of beauty. The houses were small and scattered, and across the flat commons, spite of the lofty tangle of weeds and bushes, and spite of the thickets of acacia, they needs must see the dismal old Poquelin mansion, tilted awry and shutting out the declining sun. The moon, white and slender, was hanging the tip of its horn over one of the chimneys.

"And you say," said the Secretary, "the old black man has been going by here alone? Patty, suppose old Poquelin should be concocting some mischief; he don't lack provocation; the way that clod hit him the other day was enough to have killed him. Why, Patty, he dropped as quick as *that!* No wonder

[27] *Charivari* (shä′rê·vä′rê or shĭv·à·rē′)— A bold, ribald serenade.

you haven't seen him. I wonder if they haven't heard something about him up at the drugstore. Suppose I go and see."

"Do," said his wife.

She sat alone for half an hour, watching that sudden going out of the day peculiar to the latitude.

"That moon is ghost enough for one house," she said, as her husband returned. "It has gone right down the chimney."

"Patty," said little White, "the drug clerk says the boys are going to shivaree old Poquelin tonight. I'm going to try to stop it."

"Why, White," said his wife, "you'd better not. You'll get hurt."

"No, I'll not."

"Yes, you will."

"I'm going to sit out here until they come along. They're compelled to pass right by here."

"Why, White, it may be midnight before they start; you're not going to sit out here till then."

"Yes, I am."

"Well, you're very foolish," said Mrs. White in an undertone, looking anxious, and tapping one of the steps with her foot.

They sat a very long time talking over little family matters.

"What's that?" at last said Mrs. White.

"That's the nine o'clock gun," said White, and they relapsed into a long-sustained, drowsy silence.

"Patty, you'd better go in and go to bed," said he at last.

"I'm not sleepy."

"Well, you're very foolish," quietly remarked little White, and again silence fell upon them.

"Patty, suppose I walk out to the old house and see if I can find out anything."

"Suppose," said she, "you don't do any such—listen!"

Down the street arose a great hub-bub. Dogs and boys were howling and barking; men were laughing, shouting, groaning, and blowing horns, whooping, and clanking cowbells, whinnying, and howling, and rattling pots and pans.

"They are coming this way," said little White. "You had better go in the house, Patty."

"So had you."

"No. I'm going to see if I can't stop them."

"Why, White!"

"I'll be back in a minute," said White, and went toward the noise.

In a few moments the little Secretary met the mob. The pen hesitates on the word, for there is a respectable difference, measurable only on the scale of the half century, between a mob and a *charivari*. Little White lifted his ineffectual voice. He faced the head of the disorderly column, and cast himself about as if he were made of wood and moved by the jerk of a string. He rushed to one who seemed, from the size and clatter of his tin pan, to be a leader. *"Stop these fellows, Bienvenu, stop them just a minute, till I tell them something."* Bienvenu turned and brandished his instruments of discord in an imploring way to the crowd. They slackened their pace, two or three hushed their horns and joined the prayer of little White and Bienvenu for silence. The throng halted. The hush was delicious.

"Bienvenu," said little White, "don't shivaree old Poquelin tonight; he's—"

"My fwang," said the swaying Bienvenu, "who tail you I goin' to chahivahi somebody, eh? You sink beckause I make a little playfool wiz zis tin pan zat I am *dhonk?*"

"Oh, no, Bienvenu, old fellow, you're all right. I was afraid you might not know that old Poquelin was sick, you know, but you're not going there, are you?"

"My fwang, I vay soy to tail you zat you ah dhonk as de dev'. I am *shem* of you. I ham ze servan' of ze *publique*. Zese *citoyens* [28] goin' to wickwest Jean Poquelin to give to the Ursuline [29] two hondred fifty dolla'—"

*"Hé quoi!"* [30] cried a listener. *"Cinq cent piastres, oui!"*

*"Oui!"* said Bienvenu, "and if he wiffuse we make him some lit' *musique;* ta-ra ta!" He hoisted a merry hand and foot, then frowning, added: "Old Poquelin got no bizniz dhink s'much w'isky."

"But gentlemen," said little White, around whom a circle had gathered, "the old man is very sick."

"My faith!" cried a tiny Creole, "we did not make him to be sick. W'en we have say we going make *le charivari*, do you want that we hall tell a lie? My faith! 'sfools!"

"But you can shivaree somebody else," said desperate little White.

*"Oui!"* cried Bienvenu, "et *chahivahi* Jean-ah Poquelin tomo'w!"

"Let us go to Madame Schneider!" cried two or three, and amid huzzas and confused cries, among which was heard a stentorian Celtic call for drinks, the crowd again began to move.

*"Cent piastres pour l'hôpital de charité!"* [31]

"Hurrah!"

---

[28] *Citoyens* (sē·twȧ·yȧn')—Citizens.
[29] URSULINE—The order of Ursuline nuns.
[30] *Hé quoi*, etc. (ā·kwȧ)—O, what! Five hundred pesetas, yes!
[31] *Cent piastres*, etc. (sȧn pē·ȧs'tr pûr lo-pē·tȧl dȧ shȧ·rē·tā')—One hundred pesetas for the Charity Hospital.

"One hongred dolla' for Charity hospital!"

"Hurrah!"

"Whang!" went a tin pan, the crowd yelled, and Pandemonium gaped again. They were off at a right angle.

Nodding, Mrs. White looked at the mantel clock.

"Well, if it isn't way after midnight."

The hideous noise down street was passing beyond earshot. She raised a sash and listened. For a moment there was silence. Someone came to the door.

"Is that you, White?"

"Yes." He entered. "I succeeded, Patty."

"Did you?" said Patty, joyfully.

"Yes. They've gone down to shivaree the old Dutch-woman who married her step-daughter's sweetheart. They say she has got to pay a hundred dollars to the hospital before they stop."

v

The couple retired, and Mrs. White slumbered. She was awakened by her husband snapping the lid of his watch.

"What time?" she asked.

"Half-past three. Patty, I haven't slept a wink. Those fellows are out yet. Don't you hear them?"

"Why, White, they're coming this way!"

"I know they are," said White, sliding out of bed and drawing on his clothes, "and they're coming fast. You'd better go away from that window, Patty. My! what a clatter."

"Here they are," said Mrs. White, but her husband was gone. Two or three hundred men and boys passed the place at a rapid walk straight down the broad, new street, toward the hated house of ghosts. The din was terrific. She saw little White at the head of the rabble brandishing his arms and trying

in vain to make himself heard; but they only shook their heads laughing and hooting the louder, and so passed, bearing him on before them.

Swiftly they pass out from among the houses, away from the dim oil lamps of the street, out into the broad starlit commons,[32] and enter the willowy jungles of the haunted ground. Some hearts fail and their owners lag behind and turn back, suddenly remembering how near morning it is. But the most part push on, tearing the air with their clamor.

Down ahead of them in the long, thicket-darkened way there is—singularly enough—a faint, dancing light. It must be very near the old house; it is. It has stopped now. It is a lantern, and is under a well-known sapling which has grown up on the wayside since the canal was filled. Now it swings mysteriously to and fro. A goodly number of the more ghost-fearing give up the sport; but a full hundred move onward at a run, doubling their devilish howling and banging.

Yes; it is a lantern, and there are two persons under the tree. The crowd draws near—drops into a walk; one of the two is the old African mute; he lifts the lantern up so that it shines on the other; the crowd recoils; there is a hush of all clangor, and all at once, with a cry of mingled fright and horror from every throat, the whole throng rushes back, dropping everything, sweeping past little White, and hurrying on, never stopping until the jungle is left behind, and then to find that not one in ten has seen the cause of the stampede, and not one of the tenth is certain what it was.

There is one huge fellow among them who looks capable of any villainy. He

[32] COMMONS—Grounds set aside by the city for common use.

finds something to mount on, and, in the Creole *patois*,[33] calls a general halt. Bienvenu sinks down, and vainly trying to recline gracefully, resigns the leadership. The herd gather round the speaker; he assures them they have been outraged. Their right peaceably to traverse the public streets has been trampled upon. Shall such encroachments be endured? It is now daybreak. Let them go now by the open light of day and force a free passage of the public highway!

A scattering consent was the response, and the crowd, thinned now and drowsy, straggled quietly down toward the old house. Some drifted ahead, others sauntered behind, but every one, as he again neared the tree, came to a standstill. Little White sat upon a bank of turf on the opposite side of the way looking very stern and sad. To each newcomer he put the same question:

"Did you come here to go to old Poquelin's?"

"Yes."

"He's dead." And if the shocked hearer started away he would say: "Don't go away."

"Why not?"

"I want you to go to the funeral presently."

If some Louisianian, too loyal to dear France or Spain to understand English, looked bewildered, someone would interpret for him; and presently they went. Little White led the van, the crowd trooping after him down the middle of the way. The gate, that had never been seen before unchained, was open. Stern little White stopped a short distance from it; the rabble stopped behind him. Something was moving out from under the veranda. The many whisperers stretched upward to see. The African

mute came very slowly toward the gate, leading by a cord in the nose a small brown bull, which was harnessed to a rude cart. On the flat body of the cart, under a black cloth, were seen the outlines of a long box.

"Hats off, gentlemen," said little White, as the box came in view, and the crowd silently uncovered.

"Gentlemen," said little White, "here come the last remains of Jean Marie Poquelin, a better man, I'm afraid, with all his sins,—yes a better—a kinder man to his blood—a man of more self-forgetful goodness—than all of you put together will ever dare to be."

There was a profound hush as the vehicle came creaking through the gate; but when it turned away from them toward the forest, those in front started suddenly. There was a backward rush, then all stood still again staring one way; for there, behind the bier, with eyes cast down and labored step, walked the living remains—all that was left—of little Jacques Poquelin, the long-hidden brother—a leper, as white as snow.

Dumb with horror, the cringing crowd gazed upon the walking death. They watched, in silent awe, the slow *cortège*[34] creep down the long, straight road and lessen on the view, until by and by it stopped where a wild, unfrequented path branched off into the undergrowth toward the rear of the ancient city.

"They are going to the *Terre aux Lépreux*,"[35] said one in the crowd. The rest watched them in silence.

The little bull was set free; the mute, with strength of an ape, lifted the long box to his shoulder. For a moment more the mute and the leper stood in sight, while the former adjusted his

[33] *Patois* (pà·twà)—Any French dialect.

[34] *Cortège* (kôr·tāzh′)—A funeral procession.

[35] *Terre aux Lépreux*—Land of the Lepers.

burden; then, without one backward glance upon the unkind human world, turning their faces toward the ridge in the depths of the swamp known as the Leper's Land, they stepped into the jungle, disappeared, and were never seen again.

◇◇◇◇◇◇◇◇◇◇◇◇◇◇◇◇◇◇◇◇◇◇◇◇◇◇

## FOR DISCUSSION

1. When and from whom did the United States purchase Louisiana? Do the actions of the Anglo-Americans in the story justify Creole resentment against the new regime?

2. Compare the characters of Jean and his half brother Jacques. Can you give instances from your own experience of brothers who are of opposite temperament, yet sincerely devoted to each other?

3. How does the brief account of the decline of the Poquelin fortunes bear upon the plot of the story?

4. Why do you suppose old Jean visits the cathedral daily? Does such piety fit in with the rumors and charges later made against him by "the many"?

5. Which of the two was better qualified to be a ruler of men, *le Gouverneur* or the city official? Give reasons for your choice.

6. How does little White's visit to the old mansion advance the story? What is the significance of his remark: "I understand"?

7. Why did little White keep Jean Poquelin's secret instead of revealing it to the members of the Board?

8. What was the theme the author had in mind in writing the story?

9. Explain how Jean was "a better man than all of you put together will ever be."

## STUDYING THE SHORT STORY

1. What is the single impression which the author intended to produce in "Jean-Ah Poquelin"?

2. Point out several episodes which foreshadow the end of the story, yet add to the suspense.

## WORDS

1. *Innovation* is from the Latin adjective *novus*, new. With this information can you guess the meaning of *innovation, novelty, renovate*?

2. What is the difference between *imprecation, malediction*, and *invective*? Which word more closely approximates *curse*?

3. Explain the connection between *vagary, vagrant, extravagant*.

4. When the canal was dug through the morass, its *venomous denizens* slipped away. Can the word *denizen* be applied also to human beings?

## PROJECTS

1. There is a leprosarium in Louisiana today. Learn what you can about it, and report to the class.

2. Write the conversation which you imagine might have taken place between Jean and Jacques at the time little White was watching them.

3. Draw an appropriate map, and on it trace the route which the pair might have followed on their voyage to and from the Guinea coast.

## RELATED READING

For another interesting picture of southern life, read "The Star in the Valley" in *In the Tennessee Mountains*, by Mary Noailles Murfree. The stories of Thomas Nelson Page, collected in *The Burial of the Guns* and *Bred in the Bone* are also excellent.

No one should miss the Uncle Remus Stories by Joel Chandler Harris. You will especially like "Bre'r Rabbit and the Fox."

# UNDER THE LION'S PAW

*HAMLIN GARLAND*

*Hamlin Garland spent his boyhood on a farm in Iowa. The accurate picture of the characters and their surroundings in this story is drawn from firsthand experience. The dialogue especially is unmistakably genuine.*

It was the last of autumn and first day of winter coming together. All day long the plowmen on their prairie farms had moved to and fro in their wide level fields through the falling snow, which melted as it fell, wetting them to the skin—all day, notwithstanding the frequent squalls of snow, the dripping, desolate clouds, and the muck of the furrows, black and tenacious as tar.

Under their dripping harness the horses swung to and fro silently with that marvelous uncomplaining patience which marks the horse. All day the wild geese, honking wildly as they sprawled sidewise down the wind, seemed to be fleeing from an enemy behind; and with neck outthrust and wings extended, sailed down the wind, soon lost to sight.

Yet the plowman behind his plow, though the snow lay on his ragged greatcoat and the cold, clinging mud rose on his heavy boots, fettering him like gyves, whistled in the very beard of the gale. As day passed, the snow, ceasing to melt, lay along the plowed land and lodged in the depth of the stubble, till on each slow round the last furrow stood out black and shining as jet between the plowed land and the gray stubble.

When night began to fall, and the geese, flying low, began to alight invisibly in the near cornfield, Stephen Council was still at work "finishing a land." He rode on his sulky plow [1] when going with the wind, but walked when facing it. Sitting bent and cold but cheery under his slouch hat, he talked encouragingly to his four-in-hand.

"Come round there, boys!—Round agin! We got t' finish this land. Come in there, Dan! *Stiddy*, Kate,—stiddy! None o' y'r tantrums, Kittie. It's purty tuff, but got a be did. *Tchk! tchk!* Step along, Pete! Don't let Kate git y'r singletree [2] on the wheel. Once more!"

They seemed to know what he meant and that this was the last round, for they worked with greater vigor than before.

"Once more, boys, an' then, sez I, oats an' a nice warm stall, an' sleep f'r all."

By the time the last furrow was turned on the land, it was too dark to see the house, and the snow was changing to rain again. The tired and hungry man could see the light from the kitchen shining through the leafless hedge, and he lifted a great shout, "Supper f'r a half a dozen!"

It was nearly eight o'clock by the time he had finished his chores and started for supper. He was picking his way carefully through the mud, when the

---

[1] SULKY PLOW—A plow with wheels and driver's seat attached.

[2] SINGLETREE—A swinging bar to which the traces, or straps, of a harness are fastened.

tall form of a man loomed up before him with a premonitory cough.

"Waddy ye want," was the rather startled question of the farmer.

"Well, ye see," began the stranger in a deprecating tone, "we'd like t' git in f'r the night. We've tried every house f'r the last two miles, but they hadn't any room f'r us. My wife's jest about sick, 'n' the children are cold and hungry—"

"Oh, y' want 'o stay all night, eh?"

"Yes, sir, it 'ud be a great accom—"

"Waal, I don't make it a practice t' turn anybuddy way hungry, not on sech nights as this. Drive right in. We ain't got much, but sech as it is—"

But the stranger had disappeared. And soon his steaming, weary team, with drooping heads and swinging single-trees, moved past the well to the block beside the path. Council stood at the side of the schooner [3] and helped the children out—two little half-sleeping children—and then a small woman with a babe in her arms.

"There ye go!" he shouted jovially to the children. "Now we're all right! Run right along to the house there an' tell Mam' Council you wants sumpthin' t' eat. Right this way, Mis'—keep right off t' the right there. I'll go an' git a lantern. Come," he said to the dazed and silent group at his side.

"Mother," he shouted, as he neared the fragrant and warmly-lighted kitchen, "here are some wayfarers an' folks who need sumpthin' t' eat an' a place t' snooze." He ended by pushing them all in.

Mrs. Council, a large, jolly, rather coarse-looking woman, took the children in her arms. "Come right in, you little rabbits. 'Most asleep, hey? Now here's

a drink o' milk f'r each o' ye. I'll have s'm tea in a minute. Take off y'r things and set up t' the fire."

While she set the children to drinking milk, Council got out his lantern and went out to the barn to help the stranger about his team, where his loud, hearty voice could be heard as it came and went between the haymow and the stalls.

The woman came to light as a small, timid, and discouraged-looking woman, but still pretty in a thin and sorrowful way.

"Land sakes! An' you've traveled all the way from Clear Lake t'day in this mud! Waal! waal! No wonder you're all tired out. Don't wait f'r the men, Mis'—" She hesitated, waiting for the name.

"Haskins."

"Mis' Haskins, set right up to the table an' take a good swig o' tea whilst I make y' s'm toast. Its green tea, an' it's good. I tell Council as I git older I don't seem to enjoy young hyson n'r gunpowder.[4] I want the reel green tea jest as it comes off'n the vines. Seems t' have more heart in it, some way. Don't s'pose it has. Council says it's all in m' eye."

Going on in this easy way, she soon had the children filled with bread and milk and the woman thoroughly at home, eating some toast and sweet-melon pickles and sipping the tea.

"See the little rats!" she laughed at the children. "They're full as they can stick now, and they want to go to bed. Now, don't git up, Mis' Haskins; set right where you are an' let me look after 'em. I know all about young ones, though I'm all alone now. Jane went an' married last fall. But, as I tell

[3] SCHOONER—A covered wagon.

[4] YOUNG HYSON N'R GUNPOWDER—Brands of tea.

Council, it's lucky we keep our health. Set right there, Mis' Haskins; I won't have you stir a finger."

It was an unmeasured pleasure to sit there in the warm, homely kitchen, the jovial chatter of the housewife driving out and holding at bay the growl of the impotent, cheated wind.

The little woman's eyes filled with tears, which fell down upon the sleeping baby in her arms. The world was not so desolate and cold and hopeless, after all.

"Now I hope Council won't stop out there and talk politics all night. He's the greatest man to talk politics an' read the *Tribune*—How old is it?"

She broke off and peered down at the face of the babe.

"Two months 'n' five days," said the mother, with a mother's exactness.

"Ye don't say! I want 'o know! The dear little pudzy-wudzy!" she went on, stirring it up in the neighborhood of the ribs with her fat forefinger. "Pooty tough on 'oo to go gallivant'n 'cross lots this way—"

"Yes, that's so; a man can't lift a mountain," said Council, entering the door. "Mother, this is Mr. Haskins, from Kansas. He's been eat up 'n' drove out by grasshoppers."

"Glad t' see yeh!—Pa, empty that washbasin 'n' give him a chance t' wash."

Haskins was a tall man, with a thin, gloomy face. His hair was a reddish brown like his coat and seemed equally faded by the wind and sun; and his sallow face, though hard and set, was pathetic somehow. You would have felt that he had suffered much by the line of his mouth showing under his thin, yellow mustache.

"Hain't Ike got home yet, Sairy?"

"Hain't seen 'im."

"W-a-a-l, set right up, Mr. Haskins; wade right into what we've got; 'taint much, but we manage to live on it— she gits fat on it," laughed Council, pointing his thumb at his wife.

After supper, while the women put the children to bed, Haskins and Council talked on, seated near the huge cooking stove, the steam rising from their wet clothing. In the Western fashion Council told as much of his own life as he drew from his guest. He asked but few questions, but by and by the story of Haskins' struggles and defeat came out. The story was a terrible one; but he told it quietly, seated with his elbows on his knees, gazing most of the time at the hearth.

"I didn't like the looks of the country, anyhow," Haskins said, partly rising and glancing at his wife. "I was ust t' northern Ingyannie,[5] where we have lots o' timber 'n' lots o' rain, 'n' I didn't like the looks o' that dry prairie. What galled me the worst was goin' s' far away acrosst so much fine land layin' all through here vacant."

"And the 'hoppers eat ye four years, hand runnin', did they?"

"Eat! They wiped us out. They chawed everything that was green. They jest set around waitin' f'r us t' die t' eat us, too. My God! I ust t' dream of 'em sittin' 'round on the bedpost, six feet long, workin' their jaws. They eet the fork handles. They got worse 'n' worse till they jest rolled on one another, piled up like snow in winter. Well, it ain't no use. If I was t' talk all winter, I couldn't tell nawthin'. But all the while I couldn't help thinkin' of all that land back here that nobuddy was usin' that I ought 'o had 'stead o' bein' out there in that cussed country."

"Waal, why didn't ye stop an' settle

[5] INGYANNIE—Corruption of *Indiana.*

here?" asked Ike, who had come and was eating his supper.

"For the simple reason that you fellers wanted ten 'r fifteen dollars an acre fer the bare land, and I hadn't no money fer that kind o' thing."

"Yes, I do my own work," Mrs. Council was heard to say in the pause which followed. "I'm a gettin' purty heavy t' be on m' laigs all day, but we can't afford t' hire, so I keep rackin' around somehow, like a foundered horse. S' lame—I tell Council he can't tell how lame I am, f'r I'm jest as lame in one laig as t' other." And the good soul laughed at the joke on herself as she took a handful of flour and dusted the biscuit board to keep the dough from sticking.

"Well, I hain't *never* been very strong," said Mrs. Haskins. "Our folks was Canadians an' small-boned, and then since my last child I hain't got up again fairly. I don't like t' complain. Tim has about all he can bear now—

but they was days this week when I jest wanted to lay right down an' die."

"Waal, now, I'll tell ye," said Council from his side of the stove, silencing everybody with his good-natured roar, "I'd go down and *see* Butler, *anyway*, if I was you. I guess he'd let you have his place purty cheap; the farm's all run down. He's ben anxious t' let t' somebuddy next year. It 'ud be a good chance fer you. Anyhow, you go to bed and sleep like a babe. I've got some plowin' t' do, anyhow, an' we'll see if somethin' can't be done about your case. Ike, you go out an' see if the horses is all right, an' I'll show the folks t' bed."

When the tired husband and wife were lying under the generous quilts of the spare bed, Haskins listened a moment to the wind in the eaves and then said, with a slow and solemn tone:

"There are people in this world who are good enough t' be angels, an' only haff t' die to *be* angels."

Jim Butler was one of those men called in the West "land poor." [6] Early in the history of Rock River he had come into the town and started in the grocery business in a small way, occupying a small building in a mean part of town. At this period of his life he earned all he got and was up early and late, sorting beans, working over butter, and carting his goods to and from the station. But a change came over him at the end of the second year when he sold a lot of land for four times what he paid for it. From that time forward he believed in land speculation as the surest way of getting rich. Every cent he could save or spare from his trade, he put into land at forced sale or mortgages [7] on land, which were "just as good as the wheat," he was accustomed to say.

Farm after farm fell into his hands, until he was recognized as one of the leading landowners of the country. His mortgages were scattered all over Cedar County; and as they slowly but surely fell in, he sought usually to retain the former owner as tenant.

He was not ready to foreclose; indeed, he had the name of being one of the easiest men in the town. He let the debtor off again and again, extending the time whenever possible.

"I don't want y'r land," he said. "All I'm after is the int'rest on my money— that's all. Now, if y' want 'o stay on the farm, why, I'll give y' a good chance. I can't have the land lyin' vacant." And in many cases the owner remained as tenant.

In the meantime he had sold his store; he couldn't spend time in it; he

was mainly occupied now with sitting around town on rainy days smoking and "gassin' with the boys," or in riding to and from his farms. In fishing time he fished a good deal. Doc Grimes, Ben Ashley, and Cal Cheatham were his cronies on these fishing excursions or hunting trips in the time of chickens or partridges. In winter they went to northern Wisconsin to shoot deer.

In spite of all these signs of easy life, Butler persisted in saying he "hadn't money to pay taxes on his land" and was careful to convey the impression that he was poor in spite of his twenty farms. At one time he was said to be worth fifty thousand dollars, but land had been a little slow of sale of late, so that he was not worth so much.

A fine farm, known as the Higley place, had fallen into his hands in the usual way the previous year, and he had not been able to find a tenant for it. Poor Higley, after working himself nearly to death on it in the attempt to lift the mortgage, had gone off to Dakota, leaving the farm and his curse to Butler.

This was the farm which Council advised Haskins to apply for, and the next day Council hitched up his team and drove downtown to see Butler.

"You jest let *me* do the talkin'," he said. "We'll find him wearin' out his pants on some salt barrel somew'ers; and if he thought you *wanted* a place, he'd sock it to you hot and heavy. You jest keep quiet; I'll fix 'im."

Butler was seated in Ben Ashley's store telling fish yarns when Council sauntered in casually.

"Hello, But; lyin' agin, hey?"

"Hello, Steve! how goes it?"

"Oh, so-so. Too dang much rain these days. I thought it was goin' t' freeze up f'h good last night. Tight

<hr />

[6] LAND POOR—Owning much unprofitable land; having all one's capital in land.

[7] MORTGAGES—Conditional transfers of property to one who has lent money to the original owner; upon payment of the debt ownership reverts to the original owner.

squeak if I get m' plowin' done. How's farmin' with *you* these days?"

"Bad. Plowin' ain't half done."

"It 'ud be a religious idee f'r you t' go out an' take a hand y'rself."

"I don't haff to," said Butler with a wink.

"Got anybody on the Higley place?"

"No. Know of anybody?"

"Waal, no; not eggsackly. I've got a relation back t' Michigan who's ben hot an' cold on the idee o' comin' West f'r some time. *Might* come if he could get a good layout. What do you talk on the farm?"

"Well, I d'know. I'll rent it on shares or I'll rent in money rent."

"Waal, how much money, say?"

"Well, say ten per cent on the price —two-fifty."

"Waal, that ain't bad. Wait on 'im till 'e thrashes!"

Haskins listened eagerly to his important question, but Council was coolly eating a dried apple which he had speared out of a barrel with his knife. Butler studied him carefully.

"Well, knocks me out of twenty-five dollars interest."

"My relation 'll need all he's got t' git his crops in," said Council in the safe, indifferent way.

"Well, all right; *say* wait," concluded Butler.

"All right; this is the man. Haskins, this is Mr. Butler—no relation to Ben —the hardest-working man in Cedar County."

On the way home Haskins said: "I ain't much better off. I'd like that farm; it's a good farm, but it's all run down, an' so 'm I. I could make a good farm of it if I had half a show. But I can't stock it n'r seed it."

"Waal, now, don't you worry," roared Council in his ear. "We'll pull y'

through somehow till next harvest. He's agreed t' hire it plowed, an' you can earn a hundred dollars plowin', an' y' c'n git the seed o' me an' pay me back when y' can."

Haskins was silent with emotion, but at last he said, "I ain't got nothin' t' live on."

"Now, don't you worry 'bout that. You jest make your headquarters at ol' Steve Council's. Mother'll take a pile o' comfort in havin' y'r wife an' children 'round. Y' see, Jane 's married off lately, an' Ike's away a good 'eal; so we'll be darn glad t' have y' stop with us this winter. Nex' spring we'll see if y' can't git a start agin." And he chirruped to the team, which sprang forward with the rumbling, clattering wagon.

"Say, looky here, Council, you can't do this. I never saw—" shouted Haskins in his neighbor's ear.

Council moved about uneasily in his seat and stopped his stammering gratitude by saying: "Hold on, now; don't make such a fuss over a little thing. When I see a man down, an' things all on top of 'm, I jest like t' kick 'em off an' help 'm up. That's the kind of religion I got, an' it's about the *only* kind."

They rode the rest of the way home in silence. And when the red light of the lamp shone out into the darkness of the cold and windy night, and he thought of this refuge for his children and wife, Haskins could have put his arm around the neck of his burly companion and squeezed him like a lover. But he contented himself with saying, "Steve Council, you'll git y'r pay f'r this some day."

"Don't want any pay. My religion ain't run on such business principles."

The wind was growing colder, and the ground was covered with a white frost as they turned into the gate of the

Council farm, and the children came rushing out, shouting, "Papa's come!" They hardly looked like the same children who had sat at the table the night before. Their torpidity, under the influence of sunshine and Mother Council, had given way to a sort of spasmodic cheerfulness, as insects in winter revive when laid on the hearth.

Haskins worked like a fiend, and his wife, like the heroic woman that she was, bore also uncomplainingly the most terrible burdens. They rose early and toiled without intermission till the darkness fell on the plain, then tumbled into bed, every bone and muscle aching with fatigue, to rise with the sun next morning to the same round of the same ferocity of labor.

The eldest boy drove a team all through the spring, plowing and seeding, milked the cows, and did chores innumerable, in most ways taking the place of a man.

An infinitely pathetic but common figure, this boy on the American farm, where there is no law against child labor. To see him in his coarse clothing, his huge boots, and his ragged cap, as he staggered with a pail of water from the well or trudged in the cold and cheerless dawn out into the frosty field behind his team, gave the city-bred visitor a sharp pang of sympathetic pain. Yet Haskins loved his boy and would have saved him from this if he could, but he could not.

By June, the first year, the result of such Herculean[8] toil began to show on the farm. The yard was cleaned up and sown to grass, the garden plowed and planted, and the house mended.

Council had given them four of his cows.

[8] HERCULEAN (hûr·kū′lê·ăn)—Requiring great strength and industry.

"Take 'em an' run 'em on shares. I don't want 'o milk s' many. Ike's away s' much now, Sat'd'ys and Sundays, I can't stand the bother anyhow."

Other men, seeing the confidence of Council in the newcomer had sold him tools on time; and as he was really an able farmer, he soon had round him many evidences of his care and thrift. At the advice of Council he had taken the farm for three years, with the privilege of re-renting or buying at the end of the term.

"It's a good bargain, an' y' want 'o nail it," said Council. "If you have any kind ov a crop, you c'n pay y'er debts an' keep seed an' bread."

The new hope which now sprang up in the heart of Haskins and his wife grew great almost as a pain by the time the wide field of wheat began to wave and swirl in the wind of July. Day after day he would snatch a few moments after supper to go and look at it.

"Have ye seen the wheat t' day, Nettie?" he asked one night as he rose from supper.

"No, Tim, I ain't had time."

"Well, take time now. Let's go look at it."

She threw an old hat on her head— Tommy's hat—and, looking almost pretty in her thin, sad way, went out with her husband to the hedge.

"Ain't it grand, Nettie? Just look at it."

It was grand. Level, russet here and there, heavy-headed, wide as a lake, and full of multitudinous whispers and gleams of wealth, it stretched away before the gazers like the fabled field of the cloth of gold.[9]

[9] FIELD OF THE CLOTH OF GOLD—A field near Calais where Henry VIII interviewed Francis I in 1520. The splendor of the scene was so great that the place has come to be known as the field of the cloth of gold.

"Oh, I think—I *hope* we'll have a good crop, Tim; and oh, how good the people have been to us!"

"Yes; I don't know where we'd be t'day if it hadn't been f'r Council and his wife."

"They're the best people in the world," said the little woman, with a great sob of gratitude.

"We'll be in the field on Monday, sure," said Haskins, gripping the rail on the fence as if already at the work of the harvest.

The harvest came, bounteous, glorious; but the winds came and blew it into tangles, and the rain matted it here and there close to the ground, increasing the work of gathering it threefold.

Oh, how they toiled in those glorious days! Clothing dripping with sweat, arms aching, filled with briers, fingers raw and bleeding, backs broken with the weight of heavy bundles, Haskins and his man toiled on. Tommy drove the harvester, while his father and a hired man bound on the machine. In this way they cut ten acres every day; and almost every night after supper, when the hand went to bed, Haskins returned to the field, shocking the bound grain in the light of the moon. Many a night he worked till his anxious wife came out at ten o'clock to call him in to rest and lunch.

At the same time she cooked for the men, took care of the children, washed and ironed, milked the cows at night, made the butter, and sometimes fed the horses and watered them while her husband kept at the shocking.

No slave in the Roman galleys could have toiled so frightfully and lived, for this man thought himself a free man and that he was working for his wife and babes.

When he sank into his bed with a deep groan of relief, too tired to change his grimy, dripping clothing, he felt that he was getting nearer and nearer to a home of his own and pushing the wolf of want a little farther from his door.

There is no despair so deep as the despair of a homeless man or woman. To roam the roads of the country or the streets of the city, to feel there is no rood of ground on which the feet can rest, to halt weary and hungry outside lighted windows and hear laughter and song within—these are the hungers and rebellions that drive men to crime and women to shame.

It was the memory of this homelessness and the fear of its coming again that spurred Timothy Haskins and Nettie, his wife, to such ferocious labor during that first year.

" 'M, yes; 'm, yes; first-rate," said Butler, as his eye took in the neat garden, the pigpen, and the well-filled barnyard. "You're gitt'n' quite a stock around yeh. Done well, eh?"

Haskins was showing Butler around the place. He had not seen it for a year, having spent the year in Washington and Boston with Ashley, his brother-in-law, who had been elected to Congress.

"Yes, I've laid out a good deal of money durin' the last three years. I've paid out three hundred dollars f'r fencin'."

"Um—h'm! I see. I see," said Butler while Haskins went on:

"The kitchen there cost two hundred; the barn ain't cost much in money, but I've put a lot o' time on it. I've dug a new well, and I—"

"Yes, yes, I see. You've done well. Stock worth a thousand dollars," said Butler, picking his teeth with a straw.

"About that," said Haskins modestly. "We begin to feel 's if we was gett'n' a home f'r ourselves, but we've worked hard. I tell you we begin to feel it, Mr. Butler, and we're goin' t' begin to ease up purty soon. We've been kind o' plannin' a trip back t' *her* folks after the fall plowin's done."

"*Eggs*-actly!" said Butler, who was evidently thinking of something else. "I suppose you've kind o' calc'lated on stayin' here three years more?"

"Well, yes. Fact is, I think I c'n buy the farm this fall if you'll give me a reasonable show."

"Um—m! What do you call a reasonable show?"

"Well, say a quarter down and three years' time."

Butler looked at the huge stacks of wheat which filled the yard, over which the chickens were fluttering and crawling, catching grasshoppers, and out of which the crickets were singing innumerably. He smiled in a peculiar way as he said: "Oh, I won't be hard on yeh. But what did you expect to pay f'r the place?"

"Why, about what you offered it for before, two thousand five hundred, or *possibly* three thousand dollars," he added quickly as he saw the owner shake his head.

"This farm is worth five thousand and five hundred dollars," said Butler in a careless and decided voice.

"*What!*" almost shrieked the astounded Haskins. "What's that? Five thousand? Why, that's double what you offered it for three years ago."

"Of course, and it's worth it. It was all run down then; now it's in good shape. You've laid out fifteen hundred dollars in improvements according to your own story."

"But *you* had nothin' t' do about that. It's my work an' my money."

"You bet it was; but it's my land."

"But what's to pay me for all my—"

"Ain't you had the use of 'em?" replied Butler, smiling calmly into his face.

Haskins was like a man struck on the head with a sandbag; he couldn't think; he stammered as he tried to say: "But— I never'd git the use—You'd rob me! More'n that: you agreed—you promised that I could buy or rent at the end of three years at—"

"That's all right. But I didn't say I'd let you carry off the improvements nor that I'd go on renting the farm at two-fifty. The land is doubled in value, it don't matter how; it don't enter into the question; an' now you can pay me five hundred dollars a year rent, or take it on your own terms at fifty-five hundred, or —git out."

He was turning away when Haskins, the sweat pouring from his face, fronted him, saying again:

"But *you've* done nothing to make it so. You hain't added a cent. I put it all there myself, expectin' to buy. I worked an' sweat to improve it. I was workin' for myself an' babes—"

"Well, why didn't you buy when I offered to sell? What y' kickin' about?"

"I'm kickin' about payin' you twice f'r my own things—my own fences, my own kitchen, my own garden."

Butler laughed. "You're too green t' eat, young feller. *Your* improvements! The law will sing another tune."

"But I trusted your word."

"Never trust anybody, my friend. Besides, I didn't promise not to do this thing. Why man, don't look at me like that. Don't take me for a thief. It's the law. The reg'lar thing. Everybody does it."

"I don't care if they do. It's stealin' jest the same. You take three thousand dollars of my money—the work o' my

hands and my wife's." He broke down at this point. He was not a strong man mentally. He could face hardship, ceaseless toil, but he could not face the cold and sneering face of Butler.

"But I don't take it," said Butler coolly. "All you've got to do is to go on jest as you've been a-doin', or give me a thousand dollars down and a mortgage at ten per cent on the rest."

Haskins sat down blindly on a bundle of oats near by and with staring eyes and drooping head went over the situation. He was under the lion's paw. He felt a horrible numbness in his heart and limbs. He was hid in a mist, and there was no path out.

Butler walked about, looking at the huge stacks of grain and pulling now and again a few handfuls out, shelling the heads in his hands and blowing the chaff away. He hummed a little tune as he did so. He had an accommodating air of waiting.

Haskins was in the midst of the terrible toil of the last year. He was walking again in the rain and the mud behind his plow; he felt the dust and dirt of the threshing. The ferocious husk-ing time, with its cutting wind and bit-ing, clinging snows, lay hard upon him. Then he thought of his wife, how she had cheerfully cooked and baked with-out holiday and without rest.

"Well, what do you think of it?" in-quired the cool, mocking, insinuating voice of Butler.

"I think you're a thief and a liar!" shouted Haskins, leaping up. "A black-hearted houn'!" Butler's smile mad-dened him; with a sudden leap he caught a fork in his hands and whirled it in the air. "You'll never rob another man, damn ye!" he grated through his teeth, a look of pitiless ferocity in his accusing eyes.

Butler shrank and quivered, expecting the blow; stood, held hypnotized by the eyes of the man he had a moment before despised—a man transformed into an avenging demon. But in the deadly hush between the lift of the weapon and its fall there came a gush of faint, child-ish laughter; and then across the range of his vision, far away and dim, he saw the sunbright head of his baby girl, as, with the pretty, tottering run of a two-year-old, she moved across the grass of the dooryard. His hands relaxed; the fork fell to the ground; his head lowered.

"Make out y'r deed an' mor'gage, an' git of'n my land, an' don't ye never cross my line again; if y' do, I'll kill ye."

Butler backed away from the man in wild haste and, climbing into his buggy with trembling limbs, drove off down the road, leaving Haskins seated dumbly on the sunny piles of sheaves, his head sunk into his hands.

◇◇◇◇◇◇◇◇◇◇◇◇◇◇◇◇◇◇◇◇◇◇◇◇◇◇

## FOR DISCUSSION

1. Why does the author begin with a poignant description of the hard work on an Iowa farm?

2. What is your first impression of Stephen Council? Is he a man you like at once?

3. What are some traits of Mr. and Mrs. Council? Would you say that they are humorous, generous, hospitable, industrious?

4. Do you agree with Mr. Haskins that "there are people in this world good enough t' be angels, an' only haff t' die to be angels"? Explain.

5. What did Jim Butler mean by saying that buying a mortgage on land was "just as good as the wheat"?

6. The author is careful not to arouse too much dislike for Butler when he is first introduced. Why?

7. Council's idea of religion fulfills the second great commandment: "Love thy neighbor." Does it also fulfill the first great commandment: "Thou shalt love the Lord thy God with thy whole heart"?

8. "The law will sing another tune." Is this correct? What legal steps should Haskins have taken at the time he occupied the farm in order to prevent his later difficulties with Butler?

9. It may be that Butler did not act against the law, but do you think he sinned grievously against charity?

10. Haskins' tremendous industry came from his hope of eventually owning the land. Would the lack of this hope in a communist state lessen the industry of the workers?

## TYPE STUDY—THE SHORT STORY

1. Explain the author's purpose in putting in the episode of Mr. and Mrs. Haskins' chance acquaintance with the Councils. Is this episode strictly necessary for the plot of the story? Is it helpful to the story? Explain.

2. The characters in this story are well drawn and true-to-life. But which is predominant—character or plot? Would the story be the same if Stephen Council were a weak, timid man? Explain.

## WORDS TO EXPLAIN

Explain the following similes: *tenacious as tar; fettering him like gyves; black and shining as jet; like a foundered horse.*

## PROJECTS

1. Choose five paragraphs of dialogue, and show how they differ from our ordinary way of speaking.

2. Study Garland's biography; then point out details in the story which you think are autobiographical.

## RELATED READING

Other stories by Hamlin Garland worth reading are "Mrs. Ripley's Trip," "Among the Corn Rows," and "The Return of the Private."

"A Horseman in the Sky," by Ambrose Bierce, is the poignant story of a son whose conscience forces him to fight against his father in the Civil War.

Surprise endings are featured in the famous stories, "Marjorie Daw," by Thomas Bailey Aldrich, and in "The Lady or the Tiger," by Frank R. Stockton.

# LAST ISLAND

*LAFCADIO HEARN*

"Last Island . . . is now a ghastly desolation twenty-five miles long. . . .
Lying nearly forty miles west of Grande Isle . . . it was not only the most
celebrated island of the group, but also the most fashionable watering-place
of the aristocratic South;—today it is visited by fishermen only, at long
intervals. . . . The deep channel which now cuts the island in two did not
exist while the village remained. The sea tore it out in one night—the
same night when trees, fields, dwellings, all vanished into the Gulf, leaving
no vestige of former human habitation except a few strong brick props and
foundations. . . .

"The Voice of the Sea is never one voice, but a tumult of many voices—
voices of drowned men, the muttering of multitudinous dead, the moaning
of innumerable ghosts, all rising, to rage against the living, at the great
Witch-call of storms. . . ."

Thirty years ago, Last Island lay steeped in the enormous light of . . . magical days. July was dying; for weeks no fleck of cloud had broken the heaven's blue dream of eternity; winds held their breath; slow wavelets caressed the bland brown beach with a sound as of kisses and whispers. To one who found himself alone, beyond the limits of the village and beyond the hearing of its voices—the vast silence, the vast light, seemed full of weirdness. And these hushes, these transparencies, do not always inspire a causeless apprehension: they are omens sometimes—omens of coming tempest. Nature—incomprehensible Sphinx!—before her mightiest bursts of rage ever puts forth her divinest witchery, makes more manifest her awful beauty. . . .

But in that forgotten summer the witchery lasted many long days—days born in rose-light, buried in gold. It was the height of the season. The long myrtle-shadowed village was thronged with its summer population; the big hotel could hardly accommodate all its guests; the bathing houses were too few for the crowds who flocked to the water morning and evening. There were diversions for all—hunting and fishing parties, yachting excursions, rides, music, games, promenades. Carriage wheels whirled flickering along the beach seaming its smoothness noiselessly, as if muffled. . . .

Then one great noon, when the blue abyss of day seemed to yawn over the world more deeply than ever before, a sudden change touched the quicksilver smoothness of the waters—the swaying shadow of a vast motion. First the whole sea-circle appeared to rise up bodily at the sky; the horizon-curve lifted to a straight line; the line darkened and approached—a monstrous wrinkle, an immeasurable fold of green water, moving swift as a cloud-shadow pursued by sunlight. But it had looked formidable only by startling contrast with the previous placidity of the open: it was scarcely two feet high; it curled slowly as it neared the beach, and combed itself out in sheets of woolly foam with a low, rich roll of whispered thunder. Swift in pursuit another followed—a third—a feebler fourth; then the sea only swayed a little, and stilled again. Minutes passed, and the immeasurable heaving recommenced—one, two, three, four . . . seven long swells this time—and the Gulf smoothed itself once more. Irregularly the phenomenon continued to repeat itself, each time with heavier billowing and briefer intervals of quiet, until at last the whole sea grew restless and shifted color and flickered green; the swells became shorter and changed form. Then from horizon to shore ran one uninterrupted heaving—one vast green swarming of snaky shapes, rolling in to hiss and flatten upon the sand. Yet no single cirrus-speck [1] revealed itself through all the violet heights; there was no wind!—you might have fancied the sea had been upheaved from beneath. . . .

Then the wind began to blow, with the passing of July. It blew from the northeast, clear, cool. It blew in enormous sighs, dying away at regular intervals, as if pausing to draw breath. All night it blew; and in each pause could be heard the answering moan of the rising surf—as if the rhythm of the sea moulded itself after the rhythm of the air—as if the waving of the water responded precisely to the waving of the wind, a billow for every puff, a surge for every sigh.

The August morning broke in a bright sky; the breeze still came cool and clear from the northeast. The waves were running now at a sharp angle to the shore: they began to carry fleeces, an innumerable flock of vague green shapes, wind-driven to be despoiled of their ghostly wool. Far as the eye could follow the line of the beach, all the slope was white with the great shearing of them. Clouds came, flew as in a panic against the face of the sun, and passed. All that day and through the night and into the morning again the breeze continued from the northeast, blowing like an equinoctial [2] gale. . . .

Then day by day the vast breath freshened steadily, and the waters heightened. A week later sea-bathing had become perilous: colossal breakers were herding in, like moving leviathan-backs, [3] twice the height of man. Still the gale grew, and the billowing waxed mightier, and faster and faster overhead flew the tatters of torn cloud. The gray morning of the ninth wanly lighted a surf that appalled the best swimmers: the sea was one wild agony of foam, the gale was rending off the heads of the waves and veiling the horizon with a fog of salt spray. Shadowless and gray the day remained; there were mad bursts of lashing rain. Evening brought with it a sinister apparition, looming through a cloud-rent in the west—a scarlet sun in a green sky. His sanguine disk, enor-

---

[1] CIRRUS-SPECK—Cirrus is a white, filmy variety of clouds.

[2] EQUINOCTIAL (ē′·kwĭ·nŏk′shăl)—Happening at or near the time of the equinox: that is, when the sun's center crosses the equator and night and day are everywhere of equal length: about March 21, and again about September 23.

[3] LEVIATHAN—An aquatic monster such as the whale; something huge and awe-inspiring.

mously magnified, seemed barred like the body of a belted planet. A moment, and the crimson specter vanished; and the moonless night came.

Then the Wind grew weird. It ceased being a breath; it became a Voice moaning across the world—hooting—uttering nightmare sounds—*Whoo!—whoo!—whoo!*—and with each stupendous owl-cry the moving of the waters seemed to deepen, more and more abysmally, through all the hours of darkness. From the northwest the breakers of the bay began to roll high over the sandy slope, into the salines;[4] the village bayou[5] broadened to a bellowing flood. . . . So the tumult swelled and the turmoil heightened until morning—a morning of gray gloom and whistling rain. Rain of bursting clouds and rain of wind-blown brine from the great spuming agony of the sea.

The steamer *Star* was due from Saint Mary's that fearful morning. Could she come? No one really believed it—no one. And nevertheless men struggled to the roaring beach to look for her, because hope is stronger than reason. . . .

Even today, in these Creole islands, the advent of the steamer is the great event of the week. There are no telegraph lines, no telephones; the mail-packet is the only trustworthy medium of communication with the outer world, bringing friends, news, letters. . . . And even during the deepest sleep of waves and winds there will come betimes to sojourners in this unfamiliar archipelago[6] a feeling of lonesomeness that is a fear, a feeling of isolation from the world of men—totally unlike that

sense of solitude which haunts one in the silence of mountain-heights, or amid the eternal tumult of lofty granitic coasts: a sense of helpless insecurity. The land seems but an undulation[7] of the sea-bed; its highest ridges do not rise more than the height of a man above the salines on either side; the salines themselves lie almost level with the level of the flood-tides; the tides are variable, treacherous, mysterious. But when all around and above these ever-changing shores the twin vastnesses of heaven and sea begin to utter the tremendous revelation of themselves as infinite forces in contention, then indeed this sense of separation from humanity appals. . . . Perhaps it was such a feeling which forced men, on the tenth day of August, eighteen hundred and fifty-six, to hope against hope for the coming of the *Star*, and to strain their eyes towards far-off Terrebonne. "It was a wind you could lie down on," said my friend the pilot. . . .

"Great God!" shrieked a voice above the shouting of the storm, *"she is coming!"*. . . It was true. Down the Atchafalaya,[8] and thence through strange mazes of bayou, lakelet, and pass, by a rear route familiar only to the best of pilots, the frail river-craft had toiled into Caillou Bay, running close to the main shore; and now she was heading right for the island, with the wind aft, over the monstrous sea. On she came, swaying, rocking, plunging—with a great whiteness wrapping her about like a cloud and moving with her moving—a tempest-whirl of spray—ghost-white and like a ghost she came, for her smoke-stacks exhaled no visible smoke—the

[4] SALINES—Salt deposits.
[5] BAYOU (bī′ōō)—A sluggish inlet or outlet from a lake or bay.
[6] ARCHIPELAGO (är·kĭ·pĕl′a·gō)—Any sea or broad sheet of water interspersed with islands; also, such a group of islands.

[7] UNDULATION—A wave; a waving motion.
[8] ATCHAFALAYA (ăch·a·fa·lī′a)—A bayou; the outlet of the Red River and the Mississippi River in Louisiana.

wind devoured it! The excitement on shore became wild; men shouted themselves hoarse; women laughed and cried. Every telescope and opera-glass was directed upon the coming apparition. . . .

She won! With a sonorous steam-chant of triumph the brave little vessel rode at last into the bayou, and anchored hard by her accustomed resting place, in full view of the hotel, though not near enough to shore to lower her gangplank. . . . But she had sung her swan-song. Gathering in from the northeast, the waters of the bay were already marbling over the salines and half across the island; and still the wind increased its paroxysmal power.

Cottages began to rock. Some slid away from the solid props upon which they rested. A chimney tumbled. Shutters were wrenched off; verandas demolished. Light roofs lifted, dropped again, and flapped into ruin. Trees bent their heads to the earth. And still the storm grew louder and blacker with

every passing hour. . . .

Almost every evening throughout the season there had been dancing in the great hall; there was dancing that night also. The population of the hotel had been augmented by the advent of families from other parts of the island, who found their summer cottages insecure places of shelter; there were nearly four hundred guests assembled. Perhaps it was for this reason that the entertainment had been prepared upon a grander plan than usual, that it assumed the form of a fashionable ball. . . . Perhaps in the more than ordinary merriment of that evening something of nervous exaltation might have been discerned—something like a feverish resolve to oppose apprehension with gayety, to combat uneasiness by diversion. But the hours passed in mirthfulness; the first general feeling of depression began to weigh less and less upon the guests; they had found reason to confide in the solidity of the massive building; there were no positive terrors, no outspoken fears; and the new conviction of all had found expression in the words of the host himself—*"Il n'y a rien de mieux à faire que de s'amuser!"* [9] Of what avail to lament the prospective devastation of cane-fields, to discuss the possible ruin of crops? Better to seek solace in choregraphic [10] harmonies, in the rhythm of gracious motion and of perfect melody, than hearken to the discords of the wild orchestra of storms. . . .

Night wore on: still the shining floor palpitated to the feet of the dancers; still the piano-forte pealed, and still the violins sang—and the sound of their singing shrilled through the darkness, in gasps of the gale, to the ears of Captain Smith, as he strove to keep his footing on the spray-drenched deck of the *Star*.

"A dance!" he muttered. "If that wind whips round south, there'll be another dance! . . . But I guess the *Star* will stay. . . ."

Half an hour might have passed; still the lights flamed calmly, and the violins trilled, and the perfumed whirl went on. . . . And suddenly the wind veered!

"Waltzing!" cried the captain. "God help them!—God help us all now! . . . *The Wind waltzes tonight, with the Sea for his partner!*"

O the stupendous Valse-Tourbillon! [11] O the mighty Dancer! One—two—three! From northeast to east, from east to southeast, from southeast to south: then from the south he came, whirling the Sea in his arms. . . .

Someone shrieked in the midst of the revels, some girl who found her pretty slippers wet. What could it be? Thin streams of water were spreading over the level planking—curling about the feet of the dancers. . . . What could it be? All the land had begun to quake, even as, but a moment before, the polished floor was trembling to the pressure of circling steps; all the building shook now; every beam uttered its groan. What could it be? . . .

There was a clamor, a panic, a rush to the windy night. Infinite darkness above and beyond; but the lantern-beams danced far out over an unbroken circle of heaving and swirling black water. Stealthily, swiftly, the measureless sea-flood was rising.

*"Messieurs—mesdames, ce n'est rien.* [12] Nothing serious, ladies, I assure you. . . . *Mais nous en avons vu bien souvent, les inondations comme celle-ci; ça passe vite!* [13] The water will go down in a few hours, ladies;—it never rises higher than this; *il n'y a pas le moindre danger, je vous dis! Allons! il n'y a—* [14] what is that?"

For a moment there was a ghastly hush of voices. And through that hush there burst upon the ears of all a fearful and unfamiliar sound, as of a colossal cannonade—rolling up from the south, with volleying lightnings. Vastly and swiftly, nearer and nearer it came—a ponderous and unbroken thunder-roll, terrible as the long muttering of an earthquake.

The nearest mainland—across mad Caillou Bay to the sea-marshes—lay twelve miles north; west, by the Gulf,

[9] *There is nothing better to do than to amuse oneself.*

[10] CHOREGRAPHIC (kŏ·rê·grăf'ĭk)—Dancing; the art of arranging dances.

[11] VALSE-TOURBILLON (tōōr'bĭ·yŏn)—Waltz of the Whirlwind.

[12] *Gentlemen—ladies, it is nothing.*

[13] *But we have seen them very often, floods like this; it passes quickly.*

[14] *There is not the least danger, I tell you! Come there is no—*

the nearest solid ground was twenty miles distant. There were boats, yes!— but the stoutest swimmer might never reach them now! . . .

Then rose a frightful cry—the hoarse, hideous, indescribable cry of hopeless fear—the despairing animal-cry man utters when suddenly brought face to face with Nothingness, without preparation, without consolation, without possibility of respite. . . . *Sauve qui peut!* [15] Some wrenched down the doors; some clung to the heavy banquet-tables, to the sofas, to the billiard-tables—during one terrible instant—against fruitless heroisms, against futile generosities— raged all the frenzy of selfishness, all the brutalities of panic. And then—then came, thundering through the blackness, the giant swells, boom on boom! . . . One crash!—the huge frame building rocks like a cradle, seesaws, crackles. What are human shrieks now?—the tornado is shrieking! Another! Chandeliers splinter; lights are dashed out; a sweeping cataract hurls in; the immense hall rises, oscillates,[16] twirls as upon a pivot; crepitates,[17] crumbles into ruin. Crash again!—the swirling wreck dissolves into the wallowing of another monster billow; and a hundred cottages overturn, spin in sudden eddies, quiver, disjoint, and melt into the seething. . . .

So the hurricane passed—tearing off the heads of the prodigious [18] waves, to hurl them a hundred feet in air, heaping up the ocean against the land, upturning the woods.

And over roaring Kaimbuck Pass, over the agony of Caillou Bay, the billowing tide rushed unresisted from the Gulf— tearing and swallowing the land in its course, ploughing out deep-sea channels where sleek herds had been grazing but a few hours before, rending islands in twain, and ever bearing with it, through the night, enormous vortex [19] of wreck and vast wan drift of corpses.

Day breaks through the flying wrack,[20] over the infinite heaving of the sea, over the low land made vast with desolation. It is a spectral dawn: a wan light, like the light of a dying sun.

The wind has waned and veered; the flood sinks slowly back to its abysses, abandoning its plunder, scattering its piteous waifs over bar and dune, over shoal and marsh, among the silences of the mango-swamps, over the long low reaches of sand-grasses and drowned weeds, for more than a hundred miles. . . . From their cypress groves the vultures rise to dispute a share of the feast with the shrieking frigate-birds and squeaking gulls. And as the tremendous tide withdraws its plunging waters, all the pirates of air follow the great white-gleaming retreat: a storm of billowing wings and screaming throats.

And swift in the wake of gull and frigate-bird the Wreckers come, the Spoilers of the dead—savage skimmers of the sea, hurricane-riders wont to spread their canvas-pinions in the face of storms; Sicilian and Corsican outlaws, Manila-men from the marshes, deserters from many navies, Lascars,[21] marooners, refugees of a hundred nationalities, fishers and shrimpers by name, smugglers by opportunity. . . .

There is plunder for all—birds and men. There are drowned sheep in multitude, heaped carcasses of kine. There are casks of claret and kegs of brandy

---

[15] *Let him save himself who can;* or, *Each man for himself.*
[16] OSCILLATES—Moves or swings backward and forward.
[17] CREPITATES—Crackles.
[18] PRODIGIOUS—Vast, huge; extraordinary.

[19] VORTEX—Whirlpool, eddy.
[20] WRACK—Thin flying clouds.
[21] LASCARS—East Indian native sailors.

and legions of bottles bobbing in the surf. There are billiard tables overturned upon the sand;—there are sofas, pianos, footstools and music-stools, luxurious chairs, lounges of bamboo. There are chests of cedar, and toilet-tables of rosewood, and trunks of fine stamped leather stored with precious apparel. There are *objets de luxe* innumerable. There are children's playthings: French dolls, and toy carts, and wooden horses, and wooden spades, and brave little wooden ships that rode out the gale in which the great *Nautilus* [22] went down. There is money in notes and in coin—in purses, in pocketbooks, and in pockets: plenty of it! There are silks, satins, laces, and fine linen to be stripped from the bodies of the drowned —and necklaces, bracelets, watches, finger-rings and fine chains, brooches and trinkets. . . . That ball-dress was made in Paris by—but you never heard of him, Sicilian Vicenzu. . . . Her betrothal

ring will not come off, Giuseppe; but the delicate bone snaps easily; your oyster-knife can sever the tendon. . . . Over her heart you will find it, Valentino—the locket held by that fine Swiss chain of woven hair. . . . Juan, the fastenings of those diamond eardrops are much too complicated for your peon fingers: tear them out! . . .

Suddenly a long, mighty silver trilling fills the ears of all: there is a wild hurrying and scurrying; swiftly, one after another, the overburdened luggers spread wings and flutter away.

Thrice the great cry rings rippling through the gray air, and over the green sea, and over the far-flooded shell-reefs, where the huge white flashes are—sheet-lightning of breakers—and over the weird wash of corpses coming in.

It is the steam-call of the relief boat, hastening to rescue the living, to gather in the dead.

The tremendous tragedy is over!

[22] *Nautilus*—The New York *Herald* issues of August 10–18 report that three ships went down in the storm and tidal wave: The *Star,* which only lasted out the night, the *Perseverante,* and the *Nautilus.* The last named was apparently the largest boat. Details of its final disaster were never learned. A little of its wreckage bearing its printed name was all the rescuers could discover. The catastrophe cost about 190 lives. Survivors did not reach Galveston, about a half-day's sail from Last Island, until August 16.

◇◇◇◇◇◇◇◇◇◇◇◇◇◇◇◇◇◇◇◇◇◇◇◇◇◇◇◇◇◇

FOR DISCUSSION

1. What is the total effect or impression of this narrative?

2. Do you think that the author writes in ordinary prose or does he show a poetic imagination? Point out passages to prove your judgment.

3. Cite, if you can, some illustration you have experienced of the fact that nature "before her mightiest burst of rage, ever puts forth her divinest witchery"? Is it true that nature does the same *after* a burst of rage? Discuss.

4. Have you ever experienced the sense of isolation, of lonesomeness on a boat or on an island in some vast lake or gulf? Why is it that such feelings come?

5. Was it foolishness or carelessness or a show of courage that prompted the manager of the hotel to have a fashionable ball the night of the hurricane?

6. How does human nature react in face of catastrophes? Do you think that even ordinarily heroic and unselfish men will show up poorly in the face of great disaster? Discuss.

7. What does the phrase "man . . . brought face to face with Nothingness" tell you about the author? When he speaks of Nature and "her divinest witchery," what does he tell you of his belief in God?

8. What do you think of the Wreckers and Spoilers of the dead? Can you justify their activities? Why, or why not?

9. Which is the most vivid and effective scene?

## ARTISTRY WITH WORDS

Lafcadio Hearn is a technicolor artist with words. Let the class be divided into groups and each group assigned a page or more of the text from which it will note the various words that appeal to the senses of taste, color, sound, feeling, smell.

## RELATED READING

Like a painting in its colorful beauty is *Sunrise in Louisiana*, also by Lafcadio Hearn.

◇◇◇◇◇

# SCENES ON THE MISSISSIPPI

### MARK TWAIN

Today Hannibal, Missouri, is a town of railroad shops and foundries. A century ago it was one of the centers of a more romantic trade—the Mississippi River traffic.

To this town as a child came Samuel Clemens. His 'teens found him busy in printing and newspaper shops there and in the East. But the first years of his manhood brought him back to fulfill the ambition of his boyhood. Under Captain Horace Bixby he trained to become a pilot. His LIFE ON THE MISSISSIPPI, which is almost an autobiography, gives a dramatic account of cub pilot days.

"Scenes on the Mississippi" from *Life on the Mississippi* by Mark Twain, reprinted by permission of Harper & Brothers.

513

## EARLY AMBITION

When I was a boy, there was but one permanent ambition among my comrades in our village on the west bank of the Mississippi River. That was, to be a steamboatman. We had transient ambitions of other sorts, but they were only transient. When a circus came and went, it left us all burning to become clowns; the first Negro minstrel show that ever came to our section left us all suffering to try that kind of life; now and then we had a hope that, if we lived and were good, God would permit us to be pirates. These ambitions faded out, each in its turn; but the ambition to be a steamboatman always remained.

Once a day a cheap, gaudy packet arrived upward from St. Louis, and another downward from Keokuk.[1] Before these events, the day was glorious with expectancy; after them the day was a dead and empty thing. Not only the boys, but the whole village, felt this. After all these years I can picture that old time to myself now, just as it was then: the white town drowsing in the sunshine of a summer's morning; the streets empty, or pretty nearly so; one or two clerks sitting in front of the Water Street stores, with their split-bottomed chairs tilted back against the walls, chins on breasts, hats slouched over their faces, asleep—with shingle shavings enough around to show what broke them down; a sow and a litter of pigs loafing along the sidewalk, doing a good business in watermelon rinds and seeds; two or three lonely little freight piles scattered about the "levee"; a pile of "skids" on the slope of the stone-paved wharf, and the fragrant town drunkard asleep in the shadow of them;

two or three wood flats at the head of the wharf, but nobody to listen to the peaceful lapping of the wavelets against them; the great Mississippi, the majestic, the magnificent Mississippi, rolling its mile-wide tide along, shining in the sun; the dense forest away on the other side; the "point" above the town, and the "point" below, bounding the river-glimpse and turning it into a sort of sea, and withal a very still and brilliant and lonely one.

Presently a film of dark smoke appears above one of those remote "points"; instantly a Negro drayman, famous for his quick eye and prodigious voice, lifts up the cry, "S-t-e-a-m-boat a-comin'!" and the scene changes! The town drunkard stirs, the clerks wake up, a furious clatter of drays follows, every house and store pours out a human contribution, and all in a twinkling the dead town is alive and moving. Drays, carts, men, boys, all go hurrying from many quarters to a common center, the wharf. Assembled there, the people fasten their eyes upon the coming boat as upon a wonder they are seeing for the first time. And the boat *is* rather a handsome sight, too. She is long and sharp and trim and pretty; she has two tall, fancy-topped chimneys, with a gilded device of some kind swung between them; a fanciful pilot house, all glass and "gingerbread," perched on top of the "texas" deck[2] behind them; the paddle boxes are gorgeous with a picture or with gilded rays above the boat's name; the boiler deck, the hurricane deck, and the texas deck are fenced and ornamented with clean white railings; there is a flag gallantly flying from the jack staff; the furnace doors are open and the fires glaring

[1] KEOKUK—Keokuk, Iowa, sixty miles above Hannibal on the Mississippi.

[2] "TEXAS" DECK—The *texas* was a structure on the upper or hurricane deck of a steamer, containing the officers' cabins, with the pilot house in front or on top.

bravely; the upper decks are black with passengers; the captain stands by the big bell, calm, imposing, the envy of all; great volumes of the blackest smoke are rolling and tumbling out of the chimneys—a husbanded grandeur created with a bit of pitch pine just before arriving at a town; the crew are grouped on the forecastle; the broad stage³ is run far out over the port bow, and an envied deck hand stands picturesquely on the end of it with a coil of rope in his hand; the pent steam is screaming through the gauge cocks; the captain lifts his hand, a bell rings, the wheels stop; then they turn back, churning the water to foam, and the steamer is at rest. Then such a scramble as there is to get aboard, and to get ashore, and to take in freight and to discharge freight, all at one and the same time; and such a yelling and cursing as the mates facilitate it all with! Ten minutes later the

³ BROAD STAGE—The landing stage, or gangplank.

steamer is under way again, with no flag on the jack staff and no black smoke issuing from the chimneys. After ten more minutes the town is dead again, and the town drunkard asleep by the skids once more.

My father was a justice of the peace, and I supposed he possessed the power of life and death over all men, and could hang anybody that offended him. This was distinction enough for me as a general thing; but the desire to be a steamboatman kept intruding, nevertheless. I first wanted to be a cabin boy, so that I could come out with a white apron on and shake a tablecloth over the side, where all my old comrades could see me; later I thought I would rather be the deck hand who stood on the end of the stage plank with the coil of rope in his hand, because he was particularly conspicuous. But these were only daydreams—they were too heavenly to be contemplated as real possibilities.

By and by one of our boys went away.

He was not heard of for a long time. At last he turned up as apprentice engineer or "striker" on a steamboat. This thing shook the bottom out of all my Sunday school teachings. That boy had been notoriously worldly, and I just the reverse; yet he was exalted to this eminence, and I left in obscurity and misery. There was nothing generous about this fellow in his greatness. He would always manage to have a rusty bolt to scrub while his boat tarried at our town, and he would sit on the inside guard and scrub it, where we all could see him and envy him and loathe him. And whenever his boat was laid up he would come home and swell around the town in his blackest and greasiest clothes, so that nobody could help remembering that he was a steamboatman; and he used all sorts of steamboat technicalities in his talk, as if he were so used to them that he forgot common people could not understand them. He would speak of the "labboard" side of a horse in an easy, natural way that would make one wish he was dead. And he was always talking about "St. Looy" like an old citizen; he would refer casually to occasions when he was "coming down Fourth Street," or when he was "passing by the Planter's House," or when there was a fire and he took a turn on the brakes of "the old Big Missouri"; and then he would go on and lie about how many towns the size of ours were burned down there that day. Two or three of the boys had long been persons of consideration among us because they had been to St. Louis once and had a vague general knowledge of its wonders, but the day of their glory was over now. They lapsed into a humble silence, and learned to disappear when the ruthless "cub" engineer approached. This fellow had money, too, and hair oil. Also an ignorant silver watch and a showy brass watch chain. He wore a leather belt and used no suspenders. If ever a youth was cordially admired and hated by his comrades, this one was. No girl could withstand his charms. He "cut out" every boy in the village. When his boat blew up at last, it diffused a tranquil contentment among us such as we had not known for months. But when he came home the next week, alive, renowned, and appeared in church all battered up and bandaged, a shining hero, stared at and wondered over by everybody, it seemed to us that the partiality of Providence for an undeserving reptile had reached a point where it was open to criticism.

This creature's career could produce but one result, and it speedily followed. Boy after boy managed to get on the river. The minister's son became an engineer. The doctor's and the postmaster's sons became "mud clerks"; the wholesale liquor dealer's son became a barkeeper on a boat; four sons of the chief merchant, and two sons of the county judge, became pilots. Pilot was the grandest position of all. The pilot, even in those days of trivial wages, had a princely salary—from a hundred and fifty to two hundred and fifty dollars a month, and no board to pay. Two months of his wages would pay a preacher's salary for a year. Now some of us were left disconsolate. We could not get on the river—at least our parents would not let us.

So, by and by, I ran away. I said I would never come home again till I was a pilot and could come in glory. But somehow I could not manage it. I went meekly aboard a few of the boats that lay packed together like sardines at the long St. Louis wharf, and humbly inquired for the pilots, but got only a cold shoulder and short words from mates and clerks. I had to make the best of this sort of treatment for the time being, but I had comforting daydreams of a future when I should be a great and honored pilot, with plenty of money, and could kill some of these mates and clerks and pay for them.

### I TAKE A FEW EXTRA LESSONS

During the two or two and a half years of my apprenticeship I served under many pilots, and had experience of many kinds of steamboatmen and many varieties of steamboats; for it was not always convenient for Mr. Bixby [1] to have me with him, and in such cases he sent me with somebody else. I am to this day profiting somewhat by that experience; for in that brief, sharp schooling, I got personally and familiarly acquainted with about all the different types of human nature that are to be found in fiction, biography, or history. The fact is daily borne in upon me that the average shore employment requires as much as forty years to equip a man with this sort of an education. When I say I am still profiting by this thing, I do not mean that it has constituted me a judge of men—no, it has not done that, for judges of men are born, not made. My profit is various in kind and degree, but the feature of it which I value most is the zest which that early experience has given to my later reading. When I find a well-drawn character in fiction or biography I generally take a warm personal interest in him, for the reason that I have known him before—met him on the river.

The figure that comes before me oftenest, out of the shadows of that vanished time, is that of Brown, of the steamer *Pennsylvania*. He was a middle-aged, long, slim, bony, smooth-shaven, horse-faced, ignorant, stingy, malicious, snarling, fault-hunting, mote-magnifying tyrant. I early got the habit of coming on watch with dread at my heart. No matter how good a time I might have been having with the off-watch below, and no matter how high my spirits might be when I started aloft, my soul became lead in my body the moment I approached the pilot house.

I still remember the first time I ever entered the presence of that man. The boat had backed out from St. Louis and was "straightening down." I ascended to the pilot house in high feather, and very proud to be semi-officially a member of the executive family of so fast and famous a boat. Brown was at the wheel. I paused in the middle of the room, all fixed to make my bow, but Brown did not look around. I thought he took a furtive glance at me out of the corner of his eye, but as not even this notice was repeated, I judged I had been mistaken. By this time he was picking his way among some dangerous "breaks" abreast the woodyards; therefore it would not be proper to interrupt him; so I stepped softly to the high bench and took a seat.

There was silence for ten minutes; then my new boss turned and inspected me deliberately and painstakingly from head to heel for about—as it seemed to me—a quarter of an hour. After which he removed his countenance and I saw it no more for some seconds; then it came around once more, and this question greeted me:

"Are you Horace Bixby's cub?"

"Yes, sir."

After this there was a pause and another inspection. Then:

"What's your name?"

[1] MR. BIXBY—Horace Bixby, the pilot who has taken Samuel as a cub and who is teaching him to be a pilot.

I told him. He repeated it after me. It was probably the only thing he ever forgot; for although I was with him many months he never addressed himself to me in any other way than "Here!" and then his command followed.

"Where was you born?"

"In Florida, Missouri."

A pause. Then:

"Dern sight better stayed there!"

By means of a dozen or so pretty direct questions, he pumped my family history out of me.

The leads were going now in the first crossing. This interrupted the inquest. When the leads had been laid in he resumed:

"How long you been on the river?"

I told him. After a pause:

"Where'd you get them shoes?"

I gave him the information.

"Hold up your foot!"

I did so. He stepped back, examined the shoe minutely and contemptuously, scratching his head thoughtfully, tilting his high sugar-loaf hat well forward to facilitate the operation, then ejaculated, "Well, I'll be dod derned!" and returned to his wheel.

What occasion there was to be dod derned about it is a thing which is still as much of a mystery to me now as it was then. It must have been all of fifteen minutes—fifteen minutes of dull, homesick silence—before that long horse-face swung around upon me again —and then what a change! It was as red as fire, and every muscle in it was working. Now came this shriek:

"Here! You going to set there all day?"

I lit in the middle of the floor, shot there by the electric suddenness of the surprise. As soon as I could get my voice I said apologetically: "I have had no orders, sir."

"You've had no *orders!* My, what a fine bird we are! We must have *orders!* Our father was a *gentleman*—owned slaves—and *we've* been to *school.* Yes, *we* are a gentleman, *too,* and got to have *orders!* Orders, is it? ORDERS is what you want! Dod dern my skin, *I'll* learn you to swell yourself up and blow around *here* about your dod-derned *orders!* G'way from the wheel!" (I had approached it without knowing it.)

I moved back a step or two and stood as in a dream, all my senses stupefied by this frantic assault.

"What you standing there for? Take that ice-pitcher down to the texas-tender! Come, move along, and don't you be all day about it!"

The moment I got back to the pilot house Brown said:

"Here! What was you doing down there all this time?"

"I couldn't find the texas-tender; I had to go all the way to the pantry."

"Derned likely story! Fill up the stove."

I proceeded to do so. He watched me like a cat. Presently he shouted:

"Put down that shovel! Derndest numskull I ever saw—ain't even got sense enough to load up a stove."

All through the watch this sort of thing went on. Yes, and the subsequent watches were much like it during a stretch of months. As I have said, I soon got the habit of coming on duty with dread. The moment I was in the presence, even in the darkest night, I could feel those yellow eyes upon me, and knew their owner was watching for a pretext to spit out some venom on me. Preliminarily he would say:

"Here! Take the wheel."

Two minutes later:

"*Where* in the nation you going to? Pull her down! Pull her down!"

After another moment:

"Say! You going to hold her all day? Let her go—meet her! meet her!"

Then he would jump from the bench, snatch the wheel from me, and meet her himself, pouring out wrath upon me all the time.

George Ritchie was the other pilot's cub. He was having good times now; for his boss, George Ealer, was as kind-hearted as Brown wasn't. Ritchie had steered for Brown the season before; consequently, he knew exactly how to entertain himself and plague me, all by the one operation. Whenever I took the wheel for a moment on Ealer's watch, Ritchie would sit back on the bench and play Brown, with continual ejaculations of "Snatch her! Snatch her! Derndest mud-cat I ever saw!" "Here! Where are you going *now?* Going to run over that snag?" "Pull her *down!* Don't you hear me? Pull her *down!*" "There she goes! *Just* as I expected! I *told* you not to cramp that reef. G'way from the wheel!"

So I always had a rough time of it, no matter whose watch it was; and sometimes it seemed to me that Ritchie's good-natured badgering was pretty nearly as aggravating as Brown's dead-earnest nagging.

I often wanted to kill Brown, but this would not answer. A cub had to take everything his boss gave, in the way of vigorous comment and criticism; and we all believed that there was a United States law making it a penitentiary offense to strike or threaten a pilot who was on duty. However, I could *imagine* myself killing Brown; there was no law against that; and that was the thing I used always to do the moment I was abed. Instead of going over my river in my mind, as was my duty, I threw business aside for pleasure, and killed Brown.

I killed Brown every night for months; not in old, stale, commonplace ways, but in new and picturesque ones— ways that were sometimes surprising for freshness of design and ghastliness of situation and environment.

Brown was *always* watching for a pretext to find fault; and if he could find no plausible pretext, he would invent one. He would scold you for shaving a shore, and for not shaving it; for hugging a bar, and for not hugging it; for "pulling down" when not invited, and for *not* "pulling down" when not invited; for firing up without orders, and for waiting *for* orders. In a word, it was his invariable rule to find fault with *everything* you did; and another invariable rule of his was to throw all his remarks to you into the form of an insult.

One day we were approaching New Madrid, bound down and heavily laden. Brown was at one side of the wheel, steering; I was at the other, standing by to "pull down" or "shove up." He cast a furtive glance at me every now and then. I had long ago learned what that meant; viz., he was trying to invent a trap for me. I wondered what shape it was going to take. By and by he stepped back from the wheel and said in his usual snarly way:

"Here! See if you've got gumption enough to round her to."

This was simply *bound* to be a success; nothing could prevent it; for he had never allowed me to round the boat to before; consequently, no matter how I might do the thing, he could find free fault with it. He stood back there with his greedy eye on me, and the result was what might have been foreseen: I lost my head in a quarter of a minute, and didn't know what I was about; I started too early to bring the boat around, but detected a green gleam of joy in Brown's eye, and corrected my mistake. I started around once more while too high up, but corrected myself again in time. I made other false moves, and still managed to save myself; but at last I grew so confused and anxious that I tumbled into the very worst blunder of all—I got too far *down* before beginning to fetch the boat around. Brown's chance was come.

His face turned red with passion; he made one bound, hurled me across the house with a sweep of his arm, spun the wheel down, and began to pour out a stream of vituperation upon me which lasted till he was out of breath. In the course of this speech he called me all the different kinds of hard names he could think of, and once or twice I thought he was even going to swear— but he had never done that, and he didn't this time. "Dod dern" was the

nearest he ventured to the luxury of swearing, for he had been brought up with a wholesome respect for future fire and brimstone.

That was an uncomfortable hour; for there was a big audience on the hurricane deck. When I went to bed that night, I killed Brown in seventeen different ways—all of them new.

### BROWN AND I EXCHANGE COMPLIMENTS

Two trips later I got into serious trouble. Brown was steering; I was "pulling down." My younger brother appeared on the hurricane deck, and shouted to Brown to stop at some landing or other, a mile or so below. Brown gave no intimation that he had heard anything. But that was his way: he never condescended to take notice of an under-clerk. The wind was blowing; Brown was deaf (although he always pretended he wasn't), and I very much doubted if he had heard the order. If I had had two heads, I would have spoken; but as I had only one, it seemed judicious to take care of it; so I kept still.

Presently, sure enough, we went sailing by that plantation. Captain Kline-felter appeared on the deck, and said:

"Let her come around, sir, let her come around. Didn't Henry tell you to land here?"

"No, sir!"

"I sent him up to do it."

"He *did* come up; and that's all the good it done, the dod-derned fool. He never said anything."

"Didn't *you* hear him?" asked the captain of me.

Of course I didn't want to be mixed up in this business, but there was no way to avoid it; so I said:

"Yes, sir."

I knew what Brown's next remark would be, before he uttered it. It was:

"Shut your mouth! You never heard anything of the kind."

I closed my mouth, according to instructions. An hour later Henry entered the pilot house, unaware of what had been going on. He was a thoroughly inoffensive boy, and I was sorry to see him come, for I knew Brown would have no pity on him. Brown began, straightway:

"Here! Why didn't you tell me we'd got to land at that plantation?"

"I did tell you, Mr. Brown."

"It's a lie!"

I said:

"You lie, yourself. He did tell you."

Brown glared at me in unaffected surprise; and for as much as a moment he was entirely speechless; then he shouted to me:

"I'll attend to your case in a half a minute!" then to Henry, "And you leave the pilot house; out with you!"

It was a pilot law, and must be obeyed. The boy started out, and even had his foot on the upper step outside the door, when Brown, with a sudden access of fury, picked up a ten-pound lump of coal and sprang after him; but I was between, with a heavy stool, and I hit Brown a good honest blow which stretched him out.

I had committed the crime of crimes—I had lifted my hand against a pilot on duty! I supposed I was booked for the penitentiary sure, and couldn't be booked any surer if I went on and squared my long account with this person while I had the chance; consequently I stuck to him and pounded him with my fists a considerable time. I do not know how long, the pleasure of it probably made it seem longer than it really was; but in the end he struggled free and jumped up and sprang to the wheel: a very natural solicitude, for, all

this time, here was this steamboat tearing down the river at the rate of fifteen miles an hour and nobody at the helm! However, Eagle Bend was two miles wide at this bank-full stage, and correspondingly long and deep: and the boat was steering herself straight down the middle and taking no chances. Still, that was only luck—a body *might* have found her charging into the woods.

Perceiving at a glance that the *Pennsylvania* was in no danger, Brown gathered up the big spyglass, war-club fashion, and ordered me out of the pilot house with more than Comanche bluster. But I was not afraid of him now; so, instead of going, I tarried, and criticized his grammar. I reformed his ferocious speeches for him, and put them into good English, calling his attention to the advantage of pure English over the bastard dialect of the Pennsylvania collieries whence he was extracted. He could have done his part to admiration in a cross-fire of mere vituperation, of course; but he was not equipped for this species of controversy; so he presently laid aside his glass and took the wheel, muttering and shaking his head; and I retired to the bench. The racket had brought everybody to the hurricane deck, and I trembled when I saw the old captain looking up from amid the crowd. I said to myself, "Now I *am* done for!" for although, as a rule, he was so fatherly and indulgent toward the boat's family, and so patient of minor shortcomings, he could be stern enough when the fault was worth it.

I tried to imagine what he *would* do to a cub pilot who had been guilty of such a crime as mine, committed on a boat guard-deep with costly freight and alive with passengers. Our watch was nearly ended. I thought I would go and hide somewhere till I got a chance to slide ashore. So I slipped out of the pilot house, and down the steps, and around to the texas-door, and was in the act of gliding within, when the captain confronted me! I dropped my head, and he stood over me in silence a moment or two, then said impressively:

"Follow me."

I dropped into his wake; he led the way to his parlor in the forward end of the texas. We were alone, now. He closed the after door; then moved slowly to the forward one and closed that. He sat down; I stood before him. He looked at me some little time, then said:

"So you have been fighting Mr. Brown?"

I answered meekly:

"Yes, sir."

"Do you know that that is a very serious matter?"

"Yes, sir."

"Are you aware that this boat was plowing down the river fully five minutes with no one at the wheel?"

"Yes, sir."

"Did you strike him first?"

"Yes, sir."

"What with?"

"A stool, sir."

"Hard?"

"Middling, sir."

"Did it knock him down?"

"He—he fell, sir."

"Did you follow it up? Did you do anything further?"

"Yes, sir."

"What did you do?"

"Pounded him, sir."

"Pounded him?"

"Yes, sir."

"Did you pound him much? That is, severely?"

"One might call it that, sir, maybe."

"I'm deuced glad of it! Hark ye, never mention that I said that. You have been guilty of a great crime; and don't you ever be guilty of it again, on this boat. But—lay for him ashore! Give him a good sound thrashing, do you hear? I'll pay the expenses. Now go—and mind you, not a word of this to anybody. Clear out with you! You've been guilty of a great crime, you whelp!"

I slid out, happy with the sense of a close shave and a mighty deliverance; and I heard him laughing to himself and slapping his fat thighs after I had closed his door.

When Brown came off watch he went straight to the captain, who was talking with some passengers on the boiler deck, and demanded that I be put ashore in New Orleans—and added:

"I'll never turn a wheel on this boat again while that cub stays."

The captain said:

"But he needn't come round when you are on watch, Mr. Brown."

"I won't even stay on the same boat with him. One of us has got to go ashore."

"Very well," said captain, "let it be yourself," and resumed his talk with the passengers.

During the brief remainder of the trip I knew how an emancipated slave feels, for I was an emancipated slave myself.

### A SECTION IN MY BIOGRAPHY

In due course I got my license. I was a pilot now, full-fledged. I dropped into casual employments; no misfortunes resulting, intermittent work gave place to steady and protracted engagements. Time drifted smoothly and prosperously on, and I supposed—and hoped—that I was going to follow the river the rest of my days, and die at the wheel when my mission was ended. But by and by the war came, commerce was suspended, my occupation was gone.

I had to seek another livelihood. So I became a silver-miner in Nevada; next, a newspaper reporter; next, a gold-miner in California; next, a reporter in San Francisco; next, a special correspondent in the Sandwich Islands,[2] next, a roving correspondent in Europe and the East; next, an instructional torchbearer on the lecture platform; and, finally, I became a scribbler of books, and an immovable fixture among the other rocks of New England.

In so few words have I disposed of the twenty-one slow-drifting years that have come and gone since I last looked from the windows of a pilot house.

[2] SANDWICH ISLANDS—Hawaiian Islands.

## FOR DISCUSSION

1. Enumerate the various colorful characters whom Mark Twain describes in "Scenes on the Mississippi."

2. Mark Twain referred to his experience on the Mississippi as his "high school education." Give several reasons why he considered this experience so important.

3. Why do you think the Captain was so lenient with young Clemens after his fracas with Brown?

4. Mark Twain is noted as one of America's greatest humorists. Cite four or five humorous passages from "Scenes on the Mississippi."

5. Is Mark Twain serious when he speaks of the twenty-one "slow-drifting" years after he quit the river?

## WORDS TO EXPLAIN

1. The black smoke rolling from the river steamer is called "husbanded grandeur." What is the meaning of *husbanded*? Is there any connection between *husbanded* and *husbandman*? Explain.

2. Brown is said to be "mote-magnifying." What is a *mote*?

3. Brown watched "for a pretext to spit out some venom" on his cub pilot. What is *venom*? What does the connotation of *venom* imply about the character of Brown?

## PROJECTS

1. Make a dictionary of nautical terms found in "Scenes on the Mississippi."

2. Draw a map of the Mississippi River, indicating the many riverports along her course.

## RELATED READING

You will want to read the entire book, *Life on the Mississippi*, by Mark Twain. You will find all of it as entertaining as the passage given in this book.

# DÉSIRÉE'S BABY

*KATE CHOPIN*

*The consequences of a prejudice can often be more tragic than most of us realize. The tragic elements of this story are intensified by the dramatic irony that results from the husband's prejudice.*

As the day was pleasant, Madame Valmondé drove over to L'Abri to see Désirée and the baby.

It made her laugh to think of Désirée with a baby. Why, it seemed but yesterday that Désirée was little more than a baby herself; when Monsieur in riding through the gateway of Valmondé had found her lying asleep in the shadow of the big stone pillar.

The little one awoke in his arms and began to cry for "Dada." That was as much as she could do or say. Some people thought she might have strayed there of her own accord, for she was of the toddling age. The prevailing belief was that she had been purposely left by a party of Texans, whose canvas-covered wagon, late in the day, had crossed the ferry that Coton Maïs kept, just below the plantation. In time Madame Valmondé abandoned every speculation but the one that Désirée had been sent to her by a beneficent Providence to be the child of her affection, seeing that she was without child of the flesh. For the girl grew to be beautiful and gentle, affectionate and sincere—the idol of Valmondé.

It was no wonder, when she stood one day against the stone pillar in whose shadow she had lain asleep, eighteen years before, that Armand Aubigny, riding by and seeing her there, had fallen in love with her. That was the way all the Aubignys fell in love, as if struck by a pistol shot. The wonder was that he had not loved her before; for he had known her since his father brought him home from Paris, a boy of eight, after his mother died there. The passion that awoke in him that day, when he saw her at the gate, swept along like an avalanche, or like a prairie fire, or like anything that drives headlong over all obstacles.

Monsieur Valmondé grew practical and wanted things well considered: that is, the girl's obscure origin. Armand looked into her eyes and did not care. He was reminded that she was nameless. What did it matter about a name when he could give her one of the oldest and proudest in Louisiana? He ordered the *corbeille*[1] from Paris, and contained himself with what patience he could until it arrived; then they were married.

Madame Valmondé had not seen Désirée and the baby for four weeks. When she reached L'Abri she shuddered at the first sight of it, as she always did. It was a sad looking place, which for many years had not known the gentle presence of a mistress, old Monsieur

[1] *Corbeille*—French for a basket; here, wedding presents.

Aubigny having married and buried his wife in France, and she having loved her own land too well ever to leave it. The roof came down steep and black like a cowl, reaching out beyond the wide galleries that enclosed the yellow stuccoed house. Big, solemn oaks grew close to it, and their thick-leaved, far-reaching branches shadowed it like a pall. Young Aubigny's rule was a strict one, too, and under it his negroes had forgotten how to be gay, as they had been during the old master's easy-going and indulgent lifetime.

The young mother was recovering slowly, and lay full length, in her soft white muslins and laces, upon a couch. The baby was beside her, upon her arm, where he had fallen asleep, at her breast. The yellow nurse woman sat beside a window fanning herself.

Madame Valmondé bent her portly figure over Désirée and kissed her, holding her an instant tenderly in her arms. Then she turned to the child.

"This is not the baby!" she exclaimed, in startled tones. French was the language spoken at Valmondé in those days.

"I knew you would be astonished," laughed Désirée, "at the way he has grown. The little *cochon de lait!* [2] Look at his legs, Mamma, and his hands and finger-nails—real finger-nails. Zandrine had to cut them this morning. Isn't it true, Zandrine?"

The woman bowed her turbaned head majestically, "*Mais si, Madame.*" [3]

"And the way he cries," went on Désirée, "is deafening. Armand heard him the other day as far away as La Blanche's cabin."

Madame Valmondé had never removed her eyes from the child. She

[2] *Cochon de lait*—French, a suckling pig.
[3] "*Mais si*"—French—"Yes, indeed."

lifted it and walked with it over to the window that was lightest. She scanned the baby narrowly, then looked as searchingly at Zandrine, whose face was turned to gaze across the fields.

"Yes, the child has grown, has changed," said Madame Valmondé, slowly, as she replaced it beside its mother. "What does Armand say?"

Désirée's face became suffused with a glow that was happiness itself.

"Oh, Armand is the proudest father in the parish, I believe, chiefly because it is a boy, to bear his name; though he says not—that he would have loved a girl as well. But I know it isn't true. I know he says that to please me. And Mamma," she added, drawing Madame Valmondé's head down to her, and speaking in a whisper, "he hasn't punished one of them—not one of them—since baby is born. Even Négrillon, who pretended to have burnt his leg that he might rest from work—he only laughed, and said Négrillon was a great scamp. Oh, Mamma, I'm so happy; it frightens me."

What Désirée said was true. Marriage, and later the birth of his son, had softened Armand Aubigny's imperious and exacting nature greatly. This was what made the gentle Désirée so happy, for she loved him desperately. When he frowned she trembled, but loved him. When he smiled, she asked no greater blessing of God. But Armand's dark, handsome face had not often been disfigured by frowns since the day he fell in love with her.

When the baby was about three months old, Désirée awoke one day to the conviction that there was something in the air menacing her peace. It was at first too subtle to grasp. It had only been a disquieting suggestion; an air of mystery among the blacks; unexpected visits from far-off neighbors who could hardly account for their coming. Then a strange, an awful change in her husband's manner, which she dared not ask him to explain. When he spoke to her, it was with averted eyes, from which the old love-light seemed to have gone out. He absented himself from home; and when there, avoided her presence and that of her child, without excuse. And the very spirit of Satan seemed suddenly to take hold of him in his dealings with the slaves. Désirée was miserable enough to die.

She sat in her room, one hot afternoon, in her *peignoir*,[4] listlessly drawing through her fingers the strands of her long, silky brown hair that hung about her shoulders. The baby, half naked, lay asleep upon her own great mahogany bed, that was like a sumptuous throne, with its satin-lined half-canopy. One of La Blanche's little *quadroon*[5] boys— half naked too—stood fanning the child slowly with a fan of peacock feathers. Désirée's eyes had been fixed absently and sadly upon the baby, while she was striving to penetrate the threatening mist that she felt closing about her. She looked from her child to the boy who stood beside him, and back again; over and over. "Ah!" It was a cry that she could not help; which she was not conscious of having uttered. The blood turned like ice in her veins, and a clammy moisture gathered upon her face.

She tried to speak to the little quadroon boy; but no sound would come at first. When he heard his name uttered, he looked up, and his mistress was pointing to the door. He laid aside the great, soft fan, and obediently stole away, over

the polished floor, on his bare tiptoes.

She stayed motionless, with gaze riveted upon her child, and her face the picture of fright.

Presently her husband entered the room, and without noticing her, went to a table and began to search among some papers which covered it.

"Armand," she called to him, in a voice which must have stabbed him, if he was human. But he did not notice. "Armand," she said again. Then she rose and tottered towards him. "Armand," she panted once more, clutching his arm, "look at our child. What does it mean? Tell me."

He coldly but gently loosened her fingers from about his arm and thrust the hand away from him. "Tell me what it means!" she cried despairingly.

"It means," he answered lightly, "that the child is not white; it means that you are not white."

A quick conception of all that this accusation meant for her nerved her with unwonted courage to deny it. "It is a lie; it is not true, I am white! Look at my hair, it is brown; and my eyes are gray, Armand, you know they are gray. And my skin is fair," seizing his wrist. "Look at my hand; whiter than yours, Armand," she laughed hysterically.

"As white as La Blanche's," he returned cruelly; and went away leaving her alone with her child.

When she could hold a pen in her hand, she sent a despairing letter to Madame Valmondé.

"My mother, they tell me I am not white. Armand has told me I am not white. For God's sake tell them it is not true. You must know it is not true. I shall die. I must die. I cannot be so unhappy, and live."

The answer came was brief:

"My own Désirée: Come home to Valmondé; back to your mother who loves you. Come with your child.

When the letter reached Désirée she went with it to her husband's study, and laid it upon the desk before which he sat. She was like a stone image: silent, white, motionless after she placed it there.

In silence he ran his cold eyes over the written words. He said nothing. "Shall I go, Armand?" she asked in tones sharp with agonized suspense.

"Yes, go."

"Do you want me to go?"

"Yes, I want you to go."

He thought Almighty God had dealt cruelly and unjustly with him; and felt, somehow, that he was paying Him back in kind when he stabbed thus into his wife's soul. Moreover he no longer loved her, because of the unconscious injury she had brought upon his home and his name.

She turned away like one stunned by a blow, and walked slowly towards the door, hoping he would call her back.

"Good-by, Armand," she moaned.

He did not answer her. That was his last blow at fate.

Désirée went in search of her child. Zandrine was pacing the somber gallery with it. She took the little one from the nurse's arms with no word of explanation and descending the steps, walked away, under the live-oak branches.

It was an October afternoon; the sun was just sinking. Out in the still fields the negroes were picking cotton.

Désirée had not changed the thin white garment nor the slippers which she wore. Her hair was uncovered and the sun's rays brought a golden gleam from its brown meshes. She did not take the broad, beaten road which led to the far-off plantation of Valmondé. She walked across a deserted field, where the stubble bruised her tender feet, so delicately shod, and tore her thin gown to shreds.

She disappeared among the reeds and willows that grew thick along the banks of the deep, sluggish bayou; and she did not come back again.

Some weeks later there was a curious scene enacted at L'Abri. In the center of the smoothly swept back yard was a

great bonfire. Armand Aubigny sat in the wide hallway that commanded a view of the spectacle; and it was he who dealt out to a half dozen negroes the material which kept this fire ablaze.

A graceful cradle of willow, with all its dainty furbishings, was laid upon the pyre, which had already been fed with the richness of a priceless *layette*.[6] Then there were silk gowns, and velvet and satin ones added to these; laces, too, and embroideries; bonnets and gloves; for the corbeille had been of rare quality.

The last thing to go was a tiny bundle of letters; innocent little scribblings that Désirée had sent to him during the days of their espousal. There was the remnant of one back in the drawer from which he took them. But it was not Désirée's; it was part of an old letter from his mother to his father. He read it. She was thanking God for the blessing of her husband's love:

"But, above all," she wrote, "night and day, I thank the good God for having so arranged our lives that our dear Armand will never know that his mother, who adores him, belongs to the race that is cursed with the brand of slavery."

[6] *Layette*—A complete outfit for a newborn baby.

✧✧✧✧✧✧✧✧✧✧✧✧✧✧✧✧✧✧✧✧✧✧✧✧✧

## FOR DISCUSSION

1. Why would the following words of Désirée to her husband be considered dramatic irony: "Look at my hand, whiter than yours, Armand"?

2. True love means that a person is willing to sacrifice himself for the happiness of the other rather than to obtain anything for himself. Did Armand love Désirée with a true love? Explain.

3. Marriage is a sacrament and demands certain sacrifices. Did the discovery of the fact that their child was not white remove any of these obligations? How should Armand have treated his wife after this discovery?

4. What do you think happened to Désirée and the baby at the end of the story?

5. What do you think was Armand's reaction when he read his mother's letter?

## WORDS

1. "That was the way all the Aubignys fell in love," says the author, "as if struck by a pistol shot." Can you express that suddenness better?

2. What kind of figure is a "portly figure"?

3. What difference is there between to "scan narrowly," and to "look searchingly," and to "gaze"?

4. What would be the opposite of an "imperious and exacting nature"?

5. What are "averted eyes"?

6. How does "clutching his arm" differ from "seizing his arm"?

7. What kind of courage is "unwonted courage"?

8. Can you find a reason given early in the story why the gallery was somber? From what two Latin words is the word *somber* derived?

## A PROJECT

Consider the story as being incomplete and add your own conclusion.

## RELATED READING

You will enjoy reading "A No-Account Creole" and "Beyond the Bayou" in *Bayou Folk*, by Kate Chopin. Further trustworthy pictures of life in Louisiana are given in a collection of short stories by Grace King entitled *Monsieur Motte*. Some of the best stories about the postwar South may be found in *Rodman the Keeper* by Constance Fenimore Woolson.

# TRANSITION POETRY

The Transition Period saw radical departures in poetry. The age produced two of America's most influential poets, Walt Whitman (1819–1892) and Emily Dickinson (1830–1886). Both were generations ahead of their time. Both are more popular now than they were in their own day.

It is strange to link in any way two persons so different as Walt Whitman and Emily Dickinson. She was as shy as he was aggressive. Her poems are delicate with an exquisite finish. His verses sweep all the ranges from exalted carols to self-styled "barbaric yawps." But in spite of their differences, both poets made popular a new type of verse-writing, direct and clear and powerfully imaginative.

There was nothing subtle about Whitman. Daring to be different, he flung his challenge to a smug world—

> Shut not your doors to me, proud libraries,
> For that which was lacking on all your well-
> filled shelves, yet needed most, I bring.

Into American poetry he brought the glorification of democracy and of the common man. And in this doctrine Emerson was his master. He refused to limit his subject-matter to so-called "poetic themes," and made poetry out of the most commonplace events, anything that pertained to the life of the people. For his new themes, he insisted on a new form of poetry, freed from the restraints of rhyme and meter. Hence, he introduced into American poetry the form that is called "free verse." In all these departures Whitman was variously praised and blamed during his own lifetime. And now after two generations, the world still gives a divided verdict. There are those who think Whitman was a literary trickster—a crude, not even clever egotist. There are others who would call him the first, and probably the best, great American poet. There is some justification for both views. The longest poem in *Leaves of Grass* is the "Song of Myself"—hundreds of lines which swing back and forth between nobility and tawdriness. In one line he touches immortality; in another he crashes into trivial slang.

Whitman had the poet's inborn sense of rhythm. There is a cadence to most of his lines. His poems begin with singing expressions of an imaginative idea; but they not infrequently level off into prose. Seldom did he think it worth while to sustain his poetic phrasing throughout a given passage. In the Lincoln poems and in some of the war poems he kept a uniformly high level of expression. But in more casual verse, he teases us with alternate strips of grandeur and commonplace prose. Sometimes his carelessness allowed him to leave thoughts suspended in unfinished suggestiveness.

In forming an opinion of Whitman, however, we must distinguish between his poetic skill and the doctrine he taught. It will not do to throw his book into the fire, as Whittier did, nor should we endorse his work as wholeheartedly as Emerson did. We can enjoy him for his frequent flights of high poetry, for his appreciation of nature, for his love of the common man. But we must condemn him for his pantheism, for his divinization of man, and for his contempt of the moral law. Whitman is often called "the poet of democracy," but his ideas are, in fact, basically opposed to true ideas of democracy. True democracy, as Bishop Sheen explains in "A Declaration of Dependence," must be based on a true concept of the relations between God and man. Whitman did not have a true idea either of God or of man. He did not admit a personal God, who as Creator has absolute dominion over men. Instead he thought there was no other God than nature, with man as its king. Man himself, he thought, was "part" of God, capable of infinite development if only left to follow his instincts. Thus, for all his talk about liberty, Whitman really advocated lawlessness—a condition which is hostile to democracy or any other form of government.

Whitman's false ideas of God, man, and liberty are only a few of his errors, but they are the fundamental ones. Although many of his lines sound like the most ardent plea for democracy, yet even in these lines Whitman's meaning is vitiated by his basic errors as to the nature of God and the nature of man. Fortunately, many of his ideas did not take hold upon the American people.

The only person to challenge Walt Whitman's position as the commanding poet of the later nineteenth century was a shy little lady in Amherst, Massachusetts—

Emily Dickinson. The one hint of likeness between the works of the two poets lies in a simplicity of style. But where Whitman's lines have a rugged, blatant quality, Miss Dickinson's are delicate and fragile. Her particular gifts were two: an ability to give familiar impressions a startling but delightful freshness of meaning, and an ability to compress mighty thoughts into few words. Her poems are short, often only two four-line stanzas. Her rhythms are easy. The lines are never long. Commonly the second and fourth lines rhyme; but if at any time a rhyme would not come, no matter. And yet, with all their unpretentiousness, these verses are unforgettable poetry. Emily Dickinson had a happy way of using words. She had the precise word for every need. She had a knack for translating to others her fancies. She could express the seemingly inexpressible. And she never squandered words. She used them choicely as a jeweler might his very precious stones.

But there is more to the poetry of Emily Dickinson than charming imagery. She wrote of the deep experiences of life—love, death, renunciation, immortality—and in her apparently effortless way makes them real and understandable. Linked with her impressions of death is her faith in immortality. She pictured heaven definitely, clearly.

She permitted no poems to be published during her life and requested that her manuscripts be burned when she died. But her family considered them too important. In 1890, her niece published the first volume. In the half century that has elapsed, the impression has grown that hers indeed was a genius. More and more, writers are trying to perfect an art like hers—the art of imprisoning great thoughts in slender words.

## MINOR POETS OF THE LATE NINETEENTH CENTURY

There was, of course, no special pattern which marked the works of the other late nineteenth-century poets. Most of them reflected in one way or another the tendency toward an easy style and commonplace subjects. Individual variations depended somewhat upon the locality of the writer. Men of the Far West showed in their verse the same kind of realism that characterized western fiction. Joaquin Miller, for instance, wrote narrative poems about Indians and pioneers. His verse stories have the rollicking gust of the "Wild West."

In the South, poets were more conservative. The emphasis—as is almost always true of Southern verse—was upon melody. John Bannister Tabb wrote exquisite stanzas, short like those of Emily Dickinson and often packed with meaning. He put into his poems a convert's intense appreciation of Catholic truths. Madison Cawein was a gifted Kentuckian whose poems are filled with suggestive imagery. He has something of the style of an impressionistic painter; he creates an atmosphere and does an artistic job of it. He has given us some nature poems that are different; and he has recorded in ballad style wild tales of Kentucky feuds and manhunts. The lazy, languorous rhythm of the South has found happy expression in the works of the Negro poet, Paul Laurence Dunbar. Dunbar's mellow lines mirror the joys and sorrows of the down-South colored folks.

In the Middle West two poets—Eugene Field and James Whitcomb Riley—offered a contrast to the work of the realists. Field was a newspaper poet who wrote especially pleasing child verse. Some of it was the nonsense type, like his "Dinky Bird"; some is whimsical, like the delightful lullaby, "Wynken, Blynken, and Nod." And always he will be remembered for the touching "Little Boy Blue," a heart song from his own experience. James Whitcomb Riley was the beloved poet of Indiana. In melodious stanzas—some of them in small-boy or Hoosier dialect—he wrote his *Rhymes of Childhood Days* and his reminiscences of small-town and country life. Verses like "The Days Gone By" and "The Old Swimmin' Hole" endeared him to young and old alike.

Two other Midwestern poets, Richard Hovey and Bliss Carman, wrote gay rollicking rhymes which they published jointly in the *Vagabondia* volumes. Hovey has expressed their philosophy: It is the mission of the poet "to lay open to the world the heart of man—all its heights and depths, all its glooms and glories, to reveal the beauty in things, and to breathe into his fellows a love of it."

In the East there were many verse-makers, most of them now forgotten except for a single poem here and there. One of the most promising—Stephen Crane—died in 1900; but his brief lyrics have much the style of twentieth-century verse. He liked the freedom of unrhymed verse; and he liked the suggestive and impressionistic rather than the matter-of-fact.

With almost every section of the country writing, with poets experimenting in new styles and subjects, the last decades of the nineteenth century set the stage for the flood of verse that has deluged modern America.

# I Hear America Singing

## WALT WHITMAN

*Wherever life throbbed Whitman found inspiration. In the singing of people at work he heard the voice of America itself.*

I hear America singing, the varied carols I hear;
Those of mechanics—each one singing his, as it should be, blithe and strong;
The carpenter singing his, as he measures his plank or beam,
The mason singing his, as he makes ready for work, or leaves off work;
The boatman singing what belongs to him in his boat—the deckhand singing on
    the steamboat deck;      5
The shoemaker singing as he sits on his bench—the hatter singing as he stands;
The woodcutter's song—the ploughboy's, on his way in the morning, or at the noon
    intermission, or at sundown;
The delicious singing of the mother—or of the young wife at work—or of the girl
    sewing or washing;
Each singing what belongs to him or her, and to none else;
The day what belongs to the day—at night, the party of young fellows, robust,
    friendly,      10
Singing, with open mouths, their strong melodious songs.

## FOR DISCUSSION

1. Look over the workers listed by Whitman in "I hear America Singing." What kinds of occupations are *not* listed? Why not? Are they not *singing* occupations? Or would Whitman not be likely to know about them? Discuss.

2. Do you think people are likely to sing or whistle at their work? Have you heard people sing as they work? Under what conditions?

3. What kind of songs belong to the day? What kind to the night? Do you think Whitman would still find us a singing nation? Discuss.

# Beat! Beat! Drums!

## WALT WHITMAN

*Like an actual call to arms in its strong, insistent rhythm, "Beat! Beat! Drums!" keeps alive the spirit with which the men of 1861 rallied to the colors. As in every war, drums and bugles summon men to action. Ordinary tasks and human emotions must give way to the duty of war.*

Beat! beat! drums!—Blow! bugles! blow!
Through the windows—through doors—burst like a ruthless force,
Into the solemn church, and scatter the congregation;
Into the school where the scholar is studying;
Leave not the bridegroom quiet—no happiness must he have now with his bride;   5
Nor the peaceful farmer any peace, plowing his field or gathering his grain;
So fierce you whirr and pound, you drums—so shrill you bugles blow.

Beat! beat! drums!—Blow! bugles! blow!
Over the traffic of cities—over the rumble of wheels in the streets:
Are beds prepared for sleepers at night in the houses? No sleepers must sleep in
   those beds;   10
No bargainers' bargains by day—no brokers or speculators—would they continue?
Would the talkers be talking? would the singer attempt to sing?
Would the lawyer rise in the court to state his case before the judge?
Then rattle quicker, heavier drums—you bugles wilder blow.

Beat! beat! drums!—Blow! bugles! blow!   15
Make no parley—stop for no expostulation;
Mind not the timid—mind not the weeper or prayer;
Mind not the old man beseeching the young man;
Let not the child's voice be heard, nor the mother's entreaties;
Make even the trestles to shake the dead, where they lie awaiting the hearses,   20
So strong you thump, O terrible drums—so loud you bugles blow.

20. TRESTLES—Braced frames upon which coffins could be placed.

---

FOR DISCUSSION

1. In view of Whitman's love for America, discuss the intense patriotism of this poem.

2. Is the dominant emotion of the poem one of fear or courage? Explain.

3. Show how the sound of the words enforces the emotion of the poem.

4. Point out phrases which give an impression of urgency in answering the call to war.

# O Captain! My Captain!

## WALT WHITMAN

While Whitman was in Washington from 1862 to 1865, he often saw Abraham Lincoln and formed a nodding acquaintance with him. The following poem was his first expression of personal grief at the death of his friend. It is the only poem of Whitman's in which regular meter and rhyme are used throughout.

O Captain! my Captain! our fearful trip is done,
The ship has weather'd every rack, the prize we sought is won,
The port is near, the bells I hear, the people all exulting,
While follow eyes the steady keel, the vessel grim and daring;
  But O heart! heart! heart!            5
    O the bleeding drops of red,
      Where on the deck my Captain lies,
        Fallen cold and dead.

O Captain! my Captain! rise up and hear the bells;
Rise up—for you the flag is flung—for you the bugle trills,   10
For you bouquets and ribbon'd wreaths—for you the shores a-crowding,
For you they call, the swaying mass, their eager faces turning;
  Here Captain! dear father!
    This arm beneath your head!
      It is some dream that on the deck,        15
        You've fallen cold and dead.

My Captain does not answer, his lips are pale and still,
My father does not feel my arm, he has no pulse nor will,
The ship is anchor'd safe and sound, its voyage closed and done,
From fearful trip the victor ship comes in with object won;   20
  Exult, O shores, and ring, O bells!
    But I with mournful tread,
      Walk the deck my Captain lies,
        Fallen cold and dead.

FOR DISCUSSION

1. Explain the metaphor of captain and ship which is sustained throughout the poem. What is the ship? In what sense has Lincoln been the captain of the ship? What was the "fearful trip"? Why are the crowds on shore exulting?

2. Point out lines where Whitman says that for him the joy of victory in the Civil War is overshadowed by sadness at Lincoln's death.

3. Compare this poem with Whitman's later tribute to Lincoln, "When Lilacs Last in the Dooryard Bloomed."

# *A*ssurance

## EMILY DICKINSON

*"Seeing is believing," the skeptical man is inclined to say, never realizing how many things there are that all of us believe—indeed KNOW—to be real whether we have looked at them or not. Emily Dickinson mentions two simple illustrations, and from them takes assurance for a larger faith.*

I never saw a moor,
　I never saw the sea;
Yet know I how the heather looks,
　And what a wave must be.

I never spoke with God,　　　　5
　Nor visited in heaven;
Yet certain am I of the spot
　As if the chart were given.

The poems on the following pages are selected from *The Poems of Emily Dickinson*, edited by Martha Dickinson Bianchi and Alfred Leete Hampson, and are reprinted by permission of Little, Brown & Co. The poems include: "Assurance"; "He Ate and Drank the Precious Words"; "I'm Nobody"; "They Dropped Like Flakes"; " 'Tis an Honorable Thought."

FOR DISCUSSION

1. How could Miss Dickinson know how heather looks if she had never seen it growing? If she had never seen the sea, how could she know what a wave must be? How many people in the United States, would you guess, believe that there are oceans without ever having seen one?

2. Give at least five other examples of facts that people accept or "know," without putting them to individual proof.

3. Why do you think Miss Dickinson feels so sure of God and heaven? Discuss. Are there other spiritual values, besides religious creeds, that men accept on faith? Discuss, giving definite illustrations.

4. Is it a sensible philosophy that says, "I'll believe what I can see with my own eyes, and nothing more"? Discuss.

# He Ate and Drank the Precious Words

## EMILY DICKINSON

*This poem begins as a sort of riddle. How could one "eat and drink" words? You will need to read the entire poem to find out.*

He ate and drank the precious words,
  His spirit grew robust;
He knew no more that he was poor,
  Nor that his frame was dust.

He glanced along the dingy days,     5
  And this bequest of wings
Was but a book. What liberty
  A loosened spirit brings!

❖❖❖❖❖❖❖❖❖❖❖❖❖❖❖❖❖❖❖❖❖❖❖❖❖❖❖❖❖❖❖❖❖❖❖❖❖❖❖❖❖❖❖❖❖❖

FOR DISCUSSION

1. The first line gives a picture of an avid reader. Enumerate the effects of reading mentioned in the poem.
2. What other effects can you add?

3. What is the meaning of line 5?
4. How is a book "a bequest of wings"? What kind of liberty does a "loosened spirit" bring?
5. Point out words which begin with the same letter.

❖❖❖❖❖

# I'm Nobody

## EMILY DICKINSON

*Many famous people take great trouble to avoid the glare of publicity. Emily Dickinson shunned fame all her life. In these lines she tells us why.*

I'm nobody! Who are you?
  Are you nobody too?
Then there's a pair of us—don't tell!
  They'd banish us, you know.

How dreary to be somebody!     5
  How public like a frog
To tell your name the livelong day
  To an admiring bog!

FOR DISCUSSION
1. Discuss the meaning of line 4.
2. Can you give reasons why a poet especially would find it "dreary to be somebody"?
3. Does the author imply that often enough famous people are not extremely brilliant? In what lines? Do you agree? Give instances.
4. Discuss the relation between the thought of the first stanza and that of the second.
5. Explain the meaning of "banish" and "admiring bog."

◇◇◇◇◇

# They Dropped Like Flakes

## EMILY DICKINSON

*The poetry of Emily Dickinson is noted for its deeply religious thought. Here in a few deft images she shows that, although the dead disappear from the earth, they are eternally present to God.*

They dropped like flakes, they dropped
  like stars,
Like petals from a rose,
When suddenly across the June
A wind with fingers goes.

They perish in the seamless grass,— 5
No eye could find the place;
But God on his repealless list
Can summon every face.

FOR DISCUSSION
1. Explain the figure used in lines 2–4. How can a wind have fingers?

2. What is the meaning of line 5? What is meant by God's "repealless list"? Why is the list "repealless"?

# 'Tis an Honorable Thought

## EMILY DICKINSON

*The immortal dignity of man is the theme of the following poem. One does honor to the very thought, in the same way as one honors people when meeting them on the street.*

'Tis an honorable thought,
    And makes one lift one's hat,
As one encountered gentlefolk
    Upon a daily street,

That we've immortal place,     5
    Though pyramids decay,
And kingdoms, like the orchard,
    Flit russetly away.

---

FOR DISCUSSION

1. Man's immortality is contrasted in the poem to two apparently lasting things of earth. What are these two things? Is it true that all earthly things pass away?
2. What conclusions may be drawn as to the value of any earthly glory when compared to man's eternal dignity?

THE POET'S WORDS

What does the word *russetly* in the last line mean? What part of speech is it? From what adjective is it derived?

---

# Fame

## JOHN BANNISTER TABB

*The stars, we are told, shine during the day. But it is only at night that we see their size and brilliance. The judgments of life are also best delayed, as Father Tabb points out.*

Their noonday never knows
    What names immortal are:
'Tis night alone that shows
    How star surpasseth star.

539

FOR DISCUSSION

1. Show how the "noonday" of life obscures the real worth of many great men.

2. Can you name a few great men who were not recognized as such during their lives?

3. On the other hand, are there any great men of today whom you think history will condemn?

4. Compare this poem with Emily Dickinson's "I'm Nobody." Both poems treat the same subject, fame, but each has a different thing to say. Which do you prefer? Why?

◇◇◇◇◇

# *Evolution*

## JOHN BANNISTER TABB

*The poem is a concise description of three striking changes, or in a loose sense, EVOLUTIONS, with which we are familiar. From the evening twilight comes the night; then the dawn. The silence of a cloudy sky is pierced by the song of the lark. Joy of heart is followed by the pain of sorrow. The thought of these familiar changes prepares us for the fourth, which is still to come, the resurrection of the body.*

> Out of the dusk a shadow,
>     Then, a spark;
> Out of the cloud a silence,
>     Then, a lark;
> Out of the heart a rapture,          5
>     Then, a pain;
> Out of the dead, cold ashes,
>     Life again.

FOR DISCUSSION

1. Point out in each of the four pairs of lines the two words which stand in strongest contrast.

2. Can you suggest another appropriate title for the poem?

3. Explain the following words according to their use in the poem: *spark, rapture, ashes*.

# Father Damien

## JOHN BANNISTER TABB

*Father Damien, a Belgian priest, went as a missionary to the Hawaiian Islands in 1864, and in 1873, at his own request, was made resident chaplain to six hundred lepers on the island of Molokai. After twelve years of devoted service he contracted the deadly disease and died three years later.*

> O God, the cleanest offering
> Of tainted earth below,
> Unblushing to Thy feet we bring—
> "A leper white as snow!"

4. *A leper white as snow!*—The quotation is from IV Kings 5:77. Naaman, a Syrian general was cured of leprosy through the prayers of the prophet Eliseus, who would not accept any recompense from Naaman. But his avaricious servant Giezi overtook Naaman and in the name of his master asked for and received money and garments from the Syrian. In punishment for the deceit, "the leprosy of Naaman," Eliseus tells Giezi, "shall also stick to thee, and to thy seed forever. And he went out from him a *leper as white as snow*," white, that is, with the scales of leprosy.

## FOR DISCUSSION

1. In what way is earth "tainted"? What is earth's "cleanest offering"?
2. There are two kinds of evil—physical and moral. What kind of evil is leprosy?
3. What is the meaning of the scriptural verse in line 4, as it is used by Father Tabb?

## A PROJECT

Write a short biography of Father Damien.

# God

## JOHN BANNISTER TABB

> I see Thee in the distant blue;
> But in the violet's dell of dew,
> Behold, I *breathe* and *touch* Thee too.

1. In what sense is it true to say that I see God in the distant blue? Do all men see Him there?

2. Which better suggests the nearness of an object—to see it, or to breathe and touch it?

3. What is meant by "the violet's dell of dew"?

❖❖❖❖❖

# Good Night!

## JOHN BANNISTER TABB

Good night, dear Lord! and now
  Let them that loved to keep
Thy little bed in Bethlehem
  Be near me while I sleep;
For I—more helpless, Lord—of them  5
  Have greater need than Thou.

FOR DISCUSSION

1. How does the rhythm enhance the thought of the poem? Would "Lullaby" be a good title? Why?

2. Compare this poem with "Now I Lay Me Down to Sleep." Which do you like better? Why? Which poem expresses the idea most clearly and forcefully?

❖❖❖❖❖

# Deserted

## MADISON CAWEIN

The old house leans upon a tree
  Like some old man upon a staff:
The night wind in its ancient porch
  Sounds like a hollow laugh.

The heaven is wrapped in flying clouds
  As grandeur cloaks itself in gray:  6
The starlight flitting in and out,
  Glints like a lanthorn ray.

"Deserted" from *The Vale of Tempe* by Madison Cawein, reprinted by permission of E. P. Dutton & Co., Inc.

8. LANTHORN—Lantern.

The dark is full of whispers.  Now
A foxhound howls: and through the
  night,                                    10
Like some old ghost from out its grave,
The moon comes misty white.

◇◇◇◇◇◇◇◇◇◇◇◇◇◇◇◇◇◇◇◇◇◇◇◇◇◇◇◇◇◇◇◇◇◇◇◇◇◇◇◇◇◇◇◇◇◇◇◇◇◇◇◇◇◇◇

FOR DISCUSSION

1. The second stanza gives a clear picture of the sky.  What else does it do for the poem?

2. What is the mood of the entire poem?  Point out details by which the author creates the mood.

3. What besides the house does one *see* in the poem?  What does one *hear* and *feel*?

4. Quote one line in which the idea is suggested by the sound of the words.

5. Interpret the following phrases: "hollow laugh," "grandeur cloaks itself," "the dark is full of whispers."

◇◇◇◇◇

# *When the Frost Is on the Punkin*

## JAMES WHITCOMB RILEY

*Riley was a city-bred lad who wrote poems about country folk.  The following is one of his best-known poems.  In it he views autumn with the exultant feelings of a farmer whose job for the year is done.*

When the frost is on the punkin and the fodder's in the shock,
And you hear the kyouck and gobble of the struttin' turkey-cock,
And the clackin' of the guineys, and the cluckin' of the hens,
And the rooster's hallylooyer as he tiptoes on the fence;
O, it's then's the times a feller is a-feelin' at his best,                5
With the risin' sun to greet him from a night of peaceful rest,
As he leaves the house, bareheaded, and goes out to feed the stock,
When the frost is on the punkin and the fodder's in the shock.

They's something kindo' harty-like about the atmusfere
When the heat of summer's over and the coolin' fall is here—          10
Of course we miss the flowers, and the blossums on the trees,
And the mumble of the hummin'-birds and buzzin' of the bees;
But the air's so appetizin'; and the landscape through the haze
Of a crisp and sunny morning of the airly autumn days

14. AIRLY—Early.

Is a pictur' that no painter has the colorin' to mock—     15
When the frost is on the punkin and the fodder's in the shock.

The husky, rusty russel of the tossels of the corn,
And the raspin' of the tangled leaves, as golden as the morn;
The stubble in the furries—kindo' lonesomelike, but still
A-preachin' sermuns to us of the barns they growed to fill;     20
The strawstack in the medder, and the reaper in the shed;
The hosses in theyr stalls below—the clover overhead!—
O, it sets my hart a-clickin' like the tickin' of a clock,
When the frost is on the punkin and the fodder's in the shock!

Then your apples all is gethered, and the ones a feller keeps     25
Is poured around the celler-floor in red and yeller heaps;
And your cider-makin's over, and your wimmern-folks is through
With their mince and apple-butter, and theyr souse and sausage, too! . . .
I don't know how to tell it—but ef sich a thing could be
As the Angels wantin' boardin', and they'd call around on *me*—     30
I'd want to 'commodate 'em—all the whole-indurin' flock—
When the frost is on the punkin and the fodder's in the shock!

19. FURRIES—Furrows.
21. MEDDER—Meadow.
28. SOUSE—Meat preserved in pickle brine.
31. WHOLE-INDURIN'—Everlasting.

FOR DISCUSSION

1. What signs of autumn are mentioned in the first stanza?
2. What is the meaning of line 15?
3. What sermons could the stubble preach?
4. Is the last stanza a fitting climax for a song of plenty? Do Riley's descriptions and enumerations of various foods give you a visual image?

5. Riley expressed his idea of poetry in the following couplet:

What we want, as I sense it, in the line
O' poetry is sumpn' Yours and Mine.

Show how "When the Frost Is on the Punkin" meets the requirement of these two lines.
6. How does the rhythm give a light, joyous effect to the poem?

◇◇◇◇◇

# A Vagabond Song

## BLISS CARMAN

*The frosty days of autumn in some way affect all of us. For Bliss Carman the season stirred up an insistent wanderlust.*

There is something in the Autumn that
  is native to my blood—
Touch of manner, hint of mood;
And my heart is like a rhyme,
With the yellow and purple and the
  crimson keeping time.

The scarlet of the maples can shake me
  like a cry          5
Of bugles going by.
And my lonely spirit thrills
To see the frosty asters like smoke upon
  the hills.

There is something in October sets the
  gypsy blood astir,
We must rise and follow her,    10
When from every hill of flame
She calls and calls each vagabond by
  name.

◇◇◇◇◇◇◇◇◇◇◇◇◇◇◇◇◇◇◇◇◇◇◇◇◇◇◇◇◇◇◇◇◇◇◇◇◇◇◇◇◇◇◇◇◇◇◇◇◇◇◇◇◇◇

FOR DISCUSSION

1. The first stanza has a catchy rhythm. In which lines is the lively meter most pronounced?
2. Point out lines which appeal to the sense of sight, touch, or hearing.
3. Did you notice the sound of bugles in lines 5 and 6? Explain.

4. Do you think the wanderlust expressed in the poem is more pronounced in October than at other times of the year?
5. Give interpretations for the following phrases: *native to my blood; hint of mood; scarlet of the maples; gypsy blood; hill of flame.*

# Kit Carson's Ride

## JOAQUIN MILLER

Kit Carson, famous trapper and scout, lived a picturesque and romantic life in the West and Southwest. There are many stories of his deeds and daring. While it is not known that the incident related in the poem is based on fact, the scene itself was one of the most spectacular, yet dreaded, sights to occur in the early days of the western frontier.

> Room! room to turn round in, to breathe and be free,
> To grow to be giant, to sail as at sea
> With the speed of the wind on a steed with his mane
> To the wind, without pathway or route or a rein.
> Room! room to be free where the white border'd sea          5
> Blows a kiss to a brother as boundless as he;
> Where the buffalo come like a cloud on the plain,
> Pouring on like the tide of a storm-driven main,
> And the lodge of the hunter to friend or to foe
> Offers rest; and unquestion'd you come or you go.          10
> My plains of America! Seas of wild lands!
> From a land in the seas in a raiment of foam,
> That has reached to a stranger the welcome of home,
> I turn to you, lean to you, lift you my hands.
>
> "Run? Run? See this flank, sir, and I do love him so!          15
> But he's blind, badger blind. Whoa, Pache, boy, whoa,
> No, you wouldn't believe it to look at his eyes,
> But he's blind, badger blind, and it happen'd this wise:
>
> "We lay in the grass and the sunburnt clover
> That spread on the ground like a great brown cover          20
> Northward and southward, and west and away
> To the Brazos, where our lodges lay,
> One broad and unbroken level of brown.
> We were waiting the curtains of night to come down
> To cover us trio and conceal our flight          25
> With my brown bride, won from an Indian town
> That lay in the rear the full ride of a night.

12–13—An allusion to England where Miller was at the time he wrote this poem.
15. FLANK—Side of the horse.
16. BADGER BLIND—The badger, a burrowing animal, sees better at night than in the day-time. Its difficulty in seeing in daylight has given rise to the impression that the badger is blind.
16. PACHE—The name of the horse, probably from the Indian name Apache.
22. BRAZOS—A river in southern Texas.

"Kit Carson's Ride" by Joaquin Miller, reprinted by permission of Miss Juanita Joaquina Miller.

"We lounged in the grass—her eyes were in mine,
And her hands on my knee, and her hair was as wine
In its wealth and its flood, pouring on and all over     30
Her bosom wine red, and press'd never by one.
Her touch was as warm as the tinge of the clover
Burnt brown as it reach'd to the kiss of the sun.
Her words they were low as the lute-throated dove,
And as laden with love as the heart when it beats     35
In its hot, eager answer to earliest love,
Or the bee hurried home by its burthen of sweets.

"We lay low in the grass on the broad plain levels,
Old Revels and I, and my stolen brown bride;
'Forty full miles if a foot, and the devils     40
Of red Comanches are hot on the track
When once they strike it.  Let the sun go down
Soon, very soon,' muttered bearded old Revels
As he peer'd at the sun, lying low on his back,
Holding fast to his lasso.  Then he jerk'd at his steed     45
And he sprang to his feet, and glanced swiftly around,
And then dropp'd, as if shot, with an ear to the ground;
Then again to his feet, and to me, to my bride,
While his eyes were like flame, his face like a shroud,
His form like a king, and his beard like a cloud,     50
And his voice loud and shrill, as both trumpet and reed,—
'Pull, pull in your lassoes, and bridle to steed,
And speed you if ever for life you would speed.
Aye, ride for your lives, for your lives you must ride!
For the plain is aflame, the prairie on fire,     55
And the feet of wild horses hard flying before
I heard like a sea breaking high on the shore,
While the buffalo come like a surge of the sea,
Driven far by the flame, driving fast on the three
As a hurricane comes, crushing palms in his ire.'     60

"We drew in the lassoes, seized the saddle and rein,
Threw them on, cinched them on, cinched them over again
And again drew the girth; and spring we to horse,
With head to Brazos, with a sound in the air
Like the surge of a sea, with a flash in the eye,     65
From that red wall of flame reaching up to the sky;
A red wall of flame and a black rolling sea
Rushing fast upon us, as the wind sweeping free
And afar from the desert blown hollow and hoarse.

39. OLD REVELS—A fellow scout.

"Not a word, not a wail from a lip was let fall,        70
We broke not a whisper, we breathed not a prayer,
There was work to be done, there was death in the air,
And the chance was as one to a thousand for all.
"Twenty miles! . . . thirty miles! . . . a dim distant speck . . .
Then a long reaching line, and the Brazos in sight!      75
And I rose in my seat with a shout of delight.
I stood in my stirrup, and look'd to my right—
But Revels was gone; I glanced by my shoulder
And saw his horse stagger; I saw his head drooping
Hard down on his breast, and his naked breast stooping    80
Low down to the mane, as so swifter and bolder
Ran reaching out for us the red-footed fire.
He rode neck to neck with a buffalo bull,
That made the earth shake where he came in his course,
The monarch of millions, with shaggy mane full      85
Of smoke and of dust, and it shook with desire
Of battle, with rage and with bellowings hoarse.
His keen, crooked horns, through the storm of his mane,
Like black lances lifted and lifted again;
And I looked but this once, for the fire licked through,    90
And Revels was gone, as we rode two and two.

"I look'd to my left then—and nose, neck, and shoulder
Sank slowly, sank surely, till back to my thighs,
And up through the black blowing veil of her hair
Did beam full in mine her two marvelous eyes,      95
With a longing and love yet a look of despair
And of pity for me, as she felt the smoke fold her,
And flames leaping far for her glorious hair.
Her sinking horse falter'd, plunged, fell and was gone
As I reach'd through the flame and I bore her still on.    100
On! into the Brazos, she, Pache, and I—
Poor, burnt, blinded Pache. I love him . . .
That's why."

FOR DISCUSSION

1. Miller wrote "Kit Carson's Ride" while he was in London in 1870. With this fact in mind, comment on the first fourteen lines of the poem.

2. Who is the speaker who tells the story?

3. Why was old Revels anxious for the sun to go down? How did he discover that the prairie was burning?

4. Quote the stanza which intensifies the suspense of the action.

5. What happened to old Revels and his horse? What happened to the bride's horse?

6. Who is the hero of the poem—Carson, his bride, old Revels, or Pache? Give reasons for your answer.

7. Explain the last two lines.

PROJECTS

1. Write a biographical sketch of Kit Carson.

2. Tell the story of the poem as a prose narrative.

◇◇◇◇◇

# The Defense of the Alamo

## JOAQUIN MILLER

*In San Antonio, Texas, stands an American shrine—the Alamo. Built as a mission, it was converted into a fort in 1793. Forty-three years later a small band of Texans were defending it in their fight for independence from Mexico. On February 24, 1836, Colonel William B. Travis, the officer in charge, addressed the following letter "To the People of Texas and all Americans in the world":*

FELLOW CITIZENS AND COMPATRIOTS: I am besieged by a thousand or more of the Mexicans under Santa Anna. I have sustained a continual bombardment and cannonade for twenty-four hours and have not lost a man. The enemy has demanded a surrender at discretion; otherwise the garrison are to be put to the sword if the fort is taken. I have answered the demand with a cannon shot, and our flag still waves proudly from the walls. *I shall never surrender nor retreat.* Then, I call on you in the name of liberty, of patriotism, and everything dear to the American character, to come to our aid with all dispatch. The enemy is receiving reinforcements daily and will no doubt increase to three or four thousand in four or five days. If this call is neglected, I am determined to sustain myself as long as possible and die like a soldier who never forgets what is due to his own honor and that of his country. VICTORY OR DEATH.

"The Defense of the Alamo" by Joaquin Miller, reprinted by permission of Miss Juanita Joaquina Miller.

Help could not reach the little garrison, and on March 6, 1836, Santa Anna stormed the fort. By nightfall every person within its walls had been killed. "Remember the Alamo" became a war-cry for the Texans, typical of the do-or-die attitude of the American soldier.

Santa Anna came storming, as a storm might come;
　　There was rumble of cannon; there was rattle of blade;
There was cavalry, infantry, bugle and drum—
　　Full seven thousand in pomp and parade.
The chivalry, flower of Mexico;　　　　　　　　　　　　　　5
And a gaunt two hundred in the Alamo!

And thirty lay sick, and some were shot through
　　For the siege had been bitter, and bloody, and long.
"Surrender, or die!"—"Men, what will you do?"
　　And Travis, great Travis, drew sword, quick and strong;　10
Drew a line at his feet . . . "Will you come? Will you go?
I die with my wounded, in the Alamo."

Then Bowie gasped, "Lead me over that line!"
　　Then Crockett, one hand to the sick, one hand to his gun,
Crossed with him; then never a word or a sign　　　　　　15
　　Till all, sick or well, all, all save but one,
One man. Then a woman stepped, praying, and slow
Across; to die at her post in the Alamo.

Then that one coward fled, in the night, in that night
　　When all men silently prayed and thought　　　　　　　20
Of home; of tomorrow; of God and the right,
　　Till dawn; and with dawn came Travis's cannon-shot,
In answer to insolent Mexico,
From the old bell-tower of the Alamo.

Then came Santa Anna; a crescent of flame!　　　　　　　25
　　Then the red escalade; then the fight hand to hand;
Such an unequal fight as never had name
　　Since the Persian hordes butchered that doomed Spartan band.
All day—all day and all night; and the morning? so slow,
Through the battle smoke mantling the Alamo.　　　　　　30

10. TRAVIS—Colonel William B. Travis, leader of the Texan forces.
13. BOWIE—Colonel James Bowie, a native of Georgia. The bowie knife was named for him.
14. CROCKETT—David Crockett, scout and woodsman.
28. PERSIAN HORDES . . . SPARTAN BAND—Leonidas, the king of Sparta, with a small band, defended the pass of Thermopylae against Xerxes and the Persian hosts. No Spartans survived.

Now silence! Such silence! Two thousand lay dead
 In a crescent outside! And within? Not a breath
Save the gasp of a woman, with gory gashed head,
 All alone, all alone there, waiting for death;
And she but a nurse. Yet when shall we know     35
Another like this of the Alamo?

Shout "Victory, victory, victory ho!"
 I say 'tis not always to the hosts that win!
I say that the victory, high or low,
 Is given the hero who grapples with sin,      40
Or legion or single; just asking to know
When duty fronts death in his Alamo.

---

## FOR DISCUSSION

1. According to the poet, how many men were defending the Alamo? How many were attacking? Check these figures with a historical account of the seige.

2. Who speaks the first three words of line 9? What was Travis' answer? How many decided to stay with the fort?

3. What was the crescent of flame? What was the escalade? What similarity was there between the defenders of the Alamo and the "doomed Spartan band"?

4. How many Mexicans were slain by the defenders of the fort?

5. In what respect were the defenders of the Alamo victors? Discuss. What do you think the last stanza of the poem means?

6. What other famous defensive stands in history may be compared with that of the Alamo?

7. Explain the following words and phrases: *chivalry; gaunt; insolent; or legion or single; fronts death.*

## PROJECTS

1. Look up a historical account of the defense of the Alamo, and compare it with the account given in the poem.

2. Imagine that you are a war correspondent covering the battle of Thermopylae. Write a vivid account of the one-sided struggle.

# Little Boy Blue

### EUGENE FIELD

*No death is sadder than that of a little child. The poem expresses this sadness in a touching, homelike way.*

The little toy dog is covered with dust,
   But sturdy and staunch he stands;
The little toy soldier is red with rust,
   And his musket molds in his hands.
Time was when the little toy dog was
   new,     5
And the soldier was passing fair;
And that was the time when our Little
   Boy Blue
   Kissed them and put them there.

"Now don't you go till I come," he said,
   "And don't you make any noise!"  10
So, toddling off to his trundle bed,
   He dreamt of the pretty toys;
And, as he was dreaming, an angel
   song
   Awakened our Little Boy Blue—
Oh! the years are many, the years are
   long,    15
   But the little toy friends are true!

Ay, faithful to Little Boy Blue they
   stand,
   Each in the same old place,
Awaiting the touch of a little hand,
   The smile of a little face;  20
And they wonder, as waiting the long
   years through
   In the dust of that little chair,
What has become of our Little Boy
   Blue,
   Since he kissed them and put them
   there.

◇◇◇◇◇◇◇◇◇◇◇◇◇◇◇◇◇◇◇◇◇◇◇◇◇◇◇◇◇◇◇◇◇◇◇◇◇◇◇◇◇◇◇◇◇◇◇◇◇◇◇◇◇◇◇

## FOR DISCUSSION

1. The poet leaves details of the child's appearance to the reader's imagination. Why? Does this increase the appeal of the poem?

2. About how old do you think the little boy was? Point out a line that indicates an answer to the question.

3. How is the parents' love of the child indicated in lines 5 and 6? How is the parents' grief indicated in the poem?

4. What is the meaning of lines 13–14?

# Sympathy

## PAUL LAURENCE DUNBAR

Paul Laurence Dunbar is one of the earliest and finest of our American Negro poets. His work has done much towards winning the appreciation of others for the dignity and sufferings of his race.

I know what the caged bird feels, alas!
When the sun is bright on the upland slopes;
When the wind stirs soft through the springing grass
And the river flows like a stream of glass;
When the first bird sings and the first bud opes,     5
And the faint perfume from its chalice steals—
I know what the caged bird feels!

I know why the caged bird beats his wing
Till its blood is red on the cruel bars;
For he must fly back to his perch and cling     10
When he fain would be on the bough a-swing;
And a pain still throbs in the old, old scars
And they pulse again with a keener sting—
I know why he beats his wing!

I know why the caged bird sings, ah me,     15
When his wing is bruised and his bosom sore,—
When he beats his bars and would be free;
It is not a carol of joy or glee,
But a prayer that he sends from his heart's deep core,
But a plea, that upward to Heaven he flings—     20
I know why the caged bird sings!

11. FAIN—Gladly.

"Sympathy" from *Complete Poems of Paul Laurence Dunbar*, reprinted by permission of Dodd, Mead & Company, Inc.

◇◇◇◇◇◇◇◇◇◇◇◇◇◇◇◇◇◇◇◇◇◇◇◇◇◇◇◇◇◇◇◇◇◇◇◇◇◇◇◇◇◇◇◇◇◇◇◇◇◇◇◇◇◇

## FOR DISCUSSION

1. Point out the details by which the poet brings out the feelings of the caged bird.

2. What lines in the second stanza indicate most clearly the suffering of the bird? Explain how the bird got the scars.

3. What is the meaning of the bird's song?

4. Explain why the poem is entitled "Sympathy." Explain why the poet insists that he knows why the caged bird acts as it does.

# AMERICAN FOLK LITERATURE

No one is surprised that the volume of American folk literature is slender. And the reason is not just that we are a young nation. It is true that folklore—the unstudied, unwritten stories and songs of a people—is usually a slow growth. A ballad that is once sung may be forgotten. It must catch on—be sung and resung, perhaps with additions and variations, if it is to become part of a nation's folklore. The ballads of Scotch and of German literature had been sung for centuries before any one ever thought of writing them down. But we sometimes lose sight of the fact that such tales were transmitted orally because for hundreds of generations most of the people could not write. The scholars were a small group; and their learning was too precious to spend on popular tales. With the spread of education through Europe, folk literature began to die out; and it was not until it was well on the way to being forgotten that literary men "discovered" and began collecting it.

In America conditions have been quite different. Folk literature abroad had already started its decline when Europeans began colonizing the New World. Most of the first colonists were educated people, and they believed in education for others. When bond-slaves and the poorer workers began arriving, they discovered that one of the opportunities they had gained in America was easy access to learning. Almost from the first, we have been a *literate* nation. And as we have seen, folk literature does not flourish among people who can read and write. Instead, then, of deploring the fact that we have so little folk literature, we should feel satisfaction and some pride in the conditions that have made most of our literature a cultured art. Our folk art grew up, usually, in the few situations where America had failed in her purpose of providing educational opportunities for all.

One distinct type of American folk song sprang up among the slaves of the South. When the invention of the cotton gin made slave labor profitable, many sections of the South adopted the policy of discouraging education of the Negroes—some states even passing laws prohibiting it. At the same time, the slaves found in the Christian religion a solace for their lot. The combination of the two forces—the lack of schooling and the passionate acceptance of Christianity—gave rise to a new type of folk literature—the Negro spiritual. The songs were first sung by handfuls of slaves at their prayer meetings, or in the fields where the strong rhythms made the work go faster while the words promised rest some day in "God's Heabum." After the slaves were freed, schools for the Negroes began to spring up. Sometimes the teachers were poor and the learning was indifferent; but the pupils could always sing. White visitors found the music strangely moving. When one of the really good schools—Fisk University—needed money for buildings and equipment, the treasurer conceived the idea of having the pupils sing for the funds. A band of picked musicians was sent north during the winter of 1874. Their program of spirituals proved immensely popular, and the group returned in the spring with forty thousand dollars for the school. That was how the famous Jubilee singers originated. It was also the initiation of a national and international interest in the Negro spiritual. Since that day the spiritual has come to be recognized as the richest and most original native contribution to American art.

The folk song has been found in another "blind-spot" of our educational system —in the poor mountain districts of the Southeast. Certain communities settled by early English colonists had settled down to progress-resistant living. In the nineteenth century they represented the only considerable group of illiterate whites in the country. They were fond of fiddling; and at their gatherings sang in a peculiar dialect long ballads—most of them variations of old English songs sung in the days of Queen Elizabeth. Because of their English origin, such songs are not counted "native" folklore. They are considered, rather, American developments or "variants" of English lore.

The only other literature of the folk type to develop among American white folk has grown up among men who were not always illiterate but who were isolated by their work from centers of civilization for long stretches of time—the cowboys and the lumberjacks. The cowboy, doing much of his range riding alone, would take a banjo or guitar with him for company. Before the campfire, he would twang the strings and sing himself to sleepiness with ditties, either mournful or profane. At the round-ups and rodeos the cowman exchanged songs and added fresh improvisations to old favorites. And so there has grown up a considerable stock of cowboy songs. Most of them are of the ballad type, though there is an occasional lyric among them. Radio broadcasting has helped to popularize both the words and the music of the folk song peculiar to our western plains.

The lumberjack practiced no solitary profession. His work threw him into close seasonal contact with scores of others like himself—great brawny men, usually both rough and tough. They were not a singing lot. But they did like to tell stories, the taller the better. In the shanties of the lumber camps, Paul Bunyan was born. His exploits and those of Babe, the big blue ox, were told in camps from one end of the North to the other. When oil was discovered in the Southwest, Paul was borrowed to enliven the camps, sometimes in his own name, sometimes in the name of "Pecos Bill." Bill's derivation from Paul is unmistakable. This distinction the lumbermen may claim—they have given to America her only enduring folk prose and her favorite mythical hero. Paul Bunyan is symbolic of the American notion that whatever we attempt, the bigger—the better!

## NEGRO FOLK SONGS

There are two kinds of negro folk songs—the sacred and the secular. The sacred songs, or *spirituals*, have been based on Biblical themes. The refrain may be a reference to an Old Testament story, such as "The old ark's a mover-in'" or "Go Down, Moses." It may be a "halleluja" or "jubilee" chorus. It may be a prayer, or a plaint, or a warning. Heaven is a favorite subject. Sometimes mixed with the familiar Biblical references are apparently trivial details from contemporary life. We must find explanation for them in the childlike mind of the slave. Whatever was denied him here became one of the joys awaiting him in Heaven; and so we find references to "golden slippers" and "walking canes" mingled with wings and robes. Any contrivance that seemed new or wonderful might become a symbol to the Negro. In some of the spirituals a railway train replaced the scriptural chariot as a means of carrying one from this world to the next. "Swing Low, Sweet Chariot" would be sung by one group, while another sang, "Little Black Train Is A-Comin'." But although the Negro borrowed his ideas and images from Christianity as he saw it in American dress, the music for the spirituals had the rhythms, harmonies, and undertones of Africa. It is the distinctive combination of words plus music that makes the spiritual a peculiar development in American art.

The secular folk songs include the work songs and the "blues" songs. Often the spirituals were sung as work songs; but there were other verses sung to the rhythm of plantation or levee work—verses that had no hint of the religious in their lines. They were songs that gave a swinging lift to the work of driving stakes or using picks and hammers. The "blues" songs might bewail the misfortunes of love or the plain misery of living. These secular songs have been taken over freely by white composers. They first appeared as "ragtime," then as "jazz" and "swing." They have been a dominant note in the popular music of the nation for thirty years.

# Go Down, Moses

## A SPIRITUAL

*"Go Down, Moses" outwardly speaks of the Israelites in bondage to Pharaoh, but the bondage of the Israelites is obviously parallel to the slavery of the Negroes.  A good number of the spirituals have as their theme this desire of the Negro to be freed from the yoke of slavery as well as from the yoke of sin.  They are spontaneous outcries, born of the hardships and trials of an enslaved race.  Notice the sincerity of emotion in "Go Down, Moses."  It comes from the heart of the Negro people.*

Go down, Moses,
  Way down in Egyptland;
Tell old Pharaoh,
  Let my people go.

When Israel was in Egyptland,    5
  Let my people go;
Oppressed so hard they could not stand,
  Let my people go.

Go down, Moses,
  Way down in Egyptland;    10
Tell old Pharaoh,
  "Let my people go."

"Thus saith the Lord," bold Moses said,
  "Let my people go;
If not I'll smite your first-born dead,    15
  Let my people go.

"No more shall they in bondage toil,
  Let my people go;
Let them come out with Egypt's spoil,
  Let my people go."    20

The Lord told Moses what to do,
  Let my people go;
To lead the children of Israel through,
  Let my people go.

Go down, Moses,    25
  Way down in Egyptland;
Tell old Pharaoh,
  "Let my people go!"

---

FOR DISCUSSION

1. Do you think there is an accurate parallel between the Israelites in bondage and the Negro slaves?  Explain fully the reasons for your answers.

2. Why do you think there is so much repetition in spirituals?  Remember that spirituals are folk songs to be sung by groups at work or play or in church.

3. Tell about the Biblical incident alluded to in line 15.  See Exodus, Chapter 12.

4. Do you feel sympathy for the Negro slaves as you read "Go Down, Moses"?  Explain.

## PROJECTS

1. If a member of the class has some recordings of Negro spirituals, let him arrange a short program to be presented in class.

2. Recite or sing other Negro spirituals which you happen to know. There are a number of white spirituals you may know, too.

## RELATED READING

*Songs of the Sable Harmonists*, by Stephen Foster. These are well-known songs about Negroes; they may be considered as imitation folk songs.

*The Book of American Negro Spirituals* and *The Second Book of Negro Spirituals*, edited by James Weldon Johnson.

❖❖❖❖❖

# *Little Black Train Is A-Comin'*

## A SPIRITUAL

God tole Hezykiyah
In a message from on high:
Go set yo' house in ordah,
For thou shalt sholy die.
He turned to the wall an' a-weepin',     5
Oh!  See the king in tears;
He got his bus'ness fixed all right,
God spared him fifteen years.

*Little black train is a-comin',*
*Get all yo' bus'ness right;*     10
*Go set yo' house in ordah,*
*For the train may be here tonight.*

Go tell that ballroom lady,
All filled with worldly pride,

That little black train is a-comin',     15
Prepare to take a ride.
That little black train and engine
An' a little baggage car,
With idle thoughts and wicked deeds,
Must stop at the judgment bar.     20

There was a po' young man in darkness,
Cared not for the gospel light,
Suddenly a whistle blew
From a little black train in sight.
"Oh, death, will you not spare me?     25
I'm just in my wicked plight.
Have mercy Lord, do hear me,
Pray come an' set me right."
But death had fixed his shackles
About his soul so tight,     30
Just befo' he got his bus'ness fixed,
The train rolled in that night.

1. HEZYKIYAH—Hezekiah, a strong and righteous king of Judah at the time of the prophet Isaiah.  The incident referred to in the first stanza is told in IV Kings 20:1–7.

◇◇◇◇◇◇◇◇◇◇◇◇◇◇◇◇◇◇◇◇◇◇◇◇◇◇◇◇◇◇◇◇◇◇◇◇◇◇◇◇◇◇◇◇◇◇◇◇◇◇◇◇◇◇◇◇◇

## FOR DISCUSSION

1. Relate the incident about Hezekiah as it is given in the Fourth Book of Kings.  Does this incident imply that anyone who sets his house in order will have fifteen years added to his life?

2. Explain the meaning of the "baggage car" in line 18.

# He Never Said a Mumbaling Word

## A SPIRITUAL

Oh, dey whupped him up de hill, up de hill, up de hill,
Oh, dey whupped him up de hill, and he never said a mumbaling word,
Oh, dey whupped him up de hill, and he never said a mumbaling word,
He jes' hung down his head, and he cried.

Oh, dey crowned him wid a thorny crown, thorny crown, thorny crown,    5
Oh, dey crowned him wid a thorny crown, and he never said a mumbaling word,
Oh, dey crowned him wid a thorny crown, and he never said a mumbaling word,
He jes' hung down his head, and he cried.

Well, dey nailed him to de cross, to de cross, to de cross,
Well, dey nailed him to de cross, and he never said a mumbaling word,    10
Well, dey nailed him to de cross, and he never said a mumbaling word,
He jes' hung down his head, and he cried.

Well, dey pierced him in de side, in de side, in de side,
Well, dey pierced him in de side, and de blood come a-twinkling down,
Well, dey pierced him in de side, and de blood come a-twinkling down,    15
Den he hung down his head, and he died.

---

FOR DISCUSSION

1. Point out in each stanza the two ideas which are contrasted.

2. From your knowledge of folk literature, explain why there is so much repetition in the poem.

3. Why did the Passion of Christ appeal so strongly to the Negro slaves?

# I Wish I Had Someone to Call My Own

## A BLUES SONG

I wish I had someone to call my own;
I wish I had someone to take my care.

I'm tired of coffee, an' I'm tired of tea
I'm tired of you, an' you're tired of me.

I'm tired of livin' an' I don't want to
  die;                5
I'm tired of workin' but I can't fly.

I'm so tired of livin' I don't know what
  to do;
You're tired of me, an' I'm tired of you.

I'm tired of eatin' an' I'm tired of
  sleepin':

I'm tired of yore beatin' an' I'm tired of
  yore creepin'.          10

I'm so tired of livin' I don't know what
  to do;
I'm so tired of givin' an' I've done done
  my do.

I've done done my do, an' I can't do
  no mo';
I've got no money an' I've got no hoe.

I'm so tired of livin' I don't know what
  to do;          15
You're tired of me, an' I'm tired of you.

---

FOR DISCUSSION

1. What are the chief differences between the *blues* song and the spiritual? Are there any points of resemblance? Explain.

2. Why was the blues song popular among the Negro slaves?

# It Sound Like Thunder

## A WORK SONG

I'm a man tall like a mountain,
I'm a man steddy like a fountain;
Folks all wonder what makes it thunder
When dey hear, Lawd, my hammer fall.

CHORUS

An' hit sound like thunder,    5
Lawd, hit sound like thunder
When my hammer fall.

Did yo' read it in de paper
'Bout de gov'nor an' his family?
Dey am 'cided to come to de new road
Jes' to hear, Lawd, my hammer fall.   11

Boss got money—mo' den de government
Come to town ridin' a chariot,
Drivin' forty big fine race horses
Jes' to hear, Lawd, my hammer fall.   15

FOR DISCUSSION

1. If a man sang this song while wielding a sledge hammer, what words of the song do you think would coincide with the blows of the hammer?

2. Explain the use of the word *Lawd* in the song. Do you think it is an invocation or merely an interjection?

# John Henry

## A WORK SONG

The story of John Henry is to the Negroes what the story of Paul Bunyan is to the lumbermen of the north woods. It matters little whether or not John Henry was a historical character. In song and story his mighty strength and heroic feats have been exaggerated to a point where he is now more legendary than historical. He has grown into one of the giants of American folk literature, and his story is an interesting bit of Americana.

When John Henry was a little fellow,
   You could hold him in the palm of your hand,
He said to his pa, "When I grow up

I'm gonna be a steel-driving man.
   Gonna be a steel-driving man."   5

4. STEEL-DRIVING MAN—A man who hammers the steel drill which cuts into the rock and stone.

"John Henry" from *John Henry: Tracking Down a Negro Legend* by Guy B. Johnson, reprinted by permission of Mr. Johnson and the University of North Carolina Press.

When John Henry was a little baby,
  Setting on his mammy's knee,
He said "The Big Bend Tunnel on the
    C. & O. Road
  Is gonna be the death of me,
    Gonna be the death of me."   10

One day his captain told him,
  How he had bet a man
That John Henry would beat his steam
    drill down,
  Cause John Henry was the best in the
    land,
    John Henry was the best in the
    land.   15

John Henry kissed his hammer,
  White man turned on steam,
Shaker held John Henry's trusty steel,
  Was the biggest race the world had
    ever seen,
    Lord, biggest race the world ever
    seen.   20

John Henry on the right side,
  The steam drill on the left,
"Before I'll let your steam drill beat me
    down,
  I'll hammer my fool self to death,
    Hammer my fool self to death."   25

Captain heard a mighty rumbling,
  Said "the mountain must be caving
    in,"
John Henry said to the Captain,
  "It's my hammer swinging in de wind,
    My hammer swinging in de wind."

John Henry said to his shaker,   31
  "Shaker, you'd better pray;
For if ever I miss this piece of steel,

8. THE BIG BEND TUNNEL ON THE C. & O.
ROAD—The Big Bend Tunnel, constructed by
hand labor, is on the Chesapeake and Ohio
Railroad in southern West Virginia.
18. SHAKER—The man who held the drill,
or steel, which John hammered.

Tomorrow'll be your burial day,
  Tomorrow'll be your burial day."   35

John Henry said to his captain,
  "Before I ever leave town,
Gimme a twelve-pound hammer wid a
    whale-bone handle,
  And I'll hammer dat steam driver
    down,
    I'll hammer dat steam drill on
    down."   40

John Henry said to his captain,
  "A man ain't nothin' but a man,
But before I'll let dat steam drill beat
    me down   43
  I'll die wid my hammer in my hand,
    Die wid my hammer in my hand."

The man that invented the steam drill
  He thought he was mighty fine,
John Henry drove down fourteen feet,
  While the steam drill only made nine,
    Steam drill only made nine.   50

"Oh, lookaway over yonder, captain,
  You can't see like me,"
He gave a long and loud and lonesome
    cry,
  "Lawd, a hammer be the death of me,
    A hammer be the death of me!"   55

John Henry hammering on the moun-
    tain
  As the whistle blew for half-past two,
The last words his captain heard him
    say,
  "I've done hammered my insides in
    two,
    Lawd, I've hammered my insides in
    two."   60

The hammer that John Henry swung
  It weighed over twelve pound,
He broke a rib in his left hand side
  And his intrels fell on the ground,
    And his intrels fell on the ground.

John Henry, O, John Henry,    66
  His blood is running red,
Fell right down with his hammer to the
    ground
  Said, "I beat him to the bottom but
    I'm dead,
    Lawd, beat him to the bottom but
    I'm dead."    70

When John Henry was laying there dy-
    ing,
  The people all by his side,
The very last words they heard him say,
  "Give me a cool drink of water 'fore
    I die,
    Cool drink of water 'fore I die."  75

John Henry had a little woman,
  The dress she wore was red,
She went down the track, and she never
    looked back,
  Going where her man fell dead,    79
    Going where her man fell dead.

They carried him down by the river,
  And buried him in the sand,
And everybody that passed that way,
  Said, "There lies that steel-driving
    man,
    There lies a steel-driving man."  85

They took John Henry to the river,
  And buried him in the sand,
And every locomotive come a-roaring
    by,
  Says, "There lies that steel-drivin'
    man,
    Lawd, there lies a steel-drivin'
    man."    90

Some say he came from Georgia,
  And some from Alabam,
But its wrote on the rock at the Big
    Bend Tunnel,    93
  That he was an East Virginia man,
    Lord, Lord, an East Virginia man.

FOR DISCUSSION

1. The story of John Henry may not be historically true. Nevertheless, what truth is brought out by the story? In other words, what is the point of the story?

2. What qualities of John Henry have made him so appealing to Negroes? How are these qualities similar to those which have made Paul Bunyan a folk hero?

3. What emotion is aroused by the ballad—pity, admiration, sympathy? Explain your answer.

## Cowboy Ballads

During the two decades that followed the Civil War, cattle raising was at its height in the Southwest. Stock on the open ranges had to be cared for through the winter, rounded up in the spring, branded, and herded. Many of the animals had to be driven long distances to market. Fort Dodge, Kansas, was the center for shipping the cattle, and this loading station was far north of Texas, up the famous Chisholm Trail. The cowboys enlivened the long drives with their songs. Many a ballad was made on the Trail. Even the cattle, it is said, liked the songs. Cowmen claimed that their "dogie" music kept the animals quiet and helped to prevent stampedes.

The songs sprang up spontaneously, authorship unknown. Often a group of men would get together on words and music. New stanzas were added to fit old songs, or fresh words concocted to suit a familiar tune. Sometimes the words tell a story, usually plaintive. Sometimes there is some sentimental philosophizing; sometimes a grist of advice. And of course there were songs that were funny. Their verses were careless, free as the prairie winds.

It was John A. Lomax of Dallas, Texas, who recognized in the cowboy song a new phase of American folk art. He accordingly made a study of the ballads, collecting them and preparing them for publication. In 1910 he issued his anthology, *Cowboy Songs and Other Frontier Ballads*. Since that time there have developed a great liking for cowboy music and a genuine interest in the ballads themselves.

❖❖❖❖❖

# The Cowboy's Dream

### A COWBOY BALLAD

*"The Cowboy's Dream" is like a revival hymn in cowboy language. It is based on one figure, significant to every range-rider—the branding of cattle. Because there were no fences on the great cattle plains, the animals were branded for identification. When round-up time came, the cattle were roped and divided according to their brand markings.*

Last night as I lay on the prairie,  
And looked at the stars in the sky,  
I wondered if ever a cowboy  
Would drift to that sweet by and by.

Chorus: *Roll on, roll on;* 5
*Roll on, little dogies, roll on,*
*roll on,*
*Roll on, roll on;*
*Roll on, little dogies, roll on.*

The road to that bright, happy region
Is a dim, narrow trail, so they say; 10
But the broad one that leads to perdition
Is posted and blazed all the way.

They say there will be a great round-up,
And cowboys, like dogies, will stand,
To be marked by the Riders of Judgment 15
Who are posted and know every brand.

I know there's many a stray cowboy
Who'll be lost at the great, final sale,
When he might have gone in the green pastures 19
Had he known of the dim, narrow trail.

I wonder if ever a cowboy
Stood ready for that Judgment Day,
And could say to the Boss of the Riders,
"I'm ready, come drive me away."

6. DOGIES—A dogie is a motherless calf in a range herd.

For they, like the cows that are locoed,
Stampede at the sight of a hand, 26
Are dragged with a rope to the round-up,
Or get marked with some crooked man's brand.

And I'm scared that I'll be a stray yearling,—
A maverick, unbranded on high,— 30
And get cut in the bunch with the "rusties"
When the Boss of the Riders goes by.

For they tell of another big owner
Whose ne'er overstocked, so they say,
But who always makes room for the sinner 35
Who drifts from the straight, narrow way.

They say he will never forget you,
That he knows every action and look;
So, for safety, you'd better get branded,
Have your name in the great Tally Book. 40

25. LOCOED—Poisoned with locoweed which maddened cattle.
30. MAVERICK—An unbranded animal, especially a motherless calf, usually claimed by the first one to brand it.
31. RUSTIES—Stubborn, rebellious calves or cattle.

FOR DISCUSSION

1. How would the life of a cowboy naturally give rise to the thoughts expressed in the first two stanzas of "The Cowboy's Dream"?
2. What is the meaning of the words "posted" and "blazed" in line 12?
3. Explain the cowboy's comparison of Judgment Day to a cattle round-up, stanzas 3–9.
4. What does the cowboy mean when he says, "For safety, you'd better *get branded*, have your name in the *great Tally Book*"?

## *Paul Bunyan*

The Paul Bunyan tales are usually told in straight prose, lumberjack style. But in his volume, *The People, Yes*, Carl Sandburg has not only reproduced some of the best Bunyan yarns, but has also accounted for their origin. We shall therefore let Mr. Sandburg provide both introduction and tales for Paul Bunyan of the North.

John Lee Brooks of Southern Methodist College in Texas, an authority on folklore of the Southwest, has collected stories of the exploits of Paul Bunyan in the oil fields. To show the great range of the American giant, we include a selection by Mr. Brooks.

⬥⬥⬥⬥⬥

# PAUL BUNYAN OF THE NORTH WOODS

### CARL SANDBURG

Who made Paul Bunyan, who gave him birth as a myth, who joked him into life as the Master Lumberjack, who fashioned him forth as an apparition easing the hours of men amid axes and trees, saws and lumber? The people, the bookless people, they made Paul and had him alive long before he got into the books for those who read. He grew up in shanties, around the hot stoves of winter, among socks and mittens drying, in the smell of tobacco smoke and the roar of laughter mocking the outside weather. And some of Paul came overseas in wooden bunks below decks in sailing vessels. And some of Paul is old as the hills, young as the alphabet.

The Pacific Ocean froze over in the winter of the Blue Snow and Paul Bunyan had long teams of oxen hauling regular white snow over from China. This was the winter Paul gave a party to the Seven Axmen. Paul fixed a granite floor sunk two hundred feet deep for them to dance on. And because the Seven Axmen refused to take off their hobnailed boots, the sparks from the nails of their dancing feet lit up the place so that Paul didn't light the kerosene lamps. No women being on the Big Onion river at that time the Seven Axmen had to dance with each other, the one left over in each set taking Paul as a partner. The commotion of the dancing that night brought on an earthquake and the Big Onion river moved over three counties to the east.

One year when it rained from St. Patrick's Day till the Fourth of July, Paul Bunyan got disgusted because his celebration on the Fourth was spoiled. He dived into Lake Superior and swam to where a solid pillar of water was coming down. He dived under this pillar, swam up into it and climbed with powerful swimming strokes, was gone about an hour, came splashing down, and as rain stopped, he explained, "I turned the dam thing off." This is told in the Big North Woods and on the Great Lakes, with many particulars.

Two mosquitoes lighted on one of Paul Bunyan's oxen, killed it, ate it, cleaned the bones, and sat on a grub shanty picking their teeth as Paul came along. Paul sent to Australia for two special bumble bees to kill these mosquitoes. But the bees and the mosquitoes intermarried; their children had stingers on both ends. And things kept getting worse till Paul brought a big boatload of sorghum up from Louisiana and while all the bee-mosquitoes were eating at the sweet sorghum he floated them down to the Gulf of Mexico. They got so fat that it was easy to drown them all between New Orleans and Galveston.

Paul logged on the Little Gimlet in Oregon one winter. The cook stove at that camp covered an acre of ground. They fastened the side of a hog on each snowshoe and four men used to skate on the griddle while the cook flipped the pancakes. The eating table was three miles long; elevators carried the cakes to the ends of the table where boys on bicycles rode back and forth on a path down the center of the table dropping the cakes where called for.

Benny, the Little Blue Ox of Paul Bunyan, grew two feet every time Paul looked at him, when a youngster. The barn was gone one morning and they found it on Benny's back; he grew out of it in a night. One night he kept pawing and bellowing for more pancakes, till there were two hundred men at the cook shanty stove trying to keep him fed. About breakfast time Benny broke loose, tore down the cook shanty, ate all the pancakes piled up for the loggers' breakfast. And after that Benny made his mistake; he ate the red hot stove; and that finished him. This is only one of the hot stove stories told in the North Woods.

⬦⬦⬦⬦⬦⬦⬦⬦⬦⬦⬦⬦⬦⬦⬦⬦⬦⬦⬦⬦⬦⬦⬦⬦⬦

## FOR DISCUSSION

1. To whom does Mr. Sandburg refer as "the bookless people"?

2. In what respects are the Paul Bunyan stories typical of American humor?

3. What part of Paul is "old as the hills"? How *young* is the alphabet?

4. What other exploits have you heard about Paul or his blue ox? Tell some.

⬦⬦⬦⬦⬦

# PAUL BUNYAN OF THE SOUTHWEST

### *JOHN LEE BROOKS*

Paul Bunyan, though not by any means "America's only folk-hero," is easily our most versatile. In addition to his logging, he has muscled in on other trades. He appears among the tank-builders, erecting a tank so high that a hammer dropped off the top wore out two handles before it hit the ground. Among the old-style truckers he is noted for his skill in being able to wield a forty-foot blacksnake whip out of a covered wagon. The telegraph construction men speak with great pride of his building the Mason and Dixon line and of his working so fast that his ground crew had to shoot him

"Paul Bunyan of the Southwest' by John Lee Brooks, reprinted by his permission and that of *The Saturday Review*.

the insulators out of a machine gun.

I have told elsewhere (*vide* Texas Folk-Lore Society Publication VII) how Paul came south to the oil fields and soon became a phenomenal driller and operator. He developed new methods such as rolling up the drill stem on a huge drum, and he invented new tools and equipment, giving them appropriate names like "headache post," "bull-wheel," and "calf-wheel," and "lazy-bench." Everything he did, in fact, was super-colossal!

Paul Bunyan at work was something! His rig and gears were so big that, although he lived twelve miles from the lease, he rode to the job by hopping on the rocker-arm of a pump as it went back and forth. His drilling engine had

568

a fly-wheel that took thirty days to make one revolution. The drill-stem, which was flexible, was so heavy that the engine required twenty-four gears to handle it. The derrick was appropriately large: the derrickman went up to his post as a bridegroom and was a grandfather before he came down. His meals were shot up to him out of an anti-aircraft gun. The rotary table was so wide that the backup man had a tent right on it; if he hadn't he could never have got back on time to set the slips. On one occasion Paul determined to break his record for height. He built the structure up, up, up until it became so tall that he and his crew moved to heaven and lived there while they finished their work. Paul decided to drill a well worthy of his derrick. He reached China and stopped.

When Paul attempted other types of work, he was equally terrific. The pipeliners, the roughest crew to be found in the oil fields, tell of Paul's big camp for which he laid a pipeline to furnish buttermilk for his men. According to them, his tongs were so heavy that it took four ordinary men to lift them. One day when he was setting up the joints on the twenty-four-inch buttermilk line to the camp, he absent-mindedly turned over the pump

stations for a hundred miles before he realized that the joints were tight. Work like this hardly brought the sweat, but, if the day was hot, he might wipe the perspiration off his brow with one of Barnum and Bailey's old circus tents, which was the only thing he could find adequate for a handkerchief. If he got hungry, the café manager had practically a government contract! He kept a whole batch of meal-tickets for Paul, and instead of punching them he simply tacked them on the wall and shot them with a shotgun.

These various manifestations of Paul Bunyan evidence his virility and show he is thoroughly and typically native. To American laborers in many fields, he's the super-hero—adaptable, aggressive, unstoppable, the champion at all weights.

◇◇◇◇◇◇◇◇◇◇◇◇◇◇◇◇◇◇◇◇◇◇◇◇◇◇◇◇◇

## FOR DISCUSSION

1. What does Mr. Brooks mean when he calls Paul Bunyan our most "versatile" folk hero? What examples does he give to prove his point?

2. With what sentence does Mr. Brooks sum up Paul's achievements?

3. Relate some of Paul's most spectacular feats in the oil fields.

# Further Readings in Literature of the Transition Period

## THE NOVEL

ALCOTT, LOUISA M., *Little Women*
ALLEN, JAMES LANE, *The Kentucky Cardinal*
CABLE, GEORGE WASHINGTON, *The Grandissimes*
CLEMENS, SAMUEL LANGHORNE (MARK TWAIN), *The Adventures of Huckleberry Finn; Tom Sawyer*
\* CRAWFORD, FRANCIS MARION, *Saracinesca; Don Orsino*
DAVIS, RICHARD HARDING, *Soldiers of Fortune*
EGGLESTON, EDWARD, *The Hoosier Schoolmaster*
FORD, PAUL LEICESTER, *The Honorable Peter Sterling*
FREDERIC, HAROLD, *The Damnation of Theron Ware*
HALE, EDWARD EVERETT, *The Man without a Country*
\* HARLAND, HENRY, *The Cardinal's Snuffbox*
HOWELLS, WILLIAM DEAN, *The Rise of Silas Lapham*
JACKSON, HELEN HUNT, *Ramona*
JAMES, HENRY, *The American*
MITCHELL, S. WEIR, *Hugh Wynne, Free Quaker*
SMITH, FRANCIS HOPKINSON, *Colonel Carter of Cartersville*
THOMPSON, MAURICE, *Alice of Old Vincennes*
WALLACE, LEW, *Ben Hur*
WESTCOTT, EDWARD NOYES, *David Harum, A Story of American Life*
WISTER, OWEN, *The Virginian*

## THE SHORT STORY

ALDRICH, THOMAS BAILEY, *Marjorie Daw and Other People*
BIERCE, AMBROSE, *In the Midst of Life*
BROWN, ALICE, *Meadow Grass*
BUNNER, HENRY CUYLER, *Short Sixes*
CABLE, GEORGE WASHINGTON, *Old Creole Days*
\* CHOPIN, KATE, *Bayou Folks*
CLEMENS, SAMUEL LANGHORNE (MARK TWAIN), *The Celebrated Jumping Frog of Calaveras County and Other Sketches*
COOKE, ROSE TERRY, *Somebody's Neighbors*
DAVIS, REBECCA HARDING, *Silhouettes of American Life*
FREEMAN, MARY E. WILKINS, *A New England Nun and Other Stories*
FRENCH, ALICE (OCTAVE THANET), *Stories of a Western Town*
GARLAND, HAMLIN, *Main-Traveled Roads*
\* HARRIS, JOEL CHANDLER, *Nights with Uncle Remus*
HARTE, FRANCIS BRET, *The Luck of Roaring Camp and Other Sketches*
JEWETT, SARAH ORNE, *A White Heron and Other Stories*
KING, GRACE, *Monsieur Motte*
MURFREE, MARY N. (CHARLES EGBERT CRADDOCK), *In the Tennessee Mountains*
PAGE, THOMAS NELSON, *In Ole Virginia; Marse Chan, and Other Stories*
STOCKTON, FRANK R., *The Lady or the Tiger? and Other Stories*
WOOLSON, CONSTANCE F., *Castle Nowhere; Lake-Country Sketches*

## BIOGRAPHY

CLEMENS, SAMUEL LANGHORNE (MARK TWAIN), *Autobiography*
GARLAND, HAMLIN, *A Son of the Middle Border*
GRANT, ULYSSES S., *Personal Memoirs*

HOWELLS, WILLIAM DEAN, *My Mark Twain*

JEFFERSON, JOSEPH, *Autobiography*

RIIS, JACOB, *The Making of an American*

## THE ESSAY

BURROUGHS, JOHN, *Wake-Robin; Locusts and Wild Honey*

\* DUNNE, FINLEY PETER, *Mr. Dooley in Peace and War*

HEARN, LAFCADIO, *Glimpses of Unfamiliar Japan; Chita of Last Island*

\* SPALDING, JOHN LANCASTER, *Means and Ends of Education*

\* STODDARD, CHARLES WARREN, *The Lepers of Molokai*

WARNER, CHARLES DUDLEY, *Backlog Studies; Being a Boy*

## POETRY

CARMAN, BLISS, and HOVEY, RICHARD, *Songs from Vagabondia*

CAWEIN, MADISON, *The Republic, a Little Book of Homespun Verse*

CRANE, STEPHEN, *War Is Kind*

DICKINSON, EMILY, *Poems of Emily Dickinson; Bolts of Melody*

DUNBAR, PAUL LAURENCE, *Lyrics of Lowly Life*

FIELD, EUGENE, *Little Book of Western Verse*

MILLER, JOAQUIN, *Songs of the Desert*

\* RYAN, ABRAM J., *Father Ryan's Poems*

RILEY, JAMES WHITCOMB, *The Hoosier Book of Riley Verse*

SILL, EDWARD ROWLAND, *The Hermitage and Other Poems*

\* TABB, JOHN BANNISTER, *The Poetry of Father Tabb*

WHITMAN, WALT, *Leaves of Grass*

## AMERICAN FOLK LITERATURE

BOTKIN, B. A. (ed.), *A Treasury of American Folklore*

BROWN, STERLING A., DAVIS, ARTHUR P., and LEE, ULYSSES (eds.), *The Negro Caravan*

DOBIE, J. FRANK (ed.), *Texas and Southwestern Lore*

DORSON, RICHARD M. (ed), *Davy Crockett, American Comic Legend*

GONZALES, AMBROSE E., *With Aesop Along the Black Border*

HURSTON, ZORA NEALE, *Mules and Men*

JOHNSON, GUY B., *Folk Culture on St. Helena Island, South Carolina*

LARKIN, MARGARET (ed.), *Singing Cowboy*

LOMAX, JOHN A., and LOMAX, ALAN (eds.), *Cowboy Songs and Other Frontier Ballads; American Ballads and Folk Songs*

SANDBURG, CARL, *American Song Bag*

TALLEY, THOMAS W., *Negro Folk Rhymes*

FROM M-G-M'S PRODUCTION OF THE RED BADGE OF COURAGE

# THE RED BADGE OF COURAGE

STEPHEN CRANE

Attempting an evaluation of the modern American novel is largely a case of not seeing the woods for the trees. In the midst of the forest, the critic is much more conscious of the contrasting qualities of various authors than of the similarities or the over-all pattern. Certain authors and their works stand out like redwoods, but the shape and outline of the whole trend is hard to establish. However, open to the general view are certain characteristics of the modern novel in America. Stephen Crane, in the RED BADGE OF COURAGE, set a style which has become commonplace in American literature. His work, first published in 1894, was considerably ahead of his time in this respect. He set the tone, established a literary approach, and blazed a trail which others have followed. In studying the RED BADGE, the reader will find a prototype and an exemplar for modern American novels.

First of all, Crane swung away from the romantic outlook taken by most authors of his period. This romantic approach ignores the harsher aspects of life, takes the rosy view, and culminates in the inevitable happy ending. The romantic author manipulates the plot so that good receives its just reward and evil falls into the pit. Often this is done obviously, as for example in the rags-to-riches work of Horatio Alger or in the old melodramas. Often it is done quite subtly as in the work of Bret Harte and Mark Twain. If subtly done, novels of this type give human nature at its best—life as we would like to live it.

Crane chose to depict life as it actually is, not as we would like it to be, and if all turns out for the best, the hero must still fight another day. Every boy dreams dreams of fighting heroically in the great war. Covered with glory, indefatigable to the end, he holds his ground, fights, and perchance falls, a hero to the end. The panoply of war, purple and gold, shimmers around him. As any soldier knows, this is not the way of it at all. Crane's

The Red Badge of Courage by Stephen Crane, reprinted by permission of the publishers, Appleton-Century-Crofts, Inc.

hero is three-parts coward, his motivation runs the gamut from fear of the unknown to battle hysteria. The battle, clear and glorious in dream, is a nightmare of smoke, wraiths and general chaos. His soldiers are begrimed and weary automatons. They fight shadows on a small bitter scale, not knowing the outcome of the general cause or even whether they themselves have won or lost. This is war without the medals, the parades or the triumph—it is man against the machine. Crane deals in reality, life as it is lived.

Another characteristic of the modern novel is the cynical or ironical twist which the author can give to seemingly insignificant detail. This irony shows how fate can deal a winning hand to the undeserving. The small-souled can sometimes fall into the butter-tub, and modern novels are at pains to point this out. Crane uses this device to goad his hero. For example, the youth is cracked on the head by one of his own comrades who, like himself, is running away from the fighting. Then he is received into his own camp as a hero wounded in action. He accepts the tribute of his fellows, not daring to tell the truth. A more classical example of this type of irony occurs when the young soldier is questioned by a soldier in the column of wounded. The wounded soldier asks him where his wound is and adds "It might be inside mostly an' them plays thunder." Only the reader and Henry know how "inside" his wound is. Such instances might be multiplied—they occur on every page. This device of pointing out the significance of the casual remark in the ordinary circumstance has become a standard technique in the modern novel.

Crane's novel has been called "episodic," a mere series of occurrences with chronological sequence as the only link. Although the structure is not readily apparent, there exists a more integral link than mere time-sequence. The general pattern of the book is based on contrast. Hope and despair battling for supremacy in the soldiers, war as both machine and religion, appearance and the reality beneath it—these contrasts lace the novel in a dark-light pattern. The hero is blackened by gunsmoke and shame and so is purified. The contrasting symbols and incidents in the novel are not accidents; in matter of fact, they are the meat of it.

Another characteristic of Crane's style widely copied by his successors is his use of color and figure to set a mood or depict an emotion. Crane does not merely tell the reader what emotion his characters are feeling;

he makes the reader actually feel it. He uses the poetic device of the "objective correlative"—a series of images which project an emotion—instead of the bald statement of it. For example, he is not content with telling of Henry's shame; he makes it a "great and salt reproach." He speaks of the "furnace roar" of battle and the "religious half-light" of the forest. The associations and connotations of his adjectives do more than describe, they depict. He makes the characters speak and they speak true. The colonel, in a moment of crisis, calls for a box of cigars; the reader does not have to be told how this shakes the young soldier's conception of war as Homeric, a great "blue demonstration." Biblical phraseology and the use of dialect add shades of meaning which should not be overlooked. Crane says one thing and means twenty more.

The RED BADGE OF COURAGE, at first glance, appears to be the story of a single boy and his struggle toward manhood. Actually, it is the story of human nature under pressure. No one comes to maturity without passing through the fire. If Henry Fleming's reactions seem strange, it is because the fire is still to come. Each man must finally wear his own red badge or he will go to his grave still a boy. "So it came to pass . . . his soul changed."

## CHAPTER ONE

The cold passed reluctantly from the earth, and the retiring fogs revealed an army stretched out on the hills, resting. As the landscape changed from brown to green, the army awakened, and began to tremble with eagerness at the noise of rumors. It cast its eyes upon the roads, which were growing from long troughs of liquid mud to proper thoroughfares. A river, amber-tinted in the shadow of its banks, purled at the army's feet; and at night, when the stream had become of a sorrowful blackness, one could see across it the red, eyelike gleam of hostile camp fires set in the low brows of distant hills.

Once a certain tall soldier developed virtues and went resolutely to wash a shirt. He came flying back from a brook waving his garment bannerlike. He was swelled with a tale he had heard from a reliable friend, who had heard it from a truthful cavalryman, who had heard it from his trustworthy brother, one of the orderlies at division headquarters. He adopted the important air of a herald in red and gold.

"We're goin' t' move t' morrah—sure," he said pompously to a group in the company street. "We're goin' 'way up the river, cut across, an' come around in behint 'em."

To his attentive audience he drew a loud and elaborate plan of a very brilliant campaign. When he had finished, the blue-clothed men scattered into small arguing groups between the rows of squat brown huts. A negro teamster who had been dancing upon a cracker box with the hilarious encouragement of two-score soldiers was deserted. He sat mournfully down. Smoke drifted lazily from a multitude of quaint chimneys.

"It's a lie! that's all it is—a thunderin' lie!" said another private loudly. His smooth face was flushed, and his hands were thrust sulkily into his trousers' pockets. He took the matter as an affront to him. "I don't believe the derned old army's ever going to move. We're set. I've got ready to move eight times in the last two weeks, and we ain't moved yet."

The tall soldier felt called upon to defend the truth of a rumor he himself had introduced. He and the loud one came near to fighting over it.

A corporal began to swear before the assemblage. He had just put a costly board floor in his house, he said. During the early spring he had refrained from adding extensively to the comfort of his environment because he had felt that the army might start on the march at any moment. Of late, however, he had been impressed that they were in a sort of eternal camp.

Many of the men engaged in a spirited debate. One outlined in a peculiarly lucid manner all the plans of the commanding general. He was opposed by men who advocated that there were other plans of campaign. They clamored at each other, numbers making futile bids for the popular attention. Meanwhile, the soldier who had fetched the rumor bustled about with much importance. He was continually assailed by questions.

"What's up, Jim?"

"Th' army's goin' t' move."

"Ah, what yeh talkin' about. How yeh know it is?"

"Well, yeh kin b'lieve me er not, jest as yeh like. I don't care a hang."

There was much food for thought in the manner in which he replied. He came near to convincing them by disdaining to produce proofs. They grew much excited over it.

There was a youthful private who listened with eager ears to the words of the tall soldier and to the varied comments of his comrades. After receiving a fill of discussions concerning marches and attacks, he went to his hut and crawled through an intricate hole that served it as a door. He wished to be alone with some new thoughts that had lately come to him.

He lay down on a wide bunk that stretched across the end of the room. In the other end, cracker boxes were made to serve as furniture. They were grouped about the fireplace. A picture from an illustrated weekly was upon the log walls, and three rifles were paralleled on pegs. Equipments hung on handy projections, and some tin dishes lay upon a small pile of firewood. A folded tent was serving as a roof. The sunlight, without, beating upon it, made it glow a light yellow shade. A small window shot an oblique square of whiter light upon the cluttered floor. The smoke from the fire at times neglected the clay chimney and wreathed into the room, and this flimsy chimney of clay and sticks made endless threats to set ablaze the whole establishment.

The youth was in a little trance of astonishment. So they were at last going to fight. On the morrow, perhaps, there would be a battle, and he would be in it. For a time he was obliged to labor to make himself believe. He could not accept with assurance an omen that he was about to mingle in one of those great affairs of the earth.

He had, of course, dreamed of battles all his life—of vague and bloody conflicts that had thrilled him with their sweep and fire. In visions he had seen himself in many struggles. He had imagined peoples secure in the shadow of his eagle-eyed prowess. But awake he had regarded battles as crimson blotches on the pages of the past. He had put them as things of the bygone with his thought-images of heavy crowns and high castles. There was a portion of the world's history which he had regarded as the time of wars, but it, he thought, had been long gone over the horizon and had disappeared forever.

From his home his youthful eyes had looked upon the war in his own country with distrust. It must be some sort of a play affair. He had long despaired of witnessing a Greeklike struggle. Such would be no more, he had said. Men were better, or more timid. Secular and religious education had effaced the throat-grappling instinct, or else firm finance held in check the passions.

He had burned several times to enlist. Tales of great movements shook the land. They might not be distinctly Homeric, but there seemed to be much glory in them. He had read of marches, sieges, conflicts, and he had longed to see it all. His busy mind had drawn for him large pictures extravagant in color, lurid with breathless deeds.

But his mother had discouraged him. She had affected to look with some contempt upon the quality of his war ardor and patriotism. She could calmly seat herself and with no apparent difficulty give him many hundreds of reasons why he was of vastly more importance on the farm than on the field of battle. She had had certain ways of expression that told him that her statements on the subject came from a deep conviction. Moreover, on her side, was his belief that her ethical motive in the argument was impregnable.

At last, however, he had made firm rebellion against this yellow light thrown upon the color of his ambitions. The newspapers, the gossip of the village, his own picturings, had aroused him to an uncheckable degree. They were in truth fighting finely down there. Almost every day the newspapers printed accounts of a decisive victory.

One night, as he lay in bed, the winds had carried to him the clangoring of the church bell as some enthusiast jerked the rope frantically to tell the twisted news of a great battle. This voice of the people rejoicing in the night had made him shiver in a prolonged ecstasy of excitement. Later, he had gone down to his mother's room and had spoken thus: "Ma, I'm going to enlist."

"Henry, don't you be a fool," his mother had replied. She had then covered her face with the quilt. There was an end to the matter for that night.

Nevertheless, the next morning he had gone to a town that was near his mother's farm and had enlisted in a company that was forming there. When he had returned home his mother was milking the brindle cow. Four others stood waiting. "Ma, I've enlisted," he had said to her diffidently. There was a short silence. "The Lord's will be done, Henry," she had finally replied, and had then continued to milk the brindle cow.

When he had stood in the doorway with his soldier's clothes on his back, and with the light of excitement and expectancy in his eyes almost defeating the glow of regret for the home bonds, he had seen two tears leaving their trails on his mother's scarred cheeks.

Still, she had disappointed him by saying nothing whatever about returning with his shield or on it. He had privately primed himself for a beautiful scene. He had prepared certain sentences which he thought could be used with touching effect. But her words destroyed his plans. She had doggedly peeled potatoes and addressed him as follows: "You watch out, Henry, an' take good care of yerself in this here fighting business—you watch out, an' take good care of yerself. Don't go a-thinkin' you can lick the hull rebel army at the start, because yeh can't. Yer jest one little feller amongst a hull lot of others, and yeh've got to keep quiet an' do what they tell yeh. I know how you are, Henry.

"I've knet yeh eight pair of socks, Henry, and I've put in all yer best shirts, because I want my boy to be jest as warm and comf'able as anybody in the army. Whenever they get holes in 'em, I want yeh to send 'em rightaway back to me, so's I kin dern 'em.

"An' allus be careful an' choose yer comp'ny. There's lots of bad men in the army, Henry. The army makes 'em wild, and they like nothing better than the job of leading off a young feller like you, as ain't never been away from home much and has allus had a mother, an' a-learning 'em to drink and swear. Keep clear of them folks, Henry. I don't want yeh to ever do anything, Henry, that yeh would be 'shamed to let me know about. Jest think as if I was a-watchin' yeh. If yeh keep that in yer mind allus, I guess yeh'll come out about right.

"Yeh must allus remember yer fa-

ther, too, child, an' remember he never drunk a drop of licker in his life, and seldom swore a cross oath.

"I don't know what else to tell yeh, Henry, excepting that yeh must never do no shirking, child, on my account. If so be a time comes when yeh have to be kilt or do a mean thing, why, Henry, don't think of anything 'cept what's right, because there's many a woman has to bear up 'ginst sech things these times, and the Lord 'll take keer of us all.

"Don't forgit about the socks and the shirts, child; and I've put a cup of blackberry jam with yer bundle, because I know yeh like it above all things. Good-by, Henry. Watch out, and be a good boy."

He had, of course, been impatient under the ordeal of this speech. It had not been quite what he expected, and he had borne it with an air of irritation. He departed feeling vague relief.

Still, when he had looked back from the gate, he had seen his mother kneeling among the potato parings. Her brown face, upraised, was stained with tears, and her spare form was quivering. He bowed his head and went on, feeling suddenly ashamed of his purposes.

From his home he had gone to the seminary to bid adieu to many schoolmates. They had thronged about him with wonder and admiration. He had felt the gulf now between them and had swelled with calm pride. He and some of his fellows who had donned blue were quite overwhelmed with privileges for all of one afternoon, and it had been a very delicious thing. They had strutted.

A certain light-haired girl had made vivacious fun at his martial spirit, but there was another and darker girl whom he had gazed at steadfastly, and he thought she grew demure and sad at sight of his blue and brass. As he had walked down the path between the rows of oaks, he had turned his head and detected her at a window watching his departure. As he perceived her, she had immediately begun to stare up through the high tree branches at the sky. He had seen a good deal of flurry and haste in her movement as she changed her attitude. He often thought of it.

On the way to Washington his spirit had soared. The regiment was fed and caressed at station after station until the youth had believed that he must be a hero. There was a lavish expenditure of bread and cold meats, coffee, and pickles and cheese. As he basked in the smiles of the girls and was patted and complimented by the old men, he had felt growing within him the strength to do mighty deeds of arms.

After complicated journeyings with many pauses, there had come months of monotonous life in a camp. He had had the belief that real war was a series of death struggles with small time in between for sleep and meals; but since his regiment had come to the field the army had done little but sit still and try to keep warm.

He was brought then gradually back to his old ideas. Greeklike struggles would be no more. Men were better, or more timid. Secular and religious education had effaced the throat-grappling instinct, or else firm finance held in check the passions.

He had grown to regard himself merely as a part of a vast blue demonstration.[1] His province was to look out,

as far as he could, for his personal comfort. For recreation he could twiddle his thumbs and speculate on the thoughts which must agitate the minds of the generals. Also, he was drilled and drilled and reviewed, and drilled and drilled and reviewed.

The only foes he had seen were some pickets along the river bank. They were a sun-tanned, philosophical lot, who sometimes shot reflectively at the blue pickets. When reproached for this afterward, they usually expressed sorrow, and swore by their gods that the guns had exploded without their permission. The youth, on guard duty one night, conversed across the stream with one of them. He was a slightly ragged man, who spat skillfully between his shoes and possessed a great fund of bland and infantile assurance. The youth liked him personally.

"Yank," the other had informed him, "yer a right dum good feller." This sentiment, floating to him upon the still air, had made him temporarily regret war.

Various veterans had told him tales. Some talked of gray, bewhiskered hordes who were advancing with relentless curses and chewing tobacco with unspeakable valor; tremendous bodies of fierce soldiery who were sweeping along like the Huns. Others spoke of tattered and eternally hungry men who fired despondent powders. "They'll charge through hell's fire an' brimstone t' git a holt on a haversack, an' sech stomachs ain't a-lastin' long," he was told. From the stories, the youth imagined the red, live bones, sticking out through slits in the faded uniforms.

Still, he could not put a whole faith in veterans' tales, for recruits were their prey. They talked much of smoke, fire, and blood, but he could not tell how

[1] VAST BLUE DEMONSTRATION—That is, Henry saw himself merely as one of many men in blue uniforms who were not actually doing anything real.

much might be lies. They persistently yelled, "Fresh fish!" at him, and were in no wise to be trusted.

However, he perceived now that it did not greatly matter what kind of soldiers he was going to fight, so long as they fought, which fact no one disputed. There was a more serious problem. He lay in his bunk pondering upon it. He tried to mathematically prove to himself that he would not run from a battle.

Previously he had never felt obliged to wrestle too seriously with this question. In his life he had taken certain things for granted, never challenging his belief in ultimate success, and bothering little about means and roads. But here he was confronted with a thing of moment. It had suddenly appeared to him that perhaps in a battle he might run. He was forced to admit that as far as war was concerned he knew nothing of himself.

A sufficient time before he would have allowed the problem to kick its heels at the outer portals of his mind, but now he felt compelled to give serious attention to it.

A little panic-fear grew in his mind. As his imagination went forward to a fight, he saw hideous possibilities. He contemplated the lurking menaces of the future, and failed in an effort to see himself standing stoutly in the midst of them. He recalled his visions of broken-bladed glory, but in the shadow of the impending tumult he suspected them to be impossible pictures.

He sprang from the bunk and began to pace nervously to and fro. "Good Lord, what's th' matter with me?" he said aloud.

He felt that in this crisis his laws of life were useless. Whatever he had learned of himself was here of no avail.

He was an unknown quantity. He saw that he would again be obliged to experiment as he had in early youth. He must accumulate information of himself, and meanwhile he resolved to remain close upon his guard lest those qualities of which he knew nothing should everlastingly disgrace him. "Good Lord!" he repeated in dismay.

After a time the tall soldier slid dexterously through the hole. The loud private followed. They were wrangling.

"That's all right," said the tall soldier as he entered. He waved his hand expressively. "You can believe me or not, jest as you like. All you got to do is to sit down and wait as quiet as you can. Then pretty soon you'll find out I was right."

His comrade grunted stubbornly. For a moment he seemed to be searching for a formidable reply. Finally he said: "Well, you don't know everything in the world, do you?"

"Didn't say I knew everything in the world," retorted the other sharply. He began to stow various articles snugly into his knapsack.

The youth, pausing in his nervous walk, looked down at the busy figure. "Going to be a battle, sure, is there, Jim?" he asked.

"Of course there is," replied the tall soldier. "Of course there is. You jest wait 'til tomorrow, and you'll see one of the biggest battles ever was. You jest wait."

"Thunder!" said the youth.

"Oh, you'll see fighting this time, my boy, what'll be regular out-and-out fighting," added the tall soldier, with the air of a man who is about to exhibit a battle for the benefit of his friends.

"Huh!" said the loud one from a corner.

"Well," remarked the youth, "like as

FROM M-G-M'S PRODUCTION OF THE RED BADGE OF COURAGE

not this story'll turn out jest like them others did."

"Not much it won't," replied the tall soldier, exasperated. "Not much it won't. Didn't the cavalry all start this morning?" He glared about him. No one denied his statement. "The cavalry started this morning," he continued. "They say there ain't hardly any cavalry left in camp. They're going to Richmond, or some place, while we fight all the Johnnies. It's some dodge like that. The regiment's got orders, too. A feller what seen 'em go to headquarters told me a little while ago. And they're raising blazes all over camp —anybody can see that."

"Shucks!" said the loud one.

The youth remained silent for a time. At last he spoke to the tall soldier. "Jim!"

"What?"

"How do you think the reg'ment 'll do?"

"Oh, they'll fight all right, I guess, after they once get into it," said the other with cold judgment. He made a fine use of the third person. "There's been heaps of fun poked at 'em because they're new, of course, and all that; but they'll fight all right, I guess."

"Think any of the boys 'll run?" persisted the youth.

"Oh, there may be a few of 'em run, but there's them kind in every regiment, 'specially when they first goes under fire," said the other in a tolerant way. "Of course it might happen that the hull kit-and-boodle might start and run, if some big fighting came first-off, and then again they might stay and fight like fun. But you can't bet on nothing. Of course they ain't never been under fire yet, and it ain't likely they'll lick the hull rebel army all-to-oncet the firs' time; but I think they'll fight better than some, if worse than others. That's the way I figger. They call the reg'ment 'Fresh fish' and everything; but the boys come of good stock, and most of 'em 'll fight like sin after they oncet git shootin'," he added, with a mighty emphasis on the last four words.

"Oh, you think you know—" began the loud soldier with scorn.

The other turned savagely upon him. They had a rapid altercation, in which they fastened upon each other various strange epithets.

The youth at last interrupted them. "Did you ever think you might run yourself, Jim?" he asked. On concluding the sentence he laughed as if he had meant to aim a joke. The loud soldier also giggled.

The tall private waved his hand. "Well," said he profoundly, "I've thought it might get too hot for Jim Conklin in some of them scrimmages, and if a whole lot of boys started and run, why, I s'pose I'd start and run. And if I once started to run, I'd run like the devil, and no mistake. But if everybody was a-standing and a-fighting, why, I'd stand and fight. Be jiminey, I would. I'll bet on it."

"Huh!" said the loud one.

The youth of this tale felt gratitude for these words of his comrade. He had feared that all of the untried men possessed a great and correct confidence. He now was in a measure reassured.

## CHAPTER TWO

The next morning the youth discovered that his tall comrade had been the fast-flying messenger of a mistake. There was much scoffing at the latter by those who had yesterday been firm adherents of his views, and there was even a little sneering by men who had never believed the rumor. The tall one fought with a man from Chatfield Corners and beat him severely.

The youth felt, however, that his problem was in no wise lifted from him. There was, on the contrary, an irritating prolongation. The tale had created in him a great concern for himself. Now, with the newborn question in his mind, he was compelled to sink back into his old place as part of a blue demonstration.

For days he made ceaseless calculations, but they were all wondrously unsatisfactory. He found that he could establish nothing. He finally concluded that the only way to prove himself was to go into the blaze, and then figuratively to watch his legs to discover their merits and faults. He reluctantly admitted that he could not sit still and with a mental slate and pencil derive an answer. To gain it, he must have blaze, blood, and danger, even as a chemist requires this, that, and the other. So he fretted for an opportunity.

Meanwhile he continually tried to measure himself by his comrades. The tall soldier, for one, gave him some assurance. This man's serene unconcern dealt him a measure of confidence, for he had known him since childhood, and from his intimate knowledge he did not see how he could be capable of anything that was beyond him, the youth. Still, he thought that his comrade might be mistaken about himself. Or, on the other hand, he might be a man heretofore doomed to peace and obscurity, but, in reality, made to shine in war.

The youth would have liked to have discovered another who suspected himself. A sympathetic comparison of mental notes would have been a joy to him.

He occasionally tried to fathom a comrade with seductive sentences. He looked about to find men in the proper mood. All attempts failed to bring forth any statement which looked in any way like a confession to those doubts which he privately acknowledged in himself. He was afraid to make an open declaration of his concern, because he dreaded to place some unscrupulous confidant upon the high plane of the unconfessed from which elevation he could be derided.

In regard to his companions his mind wavered between two opinions, according to his mood. Sometimes he inclined to believing them all heroes. In fact, he usually admitted in secret the superior development of the higher qualities in others. He could conceive of men going very insignificantly about the world bearing a load of courage unseen, and, although he had known many of his comrades through boyhood, he began to fear that his judgment of them had been blind. Then, in other moments, he flouted these theories, and assured himself that his fellows were all privately wondering and quaking.

His emotions made him feel strange in the presence of men who talked excitedly of a prospective battle as of a drama they were about to witness, with nothing but eagerness and curiosity apparent in their faces. It was often that he suspected them to be liars.

He did not pass such thoughts without severe condemnation of himself. He dinned reproaches at times. He was convicted by himself of many shameful crimes against the gods of traditions.

In his great anxiety his heart was continually clamoring at what he considered the intolerable slowness of the generals. They seemed content to perch tranquilly on the river bank, and leave him bowed down by the weight of a great problem. He wanted it settled forthwith. He could not long bear such a load, he said. Sometimes his anger at the commanders reached an acute stage, and he grumbled about the camp like a veteran.

One morning, however, he found himself in the ranks of his prepared regiment. The men were whispering speculations and recounting the old rumors. In the gloom before the break of the day their uniforms glowed a deep purple hue. From across the river the red eyes were still peering. In the eastern sky there was a yellow patch like a rug laid for the feet of the coming sun; and against it, black and pattern-like, loomed the gigantic figure of the colonel on a gigantic horse.

From off in the darkness came the trampling of feet. The youth could occasionally see dark shadows that moved like monsters. The regiment stood at rest for what seemed a long time. The youth grew impatient. It was unendurable the way these affairs were managed. He wondered how long they were to be kept waiting.

As he looked all about him and pondered upon the mystic gloom, he began to believe that at any moment the ominous distance might be aflare, and the rolling crashes of an engagement come to his ears. Staring once at the red eyes across the river, he conceived them to be growing larger, as the orbs [2] of a row of dragons advancing. He turned to-

[2] ORBS—Eyes.

ward the colonel and saw him lift his gigantic arm and calmly stroke his mustache.

At last he heard from along the road at the foot of the hill the clatter of a horse's galloping hoofs. It must be the coming of orders. He bent forward, scarce breathing. The exciting clickety-click, as it grew louder and louder seemed to be beating upon his soul. Presently a horseman with jangling equipment drew rein before the colonel of the regiment. The two held a short, sharp-worded conversation. The men in the foremost ranks craned their necks.

As the horseman wheeled his animal and galloped away he turned to shout over his shoulder, "Don't forget that box of cigars!" The colonel mumbled in reply. The youth wondered what a box of cigars had to do with war.

A moment later the regiment went swinging off into the darkness. It was now like one of those moving monsters wending with many feet. The air was heavy, and cold with dew. A mass of wet grass, marched upon, rustled like silk.

There was an occasional flash and glimmer of steel from the backs of all these huge crawling reptiles. From the road came creakings and grumblings as some surly guns were dragged away.

The men stumbled along still muttering speculations. There was a subdued debate. Once a man fell down, and as he reached for his rifle a comrade, unseeing, trod upon his hand. He of the injured fingers swore bitterly and aloud. A low tittering laugh went among his fellows.

Presently they passed into a roadway and marched forward with easy strides. A dark regiment moved before them, and from behind also came the tinkle of equipments on the bodies of marching men.

The rushing yellow of the developing day went on behind their backs. When the sunrays at last struck full and mellowing upon the earth, the youth saw that the landscape was streaked with two long, thin, black columns which disappeared on the brow of a hill in front and rearward vanished in a wood. They were like two serpents crawling from the cavern of the night.

The river was not in view. The tall soldier burst into praises of what he thought to be his powers of perception.

Some of the tall one's companions cried with emphasis that they, too, had evolved the same thing, and they congratulated themselves upon it. But there were others who said that the tall one's plan was not the true one at all. They persisted with other theories. There was a vigorous discussion.

The youth took no part in them. As he walked along in careless line he was engaged with his own eternal debate. He could not hinder himself from dwelling upon it. He was despondent and sullen, and threw shifting glances about him. He looked ahead, often expecting to hear from the advance the rattle of firing.

But the long serpents crawled slowly from hill to hill without bluster of smoke. A dun-colored cloud of dust floated away to the right. The sky overhead was of a fairy blue.

The youth studied the faces of his companions, ever on the watch to detect kindred emotions. He suffered disappointment. Some ardor of the air which was causing the veteran commands to move with glee—almost with song—had infected the new regiment. The men began to speak of victory as of a thing they knew. Also, the tall soldier received his vindication. They were certainly going to come around in behind the enemy. They expressed commiseration for that part of the army which had been left upon the river bank, felicitating themselves upon being a part of a blasting host.

The youth, considering himself as separated from the others, was saddened by the blithe and merry speeches that went from rank to rank. The company wags all made their best endeavors. The regiment tramped to the tune of laughter.

The blatant soldier often convulsed whole files by his biting sarcasms aimed at the tall one.

And it was not long before all the men seemed to forget their mission. Whole brigades grinned in unison, and regiments laughed.

A rather fat soldier attempted to pilfer a horse from a dooryard. He planned to load his knapsack upon it. He was escaping with his prize when a young girl rushed from the house and grabbed the animal's mane. There followed a wrangle. The young girl, with pink cheeks and shining eyes, stood like a dauntless statue.

The observant regiment, standing at rest in the roadway, whooped at once, and entered whole-souled upon the side of the maiden. The men became so engrossed in this affair that they entirely ceased to remember their own large war. They jeered the piratical private, and called attention to various defects in his personal appearance; and they were wildly enthusiastic in support of the young girl.

To her, from some distance, came bold advice. "Hit him with a stick."

There were crows and catcalls showered upon him when he retreated without the horse. The regiment rejoiced at his downfall. Loud and vociferous congratulations were showered upon the maiden, who stood panting and regarding the troops with defiance.

At nightfall the column broke into regimental pieces, and the fragments went into the fields to camp. Tents sprang up like strange plants. Camp fires, like red, peculiar blossoms, dotted the night.

The youth kept from intercourse with his companions as much as circumstances would allow him. In the evening he wandered a few paces into the gloom. From this little distance the many fires, with the black forms of men passing to and fro before the crimson rays, made weird and satanic effects.

He lay down in the grass. The blades pressed tenderly against his cheek. The moon had been lighted and was hung in a treetop. The liquid stillness of the night enveloping him made him feel vast pity for himself. There was a caress in the soft winds; and the whole mood of the darkness, he thought, was one of sympathy for himself in his distress.

He wished, without reserve, that he was at home again making the endless rounds from the house to the barn, from the barn to the fields, from the fields to the barn, from the barn to the house. He remembered he had often cursed the brindle cow and her mates, and had sometimes flung milking stools. But, from his present point of view, there was a halo of happiness about each of their heads, and he would have sacrificed all the brass buttons on the continent to have been enabled to return to them. He told himself that he was not formed for a soldier. And he mused seriously upon the radical differences between himself and those men who were dodging implike around the fires.

As he mused thus he heard the rustle of grass, and, upon turning his head, discovered the loud soldier. He called out, "Oh, Wilson!"

The latter approached and looked down. "Why, hello, Henry; is it you? What you doing here?"

"Oh, thinking," said the youth.

The other sat down and carefully lighted his pipe. "You're getting blue, my boy. You're looking thundering peaked. What the dickens is wrong with you?"

"Oh, nothing," said the youth.

The loud soldier launched then into the subject of the anticipated fight.

"Oh, we've got 'em now!" As he spoke his boyish face was wreathed in a gleeful smile, and his voice had an exultant ring. "We've got 'em now. At last, by the eternal thunders, we'll lick 'em good!"

"If the truth was known," he added, more soberly, "*they've* licked *us* about every clip up to now; but this time— this time—we'll lick 'em good!"

"I thought you was objecting to this march a little while ago," said the youth coldly.

"Oh, it wasn't that," explained the other. "I don't mind marching, if there's going to be fighting at the end of it. What I hate is getting moved here and moved there, with no good coming of it, as far as I can see, except-ing sore feet and damned short rations."

"Well, Jim Conklin says we'll get a plenty of fighting this time."

"He's right for once, I guess, though I can't see how it come. This time we're in for a big battle, and we've got the best end of it, certain sure. Gee rod! how we will thump 'em!"

He arose and began to pace to and fro excitedly. The thrill of his enthusi-asm made him walk with an elastic step. He was sprightly, vigorous, fiery in his belief in success. He looked into the future with clear, proud eye, and he swore with the air of an old soldier.

The youth watched him for a mo-ment in silence. When he finally spoke his voice was as bitter as dregs. "Oh, you're going to do great things, I s'pose!"

The loud soldier blew a thoughtful cloud of smoke from his pipe. "Oh, I don't know," he remarked with dignity; "I don't know. I s'pose I'll do as well as the rest. I'm going to try like thun-der." He evidently complimented him-self upon the modesty of this state-ment.

"How do you know you won't run when the time comes?" asked the youth.

"Run?" said the loud one; "run?— of course not!" He laughed.

"Well," continued the youth, "lots of good-a-'nough men have thought they was going to do great things before the fight, but when the time come they ske-daddled."

"Oh, that's all true, I s'pose," replied the other; "but I'm not going to skedad-dle. The man that bets on my running will lose his money, that's all." He nodded confidently.

"Oh, shucks!" said the youth. "You ain't the bravest man in the world, are you?"

"No, I ain't," exclaimed the loud sol-dier indignantly; "and I didn't say I was the bravest man in the world, neither. I said I was going to do my share of fighting—that's what I said. And I am, too. Who are you, anyhow? You talk as if you thought you was Napoleon Bonaparte." He glared at the youth for a moment, and then strode away.

The youth called in a savage voice after his comrade: "Well, you needn't git mad about it!" But the other continued on his way and made no reply.

He felt alone in space when his injured comrade had disappeared. His failure to discover any mite of resemblance in their viewpoints made him more miserable than before. No one seemed to be wrestling with such a terrific personal problem. He was a mental outcast.

He went slowly to his tent and stretched himself on a blanket by the side of the snoring tall soldier. In the darkness he saw visions of a thousand-tongued fear that would babble at his back and cause him to flee, while others were going coolly about their country's business. He admitted that he would not be able to cope with this monster. He felt that every nerve in his body would be an ear to hear the voices, while other men would remain stolid and deaf.

And as he sweated with the pain of these thoughts, he could hear low, serene sentences. "I'll bid five." "Make it six." "Seven." "Seven goes."

He stared at the red, shivering reflection of a fire on the white wall of his tent until, exhausted and ill from the monotony of his suffering, he fell asleep.

## CHAPTER THREE

When another night came the columns, changed to purple streaks, filed across two pontoon bridges. A glaring fire wine-tinted the waters of the river. Its rays, shining upon the moving masses of troops, brought forth here and there sudden gleams of silver or gold. Upon the other shore a dark and mysterious range of hills was curved against the sky. The insect voices of the night sang solemnly.

After this crossing the youth assured himself that at any moment they might be suddenly and fearfully assaulted from the caves of the lowering woods. He kept his eyes watchfully upon the darkness.

But his regiment went unmolested to a camping place, and its soldiers slept the brave sleep of wearied men. In the morning they were routed out with early energy, and hustled along a narrow road that led deep into the forest. It was during this rapid march that the regiment lost many of the marks of a new command.

The men had begun to count the miles upon their fingers, and they grew tired. "Sore feet an' damned short rations, that's all," said the loud soldier. There were perspiration and grumblings. After a time they began to shed their knapsacks. Some tossed them unconcernedly down; others hid them carefully, asserting their plans to return for them at some convenient time. Men extricated themselves from thick shirts. Presently few carried anything but their necessary clothing, blankets, haversacks, canteens, and arms and ammunition. "You can now eat and shoot," said the tall soldier to the youth. "That's all you want to do."

There was sudden change from the ponderous infantry of theory to the light and speedy infantry of practice. The regiment, relieved of a burden, received a new impetus. But there was much loss of valuable knapsacks, and, on the whole, very good shirts.

But the regiment was not yet veteran-like in appearance. Veteran regiments in the army were likely to be very small aggregations of men. Once, when the command had first come to the field, some perambulating veterans, noting the length of their column, had accosted them thus: "Hey, fellers, what brigade is that?" And when the men had replied that they formed a regiment and not a brigade, the older soldiers had laughed, and said, "O Gawd!"

Also, there was too great a similarity in the hats. The hats of a regiment should properly represent the history of headgear for a period of years. And, moreover, there were no letters of faded gold speaking from the colors. They were new and beautiful, and the color bearer habitually oiled the pole.

Presently the army again sat down to think. The odor of the peaceful pines was in the men's nostrils. The sound of monotonous axe blows rang through the forest, and the insects, nodding upon their perches, crooned like old women. The youth returned to his theory of a blue demonstration.

One gray dawn, however, he was kicked in the leg by the tall soldier, and then, before he was entirely awake, he found himself running down a wood road in the midst of men who were panting from the first effects of speed. His canteen banged rhythmically upon his thigh, and his haversack bobbed softly. His musket bounced a trifle from his shoulder at each stride and made his cap feel uncertain upon his head.

He could hear the men whisper jerky sentences: "Say—what's all this—about?" "What th' thunder—we—ske-dadlin' this way fer?" "Billie—keep off m' feet. Yeh run—like a cow." And the loud soldier's shrill voice could be heard: "What th' devil they in sich a hurry for?"

The youth thought the damp fog of early morning moved from the rush of a great body of troops. From the distance came a sudden spatter of firing.

He was bewildered. As he ran with his comrades he strenuously tried to think, but all he knew was that if he fell down those coming behind would tread upon him. All his faculties seemed to be needed to guide him over and past obstructions. He felt carried along by a mob.

The sun spread disclosing rays, and, one by one, regiments burst into view like armed men just born of the earth. The youth perceived that the time had come. He was about to be measured. For a moment he felt in the face of his great trial like a babe, and the flesh over his heart seemed very thin. He seized time to look about him calculatingly.

But he instantly saw that it would be impossible for him to escape from the regiment. It inclosed him. And there were iron laws of tradition and law on four sides. He was in a moving box.

As he perceived this fact it occurred to him that he had never wished to come to the war. He had not enlisted of his free will. He had been dragged by the merciless government. And now they were taking him out to be slaughtered.

The regiment slid down a bank and wallowed across a little stream. The mournful current moved slowly on, and from the water, shaded black, some white bubble eyes looked at the men.

As they climbed the hill on the farther side artillery began to boom. Here the youth forgot many things as he felt a sudden impulse of curiosity. He scrambled up the bank with a speed that could not be exceeded by a blood-thirsty man.

He expected a battle scene.

There were some little fields girted and squeezed by a forest. Spread over the grass and in among the tree

FROM M-G-M'S PRODUCTION OF THE RED BADGE OF COURAGE

trunks, he could see knots and waving lines of skirmishers who were running hither and thither and firing at the landscape. A dark battle line lay upon a sun-struck clearing that gleamed orange color. A flag fluttered.

Other regiments floundered up the bank. The brigade was formed in line of battle, and after a pause started slowly through the woods in the rear of the receding skirmishers, who were continually melting into the scene to appear again farther on. They were always busy as bees, deeply absorbed in their little combats.

The youth tried to observe everything. He did not use care to avoid trees and branches, and his forgotten feet were constantly knocking against stones or getting entangled in briers. He was aware that these battalions with their commotions were woven red and

startling into the gentle fabric of softened greens and browns. It looked to be a wrong place for a battle field.

The skirmishers in advance fascinated him. Their shots into thickets and at distant and prominent trees spoke to him of tragedies—hidden, mysterious, solemn.

Once the line encountered the body of a dead soldier. He lay upon his back staring at the sky. He was dressed in an awkward suit of yellowish brown. The youth could see that the soles of his shoes had been worn to the thinness of writing paper, and from a great rent in one the dead foot projected piteously. And it was as if fate had betrayed the soldier. In death it exposed to his enemies that poverty which in life he had perhaps concealed from his friends.

The ranks opened covertly to avoid the corpse. The invulnerable dead man forced a way for himself. The youth looked keenly at the ashen face. The wind raised the tawny beard. It moved as if a hand were stroking it. He vaguely desired to walk around and around the body and stare; the impulse of the living to try to read in dead eyes the answer to the Question.

During the march the ardor which the youth had acquired when out of view of the field rapidly faded to nothing. His curiosity was quite easily satisfied. If an intense scene had caught him with its wild swing as he came to the top of the bank, he might have gone roaring on. This advance upon Nature was too calm. He had opportunity to reflect. He had time in which to wonder about himself and to attempt to probe his sensations.

Absurd ideas took hold upon him. He thought that he did not relish the landscape. It threatened him. A coldness swept over his back, and it is true that his trousers felt to him that they were no fit for his legs at all.

A house standing placidly in distant fields had to him an ominous look. The shadows of the woods were formidable. He was certain that in this vista there lurked fierce-eyed hosts. The swift thought came to him that the generals did not know what they were about. It was all a trap. Suddenly those close forests would bristle with rifle barrels. Ironlike brigades would appear in the rear. They were all going to be sacrificed. The generals were stupids. The enemy would presently swallow the whole command. He glared about him, expecting to see the stealthy approach of his death.

He thought that he must break from the ranks and harangue[3] his comrades.

They must not all be killed like pigs; and he was sure it would come to pass unless they were informed of these dangers. The generals were idiots to send them marching into a regular pen. There was but one pair of eyes in the corps. He would step forth and make a speech. Shrill and passionate words came to his lips.

The line, broken into moving fragments by the ground, went calmly on through fields and woods. The youth looked at the men nearest him, and saw, for the most part, expressions of deep interest, as if they were investigating something that had fascinated them. One or two stepped with over-valiant airs as if they were already plunged into war. Others walked as upon thin ice. The greater part of the untested men appeared quiet and absorbed. They were going to look at war, the red animal—war, the blood-swollen god. And they were deeply engrossed in this march.

As he looked the youth gripped his outcry at his throat. He saw that even if the men were tottering with fear they would laugh at his warning. They would jeer him, and, if practicable, pelt him with missiles. Admitting that he might be wrong, a frenzied declamation of the kind would turn him into a worm.

He assumed, then, the demeanor[4] of one who knows that he is doomed alone to unwritten responsibilities. He lagged, with tragic glances at the sky.

He was surprised presently by the young lieutenant of his company, who began heartily to beat him with a sword, calling out in a loud and insolent voice: "Come, young man, get up into ranks there. No skulking 'll do

[3] HARANGUE (hȧ·răng′)—To speak to a multitude, usually to speak noisily and loudly.

[4] DEMEANOR (dė·mēn′ẽr)—Conduct; bearing; manner.

here." He mended his pace with suitable haste. And he hated the lieutenant, who had no appreciation of fine minds. He was a mere brute.

After a time the brigade was halted in the cathedral light of a forest. The busy skirmishers were still popping. Through the aisles of the wood could be seen the floating smoke from their rifles. Sometimes it went up in little balls, white and compact.

During this halt many men in the regiment began erecting tiny hills in front of them. They used stones, sticks, earth, and anything they thought might turn a bullet. Some built comparatively large ones, while others seemed content with little ones.

This procedure caused a discussion among the men. Some wished to fight like duelists, believing it to be correct to stand erect and be, from their feet to their foreheads, a mark. They said they scorned the devices of the cautious. But the others scoffed in reply, and pointed to the veterans on the flanks who were digging at the ground like terriers. In a short time there was quite a barricade along the regimental fronts. Directly, however, they were ordered to withdraw from that place.

This astounded the youth. He forgot his stewing over the advance movement. "Well, then, what did they march us out here for?" he demanded of the tall soldier. The latter with calm faith began a heavy explanation, although he had been compelled to leave a little protection of stones and dirt to which he had devoted much care and skill.

When the regiment was aligned in another position each man's regard for his safety caused another line of small intrenchments. They ate their noon meal behind a third one. They were moved from this one also. They were marched from place to place with apparent aimlessness.

The youth had been taught that a man became another thing in a battle. He saw his salvation in such a change. Hence this waiting was an ordeal to him. He was in a fever of impatience. He considered that there was denoted a lack of purpose on the part of the generals. He began to complain to the tall soldier. "I can't stand this much longer," he cried. "I don't see what good it does to make us wear out our legs for nothin'." He wished to return to camp, knowing that this affair was a blue demonstration; or else to go into a battle and discover that he had been a fool in his doubts, and was, in truth, a man of traditional courage. The strain of present circumstances he felt to be intolerable.

The philosophical tall soldier measured a sandwich of cracker and pork and swallowed it in a nonchalant manner. "Oh, I suppose we must go reconnoitering around the country jest to keep 'em from getting too close, or to develop 'em, or something."

"Huh!" cried the loud soldier.

"Well," cried the youth, still fidgeting, "I'd rather do anything 'most than go tramping 'round the country all day doing no good to nobody and jest tiring ourselves out."

"So would I," said the loud soldier. "It ain't right. I tell you if anybody with any sense was a-runnin' this army it—"

"Oh, shut up!" roared the tall private. "You little fool. You little damn' cuss. You ain't had that there coat and them pants on for six months, and yet you talk as if—"

"Well, I wanta do some fighting anyway," interrupted the other. "I didn't come here to walk. I could 'ave walked to home—'round an 'round the barn, if I jest wanted to walk."

The tall one, red-faced, swallowed another sandwich as if taking poison in despair.

But gradually, as he chewed, his face became again quiet and contented. He could not rage in fierce argument in the presence of such sandwiches. During his meals he always wore an air of blissful contemplation of the food he had swallowed. His spirit seemed then to be communing with the viands.

He accepted new environment and circumstance with great coolness, eating from his haversack at every opportunity. On the march he went along with the stride of a hunter, objecting to neither gait nor distance. And he had not raised his voice when he had been ordered away from three little protective piles of earth and stone, each of which had been an engineering feat worthy of being made sacred to the name of his grandmother.

In the afternoon the regiment went out over the same ground it had taken in the morning. The landscape then ceased to threaten the youth. He had been close to it and become familiar with it.

When, however, they began to pass into a new region, his old fears of stupidity and incompetence reassailed him, but this time he doggedly let them babble. He was occupied with his problem, and in his desperation he concluded that the stupidity did not greatly matter.

Once he thought he had concluded that it would be better to get killed directly and end his troubles. Regarding death thus out of the corner of his eye, he conceived it to be nothing but rest, and he was filled with a momentary

astonishment that he should have made an extraordinary commotion over the mere matter of getting killed. He would die; he would go to some place where he would be understood. It was useless to expect appreciation of his profound and fine senses from such men as the lieutenant. He must look to the grave for comprehension.

The skirmish fire increased to a long clattering sound. With it was mingled far-away cheering. A battery spoke.

Directly the youth would see the skirmishers running. They were pursued by the sound of musketry fire. After a time the hot, dangerous flashes of the rifles were visible. Smoke clouds went slowly and insolently across the fields like observant phantoms. The din became crescendo,[5] like the roar of an oncoming train.

A brigade ahead of them and on the right went into action with a rending roar. It was as if it had exploded. And thereafter it lay stretched in the distance behind a long gray wall, that one was obliged to look twice at to make sure that it was smoke.

The youth, forgetting his neat plan of getting killed, gazed spellbound. His eyes grew wide and busy with the action of the scene. His mouth was a little ways open.

Of a sudden he felt a heavy and sad hand laid upon his shoulder. Awakening from his trance of observation he turned and beheld the loud soldier.

"It's my first and last battle, old boy," said the latter, with intense gloom. He was quite pale and his girlish lip was trembling.

"Eh?" murmured the youth in great astonishment.

"It's my first and last battle, old

---

[5] CRESCENDO (krĕ·shĕn′dō)—Gradually increasing in volume; becoming louder.

FROM M-G-M'S PRODUCTION OF THE RED BADGE OF COURAGE

boy," continued the loud soldier. "Something tells me—"

"What?"

"I'm a gone coon this first time and —and I w-want you to take these here things—to—my—folks." He ended in a quavering sob of pity for himself. He handed the youth a little packet done up in a yellow envelope.

"Why, what the devil—" began the youth again.

But the other gave him a glance as from the depths of a tomb, and raised his limp hand in a prophetic manner and turned away.

## CHAPTER FOUR

The brigade was halted in the fringe of a grove. The men crouched among the trees and pointed their restless guns out at the fields. They tried to look beyond the smoke.

Out of this haze they could see running men. Some shouted information and gestured as they hurried.

The men of the new regiment watched and listened eagerly, while their tongues ran on in gossip of the battle. They mouthed rumors that had flown like birds out of the unknown.

"They say Perry has been driven in with big loss."

"Yes, Carrott went t' th' hospital. He said he was sick. That smart lieutenant is commanding 'G' Company. Th' boys say they won't be under Carrott no more if they all have t' desert. They allus knew he was a—"

"Hannises' batt'ry is took."

"It ain't either. I saw Hannises' batt'ry off on th' left not more'n fifteen minutes ago."

"Well—"

"Th' general, he ses he is goin' t' take

th' hull command of th' 304th when we go inteh action, an' then he ses we'll do sech fightin' as never another one reg'ment done."

"They say we're catchin' it over on th' left. They say th' enemy driv' our line inteh a devil of a swamp an' took Hannises' batt'ry."

"No sech thing. Hannises' batt'ry was 'long here 'bout a minute ago."

"That young Hasbrouck, he makes a good off'cer. He ain't afraid 'a nothin'.."

"I met one of th' 148th Maine boys an' he ses his brigade fit th' hull rebel army fer four hours over on th' turnpike road an' killed about five thousand of 'em. He ses one more sech fight as that an' th' war 'll be over."

"Bill wasn't scared either. No, sir! It wasn't that. Bill ain't a-gettin' scared easy. He was jest mad, that's what he was. When that feller trod on his hand, he up an' sed that he was willin' t' give his hand t' his country, but he be dumbed if he was goin' t' have every dumb bushwacker in th' kentry walkin' 'round on it. So he went t' th' hospital disregardless of th' fight. Three fingers was crunched. Th' dern doctor wanted t' amputate 'm, an' Bill, he raised a heluva row, I hear. He's a funny feller."

The din in front swelled to a tremendous chorus. The youth and his fellows were frozen to silence. They could see a flag that tossed in the smoke angrily. Near it were the blurred and agitated forms of troops. There came a turbulent stream of men across the fields. A battery changing position at a frantic gallop scattered the stragglers right and left.

A shell screaming like a storm banshee went over the huddled heads of the reserves. It landed in the grove, and exploding redly flung the brown earth. There was a little shower of pine needles.

Bullets began to whistle among the branches and nip at the trees. Twigs and leaves came sailing down. It was as if a thousand axes, wee and invisible, were being wielded. Many of the men were constantly dodging and ducking their heads.

The lieutenant of the youth's company was shot in the hand. He began to swear so wondrously that a nervous laugh went along the regimental line. The officer's profanity sounded conventional. It relieved the tightened senses of the new men. It was as if he had hit his fingers with a tack hammer at home.

He held the wounded member carefully away from his side so that the blood would not drip upon his trousers.

The captain of the company, tucking his sword under his arm, produced a handkerchief and began to bind with it the lieutenant's wound. And they disputed as to how the binding should be done.

The battle flag in the distance jerked about madly. It seemed to be struggling to free itself from an agony. The billowing smoke was filled with horizontal flashes.

Men running swiftly emerged from it. They grew in numbers until it was seen that the whole command was fleeing. The flag suddenly sank down as if dying. Its motion as it fell was a gesture of despair.

Wild yells came from behind the walls of smoke. A sketch in gray and red dissolved into a moblike body of men who galloped like wild horses.

The veteran regiments on the right and left of the 304th immediately began to jeer. With the passionate song of the bullets and the banshee shrieks of shells were mingled loud cat-calls and bits of facetious advice concerning places of safety.

But the new regiment was breathless with horror. "Gawd! Saunders's got crushed!" whispered the man at the youth's elbow. They shrank back and crouched as if compelled to await a flood.

The youth shot a swift glance along the blue ranks of the regiment. The profiles were motionless, carven; and afterward he remembered that the color sergeant was standing with his legs apart, as if he expected to be pushed to the ground.

The following throng went whirling around the flank. Here and there were officers carried along on the stream like exasperated chips. They were striking about them with their swords and with their left fists, punching every head they could reach. They cursed like highwaymen.

A mounted officer displayed the furious anger of a spoiled child. He raged with his head, his arms, and his legs.

Another, the commander of the brigade, was galloping about bawling. His hat was gone and his clothes were awry. He resembled a man who had come from bed to go to a fire. The hoofs of his horse often threatened the heads of the running men, but they scampered with singular fortune. In this rush they were apparently all deaf and blind. They heeded not the largest and longest of the oaths that were thrown at them from all directions.

Frequently over this tumult could be heard the grim jokes of the critical veterans; but the retreating men apparently were not even conscious of the presence of an audience.

The battle reflection that shone for an instant in the faces on the mad current made the youth feel that forceful hands from heaven would not have been able to have held him in place if he could have got intelligent control of his legs.

There was an appalling imprint upon these faces. The struggle in the smoke had pictured an exaggeration of itself on the bleached cheeks and in the eyes wild with one desire.

The sight of this stampede exerted a flood-like force that seemed able to drag sticks and stones and men from the ground. They of the reserves had to hold on. They grew pale and firm, and red and quaking.

The youth achieved one little thought in the midst of this chaos. The composite monster which had caused the other troops to flee had not then appeared. He resolved to get a view of it, and then, he thought he might very likely run better than the best of them.

## CHAPTER FIVE

There were moments of waiting. The youth thought of the village street at home before the arrival of the circus parade on a day in the spring. He remembered how he had stood, a small, thrillful boy, prepared to follow the dingy lady upon the white horse, or the band in its faded chariot. He saw the yellow road, the lines of expectant people, and the sober houses. He particularly remembered an old fellow who used to sit upon a cracker box in front of the store and feign to despise such exhibitions. A thousand details of color and form surged in his mind. The old fellow upon the cracker box appeared in middle prominence.

Some one cried, "Here they come!"

There was rustling and muttering among the men. They displayed a fev-

FROM M-G-M'S PRODUCTION OF THE RED BADGE OF COURAGE

erish desire to have every possible cartridge ready to their hands. The boxes were pulled around into various positions, and adjusted with great care. It was as if seven hundred new bonnets were being tried on.

The tall soldier, having prepared his rifle, produced a red handkerchief of some kind. He was engaged in knitting it about his throat with exquisite attention to its position, when the cry was repeated up and down the line in a muffled roar of sound.

"Here they come! Here they come!" Gun locks clicked.

Across the smoke-infested fields came a brown swarm of running men who were giving shrill yells. They came on, stooping and swinging their rifles at all angles. A flag, tilted forward, sped near the front.

As he caught sight of them the youth was momentarily startled by a thought that perhaps his gun was not loaded. He stood trying to rally his faltering intellect so that he might recollect the moment when he had loaded, but he could not.

A hatless general pulled his dripping horse to a stand near the colonel of the 304th. He shook his fist in the other's face. "You've got to hold 'em back!" he shouted, savagely; "you've got to hold 'em back!"

In his agitation the colonel began to stammer. "A-all r-right, General, all right, by Gawd! We-we'll do our—we-we'll d-d-do—do our best, General." The general made a passionate gesture and galloped away. The colonel, perchance to relieve his feelings, began to scold like a wet parrot. The youth, turning swiftly to make sure that the rear was unmolested, saw the commander regarding his men in a highly resentful manner, as if he regretted above everything his association with them.

The man at the youth's elbow was mumbling, as if to himself: "Oh, we're in for it now! oh, we're in for it now!"

The captain of the company had been pacing excitedly to and fro in the rear. He coaxed in schoolmistress fashion, as to a congregation of boys with primers. His talk was an endless repetition. "Reserve your fire, boys—don't shoot till I tell you—save your fire—wait till they get close up—don't be damned fools—"

Perspiration streamed down the youth's face, which was soiled like that of a weeping urchin. He frequently, with a nervous movement, wiped his eyes with his coat sleeve. His mouth was still a little way open.

He got the one glance at the foe-swarming field in front of him, and instantly ceased to debate the question of his piece being loaded. Before he was ready to begin—before he had announced to himself that he was about to fight—he threw the obedient, well-balanced rifle into position and fired a first wild shot. Directly he was working at his weapon like an automatic affair.

He suddenly lost concern for himself, and forgot to look at a menacing fate. He became not a man but a member. He felt that something of which he was a part—a regiment, an army, a cause, or a country—was in a crisis. He was welded into a common personality which was dominated by a single desire. For some moments he could not flee, no more than a little finger can commit a revolution from a hand.

If he had thought the regiment was about to be annihilated perhaps he could have amputated himself from it. But its noise gave him assurance. The regiment was like a firework that, once ignited, proceeds superior to circumstances until its blazing vitality fades. It wheezed and banged with a mighty power. He pictured the ground before it as strewn with the discomfited.[6]

There was a consciousness always of the presence of his comrades about him. He felt the subtle battle brotherhood more potent even than the cause for which they were fighting. It was a mysterious fraternity born of the smoke and danger of death.

He was at a task. He was like a carpenter who has made many boxes, making still another box, only there was furious haste in his movements. He, in his thought, was careering off in other places, even as the carpenter who as he works whistles and thinks of his friend or his enemy, his home or a saloon. And these jolted dreams were never perfect to him afterward, but remained a mass of blurred shapes.

Presently he began to feel the effects of the war atmosphere—a blistering sweat, a sensation that his eyeballs were about to crack like hot stones. A burning roar filled his ears.

Following this came a red rage. He developed the acute exasperation of a pestered animal, a well-meaning cow worried by dogs. He had a mad feeling against his rifle, which could only be used against one life at a time. He wished to rush forward and strangle with his fingers. He craved a power that would enable him to make a world-sweeping gesture and brush all back. His impotency appeared to him, and

[6] DISCOMFITED—Scattered in a fight; routed in battle; here, the dead.

made his rage into that of a driven beast.

Buried in the smoke of many rifles his anger was directed not so much against the men whom he knew were rushing toward him as against the swirling battle phantoms which were choking him, stuffing their smoke robes down his parched throat. He fought frantically for respite for his senses, for air, as a babe being smothered attacks the deadly blankets.

There was a blare of heated rage mingled with a certain expression of intentness on all faces. Many of the men were making low-toned noises with their mouths, and these subdued cheers, snarls, imprecations, prayers, made a wild, barbaric song that went as an undercurrent of sound, strange and chant-like with the resounding chords of the war march. The man at the youth's elbow was babbling. In it there was something soft and tender like the monologue of a babe. The tall soldier was swearing in a loud voice. From his lips came a black procession of curious oaths. Of a sudden another broke out in a querulous way like a man who has mislaid his hat. "Well, why don't they support us? Why don't they send supports? Do they think—"

The youth in his battle sleep heard this as one who dozes hears.

There was a singular absence of heroic poses. The men bending and surging in their haste and rage were in every impossible attitude. The steel ramrods clanked and clanged with incessant din as the men pounded them furiously into the hot rifle barrels. The flaps of the cartridge boxes were all unfastened, and bobbed idiotically with each movement. The rifles, once loaded, were jerked to the shoulder and fired without apparent aim into the smoke or at one of the blurred and shifting forms which, upon the field before the regiment, had been growing larger and larger like puppets under a magician's hand.

The officers, at their intervals, rearward, neglected to stand in picturesque attitudes. They were bobbing to and fro roaring directions and encouragements. The dimensions of their howls were extraordinary. They expended their lungs with prodigal wills. And often they nearly stood upon their heads in their anxiety to observe the enemy on the other side of the tumbling smoke.

The lieutenant of the youth's company had encountered a soldier who had fled screaming at the first volley of his comrades. Behind the lines these two were acting a little isolated scene. The man was blubbering and staring with sheeplike eyes at the lieutenant, who had seized him by the collar and was pommeling him. He drove him back into the ranks with many blows. The soldier went mechanically, dully, with his animal-like eyes upon the officer. Perhaps there was to him a divinity expressed in the voice of the other —stern, hard, with no reflection of fear in it. He tried to reload his gun, but his shaking hands prevented. The lieutenant was obliged to assist him.

The men dropped here and there like bundles. The captain of the youth's company had been killed in an early part of the action. His body lay stretched out in the position of a tired man resting, but upon his face there was an astonished and sorrowful look, as if he thought some friend had done him an ill turn. The babbling man was grazed by a shot that made the blood stream widely down his face. He clapped both hands to his head. "Oh!"

he said, and ran. Another grunted suddenly as if he had been struck by a club in the stomach. He sat down and gazed ruefully. In his eyes there was mute, indefinite reproach. Farther up the line a man, standing behind a tree, had had his knee joint splintered by a ball. Immediately he had dropped his rifle and gripped the tree with both arms. And there he remained, clinging desperately and crying for assistance that he might withdraw his hold upon the tree.

At last an exultant yell went along the quivering line. The firing dwindled from an uproar to a last vindictive popping. As the smoke slowly eddied away, the youth saw that the charge had been repulsed. The enemy were scattered into reluctant groups. He saw a man climb to the top of the fence, straddle the rail, and fire a parting shot. The waves had receded, leaving bits of dark *débris* upon the ground.

Some in the regiment began to whoop frenziedly. Many were silent. Apparently they were trying to contemplate themselves.

After the fever had left his veins, the youth thought that at last he was going to suffocate. He became aware of the foul amosphere in which he had been struggling. He was grimy and dripping like a laborer in a foundry. He grasped his canteen and took a long swallow of the warmed water.

A sentence with variations went up and down the line. "Well, we've helt 'em back. We've helt 'em back; derned if we haven't." The men said it blissfully, leering at each other with dirty smiles.

The youth turned to look behind him and off to the right and off to the left. He experienced the joy of a man who at last finds leisure in which to look about him.

Under foot there were a few ghastly forms motionless. They lay twisted in fantastic contortions. Arms were bent and heads were turned in incredible ways. It seemed that the dead men must have fallen from some great height to get into such positions. They looked to be dumped out upon the ground from the sky.

From a position in the rear of the grove a battery was throwing shells over it. The flash of the guns startled the youth at first. He thought they were aimed directly at him. Through the trees he watched the black figures of the gunners as they worked swiftly and intently. Their labor seemed a complicated thing. He wondered how they could remember its formula in the midst of confusion.

The guns squatted in a row like savage chiefs. They argued with abrupt violence. It was a grim pow-wow. Their busy servants ran hither and thither.

A small procession of wounded men were going drearily toward the rear. It was a flow of blood from the torn body of the brigade.

To the right and to the left were the dark lines of other troops. Far in front he thought he could see lighter masses protruding in points from the forest. They were suggestive of unnumbered thousands.

Once he saw a tiny battery go dashing along the line of the horizon. The tiny riders were beating the tiny horses.

From a sloping hill came the sound of cheerings and clashes. Smoke welled slowly through the leaves.

Batteries were speaking with thunderous oratorical effort. Here and there were flags, the red in the stripes dominating. They splashed bits of warm color upon the dark lines of troops.

FROM M-G-M'S PRODUCTION OF THE RED BADGE OF COURAGE

The youth felt the old thrill at the sight of the emblems. They were like beautiful birds strangely undaunted in a storm.

As he listened to the din from the hillside, to a deep pulsating thunder that came from afar to the left, and to the lesser clamors which came from many directions, it occurred to him that they were fighting, too, over there, and over there, and over there. Heretofore he had supposed that all the battle was directly under his nose.

As he gazed around him the youth felt a flash of astonishment at the blue, pure sky and the sun gleaming on the trees and fields. It was surprising that Nature had gone tranquilly on with her golden process in the midst of so much devilment.

## CHAPTER SIX

The youth awakened slowly. He came gradually back to a position from which he could regard himself. For moments he had been scrutinizing his person in a dazed way as if he had never before seen himself. Then he picked up his cap from the ground. He wiggled in his jacket to make a more comfortable fit, and kneeling relaced his shoe. He thoughtfully mopped his reeking features.

So it was all over at last! The supreme trial had been passed. The red, formidable difficulties of war had been vanquished.

He went into an ecstasy of self-satisfaction. He had the most delightful sensations of his life. Standing as if apart from himself, he viewed that last scene. He perceived that the man who had fought thus was magnificent.

He felt that he was a fine fellow. He saw himself even with those ideals which he had considered as far beyond him. He smiled in deep gratification.

Upon his fellows he beamed tenderness and good will. "Gee! ain't it hot, hey?" he said affably to a man who was polishing his streaming face with his coat sleeves.

"You bet!" said the other, grinning sociably. "I never seen sech dumb hotness." He sprawled out luxuriously on the ground. "Gee, yes! An' I hope we don't have no more fightin' till a week from Monday."

There were some handshakings and deep speeches with men whose features were familiar, but with whom the youth now felt the bonds of tied hearts. He helped a cursing comrade to bind up a wound of the shin.

But, of a sudden, cries of amazement broke out along the ranks of the new regiment. "Here they come ag'in! Here they come ag'in!" The man who had sprawled upon the ground started up and said, "Gosh!"

The youth turned quick eyes upon the field. He discerned forms begin to swell in masses out of a distant wood. He again saw the tilted flag speeding forward.

The shells, which had ceased to trouble the regiment for a time, came swirling again, and exploded in the grass or among the leaves of the trees. They looked to be strange war flowers bursting into fierce bloom.

The men groaned. The luster faded from their eyes. Their smudged countenances now expressed a profound dejection. They moved their stiffened bodies slowly, and watched in sullen mood the frantic approach of the enemy. The slaves toiling in the temple of this god began to feel rebellion at his harsh tasks.

They fretted and complained each to each. "Oh, say, this is too much of a good thing! Why can't somebody send us supports?"

"We ain't never goin' to stand this second banging. I didn't come here to fight the hull damn' rebel army."

There was one who raised a doleful cry. "I wish Bill Smithers had trod on my hand, insteader me treddin' on his'n." The sore joints of the regiment creaked as it painfully floundered into position to repulse.

The youth stared. Surely, he thought, this impossible thing was not about to happen. He waited as if he expected the enemy to suddenly stop, apologize, and retire bowing. It was all a mistake.

But the firing began somewhere on the regimental line and ripped along in both directions. The level sheets of flame developed great clouds of smoke that tumbled and tossed in the mild wind near the ground for a moment, and then rolled through the ranks as through a gate. The clouds were tinged an earthlike yellow in the sunrays and in the shadow were a sorry blue. The flag was sometimes eaten and lost in this mass of vapor, but more often it projected, sun-touched, resplendent.

Into the youth's eyes there came a look that one can see in the orbs of a jaded horse. His neck was quivering with nervous weakness and the muscles of his arms felt numb and bloodless. His hands, too, seemed large and awkward as if he was wearing invisible mittens. And there was a great uncertainty about his knee joints.

The words that comrades had uttered previous to the firing began to recur to him. "Oh, say, this is too much of a good thing! What do they take us for —why don't they send supports? I didn't come here to fight the hull damned rebel army."

He began to exaggerate the endurance, the skill, and the valor of those who were coming. Himself reeling from exhaustion, he was astonished beyond measure at such persistency. They must be machines of steel. It was very gloomy struggling against such affairs, wound up perhaps to fight until sundown.

He slowly lifted his rifle and catching a glimpse of the thickspread field he blazed at a cantering cluster. He stopped then and began to peer as best he could through the smoke. He caught changing views of the ground covered with men who were all running like pursued imps, and yelling.

To the youth it was an onslaught of redoubtable dragons. He became like the man who lost his legs at the approach of the red and green monster. He waited in a sort of a horrified, listening attitude. He seemed to shut his eyes and wait to be gobbled.

A man near him who up to this time had been working feverishly at his rifle suddenly stopped and ran with howls. A lad whose face had borne an expression of exalted courage, the majesty of he who dares give his life, was, at an instant, smitten abject.[7] He blanched like one who has come to the edge of a cliff at midnight and is suddenly made aware. There was a revelation. He, too, threw down his gun and fled. There was no shame in his face. He ran like a rabbit.

Others began to scamper away through the smoke. The youth turned his head, shaken from his trance by this movement as if the regiment was leaving him behind. He saw the few fleeting forms.

He yelled then with fright and swung about. For a moment, in the great

clamor, he was like a proverbial chicken. He lost the direction of safety. Destruction threatened him from all points.

Directly he began to speed toward the rear in great leaps. His rifle and cap were gone. His unbuttoned coat bulged in the wind. The flap of his cartridge box bobbed wildly, and his canteen, by its slender cord, swung out behind. On his face was the horror of those things which he imagined.

The lieutenant sprang forward bawling. The youth saw his features wrathfully red, and saw him make a dab with his sword. His one thought of the incident was that the lieutenant was a peculiar creature to feel interested in such matters upon this occasion.

He ran like a blind man. Two or three times he fell down. Once he knocked his shoulder so heavily against a tree that he went headlong.

Since he had turned his back upon the fight his fears had been wondrously magnified. Death about to thrust him between the shoulder blades was far more dreadful than death about to smite him between the eyes. When he thought of it later, he conceived the impression that it is better to view the appalling than to be merely within hearing. The noises of the battle were like stones; he believed himself liable to be crushed.

As he ran on he mingled with others. He dimly saw men on his right and on his left, and he heard footsteps behind him. He thought that all the regiment was fleeing, pursued by these ominous crashes.

In his flight the sound of these following footsteps gave him his one meager relief. He felt vaguely that death must make a first choice of the men who were nearest; the initial morsels for

---

[7] ABJECT (ăb′jĕkt)—Cast down in spirit; servile; ignoble.

the dragons would be then those who were following him. So he displayed the zeal of an insane sprinter in his purpose to keep them in the rear. There was a race.

As he, leading, went across a little field, he found himself in a region of shells. They hurtled over his head with long wild screams. As he listened he imagined them to have rows of cruel teeth that grinned at him. Once one lit before him and the livid lightning of the explosion effectually barred the way in his chosen direction. He groveled on the ground and then springing up went careering off through some bushes.

He experienced a thrill of amazement when he came within view of a battery in action. The men there seemed to be in conventional moods, altogether unaware of the impending annihilation. The battery was disputing with a distant antagonist and the gunners were wrapped in admiration of their shooting. They were continually bending in coaxing postures over the guns. They seemed to be patting them on the back and encouraging them with words. The guns, stolid and undaunted, spoke with dogged valor.

The precise gunners were coolly enthusiastic. They lifted their eyes every chance to the smoke-wreathed hillock from whence the hostile battery addressed them. The youth pitied them as he ran. Methodical idiots! Machine-like fools! The refined joy of planting shells in the midst of the other battery's formation would appear a little thing when the infantry came swooping out of the woods.

The face of a youthful rider, who was jerking his frantic horse with an abandon of temper he might display in a placid barnyard, was impressed deeply upon his mind. He knew that he looked upon a man who would presently be dead.

Too, he felt a pity for the guns, standing, six good comrades, in a bold row.

He saw a brigade going to the relief of its pestered fellows. He scrambled upon a wee hill and watched it sweeping finely, keeping formation in difficult places. The blue of the line was crusted with steel color, and the brilliant flags projected. Officers were shouting.

This sight also filled him with wonder. The brigade was hurrying briskly to be gulped into the infernal mouths of the war god. What manner of men were they, anyhow? Ah, it was some wondrous breed! Or else they didn't comprehend—the fools.

A furious order caused commotion in the artillery. An officer on a bounding horse made maniacal motions with his arms. The teams went swinging up from the rear, the guns were whirled about, and the battery scampered away. The cannon with their noses poked slantingly at the ground grunted and grumbled like stout men, brave but with objections to hurry.

The youth went on, moderating his pace since he had left the place of noises.

Later he came upon a general of division seated upon a horse that pricked its ears in an interested way at the battle. There was a great gleaming of yellow and patent leather about the saddle and bridle. The quiet man astride looked mouse-colored upon such a splendid charger.

A jingling staff was galloping hither and thither. Sometimes the general was surrounded by horsemen and at other times he was quite alone. He looked to be much harassed. He had the appearance of a business man whose market is swinging up and down.

The youth went slinking around this spot. He went as near as he dared trying to overhear words. Perhaps the general, unable to comprehend chaos, might call upon him for information. And he could tell him. He knew all concerning it. Of a surety the force was in a fix, and any fool could see that if they did not retreat while they had opportunity—why—

He felt that he would like to thrash the general, or at least approach and tell him in plain words exactly what he thought him to be. It was criminal to stay calmly in one spot and make no effort to stay destruction. He loitered in a fever of eagerness for the division commander to apply to him.

As he warily moved about, he heard the general call out irritably: "Tompkins, go over an' see Taylor, an' tell him not t' be in such an all-fired hurry; tell him t' halt his brigade in th' edge of th' woods; tell him t' detach a reg'ment—say I think th' center 'll break if we don't help it out some; tell him t' hurry up."

A slim youth on a fine chestnut horse caught these swift words from the mouth of his superior. He made his horse bound into a gallop almost from a walk in his haste to go upon his mission. There was a cloud of dust.

A moment later the youth saw the general bounce excitedly in his saddle.

"Yes, by heavens, they have!" The officer leaned forward. His face was aflame with excitement. "Yes, by heavens, they've held 'im! They've held 'im!"

He began to blithely roar at his staff: "We'll wallop 'im now. We'll wallop 'im now. We've got 'em sure." He turned suddenly upon an aid: "Here—you—Jones—quick—ride after Tompkins—see Taylor—tell him t' go in—everlastingly—like blazes—anything."

As another officer sped his horse after the first messenger, the general beamed upon the earth like a sun. In his eyes was a desire to chant a pæan. He kept repeating, "They've held 'em, by heavens!"

His excitement made his horse plunge, and he merrily kicked and swore at it. He held a little carnival of joy on horseback.

## CHAPTER SEVEN

The youth cringed as if discovered in a crime. By heavens, they had won after all! The imbecile line had remained and become victors. He could hear cheering.

He lifted himself upon his toes and looked in the direction of the fight. A yellow fog lay wallowing on the treetops. From beneath it came the clatter of musketry. Hoarse cries told of an advance.

He turned away amazed and angry. He felt that he had been wronged.

He had fled, he told himself, because annihilation approached. He had done a good part in saving himself, who was a little piece of the army. He had considered the time, he said, to be one in which it was the duty of every little piece to rescue itself if possible. Later the officers could fit the little pieces together again, and make a battle front. If none of the little pieces were wise enough to save themselves from the flurry of death at such a time, why, then, where would be the army? It was all plain that he had proceeded according to very correct and commendable rules. His actions had been sagacious [8]

[8] SAGACIOUS (să·gā′shŭs)—Wise; of keen judgment.

things. They had been full of strategy. They were the work of a master's legs.

Thoughts of his comrades came to him. The brittle blue line had withstood the blows and won. He grew bitter over it. It seemed that the blind ignorance and stupidity of those little pieces had betrayed him. He had been overturned and crushed by their lack of sense in holding the position, when intelligent deliberation would have convinced them that it was impossible. He, the enlightened man who looks afar in the dark, had fled because of his superior perceptions and knowledge. He felt a great anger against his comrades. He knew it could be proved that they had been fools.

He wondered what they would remark when later he appeared in camp. His mind heard howls of derision. Their destiny would not enable them to understand his sharper point of view.

He began to pity himself acutely. He was ill used. He was trodden beneath the feet of an iron injustice. He had proceeded with wisdom and from the most righteous motives under heaven's blue only to be frustrated by hateful circumstances.

A dull, animal-like rebellion against his fellows, war in the abstract, and fate grew within him. He shambled along with bowed head, his brain in a tumult of agony and despair. When he looked loweringly up, quivering at each sound, his eyes had the expression of those of a criminal who thinks his guilt and his punishment great, and knows that he can find no words.

He went from the fields into a thick wood, as if resolved to bury himself. He wished to get out of hearing of the cracking shots which were to him like voices.

The ground was cluttered with vines and bushes, and the trees grew close and spread out like bouquets. He was obliged to force his way with much noise. The creepers, catching against his legs, cried out harshly as their sprays were torn from the barks of trees. The swishing saplings tried to make known his presence to the world. He could not conciliate [9] the forest. As he made his way, it was always calling out protestations. When he separated embraces of trees and vines the disturbed foliages waved their arms and turned their face leaves toward him. He dreaded lest these noisy motions and cries should bring men to look at him. So he went far, seeking dark and intricate places.

After a time the sound of musketry grew faint and the cannon boomed in the distance. The sun, suddenly apparent, blazed among the trees. The insects were making rhythmical noises. They seemed to be grinding their teeth in unison. A woodpecker stuck his impudent head around the side of a tree. A bird flew on lighthearted wing.

Off was the rumble of death. It seemed now that Nature had no ears.

This landscape gave him assurance. A fair field holding life. It was the religion of peace. It would die if its timid eyes were compelled to see blood. He conceived Nature to be a woman with a deep aversion to tragedy.

He threw a pine cone at a jovial squirrel, and he ran with chattering fear. High in a treetop he stopped, and, poking his head cautiously from behind a branch, looked down with an air of trepidation.

The youth felt triumphant at this exhibition. There was the law, he said. Nature had given him a sign. The

[9] CONCILIATE (kŏn·sĭl´ĭ·āt)—To gain the good will of; to make friendly.

squirrel, immediately upon recognizing danger, had taken to his legs without ado. He did not stand stolidly baring his furry belly to the missile, and die with an upward glance at the sympathetic heavens. On the contrary, he had fled as fast as his legs could carry him; and he was but an ordinary squirrel, too—doubtless no philosopher of his race. The youth wended, feeling that Nature was of his mind. She reenforced his argument with proofs that lived where the sun shone.

Once he found himself almost into a swamp. He was obliged to walk upon bog tufts and watch his feet to keep from the oily mire. Pausing at one time to look about him he saw, out at some black water, a small animal pounce in and emerge directly with a gleaming fish.

The youth went again into the deep thickets. The brushed branches made a noise that drowned the sounds of cannon. He walked on, going from obscurity into promises of a greater obscurity.

At length he reached a place where the high, arching boughs made a chapel. He softly pushed the green doors aside and entered. Pine needles were a gentle brown carpet. There was a religious half light.

Near the threshold he stopped, horror-stricken at the sight of a thing.

He was being looked at by a dead man who was seated with his back against a columnlike tree. The corpse was dressed in a uniform that once had been blue, but was now faded to a melancholy shade of green. The eyes, staring at the youth, had changed to the dull hue to be seen on the side of a dead fish. The mouth was open. Its red had changed to an appalling yellow. Over the gray skin of the face ran little ants. One was trundling some sort of a bundle along the upper lip.

The youth gave a shriek as he confronted the thing. He was for moments turned to stone before it. He remained staring into the liquid-looking eyes. The dead man and the living man exchanged a long look. Then the youth cautiously put one hand behind him and brought it against a tree. Leaning upon this he retreated, step by step, with his face still toward the thing. He feared that if he turned his back the body might spring up and stealthily pursue him.

The branches, pushing against him, threatened to throw him over upon it. His unguided feet, too, caught aggravatingly in brambles; and with it all he received a subtle suggestion to touch the corpse. As he thought of his hand upon it he shuddered profoundly.

At last he burst the bonds which had fastened him to the spot and fled, unheeding the underbrush. He was pursued by a sight of the black ants swarming greedily upon the gray face and venturing horribly near to the eyes.

After a time he paused, and, breathless and panting, listened. He imagined some strange voice would come from the dead throat and squawk after him in horrible menaces.

The trees about the portals of the chapel moved soughingly in a soft wind. A sad silence was upon the little guarding edifice.

## CHAPTER EIGHT

The trees began softly to sing a hymn of twilight. The sun sank until slanted bronze rays struck the forest. There was a lull in the noises of insects as if they had bowed their beaks and were making a devotional pause. There was silence save for the chanted chorus of the trees.

Then, upon this stillness, there suddenly broke a tremendous clangor of sounds. A crimson roar came from the distance.

The youth stopped. He was transfixed by this terrific medley of all noises. It was as if worlds were being rended. There was the ripping sound of musketry and the breaking crash of artillery.

His mind flew in all directions. He conceived the two armies to be at each other panther fashion. He listened for a time. Then he began to run in the direction of the battle. He saw that it was an ironical thing for him to be running thus toward that which he had been at such pains to avoid. But he said, in substance, to himself that if the earth and the moon were about to clash, many persons would doubtless plan to get upon the roofs to witness the collision.

As he ran, he became aware that the forest had stopped its music, as if at last becoming capable of hearing the foreign sounds. The trees hushed and stood motionless. Everything seemed to be listening to the crackle and clatter and ear-shaking thunder. The chorus pealed over the still earth.

It suddenly occurred to the youth that the fight in which he had been was, after all, but perfunctory popping. In the hearing of this present din he was doubtful if he had seen real battle scenes. This uproar explained a celestial battle; it was tumbling hordes a-struggle in the air.

Reflecting, he saw a sort of humor in the point of view of himself and his fellows during the late encounter. They had taken themselves and the enemy very seriously and had imagined that they were deciding the war. Individuals must have supposed that they were cutting the letters of their names deep into everlasting tablets of brass, or enshrining their reputations forever in the hearts of their countrymen, while, as to fact, the affair would appear in printed reports under a meek and immaterial title. But he saw that it was good, else, he said, in battle every one would surely run save forlorn hopes and their ilk.[10]

He went rapidly on. He wished to come to the edge of the forest that he might peer out.

As he hastened, there passed through his mind pictures of stupendous conflicts. His accumulated thought upon such subjects was used to form scenes. The noise was as the voice of an eloquent being, describing.

Sometimes the brambles formed chains and tried to hold him back. Trees, confronting him, stretched out their arms and forbade him to pass. After its previous hostility this new resistance of the forest filled him with a fine bitterness. It seemed that Nature could not be quite ready to kill him.

But he obstinately took roundabout ways, and presently he was where he could see long gray walls of vapor where lay battle lines. The voices of cannon shook him. The musketry sounded in long irregular surges that played havoc with his ears. He stood regardant for a moment. His eyes had an awestruck expression. He gawked in the direction of the fight.

Presently he proceeded again on his forward way. The battle was like the grinding of an immense and terrible machine to him. Its complexities and powers, its grim processes, fascinated him. He must go close and see it produce corpses.

He came to a fence and clambered over it. On the far side, the ground was littered with clothes and guns. A

[10] THEIR ILK—Things like them.

newspaper, folded up, lay in the dirt. A dead soldier was stretched with his face hidden in his arm. Farther off there was a group of four or five corpses keeping mournful company. A hot sun had blazed upon the spot.

In this place the youth felt that he was an invader. This forgotten part of the battleground was owned by the dead men, and he hurried, in the vague apprehension that one of the swollen forms would rise and tell him to be gone.

He came finally to a road from which he could see in the distance dark and agitated bodies of troops, smoke-fringed. In the lane was a blood-stained crowd streaming to the rear. The wounded men were cursing, groaning, and wailing. In the air, always, was a mighty swell of sound that it seemed could sway the earth. With the courageous words of the artillery and the spiteful sentences of the musketry mingled red cheers. And from this region of noises came the steady current of the maimed.

One of the wounded men had a shoeful of blood. He hopped like a school-boy in a game. He was laughing hysterically.

One was swearing that he had been shot in the arm through the commanding general's mismanagement of the army. One was marching with an air imitative of some sublime drum major. Upon his features was an unholy mixture of merriment and agony. As he marched he sang a bit of doggerel in a high and quavering voice:

"Sing a song 'a vic'try,
A pocketful 'a bullets,
Five an' twenty dead men
Baked in a—pie."

Parts of the procession limped and staggered to this tune.

Another had the gray seal of death already upon his face. His lips were curled in hard lines and his teeth were clinched. His hands were bloody from where he had passed them upon his wound. He seemed to be awaiting the moment when he should pitch headlong. He stalked like the specter of a soldier, his eyes burning with the power of a stare into the unknown.

There were some who proceeded sullenly, full of anger at their wounds, and ready to turn upon anything as an obscure cause.

An officer was carried along by two privates. He was peevish. "Don't joggle so, Johnson, yeh fool," he cried. "Think m' leg is made of iron? If yeh can't carry me decent, put me down an' let some one else do it."

He bellowed at the tottering crowd who blocked the quick march of his bearers. "Say, make way there, can't yeh? Make way, dickens take it all."

They sulkily parted and went to the roadsides. As he was carried past they made pert remarks to him. When he raged in reply and threatened them, they told him to be damned.

The shoulder of one of the tramping bearers knocked heavily against the spectral soldier who was staring into the unknown.

The youth joined this crowd and marched along with it. The torn bodies expressed the awful machinery in which the men had been entangled.

Orderlies and couriers occasionally broke through the throng in the roadway, scattering wounded men right and left, galloping on, followed by howls. The melancholy march was continually disturbed by the messengers, and sometimes by bustling batteries that came swinging and thumping down upon them, the officers shouting orders to clear the way.

There was a tattered man, fouled with dust, blood and powder stain from hair to shoes, who trudged quietly at the youth's side. He was listening with eagerness and much humility to the lurid descriptions of a bearded sergeant. His lean features wore an expression of awe and admiration. He was like a listener in a country store to wondrous tales told among the sugar barrels. He eyed the story-teller with unspeakable wonder. His mouth was agape in yokel fashion.

The sergeant, taking note of this, gave pause to his elaborate history while he administered a sardonic comment. "Be keerful, honey, you'll be a-ketchin' flies," he said.

The tattered man shrank back abashed.

After a time he began to sidle near to the youth, and in a different way try to make him a friend. His voice was gentle as a girl's voice and his eyes were pleading. The youth saw with surprise that the soldier had two wounds, one in the head, bound with a blood-soaked rag, and the other in the arm, making that member dangle like a broken bough.

After they had walked together for some time the tattered man mustered sufficient courage to speak. "Was pretty good fight, wasn't it?" he timidly said. The youth, deep in thought, glanced up at the bloody and grim figure with its lamblike eyes, "What?"

"Was pretty good fight, wa'n't it?"

"Yes," said the youth shortly. He quickened his pace.

But the other hobbled industriously after him. There was an air of apology in his manner, but he evidently thought

that he needed only to talk for a time, and the youth would perceive that he was a good fellow.

"Was pretty good fight, wa'n't it?" he began in a small voice, and then he achieved the fortitude to continue. "Dern me if I ever see fellers fight so. Laws, how they did fight! I knowed th' boys 'd like it when they onct got square at it. Th' boys ain't had no fair chanct up t' now, but this time they showed what they was. I knowed it 'd turn out this way. Yeh can't lick them boys. No, sir! They're fighters, they be."

He breathed a deep breath of humble admiration. He had looked at the youth for encouragement several times. He received none, but gradually he seemed to get absorbed in his subject.

"I was talkin' 'cross pickets with a boy from Georgie, onct, an' that boy, he ses, 'Your fellers 'll all run like hell when they onct hearn a gun,' he ses. 'Mebbe they will,' I ses, 'but I don't b'lieve none of it,' I ses; 'an' b'jiminey,' I ses back t' 'um, 'mebbe your fellers 'll all run like hell when they onct hearn a gun,' I ses. He larfed. Well, they didn't run t'-day, did they, hey? No, sir! They fit, an' fit, an' fit."

His homely face was suffused with a light of love for the army which was to him all things beautiful and powerful.

After a time he turned to the youth. "Where yeh hit, ol' boy?" he asked in a brotherly tone.

The youth felt instant panic at this question, although at first its full import was not borne in upon him.

"What?" he asked.

"Where yeh hit?" repeated the tattered man.

"Why," began the youth, "I—I— that is—why—I—"

He turned away suddenly and slid

through the crowd. His brow was heavily flushed, and his fingers were picking nervously at one of his buttons. He bent his head and fastened his eyes studiously upon the button as if it were a little problem.

The tattered man looked after him in astonishment.

## CHAPTER NINE

The youth fell back in the procession until the tattered soldier was not in sight. Then he started to walk on with the others.

But he was amid wounds. The mob of men was bleeding. Because of the tattered soldier's question he now felt that his shame could be viewed. He was continually casting sidelong glances to see if the men were contemplating the letters of guilt he felt burned into his brow.

At times he regarded the wounded soldiers in an envious way. He conceived persons with torn bodies to be peculiarly happy. He wished that he, too, had a wound, a red badge of courage.

The spectral soldier was at his side like a stalking reproach. The man's eyes were still fixed in a stare into the unknown. His gray, appalling face had attracted attention in the crowd, and men, slowing to his dreary pace, were walking with him. They were discussing his plight, questioning him and giving him advice. In a dogged way he repelled them, signing to them to go on and leave him alone. The shadows of his face were deepening and his tight lips seemed holding in check the moan of great despair. There could be seen a certain stiffness in the movements of his body, as if he were taking infinite care not to arouse the passion of his wounds. As he went on, he seemed al-

ways looking for a place, like one who goes to choose a grave.

Something in the gesture of the man as he waved the bloody and pitying soldiers away made the youth start as if bitten. He yelled in horror. Tottering forward he laid a quivering hand upon the man's arm. As the latter slowly turned his waxlike features toward him, the youth screamed:

"Gawd! Jim Conklin!"

The tall soldier made a little commonplace smile. "Hello, Henry," he said.

The youth swayed on his legs and glared strangely. He stuttered and stammered. "Oh, Jim—oh, Jim—oh, Jim—"

The tall soldier held out his gory hand. There was a curious red and black combination of new blood and old blood upon it. "Where yeh been, Henry?" he asked. He continued in a monotonous voice, "I thought mebbe yeh got keeled over. There's been thunder t' pay t'-day. I was worryin' about it a good deal."

The youth still lamented. "Oh, Jim —oh, Jim—oh, Jim—"

"Yeh know," said the tall soldier, "I was out there." He made a careful gesture. "An', Lord, what a circus! An', b'jiminey, I got shot—I got shot. Yes, b'jiminey, I got shot." He reiterated this fact in a bewildered way, as if he did not know how it came about.

The youth put forth anxious arms to assist him, but the tall soldier went firmly on as if propelled. Since the youth's arrival as a guardian for his friend, the other wounded men had ceased to display much interest. They occupied themselves again in dragging their own tragedies toward the rear.

Suddenly, as the two friends marched on, the tall soldier seemed to be overcome by a terror. His face turned to a semblance of gray paste. He clutched the youth's arm and looked all about him, as if dreading to be overheard. Then he began to speak in a shaking whisper:

"I tell yeh what I'm 'fraid of, Henry —I'll tell yeh what I'm 'fraid of. I'm 'fraid I'll fall down—an' then yeh know —them damned artillery wagons—they like as not 'll run over me. That's what I'm 'fraid of—"

The youth cried out to him hysterically: "I'll take care of yeh, Jim! I'll take care of yeh! I swear t' Gawd I will!"

"Sure—will yeh, Henry?" the tall soldier beseeched.

"Yes—yes—I tell yeh—I'll take care of yeh, Jim!" protested the youth. He could not speak accurately because of the gulpings in his throat.

But the tall soldier continued to beg in a lowly way. He now hung babelike to the youth's arm. His eyes rolled in the wildness of his terror. "I was allus a good friend t' yeh, wa'n't I, Henry? I've allus been a pretty good feller, ain't I? An' it ain't much t' ask, is it? Jest t' pull me along outer th' road? I'd do it fer you, wouldn't I, Henry?"

He paused in piteous anxiety to await his friend's reply.

The youth had reached an anguish where the sobs scorched him. He strove to express his loyalty, but he could only make fantastic gestures.

However, the tall soldier seemed suddenly to forget all those fears. He became again the grim, stalking specter of a soldier. He went stonily forward. The youth wished his friend to lean upon him, but the other always shook his head and strangely protested. "No—no—no—leave me be—leave me be—"

His look was fixed again upon the unknown. He moved with mysterious purpose, and all of the youth's offers he brushed aside. "No—no—leave me be —leave me be—"

The youth had to follow.

Presently the latter heard a voice talking softly near his shoulders. Turning he saw that it belonged to the tattered soldier. "Ye'd better take 'im outa th' road, pardner. There's a batt'ry comin' helitywhoop down th' road an' he'll git runned over. He's a goner anyhow in about five minutes—yeh kin see that. Ye'd better take 'im outa th' road. Where th' blazes does he git his stren'th from?"

"Lord knows!" cried the youth. He was shaking his hands helplessly.

He ran forward presently and grasped the tall soldier by the arm. "Jim! Jim!" he coaxed, "come with me."

The tall soldier weakly tried to wrench himself free. "Huh," he said vacantly. He stared at the youth for a moment. At last he spoke as if dimly comprehending. "Oh! Inteh th' fields? Oh!"

He started blindly through the grass.

The youth turned once to look at the lashing riders and jouncing guns of the battery. He was startled from this view by a shrill outcry from the tattered man.

"Gawd! He's runnin'!"

Turning his head swiftly, the youth saw his friend running in a staggering and stumbling way toward a little clump of bushes. His heart seemed to wrench itself almost free from his body at this sight. He made a noise of pain. He and the tattered man began a pursuit. There was a singular race.

When he overtook the tall soldier he began to plead with all the words he could find. "Jim—Jim—what are you doing—what makes you do this way—you'll hurt yerself."

The same purpose was in the tall soldier's face. He protested in a dulled way, keeping his eyes fastened on the mystic place of his intentions. "No—no—don't tech me—leave me be—leave me be—"

The youth, aghast and filled with wonder at the tall soldier, began quaveringly to question him. "Where yeh goin', Jim? What you thinking about? Where you going? Tell me, won't you, Jim?"

The tall soldier faced about as upon relentless pursuers. In his eyes there was a great appeal. "Leave me be, can't yeh? Leave me be fer a minnit."

The youth recoiled. "Why, Jim," he said, in a dazed way, "what's the matter with you?"

The tall soldier turned and, lurching dangerously, went on. The youth and the tattered soldier followed, sneaking as if whipped, feeling unable to face the stricken man if he should again confront them. They began to have thoughts of a solemn ceremony. There was something ritelike in these movements of the doomed soldier. And there was a resemblance in him to a devotee of a mad religion, blood-sucking, muscle-wrenching, bone-crushing. They were awed and afraid. They hung back lest he have at command a dreadful weapon.

At last, they saw him stop and stand motionless. Hastening up, they perceived that his face wore an expression telling that he had at last found the place for which he had struggled. His spare figure was erect; his bloody hands were quietly at his side. He was waiting with patience for something that he had come to meet. He was at the rendezvous. They paused and stood, expectant.

There was a silence.

Finally, the chest of the doomed soldier began to heave with a strained motion. It increased in violence until it was as if an animal was within and was kicking and tumbling furiously to be free.

This spectacle of gradual strangulation made the youth writhe, and once as his friend rolled his eyes, he saw something in them that made him sink wailing to the ground. He raised his voice in a last supreme call.

"Jim—Jim—Jim—"

The tall soldier opened his lips and spoke. He made a gesture. "Leave me be—don't tech me—leave me be—"

There was another silence while he waited.

Suddenly, his form stiffened and straightened. Then it was shaken by a prolonged ague.[11] He stared into space. To the two watchers there was a curious and profound dignity in the firm lines of his awful face.

He was invaded by a creeping strangeness that slowly enveloped him. For a moment the tremor of his legs caused him to dance a sort of hideous hornpipe. His arms beat wildly about his head in expression of implike enthusiasm.

His tall figure stretched itself to its full height. There was a slight rending sound. Then it began to swing forward, slow and straight, in the manner of a falling tree. A swift muscular contortion made the left shoulder strike the ground first.

The body seemed to bounce a little way from the earth. "God!" said the tattered soldier.

The youth had watched, spellbound,

[11] AGUE (ā′gū)—A state of violent shaking.

this ceremony at the place of meeting. His face had been twisted into an expression of every agony he had imagined for his friend.

He now sprang to his feet and, going closer, gazed upon the pastelike face. The mouth was open and the teeth showed in a laugh.

As the flap of the blue jacket fell away from the body, he could see that the side looked as if it had been chewed by wolves.

The youth turned, with sudden, livid rage, toward the battlefield. He shook his fist. He seemed about to deliver a philippic.[12]

"Hell—"

The red sun was pasted in the sky like a wafer.

## CHAPTER TEN

The tattered man stood musing.

"Well, he was a reg'lar jim-dandy fer nerve, wa'n't he," said he finally in a little awe-struck voice. "A reg'lar jim-dandy." He thoughtfully poked one of the docile hands with his foot. "I wonner where he got 'is stren'th from? I never seen a man do like that before. It was a funny thing. Well, he was a reg'lar jim-dandy."

The youth desired to screech out his grief. He was stabbed, but his tongue lay dead in the tomb of his mouth. He threw himself again upon the ground and began to brood.

The tattered man stood musing.

"Look-a-here, pardner," he said, after a time. He regarded the corpse as he spoke. "He's up an' gone, ain't 'e, an' we might as well begin t' look out fer ol' number one. This here thing is all over. He's up an' gone, ain't 'e? An' he's all right here. Nobody won't

[12] PHILIPPIC (fĭ·lĭp´ĭk)—A speech full of vicious invective and name-calling.

bother 'im. An' I must say I ain't enjoying any great health m'self these days."

The youth, awakened by the tattered soldier's tone, looked quickly up. He saw that he was swinging uncertainly on his legs and that his face had turned to a shade of blue.

"Good Lord!" he cried, "you ain't goin' t'—not you, too."

The tattered man waved his hand. "Nary die," he said. "All I want is some pea soup an' a good bed. Some pea soup," he repeated dreamfully.

The youth arose from the ground. "I wonder where he came from. I left him over there." He pointed. "And now I find 'im here. And he was coming from over there, too." He indicated a new direction. They both turned toward the body as if to ask it a question.

"Well," at length spoke the tattered man, "there ain't no use in our stayin' here an' tryin' t' ask him anything."

The youth nodded an assent wearily. They both turned to gaze for a moment at the corpse.

The youth murmured something.

"Well, he was a jim-dandy, wa'n't 'e?" said the tattered man as if in response.

They turned their backs upon it and started away. For a time they stole softly, treading with their toes. It remained laughing there in the grass.

"I'm commencin' t' feel pretty bad," said the tattered man, suddenly breaking one of his little silences. "I'm commencin' t' feel pretty damn' bad."

The youth groaned. "O Lord!" He wondered if he was to be the tortured witness of another grim encounter.

But his companion waved his hand reassuringly. "Oh, I'm not goin' t' die yit! There's too much dependin' on me fer me t' die yit. No, sir! Nary die; I *can't!* Ye'd oughta see th' swad a' chil'ren I've got, an' all like that."

The youth glancing at his companion could see by the shadow of a smile that he was making some kind of fun.

As they plodded on the tattered soldier continued to talk. "Besides, if I died, I wouldn't die th' way that feller did. That was th' funniest thing. I'd jest flop down, I would. I never seen a feller die th' way that feller did.

"Yeh know Tom Jamison, he lives next door t' me up home. He's a nice feller, he is, an' we was allus good friends. Smart, too. Smart as a steel trap. Well, when we was a-fightin' this afternoon, all-of-a-sudden he begin t' rip up an' cuss an' beller at me. 'Yer shot, yeh blamed infernal!'—he swear horrible—he ses t' me. I put up m' hand t' m' head an' when I looked at m' fingers, I seen, sure 'nough, I was shot. I give a holler an' begin t' run, but b'fore I could git away another one hit me in th' arm an' whirl' me clean 'round. I got skeared when they was all a-shootin' b'hind me an' I run t' beat all, but I cotch it pretty bad. I've an idee I'd a' been fightin' yit, if t'wasn't fer Tom Jamison."

Then he made a calm announcement: "There's two of 'em—little ones —but they're beginnin' t' have fun with me now. I don't b'lieve I kin walk much furder."

They went slowly on in silence. "Yeh look pretty peaked yerself," said the tattered man at last. "I bet yeh 've got a worser one than yeh think. Ye'd better take keer of yer hurt. It don't do t' let sech things go. It might be inside mostly, an' them plays thunder. Where is it located?" But he continued his harangue without waiting for a reply. "I see' a feller git hit plum in th' head when my reg'ment was a-standin' at ease onct. An' everybody yelled out to 'im: Hurt, John? Are yeh hurt much? 'No,' ses he. He looked kinder surprised, an' he went on tellin' 'em how he felt. He sed he didn't feel nothin'. But, by dad, th' first thing that feller knowed he was dead. Yes, he was dead—stone dead. So, yeh wanta watch out. Yeh might have some queer kind 'a hurt yerself. Yeh can't never tell. Where is your'n located?"

The youth had been wriggling since the introduction of this topic. He now gave a cry of exasperation and made a furious motion with his hand, "Oh, don't bother me!" he said. He was enraged against the tattered man, and could have strangled him. His companions seemed ever to play intolerable parts. They were ever upraising the ghost of shame on the stick of their curiosity. He turned toward the tattered man as one at bay. "Now, don't bother me," he repeated with desperate menace.

"Well, Lord knows I don't wanta bother anybody," said the other. There was a little accent of despair in his voice as he replied, "Lord knows I've gota 'nough m' own t' tend to."

The youth, who had been holding a bitter debate with himself and casting glances of hatred and contempt at the tattered man, here spoke in a hard voice. "Good-by," he said.

The tattered man looked at him in gaping amazement. "Why—why, pardner, where yeh goin'?" he asked unsteadily. The youth looking at him, could see that he, too, like that other one, was beginning to act dumb and animal-like. His thoughts seemed to be floundering about in his head. "Now —now—look—a—here, you Tom Jamison—now—I won't have this—this here won't do. Where—where yeh goin'?"

The youth pointed vaguely. "Over there," he replied.

"Well, now look—a—here—now," said the tattered man, rambling on in idiot fashion. His head was hanging forward and his words were slurred. "This thing won't do, now, Tom Jamison. It won't do. I know yeh, yeh pig-headed devil. Yeh wanta go trompin' off with a bad hurt. It ain't right—now—Tom Jamison—it ain't. Yeh wanta leave me take keer of yeh, Tom Jamison. It ain't—right—it ain't —fer yeh t' go—trompin' off—with a bad hurt—it ain't—ain't—ain't right— it ain't."

In reply the youth climbed a fence and started away. He could hear the tattered man bleating plaintively.

Once he faced about angrily. "What?"

"Look—a—here, now, Tom Jamison —now—it ain't—"

The youth went on. Turning at a distance he saw the tattered man wandering about helplessly in the field.

He now thought that he wished he was dead. He believed that he envied those men whose bodies lay strewn over the grass of the fields and on the fallen leaves of the forest.

The simple questions of the tattered man had been knife thrusts to him. They asserted a society that probes pitilessly at secrets until all is apparent. His late companion's chance persistency made him feel that he could not keep his crime concealed in his bosom. It was sure to be brought plain by one of those arrows which cloud the air and are constantly pricking, discovering, proclaiming those things which are willed to be forever hidden. He admitted that he could not defend himself against this agency. It was not within the power of vigilance.

## CHAPTER ELEVEN

He became aware that the furnace roar of the battle was growing louder. Great brown clouds had floated to the still heights of air before him. The noise, too, was approaching. The woods filtered men and the fields became dotted.

As he rounded a hillock, he perceived that the roadway was now a crying mass of wagons, teams, and men. From the heaving tangle issued exhortations, commands, imprecations. Fear was sweeping it all along. The cracking whips bit and horses plunged and tugged. The white-topped wagons strained and stumbled in their exertions like fat sheep.

The youth felt comforted in a measure by this sight. They were all retreating. Perhaps, then, he was not so bad after all. He seated himself and watched the terror-stricken wagons. They fled like soft, ungainly animals. All the roarers and lashers served to help him to magnify the dangers and horrors of the engagement that he might try to prove to himself that the thing with which men could charge him was in truth a symmetrical act. There was an amount of pleasure to him in watching the wild march of this vindication.

Presently the calm head of a forward-going column of infantry appeared in the road. It came swiftly on. Avoiding the obstructions gave it the sinuous movement of a serpent. The men at the head butted mules with their musket stocks. They prodded teamsters indifferent to all howls. The men forced their way through parts of the dense mass by strength. The blunt head of the column pushed. The raving teamsters swore many strange oaths.

The commands to make way had the ring of a great importance in them. The men were going forward to the heart of the din. They were to confront the eager rush of the enemy. They felt the pride of their onward movement when the remainder of the army seemed trying to dribble down this road. They tumbled teams about with a fine feeling that it was no matter so long as their column got to the front in time. This importance made their faces grave and stern. And the backs of the officers were very rigid.

As the youth looked at them the black weight of his woe returned to him. He felt that he was regarding a procession of chosen beings. The separation was as great to him as if they had marched with weapons of flame and banners of sunlight. He could never be like them. He could have wept in his longings.

He searched about in his mind for an adequate malediction for the indefinite cause, the thing upon which men turn the words of final blame. It—whatever it was—was responsible for him, he said. There lay the fault.

The haste of the column to reach the battle seemed to the forlorn young man to be something much finer than stout fighting. Heroes, he thought, could find excuses in that long seething lane. They could retire with perfect self-respect and make excuses to the stars.

He wondered what those men had eaten that they could be in such haste to force their way to grim chances of death. As he watched, his envy grew until he thought that he wished to change lives with one of them. He would have liked to have used a tremen-

dous force, he said, throw off himself and become a better. Swift pictures of himself, apart, yet in himself, came to him—a blue desperate figure leading lurid charges with one knee forward and a broken blade high—a blue, determined figure standing before a crimson and steel assault, getting calmly killed on a high place before the eyes of all. He thought of the magnificent pathos of his dead body.

These thoughts uplifted him. He felt the quiver of war desire. In his ears, he heard the ring of victory. He knew the frenzy of a rapid successful charge. The music of the trampling feet, the sharp voices, the clanking arms of the column near him made him soar on the red wings of war. For a few moments he was sublime.

He thought that he was about to start for the front. Indeed, he saw a picture of himself, dust-stained, haggard, panting, flying to the front at the proper moment to seize and throttle the dark, leering witch of calamity.

Then the difficulties of the thing began to drag at him. He hesitated, balancing awkwardly on one foot.

He had no rifle; he could not fight with his hands, said he resentfully to his plan. Well, rifles could be had for the picking. They were extraordinarily profuse.

Also, he continued, it would be a miracle if he found his regiment. Well, he could fight with any regiment.

He started forward slowly. He stepped as if he expected to tread upon some explosive thing. Doubts and he were struggling.

He would truly be a worm if any of his comrades should see him returning thus, the marks of his flight upon him. There was a reply that the intent fighters did not care for what happened rearward saving that no hostile bayonets appeared there. In the battle-blur his face would, in a way, be hidden, like the face of a cowled man.

But then he said that his tireless fate would bring forth, when the strife lulled for a moment, a man to ask of him an explanation. In imagination he felt the scrutiny of his companions as he painfully labored through some lies.

Eventually, his courage expended itself upon these objections. The debates drained him of his fire.

He was not cast down by this defeat of his plan, for, upon studying the affair carefully, he could not but admit that the objections were very formidable.

Furthermore, various ailments had begun to cry out. In their presence he could not persist in flying high with the wings of war; they rendered it almost impossible for him to see himself in a heroic light. He tumbled headlong.

He discovered that he had a scorching thirst. His face was so dry and grimy that he thought he could feel his skin crackle. Each bone of his body had an ache in it, and seemingly threatened to break with each movement. His feet were like two sores. Also, his body was calling for food. It was more powerful than a direct hunger. There was a dull, weight-like feeling in his stomach, and, when he tried to walk, his head swayed and he tottered. He could not see with distinctness. Small patches of green mist floated before his vision.

While he had been tossed by many emotions, he had not been aware of ailments. Now they beset him and made clamor. As he was at last compelled to pay attention to them, his capacity for self-hate was multiplied. In despair, he declared that he was not like those oth-

ers. He now conceded it to be impossible that he should ever become a hero. He was a craven loon.[13] Those pictures of glory were piteous things. He groaned from his heart and went staggering off.

A certain mothlike quality within him kept him in the vicinity of the battle. He had a great desire to see, and to get news. He wished to know who was winning.

He told himself that, despite his unprecedented suffering, he had never lost his greed for a victory, yet, he said, in a half-apologetic manner to his conscience, he could not but know that a defeat for the army this time might mean many favorable things for him. The blows of the enemy would splinter regiments into fragments. Thus, many men of courage, he considered, would be obliged to desert the colors and scurry like chickens. He would appear as one of them. They would be sullen brothers in distress, and he could then easily believe he had not run any farther or faster than they. And if he himself could believe in his virtuous perfection, he conceived that there would be small trouble in convincing all others.

He said, as if in excuse for this hope, that previously the army had encountered great defeats and in a few months had shaken off all blood and tradition of them, emerging as bright and valiant as a new one; thrusting out of sight the memory of disaster, and appearing with the valor and confidence of unconquered legions. The shrilling voices of the people at home would pipe dismally for a time, but various generals were usually compelled to listen to these ditties. He of course felt no compunc-

---

[13] CRAVEN LOON—A cowardly fool.

tions for proposing a general as a sacrifice. He could not tell who the chosen for the barbs might be, so he could center no direct sympathy upon him. The people were afar and he did not conceive public opinion to be accurate at long range. It was quite probable they would hit the wrong man who, after he had recovered from his amazement would perhaps spend the rest of his days in writing replies to the songs of his alleged failure. It would be very unfortunate, no doubt, but in this case a general was of no consequence to the youth.

In a defeat there would be a roundabout vindication of himself. He thought it would prove, in a manner, that he had fled early because of his superior powers of perception. A serious prophet upon predicting a flood should be the first man to climb a tree. This would demonstrate that he was indeed a seer.

A moral vindication was regarded by the youth as a very important thing. Without salve, he could not, he thought, wear the sore badge of his dishonor through life. With his heart continually assuring him that he was despicable, he could not exist without making it, through his actions, apparent to all men.

If the army had gone gloriously on he would be lost. If the din meant that now his army's flags were tilted forward he was a condemned wretch. He would be compelled to doom himself to isolation. If the men were advancing, their indifferent feet were trampling upon his chances for a successful life.

As these thoughts went rapidly through his mind, he turned upon them and tried to thrust them away. He denounced himself as a villain. He said that he was the most unutterably selfish man in existence. His mind pictured the soldiers who would place their defiant bodies before the spear of the yelling battle fiend, and as he saw their dripping corpses on an imagined field, he said that he was their murderer.

Again he thought that he wished he was dead. He believed that he envied a corpse. Thinking of the slain, he achieved a great contempt for some of them, as if they were guilty for thus becoming lifeless. They might have been killed by lucky chances, he said, before they had had opportunities to flee or before they had been really tested. Yet they would receive laurels from tradition. He cried out bitterly that their crowns were stolen and their robes of glorious memories were shams. However, he still said that it was a great pity he was not as they.

A defeat of the army had suggested itself to him as a means of escape from the consequences of his fall. He considered, now, however, that it was useless to think of such a possibility. His education had been that success for that mighty blue machine was certain; that it would make victories as a contrivance turns out buttons. He presently discarded all his speculations in the other direction. He returned to the creed of soldiers.

When he perceived again that it was not possible for the army to be defeated, he tried to bethink him of a fine tale which he could take back to his regiment, and with it turn the expected shafts of derision.[14]

But, as he mortally feared these shafts, it became impossible for him to invent a tale he felt he could trust. He experimented with many schemes, but threw them aside one by one as flimsy.

[14] DERISION (dê·rĭzh′ŭn)—Scorn; ridicule.

He was quick to see vulnerable places in them all.

Furthermore, he was much afraid that some arrow of scorn might lay him mentally low before he could raise his protecting tale.

He imagined the whole regiment saying: "Where's Henry Fleming? He run, didn't 'e? Oh, my!" He recalled various persons who would be quite sure to leave him no peace about it. They would doubtless question him with sneers, and laugh at his stammering hesitation. In the next engagement they would try to keep watch of him to discover when he would run.

Wherever he went in camp, he would encounter insolent and lingeringly cruel stares. As he imagined himself passing near a crowd of comrades, he could hear some one say, "There he goes!"

Then, as if the heads were moved by one muscle, all the faces were turned toward him with wide, derisive grins. He seemed to hear some one make a humorous remark in a low tone. At it the others all crowed and cackled. He was a slang phrase.[15]

## CHAPTER TWELVE

The column that had butted stoutly at the obstacles in the roadway was barely out of the youth's sight before he saw dark waves of men come sweeping out of the woods and down through the fields. He knew at once that the steel fibers had been washed from their hearts. They were bursting from their coats and their equipments as from entanglements. They charged down upon him like terrified buffaloes.

Behind them blue smoke curled and clouded above the treetops, and through the thickets he could sometimes see a distant pink glare. The voices of the cannon were clamoring in interminable chorus.

The youth was horror-stricken. He stared in agony and amazement. He forgot that he was engaged in combating the universe. He threw aside his mental pamphlets on the philosophy of the retreated and rules for the guidance of the damned.

The fight was lost. The dragons were coming with invincible strides. The army, helpless in the matted thickets and blinded by the overhanging night, was going to be swallowed. War, the red animal, war, the blood-swollen god, would have bloated fill.

Within him something bade to cry out. He had the impulse to make a rallying speech, to sing a battle hymn, but he could only get his tongue to call into the air: "Why—why—what—what's th' matter?"

Soon he was in the midst of them. They were leaping and scampering all about him. Their blanched faces shone in the dusk. They seemed, for the most part, to be very burly men. The youth turned from one to another of them as they galloped along. His incoherent questions were lost. They were heedless of his appeals. They did not seem to see him.

They sometimes gabbled insanely. One huge man was asking of the sky: "Say, where de plank road? Where de plank road!" It was as if he had lost a child. He wept in his pain and dismay.

Presently, men were running hither and thither in all ways. The artillery booming, forward, rearward, and on the flanks made jumble of ideas of direction. Landmarks had vanished into the gathered gloom. The youth began to imagine that he had got into the center

[15] . . . A SLANG PHRASE—That is, his name would be used as a slang phrase for *coward*, just as Benedict Arnold's name is used as a slang phrase for *traitor*.

of the tremendous quarrel, and he could perceive no way out of it. From the mouths of the fleeing men came a thousand wild questions, but no one made answers.

The youth, after rushing about and throwing interrogations at the heedless bands of retreating infantry, finally clutched a man by the arm. They swung around face to face.

"Why—why—" stammered the youth struggling with his balking tongue.

The man screamed: "Let go me! Let go me!" His face was livid and his eyes were rolling uncontrolled. He was heaving and panting. He still grasped his rifle, perhaps having forgotten to release his hold upon it. He tugged frantically, and the youth being compelled to lean forward was dragged several paces.

"Let go me! Let go me!"

"Why—why—" stuttered the youth.

"Well, then!" bawled the man in a lurid rage. He adroitly and fiercely swung his rifle. It crushed upon the youth's head. The man ran on.

The youth's fingers had turned to paste upon the other's arm. The energy was smitten from his muscles. He saw the flaming wings of lightning flash before his vision. There was a deafening rumble of thunder within his head.

Suddenly his legs seemed to die. He sank writhing to the ground. He tried to arise. In his efforts against the numbing pain he was like a man wrestling with a creature of the air.

There was a sinister struggle.

Sometimes he would achieve a position half erect, battle with the air for a moment, and then fall again, grabbing at the grass. His face was of a clammy pallor. Deep groans were wrenched from him.

At last, with a twisting movement, he got upon his hands and knees, and from thence, like a babe trying to walk, to his feet. Pressing his hands to his temples he went lurching over the grass.

He fought an intense battle with his body. His dulled senses wished him to swoon and he opposed them stubbornly, his mind portraying unknown dangers and mutilations if he should fall upon the field. He went tall soldier fashion.[16] He imagined secluded spots where he could fall and be unmolested. To search for one he strove against the tide of his pain.

Once he put his hand to the top of his head and timidly touched the wound. The scratching pain of the contact made him draw a long breath through his clinched teeth. His fingers were dabbled with blood. He regarded them with a fixed stare.

Around him he could hear the grumble of jolted cannon as the scurrying horses were lashed toward the front. Once, a young officer on a besplashed charger nearly ran him down. He turned and watched the mass of guns, men, and horses sweeping in a wide curve toward a gap in a fence. The officer was making excited motions with a gauntleted hand. The guns followed the teams with an air of unwillingness, of being dragged by the heels.

Some officers of the scattered infantry were cursing and railing like fishwives. Their scolding voices could be heard above the din. Into the unspeakable jumble in the roadway rode a squadron of cavalry. The faded yellow of their facings shone bravely. There was a mighty altercation.

The artillery were assembling as if for a conference.

[16] . . . TALL SOLDIER FASHION—He went in a lurching, staggering fashion as the tall soldier did just before he died.

The blue haze of evening was upon the field. The lines of forest were long purple shadows. One cloud lay along the western sky partly smothering the red.

As the youth left the scene behind him, he heard the guns suddenly roar out. He imagined them shaking in black rage. They belched and howled like brass devils guarding a gate. The soft air was filled with the tremendous remonstrance. With it came the shattering peal of opposing infantry. Turning to look behind him, he could see sheets of orange light illumine the shadowy distance. There were subtle and sudden lightnings in the far air. At times he thought he could see heaving masses of men.

He hurried on in the dusk. The day had faded until he could barely distinguish place for his feet. The purple darkness was filled with men who lectured and jabbered. Sometimes he could see them gesticulating against the blue and somber sky. There seemed to be a great ruck of men and munitions spread about in the forest and in the fields.

The little narrow roadway now lay lifeless. There were overturned wagons like sun-dried boulders. The bed of the former torrent was choked with the bodies of horses and splintered parts of war machines.

It had come to pass that his wound pained him but little. He was afraid to move rapidly, however, for a dread of disturbing it. He held his head very still and took many precautions against stumbling. He was filled with anxiety, and his face was pinched and drawn in anticipation of the pain of any sudden mistake of his feet in the gloom.

His thoughts, as he walked, fixed intently upon his hurt. There was a cool, liquid feeling about it as he imagined blood moving slowly down under his hair. His head seemed swollen to a size that made him think his neck to be inadequate.

The new silence of his wound made much worriment. The little blistering voices of pain that had called out from his scalp were, he thought, definite in their expression of danger. By them he believed that he could measure his plight. But when they remained ominously silent he became frightened and imagined terrible fingers that clutched into his brain.

Amid it he began to reflect upon various incidents and conditions of the past. He bethought him of certain meals his mother had cooked at home, in which those dishes of which he was particularly fond had occupied prominent positions. He saw the spread table. The pine walls of the kitchen were glowing in the warm light from the stove. Too, he remembered how he and his companions used to go from the schoolhouse to the bank of a shaded pool. He saw his clothes in disorderly array upon the grass of the bank. He felt the swash of the fragrant water upon his body. The leaves of the overhanging maple rustled with melody in the wind of youthful summer.

He was overcome presently by a dragging weariness. His head hung forward and his shoulders were stooped as if he were bearing a great bundle. His feet shuffled along the ground.

He held continuous arguments as to whether he should lie down and sleep at some near spot, or force himself on until he reached a certain haven. He often tried to dismiss the question, but his body persisted in rebellion and his senses nagged at him like pampered babies.

At last he heard a cheery voice near his shoulder: "Yeh seem t' be in a pretty bad way, boy?"

The youth did not look up, but he assented with a thick tongue. "Uh!"

The owner of the cheery voice took him firmly by the arm. "Well," he said, with a round laugh, "I'm goin' your way. Th' hull gang is goin' your way. An' I guess I kin give yeh a lift." They began to walk like a drunken man and his friend.

As they went along, the man questioned the youth and assisted him with the replies like one manipulating the mind of a child. Sometimes he interjected anecdotes. "What reg'ment do yeh b'long teh? Eh? What's that? Th' 304th N' York? Why, what corps is that in? Oh, it is? Why, I thought they wasn't engaged t'-day—they're 'way over in th' center. Oh, they was, eh? Well, pretty nearly everybody got their share 'a fightin' t'-day. By dad, I give myself up fer dead any number 'a times. There was shootin' here an' shootin' there, an' hollerin' here an' hollerin' there, in th' damn' darkness, until I couldn't tell t' save m' soul which side I was on. Sometimes I thought I was sure 'nough from Ohier, an' other times I could a' swore I was from th' bitter end of Florida. It was th' most mixed up dern thing I ever see. An' these here hull woods is a reg'lar mess. It'll be a miracle if we find our reg'ments t'-night. Pretty soon, though, we 'll meet a-plenty of guards an' provost-guards, an' one thing an' another. Ho! there they go with an off'cer, I guess. Look at his leg a-draggin'. He's got all th' war he wants, I bet. He won't be talkin' so big about his reputation an' all when they go t' sawin' off his leg. Poor feller! My brother's got whiskers jest like that. How did yeh git 'way over here, anyhow? Your reg'-ment is a long way from here, ain't it? Well, I guess we can find it. Yeh know there was a boy killed in my comp'ny t'-day that I thought th' world an' all of. Jack was a nice feller. By ginger, it hurt like thunder t' see ol' Jack jest git knocked flat. We was a-standin' purty peaceable for a spell, 'though there was men runnin' ev'ry way all 'round us, an' while we was a-standin' like that, 'long come a big fat feller. He began t' peck at Jack's elbow, an' he ses: 'Say, where's th' road t' th' river?' An' Jack, he never paid no attention, an' th' feller kept on a-peckin' at his elbow an' sayin': 'Say, where's th' road t' th' river?' Jack was a-lookin' ahead all th' time tryin' t' see th' Johnnies comin' through th' woods, an' he never paid no attention t' this big fat feller fer a long time, but at last he turned 'round an' he ses: 'Ah, go t' hell an' find th' road t' th' river!' An' jest then a shot slapped him bang on th' side th' head. He was a sergeant, too. Them was his last words. Thunder, I wish we was sure 'a findin' our reg'ments t'-night. It's goin' t' be long huntin'. But I guess we kin do it."

In the search which followed, the man of the cheery voice seemed to the youth to possess a wand of a magic kind. He threaded the mazes of the tangled forest with a strange fortune. In encounter with guards and patrols he displayed the keenness of a detective and the valor of a gamin. Obstacles fell before him and became of assistance. The youth, with his chin still on his breast, stood woodenly by while his companion beat ways and means out of sullen things.

The forest seemed a vast hive of men buzzing about in frantic circles, but the cheery man conducted the youth without mistakes, until at last he began to chuckle with glee and self-satisfaction. "Ah, there yeh are! See that fire?"

The youth nodded stupidly.

"Well, there's where your reg'ment is. An' now, good-by, ol' boy, good luck t' yeh."

A warm and strong hand clasped the youth's languid fingers for an instant, and then he heard a cheerful and audacious whistling as the man strode away. As he who had so befriended him was thus passing out of his life, it suddenly occurred to the youth that he had not once seen his face.

## CHAPTER THIRTEEN

The youth went slowly toward the fire indicated by his departed friend. As he reeled, he bethought him of the welcome his comrades would give him. He had conviction that he would soon feel in his sore heart the barbed missiles of ridicule. He had no strength to invent a tale; he would be a soft target.

He made vague plans to go off into the deeper darkness and hide, but they were all destroyed by the voices of exhaustion and pain from his body. His ailments, clamoring, forced him to seek the place of food and rest, at whatever cost.

He swung unsteadily toward the fire. He could see the forms of men throwing black shadows in the red light, and as he went nearer it became known to him in some way that the ground was strewn with sleeping men.

Of a sudden he confronted a black and monstrous figure. A rifle barrel caught some glinting beams. "Halt! halt!" He was dismayed for a moment, but he presently thought that he recognized the nervous voice. As he stood tottering before the rifle barrel, he called out: "Why, hello, Wilson, you —you here?"

The rifle was lowered to a position of caution and the loud soldier came slowly forward. He peered into the youth's face. "That you, Henry?"

"Yes it's—it's me."

"Well, well, ol' boy," said the other, "by ginger, I'm glad t' see yeh! I give yeh up fer a goner. I thought yeh was dead sure enough." There was husky emotion in his voice.

The youth found that now he could barely stand upon his feet. There was a sudden sinking of his forces. He thought he must hasten to produce his tale to protect him from the missiles already at the lips of his redoubtable comrades. So, staggering before the loud soldier, he began: "Yes, yes. I've —I've had an awful time. I've been all over. Way over on th' right. Ter'ble fightin' over there. I had an awful time. I got separated from th' reg'-ment. Over on th' right, I got shot. In th' head. I never see sech fightin'. Awful time. I don't see how I could a' got separated from th' reg'ment. I got shot, too."

His friend had stepped forward quickly. "What? Got shot? Why didn't yeh say so first? Poor ol' boy, we must—hol' on a minnit; what am I doin'? I'll call Simpson."

Another figure at that moment loomed in the gloom. They could see that it was the corporal. "Who yeh talkin' to, Wilson?" he demanded. His voice was anger-toned. "Who yeh talkin' to? Yeh th' derndest sentinel— why—hello, Henry, you here? Why, I thought you was dead four hours ago! Great Jerusalem, they keep turnin' up every ten minutes or so! We thought we'd lost forty-two men by straight count, but if they keep on a-comin' this way, we'll git th' comp'ny all back by mornin' yet. Where was yeh?"

"Over on th' right. I got separated"—began the youth with considerable glibness.

But his friend had interrupted hastily. "Yes, an' he got shot in th' head an' he's in a fix, an' we must see t' him right away." He rested his rifle in the hollow of his left arm and his right around the youth's shoulder.

"Gee, it must hurt like thunder!" he said.

The youth leaned heavily upon his friend. "Yes, it hurts—hurts a good deal," he replied. There was a faltering in his voice.

"Oh," said the corporal. He linked his arm in the youth's and drew him forward. "Come on, Henry. I'll take keer 'a yeh."

As they went on together the loud private called out after them: "Put 'im t' sleep in my blanket, Simpson. An'—hol' on a minnit—here's my canteen. It's full 'a coffee. Look at his head by th' fire an' see how it looks. Maybe it's a pretty bad un. When I git relieved in a couple 'a minnits, I'll be over an' see t' him."

The youth's senses were so deadened that his friend's voice sounded from afar and he could scarcely feel the pressure of the corporal's arm. He submitted passively to the latter's directing strength. His head was in the old manner hanging forward upon his breast. His knees wobbled.

The corporal led him into the glare of the fire. "Now, Henry," he said, "let's have a look at yer ol' head."

The youth sat down obediently and the corporal, laying aside his rifle, began to fumble in the bushy hair of his comrade. He was obliged to turn the other's head so that the full flush of the fire light would beam upon it. He puckered his mouth with a critical air.

He drew back his lips and whistled through his teeth when his fingers came in contact with the splashed blood and the rare wound.

"Ah, here we are!" he said. He awkwardly made further investigations. "Jest as I thought," he added, presently. "Yeh've been grazed by a ball. It's raised a queer lump jest as if some feller had lammed yeh on th' head with a club. It stopped a-bleedin' long time ago. Th' most about it is that in th' mornin' yeh'll feel that a number ten hat wouldn't fit yeh. An' your head 'll be all het up an' feel as dry's burnt pork. An' yeh may git a lot 'a other sicknesses, too, by mornin'. Yeh can't never tell. Still, I don't much think so. It's jest a damn' good belt on th' head, an' nothin' more. Now, you jest sit here an' don't move, while I go rout out th' relief. Then I'll send Wilson t' take keer 'a yeh."

The corporal went away. The youth remained on the ground like a parcel. He stared with a vacant look into the fire.

After a time he aroused, for some part, and the things about him began to take form. He saw that the ground in the deep shadows was cluttered with men, sprawling in every conceivable posture. Glancing narrowly into the more distant darkness, he caught occasional glimpses of visages that loomed pallid and ghostly, lit with a phosphorescent glow. These faces expressed in their lines the deep stupor of the tired soldiers. They made them appear like men drunk with wine. This bit of forest might have appeared to an ethereal wanderer as a scene of the result of some frightful debauch.

On the other side of the fire the youth observed an officer asleep, seated bolt upright, with his back against a tree. There was something perilous in his position. Badgered by dreams, perhaps, he swayed with little bounces and starts, like an old, toddy-stricken grandfather in a chimney corner. Dust and stains were upon his face. His lower jaw hung down as if lacking strength to assume its normal position. He was the picture of an exhausted soldier after a feast of war.

He had evidently gone to sleep with his sword in his arms. These two had slumbered in an embrace, but the weapon had been allowed in time to fall unheeded to the ground. The brass-mounted hilt lay in contact with some parts of the fire.

Within the gleam of rose and orange light from the burning sticks were other soldiers, snoring and heaving, or lying deathlike in slumber. A few pairs of legs were stuck forth, rigid and straight. The shoes displayed the mud or dust of marches and bits of rounded trousers, protruding from the blankets, showed rents and tears from hurried pitchings through the dense brambles.

The fire crackled musically. From it swelled light smoke. Overhead the foliage moved softly. The leaves, with their faces turned toward the blaze, were colored shifting hues of silver, often edged with red. Far off to the right, through a window in the forest, could be seen a handful of stars lying, like glittering pebbles, on the black level of the night.

Occasionally, in this low-arched hall, a soldier would arouse and turn his body to a new position, the experience of his sleep having taught him of uneven and objectionable places upon the ground under him. Or, perhaps, he would lift himself to a sitting posture, blink at the fire for an unintelligent moment, throw a swift glance at his prostrate companion, and then cuddle down again with a grunt of sleepy content.

The youth sat in a forlorn heap until his friend, the loud young soldier, came, swinging two canteens by their light strings. "Well, now, Henry, ol' boy," said the latter, "we'll have yeh fixed up in jest about a minnit."

He had the bustling ways of an amateur nurse. He fussed around the fire and stirred the sticks to brilliant exertions. He made his patient drink largely from the canteen that contained the coffee. It was to the youth a delicious draught. He tilted his head afar back and held the canteen long to his lips. The cool mixture went caressingly down his blistered throat. Having finished, he sighed with comfortable delight.

The loud young soldier watched his comrade with an air of satisfaction. He later produced an extensive handkerchief from his pocket. He folded it into a manner of bandage and soused water from the other canteen upon the middle of it. This crude arrangement he bound over the youth's head, tying the ends in a queer knot at the back of the neck.

"There," he said, moving off and surveying his deed, "yeh look like th' devil, but I bet yeh feel better."

The youth contemplated his friend with grateful eyes. Upon his aching and swelling head the cold cloth was like a tender woman's hand.

"Yeh don't holler ner say nothin'," remarked his friend approvingly. "I know I'm a blacksmith at takin' keer 'a sick folks, an' yeh never squeaked. Yer a good un. Henry. Most 'a men would 'a been in th' hospital long ago. A shot in th' head ain't foolin' business."

The youth made no reply, but began

to fumble with the buttons of his jacket.

"Well, come, now," continued his friend, "come on. I must put yeh t' bed an' see that yeh git a good night's rest."

The other got carefully erect, and the loud young soldier led him among the sleeping forms lying in groups and rows. Presently he stooped and picked up his blankets. He spread the rubber one upon the ground and placed the woolen one about the youth's shoulders.

"There now," he said, "lie down an' git some sleep."

The youth, with his manner of dog-like obedience, got carefully down like a crone [17] stooping. He stretched out with a murmur of relief and comfort. The ground felt like the softest couch.

But of a sudden he ejaculated: "Hol' on a minnit! Where you goin' t' sleep?"

His friend waved his hand impatiently. "Right down there by yeh."

"Well, but hol' on a minnit," continued the youth. "What yeh goin' t' sleep in? I've got your—"

The loud young soldier snarled: "Shet up an' go on t' sleep. Don't be makin' a damn' fool 'a yerself," he said severely.

After the reproof the youth said no more. An exquisite drowsiness had spread through him. The warm comfort of the blanket enveloped him and made a gentle languor.[18] His head fell forward on his crooked arm and his weighted lids went slowly down over his eyes. Hearing a splatter of musketry from the distance, he wondered indifferently if those men sometimes slept. He gave a long sigh, snuggled down

---

[17] CRONE—Old woman.

[18] LANGUOR (lăng′gēr)—State of weakness or weariness.

into his blanket, and in a moment was like his comrades.

## CHAPTER FOURTEEN

When the youth awoke it seemed to him that he had been asleep for a thousand years, and he felt sure that he opened his eyes upon an unexpected world. Gray mists were slowly shifting before the first efforts of the sunrays. An impending splendor could be seen in the eastern sky. An icy dew had chilled his face, and immediately upon arousing he curled farther down into his blankets. He stared for a while at the leaves overhead, moving in a heraldic wind of the day.

The distance was splintering and blaring with the noise of fighting. There was in the sound an expression of a deadly persistency, as if it had not begun and was not to cease.

About him were the rows and groups of men that he had dimly seen the previous night. They were getting a last draught of sleep before the awakening. The gaunt, care-worn features and dusty figures were made plain by this quaint light at the dawning, but it dressed the skin of the men in corpse-like hues and made the tangled limbs appear pulseless and dead. The youth started up with a little cry when his eyes first swept over this motionless mass of men, thick-spread upon the ground, pallid, and in strange postures. His disordered mind interpreted the hall of the forest as a charnel place. He believed for an instant that he was in the house of the dead, and he did not dare to move lest these corpses start up, squalling and squawking. In a second, however, he achieved his proper mind. He swore a complicated oath at himself. He saw that this somber picture was not a fact of the present, but a mere prophecy.

He heard then the noise of a fire crackling briskly in the cold air, and, turning his head, he saw his friend pottering busily about a small blaze. A few other figures moved in the fog, and he heard the hard cracking of axe blows.

Suddenly there was a hollow rumble of drums. A distant bugle sang faintly. Similar sounds, varying in strength, came from near and far over the forest. The bugles called to each other like brazen gamecocks. The near thunder of the regimental drums rolled.

The body of men in the woods rustled. There was a general uplifting of heads. A murmuring of voices broke upon the air. In it there was much bass of grumbling oaths. Strange gods were addressed in condemnation of the early hours necessary to correct war. An officer's peremptory tenor rang out and quickened the stiffened movement of the men. The tangled limbs unraveled. The corpse-hued faces were hidden behind fists that twisted slowly in the eye sockets.

The youth sat up and gave vent to an enormous yawn. "Thunder!" he remarked petulantly. He rubbed his eyes, and then putting up his hand felt carefully of the bandage over his wound. His friend, perceiving him to be awake, came from the fire. "Well, Henry, ol' man, how do yeh feel this mornin'?" he demanded.

The youth yawned again. Then he puckered his mouth to a little pucker. His head, in truth, felt precisely like a melon, and there was an unpleasant sensation at his stomach.

"Oh, Lord, I feel pretty bad," he said.

"Thunder!" exclaimed the other. "I hoped ye'd feel all right this mornin'. Let's see th' bandage—I guess it's slipped." He began to tinker at the wound in rather a clumsy way until the youth exploded.

"Gosh-dern it!" he said in sharp irritation; "you're the hangdest man I ever saw! You wear muffs on your hands. Why in good thunderation can't you be more easy? I'd rather you'd stand off an' throw guns at it. Now, go slow, an' don't act as if you was nailing down carpet."

He glared with insolent command at his friend, but the latter answered soothingly. "Well, well, come now, an' git some grub," he said. "Then, maybe, yeh'll feel better."

At the fireside the loud young soldier watched over his comrade's wants with tenderness and care. He was very busy marshaling the little black vagabonds of tin cups and pouring into them the streaming, iron colored mixture from a small and sooty tin pail. He had some fresh meat, which he roasted hurriedly upon a stick. He sat down then and contemplated the youth's appetite with glee.

The youth took note of a remarkable change in his comrade since those days of camp life upon the river bank. He seemed no more to be continually regarding the proportions of his personal prowess. He was not furious at small words that pricked his conceits. He was no more a loud young soldier. There was about him now a fine reliance. He showed a quiet belief in his purposes and his abilities. And this inward confidence evidently enabled him to be indifferent to little words of other men aimed at him.

The youth reflected. He had been used to regarding his comrade as a blatant child with an audacity grown from his inexperience, thoughtless, headstrong, jealous, and filled with a tinsel courage. A swaggering babe accustomed to strut in his own dooryard. The youth wondered where had been born these new eyes; when his comrade had made the great discovery that there were many men who would refuse to be subjected by him. Apparently, the other had now climbed a peak of wisdom from which he could perceive himself as a very wee thing. And the youth saw that ever after it would be easier to live in his friend's neighborhood.

His comrade balanced his ebony coffee cup on his knee. "Well, Henry," he said, "what d'yeh think th' chances are? D'yeh think we'll wallop 'em?"

The youth considered for a moment. "Day-b'fore-yesterday," he finally replied, with boldness, "you would 'a' bet you'd lick the hull kit-an'-boodle all by yourself."

His friend looked a trifle amazed. "Would I?" he asked. He pondered. "Well, perhaps I would," he decided at last. He stared humbly at the fire.

The youth was quite disconcerted at this surprising reception of his remarks. "Oh, no, you wouldn't either," he said, hastily trying to retrace.

But the other made a deprecating [19] gesture. "Oh, yeh needn't mind, Henry," he said. "I believe I was a pretty big fool in those days." He spoke as after a lapse of years.

There was a little pause.

"All th' officers say we've got th' rebs in a pretty tight box," said the friend, clearing his throat in a commonplace way. "They all seem t' think we've got 'em jest where we want 'em."

"I don't know about that," the youth replied. "What I seen over on th' right makes me think it was th' other way

[19] DEPRECATE (dĕp'rẻ·kāt)—To express disapproval of.

about. From where I was, it looked as if we was gettin' a good poundin' yestirday."

"D'yeh think so?" inquired the friend. "I thought we handled 'em pretty rough yestirday."

"Not a bit," said the youth. "Why, lord, man, you didn't see nothing of the fight. Why!" Then a sudden thought came to him. "Oh! Jim Conklin's dead."

His friend started. "What? Is he? Jim Conklin?"

The youth spoke slowly. "Yes. He's dead. Shot in th' side."

"Yeh don't say so. Jim Conklin . . . poor cuss!"

All about them were other small fires surrounded by men with their little black utensils. From one of these near came sudden sharp voices in a row. It appeared that two light-footed soldiers had been teasing a huge, bearded man, causing him to spill coffee upon his blue knees. The man had gone into a rage and had sworn comprehensively. Stung by his language, his tormentors had immediately bristled at him with a great show of resenting unjust oaths. Possibly there was going to be a fight.

The friend arose and went over to them, making pacific motions with his arms. "Oh, here, now, boys, what's th' use?" he said. "We'll be at th' rebs in less'n an hour. What's th' good fightin' 'mong ourselves?"

One of the light-footed soldiers turned upon him red-faced and violent. "Yeh needn't come around here with yer preachin'. I s'pose yeh don't approve 'a fightin' since Charley Morgan licked yeh; but I don't see what business this here is 'a yours or anybody else."

"Well, it ain't," said the friend

mildly. "Still I hate t' see—"

That was a tangled argument.

"Well, he—," said the two, indicating their opponent with accusative forefingers.

The huge soldier was quite purple with rage. He pointed at the two soldiers with his great hand, extended claw-like. "Well, they—"

But during this argumentative time the desire to deal blows seemed to pass, although they said much to each other. Finally the friend returned to his old seat. In a short while the three antagonists could be seen together in an amiable bunch.

"Jimmie Rogers ses I'll have t' fight him after th' battle t'-day," announced the friend as he again seated himself. "He ses he don't allow no interferin' in his business. I hate t' see th' boys fightin' 'mong themselves."

The youth laughed. "Yer changed a good bit. Yeh ain't at all like yeh was. I remember when you an' that Irish feller—" He stopped and laughed again.

"No, I didn't use t' be that way," said his friend thoughtfully. "That's true 'nough."

"Well, I didn't mean—" began the youth.

The friend made another deprecatory gesture. "Oh, yeh needn't mind, Henry."

There was another little pause.

"Th' reg'ment lost over half th' men yesterday," remarked the friend eventually. "I thought a course they was all dead, but, laws, they kep' a-comin' back last night until it seems, after all, we didn't lose but a few. They'd been scattered all over, wanderin' around in th' woods, fightin' with other reg'ments, an' everything. Jest like you done."

"So?" said the youth.

## CHAPTER FIFTEEN

The regiment was standing at order arms at the side of a lane, waiting for the command to march, when suddenly the youth remembered the little packet enwrapped in a faded yellow envelope which the loud young soldier with lugubrious words had intrusted to him. It made him start. He uttered an exclamation and turned toward his comrade. "Wilson!"

His friend, at his side in the ranks, was thoughtfully staring down the road. From some cause his expression was at that moment very meek. The youth, regarding him with sidelong glances, felt impelled to change his purpose. "Oh, nothing," he said.

His friend turned his head in some surprise, "Why, what was yeh goin' t' say?"

"Oh, nothing," repeated the youth.

He resolved not to deal the little blow. It was sufficient that the fact made him glad. It was not necessary to knock his friend on the head with the misguided packet.

He had been possessed of much fear of his friend, for he saw how easily questionings could make holes in his feelings. Lately, he had assured himself that the altered comrade would not tantalize him with a persistent curiosity, but he felt certain that during the first period of leisure his friend would ask him to relate his adventures of the previous day.

He now rejoiced in the possession of a small weapon with which he could prostrate his comrade at the first signs of a cross-examination. He was master. It would now be he who could laugh and shoot the shafts of derision.

The friend had, in a weak hour, spoken with sobs of his own death. He had delivered a melancholy oration previous to his funeral, and had doubtless, in the packet of letters, presented various keepsakes to relatives. But he had not died, and thus he had delivered himself into the hands of the youth.

The latter felt immensely superior to his friend, but he inclined to condescension. He adopted toward him an air of patronizing good humor.

His self-pride was now entirely restored. In the shade of its flourishing growth he stood with braced and self-confident legs, and since nothing could now be discovered he did not shrink from an encounter with the eyes of judges, and allowed no thought of his own to keep him from an attitude of manfulness. He had performed his mistakes in the dark, so he was still a man.

Indeed, when he remembered his fortunes of yesterday, and looked at them from a distance he began to see something fine there. He had license to be pompous and veteran-like.

His panting agonies of the past he put out of his sight.

In the present, he declared to himself that it was only the doomed and the damned who roared with sincerity at circumstance. Few but they ever did it. A man with a full stomach and the respect of his fellows had no business to scold about anything that he might think to be wrong in the ways of the universe, or even with the ways of society. Let the unfortunates rail; the others may play marbles.

He did not give a great deal of thought to these battles that lay directly before him. It was not essential that he should plan his ways in regard to them. He had been taught that many obligations of a life were easily avoided. The lessons of yesterday had been that retribution was a laggard [20]

and blind. With these facts before him he did not deem it necessary that he should become feverish over the possibilities of the ensuing twenty-four hours. He could leave much to chance. Besides, a faith in himself had secretly blossomed. There was a little flower of confidence growing within him. He was now a man of experience. He had been out among the dragons, he said, and he assured himself that they were not so hideous as he had imagined them. Also, they were inaccurate; they did not sting with precision. A stout heart often defied, and, defying, escaped.

And, furthermore, how could they kill him who was the chosen of gods and doomed to greatness?

He remembered how some of the men had run from the battle. As he recalled their terror-struck faces he felt a scorn for them. They had surely been more fleet and more wild than was absolutely necessary. They were weak mortals. As for himself, he had fled with discretion and dignity.

He was aroused from this reverie by his friend, who, having hitched about nervously and blinked at the trees for a time, suddenly coughed in an introductory way, and spoke.

"Fleming!"

"What?"

The friend put his hand up to his mouth and coughed again. He fidgeted in his jacket.

"Well," he gulped, at last, "I guess yeh might as well give me back them letters." Dark, prickling blood had flushed into his cheeks and brow.

"All right, Wilson," said the youth. He loosened two buttons of his coat, thrust in his hand, and brought forth

[20] LAGGARD—A loiterer; one who is late or slow in coming.

the packet. As he extended it to his friend the latter's face was turned from him.

He had been slow in the act of producing the packet because during it he had been trying to invent a remarkable comment on the affair. He could conjure nothing of sufficient point. He was compelled to allow his friend to escape unmolested with his packet. And for this he took unto himself considerable credit. It was a generous thing.

His friend at his side seemed suffering great shame. As he contemplated him, the youth felt his heart grow more strong and stout. He had never been compelled to blush in such manner for his acts; he was an individual of extraordinary virtues.

He reflected, with condescending pity: "Too bad! Too bad! The poor devil, it makes him feel tough!"

After this incident, and as he reviewed the battle pictures he had seen, he felt quite competent to return home and make the hearts of the people glow with stories of war. He could see himself in a room of warm tints telling tales to listeners. He could exhibit laurels. They were insignificant; still, in a district where laurels were infrequent, they might shine.

He saw his gaping audience picturing him as the central figure in blazing scenes. And he imagined the consternation and the ejaculations of his mother and the young lady at the seminary as they drank his recitals. Their vague feminine formula for beloved ones doing brave deeds on the field of battle without risk of life would be destroyed.

## CHAPTER SIXTEEEN

A sputtering of musketry was always to be heard. Later, the cannon had entered the dispute. In the fog-filled air their voices made a thudding sound. The reverberations were continued. This part of the world led a strange, battleful existence.

The youth's regiment was marched to relieve a command that had lain long in some damp trenches. The men took positions behind a curving line of rifle pits that had been turned up, like a large furrow, along the line of woods. Before them was a level stretch, peopled with short, deformed stumps. From the woods beyond came the dull popping of the skirmishers and pickets, firing in the fog. From the right came the noise of a terrific fracas.

The men cuddled behind the small embankment and sat in easy attitudes awaiting their turn. Many had their backs to the firing. The youth's friend lay down, buried his face in his arms, and almost instantly, it seemed, he was in a deep sleep.

The youth leaned his breast against the brown dirt and peered over at the woods and up and down the line. Curtains of trees interfered with his ways of vision. He could see the low line of trenches but for a short distance. A few idle flags were perched on the dirt hills. Behind them were rows of dark bodies with a few heads sticking curiously over the top.

Always the noise of skirmishers came from the woods on the front and left, and the din on the right had grown to frightful proportions. The guns were roaring without an instant's pause for breath. It seemed that the cannon had come from all parts and were engaged in a stupendous wrangle. It became impossible to make a sentence heard.

The youth wished to launch a joke— a quotation from newspapers. He desired to say, "All quiet on the Rappahannock," but the guns refused to permit even a comment upon their uproar. He never successfully concluded the sentence. But at last the guns stopped, and among the men in the rifle pits rumors again flew, like birds, but they were now for the most part black creatures who flapped their wings drearily near to the ground and refused to rise on any wings of hope. The men's faces grew doleful from the interpreting of omens. Tales of hesitation and uncertainty on the part of those high in place and responsibility came to their ears. Stories of disaster were borne into their minds with many proofs. This din of musketry on the right, growing like a released genie of sound, expressed and emphasized the army's plight.

The men were disheartened and began to mutter. They made gestures expressive of the sentence: "Ah, what more can we do?" And it could always be seen that they were bewildered by the alleged news and could not fully comprehend a defeat.

Before the gray mists had been totally obliterated by the sunrays, the regiment was marching in a spread column that was retiring carefully through the woods. The disordered, hurrying lines of the enemy could sometimes be seen down through the groves and little fields. They were yelling, shrill and exultant.

At this sight the youth forgot many personal matters and became greatly enraged. He exploded in loud sentences. "B'jiminey, we're generaled by a lot 'a lunkheads."

"More than one feller has said that t'-day," observed a man.

His friend, recently aroused, was still very drowsy. He looked behind him until his mind took in the meaning of the movement. Then he sighed. "Oh, well, I s'pose we got licked," he remarked sadly.

The youth had a thought that it would not be handsome for him to freely condemn other men. He made an attempt to restrain himself, but the words upon his tongue were too bitter. He presently began a long and intricate denunciation [21] of the commander of the forces.

"Mebbe, it wa'n't all his fault—not all together. He did th' best he knowed. It's our luck t' git licked often," said his friend in a weary tone. He was trudging along with stooped shoulders and shifting eyes like a man who has been caned and kicked.

"Well, don't we fight like the devil? Don't we do all that men can?" demanded the youth loudly.

He was secretly dumbfounded at this sentiment when it came from his lips. For a moment his face lost its valor and he looked guiltily about him. But no one questioned his right to deal in such words, and presently he recovered his air of courage. He went on to repeat a statement he had heard going from group to group at the camp that morning. "The brigadier said he never saw a new reg'ment fight the way we fought yestirday, didn' he? And we didn't do better than any other reg'-ment, did we? Well, then, you can't say it's th' army's fault, can you?"

In his reply, the friend's voice was stern. "A course not," he said. "No man dare say we don't fight like th' devil. No man will ever dare say it. Th' boys fight like hell-roosters. But still—still, we don't have no luck."

"Well, then, if we fight like the devil

[21] DENUNCIATION (dĕ·nŭn′sĭ·ā′shŭn)—A verbal attack; a censuring.

an' don't ever whip, it must be the general's fault," said the youth grandly and decisively. "And I don't see any sense in fighting and fighting and fighting, yet always losing through some derned old lunkhead of a general."

A sarcastic man who was tramping at the youth's side, then spoke lazily. "Mebbe yeh think yeh fit th' hull battle yestirday, Fleming," he remarked.

The speech pierced the youth. Inwardly he was reduced to an abject pulp by these chance words. His legs quaked privately. He cast a frightened glance at the sarcastic man.

"Why, no," he hastened to say in a conciliating [22] voice, "I don't think I fought the whole battle yesterday."

But the other seemed innocent of any deeper meaning. Apparently, he had no information. It was merely his habit. "Oh!" he replied in the same tone of calm derision.

The youth, nevertheless, felt a threat. His mind shrank from going nearer to the danger, and thereafter he was silent. The significance of the sarcastic man's words took from him all loud moods that would make him appear prominent. He became suddenly a modest person.

There was low-toned talk among the troops. The officers were impatient and snappy, their countenances clouded with the tales of misfortune. The troops, sifting through the forest, were sullen. In the youth's company once a man's laugh rang out. A dozen soldiers turned their faces quickly toward him and frowned with vague displeasure.

The noise of firing dogged their footsteps. Sometimes, it seemed to be driven a little way, but it always returned again with increased insolence.

[22] CONCILIATE (kŏn·sĭl'ĭ·āt)—To gain good will or favor.

The men muttered and cursed, throwing black looks in its direction.

In a clear space the troops were at last halted. Regiments and brigades, broken and detached through their encounters with thickets, grew together again and lines were faced toward the pursuing bark of the enemy's infantry.

This noise, following like the yellings of eager, metallic hounds, increased to a loud and joyous burst, and then, as the sun went serenely up the sky, throwing illuminating rays into the gloomy thickets, it broke forth into prolonged pealings. The woods began to crackle as if afire.

"Whoop-a-dadee," said a man, "here we are! Everybody fightin'. Blood an' destruction."

"I was willin' t' bet they'd attack as soon as th' sun got fairly up," savagely asserted the lieutenant who commanded the youth's company. He jerked without mercy at his little mustache. He strode to and fro with dark dignity in the rear of his men, who were lying down behind whatever protection they had collected.

A battery had trundled into position in the rear and was thoughtfully shelling the distance. The regiment, unmolested as yet, awaited the moment when the gray shadows of the woods before them should be slashed by the lines of flame. There was much growling and swearing.

"Good Gawd," the youth grumbled, "we're always being chased around like rats! It makes me sick. Nobody seems to know where we go or why we go. We just get fired around from pillar to post and get licked here and get licked there, and nobody knows what it's done for. It makes a man feel like a damn' kitten in a bag. Now, I'd like to know what the eternal thunders we was

FROM M-G-M'S PRODUCTION OF THE RED BADGE OF COURAGE

marched into these woods for anyhow, unless it was to give the rebs a regular pot shot at us. We came in here and got our legs all tangled up in these cussed briars, and then we begin to fight and the rebs had an easy time of it. Don't tell me it's just luck! I know better. It's this derned old—"

The friend seemed jaded,[23] but he interrupted his comrade with a voice of calm confidence. "It'll turn out all right in th' end," he said.

"Oh, the devil it will! You always talk like a dog-hanged parson. Don't tell me! I know—"

At this time there was an interposition by the savage-minded lieutenant, who was obliged to vent some of his inward dissatisfaction upon his men. "You boys shut right up! There no need 'a your wastin' your breath in

long-winded arguments about this an' that an' th' other. You've been jawin' like a lot 'a old hens. All you've got t' do is to fight, an' you'll get plenty 'a that t' do in about ten minutes. Less talkin' an' more fightin' is what's best for you boys. I never saw sech gabbling jackasses."

He paused, ready to pounce upon any man who might have the temerity[24] to reply. No words being said, he resumed his dignified pacing.

"There's too much chin music an' too little fightin' in this war, anyhow," he said to them, turning his head for a final remark.

The day had grown more white, until the sun shed his full radiance upon the thronged forest. A sort of a gust of battle came sweeping toward that

[23] JADED—Tired; exhausted.

[24] TEMERITY (tê·mĕr'ĭ·tĭ)—Foolish courage; rashness.

part of the line where lay the youth's regiment. The front shifted a trifle to meet it squarely. There was a wait. In this part of the field there passed slowly the intense moments that precede the tempest.

A single rifle flashed in a thicket before the regiment. In an instant it was joined by many others. There was a mighty song of clashes and crashes that went sweeping through the woods. The guns in the rear, aroused and enraged by shells that had been thrown burr-like at them, suddenly involved themselves in a hideous altercation with another band of guns. The battle roar settled to a rolling thunder, which was a single long explosion.

In the regiment there was a peculiar kind of hesitation denoted in the attitudes of the men. They were worn, exhausted, having slept but little and labored much. They rolled their eyes toward the advancing battle as they stood awaiting the shock. Some shrank and flinched. They stood as men tied to stakes.

## CHAPTER SEVENTEEN

This advance of the enemy had seemed to the youth like a ruthless hunting. He began to fume with rage and exasperation. He beat his foot upon the ground, and scowled with hate at the swirling smoke that was approaching like a phantom flood. There was a maddening quality in this seeming resolution of the foe to give him no rest, to give him no time to sit down and think. Yesterday he had fought and had fled rapidly. There had been many adventures. For to-day he felt that he had earned opportunities for contemplative repose. He could have enjoyed portraying to uninitiated listeners various scenes at which he had been

a witness or ably discussing the processes of war with other proved men. Too it was important that he should have time for physical recuperation. He was sore and stiff from his experiences. He had received his fill of all exertions, and he wished to rest.

But those other men seemed never to grow weary; they were fighting with their old speed. He had a wild hate for the relentless foe. Yesterday, when he had imagined the universe to be against him, he had hated it, little gods and big gods; to-day he hated the army of the foe with the same great hatred. He was not going to be badgered of his life, like a kitten chased by boys, he said. It was not well to drive men into final corners; at those moments they could all develop teeth and claws.

He leaned and spoke into his friend's ear. He menaced the woods with a gesture. "If they keep on chasing us, by Gawd, they'd better watch out. Can't stand *too* much."

The friend twisted his head and made a calm reply. "If they keep on a-chasin' us they'll drive us all inteh th' river."

The youth cried out savagely at this statement. He crouched behind a little tree, with his eyes burning hatefully and his teeth set in a curlike snarl. The awkward bandage was still about his head, and upon it, over his wound, there was a spot of dry blood. His hair was wondrously tousled, and some straggling, moving locks hung over the cloth of the bandage down toward his forehead. His jacket and shirt were open at the throat, and exposed his young bronzed neck. There could be seen spasmodic gulpings at his throat.

His fingers twined nervously about his rifle. He wished that it was an engine of annihilating power. He felt that he and his companions were being taunted and derided from sincere convictions that they were poor and puny. His knowledge of his inability to take vengeance for it made his rage into a dark and stormy specter, that possessed him and made him dream of abominable cruelties. The tormentors were flies sucking insolently at his blood, and he thought that he would have given his life for a revenge of seeing their faces in pitiful plights.

The winds of battle had swept all about the regiment, until the one rifle, instantly followed by others, flashed in its front. A moment later the regiment roared forth its sudden and valiant retort. A dense wall of smoke settled slowly down. It was furiously slit and slashed by the knifelike fire from the rifles.

To the youth the fighters resembled animals tossed for a death struggle into a dark pit. There was a sensation that he and his fellows, at bay, were pushing back, always pushing fierce onslaughts of creatures who were slippery. Their beams of crimson seemed to get no purchase upon the bodies of their foes; the latter seemed to evade them with ease, and come through, between, around, and about with unopposed skill.

When, in a dream, it occurred to the youth that his rifle was an impotent stick, he lost sense of everything but his hate, his desire to smash into pulp the glittering smile of victory which he could feel upon the faces of his enemies.

The blue smoke-swallowed line curled and writhed like a snake stepped upon. It swung its ends to and fro in an agony of fear and rage.

The youth was not conscious that he was erect upon his feet. He did not know the direction of the ground. Indeed, once he even lost the habit of balance and fell heavily. He was up again immediately. One thought went through the chaos of his brain at the time. He wondered if he had fallen because he had been shot. But the suspicion flew away at once. He did not think more of it.

He had taken up a first position behind the little tree, with a direct determination to hold it against the world. He had not deemed it possible that his army could that day succeed, and from this he felt the ability to fight harder. But the throng had surged in all ways, until he lost directions and locations, save that he knew where lay the enemy.

The flames bit him, and the hot smoke broiled his skin. His rifle barrel grew so hot that ordinarily he could not have borne it upon his palms; but he kept on stuffing cartridges into it, and pounding them with his clanking, bending ramrod. If he aimed at some changing form through the smoke, he pulled his trigger with a fierce grunt, as if he were dealing a blow of the fist with all his strength.

When the enemy seemed falling back before him and his fellows, he went instantly forward, like a dog who, seeing his foes lagging, turns and insists upon being pursued. And when he was compelled to retire again, he did it slowly, sullenly, taking steps of wrathful despair.

Once he, in his intent hate, was almost alone, and was firing, when all those near him had ceased. He was so engrossed in his occupation that he was not aware of a lull.

He was recalled by a hoarse laugh and a sentence that came to his ears in a voice of contempt and amazement. "Yeh infernal fool, don't yeh know enough t' quit when there ain't anything t' shoot at? Good Gawd!"

He turned then and, pausing with his rifle thrown half into position, looked at the blue line of his comrades. During this moment of leisure they seemed all to be engaged in staring with astonishment at him. They had become spectators. Turning to the front again he saw, under the lifted smoke, a deserted ground.

He looked bewildered for a moment. Then there appeared upon the glazed vacancy of his eyes a diamond point of intelligence. "Oh," he said, comprehending.

He returned to his comrades and threw himself upon the ground. He sprawled like a man who had been thrashed. His flesh seemed strangely on fire, and the sounds of the battle continued in his ears. He groped blindly for his canteen.

The lieutenant was crowing. He seemed drunk with fighting. He called out to the youth: "By heavens, if I had ten thousand wild cats like you I could tear th' stomach outa this war in less'n a week!" He puffed out his chest with large dignity as he said it.

Some of the men muttered and looked at the youth in awe-struck ways. It was plain that as he had gone on loading and firing and cursing without the proper intermission, they had found time to regard him. And they now looked upon him as a war devil.

The friend came staggering to him. There was some fright and dismay in his voice. "Are yeh all right, Fleming? Do yeh feel all right? There ain't nothin' th' matter with yeh, Henry, is there?"

"No," said the youth with difficulty. His throat seemed full of knobs and burrs.

These incidents made the youth ponder. It was revealed to him that he had been a barbarian, a beast. He had fought like a pagan who defends his religion. Regarding it, he saw that it was fine, wild, and, in some ways, easy. He had been a tremendous figure, no doubt. By this struggle he had overcome obstacles which he had admitted to be mountains. They had fallen like paper peaks, and he was now what he called a hero. And he had not been aware of the process. He had slept and, awakening, found himself a knight.

He lay and basked in the occasional stares of his comrades. Their faces were varied in degrees of blackness from the burned powder. Some were utterly smudged. They were reeking with perspiration, and their breaths came hard and wheezing. And from these soiled expanses they peered at him.

"Hot work! Hot work!" cried the lieutenant deliriously. He walked up and down, restless and eager. Sometimes his voice could be heard in a wild, incomprehensible laugh.

When he had a particularly profound thought upon the science of war he always unconsciously addressed himself to the youth.

There was some grim rejoicing by the men. "By thunder, I bet this army'll never see another new reg'ment like us!"

"You bet!"

"A dog, a woman, an' a walnut tree,
    Th' more yeh beat 'em, th' better they
    be!

That's like us."

"Lost a piler men, they did. If an' ol' woman swep' up th' woods she'd git a dustpanful."

"Yes, an' if she'll come around ag'in in 'bout an' hour she'll git a pile more."

The forest still bore its burden of clamor. From off under the trees came the rolling clatter of the musketry. Each distant thicket seemed a strange porcupine with quills of flame. A cloud of dark smoke, as from smoldering ruins, went up toward the sun now bright and gay in the blue, enameled sky.

## CHAPTER EIGHTEEN

The ragged line had respite for some minutes, but during its pause the struggle in the forest became magnified until the trees seemed to quiver from the firing and the ground to shake from the rushing of the men. The voices of the cannon were mingled in a long and interminable row. It seemed difficult to live in such an atmosphere. The chests of the men strained for a bit of freshness, and their throats craved water.

There was one shot through the body, who raised a cry of bitter lamentation when came this lull. Perhaps he had been calling out during the fighting also, but at that time no one had heard him. But now the men turned at the woeful complaints of him upon the ground.

"Who is it? Who is it?"

"It's Jimmie Rogers. Jimmie Rogers."

When their eyes first encountered him there was a sudden halt, as if they feared to go near. He was thrashing about in the grass, twisting his shuddering body into many strange postures. He was screaming loudly. This instant's hesitation seemed to fill him with a tremendous, fantastic contempt, and he damned them in shrieked sentences.

The youth's friend had a geographi-cal illusion concerning a stream, and he obtained permission to go for some water. Immediately canteens were showered upon him. "Fill mine, will yeh?" "Bring me some, too." "And me, too." He departed, laden. The youth went with his friend, feeling a desire to throw his heated body onto the stream and, soaking there, drink quarts.

They made a hurried search for the supposed stream but did not find it. "No water here," said the youth. They turned without delay and began to retrace their steps.

From their position as they again faced toward the place of the fighting, they could of course comprehend a greater amount of the battle than when their visions had been blurred by the hurling smoke of the line. They could see dark stretches winding along the land, and on one cleared space there was a row of guns making gray clouds, which were filled with large flashes of orange-colored flame. Over some foliage they could see the roof of a house. One window, glowing a deep murder red, shone squarely through the leaves. From the edifice a tall leaning tower of smoke went far into the sky.

Looking over their own troops, they saw mixed masses slowly getting into regular form. The sunlight made twinkling points of the bright steel. To the rear there was a glimpse of a distant roadway as it curved over a slope. It was crowded with retreating infantry. From all the interwoven forest arose the smoke and bluster of the battle. The air was always occupied by a blaring.

Near where they stood shells were flip-flapping and hooting. Occasional bullets buzzed in the air and spanged into tree trunks. Wounded men and other stragglers were slinking through the woods.

Looking down an aisle of the grove, the youth and his companion saw a jangling general and his staff almost ride upon a wounded man who was crawling on his hands and knees. The general reined strongly at his charger's opened and foamy mouth and guided it with dexterous horsemanship past the man. The latter scrambled in wild and torturing haste. His strength evidently failed him as he reached a place of safety. One of his arms suddenly weakened, and he fell, sliding over upon his back. He lay stretched out, breathing gently.

A moment later the small, creaking calvacade was directly in front of the two soldiers. Another officer, riding with the skillful abandon of a cowboy, galloped his horse to a position directly before the general. The two unnoticed foot soldiers made a little show of going on, but they lingered near in the desire to overhear the conversation. Perhaps, they thought, some great inner historical things would be said.

The general, whom the boys knew as the commander of their division, looked at the other officer and spoke coolly, as if he were criticising his clothes. "Th' enemy's formin' over there for another charge," he said. "It'll be directed against Whiterside, an' I fear they'll break through there unless we work like thunder t' stop them."

The other swore at his restive horse, and then cleared his throat. He made a gesture toward his cap. "It'll be hell t' pay stoppin' them," he said shortly.

"I presume so," remarked the general. Then he began to talk rapidly and in a lower tone. He frequently illustrated his words with a pointing finger. The two infantrymen could hear nothing until finally he asked: "What troops can you spare?"

The officer who rode like a cowboy reflected for an instant. "Well," he said, "I had to order in th' 12th to help th' 76th, an' I haven't really got any. But there's th' 304th. They fight like a lot 'a mule drivers. I can spare them best of any."

The youth and his friend exchanged glances of astonishment.

The general spoke sharply. "Get 'em ready then. I'll watch developments from here, an' send you word when t' start them. It'll happen in five minutes."

As the other officer tossed his fingers toward his cap and, wheeling his horse, started away, the general called out to him in a sober voice: "I don't believe many of your mule drivers will get back."

The other shouted something in reply. He smiled.

With scared faces, the youth and his companion hurried back to the line.

These happenings had occupied an incredibly short time, yet the youth felt that in them he had been made aged. New eyes were given to him. And the most startling thing was to learn suddenly that he was very insignificant. The officer spoke of the regiment as if he referred to a broom. Some part of the woods needed sweeping, perhaps, and he merely indicated a broom in a tone properly indifferent to its fate. It was war, no doubt, but it appeared strange.

As the two boys approached the line, the lieutenant perceived them and swelled with wrath. "Fleming—Wilson—how long does it take yeh to git water, anyhow—where yeh been to."

But his oration ceased as he saw their eyes, which were large with great tales. "We're goin' t' charge—we're goin' t' charge!" cried the youth's friend, hastening with his news.

"Charge?" said the lieutenant. "Charge? Well, b'Gawd! Now; this is real fightin'." Over his soiled countenance there went a boastful smile. "Charge? Well, b'Gawd!"

A little group of soldiers surrounded the two youths. "Are we, sure 'nough? Well, I'll be derned! Charge? What fer? What at? Wilson, you're lyin'."

"I hope to die," said the youth's friend, pitching his tones to the key of angry remonstrance. "Sure as shooting, I tell you."

And the youth spoke in re-enforcement. "Not by a blame sight, he ain't lyin'. We heard 'em talkin'."

They caught sight of two mounted figures a short distance from them. One was the colonel of the regiment and the other was the officer who had received orders from the commander of the division. They were gesticulating at each other. The soldier, pointing at them, interpreted the scene.

One man had a final objection: "How could yeh hear 'em talkin'?" But the men, for a large part, nodded, admitting that previously the two friends had spoken truth.

They settled back into reposeful attitudes with airs of having accepted the matter. And they mused upon it, with a hundred varieties of expression. It was an engrossing thing to think about. Many tightened their belts carefully and hitched at their trousers.

A moment later the officers began to bustle among the men, pushing them into a more compact mass and into a better alignment. They chased those that straggled and fumed at a few men who seemed to show by their attitudes that they had decided to remain at that spot. They were like critical shepherds struggling with sheep.

Presently, the regiment seemed to draw itself up and heave a deep breath. None of the men's faces were mirrors of large thoughts. The soldiers were bended and stooped like sprinters before a signal. Many pairs of glinting eyes peered from the grimy faces toward the curtains of the deeper woods. They seemed to be engaged in deep calculations of time and distance.

They were surrounded by the noises of the monstrous altercation between the two armies. The world was fully interested in other matters. Apparently, the regiment had its small affair to itself.

The youth, turning, shot a quick, inquiring glance at his friend. The latter returned to him the same manner of look. They were the only ones who possessed an inner knowledge. "Mule drivers—hell t' pay—don't believe many will get back." It was an ironical secret. Still, they saw no hesitation in each other's faces, and they nodded a mute and unprotesting assent when a shaggy man near them said in a meek voice: "We'll git swallowed."

## CHAPTER NINETEEN

The youth stared at the land in front of him. Its foliage now seemed to veil powers and horrors. He was unaware of the machinery of orders that started the charge, although from the corners of his eyes he saw an officer, who looked like a boy a-horseback, come galloping, waving his hat. Suddenly he felt a straining and heaving among the men. The line fell slowly forward like a toppling wall, and, with a convulsive gasp that was intended for a cheer, the regiment began its journey. The youth was pushed and jostled for a moment before

FROM M-G-M'S PRODUCTION OF THE RED BADGE OF COURAGE

he understood the movement at all, but directly he lunged ahead and began to run.

He fixed his eye upon a distant and prominent clump of trees where he had concluded the enemy were to be met, and he ran toward it as toward a goal. He had believed throughout that it was a mere question of getting over an unpleasant matter as quickly as possible, and he ran desperately, as if pursued for a murder. His face was drawn hard and tight with the stress of his endeavor. His eyes were fixed in a lurid glare. And with his soiled and disordered dress, his red and inflamed features surmounted by the dingy rag with its spot of blood, his wildly swinging rifle and banging accouterments, he looked to be an insane soldier.

As the regiment swung from its position out into a cleared space the woods and thickets before it awakened. Yellow flames leaped toward it from many directions. The forest made a tremendous objection.

The line lurched straight for a moment. Then the right wing swung forward; it in turn was surpassed by the left. Afterward the center careered to the front until the regiment was a wedge-shaped mass, but an instant later the opposition of the bushes, trees, and uneven places on the ground split the command and scattered it into detached clusters.

The youth, light-footed, was unconsciously in advance. His eyes still kept note of the clump of trees. From all places near it the clannish yell of the enemy could be heard. The little flames of rifles leaped from it. The song of the bullets was in the air and shells snarled among the tree-tops. One tumbled directly into the middle of a hurrying group and exploded in crimson fury. There was an instant's spectacle of a man, almost over it, throwing up his hands to shield his eyes.

Other men, punched by bullets, fell in grotesque agonies. The regiment left a coherent trail of bodies.

They had passed into a clearer atmosphere. There was an effect like a revelation in the new appearance of the landscape. Some men working madly at a battery were plain to them, and the opposing infantry's lines were defined by the gray walls and fringes of smoke.

It seemed to the youth that he saw everything. Each blade of the green grass was bold and clear. He thought that he was aware of every change in the thin, transparent vapor that floated idly in sheets. The brown or gray trunks of the trees showed each roughness of their surfaces. And the men of the regiment, with their starting eyes and sweating faces, running madly, or falling, as if thrown headlong, to queer, heaped-up corpses—all were comprehended. His mind took a mechanical but firm impression, so that afterward everything was pictured and explained to him, save why he himself was there.

But there was a frenzy made from this furious rush. The men, pitching forward insanely, had burst into cheerings, moblike and barbaric, but tuned in strange keys that can arouse the dullard and the stoic. It made a mad enthusiasm that, it seemed, would be incapable of checking itself before granite and brass. There was the delirium that encounters despair and death, and is heedless and blind to the odds. It is a temporary but sublime absence of selfishness. And because it was of this order was the reason, perhaps, why the youth wondered, afterward, what reasons he could have had for being there.

Presently the straining pace ate up the energies of the men. As if by agreement, the leaders began to slacken their speed. The volleys directed against them had had a seeming windlike effect. The regiment snorted and blew. Among some stolid trees it began to falter and hesitate. The men, staring intently, began to wait for some of the distant walls of smoke to move and disclose to them the scene. Since much of their strength and their breath had vanished, they returned to caution. They were become men again.

The youth had a vague belief that he had run miles, and he thought, in a way, that he was now in some new and unknown land.

The moment the regiment ceased its advance the protesting splutter of musketry became a steadied roar. Long and accurate fringes of smoke spread out. From the top of a small hill came level belchings of yellow flame that caused an inhuman whistling in the air.

The men halted, had opportunity to see some of their comrades dropping with moans and shrieks. A few lay under foot, still or wailing. And now for an instant the men stood, their rifles slack in their hands, and watched the regiment dwindle. They appeared dazed and stupid. This spectacle seemed to paralyze them, overcome them with a fatal fascination. They stared woodenly at the sights, and, lowering their eyes, looked from face to face. It was a strange pause, and a strange silence.

Then, above the sounds of the outside commotion, arose the roar of the lieutenant. He strode suddenly forth, his infantile features black with rage.

"Come on, yeh fools!" he bellowed. "Come on! Yeh can't stay here. Yeh must come on." He said more, but much of it could not be understood.

He started rapidly forward, with his head turned toward the men. "Come on," he was shouting. The men stared with blank and yokel-like eyes at him. He was obliged to halt and retrace his steps. He stood then with his back to the enemy and delivered gigantic curses into the faces of the men. His body vibrated from the weight and force of his imprecations. And he could string oaths with the facility of a maiden who strings beads.

The friend of the youth aroused. Lurching suddenly forward and dropping to his knees, he fired an angry shot at the persistent woods. This action awakened the men. They huddled no more like sheep. They seemed suddenly to bethink them of their weapons, and at once commenced firing. Belabored by their officers, they began to move forward. The regiment, involved like a cart involved in mud and muddle, started unevenly with many jolts and jerks. The men stopped now every few paces to fire and load, and in this manner moved slowly on from trees to trees.

The flaming opposition in their front grew with their advance until it seemed that all forward ways were barred by the thin leaping tongues, and off to the right an ominous demonstration could sometimes be dimly discerned. The smoke lately generated was in confusing clouds that made it difficult for the regiment to proceed with intelligence. As he passed through each curling mass the youth wondered what would confront him on the farther side.

The command went painfully forward until an open space interposed between them and the lurid lines. Here, crouching and cowering behind some trees, the men clung with desperation, as if threatened by a wave. They looked wild-eyed, and as if amazed at this furious disturbance they had stirred. In the storm there was an ironical expression of their importance. The faces of the men, too, showed a lack of a certain feeling of responsibility for being there. It was as if they had been driven. It was the dominant animal failing to remember in the supreme moments the forceful causes of various superficial qualities. The whole affair seemed incomprehensible to many of them.

As they halted thus the lieutenant again began to bellow profanely. Regardless of the vindictive threats of the bullets, he went about coaxing, berating, and bedamning. His lips, that were habitually in a soft and childlike curve, were now writhed into unholy contortions. He swore by all possible deities.

Once he grabbed the youth by the arm. "Come on, yeh lunkhead!" he roared. "Come on! We'll all git killed if we stay here. We've on'y got t' go across that lot. An' then"—the remainder of his idea disappeared in a blue haze of curses.

The youth stretched forth his arm. "Cross there?" His mouth was puckered in doubt and awe.

"Certainly. Jest 'cross th' lot! We can't stay here," screamed the lieutenant. He poked his face close to the youth and waved his bandaged hand. "Come on!" Presently he grappled with him as if for a wrestling bout. It was as if he planned to drag the youth by the ear on to the assault.

The private felt a sudden unspeakable indignation against his officer. He wrenched fiercely and shook him off.

"Come on yerself, then," he yelled. There was a bitter challenge in his voice.

FROM M-G-M'S PRODUCTION OF THE RED BADGE OF COURAGE

They galloped together down the regimental front. The friend scrambled after them. In front of the colors the three men began to bawl: "Come on! come on!" They danced and gyrated like tortured savages.

The flag, obedient to these appeals, bended its glittering form and swept toward them. The men wavered in indecision for a moment, and then with a long, wailful cry the dilapidated regiment surged forward and began its new journey.

Over the field went the scurrying mass. It was a handful of men splattered into the faces of the enemy. Toward it instantly sprang the yellow tongues. A vast quantity of blue smoke hung before them. A mighty banging made ears valueless.

The youth ran like a madman to reach the woods before a bullet could discover him. He ducked his head low, like a football player. In his haste his eyes almost closed, and the scene was a wild blur. Pulsating saliva stood at the corners of his mouth.

Within him, as he hurled himself forward, was born a love, a despairing fondness for this flag which was near him. It was a creation of beauty and invulnerability. It was a goddess, radiant, that bended its form with an imperious gesture to him. It was a woman, red and white, hating and loving, that called him with the voice of his hopes. Because no harm could come to it he endowed it with power. He kept near, as if it could be a saver of lives, and an imploring cry went from his mind.

In the mad scramble he was aware that the color sergeant flinched suddenly, as if struck by a bludgeon. He faltered, and then became motionless, save for his quivering knees.

He made a spring and a clutch at the pole. At the same instant his friend grabbed it from the other side. They jerked at it, stout and furious, but the color sergeant was dead, and the corpse would not relinquish its thrust. For a moment there was a grim encounter. The dead man, swinging with bended back, seemed to be obstinately tugging, in ludicrous and awful ways, for the possession of the flag.

It was past in an instant of time. They wrenched the flag furiously from the dead man, and, as they turned again, the corpse swayed forward with bowed head. One arm swung high, and the curved hand fell with heavy protest on the friend's unheeding shoulder.

## CHAPTER TWENTY

When the two youths turned with the flag they saw that much of the regiment had crumbled away, and the dejected remnant was coming back. The men, having hurled themselves in projectile fashion, had presently expended their forces. They slowly retreated, with their faces still toward the spluttering woods, and their hot rifles still replying to the din. Several officers were giving orders, their voices keyed to screams.

"Where in hell yeh goin'?" the lieutenant was asking in a sarcastic howl. And a red-bearded officer, whose voice of triple brass could plainly be heard, was commanding: "Shoot into 'em! Shoot into 'em, Gawd damn their souls!" There was a mêlée of screeches, in which the men were ordered to do conflicting and impossible things.

The youth and his friend had a small scuffle over the flag. "Give it t' me!"

"No, let me keep it!" Each felt satisfied with the other's possession of it, but each felt bound to declare, by an offer to carry the emblem, his willingness to further risk himself. The youth roughly pushed his friend away.

The regiment fell back to the stolid trees. There it halted for a moment to blaze at some dark forms that had begun to steal upon its track. Presently it resumed its march again, curving among the tree trunks. By the time the depleted regiment had again reached the first open space they were receiving a fast and merciless fire. There seemed to be mobs all about them.

The greater part of the men, discouraged, their spirits worn by the turmoil, acted as if stunned. They accepted the pelting of the bullets with bowed and weary heads. It was of no purpose to strive against walls. It was of no use to batter themselves against granite. And from this consciousness that they had attempted to conquer an unconquerable thing there seemed to arise a feeling that they had been betrayed. They glowered with bent brows, but dangerously, upon some of the officers, more particularly upon the red-bearded one with the voice of triple brass.

However, the rear of the regiment was fringed with men, who continued to shoot irritably at the advancing foes. They seemed resolved to make every trouble. The youthful lieutenant was perhaps the last man in the disordered mass. His forgotten back was toward the enemy. He had been shot in the arm. It hung straight and rigid. Occasionally he would cease to remember it, and be about to emphasize an oath with a sweeping gesture. The multiplied pain caused him to swear with incredible power.

The youth went along with slipping, uncertain feet. He kept watchful eyes rearward. A scowl of mortification and rage was upon his face. He had thought of a fine revenge upon the officer who had referred to him and his fellows as mule drivers. But he saw that it could not come to pass. His dreams had collapsed when the mule drivers, dwindling rapidly, had wavered and hesitated on the little clearing, and then had recoiled. And now the retreat of the mule drivers was a march of shame to him.

A dagger-pointed gaze from without his blackened face was held toward the enemy, but his greater hatred was riveted upon the man, who not knowing him, had called him a mule driver.

When he knew that he and his comrades had failed to do anything in successful ways that might bring the little pangs of a kind of remorse upon the officer, the youth allowed the rage of the baffled to possess him. This cold officer upon a monument, who dropped epithets unconcernedly down, would be finer as a dead man, he thought. So grievous did he think it that he could never possess the secret right to taunt truly in answer.

He had pictured red letters of curious revenge. "We *are* mule drivers, are we?" And now he was compelled to throw them away.

He presently wrapped his head in the cloak of his pride and kept the flag erect. He harangued his fellows, pushing against their chests with his free hand. To those he knew well he made frantic appeals, beseeching them by name. Between him and the Lieutenant, scolding and near to losing his mind with rage, there was felt a subtle fellowship and equality. They sup-

ported each other in all manner of hoarse, howling protests.

But the regiment was a machine run down. The two men babbled at a forceless thing. The soldiers who had heart to go slowly were continually shaken in their resolves by a knowledge that comrades were slipping with speed back to the lines. It was difficult to think of reputation when others were thinking of skins. Wounded men were left crying on this black journey.

The smoke fringes and flames blustered always. The youth, peering once through a sudden rift in a cloud, saw a brown mass of troops, interwoven and magnified until they appeared to be thousands. A fierce-hued flag flashed before his vision.

Immediately, as if the uplifting of the smoke had been prearranged, the discovered troops burst into a rasping yell, and a hundred flames jetted toward the retreating band. A rolling gray cloud again interposed as the regiment doggedly replied. The youth had to depend again upon his misused ears, which were trembling and buzzing from the *mêlée* of musketry and yells.

The way seemed eternal. In the clouded haze men became panicstricken with the thought that the regiment had lost its path, and was proceeding in a perilous direction. Once the men who headed the wild procession turned and came pushing back against their comrades, screaming that they were being fired upon from points which they had considered to be toward their own lines. At this cry a hysterical fear and dismay beset the troops. A soldier, who heretofore had been ambitious to make the regiment into a wise little band that would proceed calmly amid the huge-appearing difficulties, suddenly sank down and buried his face in his arms with an air of bowing to a doom. From another a shrill lamentation rang out filled with profane illusions to a general. Men ran hither and thither, seeking with their eyes roads of escape. With serene regularity, as if controlled by a schedule, bullets buffeted into men.

The youth walked stolidly into the midst of the mob, and with his flag in his hands took a stand as if he expected an attempt to push him to the ground. He unconsciously assumed the attitude of the color bearer in the fight of the preceding day. He passed over his brow a hand that trembled. His breath did not come freely. He was choking during this small wait for the crisis.

His friend came to him. "Well, Henry, I guess this is good-by—John."

"Oh, shut up, you damned fool!" replied the youth, and he would not look at the other.

The officers labored like politicians to beat the mass into a proper circle to face the menaces. The ground was uneven and torn. The men curled into depressions and fitted themselves snugly behind whatever would frustrate a bullet.

The youth noted with vague surprise that the lieutenant was standing mutely with his legs far apart and his sword held in a manner of a cane. The youth wondered what had happened to his vocal organs that he no more cursed. There was something curious in this little intent pause of the lieutenant. He was like a babe which, having wept its fill, raises its eyes and fixes them upon a distant toy. He was engrossed in this contemplation, and the soft underlip quivered from self-whispered words.

Some lazy and ignorant smoke curled slowly. The men, hiding from the bullets, waited anxiously for it to lift and disclose the plight of the regiment.

The silent ranks were suddenly thrilled by the eager voice of the youthful lieutenant bawling out: "Here they come! Right on to us, b'Gawd!" His further words were lost in a roar of wicked thunder from the men's rifles.

The youth's eyes had instantly turned in the direction indicated by the awakened and agitated lieutenant, and he had seen the haze of treachery disclosing a body of soldiers of the enemy. They were so near that he could see their features. There was a recognition as he looked at the types of faces. Also he perceived with dim amazement that their uniforms were rather gay in effect, being light gray, accented with a brilliant-hued facing. Moreover, the clothes seemed new.

These troops had apparently been going forward with caution, their rifles held in readiness, when the youthful lieutenant had discovered them and their movement had been interrupted by the volley from the blue regiment. From the moment's glimpse, it was derived that they had been unaware of the proximity of their dark-suited foes or had mistaken the direction. Almost instantly they were shut utterly from the youth's sight by the smoke from the energetic rifles of his companions. He strained his vision to learn the accomplishment of the volley, but the smoke hung before him.

The two bodies of troops exchanged blows in the manner of a pair of boxers. The fast angry firings went back and forth. The men in blue were intent with the despair of their circumstances and they seized upon the revenge to be had at close range. Their thunder swelled loud and valiant. Their curving front bristled with flashes and the place resounded with the clangor of their ramrods. The youth ducked and dodged for a time and achieved a few unsatisfactory views of the enemy. There appeared to be many of them and they were replying swiftly. They seemed moving toward the blue regiment, step by step. He seated himself gloomily on the ground with his flag between his knees.

As he noted the vicious, wolflike temper of his comrades he had a sweet thought that if the enemy was about to swallow the regimental broom as a large prisoner, it could at least have the consolation of going down with bristles forward.

But the blows of the antagonist began to grow more weak. Fewer bullets ripped the air, and finally, when the men slackened to learn of the fight, they could see only dark, floating smoke. The regiment lay still and gazed. Presently some chance whim came to the pestering blur, and it began to coil heavily away. The men saw a ground vacant of fighters. It would have been an empty stage if it were not for a few corpses that lay thrown and twisted into fantastic shapes upon the sward.

At sight of this tableau, many of the men in blue sprang from behind their covers and made an ungainly dance of joy. Their eyes burned and a hoarse cheer of elation broke from their dry lips.

It had begun to seem to them that events were trying to prove that they were impotent. These little battles had evidently endeavored to demonstrate that the men could not fight well. When on the verge of submission to these opinions, the small duel had showed them that the proportions were not impossible, and by it they had revenged themselves upon their misgivings and upon the foe.

The impetus of enthusiasm was theirs again. They gazed about them with looks of uplifted pride, feeling new trust in the grim, always confident weapons in their hands. And they were men.

## CHAPTER TWENTY-ONE

Presently they knew that no fighting threatened them. All ways seemed once more opened to them. The dusty blue lines of their friends were disclosed a short distance away. In the distance there were many colossal noises, but in all this part of the field there was a sudden stillness.

They perceived that they were free. The depleted band drew a long breath of relief and gathered itself into a bunch to complete its trip.

In this last length of journey the men began to show strange emotions. They hurried with nervous fear. Some who had been dark and unfaltering in the grimmest moments now could not conceal an anxiety that made them frantic. It was perhaps that they dreaded to be killed in insignificant ways after the times for proper military deaths had passed. Or, perhaps, they thought it would be too ironical to get killed at the portals of safety. With backward looks of perturbation, they hastened.

As they approached their own lines there was some sarcasm exhibited on the part of a gaunt and bronzed regiment that lay resting in the shade of trees. Questions were wafted to them.

"Where th' hell yeh been?"

"What yeh comin' back fer?"

"Why didn't yeh stay there?"

"Was it warm out there, sonny?"

"Goin' home now, boys?"

One shouted in taunting mimicry:

"Oh, mother, come quick an' look at th' so'jers!"

There was no reply from the bruised and battered regiment, save that one man made broadcast challenges to fist fights and the red-bearded officer walked rather near and glared in great swashbuckler style at a tall captain in the other regiment. But the lieutenant suppressed the man who wished to fist fight, and the tall captain, flushing at the little fanfare of the red-bearded one, was obliged to look intently at some trees.

The youth's tender flesh was deeply stung by these remarks. From under his creased brows he glowered with hate at the mockers. He meditated upon a few revenges. Still, many in the regiment hung their heads in criminal fashion, so that it came to pass that the men trudged with sudden heaviness, as if they bore upon their bended shoulders the coffin of their honor. And the youthful lieutenant, recollecting himself, began to mutter softly in black curses.

They turned when they arrived at their old position to regard the ground over which they had charged.

The youth in this contemplation was smitten with a large astonishment. He discovered that the distances, as compared with the brilliant measurings of his mind, were trivial and ridiculous. The stolid trees, where much had taken place, seemed incredibly near. The time, too, now that he reflected, he saw to have been short. He wondered at the number of emotions and events that had been crowded into such little spaces. Elfin thoughts must have exaggerated and enlarged everything, he said.

It seemed, then, that there was bitter justice in the speeches of the gaunt and bronzed veterans. He veiled a glance of disdain at his fellows who strewed the ground, choking with dust, red from perspiration, misty-eyed, disheveled.

They were gulping at their canteens, fierce to wring every mite of water from them, and they polished at their swollen and watery features with coat sleeves and bunches of grass.

However, to the youth there was a considerable joy in musing upon his performances during the charge. He had had very little time previously in which to appreciate himself, so that there was now much satisfaction in quietly thinking of his actions. He recalled bits of color that in the flurry had stamped themselves unawares upon his engaged senses.

As the regiment lay heaving from its hot exertions the officer who had named them as mule drivers came galloping along the line. He had lost his cap. His tousled hair streamed wildly, and his face was dark with vexation and wrath. His temper was displayed with more clearness by the way in which he managed his horse. He jerked and wrenched savagely at his bridle, stopping the hard-breathing animal with a furious pull near the colonel of the regiment. He immediately exploded in reproaches which came unbidden to the ears of the men. They were suddenly alert, being always curious about black words between officers.

"Oh, thunder, MacChesnay, what an awful bull you made of this thing!" began the officer. He attempted low tones, but his indignation caused certain of the men to learn the sense of his words. "What an awful mess you made! Good Lord, man, you stopped a hundred feet this side of a very pretty success! If your men had gone a hundred feet farther you would have made a great charge, but as it is—what a lot of mud diggers you've got anyway!"

The men, listening with bated breath, now turned their curious eyes upon the colonel. They had a ragamuffin interest in this affair.

The colonel was seen to straighten his form and put one hand forth in oratorical fashion. He wore an injured air; it was as if a deacon had been accused of stealing. The men were wiggling in an ecstasy of excitement.

But of a sudden the colonel's manner changed from that of a deacon to that of a Frenchman. He shrugged his shoulders. "Oh, well, general, we went as far as we could," he said calmly.

"As far as you could? Did you, b'Gawd?" snorted the other. "Well, that wasn't very far, was it?" he added, with a glance of cold contempt into the other's eyes. "Not very far, I think. You were intended to make a diversion in favor of Whiterside. How well you succeeded your own ears can now tell you." He wheeled his horse and rode stiffly away.

The colonel, bidden to hear the jarring noises of an engagement in the woods to the left, broke out in vague damnations.

The lieutenant, who had listened with an air of impotent rage to the interview, spoke suddenly in firm and undaunted tones. "I don't care what a man is—whether he is a general or what—if he says th' boys didn't put up a good fight out there he's a damned fool."

"Lieutenant," began the colonel, severely, "this is my own affair, and I'll trouble you—"

The lieutenant made an obedient gesture. "All right, colonel, all right," he said. He sat down with an air of being content with himself.

The news that the regiment had been reproached went along the line. For a time the men were bewildered by it. "Good thunder!" they ejaculated, staring at the vanishing form of the general. They conceived it to be a huge mistake.

Presently, however, they began to believe that in truth their efforts had been called light. The youth could see this conviction weigh upon the entire regiment until the men were like cuffed and cursed animals, but withal rebellious.

The friend, with a grievance in his eye, went to the youth. "I wonder what he does want," he said. "He must think we went out there an' played marbles! I never see sech a man!"

The youth developed a tranquil philosophy for these moments of irritation. "Oh, well," he rejoined, "he probably didn't see nothing of it at all and got mad as blazes, and concluded we were a lot of sheep, just because we didn't do what he wanted done. It's a pity old Grandpa Henderson got killed yesterday—he'd have known that we did our best and fought good. It's just our awful luck, that's what."

"I should say so," replied the friend. He seemed to be deeply wounded at an injustice. "I should say we did have awful luck! There's no fun in fightin' fer people when everything yeh do—no matter what—ain't done right. I have a notion t' stay behind next time an' let 'em take their ol' charge an' go t' th' devil with it."

The youth spoke soothingly to his comrade. "Well, we both did good. I'd like to see the fool what'd say we both didn't do as good as we could!"

"Of course we did," declared the friend stoutly. "An' I'd break th' feller's neck if he was as big as a church. But we're all right, anyhow, for I heard one feller say that we two fit th' best in th' reg'ment, an' they had a great argument 'bout it. Another feller, 'a course, he had t' up an' say it was a lie—he seen all what was goin' on an' he never seen us from th' beginnin' t' th' end. An' a lot more struck in an' ses it wasn't a lie—we did fight like thunder, an' they give us quite a send-off. But this is what I can't stand—these everlastin' ol' soldiers, titterin' an' laughin', an' then that general, he's crazy."

The youth exclaimed with sudden exasperation: "He's a lunkhead! He makes me mad. I wish he'd come along next time. We'd show 'im what—"

He ceased because several men had come hurrying up. Their faces expressed a bringing of great news.

"O Flem, yeh jest oughta heard!" cried one, eagerly.

"Heard what?" said the youth.

"Yeh jest oughta heard!" repeated the other, and he arranged himself to tell his tidings. The others made an excited circle. "Well, sir, th' colonel met your lieutenant right by us—it was damnedest thing I ever heard—an' he ses: 'Ahem! ahem!' he ses. 'Mr. Hasbrouck!' he ses, 'by th' way, who was that lad what carried th' flag?' he ses. There, Flemin', what d' yeh think 'a that? 'Who was th' lad what carried th' flag?' he ses, an' th' lieutenant, he speaks up right away: 'That's Flemin', an' he's a jimhickey,' he ses, right away. What? I say he did. 'A jimhickey,' he ses—those 'r his words. He did, too. I say he did. If you kin tell this story better than I kin, go ahead an' tell it. Well, then, keep yer mouth shet. Th' lieutenant, he ses: 'He's a jimhickey,' an' th' colonel, he ses: 'Ahem! ahem! he is, indeed, a very good man t' have, ahem! He kep' th' flag 'way t' th'

front. I saw 'im. He's a good un,' ses th' colonel. 'You bet,' ses th' lieutenant, 'he an' a feller named Wilson was at th' head 'a th' charge, an' howlin' like Indians all th' time,' he ses. 'Head a' th' charge all th' time,' he ses. 'A feller named Wilson,' he ses. There, Wilson, m'boy, put that in a letter an' send it hum t' yer mother, hay? 'A feller named Wilson,' he ses. An' th' colonel, he ses: 'Were they, indeed? Ahem! ahem! My sakes!' he ses. 'At th' head a' th' reg'ment?' he ses. 'They were,' ses th' lieutenant. 'My sakes!' ses th' colonel. He ses: 'Well, well, well,' he ses, 'those two babies?' 'They were,' ses th' lieutenant. "Well, well,' ses th' colonel, 'they deserve t' be major generals,' he ses. 'They deserve t' be major generals.' "

The youth and his friend had said: "Huh!" "Yer lyin', Thompson." "Oh, go t' blazes!" "He never sed it." "Oh, what a lie!" "Huh!" But despite these youthful scoffings and embarrassments, they knew that their faces were deeply flushing from thrills of pleasure. They exchanged a secret glance of joy and congratulation.

They speedily forgot many things. The past held no pictures of error and disappointment. They were very happy, and their hearts swelled with grateful affection for the colonel and the youthful lieutenant.

## CHAPTER TWENTY-TWO

When the woods again began to pour forth the dark-hued masses of the enemy the youth felt serene self-confidence. He smiled briefly when he saw men dodge and duck at the long screeching of shells that were thrown in giant handfuls over them. He stood, erect and tranquil, watching the attack begin against a part of the line that made a blue curve along the side of an adjacent hill. His vision being unmolested by smoke from the rifles of his companions, he had opportunities to see parts of the hard fight. It was a relief to perceive at last from whence came some of these noises which had been roared into his ears.

Off a short way he saw two regiments fighting a little separate battle with two other regiments. It was in a cleared space, wearing a set-apart look. They were blazing as if upon a wager, giving and taking tremendous blows. The firings were incredibly fierce and rapid. These intent regiments apparently were oblivious of all larger purposes of war, and were slugging each other as if at a matched game.

In another direction he saw a magnificent brigade going with the evident intention of driving the enemy from a wood. They passed in out of sight and presently there was a most awe-inspiring racket in the wood. The noise was unspeakable. Having stirred this prodigious uproar, and, apparently, finding it too prodigious, the brigade, after a little time, came marching airily out again with its fine formation in nowise disturbed. There were no traces of speed in its movements. The brigade was jaunty and seemed to point a proud thumb at the yelling wood.

On a slope to the left there was a long row of guns, gruff and maddened, denouncing the enemy, who, down through the woods, were forming for another attack in the pitiless monotony of conflicts. The round red discharges from the guns made a crimson flare and a high, thick smoke. Occasional glimpses could be caught of groups of the toiling artillerymen. In the rear of this row of guns stood a house, calm and white, amid bursting shells. A congregation of horses, tied to a long railing, were tugging frenziedly at their bridles. Men were running hither and thither.

The detached battle between the four regiments lasted for some time. There chanced to be no interference, and they settled their dispute by themselves. They struck savagely and powerfully at each other for a period of minutes, and then the lighter-hued regiments faltered and drew back, leaving the dark-blue lines shouting. The youth could see the two flags shaking with laughter amid the smoke remnants.

Presently there was a stillness, pregnant with meaning. The blue lines shifted and changed a trifle and stared expectantly at the silent woods and fields before them. The hush was solemn and churchlike, save for a distant battery that, evidently unable to remain quiet, sent a faint rolling thunder over the ground. It irritated, like the noises of unimpressed boys. The men imagined that it would prevent their perched ears from hearing the first words of the new battle.

Of a sudden the guns on the slope roared out a message of warning. A spluttering sound had begun in the woods. It swelled with amazing speed to a profound clamor that involved the earth in noises. The splitting crashes swept along the lines until an interminable roar was developed. To those in the midst of it it became a din fitted to the universe. It was the whirring and thumping of gigantic machinery, complications among the smaller stars. The youth's ears were filled up. They were incapable of hearing more.

On an incline over which a road wound he saw wild and desperate rushes of men perpetually backward and forward in riotous surges. These parts of the opposing armies were two long waves that pitched upon each other madly at dictated points. To and fro they swelled. Sometimes, one side by its yells and cheers would proclaim decisive blows, but a moment later the other side would be all yells and cheers. Once the youth saw a spray of light forms go in houndlike leaps toward the waving blue lines. There was much howling, and presently it went away with a vast mouthful of prisoners. Again, he saw a blue wave dash with such thunderous force against a gray obstruction that it seemed to clear the earth of it and leave nothing but trampled sod. And always in their swift and deadly rushes to and fro the men screamed and yelled like maniacs.

Particular pieces of fence or secure positions behind collections of trees were wrangled over, as gold thrones or pearl bedsteads. There were desperate lunges at these chosen spots seemingly every instant, and most of them were bandied like light toys between the contending forces. The youth could not tell from the battle flags flying like crimson foam in many directions which color of cloth was winning.

His emaciated regiment bustled forth with undiminished fierceness when its time came. When assaulted again by bullets, the men burst out in a barbaric cry of rage and pain. They bent their heads in aims of intent hatred behind the projected hammers of their guns. Their ramrods clanged loud with fury as their eager arms pounded the cartridges into the rifle barrels. The front of the regiment was a smoke-wall penetrated by the flashing points of yellow and red.

Wallowing in the fight, they were in an astonishingly short time resmudged. They surpassed in stain and dirt all their previous appearances. Moving to and fro with strained exertion, jabbering the while, they were, with their swaying bodies, black faces, and glowing eyes, like strange and ugly friends jigging heavily in the smoke.

The lieutenant, returning from a tour after a bandage, produced from a hidden receptacle of his mind new and portentous oaths suited to the emergency. Strings of expletives he swung lashlike over the backs of his men, and it was evident that his previous efforts had in nowise impaired his resources.

The youth, still the bearer of the colors, did not feel his idleness. He was deeply absorbed as a spectator. The crash and swing of the great drama made him lean forward, intent-eyed, his face working in small contortions. Sometimes he prattled, words coming unconsciously from him in grotesque exclamations. He did not know that he breathed; that the flag hung silently over him, so absorbed was he.

A formidable line of the enemy came within dangerous range. They could be seen plainly—tall, gaunt men with excited faces running with long strides toward a wandering fence.

At sight of this danger the men suddenly ceased their cursing monotone. There was an instant of strained silence before they threw up their rifles and fired a plumping volley at the foes. There had been no order given; the men, upon recognizing the menace, had immediately let drive their flock of bullets without waiting for word of command.

But the enemy were quick to gain the protection of the wandering line of fence. They slid down behind it with remarkable celerity, and from this position they began briskly to slice up the blue men.

These latter braced their energies for a great struggle. Often, white clinched teeth shone from the dusky faces. Many heads surged to and fro, floating upon a pale sea of smoke. Those behind the fence frequently shouted and yelped in taunts and gibelike cries, but the regiment maintained a stressed silence. Perhaps, at this new assault the men recalled the fact that they had been named mud diggers, and it made their situation thrice bitter. They were breathlessly intent upon keeping the ground and thrusting away the rejoicing body of the enemy. They fought swiftly and with a despairing savageness denoted in their expressions.

The youth had resolved not to budge whatever should happen. Some arrows of scorn that had buried themselves in his heart had generated strange and unspeakable hatred. It was clear to him that his final and absolute revenge was to be achieved by his dead body lying, torn and gluttering, upon the field. This was to be a poignant retaliation upon the officer who had said "mule drivers," and later "mud diggers," for in all the wild graspings of his mind for a unit responsible for his sufferings and commotions he always seized upon the man who had dubbed him wrongly. And it was his idea, vaguely formulated, that his corpse would be for those eyes a great and salt reproach.[25]

The regiment bled extravagantly. Grunting bundles of blue began to drop. The orderly sergeant of the youth's company was shot through the cheeks. Its supports being injured, his jaw hung afar down, disclosing in the wide cavern of his mouth a pulsing

[25] SALT REPROACH—A reproach which would sting sharply, like salt in an open wound.

mass of blood and teeth. And with it all he made attempts to cry out. In his endeavor there was a dreadful earnestness, as if he conceived that one great shriek would make him well.

The youth saw him presently go rearward. His strength seemed in nowise impaired. He ran swiftly, casting wild glances for succor.

Others fell down about the feet of their companions. Some of the wounded crawled out and away, but many lay still, their bodies twisted into impossible shapes.

The youth looked once for his friend. He saw a vehement young man, powder-smeared and frowzled, whom he knew to be him. The lieutenant, also, was unscathed in his position at the rear. He had continued to curse, but it was now with the air of a man who was using his last box of oaths.

For the fire of the regiment had begun to wane and drip. The robust voice, that had come strangely from the thin ranks, was growing rapidly weak.

## CHAPTER TWENTY-THREE

The colonel came running along back of the line. There were other officers following him. "We must charge'm!" they shouted. "We must charge'm!" they cried with resentful voices, as if anticipating a rebellion against this plan by the men.

The youth, upon hearing the shouts, began to study the distance between him and the enemy. He made vague calculations. He saw that to be firm soldiers they must go forward. It would be death to stay in the present place, and with all the circumstances to go backward would exalt too many others. Their hope was to push the galling foes away from the fence.

He expected that his companions,

weary and stiffened, would have to be driven to this assault, but as he turned toward them he perceived with a certain surprise that they were giving quick and unqualified expressions of assent. There was an ominous, clanging overture to the charge when the shafts of the bayonets rattled upon the rifle barrels. At the yelled words of command the soldiers sprang forward in eager leaps. There was new and unexpected force in the movement of the regiment. A knowledge of its faded and jaded condition made the charge appear like a paroxysm, a display of the strength that comes before a final feebleness. The men scampered in insane fever of haste, racing as if to achieve a sudden success before an exhilarating fluid should leave them. It was a blind and despairing rush by the collection of men in dusty and tattered blue, over a green sward and under a sapphire sky, toward a fence, dimly outlined in smoke, from behind which spluttered the fierce rifles of enemies.

The youth kept the bright colors to the front. He was waving his free arm in furious circles, the while shrieking mad calls and appeals, urging on those that did not need to be urged, for it seemed that the mob of blue men hurling themselves on the dangerous group of rifles were again grown suddenly wild with an enthusiasm of unselfishness. From the many firings starting toward them, it looked as if they would merely succeed in making a great sprinkling of corpses on the grass between their former position and the fence. But they were in a state of frenzy, perhaps because of forgotten vanities, and it made an exhibition of sublime recklessness. There was no obvious questioning, nor figurings, nor diagrams. There was, apparently, no considered loop-

holes. It appeared that the swift wings of their desires would have shattered against the iron gates of the impossible.

He himself felt the daring spirit of a savage religion-mad. He was capable of profound sacrifices, a tremendous death. He had no time for dissections,[26] but he knew that he thought of the bullets only as things that could prevent him from reaching the place of his endeavor. There were subtle flashings of joy within him that thus should be his mind.

He strained all his strength. His eyesight was shaken and dazzled by the tension of thought and muscle. He did not see anything excepting the mist of smoke gashed by the little knives of fire, but he knew that in it lay the aged fence of a vanished farmer protecting the snuggled bodies of the gray men.

As he ran a thought of the shock of contact gleamed in his mind. He expected a great concussion when the two bodies of troops crashed together. This became a part of his wild battle madness. He could feel the onward swing of the regiment about him and he conceived of a thunderous, crushing blow that would prostrate the resistance and spread consternation and amazement for miles. The flying regiment was going to have a catapultian effect. This dream made him run faster among his comrades, who were giving vent to hoarse and frantic cheers.

But presently he could see that many of the men in gray did not intend to abide the blow. The smoke, rolling, disclosed men who ran, their faces still turned. These grew to a crowd, who retired stubbornly. Individuals wheeled frequently to send a bullet at the blue wave.

[26] . . . NO TIME FOR DISSECTIONS—He had no time to stop and examine the situation.

But at one part of the line there was a grim and obdurate group that made no movement. They were settled firmly down behind posts and rails. A flag, ruffled and fierce, waved over them and their rifles dinned fiercely.

The blue whirl of men got very near, until it seemed that in truth there would be a close and frightful scuffle. There was an expressed disdain in the opposition of the little group, that changed the meaning of the cheers of the men in blue. They became yells of wrath, directed, personal. The cries of the two parties were now in sound an interchange of scathing insults.

They in blue showed their teeth; their eyes shone all white. They launched themselves as at the throats of those who stood resisting. The space between dwindled to an insignificant distance.

The youth had centered the gaze of his soul upon that other flag. Its possession would be high pride. It would express bloody minglings, near blows. He had a gigantic hatred for those who made great difficulties and complications. They caused it to be as a craved treasure of mythology, hung amid tasks and contrivances of danger.

He plunged like a mad horse at it. He was resolved it should not escape if wild blows and darings of blows could seize it. His own emblem, quivering and aflare, was winging toward the other. It seemed there would shortly be an encounter of strange beaks and claws, as of eagles.

The swirling body of blue men came to a sudden halt at close and disastrous range and roared a swift volley. The group in gray was split and broken by this fire, but its riddled body still fought. The men in blue yelled again and rushed in upon it.

The youth, in his leapings, saw, as through a mist, a picture of four or five men stretched upon the ground or writhing upon their knees with bowed heads as if they had been stricken by bolts from the sky. Tottering among them was the rival color bearer, whom the youth saw had been bitten vitally by the bullets of the last formidable volley. He perceived this man fighting a last struggle, the struggle of one whose legs are grasped by demons. It was a ghastly battle. Over his face was the bleach of death, but set upon it were the dark and hard lines of desperate purpose. With this terrible grin of resolution he hugged his precious flag to him and was stumbling and staggering in his design to go the way that led to safety for it.

But his wounds always made it seem that his feet were retarded, held, and he fought a grim fight, as with invisible ghouls fastened greedily upon his limbs. Those in advance of the scampering blue men, howling cheers, leaped at the fence. The despair of the lost was in his eyes as he glanced back at them.

The youth's friend went over the obstruction in a tumbling heap and sprang at the flag as a panther at prey. He pulled at it and, wrenching it free, swung up its red brilliancy with a mad cry of exultation even as the color bearer, gasping, lurched over in a final throe and, stiffening convulsively, turned his dead face to the ground. There was much blood upon the grass blades.

At the place of success there began more wild clamorings of cheers. The men gesticulated and bellowed in an ecstasy. When they spoke it was as if they considered their listener to be a mile away. What hats and caps were left to them they often slung high in the air.

At one part of the line four men had been swooped upon, and they now sat as prisoners. Some blue men were about them in an eager and curious circle. The soldiers had trapped strange birds, and there was an examination. A flurry of fast questions was in the air.

One of the prisoners was nursing a superficial wound in the foot. He cuddled it, babywise, but he looked up from it often to curse with an astonishing utter abandon straight at the noses of his captors. He consigned them to red regions; he called upon the pestilential wrath of strange gods. And with it all he was singularly free from recognition of the finer points of the conduct of prisoners of war. It was as if a clumsy clod had trod upon his toe and he conceived it to be his privilege, his duty, to use deep, resentful oaths.

Another, who was a boy in years, took his plight with great calmness and apparent good nature. He conversed with the men in blue, studying their faces with his bright and keen eyes. They spoke of battles and conditions. There was an acute interest in all their faces during this exchange of viewpoints. It seemed a great satisfaction to hear voices from where all had been darkness and speculation.

The third captive sat with a morose countenance. He preserved a stoical and cold attitude. To all advances he made one reply without variation, "Ah, go t' hell!"

The last of the four was always silent and, for the most part, kept his face turned in unmolested directions. From the views the youth received he seemed to be in a state of absolute dejection. Shame was upon him, and with it profound regret that he was, perhaps, no more to be counted in the ranks of his fellows. The youth could detect no expression that would allow him to believe that the other was giving a thought to his narrowed future, the pictured dungeons, perhaps, and starvations and brutalities, liable to the imagination. All to be seen was shame for captivity and regret for the right to antagonize.

After the men had celebrated sufficiently they settled down behind the old rail fence, on the opposite side to the one from which their foes had been driven. A few shot perfunctorily at distant marks.

There was some long grass. The youth nestled in it and rested, making a convenient rail support the flag. His friend, jubilant and glorified, holding his treasure with vanity, came to him there. They sat side by side and congratulated each other.

## CHAPTER TWENTY-FOUR

The roarings that had stretched in a long line of sound across the face of the forest began to grow intermittent and weaker. The stentorian speeches of the artillery continued in some distant encounter, but the crashes of the musketry had almost ceased. The youth and his friend of a sudden looked up, feeling a deadened form of distress at the waning of these noises, which had become a part of life. They could see changes going on among the troops. There were marchings this way and that way. A battery wheeled leisurely. On the crest of a small hill was the thick gleam of many departing muskets.

The youth arose. "Well, what now, I wonder?" he said. By his tone he seemed to be preparing to resent some new monstrosity in the way of dins and smashes. He shaded his eyes with his grimy hand and gazed over the field.

His friend also arose and stared. "I bet we're goin' t' git along out of this an' back over th' river," said he.

"Well, I swan!" said the youth.

They waited, watching. Within a little while the regiment received orders to retrace its way. The men got up grunting from the grass, regretting the soft repose. They jerked their stiffened legs, and stretched their arms over their heads. One man swore as he rubbed his eyes. They all groaned "O Lord!" They had as many objections to this change as they would have had to a proposal for a new battle.

They trampled slowly back over the field across which they had run in a mad scamper.

The regiment marched until it had joined its fellows. The reformed brigade, in column, aimed through a wood at the road. Directly they were in a mass of dust-covered troops, and were trudging along in a way parallel to the enemy's lines as these had been defined by the previous turmoil.

They passed within view of a stolid white house, and saw in front of it groups of their comrades lying in wait behind a neat breastwork. A row of guns were booming at a distant enemy. Shells thrown in reply were raising clouds of dust and splinters. Horsemen dashed along the line of intrenchments.

At this point of its march the division curved away from the field and went winding off in the direction of the river. When the significance of this movement had impressed itself upon the youth he turned his head and looked over his shoulder toward the trampled and *débris*-strewed ground. He breathed a breath of new satisfaction.

He finally nudged his friend. "Well, it's all over," he said to him.

His friend gazed backward. "B'Gawd, it is," he assented. They mused.

For a time the youth was obliged to reflect in a puzzled and uncertain way. His mind was undergoing a subtle change. It took moments for it to cast off its battleful ways and resume its accustomed course of thought. Gradually his brain emerged from the clogged clouds, and at last he was enabled to more closely comprehend himself and circumstance.

He understood then that the existence of shot and counter-shot was in the past. He had dwelt in a land of strange, squalling upheavals and had come forth. He had been where there was red of blood and black of passion, and he was escaped. His first thoughts were given to rejoicings at this fact.

Later he began to study his deeds, his failures, and his achievements. Thus, fresh from scenes where many of his usual machines of reflection had been idle, from where he had proceeded sheeplike, he struggled to marshal all his acts.

At last they marched before him clearly. From this present viewpoint he was enabled to look upon them in spectator fashion and to criticize them with some correctness, for his new condition had already defeated certain sympathies.

Regarding his procession of memory he felt gleeful and unregretting, for in it his public deeds were paraded in great and shining prominence. Those performances which had been witnessed by his fellows marched now in wide purple and gold, having various deflections. They went gayly with music. It was pleasure to watch these things. He spent delightful minutes viewing the gilded images of memory.

He saw that he was good. He recalled with a thrill of joy the respectful comments of his fellows upon his conduct.

Nevertheless, the ghost of his flight from the first engagement appeared to him and danced. There were small shoutings in his brain about these matters. For a moment he blushed, and the light of his soul flickered with shame.

A specter of reproach came to him. There loomed the dogging memory of the tattered soldier—he who, gored by bullets and faint for blood, had fretted concerning an imagined wound in another; he who had loaned his last of strength and intellect for the tall soldier; he who, blind with weariness and pain, had been deserted in the field.

For an instant a wretched chill of sweat was upon him at the thought that he might be detected in the thing. As he stood persistently before his vision, he gave vent to a cry of sharp irritation and agony.

His friend turned. "What's the matter, Henry?" he demanded. The youth's reply was an outburst of crimson oaths.

As he marched along the little branch-hung roadway among his prattling companions this vision of cruelty brooded over him. It clung near him always and darkened his view of these deeds in purple and gold. Whichever way his thoughts turned they were followed by the somber phantom of the desertion in the fields. He looked stealthily at his companions, feeling sure that they must discern in his face evidences of this pursuit. But they were plodding in ragged array, discussing with quick tongues the accomplishments of the late battle.

"Oh, if a man should come up an' ask me, I'd say we got a dum good lickin'."

"Lickin'—in yer eye! We ain't licked, sonny. We're going down here aways, swing aroun', an' come in behint 'em."

"Oh, hush, with your comin' in behint 'em. I've seen all 'a that I wanta. Don't tell me about comin' in behint—"

"Bill Smithers, he ses he'd rather been in ten hundred battles than been in that heluva hospital. He ses they got shootin' in th' nighttime, an' shells dropped plum among 'em in th' hospital. He ses sech hollerin' he never see."

"Hasbrouck? He's th' best off'cer in this here reg'ment. He's a whale."

"Didn't I tell yeh we'd come aroun' in behint 'em? Didn't I tell yeh so? We—"

"Oh, shet yer mouth!"

For a time this pursuing recollection of the tattered man took all elation from the youth's veins. He saw his vivid error, and he was afraid that it would stand before him all his life. He took no share in the chatter of his comrades, nor did he look at them or know them, save when he felt sudden suspicion that they were seeing his thoughts and scrutinizing each detail of the scene with the tattered soldier.

Yet gradually he mustered force to put the sin at a distance. And at last his eyes seemed to open to some new ways. He found that he could look back upon the brass and bombast of his earlier gospels and see them truly. He was gleeful when he discovered that he now despised them.

With the conviction came a store of assurance. He felt a quiet manhood, non-assertive but of sturdy and strong blood. He knew that he would no more quail before his guides wherever they should point. He had been to touch the great death, and found that, after all, it was but the great death. He was a man.

So it came to pass that as he trudged from the place of blood and wrath his soul changed. He came from hot plowshares to prospects of clover tranquilly, and it was as if hot plowshares were not. Scars faded as flowers.

It rained. The procession of weary soldiers became a bedraggled train, despondent and muttering, marching with churning effort in a trough of liquid brown mud under a low, wretched sky. Yet the youth smiled, for he saw that the world was a world for him, though many discovered it to be made of oaths and walking sticks. He had rid himself of the red sickness of battle. The sultry nightmare was in the past. He had been an animal blistered and sweating in the heat and pain of war. He turned now with a lover's thirst to images of tranquil skies, fresh meadows, cool brooks—an existence of soft and eternal peace.

Over the river a golden ray of sun came through the hosts of leaden rain clouds.

❖❖❖❖❖❖❖❖❖❖❖❖❖❖❖❖❖❖❖❖❖❖❖❖❖

## FOR DISCUSSION

### CHAPTER I

1. What was the tall man's rumor? How was it received by his comrades? What was Henry's first reaction? Why?

2. What was Henry's motive for enlisting? What was his mother's attitude? Which attitude was the more realistic?

3. Did Henry's initial training, a "blue demonstration," strengthen his attitude toward soldiering? How?

4. What problem was Henry pondering on his bunk? Was this reflection healthy or unhealthy? Why?

5. What was Henry's attitude toward the tall soldier? Why does the tall soldier's reaction to "running" reassure the new recruit?

### CHAPTER II

1. Why did Henry fret over the failure of the immediate materialization of the rumor?

2. What mood does the author attempt to establish during the preparations for battle? What words exemplify this mood?

3. What effect does the author achieve with the "box of cigars" remark?

4. What psychological effect does the first light of dawn and the marching have on the troops?

5. How do Henry's doubts about his courage affect his actions? Is this a normal reaction?

6. Is the loud soldier a new recruit or a veteran? How can you tell? What makes Henry's suffering very poignant?

### CHAPTER III

1. Notice the author's use of color to intensify moods. What is the mood established in the first paragraph of this chapter?

2. How does the discarding of equipment indicate a maturing of the regiment?

3. How does Henry's introduction to the battleground at first revise his outlook on the "blue demonstration"?

4. What is Henry's first impression of the battlefield? What does this indicate about the private soldier's idea of war?

5. What is the "question" Henry wishes to read in the eyes of the dead Confederate?

6. Is the author's approach to war realistic or romantic? In what words does he define this attitude?

7. What indication do the different barriers and fox holes give about the experience of the soldiers?

8. Why does a march into a "new region" unsettle Henry?

9. What happens to the morale of the loud soldier under stress of the first gunfire? What does this indicate about his loudness?

CHAPTER IV

1. Why do the soldiers gossip, with the fighting near at hand?

2. Does the battle begin with a crash? What impression does the author create at the outset of the fight?

3. What do the contrasting reactions of the new and veteran regiments tell about the first retreat?

4. Curiosity strikes the youth with regard to the enemy. What causes this curiosity?

CHAPTER V

1. In the first paragraph what similarity does the circus parade have with the battle in Henry's mind? Why?

2. What does the brown of the Southern uniforms tell of their condition? Are they veterans?

3. How does the battle tension express itself in the various officers? The Colonel? The Captain?

4. From what does Henry's feeling of being part of a whole stem? How is he like a workman, a carpenter?

5. Battle fury takes possession of the boy. Why? Does the attitude of the men fit Henry's former picture? Explain.

6. How do the wounded and the dead fall? Heroically? What impressions does the author give of dead in battle?

7. What psychological effect does the flag have on the soldier?

8. Does he have any real idea of the progress of the battle? What contrast does the author point out at the end of the chapter?

CHAPTER VI

1. Has the first assault tested Henry? Why?

2. What reaction does the second charge cause among the new regiment? Why?

3. What sense has the youth lost which causes his flight? How does flight affect him? Why?

4. What reaction does the youth reveal to those holding their ground or coming up? What does this show about his own condition?

5. What contrast does the general make with the youth? How is it significant?

CHAPTER VII

1. Notice the ironical note in the young soldier's reflections. How does the author achieve this irony?

2. How does Nature support Henry's logic? What effect does it have on him?

3. The chapel in the woods creates a contrast with Henry's feelings about Nature. Why?

CHAPTER VIII

1. Why does Henry return to the battle? Pride? Curiosity? Shame?

2. Does the depiction of different types of wounded in the column help for realism? Why? Notice the contrast between the different types of wounded. What effect does this produce?

3. War is the "machine." Is this a romantic or realistic view? Why does Henry join the column of wounded?

4. Talk of the way "they fit" has what effect on the boy? What impression does the author intend to create?

CHAPTER IX

1. Notice the author's use of descriptive epithets rather than names—the "loud soldier," "spectral soldier," "tattered soldier." Why does he employ these?

2. Henry wants a "red badge of courage." Would he really have merited it? What is courage? Who is the "spectral soldier"? Of what is Jim afraid? How is this fear ironical?

3. Why did Jim go doggedly on? What supported him?

4. Notice the comparison of Jim to a devotee of a religion and the expletives of the soldiers—God, Hell! In the light of these what is the significance of the image "red sun pasted like a wafer"?

CHAPTER X

1. How do the reactions of the tattered soldier to Jim's death compare with Henry's? What does this comparison show?

2. What is the significance of the tattered soldier's remark, "It might be inside mostly, and them plays thunder"? How does it apply to the youth?

3. Why does the tattered soldier call Henry "Tom Jamison"? What implicit blame does this call down on Henry?

4. Why does Henry leave the column of wounded?

CHAPTER XI

1. The contrasting pictures of retreat and advance call up contrasting emotions in the young soldier. Why?

2. How does taking thought about joining the regiment affect Henry? Is this a common phenomenon?

3. Henry wants to feel one of the group. How does this feeling express itself?

4. Why does he allow himself to consider the possibility of defeat and finally to desire it?

CHAPTER XII

1. What comes of Henry's attempt to stop the retreating soldier? How is this ironical?

2. What is the cause of Henry's thoughts of home? About what are they centered?

3. What fact comes out of the "cheery voice's" ranklings? What is the significance of Henry's never having "seen his face"?

CHAPTER XIII

1. How do the greetings of his friends affect Henry? What does he say?

2. What effect does the author achieve in his descriptions of the sleeping soldiers?

3. What caused the loud soldier's reproof? Was he really angry?

CHAPTER XIV

1. How was Henry's first view of the sleeping camp a prophecy?

2. What caused the change in the loud soldier? How does the change explain his former loudness?

CHAPTER XV

1. How do the first few paragraphs of this chapter show that the youth remains unchanged in spite of his wound, the red badge? On what does his confidence depend? Can a soldier really flee with "discretion and dignity"?

2. Henry is coloring yesterday's exploits with self-pride; a natural tendency. How does this affect the reader's attitude toward him?

CHAPTER XVI

1. What is significant about the gunfire drowning out the young soldier's joke?

2. Notice the reversal of attitude in Henry and the erstwhile loud soldier. How is this significant?

3. Why does Henry suddenly become modest? How long does this last?

4. Does Henry stand up to the lieutenant? Why not?

5. How does the present attitude of the soldiers of the regiment contrast with their former attitude on going into battle?

CHAPTER XVII

1. Henry has come to believe in his courageous pose. How does the author bring this out?

2. What accounts for Henry's spirit of frenzy? Does it prove him courageous?

3. The regiment is cocky after the first assault. Have they proved themselves now?

CHAPTER XVIII

1. What effect does the wounded man have on the morale of the regiment? Why?

2. Do the two soldiers looking for water have any idea of the larger picture of the battle? Explain.

3. The general's conference in the woods brings out what fact about Henry's regiment?

4. How does the news affect the young soldier? What painful fact does he learn for the first time?

5. What is the significance of Henry's secret—that his regiment are considered "mule-drivers"?

CHAPTER XIX

1. Why does Henry fling himself into the charge?

2. How are Henry's first impressions in this battle different from those of yesterday?

3. What halts the charge of the regiment? How does Henry's friend Wilson prove himself?

4. Why does Henry help lead the charge? Why does he leap to recover the colors?

CHAPTER XX

1. What is the significance of Henry and his friend struggling over the flag?

2. When does Henry begin to accept the mule-driver remark of the officer?

3. What moves Henry to exhort his comrades?

4. What is the deciding factor in their retreat?

5. What does Henry's reply to his friend—"don't be a damned fool"—indicate about his attitude? Whom does he resemble here?

6. Why does the regiment take heart at the appearance of the enemy? Why do they stand fast?

CHAPTER XXI

1. Why does the author record the remarks of the veteran soldiers? Henry finally accepts these remarks as just. Why?

2. What is the ironic note in the disheveled officer's reprimand? Why are the soldiers bewildered?

3. Notice how Henry and his friend are condemning the general and his staff. What contrast is drawn by the report of the colonel's conversation?

CHAPTER XXII

1. How do you explain the change that has taken place in the youth, who now can watch an attack, "erect and tranquil"?

2. The author uses the striking, unexpected adjective. Discuss "yelling wood," "unimpressed boys," "perched ears."

3. How does the youth's regiment go to battle this time? How does the "great and salt reproach" spur them on?

CHAPTER XXIII

1. How does the regiment react to the command to charge? Why? What psychological effect does the charge have?

2. Notice the repeated reference to religious-like fervor of the soldiers? Why does the author bring this up again?

3. How does this battle differ in tactics from the others in which the regiment has engaged? Why? The contrasting attitudes of the captured Rebels add realism to the scene. Why? Does the young soldier reach maturity here? Or has he reached it earlier, so that this bravery is but the result of it?

CHAPTER XXIV

1. How accurate an idea do the soldiers have of the progress of the battle?

2. After the battle the youth feels gleeful and ashamed. How are these conflicting emotions possible?

3. "Deeds in purple and gold" means what?

4. Why does the author add the seemingly disconnected remarks of the battle-weary soldiers?

5. Assurance comes to the youth from the thought that it is "but the great death." What does this signify?

6. How has Henry become a man? If the army had been defeated, would he still have reached manhood? How does the last line of the story point the significance of the book?

# Meet the Authors

HENRY ADAMS (1838–1918). Great-grandson of President John Adams, grandson of President John Quincy Adams, son of a distinguished ambassador to England —such was the rich heritage of Henry Brooks Adams. He grew up in Boston and like many distinguished Bostonians he went to Harvard. After graduation from Harvard, he went to Germany to further studies in civil law; but he soon lost interest in this pursuit, and spent most of his time traveling on the continent.

In 1870, he accepted a professorship in history at Harvard and at the same time became editor of the *North American Review*. Although he was a stimulating teacher, his heart was not in the work. He resigned in 1877 and returned to Washington where he devoted himself to study and writing. His drawing room was the most brilliant in the nation's capital. In 1885, however, his wife died suddenly; and this tragedy deeply wounded Henry Adams. In order to forget his sorrow, he took a long trip to Japan and spent some time traveling in the Orient. On his return to Washington, he busied himself in finishing his *History of the United States of America during the Administrations of Jefferson and Madison*, which was finally completed in 1891.

Much of the next ten years was spent traveling in America and Europe. As a result of these years of thought and observation, Adams produced the two books on which his fame chiefly rests. *Mont-Saint-Michel and Chartres*, published in 1904, was a study of the Middle Ages, which the author regarded as the highest point of human culture. Still more famous is *The Education of Henry Adams*, really an autobiography, but intended as an expression of the enigma facing the twentieth-century man.

ALFRED J. BARRETT, S.J. (1906– ) was born in Flushing, New York, and educated at St. Francis Xavier College. In 1924, immediately after graduation, he entered the Society of Jesus at St. Andrew-on-Hudson, New York. During his thirteen years of training as a Jesuit, he acquired his Bachelor's and Master's degrees at Woodstock College in Maryland. Ordained in 1937, he spent a year at the Jesuit Martyrs' Shrine at Auriesville, New York, and then taught poetry at Canisius College, Buffalo. This life of comparative solitude was broken when he volunteered as chaplain at the outbreak of World War II in 1941. Since his release he has taught English at Fordham University, New York City. His main work is a short book of poems entitled, *Mint by Night*.

STEPHEN VINCENT BENÉT (1898–1943). Younger brother of William Rose Benét, Stephen Vincent Benét liked to trace his ancestry back to a Mexican bandit. At seventeen he published his first volume of poetry, then turned to the more lucrative field of short story writing. While studying in Paris, he wrote his most famous poem, *John Brown's Body*, a story of the American Civil War.

WILLIAM BRADFORD (1590–1657), who was born in Yorkshire, England, was one of the Mayflower Pilgrims and a tower of strength in the new community. When Governor Carver died in 1621, Bradford was elected governor and except for five years—at scattered intervals—he held the office until his death thirty-six years later.

HEYWOOD BROUN (1888–1939) was a newspaper man by vocation and by avocation. After his graduation from Harvard in 1910, he held many journalistic jobs, progressing from reporter to correspondent, to critic, to columnist and feature writer. From 1928 to 1939 he was employed by the Scripps-Howard papers. He transferred to the *New York Post* only two weeks before his death. "It Seems to Me" was his popular column. He was also a lecturer on the drama and dramatic critic for *Vanity Fair.*

Because of his prominence as a columnist and because of his long association with radical movements, his conversion to the Catholic Church in May, 1939, created a sensation.

WILLIAM CULLEN BRYANT (1794–1878) was born and grew to manhood in the Berkshire Hills of New England. His parents were Puritans, and he was brought up in the rigid religious atmosphere of the time.

He was prepared for college by the local preacher, and in his sixteenth year entered Williams College in the sophomore class. After two terms he had to leave, for his father had no money to give him. He was heartbroken; and while grieving over this and over his poor health, wrote "Thanatopsis." He wanted to devote his time to poetry, but he knew that poetry would earn him no living. He had an ambition to become an editor, but editorial openings were few. He turned to the study of law, but his heart was not in it. However, he had to earn his living, so he persisted in his studies and was admitted to the bar when he was twenty-one. He continued his law practice for a time and then became connected with the New York *Evening Post* which he edited for forty-nine years.

Four-fifths of his poetry deals with death or nature, both subjects coming naturally from the stern, unrelenting environment of the Puritans, from which his early training never let him entirely escape. The Puritans had always looked upon death with great interest. Two of the books which they read were *Paradise Lost* and *Pilgrim's Progress*, both of which are concerned with life hereafter. It is not

so surprising, therefore, that Bryant's thoughts turned to the theme of death.

KATHERINE BURTON (1890–    ) was born in Cleveland, Ohio, and educated at Lakewood High School and Western Reserve University. Always interested in writing, she has been associate editor for *McCall's* magazine and *Redbook.* Since 1934 she has been the woman's editor for *The Sign.* Mrs. Burton is a convert from Episcopalianism and has written several biographies of American converts who have become outstanding members of the Catholic Church. In 1937 she wrote *Sorrow Built a Bridge*, a beautifully written portrait of Rose Hawthorne, daughter of Nathaniel Hawthorne. In 1940 she finished *His Dear Persuasion*, a life of Mother Seton.

GEORGE WASHINGTON CABLE (1844–1925). The first interpreter of the South was George Washington Cable, portrayer of life in early New Orleans.

Cable was born in New Orleans in 1844. His father was a Virginian and his mother a New Englander. When he was fourteen, his father died and the boy worked at odd jobs to support his mother and sisters. During the Civil War he enlisted in the 4th Mississippi Cavalry. His desire for learning was so great that even during his enlistment he studied Latin and the Bible. At the close of the war he helped survey along the Atchafalya River. Here he contracted malaria and for two years was unable to do physical work. He began to write at this time for newspapers. His column received such favorable attention that he was made a reporter. However, his religious convictions would not permit him to attend the theater and write up the press notices, so he was forced to leave the paper. These same religious convictions made him an active advocate of prison reforms and of justice for the Negro. After his experience at newspaper work he became a clerk for a company dealing in cotton. Still his desire for learning was unsatisfied and even after his marriage and the birth of his children, he got up at four o'clock in the morning to study. When he had mastered French, he became extremely interested in the old records and archives of New Orleans. As Hawthorne had brooded over Puritan traditions, so did Cable brood over those of Louisiana, and at length put them into story form.

BLISS CARMAN (1861–1929) is always associated with Richard Hovey, for the two instituted the "open road" school of poetry with their *Songs from Vagabondia*. Bliss Carman was a Canadian but he spent most of his life in the United States, studying law, teaching school, and working at field engineering before he achieved success as a poet.

WILLA CATHER (1876–1947). Although born in Virginia, Willa Cather spent her childhood in Nebraska where she grew up with the children of pioneer Germans, Scandinavians, and Bohemians. Tutored at home and steeped in the English classics, Miss Cather had no formal education until high school. Later she attended the University of Nebraska, where she wrote for the college newspaper. At various times she was English teacher, magazine editor, and free lance writer before she concentrated on the writing of novels.

MADISON CAWEIN (1865–1914), like many poets, began his verse-writing career as an avocation. His vocation as a cashier in Louisville, Kentucky, seems scarcely conducive to nature lyrics, but his first six books were written after his working day from 8 A.M. to 10 P.M. was over. His works can be classed under two headings: those dealing with nature and those dealing with feuds, lynchings, and man-hunts of the older life of Kentucky.

PADDY CHAYEFSKY (1922–    ). Born and raised in a Jewish-Italian section of the Bronx, New York, Paddy Chayefsky has the knack of finding his stories in the everyday situations of the people with whom he has lived most of his life, those in the big city. Among the more promising television writers in America today, Chayefsky's knack of portraying the average man as he actually is has all television viewers singing his praises. On the NBC's "Television Playhouse," his *Marty* was considered a prize-winner in 1954. In 1955 it was made into a movie, and at the annual Film Festival at Cannes, France, in 1955, *Marty* was one of two American films shown.

KATE CHOPIN (1851–1904) was a sympathetic interpreter of Southern life, who, like Cable, wrote of the Louisiana Creoles. Her best known works are *Bayou Folk* and *A Night in Acadie*, collections of sketches and stories of the people of Natchitoches Parish, whom she came to know and love during the years which she spent on her husband's plantation on the Red River.

Kate Chopin was born in St. Louis in 1851. Her father, a successful business man, died while she was but a child. Her formal schooling was received at the Sacred Heart Convent in St. Louis; a more influential part of her education she gathered in the attic of her home, whither she fled for uninterrupted reading of her favorite authors.

In 1870 she married a native of Louisiana, Oscar Chopin, and after a honeymoon in Europe the couple moved to New Orleans, where for the next ten years Mr. Chopin engaged in the cotton trade. It was his decision to assume the personal management of his own plantation and his sister's on the Red River that brought his wife to the section of Louisiana which she was to portray so realistically in her stories.

SAMUEL LANGHORNE CLEMENS (MARK TWAIN) (1835–1910). The general background of Mark Twain's growing up was the happy-go-lucky environment of a Missouri river town. His mother, a good woman, was a wholesome influence, but the family was poor. When the father died, Samuel's regular schooling stopped. He was apprenticed to a printer, and before long was a wage-earner in the family. This apprenticeship he later termed his "high school course"; and a subsequent four-year period as apprentice and pilot on the river, his "university career."

Samuel might have remained a river pilot had not the Civil War stopped navigation on the lower river. Uncertain days followed, but eventually he went with his brother, who had a secretarial position, to the territory of Nevada. Experiences in the far West furnished material for his first sketches; and with the publication of a series of humorous letters which were the result of a tour of Europe as a newspaper correspondent, he knew success as a journalist, humorist, and lecturer.

When he was sixty, the failure of a printing firm in which he had invested heavily swept away what money he had accumulated. Courageously, he continued writing and speaking to win back a competence for his family. His last years were spent in the New England states, and even in that conservative stronghold he commanded respect and admiration.

MARCUS CONNELLY (1890–    ) is a dramatist who learned the hard way. Educated in Washington, Pennsylvania, he went to Pittsburgh in 1910 and until 1915 divided his time and his talents among that city's *Sun*, *Dispatch*, and *Gazette-Times*. But in 1915 Mr. Connelly journeyed to New York to see a musical comedy in which he had invested a few lyrics. The play failed, and Connelly was stranded. His penniless straits, however, forced him to try his hand at making a quick dollar, and in the next few years his verse, short stories, and lyrics were read and heard by countless New Yorkers. Then he met George Kaufman. This team promptly turned out such successful hits as *Beggar on Horseback*, *Merton of the Movies*, *Helen of Troy, N. Y.*, and *Be Yourself*. Connelly's first solo effort was *The Wisdom Tooth*, a great play of 1926. He was branching out now and directed *Berkeley Square* (1929–30), and wrote short stories and verse for the *New Yorker*, a magazine he helped to found. In 1930, after months spent in Louisiana obtaining local color, he produced *The Green Pastures* which received the Pulitzer Prize of that year.

MYLES CONNOLLY (1897–    ) is better known as a novelist than as a poet. Born and raised a Catholic in Boston, he received his degree from Boston College in 1918. He served in the United States Navy for several years. Returning to civilian life, he turned to newspaper reporting and short story writing. From 1924 until 1930 he was editor of *Columbia*, the Knights of Columbus magazine. He married Agnes Bevington, the concert pianist. Living with his wife and five children in California, he now spends a good deal of his time writing stories for motion pictures, many of which have become famous movies. *The Reason for Ann* is a collection of some of his short stories that have been published in various periodicals. Some of his novels are: *The Bump on Brannigan's Head*, *Dan England and the Noonday Devil*, and *Mr. Blue*.

STEPHEN CRANE (1871–1900) was born in Newark, New Jersey, the son of a Methodist minister. He was educated at the Hudson River Institute at Claverack, New York, and spent a year each at Lafayette College and Syracuse University, paying more attention throughout to playing baseball than to education.

Crane was a devoted student of literary art all his life. After finishing his years of college he went to New York to start his career as author and newspaper reporter. His first novel—its printing paid for partly with money borrowed from his brother—

did not sell. Then, after study of war accounts, and painstaking toil to perfect his writing, he published *The Red Badge of Courage* in 1895. Its instant success assured his literary reputation. For the rest of his short life, Crane was engaged as a war correspondent by various American and English periodicals. He was sent to report a Cuban revolution. The ship he was on sank, and with other passengers Crane was in a lifeboat two days before being rescued. From this experience he wrote his most famous short story, "The Open Boat." He reported the Greco-Turkish War, and went back to Cuba a second time to report the Spanish-American War. After finally seeing battle at first hand, he was happy to be able to say to a friend, "*The Red Badge of Courage* is all right."

Crane's later books include novels; volumes of short stories and other brief sketches; and two collections of poems.

COUNTÉE CULLEN (1903–1946). When Countée Cullen was only twenty-two years old he published a volume of poems that at once gave him a place among contemporary American poets. His early life was spent in New York City, his birthplace. He attended the city public schools and was graduated from New York University. Later he went to Harvard.

JAMES J. DALY, S.J. (1872–1953) was born in Chicago in 1872; received his college training at St. Ignatius College in that city; entered the Society of Jesus at Florissant, Missouri, in 1890; and was ordained to the priesthood in 1905. He has taught English in several Jesuit colleges in the Middle West, and has been literary editor of three Catholic periodicals, *America*, the *Queen's Work*, and *Thought*.

MAUREEN DALY (1921–    ). At the age of three Maureen Daly came to the United States from Ireland to live in Fond du Lac, Wisconsin, where her father had set up business. Her early education was received at St. Mary's Springs Academy in Fond du Lac, after which she entered Rosary College, River Forest, Illinois, graduating in 1942 with an A.B. degree.

She began writing at an early age, placing fourth in a short-story contest in a national magazine when she was only fifteen years old. The following year she won first prize. In college she majored in English and Latin, edited the school paper, and wrote for a number of magazines. In 1941 her novel *Seventeenth Summer* was judged the first winner of the Dodd, Mead Intercollegiate Literary Fellowship annual prize contest by the unanimous choice of the judges.

JOSEPH GERARD DEVER (1919–    ) is a young Catholic writer with great ambitions and a vast capacity for hard work. He entered the writing field at an early age, and as a student editor of the Boston College magazine he turned it into one of the best college magazines in the country. After graduating from college in 1942, he was in the United States Air Force from 1943 until 1946. Even in the army he did not stop writing. Part of his time he spent editing one of the camp papers and made many contributions to *Yank, the Army Weekly*. After the war he taught at Marquette University, became an editor of the Bruce Publishing Co., and at present is devoting most of his time to writing.

EMILY DICKINSON (1830–1886) was a modernist who had no business being a modernist. Her early life in Amherst, Massachusetts, surrounded by propriety and conventions, her education at the South Hadley Female Seminary, and her debut as a village belle might lead one to expect a prettily sentimental birthday message on a hand-painted card, but little more than that. Instead, Emily Dickinson, although she wrote in the 1860's, is one of the leading poets of the twentieth century.

In her early twenties a tragic love affair ruined her chances for a happy life. From then on, she became more and more a recluse. Her writing absorbed her and she wrote hundreds of verses for herself and her friends. Some of these verses were enclosed in letters; some went with flowers to a friend or with some delicacy to a neighbor. She was not unhappy as she went about her "little toil of love" in the kitchen or in her garden. Her sister, sensing something of her genius, helped to shield her from the world. For two years before her death, she was a helpless invalid. She died in May, 1886.

JOHN DUFFY, C.SS. R. (1914– ) grew up in Roxbury, a section of Boston, Massachusetts, and attended the parochial school of the Redemptorist Parish. He completed his high school and college studies at the Redemptorist Juvenate in North East, Pennsylvania, and then entered the novitiate of the same order. After one year of novitiate and six years of philosophy and theology, he was ordained to the priesthood in 1940. In 1944, he took his doctor's degree in philosophy at The Catholic University of America. Since then, he has been teaching English at the Redemptorist Juvenate. He is the author of a volume of poems, *Thou and I.*

PAUL LAURENCE DUNBAR (1872– 1906) was one of the first Negro writers to win literary honors. Both his father and mother were escaped slaves and Paul early learned of the life of the slave people before and after the war. Graduating from the high school at Dayton, Ohio, he went to work running an elevator at four dollars a week, writing his verse at night, getting it published privately, and slowly winning the attention of the critics.

JONATHAN EDWARDS (1703–1758) was the last and probably the greatest of a famous group of Puritan preachers of early America. The son and grandson of New England ministers, he chose the same vocation for himself. From his earliest youth he showed signs of genius. When he graduated from Yale in 1720, he was recognized as a person of brilliant promise. As pastor of the Congregational Church in Northampton, Massachusetts, for over twenty years, his fame as a preacher grew. Trained in stern Calvinistic theology, he stressed the wrath rather than the mercy of God and preached what he called the "pleasant, bright, and sweet" doctrine of damnation.

RALPH WALDO EMERSON (1803– 1882). "The great man is he who in a crowd keeps with perfect sweetness, the independence of solitude." This sentence from *Self-Reliance* almost reflects Emerson's life. We see him, a tall, erect figure moving about the streets of Concord —honored, beloved by all—yet somehow alone. That it is a spiritual aloneness, he himself confesses: "I have no social talent; most of the persons whom I see, I see across a gulf. I can not go to them, nor they come to me." But the perfect sweetness was there.

Emerson's philosophy explains his life better than his life explains his philosophy —for Emerson did not choose the easiest way. After a boyhood of hardship and self-sacrifice, young Ralph found himself established as pastor of the Old North Church of Boston. Here life might have fallen into easy, pleasant ways, for he was an eloquent speaker and his pastorate enjoyed him. However, he was troubled by doctrinal doubts. The creed of his church he could not fully accept. A persistent inner voice said, "Trust thyself. Speak thy latent conviction." Emerson obeyed the voice. He resigned his position and renounced the ministry.

He had married the daughter of a merchant. Mrs. Emerson received a share in her father's estate, and after her tragically early death, this small income continued to provide Emerson with means for a living.

Emerson was the inspiration of all the

Concord group. He was an idealist and poet as well as a philosopher. His favorite theme was the importance of the individual and the need for faith in oneself. He rebelled against the complexity of civilization. He pleaded for less hurry and more inspiration, more meditation and communion with nature. This doctrine colors the writings of his associates.

THOMAS BUTLER FEENEY, S.J. (THOMAS BUTLER) (1899–    ) spent his boyhood in Lynn, Massachusetts. After graduating from Boston College High School, he entered the Society of Jesus in 1918 at St. Andrew-on-Hudson, Poughkeepsie, New York. He was ordained to the priesthood at Weston, Massachusetts, in 1931. For his final year of training (the tertianship), he went to Tronchiennes, Belgium. Since completing his course, Father Feeney has been engaged in teaching English Literature at Boston College High School and Boston College.

EUGENE FIELD (1850–1895) was born in Missouri. He was educated in the East, but he always loved his West and preferred to live there. He is known chiefly as a poet of childhood, but is also known for a book of western verse which has been very popular with the American public.

BENJAMIN FRANKLIN (1706–1790). It has often been said that Benjamin Franklin typifies the age in which he lived. Yet this same Franklin has been the choice of a recent writer as the man who could do the most for and with the America of today. The truth is that Franklin had those qualities which would make him thrive in any age. He was intelligent and ambitious. Besides that, he had common sense, an understanding of human nature plus a knack of getting along with folks, and a shrewd good humor. Above all, he was a tireless worker. As we read the list of his achievements, we are divided in wonder between the number of different kinds of things he could do and the prodigious amount of things that he accomplished. How could one man possibly do so much so well? Consider a partial list:

Although almost penniless at seventeen, he had made a fortune sufficient to retire on by the time he was forty.

He founded one of the first newspapers in the colonies, and so solidly that it survives today as one of the most widely read periodicals in the world—a magazine now, but with a keen eye to current affairs.

Although he had only two years of schooling, for twenty-five years he circulated the most popular piece of reading matter through the colonies—*Poor Richard's Almanac.*

He founded the school that later became the University of Pennsylvania.

He was respected throughout the civilized world for his writings and his scientific studies.

He invented the Franklin stove which pointed the way to our modern systems of heating by radiation.

He identified electricity and proposed a theory in explanation of it to which scientists have returned, naming the "particles" Franklin talked about, "electrons."

He organized in Philadelphia an efficient, paying, postal system which became the model for the postal system of the United States.

He organized the first police force in the colonies, the first fire company, the first state militia, and established the first public library.

Self-taught, he became our most pleasing and successful representative in London and Paris.

He was the only American to sign the four great documents of his age—the Declaration of Independence, the Treaty of Alliance with France, the Peace Treaty with Great Britain, and the Constitution of the United States.

PHILIP FRENEAU (1752–1832). The one really lyric poet of the Revolutionary Period was an ardent soldier and politician—Philip Freneau. The two parties of the period were the Whigs and the Tories. Freneau threw himself wholeheartedly into the cause of the Whigs. He denounced the Tories in scathing verse. His versatile life had given him a background to make his sallies the more effective. After graduating from Princeton, he had taught school, tried his wits at law, and traveled extensively. He fitted out a vessel which he himself commanded, but he was captured and thrown into a British prison ship. Throughout the war he penned verses to rail at the British and hearten the colonists. But after the war was over and peace established, Freneau wrote verses of another sort—simple poems of men and nature. It is for these lyrics that he is remembered today.

ROBERT LEE FROST (1875–    ). Robert Frost's ancestors for nine generations were New Englanders and lived in Lowell, Massachusetts. Frost had a rather meager education, for he never seemed to want to stay in school. He attended Dartmouth for a few months, but college was not to his liking and he left it to work as bobbin boy in a cotton mill. After his marriage he attended Harvard for two years, but he still found college uncongenial and left without a degree to earn a living for his growing family. In 1900 his grandfather bought him a farm in New Hampshire from which he wrested a living, supplemented by teaching, for twelve years. From the standpoint of his poetry, this is no doubt an important period in his development, for he is distinctly and almost exclusively the poet of the New England countryside and country people.

JAMES J. GALVIN, C.SS. R. (1911–    ). Father Galvin is a native of Boston. He attended the Redemptorist parish school in Roxbury, and then entered the Redemptorist Juvenate at North East, Pennsylvania. He was ordained to the priesthood in 1937. Since then he has spent several years in the missions in Puerto Rico. Now stationed at Esopus, New York, he is editor of *Perpetual Help*.

HAMLIN GARLAND (1860–1940) was the chief interpreter of the region of the Middle West. He was born in Wisconsin, the son of a typical pioneer whose restless spirit, with its visions and hopes of better soil and bigger crops farther west, urged him continually to move on to new land. When Garland was still a small boy the family moved from Wisconsin to Minnesota, from Minnesota to Iowa, and from Iowa to Dakota. He attended school in winter and worked on the farm in summer. He attended the Cedar Valley Seminary in Osage, Iowa, for five winters and later became a country school teacher in Illinois. The call of the border was too strong to be resisted, however, and in 1883 he took up a claim in Dakota. This he sold in 1884 and went to Boston, the home of his ancestors, where he lived for several years, supporting and educating himself as best he could with the meager resources at his command. It was on a summer visit to his "Middle Border" home that he saw with new eyes the grinding toil and crushing burden of the border farmer. This visit started him upon a series of stories depicting farm life as he knew it and had lived it. This series, under the title of *Main-Travelled Roads*, was a group of realistic, almost grim, sketches of farm life picturing the overburdened, hard-worked farmer.

In later writings he turned to biographical and autobiographical material and here his style was less grim and harsh. His own life was written in A *Son of the Middle Border*, and the story of the girl who later became his wife in A *Daughter of the Middle Border*.

JAMES M. GILLIS, C.S.P. (1876–    ). Father Gillis was born in Boston in 1876. After graduation from the Boston Latin School he continued his education at St. Charles College, Catonsville, Maryland, St. John's Seminary, Brighton, Massachusetts, and Catholic University, Washington. He joined the Paulist Fathers in 1900 and was ordained priest in 1901. From 1922 to 1948 he was editor of the *Catholic World*.

LOUISE IMOGEN GUINEY (1861–1920) was born in Boston, the daughter of Major General Patrick R. Guiney, a hero of the Civil War. She was educated at Elmhurst, the convent school of the Religious of the Sacred Heart in Providence, Rhode Island. Although she early made a name for herself in Boston literary circles, Miss Guiney still had to earn a livelihood for herself and mother, and for three years was postmistress at Auburndale, Massachusetts. Later she was employed in the Boston Public Library. But two visits to England had made her yearn to live and labor there. In 1901 the opportunity came, and thereafter she made her home at Oxford, where she devoted the rest of her life to writing and research.

ARTHUR GUITERMAN (1871–1943) was born of American parents in Vienna, Austria. He was educated at the College of the City of New York where he won acclaim as a member of the rowing team, as class secretary and poet, and as the leading light of the dramatic club. He went immediately into newspaper work, writing for magazines and contributing verse to the New York *Times*.

NATHANIEL HAWTHORNE (1804–1864). To understand Hawthorne's writings we must consider him in the light of his background. Born in 1804, he lived a lonely, unnatural childhood. After the death of his father, his mother became a recluse. Every curtain was drawn, every shutter was closed, and she lived in her own room. In this atmosphere the boy grew shy, sensitive, and imaginative. His years at Bowdoin College furnished almost the first bright and natural spot in his life, but after his graduation he again went into seclusion. In 1837 he collected a number of short stories he had written, and, with their publication under the title of *Twice-Told Tales*, he became known as a writer and began to emerge into the world of affairs. His marriage was a happy one and his wife encouraged his writing. Besides his novels he produced more than a hundred short stories.

LAFCADIO HEARN (1850–1904). Born of Irish and Greek parents under the blue sky of an island in the Ægean Sea, educated in France and England, living for brief periods in Cincinnati and New Orleans where he poured into the local newspapers his astonishing vivid sketches, finally becoming a citizen of Japan, even to adopting its dress, manners and religion —these are the high points in the life of Lafcadio Hearn.

His father, member of an ancient Irish family, had accompanied his regiment as surgeon-major to Corfu. Becoming infatuated with a beautiful Grecian girl, Rosa Cerigote, he married her. They named their first son for the island where he was born, his mother's home, Leucadia, in modern Greek, Lefcadia.

The facts of Hearn's life are very imperfectly known. His mother spent some time in Ireland and then, when Lafcadio was only seven, she went away to Smyrna, never to return. Now the boy stayed for a time with an aunt in Ireland, and then spent some time in school in France and England. It was while he was in school that an accident almost completely blinded him for the rest of his life.

For some time he lived in the slums of

London, hungry and sick, restless and ambitious. At nineteen he was in New York, reading omnivorously, despite his feeble vision, in the public library. He drifted to Cincinnati where his intensely vivid account of a murder made the city gasp with horror and won him a place on the *Enquirer*. His wanderings brought him to New Orleans where for the first time in his life he found congenial surroundings, where his knowledge of French was of genuine service to him, and where he could support himself by reporting for the *Times-Democrat*.

After several years, armed with a commission from *Harper's Magazine*, he went to Japan. Here he promptly forgot his commission in his delight over this new world of sensation. His later writings, beginning with *Glimpses of Unfamiliar Japan*, published in 1894, are attempts to interpret the country of his adoption, vivid impressions of a romantic country which he saw with equally romantic eyes.

PATRICK HENRY (1736–1799) was one of the liberty-loving orators who set the flame of freedom burning. He was born in Hanover County, Virginia, of Scotch and Welsh descent. After a somewhat irregular schooling he decided to study law and was licensed in 1760. His natural fire and eloquence made him almost immediately successful.

In 1765 he became a member of the House of Burgesses. Insignificant and unknown, he created a furor by offering a resolution declaring that the Burgesses and the Governor had the exclusive right to impose taxes in Virginia, and that all attempts of the British Parliament to tax the colonies were unconstitutional. In the stormy debate that followed he scandalized even his friends when he cried, "Caesar had his Brutus, Charles the First his Cromwell, and George the Third—[here he was stopped by cries of "Treason! treason!", but calmly proceeded] may profit by their example. If this be treason, make the most of it." His resolution was adopted, and Patrick Henry was recognized as a power in the colony.

DUBOSE HEYWARD (1885–1940) was born in South Carolina of an aristocratic family. When he was an infant, his father died, leaving the family in financial straits. At nine years of age he helped support the family by selling newspapers and at fourteen he left high school and worked in a hardware store. He became ill from too much hard work and was unable to do much for several years. This period was spent in reading, and in this way he educated himself. Then he went to work on the wharves in Charleston and was thrown into contact with the Negroes. Later he moved to North Carolina and devoted his time to writing about the Negroes and hardy mountaineers he had come to know and admire.

OLIVER WENDELL HOLMES (1809–1894). Can you picture a twinkling-eyed physician who preferred making puns to writing out prescriptions? Or a Harvard professor who would rather scribble verses than lecture to his students? Or an authority on anatomy who proved to be the most delightedly-read magazine writer of his day? That was the kind of man Holmes proved to be. For nearly forty years he was professor of anatomy at Harvard; yet for over sixty years he delighted readers in America and England with his verses and essays.

He was born in 1809—the same year as Lincoln and Poe—and was educated at Harvard. When he was twenty-one, to save the ship *Constitution* from being scrapped, he wrote "Old Ironsides." The verses saved the ship and made Holmes famous. For the remaining sixty-odd years of his life he wrote poetry, both serious and humorous, as a kind of sideline. And when he was nearly fifty he began writing some whimsical essays for the *Atlantic Monthly*, the new magazine which Lowell was editing. The first series was called the *Autocrat of the Breakfast Table*.

Into these chatty papers Holmes inserted many of his best poems.

## WASHINGTON IRVING (1783–1859).

Irving's years span the interesting period between the presidency of Washington (for whom he was named) and the election of Lincoln. He was born in New York City in April, 1783, the eleventh and youngest child of well-to-do parents. His schooling was mostly private and somewhat intermittent. In his twenty-first year he was threatened with consumption and was sent abroad for his health. In two years' time he returned cured, to spend his next twelve years in America. It was during this period that he undertook the publication of the *Salmagundi Papers* with his brother William as one of the co-editors, and that he brought out the rollicking Knickerbocker history.

In 1815 he sailed for England where at first he traveled at will, making friends with many writers—among them, Sir Walter Scott. In 1819, his brothers' business failed, and Irving began to write in earnest. *The Sketch Book of Geoffrey Crayon, Gent.* was the first book to appear. When it proved successful in England as well as in America, his literary career was assured.

## THOMAS JEFFERSON (1743–1826).

It is curious that Thomas Jefferson, who of all our statesmen was most completely devoted to the cause of the common man, should have been born of an aristocratic family and have enjoyed all the advantages of a cultural background. He was born at Shadwell of a good Virginia family. His mother fostered in him a knowledge and love of good literature while his father encouraged the more practical side of his training. Then he was sent to William and Mary College where he took, first, the regular academic subjects, and then five years of law. When he entered the Virginia House of Burgesses in 1769, he began a series of unbroken activities for the people and their government which culminated in his fulfillment of two terms as President of the United States.

No brief discussion can do justice to a man so many sided and productive as Jefferson. The student of literature makes acknowledgment to his idealism, to his craftsmanship, and to his sincerity. Jefferson was not content to be a mere spokesman for the rights of man. He devoted his life to securing these rights in actual fact for the citizens of the United States.

## JAMES WELDON JOHNSON (1871–1938).

A tragic railroad-crossing accident cut off in its prime the highly useful career of a great American Negro, James Weldon Johnson. Scholar, writer, lecturer, educator, lawyer, social worker, and diplomat, Johnson was born in Jacksonville, Florida. He attended Atlanta University, and later did graduate work in literature and drama at Columbia University. While serving as principal in a Jacksonville high school, the energetic Johnson read law on the side and was admitted to the Florida bar (1897), the first Negro attorney since the Civil War.

From 1906 to 1913 Johnson served with distinction as American Consul in Venezuela, and then in Nicaragua, where he became involved in the typical political turmoil of revolution and counterrevolution. While in Nicaragua he published anonymously his novel, *The Autobiography of an Ex-Colored Man*, without acknowledging authorship until 1927. This novel was the first work of its kind, attempting to give a real cross-section of Negro life—a departure from the stereotyped emotionalism of *Uncle Tom's Cabin*. Although the story drew heavily on the varied experiences of the author, it was fiction. The real autobiography of Johnson, *Along This Way*, appeared in 1934.

Several volumes of poetry are credited to him: *Fifty Years and Other Poems; God's Trombones*, a creative and powerful interpretation of typical Negro sermons; "St. Peter Relates an Incident of the Resurrection Day"; *The Book of American Negro Spirituals* (2 vols.). His *Book of American Negro Poetry* stimulated the efforts of many young writers.

BLANCHE MARY KELLY (1881– ) was born in Troy, New York, and educated at the Sacred Heart Convent in Albany, New York. She served on the staff of the *Catholic Encyclopedia* and of the *Catholic Dictionary*. A frequent contributor of both prose and poetry to Catholic periodicals in the United States and England, she is perhaps best known for her volume of poetry, *The Valley of Vision*, from which "The Housewife's Prayer" is taken. Her *The Well of English* is a critical study of the influence of the Catholic tradition on English literature. Miss Kelly is now professor emeritus of English, Mount St. Vincent College, New York City.

ALINE KILMER (1888–1941) was born at Norfolk, Virginia, and educated at Rutgers Preparatory School, Brunswick, New Jersey, and at the Vail-Deane School, Elizabeth, New Jersey. She was married to Joyce Kilmer in 1908, and with him embraced Catholicism in 1913.

JOYCE KILMER (1886–1918) is known to most high school students as the author of the poem, "Trees," and as the American soldier-poet killed in action. Actually, despite his brief thirty-two years, Joyce Kilmer accomplished a full span of writing. As an undergraduate at Columbia University he was active in public speaking and journalism. After graduation, he became an editorial assistant on a revision of a dictionary and began publishing his own verse in 1911. Later he interviewed celebrities for the New York *Times*, "luring his subjects into provocative statements" through his personal charm, lectured on poetry before literary groups, and wrote furiously—poetry, prose, and criticism. Three weeks after America entered the war Mr. Kilmer enlisted as a private.

In France he asked to be transferred from his "bullet proof" job as statistician and insisted on being sent on the most dangerous missions. He was killed in action, July, 1918. In his death America lost a poet of rare accomplishment and great promise.

S. I. KISHOR ( – ). Although Miss Kishor was born in London, England, she came to the United States as a child and is an American citizen. She was educated in London and in New York City at Hunter College and Columbia University. Miss Kishor is the author of *American Promise* and *Magnificent Hadrian*, as well as a variety of short stories and poems.

SARAH KEMBLE KNIGHT (1666–1727) was born in Boston when the town was thirty-six years old. Like most colonial women she married young. In 1703 her husband died, and three years later she opened a school. Benjamin Franklin became one of her pupils. It would seem that they must have had equal enjoyment in each other—she in the serious industry of the small boy and he in the capability and wit of his instructor.

The diary in which Madame Knight recorded her journey on horseback from Boston to New York is one of the most entertaining bits of colonial writing. The account reveals Sarah Knight as a woman well able to take care of herself, not afraid of doing the unconventional.

SIDNEY LANIER (1842–1881) was a soldier of the South. From the war he reaped poverty, a broken career, sickness, and death. To his homeland he had given service—hard fighting in the ranks, dangerous duty with the blockade-runners, imprisonment at Fort Lookout. When the struggle ended, he tramped five hundred miles back home penniless and sick. And without bitterness he took up the fight for life and a living. He was ready to take any kind of job to support his family. As a child he had shown unusual musical ability. He could play any instrument; and his flute had been his best companion through the war. When he finally secured a position with the Baltimore symphony orchestra, he came close to complete happiness. But then came the hindrance of failing health. From 1865 until his death in 1881, he tried to find a climate and a cure for tuberculosis, the aftermath of his camp life.

ABRAHAM LINCOLN (1809–1865). The story of Abraham Lincoln's rise from son of an illiterate, shiftless frontier family to war president of the United States would read like a fantastic legend, the rise of an epic hero, were it not for his own writings, which are full of earthiness and solid common sense touched with the peculiarly American flavor of his humor.

Lincoln, to express his opinions, depended largely upon letters addressed to individuals or delegations, but intended for public consumption. It is for this reason that we have an unusual amount of his writing. His was not an easy life nor a happy one. Although he now "belongs to the ages" his writings bring him to us as he was—a hard-working, clear-eyed realist —but a realist who knew that there are "things not seen" which are the *eternal realities.*

NICHOLAS VACHEL LINDSAY (1879–1931) ranks as one of the outstanding poets of our day, and one of the most singular. Springfield, Illinois, where Abraham Lincoln lived and lies buried, was his birthplace and lifelong home and it was there he died in 1931. He was educated at the Springfield High School and at Hiram College.

The verse form which he employs is wholly original. The rhythm of his poetry is a kind of syncopated movement, chosen deliberately to attract the attention of the public, but developed by him quite beyond anyone else's power to imitate. His poetry must be read aloud.

HENRY WADSWORTH LONGFELLOW (1807–1882) was born in Maine and received his education in his home state. He has been called "the household poet," but we could with truth call him "the universal poet," for he writes of nature, love, home, children, of various emotions, of historical incidents; and not content with writing the legends of his own country, he appropriates literary gems from Europe and writes about them.

He was a man of culture and refinement whose interests were largely in books. Sorrow he knew, but never hardship. He was of a calm and gentle nature. It is difficult to imagine him as ever in bitter mood, or in violent passion. Certainly his poetry never reveals him in such light. In fact, though it is invariably graceful, it is generally lacking in the intensity of feeling which is to be sensed in the poems of Whittier. He had wonderful ability to tell a story in verse, an ability equaled by few men in literature. Some of his best known story-poems are "The Courtship of Miles Standish," "Hiawatha," "Evangeline," "Paul Revere's Ride," and "The Birds of Killingworth."

AMY LOWELL (1874–1925) was born in Massachusetts and maintained her residence in that state throughout her life. She was a member of the distinguished Lowell family of New England.

She had wealth, social position, and every cultural advantage. This assuredness of position is reflected in her life and works. She was afraid of no criticism or opposition and threw her unlimited energy into battling for the supremacy of the new poetry. She was indefatigable in her interest in technique and declared that "a poet must learn his trade in the same manner and with the same painstaking care as a cabinet maker." She is the best known, and the best, of the so-called "Imagist" poets, who contend that poetry should present an image in clear, definite tones, without dealing in vague generalities.

JAMES RUSSELL LOWELL (1819–1891) was born in Cambridge, Massachusetts, ten years after Oliver Wendell Holmes. They were always the greatest of friends. Lowell came from an old New England family distinguished through generations for the number of able men which it had produced. As in his ancestry, so in the outward facts of his life he resembles many another famous son of New England. His father was a clergyman of note. He was brought up in a home where learning was valued, where books were known and appreciated, and where literary aspirations were encouraged. He was given a good education begun at a dame school, and continued at a Cambridge day school and Harvard, which he entered at the age of fifteen. Like Holmes he studied law, and even opened an office; but he soon gave it up for literature.

After Longfellow resigned his professorship in Harvard, Lowell was called upon to take his place. He was at this time also editor of the *Atlantic Monthly*. When he was nearly fifty, he was appointed American minister to Spain, and three years later he was sent as minister to England. Lowell had an intense interest in politics. We see this in his *Biglow Papers*, which were a series of political tracts. Besides his interest in politics Lowell loved nature. His nature writings are not as spontaneous as Whittier's, but some of them are appealing and beautiful. His best known poem is perhaps "The Vision of Sir Launfal."

ROBERT LOWELL (1917–     ) was born of the famous Lowell family of Boston. Though steeped in the Puritan traditions of his family, Robert was of a rebellious spirit. He entered Harvard, the family school, but soon transferred to Kenyon College to receive his B.A. degree. In 1940 he threw over all the traditions of his family and entered the Catholic Church. Several times after the beginning of the Second World War he tried to enlist in the armed services but was re-jected. When the draft finally caught up with him, he had become convinced that there was no longer any reason for fighting, since war can never change the Old Man into the New. Because of his conviction, he spent five months in a Federal prison.

Robert Lowell is one of the more promising of the modern young poets. His poetry has much of the Old Testament sombreness about it. Christ and the wrathful God of the Old Testament dominate a world bathed in blood. Image after image suggest that "innocence is lost, that man has fallen, that chaos has come, that humanity is sinful." For Lowell, Christianity has come to the end of another cycle and is ready to begin anew with the vigor of the early Christians. Though a modern metaphysical poet, Lowell has retained the familiar forms of poetry. However, his tight, allusion-packed images frequently tend to obscure his meaning, and erudition many times defeats emotion.

Of all his poetry, the Pulitzer Prize winning volume, *Lord Weary's Castle*, is best known. Besides two other volumes, *Land of Unlikeness* and *The Mills of the Kavanaughs*, he has published poems in periodicals.

ARCHIBALD MacLEISH (1892–     ) was born at Glencoe, Illinois. His father was an emigrant merchant from Scotland; his mother came from a Connecticut seafaring family. At Yale, MacLeish distinguished himself both as athlete and scholar. Proficient at swimming and football, he won the coveted Phi Beta Kappa key for scholarship. During the First World War he served in the field artillery, and possessed the rank of Captain at the end of the war.

After the armistice he taught for a year at the Harvard Law School and practiced law in Boston for three years. In 1923 he went abroad with his wife and two children to broaden his education by travel. One of the results of these travels was

"Conquistador," which brought him the Pulitzer Prize for poetry in 1933.

JOHN GILLESPIE MAGEE, JR. (1922–1941). Born in Shanghai of missionary parents, John Gillespie Magee, Jr., was educated in Connecticut and attended the famous Rugby school in England. He won a scholarship to Yale University, but never attended, choosing instead to enlist in the Royal Canadian Air Force. Always idealistic, he believed intensely in the cause of freedom, and was particularly impressed by the heroism and gallantry of his companions in service.

SISTER MARIS STELLA, C.S.J. (1899– ) is a native of Iowa, and her poems about children have Des Moines and Okoboji as backgrounds. At sixteen she entered the preparatory school of the College of St. Catherine in St. Paul. At twenty she entered the novitiate of the Sisters of St. Joseph. She teaches literature and creative writing at St. Catherine's where she is also chairman of the Department of English.

Her poems have appeared in a number of periodicals, including *America*, *Commonweal*, *The Sign*, *Poetry*, and *Spirit*. In 1939, she published a volume of poetry, *Here Only a Dove*; and ten years later, a second volume containing both earlier and later works. Her latest book is entitled *Frost for Saint Brigid and Other Poems*.

EDWIN MARKHAM (1852–1940) was the child of pioneer parents who were among Oregon's early settlers. His mother was the earliest woman writer in Oregon. As a growing boy he knew hardship and hard work—farming, blacksmithing, and working on ranches. Encouraged by a teacher who recognized his poetic possibilities, Markham read widely and became a teacher in the California schools. He was principal of a school in Oakland when, in 1899, he published "The Man with the Hoe," the poem which brought him fame.

SISTER MARY JEREMY, O.P. was born in Chicago. She attended Saint Thomas the Apostle High School, Chicago Teachers' College, and the University of Chicago. At the last named institution she received the John Billings Fiske award for poetry. After taking her master's degree at the University of Chicago, she entered the congregation of the Dominican Sisters at Saint Clara Convent, Sinsinawa, Wisconsin, where for several years she taught in Saint Clara Academy. From 1939 to 1942 she studied for her doctorate in English at Yale University. Then she became a professor of English at Rosary College, River Forest, Illinois. For three years she was also on the summer school faculty of The Catholic University of America.

Poetry by Sister Jeremy has appeared in the *Saturday Review of Literature*, *America*, *Spirit*, and other periodicals. A volume of her poems entitled *Dialogue with an Angel* was published in 1949. She has found time, too, for writing articles on medieval literature for such journals as *Medieval Studies*, *Modern Language Notes*, and *Speculum*.

SISTER MARY MADELEVA, C.S.C. (1887– ), in the words of Katherine Brégy "the Lady Abbess of our singing sisterhoods today," was born in Cumberland, Wisconsin. She received her Bachelor of Arts degree in 1909 from St. Mary's College, Notre Dame, Indiana. For her Doctor of Philosophy degree (1925) she moved westward to the University of California. She was president of St. Mary-of-the-Wasatch College in Salt Lake City, Utah, from 1926 to 1933. In 1934 she returned to St. Mary's College, Notre Dame, to become its president.

SISTER MARY ST. VIRGINIA, B.V.M. (1907– ). Born in Iowa, Sister Mary St. Virginia received her bachelor's degree from Mount Mary College, Milwaukee, where she was elected to membership in the national Catholic honor society,

Kappa Gamma Pi. In 1935 she made her First Profession in the Congregation of the Sisters of Charity of the Blessed Virgin Mary, and since then she has taught successively at The Immaculata, a school for girls in Chicago, and at Clarke College, Dubuque, Iowa; she also served as Secretary-General of her Congregation for four years. She holds a master's degree from Fordham University, where she is presently engaged in further studies in English literature.

Sister Mary St. Virginia's poetry has been published in *America, The Commonweal, Poetry, The Saturday Review, The Sewanee Review, Thought,* and other periodicals.

EDGAR LEE MASTERS (1869–1950) was born in Kansas, but spent his boyhood in Illinois not far from the Spoon River which he later made famous in his poetry. Encouraged by one of his high school English teachers, Masters read widely in all types of literature and later at Knox College, Illinois, developed a taste for foreign languages, particularly Greek. He published a few poems which attracted little or no attention and then began the practice of law in Chicago. He did not lose his interest in writing, however, and at the suggestion of a friend he read the *Greek Anthology,* a collection of brief poetic sketches. Using this idea, he wrote the *Spoon River Anthology,* a collection of sketches which are the confessions after death of some two hundred men and women of a small mid-west town. The publication of this book produced a furor in literary circles and established Masters' reputation.

PHYLLIS McGINLEY (1905–    ). Living in Larchmont with her husband and two daughters, Mrs. Charles Hayden is better known in literary circles by her maiden name of Phyllis McGinley. For it is under that name that her poetry has been appearing for over twenty-five years in various popular and literary magazines.

She began her literary career writing serious poetry, but discovered that her light verse was more popular. When given a contract that paid more for her humorous than her serious poetry, she merged the two. As she said, "I sort of tricked them, I think, into letting me write things that were outwardly amusing but inwardly serious." And that has been her purpose ever since. "What I have been consciously trying to do," she says, "is to narrow the gulf between 'light' and 'serious' verse. One other thing: I always try to share with my readers the immediacy of my own delight or despair of the world as I see it through my window." The growing popularity of her poems is a proof of the achievement of her purpose.

HERMAN MELVILLE (1819–1891) once said that a whaling ship had been his "Harvard and Yale College." There is more truth in that statement than one would at first suspect. Born in New York City and left fatherless at the age of thirteen, he had only a few years of formal schooling. At the age of eighteen he found himself on the seas, and at the age of twenty-five, relying upon his experiences at sea and among cannibals, he began writing his novels. His masterpiece is *Moby Dick,* the story of the pursuit of the white whale by the half mad ship-captain Ahab. It is one of the greatest sea stories of all time.

THOMAS MERTON (1915–    ). The background of the ordinary Trappist monk is usually varied. That of Thomas Merton, a Trappist monk, outdoes them all. He was born in Southern France, was educated in a French Lycée, and has lived in Paris, Bermuda, England, the West Indies, and the United States. His education outside of France was in an English Public School, at Cambridge University, and at Columbia University. After teaching at St. Bonaventure College and Seminary, he became a Trappist monk in the monastery of Our Lady of Gethsemani, Kentucky.

Merton's poetry mirrors his wide experience. It is rich, intelligent, merry, and melancholy. A far better poet and thinker than many of his contemporaries, Merton has also been able to add to his poetry the unifying and leavening effect of his Catholic Faith. His autobiography, *Seven Storey Mountain,* was published in 1948.

SISTER M. THÉRÈSE, SOR.D.S. (1902–     ) is particularly well qualified to write of "God's organ," for even before receiving her bachelor's degree from Marquette University in 1933, and her master's degree in 1937, she had in 1928 received the Diploma in Piano from the Wisconsin Conservatory of Music. She was born in Oconto Falls, Wisconsin, in 1902, and entered the Congregation of the Sisters of the Divine Savior in 1923. She was director of music at the Sisters' Training School of St. Mary's Convent, Milwaukee, from 1928 to 1938, and since 1933 has taught English there. In 1933 she was appointed poet laureate of Marquette University. Besides contributing to numerous reviews, Sister M. Thérèse has published several volumes of poetry, of which V*ox Jubilantium* is best known.

JOAQUIN MILLER (1841–1913) was born, quite appropriately, in a "covered wagon, pointed west" somewhere near the Indiana-Ohio line. When he was twelve years old, the family made a 3,000 mile trek overland to Oregon. It took them seven months and five days to make the journey, which was a constant struggle with cholera, tornadoes, and Indians. At thirteen he cooked in a lumber camp, soon ran off with a horse dealer, and was taken and kept by the Indians. He rode the pony express, prospected successfully for gold, and during the Civil War published a newspaper which was suppressed for alleged treason.

CHARLES L. O'DONNELL, C. S. C. (1884–1934) was born in Greenfield, Indiana; entered the Holy Cross Seminary at Notre Dame in 1899; and was graduated from the University in 1906. In the year 1910, that of his ordination to the priesthood, he received the degree of Doctor of Philosophy at the Catholic University in Washington. After a biennium of teaching in the English department of Notre Dame University he became associate editor of *Ave Maria.* Father O'Donnell was a chaplain with the A. E. F. first in France, and then in Italy. The war over, after filling various executive positions in the Holy Cross Order, he became president of the University of Notre Dame in 1928.

FULTON OURSLER (1893–1952). "For nearly thirty-five years I was an unbeliever," said Oursler. "I disbelieved in the existence of Jesus Christ, whom I considered the figure of a beautiful myth, and in Christianity, which I regarded as based upon mere legends. At the age of forty-five, a kindly skeptic as it were, I had absolutely no religious faith." Then while on a vacation he made a visit to the Holy Land. "When I got back to New York I sat down and quickly wrote a book, *A Skeptic in the Holy Land.* By the time I finished the last chapter, I was really no longer a skeptic." That was the turning point in his life. After that, his life and his works acquired a deep religious significance. Perhaps his greatest achievement is his trilogy on the Bible, for there his genius for storytelling is at its best. His radio dramatization of episodes in the life of Christ, *The Greatest Story Ever Told,* reached a radio audience of twenty million listeners each week.

THOMAS PAINE (1737–1809) was not an American. In fact, he had no country. In 1774 he had fled from England to the colonies. Here he threw himself into the fight for freedom, serving in the army under Washington, and using his pen to compose pamphlets like "Common Sense" and "The Crisis." His fiery words were timely, giving courage when the cause seemed most desperate. After the Revolution was won, the United States gave him an estate in New Rochelle. But the outbreak of the French Revolution lured him to Europe. He wrote *The Rights of Man* in support of the French Revolutionists. England tried and convicted him of treason, outlawing him for life. He found refuge in France, but later alienated himself from his remaining friends by writing the atheistic *Age of Reason*. He returned to America in 1802 and died here in 1809 —a strange, violent man of great ability but with no anchorage.

FRANCIS PARKMAN (1823–1893). Fortunately for students of the early French and English colonial period in America, Francis Parkman did not elect to take the bar examination after being awarded his law degree from Harvard in 1846. Sprung from a prominent Boston family, he showed an early interest in frontier life and made many excursions to the northern woods to study Indian life. In 1846 he went west for the dual purpose of restoring his health and continuing his studies of Indian customs. From St. Louis he set out by steamboat and horseback to Fort Laramie, Wyoming, following the Oregon Trail. The trip left him less robust than when he started, but with material for his best known book, *The Oregon Trail*, published in 1849.

In spite of his ill health, Parkman began a long series of histories of the French and English struggle for colonial America. Among these works are *The Conspiracy of Pontiac* (1851) and *Montcalm and Wolfe* (1884).

WESTBROOK PEGLER (1894–     ), one of America's most bellicose journalists, was born in Minneapolis Minnesota, and educated at Lane Technical School and Loyola Academy, Chicago. During the First World War he was battle correspondent for the United Press, reporting the maneuvers of the A.E.F. during 1917–18. He later did the same work for the Navy. Because action is what he loves, he satisfied a boyhood ambition by becoming a sports writer and editor, a job he held from 1919 to 1925. But gradually the glamorous yet tedious round of ball games, boxing shows, and football struggles began to pall, and he turned his sports-eye to politics and the Washington "playing field." Since then, many an unscrupulous statesman has trembled when Pegler has trained his guns on him.

EDGAR ALLAN POE (1809–1849). The general outlines of Poe's life are pretty well known—that his parents were actors of Southern descent, that he was born in Boston, and that upon the early death of his parents he was adopted by the Allans, a wealthy family in Richmond, Virginia. We know, too, the story of his failure at school and work. The Allans, who had been too lenient with the attractive child, found him too difficult a problem as a young man and finally disowned him.

Business proved as distasteful as school; and he drifted into newspaper work, getting a position as assistant editor of the *Southern Literary Messenger*, a magazine published in Richmond. When he was twenty-six, he married his young cousin, Virginia Clemm, whom he idolized. His writings were beginning to attract attention, and the future seemed bright.

But Poe had no stability. His temperament unfitted him for making a practical success. He worked hard at his writing; but he could not get along with men. Mrs. Clemm took in boarders to help out, but things went from bad to worse. When Virginia was ill, Poe wrote "The Raven." The success that it won was not enough to relieve the distress of the family. In 1847, Virginia died. She was then only twenty-six and had been married twelve years. Poe still loved her devotedly, and her death left him desolate. There were two more years of wretched living; and then when it seemed that his fortunes had a chance to mend, Poe died suddenly. The monument erected in his memory at Baltimore quotes these lines from his poem, "For Annie"——

"And the fever called Living
Is conquered at last."

WILLIAM SYDNEY PORTER (O. HENRY) (1862–1910). The story of William Sydney Porter, who in prison took the pen name, O. Henry, reads like one of his own famous stories, spiced with the ironic twists he doted on in his own work. Born in North Carolina, he left school at fifteen and began work in a drug store and pharmacy. Later he was to practice pharmacy in prison and thus be allowed more privileges than the ordinary inmate. In 1882 O. Henry went to Texas because of illness, his reputation at this time resting on cartoons and caricatures. Successful in his public and private life in Austin, he became teller in a bank, newspaper editor, and husband of one of the Austin belles. He had just embarked on his journalistic career with a Houston paper when he was summoned back to Austin for trial on the charge of embezzling funds. According to all evidence he was innocent, but for some reason, after leaving Houston for Austin, he boarded a fruit ship and sailed for Honduras. Then began a period in the company of two robbers, the Jennings brothers, roaming from Mexico to South America and back. Receiving word that his wife was dying, O. Henry returned to Austin, stood trial and was sentenced to five years in prison. It was there that he began writing short stories. Upon his release he went to New York and agreed to a contract with the New York World for a story a week at a hundred dollars a story.

J. F. POWERS (1917–     ). Catholics can well feel elated with the appearance of Mr. Powers on the literary scene. He is among the very few writers of fiction who can write of highly spiritual themes with an artistry that gives him a place among the best of story tellers. His approach to the supernatural is genuinely Catholic and his style of writing is equal to his subject. Stories by J. F. Powers have appeared in many magazines—among them, *Accent, Commonweal, The Rocky Mountain Review*, and *Opportunity: A Journal of Negro Life*. His *Prince of Darkness* has placed him high in the ranks of short story writers.

Mr. Powers was born in Jacksonville, Illinois. He attended the parochial schools at Rockford and Quincy, and then the Quincy College Academy, which is conducted by the Franciscans. He studied, too, at the evening school of Northwestern University in Chicago.

ERNIE PYLE (1901–1945). "I try not to take foolish chances, but . . ." was the message Ernie Pyle wrote to his wife three weeks before a Jap machine-gunner's bullet put an end to his job and his life. Pyle was a quiet, shy man. Not very tall, slim-figured, wiry, shaggy-browed, with deep-set eyes, Pyle looked hard and tough. Yet he was not a dashing, devil-may-care figure, as newsmen are often described, but a war correspondent who took a serious job seriously. The news copy he wired back to the states was tragic or humorous at times, but always artfully simple. President Truman said of him, "No man in this war has so well told the story of the American fighting man as American fighting men would want it told." *Here Is Your War* and *Brave Men* were read by over a million people. Your own father or brother may have seen Ernie Pyle covering his beat in the battle zones, where (as Pyle once wrote) "war to an individual is hardly ever bigger than a hundred yards on each side of him." During World War II Pyle covered the London Blitz, the North African Invasion; landed at Sicily; was wounded at Anzio (Italy); hit the Normandy beach with the first invaders; and was finally stopped on the Pacific side of the world on a small island, Ie Shima. "At this spot the 77th Infantry lost a buddy—Ernie Pyle—18 April, 1945."

QUENTIN JAMES REYNOLDS (1902–  ). Another popular Catholic writer of today is Quentin Reynolds. Born in Brooklyn, New York, he had many of his articles published before he had even finished Brooklyn Law School. He has attempted and succeeded in practically every field of writing. At various times he has been a reporter, sports writer, columnist, foreign correspondent, novelist, short story writer, historian, and motion picture writer. His book about the war in France, *The Wounded Don't Cry*, was a best seller. His suspense-filled novel, *The Man Who Wouldn't Talk*, is a realistic portrayal of a British spy in German-held territory during the Second World War. Some other books by him are: *The Curtain Rises, London Diary*, and *Courtroom*.

JAMES WHITCOMB RILEY (1849–1916) was the beloved poet of Indiana and is known as "the Hoosier poet." Most of his poems are reminiscent of childhood. Riley had marvelous ability in the writing of simple things which have a universal appeal and could incite the reader to tears or laughter as he willed. His early life gave him unusual opportunity to understand people. His father was a lawyer and a speaker of ability. Riley often accompanied him to the courthouse where he came in contact with country people and came to know their manner of speech, their feelings, and their ways of looking at things. His father wanted him to study law, but Riley found it hard to settle down to an ordered life. For a time he wandered about the country doing any odd job he could find to earn his living. He painted signs, acted as an extra man for a party of traveling players, and finally joined a traveling medicine troup where he played the banjo for the entertainment of the patrons of the show. This mingling with people gave him the understanding

and human interest which, when put into poetry, endeared him to the hearts of his readers.

EDWIN ARLINGTON ROBINSON (1869–1935) was born in Maine. After studying at Harvard he lived in New York City for a number of years, working at various occupations to make a living. During this period he persistently kept at his writing although he was seriously handicapped by lack of funds. Theodore Roosevelt became interested in the poet and wrote in terms of high praise of his poetry in the *Outlook* magazine. This recognition helped to make Robinson better known, and after a few more years he was able to devote his entire time to writing. Robinson did not concern himself with social problems. On the contrary, he portrayed characters with whom he came in contact during his years of poverty—many of them men who were failures. He seems to have been more interested in failures than in successes. He tried to find out the reason for the failure and went upon the assumption that when one knows the underlying reasons for apparent failure, one understands and thinks more kindly of the character portrayed.

ABRAM J. RYAN (1838–1886) was a Virginian. He had been ordained to the priesthood a few years before the Civil War, and he became a chaplain in the Confederate army. He wrote a great many patriotic poems under the pen name "Moina." His post-war lyrics reflect the despair of the South at her tremendous losses; but there is in most of them also a hint of strong faith.

CARL SANDBURG (1878–   ) was born in Illinois. His rise in the field of literature is evidence of the progress America has made in her sympathetic relations with immigrants. Both of Sandburg's parents were born in Sweden and came to this country with practically no education. Sandburg himself was driver of a milk wagon, porter in a barber shop, and truck operator at a brick kiln before he was seventeen. Then he rode "blind baggage" and went west where he washed dishes in hotels and sold stove polish. He had left school at thirteen; but after the Spanish-American War, in which he had volunteered his services, he went to Lombard College with the little money he had saved from his soldier's pay, and after graduation became an editorial writer on the Chicago *Daily News*. His poem "Chicago" which appeared in 1914 marked him as the poet of industrial America, and as a modernist in his use of free verse and in his experimentation with words and rhythms.

FULTON J. SHEEN (1895–    ). A happy marriage between eloquence and scholarship is rare. A successful union of the emotional warmth essential to true eloquence and of the impersonal objectivity indispensable for true scholarship is difficult to achieve. Either the heart runs away with the head, or the head chills the heart. Because Bishop Sheen represents the accomplishment of this difficult combination he is, according to a modern secular periodical, "perhaps the most famous preacher in the United States, certainly America's best known Roman Catholic priest." Another periodical asserts that he is the "most influential voice in Christendom next to that of Pius XII."

Bishop Sheen was born in El Paso, Illinois. After graduating from Saint Viator's College, he continued his studies at Saint Paul Seminary, the Catholic University of America, the University of Louvain, Belgium, and Angelico University, Rome. In 1926 the University of Louvain awarded him the Cardinal Mercier prize for International Philosophy, the first time this honor was ever given to an American. He has twelve college degrees and is the author of over forty full length books.

Since 1926 he has been on the faculty of the Catholic University, and has been broadcasting for over twenty-five years. In addition to his well known television

program, he delivers over a hundred lectures and sermons a year, edits two magazines, writes two syndicated columns a week, and is National Director of the Society for the Propagation of the Faith.

SEYMOUR ST. JOHN (1912–    ). After several years of study in Switzerland, Seymour St. John returned to America and obtained his Bachelor of Arts degree from Yale, his Master of Arts from Columbia, and his Doctorate in the Humanities from Tufts. He was ordained an Episcopalian minister in 1942, and as a chaplain was a Lieutenant Commander in the navy. At present he is headmaster at Choate School in Connecticut.

JOHN BANNISTER TABB (1845–1909) had the unique distinction of turning from blockade-running to the priesthood. A Virginian, he served as a blockade-runner during the War Between the States and was captured and imprisoned in Maryland. In the next cell he discovered the Southern poet, Sidney Lanier. They became close friends and soon Tabb began writing verse in earnest. Upon his release he turned to the Catholic faith, later teaching English in Catholic boys' schools in Richmond and Baltimore.

FRANCIS X. TALBOT, S.J. (1889–1953) was born in Philadelphia in 1889 and received his A.B. from St. Joseph's College in that city in 1909. Literary editor of *America* from 1922 to 1936, he was editor-in-chief of that journal from 1936 to 1944. Father Talbot is widely known for his work in the field of Catholic journalism and for his active promotion of the Catholic Book Club and the Spiritual Book Associates.

EDWARD TAYLOR (1645?–1729). In 1937 the dusty manuscripts of Edward Taylor, an early Colonial poet, were discovered in the Yale University library. We know very little about this devout seventeenth-century writer except for the picture of his character and soul as reflected in these poems. He was born in Coventry, England, about 1645, and when twenty-three years of age, he boarded a ship for the "new land of freedom." After a successful course at Harvard College, he settled down as pastor and physician in the quiet little town of Westfield, Massachusetts. In these peaceful environs for fifty-six years he dedicated himself to the spiritual and physical health of his tiny flock. The majority of his poems were probably composed from time to time over the course of these uneventful years in Westfield. He did not write for publication, and it must have been his grandson, Ezra Stiles (president of Yale, 1778–1795), who was responsible for putting the poet's work in the University library, where it was uncovered in 1937.

SARA TEASDALE (1884–1933). Born into a wealthy Missouri family, Sara Teasdale led a life of comparative ease and quiet—traveling, writing, and reading. From such a milieu came exquisite lyrics, favorites of the young at heart the world over. At college Miss Teasdale began her first verse writing with translations from the French. Proceeding into original verse for magazine publication, she also edited an exclusive magazine. With the publication of *Love Songs* in 1917, her reputation was established.

DOROTHY THOMPSON (1894–    ). The daughter of a Methodist minister, Dorothy Thompson was born in Lancaster, New York. She attended the Lewis Institute in Chicago, and later, in 1914, received her A.B. degree at Syracuse University. For postgraduate work she went to the University of Vienna. She has received honorary degrees from six universities, including Columbia and Dartmouth.

Miss Thompson is best known for her syndicated column "On the Record," which is read daily by an estimated 7,500,-000 people. She began her newspaper career as a correspondent for the Philadelphia *Public Ledger* and the New York *Evening Post*. From 1920 to 1928 she reported from Vienna and Berlin, where she witnessed the turmoil preceding Hitler's Germany. In 1936 she became political commentator for the New York *Herald Tribune*. She also writes a monthly editorial for the *Ladies' Home Journal*.

HENRY DAVID THOREAU (1817–1861). Emerson, who knew him intimately, best summarized Thoreau's character when he said, "He was bred to no profession; he never married; he lived alone; he never went to church; he never voted; he refused to pay a tax to the State; he ate no flesh, he drank no wine, he never knew the use of tobacco; and though a naturalist, he used neither trap nor gun."

But in spite of his oddity, Thoreau was gifted in mind and character. Born at Concord, Massachusetts, he graduated from Harvard in 1837. Although he at first successfully carried on his father's pencil business, he soon abandoned the work saying "his life was too valuable to him to put what remained of it into pencil." He taught school for a while, surveyed land, and also lectured occasionally. He was a member of the famous group of American men of letters who made their home in Concord.

HENRY TIMROD (1828–1867) was born in Charleston, on December 8, 1828. As a boy he was active in outdoor sports and games. At seventeen he entered the University of Georgia, but was not able to complete his course for lack of funds. He returned to his home in Charleston and entered a law office, but the work was distasteful to him and he turned to teaching.

Timrod early showed ability in writing. In college he was fond of the classics, and did some verse writing at that time. In later life, he contributed to *Russell's Maga-*

*zine* and the *Southern Literary Messenger.* Then when the Civil War broke out, since he was not physically strong enough to bear arms, he entered the war as a correspondent for the *Charleston Mercury.* His verse and songs at this time won him a place as a foremost Southern poet.

After the war, his fortune gone, his health broken and tuberculosis fastened upon him, he faced a hopeless battle. Just before his death he wrote the "Ode to the Confederate Dead" which is his finest poem. This is said to be perfect in tone and workmanship.

GEORGE WASHINGTON (1732–1799). It would seem that the tradition which pictures Washington as growing up in aristocratic ease and affluence on a broad Virginia plantation is in need of revision. It is true that he came of an old family and that his father was a wealthy man, but the latter's property went to the children of his first wife— George's half-brothers. The father died when George was eleven and the mother removed to Fredericksburg where she lived apparently in modest, if not somewhat straitened, circumstances.

At Fredericksburg he attended the school of the Reverend James Mayre. Washington's master was one who firmly believed that "manners maketh man." Part of the education which Washington received was in *Rules of Civility and Decent Behaviour*—a hundred and ten of them which he copied carefully in an even, well-written, legible hand. The first of the rules is as follows: "Every Action done in Company, ought to be with Some Sign of Respect to those that are Present."

When Washington was about sixteen, his schooling ended. Then began a period of about five years during which he surveyed the vast holdings of Lord Fairfax and gained, especially in the ways of the frontier, a valuable experience. From this time on the facts of his life are well known.

DANIEL WEBSTER (1782–1852) is without doubt America's greatest orator and one of the world's greatest. He was born in Salisbury, New Hampshire, was educated at Dartmouth College, studied law, and entered the House of Representatives from Massachusetts in 1813. Few lawyers have been so able that their speeches to a jury live after the case has been decided. Yet Webster's speech in the White murder case is still read and declaimed, and passages from the *Dartmouth College Case* speech, made before the Supreme Court, are still quoted. His "First Bunker Hill Oration," "Second Bunker Hill Oration," "Reply to Hayne," "Seventh of March Speech"—all show his unusual ability, and these are read today with interest and appreciation.

WALT WHITMAN (1819–1892). Today the world is still piecing out the facts of Walt Whitman's life, reading his poetry, and trying to see the person of the poet. Was he a sham or a genius? A tramp? A martyr? He sounds loud-mouthed and boastful, but we know that he was compassionate. He did not always support himself. But he was not afraid of work. One winter he took the place of an ailing cab-driver and gave all his earnings to the cabby's family. He glorified democracy, and he lived as a democratic brother to all the world; yet democracies could not survive were all citizens as spasmodic as he in accepting their obligations. So the riddle remains.

It is generally understood that Whitman was a vagabond of sorts. He had no regular job, no family to support. He had only common school education. At sixteen he was teaching country school and writing for newspapers. He dabbled at other professions, but stuck to journalism for fifteen years, editing papers from Brooklyn to New Orleans. He was not at all concerned about making money. And then when he was thirty-five he published a book of unrhymed verse, *Leaves of Grass.* At first the book was utterly condemned.

But it was read. Other writers adopted Whitman's vigorous language and careless style. The fashion of free verse "caught on." Whitman himself seemed unaffected by the praise and blame that swirled about him. In his writing as in his life, he was putting into practice Emerson's principles of self-reliance and individualism. He admitted obligations to no living soul. Even when the war broke, he felt no call to fight. But a brother was in the Union army, and in 1862 was wounded. Walt went to Washington to visit him. What he saw in that army hospital stirred him to volunteer in the hardest, most unselfish service of his life —months and months of duty as a nurse to the sick and wounded men. He was wonderfully tender with them, and they loved him.

When the war ended, he was offered a clerkship in a government office. In the meantime he continued to write. In 1873 a stroke of paralysis ended his physical activity. For the last nineteen years of his life he was an invalid. He was taken to Camden, New Jersey, where for three years he was neglected and miserable. Then news of his misfortune and his need spread abroad. Generous contributions were made for his relief, especially by friends in England, where his poetry was much admired. During his last years the cottage at Camden became a shrine which brought friends and admirers from every walk of life to Whitman's bedside.

JOHN GREENLEAF WHITTIER (1807–1892) was born near Haverhill, Massachusetts, on a farm which his great-great-grandfather had cleared in the wilderness in 1647, and in the house which his ancestor had built some forty years later. He had chance for only a little education, and not much encouragement for writing. His parents were Quakers with no literary interests, and the farm was poor. After some country schooling, he had two terms at Haverhill Academy. For those two terms he paid his own way,

making and selling slippers. Early and late he was busy on the farm.

He was still a young man when he became interested in the Abolitionist movement. Most people considered the antislavery leaders as troublemakers; and Whittier realized that he was helping an unpopular cause. He had shown some liking for politics, and might have been elected to Congress in 1832 if he had been able to stifle his conscience. But for him there was no choice. For the next thirty years he sacrificed everything else to the Abolitionist cause. That the issue had to be settled by war was a great sorrow to him. But he lived to see the slaves freed, the Union saved, and the war ended.

Then he settled back to peaceful living at Amesbury, Massachusetts. Whittier had never married, but a favorite niece, Elizabeth, kept house for him. In the years between 1865 and his death in 1892, he wrote his best poems—most of them New England idylls and lyrics reminiscent of his youth.

WILLIAM CARLOS WILLIAMS (1883–    ), a physician, was born in Rutherford, New Jersey. His education was, more or less, a travelogue. From New Jersey and New York to Switzerland and Leipzig, Germany, Williams found courses to further his education in medicine. In these educational travels Williams formed lifelong friendships with many literary artists—a cause, no doubt, of his deep interest in poetry.

After his studies were completed, Dr. Williams published his first poems in 1909. Since that time he has produced many important works.

Williams is an imagist whose subject matter is the observations of a practicing physician; a modernist whose thought is not too readily seen in just one reading of his works. Like most literary men of his era, Williams is seeking to find better social conditions for the people he knows so well as a doctor.

JOHN WINTHROP (1588–1649). Much like William Bradford in character and history was the first governor of the Massachusetts Bay colony, John Winthrop. Winthrop, too, was a man of culture and importance in old England. Dissatisfied with conditions there, he led a large band of Puritans to the New World in 1630. He kept a record of the events of the journey, of the founding of the colony, and of the life that developed in what was to become the city of Boston. Winthrop had the same high morality that characterized Bradford; but he had a more credulous nature. He believed every wonder that was reported to him; and all sorts of curious odds and ends found their way into his journal. He was especially interested in instances of God's Providence; in fact, in the simplest incidents of daily life he found evidences of Divine care. His journal, which is commonly called *The History of New England*, is an 800-page collection of miscellaneous information, much of it hastily written as personal memoranda.

ELINOR WYLIE (1885–1928). In private life Elinor Wylie was the wife of the poet William Rose Benét, but she used for writing the name of her former husband, Horace Wylie. She was born in New Jersey but spent most of her girlhood in Washington. She began writing poetry at an early age and was known in school as "the infant Keats." After finishing her education at Holton Arms School in Washington and traveling in Europe, she began her literary career in New York City. Her father, Henry Hoyt, was Solicitor-General in Theodore Roosevelt's administration. Her brother Henry was a painter of some note, and her sister Nancy a novelist.

# For Appreciation
## of Poetry

## THE ORNAMENTS OF POETRY

Since most of the classifications of poetry are made on the basis of form, it is well for the student to be familiar with the various ornaments of poetry and the vocabulary of versification.

Poems are read from the printed page, either silently or aloud. Thus they appeal both to the eye and to the ear. To please the eye, poetry is spaced differently from prose. Poems are set off in lines or stanzas rather than paragraphs. The lines emphasize the devices of rhyme and rhythm. Their lengths are determined by the number of accented and unaccented syllables. Each line of a poem usually begins with a capital letter. A single line is called a *verse*. A group of verses forming a poetic unit is a *stanza*. Stanzas are set off as units of form, regardless of whether or not the thought is complete. Lines within a stanza are often indented to indicate correspondence in length or in rhyme. These mechanics of arrangement make it easier to read poetry with full appreciation of its melody.

### Rhythm

To please the ear, poetry uses musical words arranged in special sound patterns. The most important of the sound devices is *rhythm*, or the arrangement of words so that the accented syllables come at regular intervals. The spacing of accented and unaccented syllables gives poetry its movement and much of its melody. Notice the effects produced by the sound of the following lines:

> To *him* who *in* the *love* of *nature holds*
> Communion *with* her *visible forms* she *speaks*
> A *various language.*
> > —Bryant's "Thanatopsis"

> But *now* his *nose* is *thin,*
> And it *rests* upon his *chin*
> > Like a *staff,*
> And a *crook* is *in* his *back,*
> And a *melancholy crack*
> > In his *laugh.*
> > > —Holmes's "The Last Leaf"

689

Some of these lines sound solemn; some sound jolly. Other rhythmic patterns may be discovered which sound strong or lively or dancing. Poets do not always use the same rhythm all the way through a poem; but usually a fairly regular pattern emerges after the accented syllables have been marked. Special names have been given to the different rhythmic patterns. For instance, an arrangement like that in "Thanatopsis" in which every second syllable is accented is called *iambic*. It is the rhythm used most often in English verse. A group of syllables containing one accent is called a *foot*. A line of one foot, like lines 3 and 6 from "The Last Leaf," is called *monometer*. A line of two feet is *dimeter*; three feet, *trimeter*; four feet, *tetrameter*; five feet, *pentameter*. The best known line in English poetry is *iambic pentameter*, the line used by Bryant in "Thanatopsis" and the line used in all sonnets. It is possible, however, to appreciate the various rhythmic patterns without knowing all their names.

### Rhyme

The second most important device is rhyme, or the similarity in sound of the last accented syllables in two or more lines of verse. Rhyming schemes are indicated by letters of the alphabet, using the same letter for each of a set of rhyming lines. The rhyming scheme for "The Last Leaf" is *a a b c c b*, because the first and second lines rhyme; the third and sixth lines rhyme; and the fourth and fifth lines rhyme. You will notice that there is no rhyme in the selection from "Thanatopsis." Unrhymed verse usually sounds more dignified than rhymed verse. The greater the number of rhymes within a set of verses, the merrier it sounds. Some very musical poems are without rhyme, but in these poems, the authors have used other kinds of sound repetition. Longfellow's "Song of Hiawatha" is a good example of such verse. Sometimes a poet, for added melody, has a word within a line rhyme with a word at the end of the line. Poe was fond of this device and used it in such poems as "The Raven."

### Alliteration

A third device, much used in English poetry, is *alliteration*, or the use of two or more words beginning with the same consonant in one line or in adjoining lines. Lanier's "Revenge of Hamish" illustrates the skillful use of alliteration:

> In the print of her velvet flank on the velvet fern
> She reared, and rounded her ears in turn.

Poe took particular delight in the use of alliteration. Note these lines from "The Bells"—

> Brazen bells!
> What a tale of terror now their turbulency tells!

*Assonance*

A fourth device, not so noticeable in English verse, is *assonance,* or the repetition of the same vowel sound within a line or adjoining lines of poetry. The following lines from Lowell illustrate the repetition of the long *o.*

> Down swept the chill wind from the mountain peak,
> From the snow five thousand summers old;
> On open wold and hilltop bleak
> It had gathered all the cold.

*Onomatopoeia*

A fifth device, and the last to be considered, is *onomatopoeia,* or the use of words which sound like the idea they denote. Practically all our names for sounds and many of our words for movement are examples of onomatopoeia: *hum, buzz, thud, crash, wiggle, zigzag,* and the like. Most poets make considerable use of the figure.

It is by means of these five sound effects in various combinations that writers construct poetic forms pleasing to the ear.

## THE TYPES OF POETRY

*Narrative poetry*

Like prose, poetry is usually divided into two main classifications depending on whether or not it tells a story. Story-telling verse is called *narrative* poetry. It again is divided into classifications dependent largely on length.

An extremely long narrative poem in dignified style on a traditional or legendary subject is an *epic.* There is no true American epic. However, Bryant translated the two Greek epics, *The Iliad* and *The Odyssey,* into excellent English verse.

A moderately long narrative poem written in simple or romantic style on a theme from home or country life is an *idyl.* American poets, particularly Longfellow and Whittier, have been fond of the idyl. "Evangeline," "Maud Muller," and "Snow-bound" are good examples of this type of narrative poem.

The *ballad* is a short narrative poem originally composed to be sung. The *folk ballad* is a story-telling song which has grown up among people—people often illiterate or poorly educated. Such a ballad uses commonplace words or dialect. Its authorship is usually unknown. The best American folk ballads are the cowboy songs. The *literary ballad* is a story-telling poem—usually an artistic imitation of the folk ballad. All types of ballads use a simple verse form with a recurring refrain. When sung, a soloist gives the story lines while every one joins in on refrains.

There are other poems which tell stories that are difficult to classify. Longfellow's "Song of Hiawatha" is legendary in subject, but not sober and dignified enough in form for an epic. It is like a group of narratives written in a rather lyric style. Stephen Vincent Benét's long poem, *John Brown's Body,* is like a novel in verse. And there are other poems which we simply describe as *narrative* for lack of any more specific name.

### Lyric poetry

Most poetry which tells no story is classified as *lyric*. The word lyric is derived from *lyre*, and originally it denoted a short poem to be sung to the accompaniment of the lyre. It was an expression of feeling—of joy, or praise, or grief, or love. Today its meaning has been expanded to include any poem of distinctly musical form, revealing the feelings or fancy of the writer. There are many specialized types of lyrics, such as the *elegy*, the *ode*, and the *sonnet*.

An *elegy* is a lyric written in praise of some one who has died. It may be in honor of an individual, like the many poems written for Lincoln after his assassination; or it may be in honor of a group of people like Joyce Kilmer's "Rouge Bouquet," written for a company of Irish soldiers buried in their dugout by an exploding shell in the first World War. A short poem designed to be inscribed on a tombstone is called an *epitaph*. Edgar Lee Masters' *Spoon River Anthology* is a collection of imaginary epitaphs.

An *ode* is a lyric on a serious subject, characterized by nobility of sentiment and dignity of style. It is usually a rather long poem, and sometimes as in the case of Lowell's "Commemoration Ode," it has the same sort of subject as an elegy. It is merely longer and more elaborate.

A *sonnet* is a lyric of fourteen iambic pentameter lines. There are two kinds of sonnets, the Italian, and the Shakespearean, sometimes also called the Elizabethan. In the Italian sonnet the first eight lines rhyme a b b a a b b a; the last six lines may rhyme in several ways using three rhymes, such as c d e c d e. The first eight lines present a problem or state a case or introduce a subject; the last six lines solve the problem or draw a conclusion. In the Shakespearean sonnet, there are three sets of four lines and a closing couplet, with the rhyming scheme a b a b, c d c d, e f e f, g g. In the Elizabethan sonnet the closing couplet should contain the most striking thought of the poem; and in any sonnet the last line should represent a climax of beauty and significance. Sonnets are invariably on a serious, thoughtful subject and present an experience or impression of unusual beauty. Because the form is so exacting, the subject of the sonnet should be worth while.

One other type of lyric should be mentioned—the *song*. It is the true lyric. Our American songs range from the patriotic anthem, the soldier's ditty, the home song, the hymn, through the folk song of the Indian, cowboy, and Negro. The words of the true song are usually simple and singable, with a direct appeal to the heart.

There are other lyric forms, many of them; but those which we have defined are the ones most often used and the types usually referred to by name. You will need to remember their names and characteristics if you wish to be able to discuss lyric verse.

## FIGURES OF SPEECH

Figurative language, which uses words, not literally but imaginatively, is part of all our speech. Everyday talk is full of such non-literal expressions as "My teeth were clicking like castanets" or "The pitcher burned a hot one across the plate." Slang, except for ejaculations is made up almost entirely of figures of speech like, "Don't be an apple-polisher" and "He thumbed a ride home."

But figures of speech are most effective when they add vividness or beauty to poetry and to literary prose. In fact, figurative language is so much a part of poetry that an acquaintance with the most common figures of speech is necessary for a complete appreciation of the art.

### Simile

A *simile* is an expressed comparison between two things of unlike nature. The simile is usually indicated by the comparative adverbs *like, as,* or *than.*

> Helen, thy beauty is to me
> Like those Nicean barks of yore.
> > —Poe's "To Helen"

> As a twig trembles, which a bird
> Lights on to sing, then leaves unbent,
> So is my memory thrilled and stirred;
> I only know she came and went.
> > —Lowell's "She Came and Went"

### Metaphor

A *metaphor* is an *implied* comparison between two things of unlike nature. *Like, as,* or *than* are omitted.

> My father, he was a mountaineer,
> His fist was a knotty hammer.
> > —Bénet's "Ballad of William Sycamore"

> You are the little room in Nazareth
> Wherein He dreamed.
> > —Sister Mary St. Virginia's "To Catherine"

### Personification

*Personification* gives to the lower animals, to inanimate objects, or to abstract ideas the characteristics of persons. It is a specialized metaphor.

> Bid Time and Nature gently spare
> The shaft we raise to them and thee.
> > —Emerson's "The Concord Hymn"

> My apple trees will never get across
> And eat the cones under his pine trees.
> > —Frost's "Mending Wall"

*Apostrophe*

*Apostrophe* is an address to the dead as if living, to the absent as if present, **and** to animals, objects, or ideas as if they were persons.

> Rhodora! if the sages ask thee why
> This charm is wasted on the earth and sky,
> Tell them, dear, that if eyes were made for seeing,
> Then beauty is its own excuse for being.
> —Emerson's "The Rhodora"

*Hyperbole*

*Hyperbole* is obvious exaggeration.

Wouter Van Twiller was exactly five feet six inches high and *six feet five inches in circumference.*
—Irving's "Wouter Van Twiller"

> Here once the embattled farmers stood
> And fired the shot heard round the world.
> —Emerson's "The Concord Hymn"

*Irony*

*Irony* is an expression in which the writer says the opposite of what he means.

> I *care not much for gold or land;*—
> Give me a mortgage here and there,—
> Some good bank stock,—some note of hand;—
> Or trifling railroad share;—
> I only ask that Fortune send
> A *little* more than I can spend.
> —Holmes's "Contentment"

*Analogy*

An *analogy* is something like a metaphor. One situation is described; then a second situation is stated, the inference being that the second is true because it is like the first, which is known to be true. Analogy is often used in debates and arguments. John Bannister Tabb's poem "Fame" combines metaphor and analogy. Emily Dickinson's "Assurance" is another example of the figure.

# GLOSSARY

◇◇◇◇◇◇◇◇◇◇◇◇◇◇◇◇◇◇◇◇◇◇◇◇◇◇◇◇◇◇◇◇◇◇◇◇◇◇◇◇◇◇◇◇◇◇

## A

**abscond** (ăb·skŏnd'). To run away secretly.

**abysmal** (a·bĭz'măl). Of or like an abyss; unending; profound.

**accede** (ăk·sēd'). To agree; to assent.

**acquiesce** (ăk'wĭ·ĕs'). To accept or agree passively.

**acquisition** (ăk'wĭ·zĭsh'ŭn). A thing acquired or gained.

**acrid** (ăk'rĭd). Sharp; irritating.

**adherent** (ăd·hēr'ĕnt). A follower; a supporter.

**adjunct** (ăj'ŭngkt). Associate.

**admonition** (ăd'mô·nĭsh'ŭn). A gentle reproof; a mild warning.

**aeon** (ē'ŏn). An immeasurably long period of time.

**agate** (ăg'ĭt; ăg'át). A striped variety of translucent quartz.

**alienate** (āl'yĕn·āt; ā'lĭ·ĕn·āt). To make unfriendly; to divert affection or confidence.

**altercation** (ôl'tēr·kā'shŭn). A verbal dispute; an argument.

**amicably** (ăm'ĭ·ka·b'lĭ). In a friendly or cordial manner.

**amity** (ăm'ĭ·tĭ). Harmony; peace.

**amoral** (â·mŏr'ăl). Without a sense of moral responsibility.

**anecdote** (ăn'ĕk·dōt). A short account of some interesting incident or event.

**animated** (ăn'ĭ·māt'ĕd). Made vigorous and active.

**animosity** (ăn'ĭ·mŏs'ĭ·tĭ). Ill will.

**annihilated** (a·nī'ĭ·lāt'ĕd). Reduced to nothing.

**antagonism** (ăn·tăg'ô·nĭz'm). Active opposition or resistance.

**apathetic** (ăp'a·thĕt'ĭk). Unemotional; indifferent.

**aperture** (ăp'ēr·tụr). An opening; a hole.

**apparition** (ăp'a·rĭsh'ŭn). An appearance of something strange or unexpected.

**appeased** (a·pēzd'). Satisfied; calmed.

**appelation** (ăp'ē·lā'shŭn). A name or designation.

**appellative** (a·pĕl'a·tĭv). A descriptive name.

**appertaining** (ăp'ēr·tān'ĭng). Belonging.

**approbation** (ăp'rô·bā'shŭn). Approval; sanction.

**appropriating** (a·prō'prĭ·āt·ĭng). Setting apart; allotting.

**appurtenance** (a·pûr'tê·năns). Something incident to a chief or principal thing.

**arabesque** (ăr'a·bĕsk'). An elaborate or fanciful design of flowers, leaves, geometrical figures, *etc.*

**ardor** (är'dēr). Warmth; spirit; zeal.

**arduous** (är'dụ·ŭs). Difficult and laborious.

**arrogant** (ăr'ô·gănt). Contemptuous and proud.

**artifice** (är'tĭ·fĭs). Trickery.

**ascend** (a·sĕnd'). To climb.

**assail** (a·sāl'). To attack with violence.

**assuage** (a·swāj'). To soften; to ease.

**audacity** (ô·dăs'ĭ·tĭ). Boldness; impudence.

**augmented** (ôg·mĕn'tĕd). Increased.

**aureole** (ô'rê·ōl). A halo, actual or figurative.

**auroral** (ô·rō'răl). Pertaining to the dawn or the aurora borealis; rosy; radiant.

**auspices** (ôs'pĭ·sĕz). Guidance; direction; care.

**auspicious** (ôs·pĭsh'ŭs). Favorable; fortunate.

**averse** (a·vûrs'). Unwilling; opposed.

**aversion** (a·vûr'zhŭn). A settled dislike.

**awaft** (a·wàft'). Adrift; afloat.

**awry** (a·rī'). Crooked.

## B

**badgering** (băj'ēr·ĭng). Teasing; annoying.

**bairn** (bârn). A child.

**bating** (bāt'ĭng). Lessening; reducing.

**bauble** (bô'b'l). A gay and showy trinket.

**bequeath** (bê·kwēth'). To give when one dies.

**bigoted** (bĭg'ŭt·ĕd). Prejudiced and unreasonably narrow-minded.

**blanched** (blàncht). Bleached; whitened.

**bland** (blănd). Smooth.

**blatant** (blā'tănt). Demanding attention in a vulgar or tasteless manner.

**brim** (brĭm). The edge.

**broker** (brō'kēr). A person who buys and sells stocks, bonds, etc., for other people; an agent.

**buffet** (bŭf'ĕt). A blow.

**bulwark** (bool'wērk). 1. A solid wall-like defensive structure. 2. A breakwater for protection against the force of the waves.

**buxom** (bŭk'sŭm). Plump and rosy.

## C

**cabalistic** (kăb'a·lĭs'tĭk). Mysterious; secret.

**cadaver** (ka·dăv'ēr). A corpse.

**cadence** (kā'dĕns). A regular rise and fall; rhythm.

**capacious** (ka·pā'shŭs). Able to contain much; large.

**capering** (kā'pēr·ĭng). Leaping and jumping about in a gay manner.

**chalice** (chăl'ĭs). 1. A drinking cup; a goblet. 2. A flower cup.

**chanticleer** (chăn'tĭ·klēr). A rooster.

**chaste** (chāst). Pure and simple in design.

**chivalric** (shĭv'ăl·rĭk). Courteous and gallant, as a knight.

**churlish** (chûr'lĭsh). Rude, rough and unmannerly.

**cinched** (sĭncht). Tightly secured.

**circumscribing** (sûr'kŭm·skrīb'ĭng). Encircling.

āte, châotic, dàre, ădd, ăccuse, bär, càsk, áfar; ēat, dĕar, êlude, ĕgg, quiĕt, centēr; īdle, ĭf, activĭty; ōpen, ôbey, ôr, ŏrange, ŏffer, ŏccur, cōol, cŏok; our, boil; cūte, ûnite, bûrn, cŭt, ŭnless, menü; check; goat, sing, this, thick, scriptụre, verdụre.

**circumvented** (sûr′kŭm·věnt′ĕd). Gained advantage over; cheated.

**clangor** (klăng′gĕr). A sharp, harsh, ringing sound.

**claret** (klăr′ĕt). A red table wine.

**clime** (klīm). Climate (poetic).

**complaisant** (kŏm·plā′zănt). Courteous and obliging.

**complicity** (kŏm·plĭs′ĭ·tĭ). Partnership in wrongdoing.

**comport** (kŏm·pōrt′). 1. To behave. 2. To agree.

**composite** (kŏm·pŏz′ĭt). Made up of many parts.

**conciliated** (kŏn·sĭl′ĭ·āt′ĕd). Won over; soothed; brought into harmony.

**concurrency** (kŏn·kûr′ĕn·sĭ). 1. A coming together. 2. Agreement in action. 3. A meeting of minds.

**condone** (kŏn·dōn′). Pardon or forgive.

**conical** (kŏn′ĭ·kăl). Cone-shaped.

**conjecture** (kŏn·jĕk′tûr). A guess.

**consternation** (kŏn′stĕr·nā′shŭn). Dismay.

**contemplate** (kŏn′tĕm·plāt). Meditate; consider.

**contending** (kŏn·těnd′ĭng). Struggling.

**contingency** (kŏn·tĭn′jĕn·sĭ). A possible event.

**contortion** (kŏn·tôr′shŭn). A twisted condition.

**controversy** (kŏn′trō·vûr′sĭ). Argument.

**convulsion** (kŏn·vŭl′shŭn). A violent contraction of the muscles; a fit.

**coquetry** (kō′kĕ·trĭ). Flirting.

**cordial** (kôr′jăl). A liqueur.

**cordiality** (kôr·jăl′ĭ·tĭ). Warmth of regard; friendliness.

**corpulent** (kôr′pū·lĕnt). Bulky; very stout.

**corroborated** (kŏ·rŏb′ô·rāt′ĕd). Confirmed.

**countenance** (koun′tĕ·năns). Face.

**cower** (kou′ĕr). To crouch or shrink in fear or shame.

**crannies** (krăn′ĭz). Cracks or chinks, as in a wall.

**crevasse** (krĕ·văs′). A break in a dam or dyke or levee, hence, a flood.

**crevice** (krĕv′ĭs). A narrow opening resulting from a split or crack.

**cringe** (krĭnj). To shrink; to crouch in fear.

**crypt** (krĭpt). A vault, usually wholly or partly underground.

**crystalline** (krĭs′tăl·ĭn). 1. Made of crystal. 2. Resembling crystal.

**D**

**damask** (dăm′ȧsk). A linen, wool, or silk fabric.

**debasement** (dĕ·bās′mĕnt). A state of low esteem.

**debauch** (dĕ·bôch′). A period of sensual indulgence.

**debonair** (dĕb′ô·nâr′). Graceful and gay.

**decorous** (dĕk′ô·rŭs). Well behaved; suitable and dignified.

**decorum** (dĕ·kō′rŭm). Decency; seemliness.

**decrepitude** (dĕ·krĕp′ĭ·tūd). Weakness or feebleness of old age.

**defile** (dĕ·fīl′). To march off in a line, file by file.

**deific** (dĕ·ĭf′ĭk). God-like.

**deluded** (dĕ·lūd′ĕd). Misled.

**demeaned** (dĕ·mēnd′). Lowered in dignity or standing.

**denizen** (dĕn′ĭ·zĕn). Inhabitant.

**depravity** (dĕ·prăv′ĭ·tĭ). Corruption.

**depreciate** (dĕ·prē′shĭ·āt). To undervalue; to belittle.

**deputation** (dĕp′ū·tā′shŭn). A delegation.

**despotism** (dĕs′pŏt·ĭz′m). Tyranny.

**devoid** (dĕ·void′). Empty.

**dexterous** (dĕk′stĕr·ŭs). Skillful; expert.

**diffuse** (dĭ·fūz′). To spread out.

**digression** (dĭ·grĕsh′ŭn). Departure from a subject.

**disbursement** (dĭs·bûrs′mĕnt). Funds paid out.

**discordant** (dĭs·kôr′dănt). Harsh and jarring.

**discreet** (dĭs·krēt′). Showing good judgment in conduct and especially in speech.

**disdain** (dĭs·dān′). To reject or scorn.

**dishevelled** (dĭ·shĕv′ĕld). Rumpled; untidy.

**dispassionately** (dĭs·păsh′ŭn·ĭt·lĭ). Calmly; not carried away by emotions.

**disputed** (dĭs·pūt′ĕd). Opposed by argument.

**disrelish** (dĭs·rĕl′ĭsh). Distaste.

**dissension** (dĭ·sĕn′shŭn). Disagreement.

**dissever** (dĭ·sĕv′ĕr). To cut in parts; to separate.

**dissipation** (dĭs′ĭ·pā′shŭn). Idle, wasteful, or harmful diversion.

**distended** (dĭs·tĕnd′ĕd). Stretched; expanded.

**docile** (dŏs′ĭl). Gentle and easily managed.

**doggedly** (dŏg′ĕd·lĭ). Stubbornly; determinedly.

**dotage** (dōt′ĭj). Feeble-mindedness, especially in old age.

**dower** (dou′ĕr). A gift.

**draught** (drȧft). A drink.

**drudgery** (drŭj′ĕr·ĭ). Wearisome toil.

**dun** (dŭn). Dingy or dull greyish-brown.

**dunderpate** (dŭn′dĕr·pāt). A dunce; a blockhead.

**dupe** (dūp). One who has been, or is, easily deceived.

**dyspepsia** (dĭs·pĕp′shȧ). Indigestion.

**E**

**ebbed** (ĕbd). Grown less or weaker; declined.

**ecstatic** (ĕk·stăt′ĭk). Great joy and rapture.

**edifice** (ĕd′ĭ·fĭs). A large or massive building.

**effaced** (ĕ·fāst′). Erased; rubbed out.

**effervesce** (ĕf′ĕr·vĕs′). To bubble, hiss and foam, as carbonated water.

**efficacy** (ĕf′ĭ·kȧ·sĭ). The power to produce effects; as the *efficacy* of prayer.

**effrontery** (ĕ·frŭn′tĕr·ĭ). Impudence; boldness.

**egregious** (ĕ·grē′jŭs). Conspicuous for bad quality.

**emaciated** (ĕ·mā′shĭ·āt′ĕd). Very thin.

**embodiment** (ĕm·bŏd′ĭ·mĕnt). A person or thing symbolizing some idea or quality.

**empyrean** (ĕm′pĭ·rē′ăn). Celestial; sublime.

**enamoured** (ĕn·ăm′ĕrd). Fondly in love; charmed; captivated.

**endowment** (ĕn·dou′mĕnt). Gifts of nature.

āte, châotic, dâre, ădd, ȧccuse, bär, càsk, ȧfar; ēat, dĕar, ĕlude, ĕgg, quiĕt, centēr; īdle, ĭf; actĭvĭty; ōpen, ȯbey, ȯr, ŏrange, ŏffer, ŏccur.

**engross** (ĕn·grōs′). Occupy wholly.

**enmity** (ĕn′mĭ·tĭ). Ill will on one side or both; hate.

**epigram** (ĕp′ĭ·grăm). A short, pointed saying.

**episode** (ĕp′ĭ·sōd). A single happening or a group of happenings in real life or story.

**equity** (ĕk′wĭ·tĭ). Fairness; justice.

**escalade** (ĕs′ka·lād′). An attack on a fortified place in which ladders are used.

**ethereal** (ê·thĕr′ê·ăl). Spiritlike; airy.

**exacted** (ĕg·zăkt′ĕd). Required.

**exaltation** (ĕg′zŏl·tā′shŭn). High emotion; rapture.

**exhalation** (ĕks′ha·lā′shŭn). Something exhaled; air, vapor, smoke, odor, *etc.*

**exhilaration** (ĕg·zĭl′a·rā′shŭn). Gaiety and merriment.

**expedient** (ĕks·pē′dĭ·ĕnt). A means to an end.

**expiration** (ĕk′spĭ·rā′shŭn). A coming to a close; end.

**expletive** (ĕks′plê·tĭv). An oath or exclamation.

**explicit** (ĕks·plĭs′ĭt). Distinctly stated; plain in language; clear.

**exuberant** (ĕg·zū′bĕr·ănt). Overflowing.

## F

**fabricated** (făb′rĭ·kāt′ĕd). Constructed.

**facilitate** (fa·sĭl′ĭ·tāt). To make easy or less difficult.

**fagot** (făg′ŭt). A bundle of sticks or twigs used for fuel; specif. a fagot formerly used to burn a heretic alive.

**fastidiously** (făs·tĭd′ĭ·ŭs·lĭ). Delicately; overnicely.

**felicity** (fê·lĭs′ĭ·tĭ). State of being happy; bliss; well-being.

**fervor** (fûr′vēr). Intensity of feeling; ardor.

**festoon** (fĕs·tōōn′). Flowers, leaves, ribbons, *etc.*, hanging in a curve.

**fetid** (fĕt′ĭd). Having an offensive odor.

**fettered** (fĕt′ērd). Enchained; shackled.

**firmament** (fûr′ma·mĕnt). The heavens.

**flagrant** (flā′grănt). Glaring; notorious.

**foible** (foi′b′l). A weak point; a fault.

**formidable** (fôr′mĭ·da·b′l). Hard to overcome or deal with; that which is to be dreaded.

**forspent** (fŏr·spĕnt′). Exhausted.

**fortissimo** (fôr·tĭs′ĭ·mō). Very loud.

**fortitude** (fôr′tĭ·tūd). Resolute endurance; courage.

**fratricidal** (frăt′rĭ·sīd′ăl). Pertaining to the killing of one's brothers.

**frenzy** (frĕn′zĭ). Very great excitement, almost madness.

**fretted** (frĕt′ĕd). Worn away; chafed.

**furl** (fûrl). To wrap or roll tightly.

## G

**galling** (gôl′ĭng). Irritating.

**gambol** (găm′bŭl). A skipping or leaping about in frolic.

**garnished** (gär′nĭsht). Decorated.

**gauntleted** (gônt′lĕt·ĕd). Wearing a glovelike leather and metal protection for the hand.

**gemmary** (jĕm′a·rĭ). Of or pertaining to gems.

**gesticulation** (jĕs·tĭk′ú·lā′shŭn). A lively or excited movement or gesture.

**gibe** (jīb). A sarcastic, scornful joke.

**girt** (gûrt). Clothed.

**gloss** (glŏs). Brightness or luster.

**gluttonous** (glŭt′n·ŭs). Greedy.

**gout** (gout). A disease in which the joints become swollen and inflamed.

**granitic** (gra·nĭt′ĭk). 1. Of or pertaining to granite. 2. Hard and unyielding as granite.

**gratulation** (grăt′ú·lā′shŭn). Joyful congratulation.

**gravity** (grăv′ĭ·tĭ). Solemnity.

**grizzled** (grĭz′′ld). Sprinkled or streaked with grey.

**gumption** (gŭmp′shŭn). 1. Common-sense. 2. Courage; initiative; enterprise.

**guttural** (gŭt′ēr·ăl). Sounded in the throat; harsh; rasping.

**gyrated** (jī′rāt·ĕd). Revolved.

**gyves** (jīvs). Shackles.

## H

**haggard** (hăg′ērd). Wild-looking from pain, worry, fatigue, hunger, *etc.*; careworn.

**harassed** (hăr′ăst). Troubled by repeated attacks; disturbed.

**harrowed** (hăr′ōd). Tormented; lacerated.

**haunched** (hôncht). Squatted on one's haunches.

**headland** (hĕd′lănd′). Cape; promontory.

**henchman** (hĕnch′măn). An active follower and supporter.

**heraldry** (hĕr′ăld·rĭ). The science or art dealing with coats of arms.

**heterogeneous** (hĕt′ēr·ô·jê′nê·ŭs). Not alike; varied.

**hewn** (hūn). Chopped down.

**hoary** (hōr′ĭ). White or grey with age.

**Homeric** (hô·mĕr′ĭk). Characteristic or suggestive of the Greek epic poet, Homer, his style, his age, *etc.* Used to suggest epic qualities: great size, superb courage, *etc.*

**husbanded** (hŭz′bănd·ĕd). Cared for with frugality; saved carefully.

**hypothesis** (hī·pŏth′ê·sĭs). A theory; a supposition.

## I

**illimitable** (ĭl·lĭm′ĭt·a·b′l). Incapable of being limited; immeasurable.

**illusion** (ĭ·lū′zhŭn). An unreal or misleading image; a deceptive appearance.

**imbued** (ĭm·būd′). Tinged deeply; saturated.

**immemorial** (ĭm′mê·mō′rĭ·ăl). Extending back beyond the bounds of memory; indefinitely ancient.

**impending** (ĭm·pĕnd′ĭng). Threatening.

**imperious** (ĭm·pēr′ĭ·ŭs). 1. Over-bearing. 2. Urgent and compelling.

**impetuous** (ĭm·pĕt′ú·ŭs). Impulsive; rashly energetic.

**implacable** (ĭm·plā′ka·b′l). Unyielding.

**imposture** (ĭm·pŏs′tŭr). A fraud or deception.

**impotent** (ĭm′pô·tĕnt). Powerless.

cōōl, cŏŏk; our, boil; cūte, ûnite, bûrn, cŭt, ŭnless, menü; check; goat, sing, ~~this~~, thick, scriptŭre, verdŭre.

**imprecation** (ĭm′prê·kā′shŭn). A curse.
**impunity** (ĭm·pū′nĭ·tĭ). Freedom from punishment.
**imputed** (ĭm·pūt′ĕd). Considered as belonging; charged; blamed.
**inarticulate** (ĭn′är·tĭk′û·lât). Not distinct; not like regular speech.
**incantation** (ĭn′kăn·tā′shŭn). A set of words spoken as a magic charm.
**incessant** (ĭn·sĕs′ănt). Unceasing.
**incompatible** (ĭn′kŏm·păt′ĭ·b'l). Opposed in character.
**inconsequential** (ĭn·kŏn′sê·kwĕn′shăl). Unimportant.
**incubus** (ĭn′kŭ·bŭs). 1. An evil spirit supposed to lie upon persons in their sleep. 2. Any person or thing that oppresses or burdens.
**inculcated** (ĭn·kŭl′kāt·ĕd). Taught; impressed.
**indemnify** (ĭn·dĕm′nĭ·fĭ). Repay; make good.
**indolence** (ĭn′dô·lĕns). Laziness.
**ineffable** (ĭn·ĕf′å·b'l). Not to be expressed in words; too great to be expressed in words.
**infamous** (ĭn′fà·mŭs). 1. Wicked. 2. Having a bad reputation.
**iniquity** (ĭn·ĭk′wĭ·tĭ). Injustice; wickedness.
**in lieu** (ĭn lū′). In place of.
**inordinate** (ĭn·ôr′dĭ·nĭt). Immoderate.
**insidious** (ĭn·sĭd′ĭ·ŭs). 1. Wily; crafty. 2. Working secretly or subtly.
**instigate** (ĭn′stĭ·gāt). To stimulate; to incite.
**insurrection** (ĭn′sŭ·rĕk′shŭn). Uprising; revolt.
**intermittent** (ĭn′tēr·mĭt′ĕnt). Coming and going at intervals.
**interposition** (ĭn′tēr·pô·zĭsh′ŭn). Interference in order to help.
**intimate** (ĭn′tĭ·mĭt). n-. A close friend.
**intimate** (ĭn′tĭ·māt). v-. To suggest indirectly.
**intrepidly** (ĭn·trĕp′ĭd·lĭ). Fearlessly.
**intuition** (ĭn′tû·ĭsh′ŭn). Perception of truths, facts, etc., without reasoning.
**invective** (ĭn·vĕk′tĭv). Vocal abuse.
**inveterate** (ĭn·vĕt′ĕr·ĭt). Fixed; confirmed in a habit, practice, feeling, etc.
**invigorate** (ĭn·vĭg′ĕr·āt). To give vigor, life, or energy to.
**inviolable** (ĭn·vī′ô·lå·b'l). Sacred; not to be violated or disturbed.
**ire** (īr). Anger.
**irksome** (ûrk′sŭm). Wearisome.
**iterated** (ĭt′ēr·āt·ĕd). Repeated.

**J**

**jasmin** (jăs′mĭn). A shrub or vine with clusters of fragrant flowers.
**jeopardy** (jĕp′ēr·dĭ). Danger.
**jower** (jou′ēr). Quarrel.
**judicial** (jōō·dĭsh′ăl). Pertaining to judges; having to do with a court of law or the administration of justice.
**judicious** (jōō·dĭsh′ŭs). Wise; prudent.

**K**

**ken** (kĕn). That which is within the range of sight or of knowledge.
**kindred** (kĭn′drĕd). 1. adj.- Related to. 2. n-. Relatives.

**L**

**lank** (lăngk). Shrunken; lean.
**lavish** (lăv′ĭsh). 1. v-. Squander; waste. 2. adj.- Very abundant; more than is needed.
**lay** (lā). 1. A song; a simple lyric or short narrative poem. 2. A melody.
**legacy** (lĕg′å·sĭ). Money or property left to a person by someone who has died.
**leonine** (lē′ô·nīn). Characteristic of a lion.
**licentiousness** (lī·sĕn′shŭs·nĕss). Lawlessness; immorality.
**lintel** (lĭn′tĕl). A horizontal beam or stone above a door or window to support the structure above it.
**livid** (lĭv′ĭd). 1. Ashy pale. 2. Discolored.
**longitudinal** (lŏn′jĭ·tū′dĭ·năl). Running lengthwise.
**lucid** (lū′sĭd). Shining and clear.
**lurid** (lū′rĭd). Appearing like glowing fire seen through cloud or smoke.

**M**

**machination** (măk′ĭ·nā′shŭn). Artful design or plot.
**magnanimous** (măg·năn′ĭ·mŭs). Noble in soul and mind; above pettiness.
**mail** (māl). A flexible fabric of interlocked metal rings used as a defensive armor.
**maize** (māz). Indian corn.
**malady** (măl′å·dĭ). Any disease of the human body.
**malediction** (măl′ê·dĭk′shŭn). A curse.
**malice** (măl′ĭs). Spite; active ill-will.
**malignant** (må·lĭg′nănt). Very evil; very hateful.
**manifest** (măn′ĭ·fĕst). Open and visible.
**massy** (măs′ĭ). Having bulk or weight and substance; massive.
**maze** (māz). 1. A network of paths through which it is difficult to find one's way. 2. Confusion of thought.
**melee** (mâ·lā′). A confused fight between a number of combatants.
**mendicant** (mĕn′dĭ·kănt). A beggar.
**meteorological** (mē′tê·ôr·ô·lŏj′ĭ·kăl). Having to do with the atmosphere and weather.
**misapprehension** (mĭs′ăp·rê·hĕn′shŭn). A misunderstanding.
**mitigate** (mĭt′ĭ·gāt). To make or become less severe, harsh, etc.
**mollify** (mŏl′ĭ·fĭ). To soften.
**mote** (mōt). A small particle, as of floating dust.
**mottled** (mŏt′'ld). Spotted or streaked with different colors.
**multitudinous** (mŭl′tĭ·tū′dĭ·nŭs). Very numerous.
**myriad** (mĭr′ĭ·ăd). An indefinitely large number.
**mythical** (mĭth′ĭ·kăl). Unreal; existing only in legend.

**N**

**negligent** (nĕg′lĭ·jĕnt). Careless.
**nether** (nĕth′ēr). Lower.
**niche** (nĭch). A recess or hollow in a wall.
**niter** (nī′tēr). 1. Potassium nitrate. 2. Sodium nitrate.

āte, châotic, dâre, ădd, ăccuse, bär, càsk, áfar; ēat, dęar, ĕlude, ĕgg, quiĕt, centēr; īdle, ĭf, activĭty; ōpen, ôbey, ôr, ŏrange, ŏffer, ŏccur.

**nocturne** (nŏk'tûrn). 1. A dreamy or pensive musical piece. 2. A painting of a night scene.

**noisome** (noi'sŭm). Offensive; disgusting.

**nondescript** (nŏn'dĕ·skrĭpt). *n-*. A person or thing of no particular class or kind.

**noxious** (nŏk'shŭs). Unwholesome.

**nucleus** (nū'klĕ·ŭs). A central point about which matter is gathered; a core.

## O

**obliterated** (ŏb·lĭt'ĕr·āt·ĕd). Erased; blotted out; completely destroyed.

**oblivious** (ŏb·lĭv'ĭ·ŭs). Forgetful; not mindful.

**obstructed** (ŏb·strŭkt'ĕd). Barred; checked.

**ocular** (ŏk'ū·lēr). Visual.

**odium** (ō'dĭ·ŭm). 1. Hatred; dislike. 2. Reproach; blame.

**oleograph** (ō'lĕ·ô·grȧf'). An imitation oil painting.

**ominous** (ŏm'ĭ·nŭs). Of bad omen; unfavorable; threatening.

**opprobrium** (ŏ·prō'brĭ·ŭm). The disgrace that follows shameful conduct.

**opulence** (ŏp'ū·lĕns). Wealth; riches; plenty.

**orgy** (ôr'jĭ). Excessive indulgence in some activity.

**ostensibly** (ŏs·tĕn'sĭ·blĭ). Avowedly; apparently.

**ostentatious** (ŏs'tĕn·tā'shŭs). That which is done for display; intended to attract notice.

**overweening** (ō'vēr·wēn'ĭng). Excessive self-importance.

## P

**pæan** (pē'ăn). A song of joy, praise, triumph or the like.

**palladium** (pȧ·lā'dĭ·ŭm). That which affords security; a safeguard.

**pallid** (păl'ĭd). Pale.

**pallor** (păl'ēr). Deficiency of color; paleness.

**palpitated** (păl'pĭ·tā'tĕd). Beat rapidly; throbbed.

**paraphernalia** (păr'ȧ·fēr·nā'lĭ·ȧ). 1. Personal belongings. 2. Outfit.

**paroxysmal** (păr'ŏx·sĭz'măl). That which is characterized by sudden violent and uncontrollable action.

**partition** (pär·tĭsh'ŭn). A division.

**pathos** (pā'thŏs). The quality in speech, writing, music, *etc.*, that arouses a feeling of pity or sadness.

**patriarch** (pā'trĭ·ärk). 1. The father or ruler of a family or tribe. 2. A venerable old man.

**patronizing** (pā'trŭn·ĭz·ĭng). Giving protection or support to.

**pavilion** (pȧ·vĭl'yŭn). A tent; esp. a large tent with a peaked or rounded top.

**pecuniary** (pê·kū'nĭ·ĕr'ĭ). Consisting of, or related to, money.

**pelt** (pĕlt). A skin.

**pendant** (pĕn'dănt). Suspended; hanging.

**pensive** (pĕn'sĭv). Thoughtful in a serious or sad way.

**pent** (pĕnt). Penned or shut up; confined.

**peremptory** (pēr·ĕmp'tô·rĭ). 1. Decisive; final; absolute. 2. Allowing no denial or refusal.

**perfidy** (pûr'fĭ·dĭ). Faithlessness.

**perfunctorily** (pēr·fŭngk'tô·rĭ·lĭ). Mechanically; indifferently.

**pernicious** (pēr·nĭsh'ŭs). Wicked and deadly.

**perpetrated** (pûr'pê·trāt·ĕd). That which is done or committed, as a crime, fraud, trick, or anything bad or foolish.

**perturbation** (pûr'tēr·bā'shŭn). An uneasy or troubled condition.

**pervade** (pēr·vād'). Go or spread throughout.

**pestilence** (pĕs'tĭ·lĕns). Any disease that spreads rapidly, causing many deaths.

**petulant** (pĕt'ū·lănt). Fretful and peevish.

**phenomenon** (fê·nŏm'ê·nŏn). An extraordinary or remarkable event.

**pianissimo** (pē'ȧ·nĭs'ĭ·mō). In music: 1. Very soft. 2. Very softly.

**pinion** (pĭn'yŭn). A wing.

**pique** (pēk). Some feeling of anger at being slighted; wounded pride.

**pithy** (pĭth'ĭ). Full of substance, meaning, force or vigor.

**placate** (plā'kāt). To soothe or satisfy; to make peaceful.

**plausible** (plô'zĭ·b'l). Appearing true, reasonable or fair.

**plight** (plīt). Condition; state.

**poignant** (poin'yănt). Keen; painfully moving or touching.

**ponderous** (pŏn'dēr·ŭs). 1. Very heavy. 2. Heavy and clumsy.

**poniard** (pŏn'yērd). A kind of dagger, usually slender with a triangular or square blade.

**portentous** (pōr·tĕn'tŭs). 1. Indicating evil to come; threatening. 2. Amazing; extraordinary.

**posterity** (pŏs·tĕr'ĭ·tĭ). Offspring to the furthest generation; descendants.

**practicability** (prăk'tĭ·kȧ·bĭl'ĭ·tĭ). Capability of being accomplished or put into practice.

**precedent** (prĕs'ê·dĕnt). Action that may serve as an example to justify or authorize later action.

**predicament** (prê·dĭk'ȧ·mĕnt). An unpleasant, trying, or dangerous situation.

**premonitory** (prê·mŏn'ĭ·tō'rĭ). Warning.

**prentice** (prĕn'tĭs). Inexperienced; not fully skilled.

**preoccupation** (prê·ŏk'û·pā'shŭn). A state of being lost in thought.

**preposterous** (prê·pŏs'tĕr·ŭs). Contrary to nature, reason, or common sense; absurd.

**preternatural** (prē'tēr·năt'û·răl). Beyond normal; not miraculous, but strange and not to be explained.

**pristine** (prĭs'tēn). Original; primitive.

**prodigious** (prô·dĭj'ŭs). 1. Huge; vast. 2. wonderful; marvelous.

**proffer** (prŏf'ēr). To offer for acceptance.

**promiscuous** (prô·mĭs'kû·ŭs). Mixed and in disorder.

**propensities** (prô·pĕn'sĭ·tĭz). Natural inclinations.

**propriety** (prô·prī'ĕ·tĭ). Proper behavior.

**prostrate** (prŏs'trāt). Reclining flat; thrown down; fallen prone.

**provender** (prŏv'ĕn·dēr). Food for animals.

**pulsating** (pŭl'sāt·ĭng). Beating or throbbing.

cōol, cŏok; our, boil; cūte, ûnite, bûrn, cŭt, ŭnless, menü; check; goat, sing, ~~this~~, thick, scriptŭre, verdŭre.

**puncheon** (pŭn′chŭn). 1. A split log or a heavy slab with the face smoothed. 2. A large cask.

**purl** (pûrl). To run swiftly round, as a small stream among obstructions; to eddy, swirl; also, to make a murmuring sound.

**purloin** (pûr·loin′). Steal.

## Q

**quaffed** (kwȧft). Drank.

**quartz** (kwôrts). A very hard mineral composed of silica.

**quibble** (kwĭb′'l). An unfair and petty evasion of the point or truth by using words with a double meaning.

## R

**rabble** (răb′'l). A disorderly crowd; a mob.

**rack** (răk). Torment.

**railing** (rāl′ĭng). A harsh scolding.

**raiment** (rā′mĕnt). Clothing.

**rankness** (răngk′nĕs). Offensiveness; grossness.

**rapacious** (rȧ·pā′shŭs). Plundering; seizing by force.

**raucous** (rô′kŭs). Disagreeably harsh.

**ravenous** (răv′ĕn·ŭs). Eager for food, satisfaction, or gratification.

**ravine** (rȧ·vēn′). A depression worn out by running water, larger than a gully and smaller than a valley.

**rebuff** (rė·bŭf′). 1. n-. Snub; a curt refusal to meet an advance. 2. v-. To drive or beat back.

**recluse** (rė·kloōs′). A person who lives in seclusion.

**recompense** (rĕk′ŏm·pĕns). Reward.

**reconnoitring** (rĕk′ŏ·noi′tēr·ĭng). Making a preliminary examination.

**rectitude** (rĕk′tĭ·tūd). Moral uprightness.

**recumbent** (rė·kŭm′bĕnt). Lying; resting.

**redolent** (rĕd′ō·lĕnt). Odorous; fragrant.

**redoubtable** (rė·dout′ȧ·b'l). That which should be feared or dreaded.

**redress** (rė·drĕs′). Amends; reparation of wrongs.

**reeking** (rēk′ĭng). Sending out vapor or an unpleasant smell.

**reflux** (rē′flŭks). A flowing back; ebb.

**regalia** (rė·gā′lĭ·ȧ). Finery; special dress.

**reminiscence** (rĕm′ĭ·nĭs′ĕns). Recollection.

**remonstrate** (rė·mŏn′strāt). To protest; to reprove.

**repining** (rė·pīn′ĭng). Complaining; grumbling.

**repudiate** (rė·pū′dĭ·āt). To refuse to acknowledge; to reject.

**requisite** (rĕk′wĭ·zĭt). Required by circumstances; necessary.

**resinous** (rĕz′ĭ·nŭs). Odor given off by the sticky substance that flows from some trees.

**respiration** (rĕs′pĭ·rā′shŭn). 1. Act of breathing. 2. A breath.

**retaliate** (rė·tăl′ĭ·āt). To pay back wrong, injury, etc.; return like for like, usually to return evil for evil.

**retention** (rė·tĕn′shŭn). Holding back; the ability to keep things in the mind; to remember.

**retrospect** (rĕt′rȯ·spĕkt). A looking back on things past.

**rhetoric** (rĕt′ȯ·rĭk). Skillful or artistic use of speech.

**rigorous** (rĭg′ēr·ŭs). Harsh and severe.

**robust** (rȯ·bŭst′). Strong and healthy.

**rood** (roōd). Measure of land.

**rude** (roōd). Rugged; sturdy; vigorous.

**rudiment** (roō′dĭ·mĕnt). That which is undeveloped; an unfinished beginning.

**russet** (rŭs′ĕt). Yellowish-brown; reddish-brown.

**ruthless** (roōth′lĕs). Cruel; pitiless.

## S

**sagacity** (sȧ·găs′ĭ·tĭ). Keenness of judgment.

**salubrity** (sȧ·lū′brĭ·tĭ). Wholesomeness; health.

**salutary** (săl′ů·tĕr′ĭ). That which is good for the health; wholesome.

**sanguine** (săng′gwĭn). Optimistic.

**sceptre** (sĕp′tēr). The rod or staff carried by a ruler as a symbol of royal power or authority.

**scion** (sī′ŭn). A descendant.

**scoffing** (skŏf′ĭng). Scornful teasing.

**sconce** (skŏns). A bracket candlestick secured to a wall.

**scrupulous** (skroō′pů·lŭs). Careful; exact; painstaking.

**sedentary** (sĕd′ĕn·tĕr′ĭ). Characterized by sitting; settled; not active.

**seepage** (sēp′ĭj). Trickling; oozing; leakage; slow passing through.

**seer** (sē′ēr). One who foresees events; a prophet.

**seethe** (sēth). Boil; bubble and foam.

**serpentine** (sûr′pĕn·tēn). Of or like a serpent; winding; twisting.

**sheen** (shēn). Brightness; luster.

**shrouded** (shroud′ĕd). Covered.

**simper** (sĭm′pēr). To smile in a silly way.

**simulated** (sĭm′ů·lāt′ĕd). Assumed the appearance of without the reality.

**singular** (sĭng′gů·lēr). Unusual; strange.

**smatterer** (smăt′ēr·ēr). A person with only a slight knowledge of a particular subject.

**smiting** (smīt′ĭng). Striking.

**snipe** (snīp). A marsh bird.

**solace** (sŏl′ĭs). Comfort; relief.

**solicitude** (sȯ·lĭs′ĭ·tūd). Concern; anxiety.

**sonorous** (sȯ·nō′rŭs). Giving out a deep, loud sound.

**sorghum** (sôr′gŭm). A kind of molasses or thick syrup.

**spasmodic** (spăz·mŏd′ĭk). With sudden spurts of energy or violence.

**specter** (spĕk′tēr). A ghost; an apparition.

**speculate** (spĕk′ů·lāt). To reflect; meditate; consider; conjecture.

**speculation** (spĕk′ů·lā′shŭn). Buying or selling at a large risk with the hope of making a profit from future price changes.

**squall** (skwôl). A sudden, violent gust of wind, often with rain, snow, or sleet.

**squalor** (skwŏl′ēr). Filth; misery and dirt.

**stalactite** (stȧ·lăk′tīt). A formation of lime, shaped like an icicle, hanging from the roof of a cave.

āte, châotic, dâre, ădd, ȧccuse, bär, cȧsk, ȧfar; ēat, dẹar, ėlude, ĕgg, quїĕt, centēr; ĭdle, ℸ, actĭvĭty; ōpen, ȯbey, ôr, ŏrange, ŏffer, ŏccur.

**statuary** (stăt′ụ̇·ĕr′ĭ). One who makes statues.

**staunch** (stônch). Strong; firm; reliable.

**stentorian** (stĕn·tō′rĭ·ăn). Extremely loud.

**stigma** (stĭg′mȧ). 1. A brand, as upon a slave or a criminal. 2. Any mark of infamy or disgrace.

**strait** (strāt). Narrow; strict.

**suasion** (swā′zhŭn). A convincing or persuading.

**suave** (swäv). Worldly; sophisticated.

**subjugation** (sŭb′jŏŏ·gā′shŭn). Conquest; subjection.

**subsistence** (sŭb·sĭs′tĕns). A means of keeping alive; food.

**subvert** (sŭb·vûrt′). To overthrow; overturn; ruin utterly.

**succor** (sŭk′ẽr). Help; assistance; relief.

**succumbed** (sŭ·kŭmd′). To yield; give up; specif. to die.

**suffusion** (sŭ·fū′zhŭn). Tinge.

**sulphurous** (sŭl′fū·rŭs). Fiery; scorching.

**sultry** (sŭl′trĭ). Very hot and moist; close and oppressive.

**superficial** (sū′pēr·fĭsh′ăl). That which affects only the surface.

**superfluous** (sū·pûr′flŏŏ·ŭs). More than is needed; unnecessary.

**supine** (sū·pīn′). 1. Lying on the back. 2. Mentally or morally lethargic; without stamina; abject.

**surly** (sûr′lĭ). Ill-natured and rude.

**swain** (swān). A young peasant.

**sward** (swôrd). The grassy surface of land; turf.

**swound** (swound). *Archaic*, swoon; faint.

## T

**tableau** (tăb′lō). 1. Picture; striking scene. 2. A representation of a picture, statue, scene, *etc.*, by persons.

**tangible** (tăn′jĭ·b′l). Capable of being touched or felt by touch.

**tawny** (tô′nĭ). Of a brownish-red color.

**temerity** (tḗ·mĕr′ĭ·tĭ). Rashness.

**tempestuous** (tĕm·pĕs′tụ̇·ŭs). Stormy; violent.

**throng** (thrŏng). A multitude of persons crowded together.

**tier** (tēr). Layer.

**torpidity** (tôr·pĭd′ĭ·tĭ). Sluggishness.

**tractable** (trăk′tȧ·b′l). Capable of being easily led, taught, or controlled.

**tranquil** (trăng′kwĭl). Calm and undisturbed.

**transient** (trăn′shĕnt). Short-lived.

**transmute** (trăns·mūt′). Convert; change.

**tremulous** (trĕm′ụ̇·lŭs). 1. Quivering; shaking. 2. Timid.

**trepidation** (trĕp′ĭ·dā′shŭn). 1. Fear; fright. 2. Trembling.

**tribulation** (trĭb′ụ̇·lā′shŭn). Affliction; severe trial; great trouble.

**tribunal** (trī·bū′năl). A court of justice; a place of judgment.

**tribute** (trĭb′ūt). An acknowledgment of thanks or respect; a compliment.

**troll** (trōl). To sing loudly; to celebrate in song.

**trysting** (trĭst′ĭng). Meeting.

**tuition** (tṳ·ĭsh′ŭn). Teaching; instruction.

## U

**unbridled** (ŭn·brī′d′ld). Unrestrained.

**undefiled** (ŭn·dḗ·fīld′). Pure; not corrupt.

**undue** (ŭn·dū′). Excessive.

**unencumbered** (ŭn·ĕn·kŭm′bẽrd). Unobstructed.

**unhallowed** (ŭn·hăl′ōd). Unholy.

**unremunerative** (ŭn·rḗ·mū′nẽr·āt·ĭv). Unprofitable.

**unrequited** (ŭn·rḗ·kwīt′ĕd). Unpaid.

**unsavory** (ŭn·sā′vẽr·ĭ). Tasteless; unpleasant.

**unscrupulous** (ŭn·skrŏŏ′pụ̇·lŭs). Not careful about right or wrong.

**usurpation** (ū′zŭr·pā′shŭn). Forcible seizure; uprising.

## V

**vagaries** (vȧ·gâr′ĭz). Fanciful notions.

**vassalage** (văs′ăl·ĭj). The state of being a servant rather than a free person; servitude, especially, political dependence.

**veered** (vērd). Changed direction; shifted.

**vehemently** (vē′ḗ·mĕnt·lĭ). Eagerly; forcibly.

**venerable** (vĕn′ẽr·ȧ·b′l). 1. Old. 2. Revered.

**venerate** (vĕn′ẽr·āt). To regard with respect, admiration, or reverence.

**veracious** (vḗ·rā′shŭs). Truthful; honest.

**versatile** (vûr′sȧ·tĭl). Turning with ease from one thing to another; skilful at many things.

**viand** (vī′ănd). An article of food.

**vicissitude** (vĭ·sĭs′ĭ·tūd). Irregular change, usually of fortune or luck.

**vindication** (vĭn′dĭ·kā′shŭn). Justification.

**vindictive** (vĭn·dĭk′tĭv). Bearing a grudge; wanting revenge.

**virility** (vĭ·rĭl′ĭ·tĭ). Manly vigor.

**visage** (vĭz′ĭj). Face; countenance.

**vista** (vĭs′tȧ). 1. A long view seen through a narrow opening or passage. 2. A mental view.

**vituperation** (vī·tū′pēr·ā′shŭn). Wordy abuse.

**vociferous** (vō·sĭf′ẽr·ŭs). Loud and noisy; shouting; clamorous.

**vogue** (vōg). That which is in fashion.

**volleying** (vŏl′ĭ·ing). A simultaneous discharge; a burst or emission of many things at once.

**vouchsafe** (vouch·sāf′). To bestow; to guarantee; to condescend; to grant.

## W

**waned** (wānd). Decreased; diminished.

**wanton** (wŏn′tŭn). 1. Undisciplined. 2. Having no just provocation; willfully malicious.

**waxed** (wăkst). Grew; increased.

**weal** (wēl). Well-being.

**wily** (wīl′ĭ). Crafty and cunning.

**winded** (wīnd′ĕd). Blew.

**wreak** (rēk). Inflict (vengeance, punishment, *etc.*) on another.

---

cōōl, cŏŏk; our, boil; cūte, ûnite, bûrn, cŭt, ŭnless, menü; check; goat, sing, ~~this~~, thick, scriptụre, verdụre.

# INDEX